MASTERPLOTS II

POETRY SERIES
REVISED EDITION

MASTERPLOTS II

POETRY SERIES
REVISED EDITION

3

The Drunken Boat–Heritage

Editor, Revised Edition
PHILIP K. JASON

Project Editor, Revised Edition
TRACY IRONS-GEORGES

Editors, Supplement
JOHN WILSON   **PHILIP K. JASON**

Editor, First Edition
FRANK N. MAGILL

SALEM PRESS

Pasadena, California   Hackensack, New Jersey

Editor in Chief: Dawn P. Dawson

Project Editor: Tracy Irons-Georges   *Research Supervisor:* Jeffry Jensen
Production Editor: Cynthia Beres   *Research Assistant:* Jeff Stephens
Copy Editor: Lauren Mitchell   *Acquisitions Editor:* Mark Rehn

Some of the essays in this work originally appeared in *Masterplots II, Poetry Series*, edited by Frank N. Magill (Pasadena, Calif.: Salem Press, Inc., 1992), and in *Masterplots II, Poetry Series Supplement*, edited by John Wilson and Philip K. Jason (Pasadena, Calif.: Salem Press, Inc., 1998).

∞ The paper used in these volumes conforms to the American National Standard for Permanence of Paper for Printed Library Materials, Z39.48-1992 (R1997).

Library of Congress Cataloging-in-Publication Data
Masterplots II. Poetry series.— Rev. ed. / editor, Philip K. Jason ; project editor, Tracy Irons-Georges
    p. ; cm.
Rev. ed.: Masterplots two / Frank Northen Magill, 1992-1998.
Includes bibliographical references and indexes.
    ISBN 1-58765-037-1 (set : alk. paper) — ISBN 1-58765-040-1 (vol. 3 : alk. paper) —
    1. Poetry — Themes, motives. I. Title: Masterplots two. II. Title: Masterplots 2. III. Jason, Philip K., 1941-   . IV. Irons-Georges, Tracy.

PN1110.5 .M37 2002
809.1—dc21
                                                          2001055059

Second Printing

PRINTED IN THE UNITED STATES OF AMERICA

TABLE OF CONTENTS

TABLE OF CONTENTS

TABLE OF CONTENTS

MASTERPLOTS II

POETRY SERIES
REVISED EDITION

THE DRUNKEN BOAT

Author: Arthur Rimbaud (1854-1891)
Type of poem: Narrative
First published: 1883, as "Le Bateau ivre"; collected in *Poésies complètes d'Arthur Rimbaud*, 1895; English translation collected in *Complete Works, Selected Letters*, 1966

The Poem

"The Drunken Boat" was written by the sixteen-year-old Arthur Rimbaud as a demonstration of his poetic skills for the audience of poets that he expected to meet in Paris in 1871. The one hundred lines of the poem are divided into twenty-five quatrains, Alexandrines rhymed *abab*, which are quite traditional and conventional. Beneath the controlled surface, however, seethes a turmoil of complex and conflicting, but interdependent, thoughts and feelings. The poem is a statement of adolescent rebellion and a hymn to liberation and independence. It expresses the young Rimbaud's personal longing for freedom, adult life, and mature experience.

The poem is a narrative related by a boat that has somehow escaped its moorings and run alone, without control or guidance, down a river to the sea. The "drunken" boat of the title is not intoxicated with alcohol or drugs but with uncontrolled and aimless liberty, an abandonment to whatever forces drive it toward an unknown destination. The boat, lacking haulers, rudder, or grappling hook, finds total freedom in its mad and senseless frolic in the sea. During this long journey—time and the cause of the liberation are never specific—the boat experiences many adventures and encounters previously unknown sights, sounds, and sensations. At the end of the voyage, the boat, weary and deteriorating physically, longs for release from the exhaustion of experience. It seeks tranquillity and rest at the bottom of the sea.

Although there are no formal divisions into parts within the text, the poem breaks rhetorically into five sections. In the first two stanzas, the boat tells of its magical liberation from the control of its haulers and the burdens placed on it by commerce. The next three stanzas describe its physical initiation into the sea world. With triumphant exhilaration, it rushes to unite itself with the element of water, which washes away the traces of the human world and purifies it of both wine and vomit. In the long central section of the poem, which consists of twelve stanzas, the boat elliptically and chaotically relates some of its most startling adventures. Some experiences are acute perceptions of dawn and sunset, as well as of the play of light on the surface of the water. Others describe strange new lands, exotic flowers, and monstrous, fabulous beasts; tropical fish and bizarre marine birds entice the boat onward as it continues its reckless and irregular pursuit of drunken freedom. Gradually becoming sated with freedom and new experience, however, the boat begins to feel languorous and weary. The next four stanzas—one rigorously organized sentence—summarize the boat's total sea experiences, which have produced a disillusioned homesickness. The last four stanzas express the boat's disgust with its previous aspirations, its sense of physical weakness and gradual disintegration, and finally its longing for death. Having enjoyed the ecstasy of new physical and spiritual sensations, the boat hopes either to return to its abandoned home or to sink to the bottom of the sea.

Forms and Devices

Although conventional in conception (narrative) and in structure (rhymed quatrains), "The Drunken Boat" broke entirely new ground in Rimbaud's invention of poetic images adequate to convey the intensity of the boat's emotional reactions to its various experiences. Some of Rimbaud's images, quite simple and conventional, speak to the reader directly with their power and beauty. "Lighter than a cork I danced on the waves," the boat reveals, and "—from then on I bathed in the Poem/ Of the Sea—." Throughout the poem, Rimbaud refers to nature in terms that might have been used by many earlier poets: "I know the evening,/ The dawn as exalted as a flock of doves" and "Glaciers, suns of silver, nacreous waves, skies of embers." Emotions are conveyed through common references: "And I remained, like a woman on her knees" expresses the boat's sense of reverence for the beauty of exotic sea life, while "Every moon is atrocious and every sun bitter" reveals the boat's disgust as it approaches the end of its mad journey. The image of a child releasing a boat as "fragile as a May butterfly" into a black, cold puddle is impressive for the simplicity of its tone and for its expressiveness.

Mingled among these simple images, however, are many others whose significance is neither apparent nor rational and logical. For example, the boat sees the low sun "spotted with mystic horrors" striking the sea so that the waves seem to be "rolling far off their quivering of shutters"; the boat has dreamed of "the yellow and blue awakening of singing phosphorus." With a willing imagination, a reader may decide that the word "mystic" contributes an aura of mystery to the apprehensions attendant upon the approach of night, while the shutters may allude to Venetian blinds moving in the breeze as the sun sets. Images of exotic marine life complete this striking description of the sea as threatening night descends.

A third kind of image, one which defies efforts at logical analysis, appears frequently in the central section of the poem. The boat notices in "hideous strands" that "giant serpents devoured by bedbugs/ Fall, from gnarled trees, with black scent!" It endures "the quarrels/ And droppings of noisy birds with pale yellow eyes," and, near the end, describes itself as "spotted with small electric moons,/ A wild plank, escorted by black seahorses." Such conjunctions of meaning lose logical coherence because they transcend reason to achieve meaning in the realm of the emotions. They suggest fantastic visual images and sensations burdened with intense emotion. Serpents covered with bedbugs, yellow-eyed birds, and electric moons suggest paintings by Salvador Dalí and Marc Chagall. Rimbaud has pressed words and their meanings from the real through the unreal to the surreal by linking concepts that reflect spiritual rather than physical reality. Connotation has taken precedence over denotation; implications and suggestions prevail over literal significations. A new way of forming poetic images was invented, one which served poets and other artists for many generations to come. Perhaps Rimbaud cannot quite be called a Surrealist, but "The Drunken Boat" clearly introduces new poetic techniques.

Themes and Meanings

Numerous allegorical interpretations can be generated by the poem, but none is so coherent as to exclude all others or to provide a definitive explanation of all details: "The Drunken Boat" is not a structure of simple symbols which can be translated into single concepts. A rational order cannot be pressed upon it, and it is useless to insist that the poem conform to the mental restraints of clarity and coherence. Its images bristle with suggestions and resonances that must be understood on their own terms while being integrated into the whole poetic structure. Rimbaud's poem is not an enigma to be solved but rather a complex structure of episodes, details, and emotions which the reader must explore carefully.

"The Drunken Boat" is an extraordinary example of a Symbolist poem, astonishing in the perfection of its conception and execution. The structure rests on the presentation and elaboration of one term of a metaphor—the symbolic one. The reader, after comprehending various aspects of the symbol, is left to perceive their relationships to an unnamed term which is the true subject of the poem. Charles Baudelaire and the Parnassian poets Paul Verlaine and Théodore de Banville had been working in this mode of poetry for some years, experimenting with techniques that would reveal the subject without disclosing it, leading the reader to discover the significance of the poem through a thoughtful interpretation of the symbol. Rimbaud's boat, telling of its reckless, aimless voyage and referred to always in terms appropriate to a boat, implies a corresponding term of a metaphor relating to humankind. The boat—sentient, thoughtful, capable of feelings—conceals within it the image of all those who break the ties that bind them in their quest for both physical and spiritual fulfillment.

"The Drunken Boat" is an autobiographical poem about growing up. Ernest Delahaye, a schoolmate of Rimbaud, wrote that, as a child, the young poet liked to play in a rowboat tied in the Meuse river near his home, dreaming of the freedom and adventures that it represented. This small boat probably inspired Rimbaud to imagine a magical freighter escaping from the stability of its moorings to pursue extravagant and exotic adventures on the oceans of the world. Provoked by his feelings of constraint and confined within the repressive atmosphere of middle-class values and views represented by his mother, his teachers, and the clergy in Charleville where he was born, Rimbaud embodied in the symbol of the boat his dream of reckless independence. Sometimes clouded by fear and apprehension, the boat nevertheless established its identity—"Free, smoking, topped with violet fog"—as the young poet himself was soon to do.

Raymond M. Archer

THE DUKE ELLINGTON DREAM

Author: Paul Zimmer (1934-   )
Type of poem: Narrative
First published: 1983, in *Family Reunion: Selected and New Poems*

The Poem

A twenty-three-line poem, Paul Zimmer's "The Duke Ellington Dream" consists of four stanzas of varying lengths. In free verse that organically echoes the modulating rhythms and tempos of the very jazz it describes, the poem relates a "dream" of the persona, here—as in many of Zimmer's poems—Zimmer, a daydream in which he plays with Duke Ellington's band. As in any dream of heroism or excellence, in this fantasy Zimmer is not only a part of the band, he is in the spotlight. To effect this feat, he must also be the one who walks his own way to his own beat, although it both dismays and delights (albeit grudgingly) his idol, mentor, and leader; he must be the perfect but intractable student who learns the lesson so well he outstrips and outshines his teacher and does it with an illimitable supply of "cool."

The dream begins when Zimmer saunters into a club where arguably the most famous jazz composer and musician of the twentieth century, Duke Ellington, is playing with his band. In his dream, Zimmer is a member of Ellington's band or perhaps a guest soloist, although that option might be less probable because of Ellington's obvious disapproval of the way Zimmer casually strolls in late to join in the gig. As Zimmer puts it, "Duke was pissed." Despite Ellington's continuing annoyance with him and in clear and unabashed defiance of the bandleader's huff, Zimmer takes his place with his tenor sax as the other band members quietly but surely move to make room for him. Though the band has evidently been playing for some time, the whole place suddenly comes alive when Zimmer begins to wail Ellington's tunes from his saxophone while Ellington himself remains stoic and visibly unappeased. Nonetheless, Zimmer's performance of each song is definitive; he "blew them so they would stay played."

When he is finished, he calmly packs up his horn to leave only to have Ellington abruptly stop him—the word Zimmer uses is "collar" him—and growl, "'Zimmer . . . You most astonishing ofay!/ You have shat upon my charts,/ But I love you madly.'" The dream, which threatened momentarily to become a nightmare, thus ends in the hippest, coolest (to use the jargon of jazz) fashion possible—not with a saccharine approval by Ellington, but with his physical, semiviolent, and almost obscene explosion of appreciation and approbation. The dream is completely satisfactory, psychologically honest, and vividly evocative of the hot and cool ranges traversed by both fantasy and jazz.

Forms and Devices

From the first line of "The Duke Ellington Dream," Zimmer mimics the tone, mood, and rhythms of jazz. "Of course Zimmer was late for the gig," with its sinuous meter and liquid sounds, provides a jaded and irreverent counterpoint to the guttural notes and sibilance of the second line, with its hard-hammered meter: "Duke was pissed and growling at the piano." The continual shifting of meter throughout the poem mirrors the ever-changing rhythms of jazz, virtually imitating the various solos of the jazz musicians, from the slamming downbeat of Ellington's piano to the staccato riffs of the drummers to the curving, circuitous rhythms of Zimmer's tenor sax. Even the recital of the names of the bandmembers—"Jeep, Brute, Rex, Cat and Cootie"—helps to evoke the sounds and rhythms of the band as they reinforce the aspect of "coolness," epitomized by Zimmer's late arrival and the affirmation at the end of the stanza that "the boss had arrived." Each of these rhythms, sound devices, and tones are present within the first stanza alone, though its overall effect is more laidback than succeeding ones, taking its note from Zimmer's unhurried, and apparently deliberate, entrance.

The tempo steps up in the second stanza as the focus moves from Zimmer himself to his playing and the impact it has on the "whole joint," which immediately begins "jiving." Word choice is important in terms of evocation of atmosphere as well as sound: for instance, the choice of "chicks" for women and "lovelies" for breasts. Significantly, in this stanza the emphasis also moves from softer consonants (s, t, g, p, w, m, b), which dominate the first stanza, to harsher ones (k, st, j, ch), indicative of the increased activity. Only when the focus reverts to Ellington does the beat in this stanza slow down.

By the third stanza, made up almost entirely of the titles of some of Duke Ellington's most famous songs, "Satin Doll," "Do Nothing Till You Hear From Me," "Warm Valley," and "In A Sentimental Mood," the rhythm mellows out, sliding easily and effortlessly like the notes from Zimmer's sax, which "blew them so they would stay played." Similarly, the vowels and consonants in this stanza are soft and smooth; the only fricatives are softened by close proximity to sibilant or liquid consonants.

The final stanza presents a contrast in its short, businesslike "packing up" at the end of the gig. Once again, the appearance of Ellington alters the rhythm, reintroducing passion with the harsh k sound of "came" and "collared," the fricative of "ofay," (a derogatory term for whites), and the hilariously formal past-tense "shat," which spits out not one but two harsh consonant sounds, the *sh* and the emphatic final t sound. The final line of the poem, "But I love you madly," visually the briefest line in the entire poem, which zigzags its way across the page like musical notes on a score, is composed of six syllables, the first five of which must be stressed almost equally to recreate Ellington's tone and emotion accurately. The poem thus masterfully conjoins meter and sound to sense.

Themes and Meanings

The nonchalance of Zimmer's entrance counterpoints the obvious professionalism with which Ellington conducts the gig, setting up the first of the tensions that pervade the poem. Naturally, Zimmer chooses the tenor sax as his instrument; after all, it has been called the sexiest of all instruments, not to mention that it is the instrument closest in sound and ability to the human voice and the one that most often serves for the competition with which the jazz singer "duels." Here the duel, or battle of wills, is not between singer and saxophonist but is the age-old struggle between mentor and student, age and youth, made concrete in the conflict between bandleader and soloist, pianist and saxophonist, composer and musician, Ellington and Zimmer.

In line with the defiant tone of one of Zimmer's most frequently anthologized poems, "The Day Zimmer Lost Religion," "The Duke Ellington Dream" carries the encounter further by having the authority figure—Ellington—actually approach Zimmer with indignation and anger, which the timorous Christ fails to do in "The Day Zimmer Lost Religion." Rather than ending with separation and alienation from the authority figure, however, this poem ends with Ellington's passionate approbation of Zimmer, faults included. His anger at Zimmer for his tardiness cannot match his love for his ability to make the music live.

Another major tension of the poem rests on the improvisatory nature of jazz. Here it should be noted that jazz is one of the enduring topics of Zimmer's poetry. All music is a transient art form that can never be exactly reproduced, but jazz defines itself on the re-creation of tunes and chords through improvisation so that it not only cannot be exactly reproduced but also does not wish to be. Zimmer's belief that he "blew" Ellington's songs "so they would stay played" is counter to the belief that jazz should be ever-changing, ever-evolving. The image of a musical composition being caught in stasis is anathema to jazz, though the idea that a particular rendition might be unsurpassable is every jazz musician's dream; therein lies the tension.

Ellington's attitude similarly points up a tension in terms of his art form and his personal art. His obvious consternation at Zimmer's tardiness is not the problem he confronts Zimmer with when he nabs him at the end of the gig. Although in Ellington's name-calling, the "astonishing" in the phrase "most astonishing ofay" might refer to Zimmer's cheekiness, the next line—"You have shat upon my charts"—gives it an optional reading or at least stretches Zimmer's audacity to include his wholesale rejection of Ellington's arrangements in favor of his own conception of the music. His anger at Zimmer's improvisation is in direct contrast to the nature of jazz, but Ellington's loyalty to his art form over his own personal expression of it and his recognition of genius even though it might run counter to his own vision is tantamount in his final avowal to Zimmer, "But I love you madly."

Humorous as many of Zimmer's poems are, often primarily because of his habit of referring to himself in the third person, this poem nonetheless addresses significant themes in a significant way. Vigorous, bold, third-person, Walter Mitty-ish, "The Duke Ellington Dream" vividly expresses the desire for excellence, a desire as intense and gratifying as any other.

Jaquelyn W. Walsh

EACH AND ALL

Author: Ralph Waldo Emerson (1803-1882)
Type of poem: Lyric
First published: 1839; collected in *Poems,* 1847

The Poem

"Each and All" is usually treated as one of Ralph Waldo Emerson's best nature poems. It seems to have developed from a journal passage Emerson recorded in 1834 about recalling seeing seashells on the shore when he was a boy. He picked some up and took them home. When he got them there and looked at them, they appeared "dry and ugly." From that episode, he said in the journal passage, he learned that what he called "Composition"—things in arrangement with other things—was more important than the beauty of anything alone in terms of its effect on the viewer.

The poem recounts the process through which the first-person narrator, who seems to be a version of Emerson himself, becomes aware of "the perfect whole." It begins with the observation that "yon red-cloaked clown," apparently a man standing in a field, does not think about the observer looking at him, nor does the heifer think of the person who hears it lowing. It then refers to a sexton ringing his church bell without thinking of Napoleon listening. Emerson is alluding to Napoleon Bonaparte, emperor of France from 1804 to 1815, about whom Emerson wrote an essay in his book *Representative Men* (1850). Emerson had read that Napoleon paused whenever he heard the bell of a parish church because, Napoleon himself said, the sound reminded him of a period from his youth when he was happy. In "Each and All," the narrator speaks of Napoleon stopping his horse while his armies march through the Alps. Napoleon listens to the church bells ringing even though the sexton who rings them is unaware that he is there. From these episodes, the narrator concludes that one cannot know how one's life influences other people's lives and beliefs. In fact, the narrator says that each one is needed by every other one: "Nothing is fair or good alone."

The narrator then recounts a series of episodes in which he learns the truth of this conclusion. First, he tells of hearing a sparrow sing magnificently and bringing the bird home. There, the bird sings the same song it sang when it was free, but it no longer "cheers" the narrator, for, he says, he did not bring home the river and sky where the bird first sang. These parts of the bird's natural setting, he says, sang to his eye, while the bird in captivity sings only to his ear. The narrator next recounts an episode similar to the one Emerson recounts in his journal involving the seashells. The narrator brings home beautiful shells, which, when taken from the shore, become "poor, unsightly, noisome things." Their beauty remains, he feels, on the shore "With the sun and the sand and the wild uproar."

The next episode the narrator recounts involves a lover who "watched his graceful maid," knowing that "her beauty's best attire/ Was woven still by the snow-white choir." Just as the narrator puts the bird in a cage, so the lover marries the maid and takes her to his "hermitage"—his home. There he notices that even though she becomes "a gentle wife," she no longer seems to be a fairylike creature. Her ability to enchant the lover resulted, the narrator believes, largely from her being among her friends. When she was separated from her friends, the "enchantment was undone."

As a result of these episodes, in each of which something loses beauty when separated from its setting, the narrator decides that beauty is a "cheat." Consequently, the narrator decides that he covets nothing but truth. He declares that he will leave beauty behind just as he left behind his youthful games. Yet even as he makes this declaration, he finds himself in the midst of a beautiful natural scene that he describes in detail. He sees the ground-pine curling in a wreathlike shape as it runs "over the club-moss burrs"; he inhales the aroma of the violet; he sees oaks and firs, and the pine cones and acorns from which new trees will grow. The sky soars above him; he sees and hears "the rolling river" and "the morning bird." He concludes the poem, "Beauty through my senses stole;/ I yielded myself to the perfect whole."

Forms and Devices

"Each and All" consists primarily of four-stress couplets. The poem's fairly regular rhythm and rhymes, some people feel, are supposed to imitate the patterns Emerson claims to find in nature. According to this theory, the fact that the poem contains some lines that are written in an *abab* pattern, one line (ending with "shore") that rhymes only with lines separated from it by a number of lines, and one line (ending with "ground") that rhymes with no other line—as well as the poem's having an odd number of lines—indicates that the symmetry Emerson finds in nature is not exact.

Most readers of the poem see it as being divided into three parts. The first consists of four images or episodes followed by a conclusion about all things needing other things (lines 1-12). The second consists of three more images or episodes (lines 13-36). In the final part, the poet arrives at a conclusion about the earlier material, only to discover that his conclusion is incorrect (lines 37-51).

Critics often accuse Emerson of being more interested in nature as an idea than in nature itself. Thus, critics say, his writing about nature tends to be rather vague. Although "Each and All" contains several images drawn from human interaction with other humans, such as the episodes involving the "clown," Napoleon, and the wife, the poem is for the most part dependent on imagery drawn from nature. Emerson deals with several specific parts of nature and specific ideas about nature. The images he uses—the seashells, the birds, the trees—place the reader in a familiar world of experience, a world in which the reader can participate through the vividness of the images.

The poem itself takes the form of a mental journey of discovery. One critic writes of its "dramatic" structure, a term that implies that the parts of the poem interact with one another, just as the parts of nature that Emerson treats within the poem interact with one another. The narrator begins his journey with generalizations about relationships between things. Then he observes the results of separation of things. He then draws the logical but wrong conclusion that beauty is a "cheat," a childhood thing to be outgrown, and that he, now that he is mature, will no longer be concerned with beauty. However, nature leads him, in spite of himself, to an appreciation of beauty again, which, as in most of Emerson's writing, cannot be separated from truth. In his first book, *Nature* (1836), Emerson says that beauty and truth "are but different faces of the same All." The narrator of "Each and All" reaches this truth not through logical processes but through a moment of insight in which he recognizes that nature forms a "perfect whole."

Themes and Meanings

"Each and All" echoes the idea—which Emerson voices in many places—that things by themselves are unaffecting and even ugly but that when placed in context, usually their natural context, they become beautiful. Even putrefaction, Emerson writes, is beautiful when seen as the source of new life.

Central to the poem is the speaker's interaction with the parts of nature. At the poem's end, in spite of himself, the speaker interacts with the natural world—he sees the parts of nature around him, inhales the violet's odor, and sees and hears "the rolling river, the morning bird." Consequently, he once again becomes aware of beauty and recognizes that he is a part of "the perfect whole." Emerson seems to be saying here that reason alone is not a sufficient guide for understanding the world of nature and humankind's relationship to that world. The poem is also about human interaction with other humans. At least in part it deals with the idea that the interactions are so extensive that people affect other people of whose lives they are not even aware.

Central to the poem is Emerson's idea that truth often cannot be attained through logical means or even through experience and reflection on experience. In fact, for Emerson, experience is decidedly not the best teacher. Instead, as Emerson writes in work after work, insight or intuition is often a better guide to truth than experience is. Thus, logical processes based on experience lead the narrator of "Each and All" astray. A moment of intuition communicates to him the truth: that beauty and truth are inseparable parts of the unity of nature.

Richard Tuerk

AN EARLY AFTERLIFE

Author: Linda Pastan (1932-   )
Type of poem: Lyric
First published: 1995, in *An Early Afterlife*

The Poem

Linda Pastan's "An Early Afterlife" is a free-verse poem consisting of two twelve-line stanzas. The poem is preceded by an epigraph from Horace, stating that "a wise man in time of peace, shall make the necessary preparations for war." In the poem itself, Pastan transposes the peace-war opposition into an opposition between life and "afterlife," that part of life that occurs—in Pastan's special definition—between official leave-taking and death. In Pastan's analogy, in good years (the time of peace) one should make oneself ready for the bad years of decline and death (war).

The poem begins by asking, "Why don't we say goodbye right now," while life, presumably, is still good. There follow three sentences beginning with the phrase "We could. . . ." Each succeeding sentence describes something advantageous the subject could do if he or she were to say good-bye right now. Point by point, the speaker argues that the good-byes said now could be expressed at leisure, more perfectly, more elegantly, than if they were to occur under forced circumstances.

Yet, in what seems at first like a contradiction, Pastan cites an example of forced good-byes as the example of what she wants. She alludes to the characters in Nevil Shute's 1957 novel *On the Beach* and its 1959 film adaptation, who, on the shores of Australia, await the arrival of a radiation cloud from the hydrogen bombs that have wiped out the rest of the planet's population. These characters, anticipating an imminent death, are able to "perfect [their] parting." They are able to do this, one may infer, because of the critically adjusted time window they have: long enough to say good-bye, but not so long that they let any distractions keep them from saying good-bye.

Most people, it may be supposed, forget about or block out thoughts of eventual death. Life is passing agreeably, mortgages are paid, and children are in school, and humans simply forget about the fact that they will eventually die. It is to these people that Pastan especially addresses herself, arguing that now—before it is absolutely necessary, before it is too late to do it correctly—is the time to say good-bye.

The second stanza describes in detail the afterlife following this proposed perfect good-bye. The arteries start closing down, or the "rampant cells" stampede, as in cancer, but, according to the speaker, it "wouldn't matter." However, "we would bask/ in an early afterlife of ordinary days" because "Nothing could touch us." It is as if, having given the perfect good-bye, having rejected this life by choice, any additional life is a sort of bonus. If one has no expectations, nothing in life can disappoint. Thus, Pastan's poem proposes a hypothetical way to increase the pleasure and diminish the pain of life.

Forms and Devices

The form of the poem strongly reinforces its content. As previously stated, the poem is divided into symmetrical halves. The first twelve lines call for an early good-bye to this life and describe the ideal nature of this good-bye; the second twelve lines describe the afterlife and its imperviousness to tragedy. Thus the poem embodies the life-afterlife division it advocates.

As is her trademark, Pastan devises interesting language to maximize the impact of her ideas. In the second line she alerts us to the "fallacy of perfect health." This suggestive phrase implies that perfect health is an oxymoron, since even the most healthy individual is—from a long-term perspective—dying. In the second stanza, picturing the body's decline, Pastan uses the simile of "arteries closing like rivers silting over" and the metaphor of "rampant cells stampeding us to the exit." One can understand why doctors prefer terms such as "arteriosclerosis" and "inoperable cancer," but Pastan's ability to translate deadly mutations of the body into powerful figures that strike the imagination helps to make this a significant poem. There is an interesting contrast in the two figures mentioned above: The silting river suggests a slow, almost imperceptible danger; the rampant cells suggest panic in a theater. Yet fast or slow, the body's ways of declining are equally deadly.

It is interesting that Pastan's speaker consistently addresses the reader with the pronoun "we," as in the line "Why don't we say goodbye right now." If the speaker had used the pronoun "I" the reader might be likely to dismiss any of the reflections as having personal relevance. If the speaker had used "you" the poem would turn into an obnoxious set of instructions from a disembodied and patronizing superior. However, the consistent use of "we"—it is used eight times in the poem—creates a bond, a closeness, even a tenderness, between speaker and reader. An idea that might be received indifferently, or rejected out of hand, becomes appealing because of this bond, introducing someone who will share the experience with the reader. In fact, the speaker goes so far as to imagine having sat with the reader through the film version of *On the Beach*, holding his or her hand while watching this set of characters say good-bye. Pastan's poem itself creates a similiar experience, reminding readers of their fate but also making that knowledge the catalyst for an instant bond of considerable depth with a similarly fated human being.

Themes and Meanings

The realities of old age and death have depressed many poets, and Pastan ranks among those who have treated this subject extensively, in poems such as "Ethics," "after minor surgery," "November," and "In the Kingdom of Midas." She even wrote a poem, "1932-," which meditates upon seeing her name in print with the birth date denoted and the death date yet to come. One traditional response to eventual demise is *carpe diem*, a Latin term translated as "seize the day." If one will soon grow old, the thinking goes, one should enjoy life now. One of the most well-known poetic examples of this response may be found in Andrew Marvell's "To His Coy Mistress" (1681), in which the speaker implores his mistress to give up her chastity while they are young and full of ardor. "An Early Afterlife" has a different twist: Instead of ignoring decline and death, the poet anticipates it, gets the worst over right away, so to speak, and then, having paid for a sort of insurance policy, can go on living without any specter of evil days to come.

One might look at the parting as being a vaccination, in which a small, but not harmful, dosage of the dread disease is taken into the system, which then produces an antibody, so that when the real thing comes the body can fight it off. In this respect the poem is like A. E. Housman's "Terence, This Is Stupid Stuff" (1896), which ends by retelling the story of Mithridates, King of Pontus, who builds up a tolerance to poison by eating small daily dosages, thus training himself to ingest large quantities without harm when his enemies eventually try to poison him.

Pastan's poem implies that people can have a certain control over the afterlife. Rather than spending life fearing death and what it will bring, one may renounce life and its pleasures and thus have nothing to fear from old age and death. In fact, one may find a special appreciation for the pleasures life offers, undiluted by a backdrop of decline and death, or, as Pastan euphemistically puts it, "the inclement weather/ already in our long-range forecast."

The irony is that Pastan's solution would not actually work in real life—one cannot bypass the evil day, no matter the mental gymnastics used—and the recognition that this is so simply reinforces death's power. On the other hand, poets and other artists have often found a measure of consolation in putting terrible realities into artistic form, as in Pablo Picasso's famous painting *Guernica* (1937). This does not change the reality, but it gives it a certain perspective that makes it more bearable.

Scott E. Moncrieff

EARTH AND I GAVE YOU TURQUOISE

Author: N. Scott Momaday (1934-   )
Type of poem: Elegy
First published: 1972; collected in *Angle of Geese and Other Poems*, 1974

The Poem

   N. Scott Momaday's poem "Earth and I Gave You Turquoise" is an elegy consisting of five sestet stanzas. In this poem, the speaker pays tribute to a deceased love and makes plans to join her in the afterlife. The first stanza establishes the relationship between the speaker, "I," and the subject, "you." Written in the past tense, the opening lines of the poem tell the reader that the happy life experienced by the speaker and the subject ended when the subject became ill. The reader infers that the subject died after becoming "ill when the owl cried." The first stanza reveals the speaker's plans to join his loved one on Black Mountain, most likely her final resting place, the entrance point into the afterlife.

   In stanza 2, the reader learns what will happen when the speaker and subject reunite in the next life. Each with a specific role, they will make a new life together. The speaker "will bring corn for planting," and together they will make a fire, signifying that once again they will have a home. In discussing their new life together, Momaday expands the feminine companion role of the subject in healing the speaker's heart to a maternal one, with children coming to her breast. Attesting to his love for her, the speaker tells his love that not only does he remember her but also does nature, as exemplified by "the wild cane."

   The third stanza shifts the setting to the speaker's brother's house, the scene of sad songs, a place where "we have not spoken of you." This signifies that the family still mourns her loss. It is here, midway through the poem, that the speaker reveals when he plans to join his love on Black Mountain. He will follow the current moon's path, her "white way" as she travels the sky. Separating himself from the present life, having already joined his love in spirit, the speaker tells his love at the close of stanza 4 that "you and I will not be there" for the dancing near Chinle. The reader knows this place to be their former home, for it is here that her "loom whispered beauty." In Native American cultures of the Southwest, particularly the Navajo, women were well known for their weaving, which was an integral part of their lives.

   The speaker's memory of his love is triggered by several places and things within the poem. Even the sight of a crow in a familiar location, Red Rock, reminds him of his love's black hair. However, even though the "years are heavy" for the speaker, he will join his love as a young man on a swift horse. From her place on Black Mountain, the subject will hear the "drumming hooves" of her love's horse as he joins her and they begin a new life together in another world.

Forms and Devices

"Earth and I Gave You Turquoise" has no apparent rhyme scheme and is devoid of any punctuation. Each of the five stanzas is written with the same mixed rhythms. The first four lines of each stanza are pairs of iambic hexameter and iambic pentameter. Each six-line stanza closes with a couplet of iambic hexameter. Places are named, such as Black Mountain, Chinle, and Red Rock, which establish the location of the poem in Navajo country in present-day Arizona. Even though the speaker declares in stanza 2, "I speak your name many times," Momaday does not reveal her name, nor the name of the speaker's brother, nor the children who come to the subject's breast. As with the naming of the landscape, the moon is treated with the personification of "Moon Woman."

There is marked significance to line 3 of each stanza. In stanzas 1 and 3, the subject of the third line is "we" with a different collective subject. The "we" of stanza 1 is the speaker and the object of the poem, his lost love. The line "We lived laughing in my house" tells the reader that they were married. In stanza 3 however, the "we" is composed of the speaker and those gathered in his brother's house. "We have not spoken of you" is a signifier of the cultural custom of not mentioning aloud the name of a deceased family member. This practice is symbolic of one of the ways in which many American Indian societies honor the dead. In stanzas 2, 4, and 5, line 3 reveals something about the "you" to whom the speaker refers. Respectively, Momaday uses "your breast," "your loom," and "your hair" in the middle of these stanzas as he continues to describe the woman who is the object of this elegiac poem.

The beauty of "Earth and I Gave You Turquoise" lies in its implied action. The reader can only surmise the speaker's intentions and actions through Momaday's magnificent use of words and cultural symbols. Signifiers of Native American culture in the Southwest within the poem are turquoise, which comes from the sacred earth; the loom, which whispers beauty; mutton, which is part of a festive gathering; and the old stories the lovers tell together.

Momaday has the speaker indicate his intentions to join his dead love in the last line of stanza 1, "We will meet on Black Mountain." He lets the reader know when this is to take place at the end of stanza 3: "When Moon Woman goes to you/ I will follow her white way." Finally, the reader finds out how the speaker intends to carry out his plan to join his love in the last lines of the poem. Whether or not he really rides the swiftest horse to Black Mountain is known only to Momaday, the speaker, and his love, as well as to the reader, who will perhaps also hear the drumming hooves of his horse.

Themes and Meanings

The first line of this poem, which is also the title, "Earth and I gave you turquoise," lets the reader know the value of the relationship and hints at the geographical location of the setting. In the American Southwest, turquoise is a highly valued stone, often combined with silver in beautiful adornments. In some southwestern Native American cultures, such as the Zuni, the god of turquoise followed his wife, the goddess of salt, to a new location, leaving behind turquoise footsteps in the desert. Historically, turquoise was valued not only for its beauty but also for its trade value.

As with much Native American literature, time does not play a crucial role in this poem except to inform the reader that the years since the subject's death weigh heavily on the speaker. His family, on the other hand, although their songs are sad, are preparing to dance. This is a sign that only the speaker remains deep in mourning, reaffirming that he has lost his life companion.

Momaday uses key words and phrases to establish the past, present, and future mood for the speaker of this poem. For example, in stanza 1, the reader learns that the speaker's life and times together with his love were pleasant. The use of the words "singing" and "laughing" are indicators of a happier time, when the speaker shared his life with the subject. The mood of stanzas 2 and 3 is one of overwhelming sadness in the present, as the reader becomes aware of the speaker's broken heart. "Our songs are sad," recites the speaker, and yet there is hope when he says, "You will heal my heart." This mood of hope is in the future, in a time when the speaker will be joining his love in the afterlife on Black Mountain.

While the reader knows that the speaker's family also mourns her loss because they do not speak her name, they are ready to move into a more festive time as they prepare to dance, "eat mutton/ and drink coffee till morning." Momaday removes the speaker from the present—"You and I will not be there"—placing him with the subject at the end of stanza 4. In stanza 5, the reader experiences the difficult time of the "heavy" years for the speaker without his love and also feels a sense of relief in the closing two lines of the poem. Closing the poem in the future tense, Momaday leaves the speaker, his love, and the reader on a positive emotional plane. The lovers not only are reunited on Black Mountain but also return to the beauty and excitement of their youth as the speaker rides "the swiftest horse" and his love hears "the drumming hooves" as he approaches her.

Susan Dominguez

EASTER 1916

Author: William Butler Yeats (1865-1939)
Type of poem: Lyric
First published: 1920, in *Michael Robartes and the Dancer*

The Poem

"Easter 1916" is a poem of four stanzas, with sixteen lines in the first and third, and twenty-four lines in the second and fourth. One of William Butler Yeats's best-known political poems, it was written shortly after the Irish Republican uprising against the British government in April of 1916, although it was not published until 1920. "Easter 1916" is one of several poems that Yeats composed during the Irish national struggle against the English, which lasted until an independent Irish state was created in 1922.

In a first-person voice that conveys Yeats's personal beliefs, the opening stanza confesses disillusionment with a shallow existence before the Easter uprising. Dublin is a "motley" place centered in the past and the "grey/ Eighteenth-century houses" refer to the last time that Ireland had its own parliament. The future revolutionaries are dismissed with "polite meaningless words" and made fun of "around the fire at the club." The stanza concludes with the ominous yet thrilling discovery that, because of the uprising, "All changed, changed utterly:/ A terrible beauty is born." This phrase, with some variation, becomes a refrain for the poem.

The second stanza describes the history and character of several of the rebels, though not identifying them by name. Yeats's contemporaries would have recognized Countess Constance Markiewicz, a childhood friend from County Sligo, the schoolmaster Patrick Pearse, and John MacBride, the husband of Maud Gonne, Yeats's own great love. With their varied accomplishments and failings, all were "transformed utterly" by their Easter sacrifice.

In the third stanza, Yeats contemplates the single-mindedness of the rebels, those "Hearts with one purpose alone." A stone metaphorically represents those who refuse to sacrifice their ideals to the "living stream." Maud Gonne many years before had referred to herself as a stone in her refusal to marry Yeats, claiming that she could not surrender her political mission in order to lead an ordinary life. As symbols of the transitory nature of such a life, the horses and riders, clouds and streams, moor-cocks and moor-hens of the third stanza live "minute by minute," but "The stone's in the midst of all," unchanged and immovable.

In the final stanza, Yeats notes the possible results of such commitment and dedication. He fears that "Too long a sacrifice/ Can make a stone of the heart," intimating that the purpose that drove the martyrs may have "bewildered" them as well. Perhaps the English would have granted freedom without the bloodshed of the Easter rising; all that can be known is that "they dreamed and are dead." It remains for those who survive to chronicle the effect of their dreams, "To murmur name upon name":

"I write it out in a verse—/ MacDonagh and MacBride/ And Connolly and Pearse." Their deaths changed the course of Irish history by uniting the country in the fight for independence; the dead men, "Wherever green is worn/ Are changed, changed utterly:/ A terrible beauty is born."

Forms and Devices

"Easter 1916" is one of Yeats's most popular and often quoted poems; its subject matter—the revolt of the rebels and their resulting martyrdom—is inspiring and accessible. Yeats gives the poem a balladlike quality, telling the story conversationally while exploring his feelings about it. Written in irregular meter with alternate rhyming lines, "Easter 1916" lacks the poetic artifices of many of Yeats's other poems; it has few complex images or metaphors.

Yeats uses his interest in myth and folktales to create a modern myth from recent history. He recognized the event's transcendent significance; although most Irish had initially disapproved of the rebels, public opinion swiftly rallied when the British sentenced them to death. While the executions were taking place, Yeats wrote that "I feel that all the work of years has been overturned, all the bringing together of classes, all the freeing of Irish literature and criticism from politics." Revolutionary politics returned with a vengeance.

Yeats also drew on his own experience; he knew many of the rebels and, in the poem reveals his own doubts and antipathies to them and their cause. They serve as symbols of a certain type of driven personality, and he exposes the contradictions between their dreams and their characters. Countess Markiewicz, whose "ignorant good-will" made "her voice grow shrill," epitomizes the upper classes' patronizing sense of *noblesse oblige*. Pearse, the revolutionary schoolteacher, was an intellectual playing at romantic violence who allowed his belief in heroic Irish myths, "the wingèd horse," to alienate him from ordinary life. MacBride, Maud Gonne's estranged husband, for whom Yeats had only disgust and envy, is portrayed as "a drunken, vainglorious lout." Yeats questions their motives and characters, but he also examines his own contradictory feelings of doubt and admiration.

These conflicting thoughts are reflected in Yeats's use of colors. Dublin is "grey" before the Easter uprising; it is a "motley" world, mixed and heterogeneous, lacking in noble ideals. Afterward, the grey and motley are replaced by a single hue of green, representing the renewed and unified spirit of the people. Green is the national color of Ireland and a universal symbol of spring; in the poem, it represents the resurrection of Ireland. A subtle contradiction remains, however, for the ubiquitous use of green by strident nationalists had made it also a symbol of decadence rather than renewal. In his color imagery, Yeats implies that the changes wrought by the uprising were a mixed blessing.

The stone imagery continues these contradictions, as Yeats weighs the achievements of the revolt against the costs. In contrasting the rebels' stonelike steadfastness with the "living stream" which changes "minute by minute," Yeats indicates a reluctant admiration for their dedication; the permanence of their cause contrasts with the transitory nature of ordinary life. Yet Yeats also warns that the revolutionaries risk a loss of their own humanity, allowing their hearts to harden to stone.

The result is that—as the poem's refrain reminds the reader—"A terrible beauty is born," an oxymoron deriving its power from the obvious contrast between the terms. The Easter uprising was terrible because "not night but death" awaited the rebels and many innocent victims, a "needless death" if England would have granted independence without the violence of 1916. There was nevertheless a transforming beauty that took the rebels, and perhaps many others, out of their lives of "casual comedy" into the tragic drama of life.

Themes and Meanings

There are two interrelated themes in "Easter 1916," one political and public, the other personal and private. The poem is based on a historic event: A small group of Irish rebels, under the leadership of Patrick Pearse and James Connolly, led an armed uprising against British rule despite the fact that even the rebels themselves knew they would fail. In spite of the rebellion being crushed by British troops within a week, "a terrible beauty [was] born"; the executions of the leaders made them martyrs and unified the nation in the fight for independence. The poem also explores Yeats's personal response to the failed rebellion and to the costs of such sacrifice.

Yeats was pessimistic about the character of his countrymen. In "September 1913" he complained that "Romantic Ireland's dead and gone," replaced by greed and superficial piety. The first stanza of "Easter 1916" makes the same charges, accusing the rebels—who lead safe lives behind "counter or desk"—of lacking the stature to restore Ireland's revolutionary drive. In proving themselves willing to die for their beliefs, however, the rebels succeeded in reuniting the nation, and Yeats had to grant them grudging admiration for their commitment to their dreams. Their common lives became heroic inspiration.

If MacDonagh, MacBride, Connolly, and Pearse had been "transformed utterly," Yeats's own feelings were more ambivalent. The rebels had become martyrs for Ireland; their courage was not in doubt, and the poem recognizes their accomplishments. Nor did Yeats dismiss their impact on the future. He does question the costs of the Easter rebellion, however, wondering if the same results could have been achieved without the bloodshed. The rebels, in their Easter rising, as symbolic as it is in a Christian sense, paid a price that was perhaps too great. Death is final—"No, no, not night but death"—and Yeats laments what was lost by those deaths in his discussion of one of the rebels: "He might have won fame in the end,/ So sensitive his nature seemed/ So daring and sweet his thought." The poem's refrain, the "terrible beauty" of the uprising, is made even more moving by Yeats's refusal to resolve its ambiguity; one never knows whether it is the beauty or the terror that is triumphant. In "Easter 1916," one feels Yeats's own awe and trembling in the face of this event.

Eugene Larson

EASTER 1984

Author: Les A. Murray (1938-   )
Type of poem: Lyric
First published: 1987, in *The Daylight Moon*

The Poem

"Easter 1984" is a short lyric on the subject of the role of Jesus Christ and Christianity in human history. The first section of the poem evokes the crucifixion of Christ. Christ is referred to in the first couplet as "human dignity," the humanity of the Savior healing people "in the middle of the day"—not only referring to the time of day but also meaning in the open rather than in secret.

The second couplet relates humankind's hostile, uncomprehending response to Jesus' generosity: "we moved in on him slowly," too used to old systems of law, vengeance, and the strange mixture of anarchy and retribution that is at the root of purely human systems of justice: "If this was God, we would get even." The Crucifixion, it is implied, was an act of fear, of humans fearing their own potential, fearing the opportunities that Christ's healing would have brought them. Christ's dual divine-human nature redeems humankind, yet humankind fears being redeemed, wanting instead to continue the normal state of affairs. "We'd send it to be abstract again," the poem says, suggesting that by crucifying Jesus humankind had made divinity once again abstract, loosed it from being incarnated in humanity. Therefore, a hesitant and uncomprehending humankind falsely feels liberated.

However, as the second section of the poem suggests, this was not the end of the story. The killing of Christ did not extinguish the qualities he brought to the world. "It would not stop being human"; in other words, the divinity did not totally fade from humankind. Christ's gifts were now a permanent part of the human character. Eventually, this process of evolution will result in humankind's total redemption and the fading of the need ever to torture or kill anyone again.

The third stanza is the most difficult of the poem. "The day when life increased" is Easter—the first Easter, the day of Christ's resurrection. On Easter, human life attained an unprecedented dignity, became "haloed in poignancy." For once, the guards, who usually arrest people, were themselves arrested, and human liberty and potential were at last released. The lines "Four have been this human/ night and day, steadily" refer to the four canonical Gospels of Matthew, Mark, Luke, and John, through which the message of Christ has been communicated. "Three fell, two went on" refers to the historical fortunes of the religion Christ founded. As the Christian church grew, five principal patriarchates, where the main leaders of the church lived, were established. These were located in Antioch, Alexandria, Jerusalem, Constantinople, and Rome. Three of these cities fell to Islam in the seventh century, but two, Constantinople and Rome, "went on," yielding today's Eastern Orthodox Church and Roman Catholic Church, respectively. The poet then refers to the Shroud of Turin, once thought to be an actual relic of the Crucifixion but found unauthentic through a scientific laser probe. The implication is that if the shroud had been real, the laser would have revealed what Christians know already: that Christ made human dignity no longer something to be futilely strived for but an essential part of human identity.

Forms and Devices

The poem is written in three sections of seven couplets each. Les Murray's choice of a couplet form is unusual, because in English this mode of versification is usually associated with satire. Perhaps Murray was influenced by the ghazal, an Urdu poetic form whose couplets have a generally spiritual and lofty tone. Also, unlike the traditional English couplet, the lines of "Easter 1984" do not rhyme directly; at most they are linked by a sort of off-rhyme that does not intrude upon the reader. Off-rhymes such as "dignity" and "day" at the beginning of the first section, "again" and "risen" in the last couplet of the first section, or "human" and "on" in the fourth couplet of the third section are very close in sound even though they do not completely rhyme. Alternately, there are some true rhymes such as "him" and "limb" in the fifth couplet of the first section, as well as one instance (increased/poignancy/ecstasy/released) at the beginning of the third section where there is an *abba* rhyme scheme stretched across two couplets. Sometimes these almost-rhymes have definite undertones of meaning, as in "forgotten" and "human" in the last couplet of the poem, where the first word represents a deprivation that is healed by the second.

It is not symbol-hunting in a Christian poem to hypothesize that the three sections of the poem allude to the Holy Trinity. (Equally, the couplet form could be expressing the dual divine-human nature of Christ.) The "O" placed at the beginning of each of the last two sections is also worthy of note. "O" traditionally begins an invocation or prayer in Christian worship. It is a call, whether it be a call to God, to Christ, or to the speaker's fellow worshippers. It is not only the meaning but also the verbal shape of the "O" that matters. "O" connotes roundness, a kind of perfection, much as God is perfect and is as inaccessible to human reason as a circle is to purely rectilinear geometry. In this way, the poem can suggest the fullness of God even though, as an imperfect verbal artifact, it cannot completely convey it. Murray thus joins much earlier Christian poets in English such as George Herbert in using the shape of a poem to aid him in fashioning his sacral verse.

The diction of the poem is an interesting mixture of traditional religious language and colloquial speech. Murray is not afraid to make allusions that puzzle the reader, as with the different numbers (four, then the seemingly incompatible three and two) in the third section, or to be unabashedly sentimental. "Human," drastically overexposed as an adjective, gains new force from the way Murray explores the willingness of many humans to disallow any sense of divinity in their ideas of humanity.

Themes and Meanings

"Easter 1984" is at once a traditional devotional poem and a departure from the mainstream of religious poetry as it was written for much of the twentieth century.

Most of this poetry, as typified by the work of T. S. Eliot or W. H. Auden, starts from a position of alienation or despair and then reaches a position suggesting wholeness or redemption. Murray, on the other hand, starts from the position that Christ's victory has already been won and that the task of humanity is to understand the nature and terms of this victory.

The Easter theme is explicitly elaborated in the poem, but why is it titled "Easter 1984"? Murray may simply have written the poem in 1984, but there seem to be larger reverberations. To most "literary" readers, "1984" is most likely to suggest George Orwell's novel of that name (published in 1949), which depicts a Soviet-style totalitarian system in which Christianity, or any religion, has no place. Murray, writing from the vantage point of the "real" 1984, does not have so pessimistic a vision. Christianity, though hardly triumphant, has persisted and endured. This is the thrust of the mysterious "Three fell, two went on" line, which expands the poem from a consideration of the Crucifixion as such to include the course of Christian history. By going into the historic fate of humanity's belief in Christ, Murray includes both the defeats and victories of Christianity on the worldly level.

Murray is a convert to Roman Catholicism, but this poem seems less an extension or application of religious dogma—which, characteristically, the zeal of the convert poet might produce—than an expression of religious feeling. Murray wishes to bear witness to the beauty and majesty of Christ's resurrection, not to castigate those who are indifferent to it. His treatment of the theme of "humanity" is crucial. Human nature—human "meanness," for lack of a better word—is what makes people refuse the challenge of the redemption Christ offers them. At the end Christ's love becomes "the baseline of the human" instead of being completely above the here-and-now. Christianity is a higher humanism, so it can still have relevance to humankind, just as Murray's references have made clear that Christianity is a force in human history as well as spirituality.

Murray's Australian nationality may contribute to his unusually forceful exposition of the Christian theme. Unlike the United States, so long ideologically anchored by the Puritan vision of the "New Jerusalem," Australia has had no founding or sustaining religious myth. Against this background, the function of religious poetry is somewhat different. Although Murray is very much his own person as a poet and should not be considered a part of a general Australian trend, his preference for testifying to Christ's glory rather than proclaiming the authority of his dogma may well reflect his nationality.

Nicholas Birns

EASTER MORNING

Author: A. R. Ammons (1926-2001)
Type of poem: Meditation
First published: 1981, in *A Coast of Trees*

The Poem

The title of "Easter Morning" refers not only to the Easter-morning walk taken near the end of the poem but also to the spiritual and seasonal renewal that the phrase suggests. The "letter-perfect" Easter morning of the poem comes when the poem shifts from what seems to be a dead end of insurmountable incompletions to a scene in nature that suggests a renewal and rebirth.

The speaker of the poem is clearly the poet himself; A. R. Ammons usually writes in his own voice, and his repeated subject is nature and its processes. "Easter Morning" begins with a startling declaration: "I have a life that did not become/ that turned aside and stopped,/ astonished." Ammons compares it to a "pregnancy" or a child "on my lap" that did not grow. It is the potential life that he might have lived, the path he might have taken, or perhaps the child he left behind when he grew up and began to think and act as an adult. He returns to the "grave" of this child that is within him and will die with him; the grave "will not heal." The grave is an end, not a new beginning or an answer to his dilemma.

He returns to his "home country" and finds a similar "return" that also will not heal. He returns to visit all of his uncles and aunts, and his mother and father. The closeness between them is movingly expressed; they are as close as "burrowing under skin." They are, however, "all in the graveyard/ assembled, done for, the world they/ used to wield, have trouble and joy/ in, gone." The pattern repeats itself; there is another "return" and another grave, another finality. There seems to be no way out.

The next part of the poem brings child and parents together in a kind of summation and evaluation. "The child in me that could not become" was not ready for the others to go, to change. That child seems to wish for an impossible stasis of his world; it is attractive to imagine such a world, but to do so is to deny every movement and process of nature on which Ammons has written so precisely over the years. Now the failure to overcome the destruction of change makes his life and world seem filled with negatives. All that he has are "incompletions," not "completions, not rondures the fullness/ has come into." There are "knots of horror" that cannot be undone.

Suddenly, the poem changes direction. It is a "picture-book, letter-perfect/ Easter morning," the "wind is tranquil: the brook/ works without flashing in an abundant/ tranquility." Above all, the speaker observes "two great birds/ maybe eagles" in their flight, and he sees "something I had never seen before." The eagles fly together for a while and one bird deviates from his route; the other one "seeming/ not to notice for a minute." The wayward eagle then comes back and they are rejoined. The speaker explains the significance: "the having/ patterns and routes, breaking/ from them to explore other patterns or/ better ways to routes, and then the/ return." This return, in contrast to that of the "child within me that died" and to the family in his home country, does heal. Routes can be both varied and returned to.

Forms and Devices

"Easter Morning" is written in free verse and is divided into verse paragraphs. It is true free verse; there is no syllabic pattern, and there are many run-on lines. The lines are usually short, and at times Ammons isolates one word as a line of verse. Ammons also ignores conventional grammar; there are few periods, and sometimes a sentence runs over a whole verse paragraph. He tends to use the colon as a way of separating sections, ignoring other conventions of punctuation. There is considerable repetition, especially of key words such as "return." The verse paragraphs are divided into separate parts, and the poem itself is also clearly divided into three parts. There is a section on the child who died, a section on the speaker's return to his "home country," and the climactic appearance of the eagles on Easter morning.

The most important device in the poem is the pattern of imagery. The first and second parts of the poem are filled with such negative images as the "stump/ of a child," the "grave," "knots," "incompletions." Even nature seems dead. The reader sees the barrenness of the air and the "flash high-burn/ momentary structure of ash." In contrast, there are images of tranquillity in the "wind," the "brook/ works," and "the birds are lively with voice." There is also the closeness of the family, which is seen as "burrowing under skin," but it is contrasted with the finality of "gone."

Another important technique used by Ammons is paradox. A group of paradoxes mirrors the incompletions he has found and cannot overcome. He cannot leave this place, which is "the dearest and the worst," "nearest to life which is/ life lost"; here he must "stand and fail." Ammons does not show how these paradoxes can be resolved, but he does provide an alternative to them with the eagles at the end of the poem.

The most important symbolic aspect of the poem is the two eagles. Their flight, which breaks from the established route, manages to recover and return successfully, something neither the child nor the family in the "home country" could do. Nature clearly shows Ammons a way out of the "incompletions." The natural images of the last part of the poem support the dazzling return and rejoining of the two eagles. It is as "permanent in its descriptions/ as the ripples round the brook's/ ripplestone: fresh as this particular/ flood of burn breaking across us now/ from the sun." The permanence of nature seems to be an answer to the human dilemmas the poet failed to overcome earlier. It is seen as a visible annual renewal; it is never incomplete or exhausted, and it is constantly changing.

Themes and Meanings

The theme of change is one of the most interesting aspects of the poem. Ammons presents a world from the point of view of a child who cannot change or grow. The child is seeking a stasis and sameness that is very comforting, but this is only a fantasy. A world without change would be a dead or frozen one, a parody of the real world. It would be, literally, a childish world. Nature must change; change is the law of its being. The human cannot remain a child, and the family cannot be there for solace and sustenance.

Another central theme is the return. The first two returns in the poem lead to dead ends; the one dealing with the eagles clearly is possible and fulfilling. It is a symbol of the workings of nature. One of the eagles returns to what it has abandoned and rejoins the one it has left. The choice of another direction or route need not be final; the past and the present, the original position and the new discovery, can be united.

There remains a question about the final meaning of the poem. Nature clearly is capable of renewing itself. The seasonal growth, decay, death, and rebirth of nature show that. Ammons offers a symbol of two eagles as a way of overcoming the problem of the return; he does not, however, say anything about humans. Humankind differs from nature; a human being's death cannot be renewed without an afterlife. People leave the children within them behind, and those they love will die and not return. The example of the eagles does not overcome this finality or provide a way out of the dead end.

There is a suggestion of renewal, however, in placing the climactic part of the poem on Easter morning. It is natural to associate the idea of rebirth and renewal with Easter; in addition, the speaker does not seem to be downcast at the end of the poem. The eagles point a way to renewal that is echoed by nature.

One other theme that needs comment is the tradition of the child in literature. William Wordsworth, whose approach is close to but different from that of Ammons, portrays the child as close to nature or God. He sees the growth from child to adult as a beneficial one, since the human being moves from an animal approach to nature to a moral and spiritual one. Ammons gives the child no special characteristics; his child's only demand is that everything remain the same. This is much closer to the true nature of a child than Wordsworth's attempt to add spiritual and philosophical significance.

James Sullivan

EASTER WINGS

Author: George Herbert (1593-1633)
Type of poem: Lyric
First published: 1633, in *The Temple*

The Poem

George Herbert's "Easter Wings" is a celebration of Christ's resurrection, which is presented as the means by which humankind overcomes sin and attains freedom. The poem consists of two ten-line stanzas of varying line lengths, which in their printed form on the page resemble the wings of a bird.

The poem is addressed directly to God or Christ ("Lord"). The first stanza begins by emphasizing how complete humankind was when first created by God. People had "wealth and store," meaning that they were created in the image of God and were meant to preside over the natural world, which existed only to serve them. They had everything they needed, in abundance.

In line 2, the poet points out that humankind lost its wealth. This is a reference to the Fall of Man described in the book of Genesis, a doctrine that is an essential part of the Christian faith. This line also emphasizes that the Fall was the result of human foolishness, a reference to Adam and Eve's disobedience of God's instructions not to eat of the fruit on the tree of the knowledge of good and evil in the Garden of Eden. The blame for humanity's loss of its original "wealth" therefore lies not with God but with people. As a result of the Fall, as line 3 shows, the human condition deteriorated. Humans "fell" further and further into sin, continually "decaying" from their original purity, until they reached the lowest point in their fortunes ("Most poore").

In line 6, the poet begins his request that he may be allowed to rise again with the resurrected Christ, who was sent by God to save humanity. The reference is to the Christian belief that after Christ had been crucified, he rose from the dead three days later. The poet asks that he may rise like a lark and sing of how Christ has vanquished death. The last line of the first stanza, "Then shall the fall further the flight in me," refers to the Christian notion of the Fortunate Fall. If it had not been for the Fall, there would have been no need for salvation, and so no need for the incarnation of Christ as human. Because of the greatness of the Redeemer, humans are therefore better off than they would have been had they not sinned.

Stanza 1 began with a general statement about humans' first disobedience; in stanza 2, the poet makes this statement personal. Like all men, the poet was born into sin, so even as a child his life was full of sorrow. God punished him with sickness and shame for his sins until he became "most thinne." The two-word line 15— "Most thinne"—parallels the "Most poore" of stanza 1, but it is applied to the personal life of the poet rather than to humankind as a whole. As in stanza 1, the lines then get longer, and the poet requests that he be allowed to join with Christ and so participate in Christ's victory over death. To convey this idea he uses a term from falconry; to "imp" means to engraft feathers in the damaged wing of a bird to enable it to fly again. If the poet is able to "imp" his "wing" with that of God, "Affliction shall advance the flight in me." This line is similar in meaning to the final line of stanza 1. The poet says that all his sufferings will have had a purpose and will even have advanced his spiritual progress.

Forms and Devices

"Easter Wings" is in the tradition of pattern poetry, also known as shaped verse, in which the lines are arranged on the printed page so that they in some way illustrate the subject of the poem. Herbert wrote other pattern poems, including "The Altar," in which the printed words are shaped like an altar. The device has been used by many other poets, including such modern poets as Dylan Thomas in "Vision and Prayer."

Since "Easter Wings" is set in the spring and contains a simile in which human spiritual freedom is compared to the lark singing in the morning, the arrangement of each stanza in the shape of two wings of a bird is thematically appropriate. The poet gains another thematic resonance from this pattern because the shorter lines refer to humanity's most cramped, afflicted state. Just as humanity has squandered its wealth, the poet too has only the fewest of words at his disposal and must make whole lines out of "Most poore" and "Most thinne." Then the lines lengthen as the wings begin to beat and the soul expands in freedom, like the wider wingspan of a bird in flight.

In early editions of *The Temple*, the lines of "Easter Wings" were arranged vertically rather than horizontally on the page. When this is done, the pattern of birds' wings becomes even more visually striking since the words cannot be read; the pattern is all the reader sees.

The rhyme scheme of the poem is the same in both stanzas and can be represented as *ababacdcdc*. This means that line 1 rhymes with lines 3 and 5 (*a*); line 2 rhymes with line 4 (*b*); line 6 rhymes with lines 8 and 10 (*c*); and line 7 rhymes with line 9 (*d*). The enclosing of the poem in this regular rhyme scheme conveys a sense of structure and order and reinforces the idea that the universe and humankind are under divine protection, even though humans have sinned and suffered. The splitting of the rhymes into the two distinct halves of the stanza is appropriate for the theme, since the first half of each stanza describes humanity's sin and loss and the second half describes salvation through Christ.

In the last line of each stanza the poet also makes use of alliteration to drive home the idea of the Fortunate Fall. In the last line of stanza 1, the triple repetition of the consonant *f* in "fall further the flight," reinforces the meaning by linking the fall to the redemption through Christ; the latter would not have been possible without the former. A similar idea is conveyed in the last line of the poem, in the alliteration of the two consonants *fl* contained in "affliction" and "flight"; this creates at the level of sound the link between suffering and liberation that the sense of the line conveys.

The inspiration for much of the imagery of "Easter Wings" is biblical. The central image, of the soul compared to a bird ascending in flight, has several examples in scripture. Isaiah 40:31 for example, reads, "They that wait upon the Lord . . . shall mount up with wings as eagles"; Malachi 4:2 states, "unto you that fear my name shall the Sun of righteousness arise with healing in his wings."

Themes and Meanings

"Easter Wings" is the work of a poet who accepted the truths of the Christian religion with piety, reverence, and humility. Often in Herbert's work this attitude of quiet acceptance finds expression in poetry that is at once simple in theme and subtly inventive in poetic style and form. This combination makes Herbert not only one of England's finest devotional poets but also one of its most admired metaphysical poets.

Although the typographical form of "Easter Wings" is unusual, its theme is not. Central to the poem is the Christian belief that humans were born into the paradise of the Garden of Eden, that they sinned, and that because of this first failure every human is born in a state of Original Sin. God continues to punish humanity because of sin, but humans are redeemed through the saving death of Christ, the Son of God. Humans cannot save themselves by their own efforts. Left to their own devices, they will sink deeper and deeper into sin; they need divine aid. When people sincerely call on God, it does not matter how low they have previously sunk, how far they have fallen from the original perfection. Their souls can soar once again if they are joined with Christ.

Within the orthodox Christian framework, the main theme of "Easter Wings" is that of the Fortunate Fall. This is a common Christian idea. It is found, for example, in the Catholic Latin mass recited at Easter: "*O felix culpa quae talem et tantum meruit habere redemptorum,*" which means, "O blessed sin, which received as its reward so great and so good a Redeemer." The same idea is found in John Milton's epic poem *Paradise Lost* (1667, 1674). When Adam learns of the divine plan he says, "O goodness infinite, goodness immense!/ That all this good of evil shall produce,/ And evil turn to good; more wonderful/ Than that which by creation first brought forth/ Light out of darkness!"

The idea is that humans are better off as a result of the outpouring of divine grace that occurred when God sent Christ to save the world than they would ever have been had they remained without sin in the Garden of Eden. The Fortunate Fall does not mean that it was or is a good thing to commit sin, since sin brought suffering into the world. The point is that God was able to use the fact of human sin to bring forth his plan of salvation, which is something even greater than the creation of the world. Therefore sin was necessary, since the Fall that occurred as a result of it was a necessary precondition for the movement of grace in human history.

Bryan Aubrey

EATING POETRY

Author: Mark Strand (1934-   )
Type of poem: Lyric
First published: 1968, in *Reasons for Moving*

The Poem

"Eating Poetry" is a short poem in free verse, its eighteen lines divided into six stanzas. The title suggests either comedy or surrealism, and the poem contains elements of both. Mark Strand uses the first person to create a persona whose voice is Strand's but whose experience is imaginary; indeed, the fact that the poem is a work of imagination is the main point.

The story of "Eating Poetry" is simple enough. The speaker is in a library, where he is eating, not reading, poetry. After he has eaten "The poems," the speaker is confronted by a librarian, and dogs start on their way up from the basement; the speaker himself begins to behave like a dog. Eating the poetry seems to have changed the speaker.

The first sentence of the poem's opening stanza carries the reader into a strange world. Not only is eating poetry an unlikely (even surreal) activity, but Strand's description of the immediate physical result is also extraordinary. The ink in books of poetry is not usually runny, but if one can eat poetry, strange things may happen. "Eating Poetry" begins with an image confirming the title: "Ink runs from the corners of my mouth." The image plays on the familiar metaphor "a voracious reader," which suggests a hungry consumer of books. Strand takes the idea of consuming poetry literally. Instead of simply reading poetry voraciously, the speaker is actually eating it—and enjoying it.

The speaker's childlike happiness in the first stanza is interrupted by the appearance of the librarian in the second stanza. Like the reader who may feel disoriented by the events in the poem, the incredulous librarian "does not believe what she sees." Her sad eyes contrast sharply with the happiness of the narrator. In the third stanza, the focus of the poem shifts slightly from the speaker and the librarian to the setting. "The poems are gone," and "The light is dim." A pack of dogs is on its way up from the basement. By mentioning "the basement stairs," Strand gives a detail that almost gives plausibility to the poem's events.

The fourth stanza describes the dogs, which have rolling eyeballs and "blond legs" that "burn like brush." The librarian, a woman, becomes agitated. The speaker's having eaten the poems seems somehow to have unleashed the dogs from the basement of the library, or from the speaker's mind. When, in the fourth stanza, the librarian—again, perhaps like the reader—"does not understand," the speaker behaves like a dog himself and licks her hand, which makes her scream.

By the end of the poem, the speaker has been transformed into "a new man," one who behaves like an excited dog. The lights have apparently completely gone out, so no one can read, but the speaker, doglike, romps with joy.

Forms and Devices

"Eating Poetry" is based on such simple statements and such straightforward language that its mysteriousness is hard to pin down, but it is precisely these simple statements in ordinary language that create the surrealistic atmosphere of the poem. Taken together with the title, the first sentence describes an implausible cause and effect. After that sentence, nothing in the poem is impossible. Each sentence in isolation makes perfect sense and describes a strange, but hardly impossible, situation. The strangeness of the poem, which rests in neither sentence structure nor diction, is the strangeness of imagination.

The free verse of "Eating Poetry" uses the rhythm of subject-verb-object sentence structure. "Eating Poetry" has no adverbs, few adjectives, and only the simplest verbs. Forms of "to be" are the most commonly used verbs in the poem. The lines are of unequal length, and the poem is not particularly musical in its sound effects.

Surrealism can be explained as a style of art—whether painting, literature, or music—in which things happen that defy the laws of physics. Ink dribbling from the mouth of someone who has eaten poems is a surrealistic image. Surrealist works often have much in common with dreams; in dreams, time and space operate by a different logic than that of one's waking hours. Indeed, perhaps it is best not to categorize Strand's poem as surrealism, but to think of it as a kind of a dream.

"Eating Poetry" contains no difficult or unusual vocabulary. The simple diction and sentence structure give the poem a childlike quality, and at the same time an assertive voice. Like events in a dream, the events of the poem happen one by one, and the speaker never explains the connections between them. The sentences that make up the poem are so straightforward that they can hardly be paraphrased; to paraphrase them is to be tempted to augment them to explain causes and effects which the poem does not explain. Are the lights dim and the dogs on their way because the speaker has eaten poetry, or because "The poems are gone"? The poem's simple sentences do not say.

Strand uses the definite article to identify "the poems" and "the dogs" as if they were specific, but he never says what poems he ate or what kind of dogs are coming up from the basement. Because the poems are gone by the third stanza, the implication is that the speaker has eaten all the poems in the library.

Perfect rhymes appear in only two places—"understand" and "hand" in the fifth stanza, and "bark" and "dark" in the last two lines of the poem. These rhymes emphasize two important points in the poem. The climax of this poem occurs when the speaker licks the librarian's hand, which he recognizes she does not understand. In the end, poetry is as wild and as ambiguous as the dog's joyous bark in the dark.

Themes and Meanings

"Eating Poetry" is a poem about imagination. Everything in it is imaginary. It uses commonplace notions about the readers of poetry and librarians to dramatize the waywardness of imagination. Librarians are supposed to maintain order, and poetry readers are supposed to be harmless people. Strand wants the reader to see that poetry may be dangerous: To consume it is to run the risk of being transformed.

The poem takes place in imagination. Poets and readers of poetry live by imagination. Poems do not only yield "meaning," they also offer experiences. Like a reader with limited expectations for poetry, the librarian "does not believe what she sees" and "does not understand" the speaker's transformation. Her bewilderment elicits more and more doglike behavior from the speaker, until he licks her hand.

Because poetry is generous, the speaker understands the librarian better than she understands him. The speaker's licking the librarian's hand is a gentle act of communication from a dog, but from a man—who should be able to use words to explain himself—the action is so bizarre it makes the imaginary librarian scream.

Like the speaker licking the librarian's hand, "Eating Poetry" arouses the senses. From dripping ink to snarling and romping dogs, poems are more than simple information that librarians can maintain between the covers of books for orderly reference. One of the most striking images in the poem is that of the dogs with rolling eyeballs and "blond legs" that "burn like brush." The idea of the dogs' legs burning suggests that poetry incites the imagination with disturbing images. This image may unsettle the reader just as the librarian is unsettled when the dogs from the basement of the speaker's imagination arrive and he himself becomes doglike.

"Eating Poetry," however, does not take itself too seriously. It would be a mistake to miss the poem's humor. The speaker does not become a tiger. His mouth drips ink, not blood. Poetry transforms him, but into an unruly domestic creature rather than into a powerful violent animal. Even though he may "snarl and bark" at the librarian, the speaker has sympathy for her. He recognizes her feelings from her face ("She does not believe what she sees") and refers to her as "The poor librarian."

In the third stanza, halfway through the poem, the light becomes dim; by the end of the poem, the speaker is romping "with joy" in the dark. Libraries, this implies, are not entirely bad places for poetry. Poetry also includes light, the light of reason or truth, but here poetry seems to make the light go out. More precisely, perhaps, after the poetry is eaten, the library's artificial light is gone. The tone of "Eating Poetry," teasing yet earnest, might best be described as exultant. Happy at the beginning of the poem and joyous at the end, the speaker's mood does not really change. The poem certainly ends on a note of renewal and joy, two results of the revivification of imagination through poetry.

Thomas Lisk

THE ECSTASY

Author: John Donne (1572-1631)
Type of poem: Lyric
First published: 1633, in *Poems, by J. D.: With Elegies on the Authors Death*

The Poem

Although "The Ecstasy" was initially printed without stanza breaks, a number of manuscripts suggest that John Donne conceived of this poem as containing nineteen separate quatrains of iambic tetrameter that trace the movement of lovers' souls from their bodies and the souls' union in that incorporeal state. "The Ecstasy" opens with the lovers sitting in an erotic pastoral landscape. The violets suggest springtime, the season of love. Though the lover and his lass are "one another's best," they have not yet consummated their relationship. Their only union thus far is the physical joining of palms, which are sweaty, and the spiritual linking of eyebeams. During the Renaissance, it was thought that love was engendered by beams shot from the eyes of the beloved; these beams then entered the eyes of the lover and traveled to the heart, where they inflamed the blood, causing such symptoms of affection as perspiration and blushing.

Reinforcing this theme of nonsexual union are references to horticulture and mirrors. One may propagate plants asexually through grafting, and one may reproduce oneself by looking into a mirror. In this poem, the eye is both the transmitter and the reflector of light, acting as a glass wherein each lover sees his or her own image.

The lovers' souls now leave their bodies, reducing the lovers to lifeless figures one finds on tombs. They therefore no longer sit but lie. The souls may initially seek conquest—hence the military allusions—but quickly turn to peaceful parleying, perhaps because they recognize their equality and therefore the impossibility of the triumph of one over the other. Before presenting to the reader these two souls standing apart from their bodies—the literal meaning of the poem's title—Donne introduces a platonic listener, one who is "all mind" and hence has rejected physical love. This third person will benefit from his eavesdropping by learning something more about the nature of love.

With line 29, the poem begins the "dialogue of one," a conversation between the souls in which both say the same thing. In their disembodied state, the souls recognize that they are attracted to each other not through sexual desire but through spiritual love. This love allows their separate, flawed, ignorant souls to unite and compensate for each other's deficiencies. To explain this abstract concept, Donne refers again to the violet, which, when it is transplanted, grows with increased vigor. So, too, the fusion of the lovers' souls produces a new, "abler soul" that knows itself and is perfect. Because this new soul has no deficiencies, it transcends mortality.

In line 49, the souls, having fused and so attained knowledge and perfection, resolve for a variety of reasons to return to their bodies. The first argument they offer is their responsibility to do so; they are like the angels that guide the planets (according to medieval cosmologists) or the celestial "intelligences" supposedly in charge of each of the spheres that comprise the cosmos (lines 51-52). A second reason to return is that the bodies deserve thanks for first bringing the lovers together (lines 53-56). Bodies are not impediments to love; on the contrary, physical love strengthens the spiritual. Just as planets affect people through the air rather than through direct influence, so spirits must act through bodies. If love is to be free, it requires physical as well as spiritual outlets.

The last eight lines offer the final reason for the souls to reembody themselves: to instruct the uninitiated in the nature of love. Those who do not understand spiritual love need sensual evidence, and even the platonic lover who appeared earlier in the poem will learn that his understanding was incomplete because it excluded the physical.

Forms and Devices

The imagery in the poem repeatedly mediates between the sexual and the spiritual. The opening references to pillow, bed, and pregnancy suggest sexuality, but all these words refer to the landscape. In "To His Coy Mistress," Andrew Marvell refers to his "vegetable [asexual] love," the only kind that Donne's couple has so far enjoyed. The violet, which in the language of flowers represents true love, again symbolizes the lovers of the poem, faithful to each other but not physical lovers. The doubling of the violet's petals through transplantation reinforces the sense of vegetable love.

Grafting and transplanting provide asexual means of propagation; they also can improve plants, just as the union of the lovers' souls improves the lovers. Alchemy offers another way to create and to perfect; such scientific imagery also appears in the poem. Though one associates alchemy with charlatans—a linkage relevant to this poem— the desire to transmute baser elements into gold was viewed also as a means of improving the world by producing a literal as well as metaphoric golden age and reversing the Fall (when metals grew baser). The platonic lover who has "grown all mind" has been "refined" already in an alchemical process, but he will be further improved by his encounter with the lovers in the poem because he will recognize the imposture and inadequacy of purely spiritual love. The union of the lovers' souls, like the compounding of two chemicals, yields a purer product than either of its components; the fusion of body and soul strengthens spiritual love.

A third set of images involves astronomy/astrology. Donne often compares people to planets or to the cosmos, drawing on the medieval and Renaissance view that each individual, the microcosm, is like the universe, the macrocosm. So he compares bodies to planets and souls to the angels that control the motions of these objects. Later he uses the idea that stars and planets influence people's lives, but they do so through the intermediary of air. Such conceits clarify the theory that body and soul are interdependent.

Themes and Meanings

Interpretations of "The Ecstasy" have ranged from Pierre Legouis's view that it is a seduction poem to Ezra Pound's assertion that it represents "Platonism believed," at least to the extent that Donne accepts "the existence of an extra-corporal soul, and its . . . incarnation." Both of these observations contain partial truths, but neither adequately expresses Donne's concept of human love. The fusion of sexual and vegetative metaphors in the first quatrain indicates Donne's belief in the necessity of both physical and spiritual love. The rejection of purely platonic love is implicit again in the discussion of the eavesdropper who has refined away the body.

Yet what can be purer than platonic love? Donne maintains that spiritual love alone is actually less pure than when it is joined with sex. As the alchemical imagery demonstrates, the physical improves rather than diminishes the spiritual. Line 68 again plays with this seeming paradox by alluding to the traditional view that the soul lies imprisoned in the body and longs to escape from that impurity. Donne reverses this convention by declaring that unless lovers' bodies join as well as their souls, love becomes a prisoner lacking the freedom to express itself as it would.

If the poem emphasizes the sexual more than the spiritual, the reason may well lie in the recognition that the lovers' souls are already united. Contrary to the received opinion that love begins with physical attraction, or lust, and then grows into a marriage of true minds, Donne posits that, at least in the circumstances of the poem, the desire for sex does not bring the couple together. They began as soul-mates, but because they are human their love remains incomplete until it is consummated physically. The poem recognizes, too, that religion, poetic convention, and the intellectual vogue of the court of Charles I all conspire to glorify nonsexual love. Such an attitude is fine as far as it goes, but it does not go far enough in accepting the distinction between mortals and angels.

Though the poem could provide arguments for seducers, it does not celebrate physical love alone any more than it does spiritual love divorced from sex. As an individual consists of body and soul, so human love must combine both. Only when sexual love expresses the spiritual will an impartial observer be unable to distinguish between the two; to insist on either one without the other is to ignore "that subtle knot, which makes us" human.

Joseph Rosenblum

EDGE

Author: Sylvia Plath (1932-1963)
Type of poem: Lyric
First published: 1965, in *Ariel*

The Poem

"Edge" is a short poem in free verse; its twenty lines are divided into ten couplet stanzas. The title suggests a border, perhaps between life and death. One of the last two poems written by Sylvia Plath before her suicide, "Edge" is a meditation on the death of a woman.

Written in the third person, the poem may give the impression of offering a detached judgment of the dead woman. This point of view usually suggests a less subjective perspective than the first person. The apparently objective imagery of the poem, however, disguises a high degree of subjectivity on the part of the poet.

"Edge" begins with an implied thesis: A woman is "perfected" by death. It is not difficult to see at least three ways in which the woman has been "perfected." To "perfect" means to complete, to master, or to make flawless. While literally true that the woman has completed her life, "perfected" also suggests that the woman has mastered womanhood and has been made flawless through her death. These notions of completion, mastery, and achieved excellence are linked to death in the brief second line, "Her dead," which provides an approximate rhyme with the first line.

The second stanza notes "the smile of accomplishment" that adorns the dead body, suggesting that the woman is pleased by the perfection she has achieved. The poet then hints that the woman has achieved death through suicide. The "Greek necessity" that one imagines flowing "in the scrolls of her toga" strongly suggests the ritual suicides demanded of disgraced individuals in the classical world. Although most readers are familiar with the self-inflicted death by hemlock of the Greek philosopher Socrates, ritual suicide (like the toga) is actually associated with imperial Rome. Nevertheless, Plath is able to allude to her own writing through the clever description of the folds of the toga as "scrolls." The third and fourth stanzas explain the meaning of the woman's bare feet. They have taken her the length of her life with all its obstacles, but now "it is over." The sense of relief at journey's end is apparent.

A new and ominous element is introduced in the fifth stanza. Dead children, presumably the woman's own children, are described as white serpents. Each is coiled before a small "pitcher of milk," which is "now empty." Apparently, the children have each drunk the milk and coiled, fetuslike, at each pitcher; they are pale, or white, with death. One must consider the possibility that the children have been poisoned by their mother.

The sixth through eighth stanzas confirm this suspicion. The woman has "folded/ them back into her body." She is their mother, and she has taken her children with her into death. The first line of the poem, "The woman is perfected," now takes on yet another meaning: She becomes whole or complete as all the life that went forth from her is returned to her in death. The poet defends the murder of the children as the mere closing of a flower at the approach of night. The rose draws in its petals (as the mother draws in her children) when the chill of the evening (or, in the case of the woman, death) descends upon the garden. The sensual but ghastly image of the night as a many-throated flower that "bleeds" its odors transforms the traditional literary meaning of flowers and gardens as emblems of love into omens of death.

From the lush imagery of the garden at nightfall, the ninth stanza turns to the stark moon of the night sky. The poet imagines the moon's view of the grisly tableau of the dead bodies of mother and children. Like a nun in a white cowl, the moon in "her hood of bone" surveys the scene without sadness.

The final stanza of the poem explains the moon's indifference: "She is used to this sort of thing." The dead woman has reenacted an ancient tragedy that the moon has witnessed over and over again. Further, the poem concludes with the hint that the moon bears some responsibility for the deaths. The moon's "blacks crackle and drag." The effect of the moon on the earth (dragging the oceans back and forth across the planet in tides) and on the menses of women account for the final verb. "Crackle," however, suggests something more like sunspots, casting interference and static into the atmosphere and, perhaps, troubling individuals. Such a relationship between the moon and human behavior is acknowledged in folklore (the werewolf is transformed under the light of a full moon) and even in our vocabulary ("lunatic" derives from the same root as "lunar"). The moon, it is implied, may have influenced the terrible events that "she" then observes impassively.

Forms and Devices

As Linda Wagner-Martin points out in *Sylvia Plath: A Biography* (1987), "Edge" was drawn together from previous drafts of poems. The poem's title and some of its most important images first appeared in a draft of "Mystic," a poem that includes images of the demanding life of nuns. Coincidentally, "Nuns in Snow" was the working title of "Edge." The image of the moon with "her hood of bone" (suggesting the cowl of a nun's habit) seems the only trace of this religious motif in the final version of the poem.

The moon's hood is not the only image of clothing in the poem. The dead body of the woman "wears" a smile; she is clothed, first of all, by her sense of satisfaction in her suicide. More graphically, her blood flows down her "toga." As one descends from her lips to her body, one comes to her feet, which are bare. She wears no more than a nightgown.

The shocking image of her dead children coiled like white serpents before little pitchers that had held poisoned milk reveals the troubled mind that describes the scene. (The fragmentary couplets and unexpected enjambments heighten this impression of a disordered and unbalanced narrator.) This highly subjective imagery conveys repugnance for the children. It may also allude to the whitish umbilical cords that linked them to their mother.

Their fetal posture in death seems to return the children to their mother, who "has folded/ them back into her body." The image of a body closing in on itself is developed through the image of the rose drawing its petals shut against the night. The garden "stiffens," and odors "bleed," as does the corpse, when the flower of night (traditionally symbolic of death) opens. Poets have employed the flower and the garden as images of sexual love as long as poetry has been written. The floral imagery here, however, suggests another tradition: death as an alluring and intoxicating temptation. This depiction of death through erotic imagery also has a long history. "La Belle Dame sans Merci," by John Keats, is one of the most famous examples of this tradition.

The most powerful "beautiful lady without mercy" in Greek mythology (the fourth line of the poem alludes to the Greeks) is Artemis, whose attribute is the moon. This virgin goddess, unconquered by love, slew those who attacked her chastity. Sudden deaths of all sorts, but especially among women, were blamed on her arrows. The description of the moon in the virginal habit of a nun modernizes the myth, but the implication of the lines that the moon is responsible, in some fashion, for the woman's death harks back to the implacable Artemis herself.

Themes and Meanings

Written only six days before the author's suicide, "Edge" has sometimes been viewed as a formal suicide note. Such a hasty conclusion deprives the poem of its significance as a work of art. As mentioned above, "Edge" was carefully constructed through a series of drafts. A close inspection of its form and imagery confirms an artistic intent, so one must look for the meaning of the poem not in Plath's biography, but in the poem itself.

The poem argues that the woman who is the subject of the poem is "perfected" in death, which alone offers release from her unhappiness. She smiles in death at the conclusion of an obviously painful journey through life. The description of her children suggests the malevolent role they have played in her life. She imagines them back within her as her body closes like a chilled rose. The woman seeks to return to the condition of the virgin, and it is to the virgin goddess, Artemis, that the poet turns for consolation. The solitary, pure white, perfect female offers no sympathy; the suicide has endured the ancient destiny of women. Only the woman who can hold herself aloof from love and its demands can escape a similar fate.

It is difficult to imagine a bleaker view of human experience than that which Plath expresses in "Edge." She suggests that one can find happiness only in absolute solitude, the solitude of death.

John Biguenet
Geri Johnson

THE EEL

Author: Eugenio Montale (1896-1981)
Type of poem: Lyric
First published: 1956, as "L'anguilla," in *La bufera e altro*; English translation collected in *The Storm and Other Things*, 1985

The Poem

"The Eel" is a lyric in free verse. It is contained in one stanza of thirty lines. The title directs the reader to the eel, whose journey is related by the poem, and raises the question of the significance of the eel, prompting the reader to ask what the poet means by centering attention upon it.

The first sixteen lines describe the journey of the eel. The eel is described leaving the cold reaches of the Baltic Sea and plunging south into Europe, eventually to reach "these shores of ours"—the Italy in which the poet is writing. The poem mentions the marshes, wetlands, and rivers of Italy even before the beginning of the eel's journey is told, thus already focusing attention on the creature's destination. As the eel goes upstream, her journey becomes less smooth, more of a struggle. The eel is no longer moving in elements that are natural and friendly to her. Instead, she is involved in a frenzied battle with powerful and awesome forces of nature. The eel is not a slimy, inert natural object. Her movement against nature arouses the reader's human sympathies.

The Alps are natural barriers to any creature, or for that matter any man-made artifact such as a boat, seeking to journey by river from the north to the south of Europe. Yet the eel, by the sheer force of her lowly, earthy will, bursts her way through "stone interstices of slime" until she miraculously comes out on the other side. Her entry into the Italian landscape is described as a blaze of light. She appears, quite contrary to one's usual expectations of what an eel is like, to be a source of revelation.

The last seventeen lines of the poem describe how the poet perceives the eel. His tone is celebratory, so much so that one wonders if it can really be an eel he is talking about. He praises the eel as "arrow of Love on earth" and several times suggests that it embodies the principle of life itself. The eel seeks life even in the midst of "drought, desolation." She is depicted as the spark of life, which does not always flourish on earth, but needs to go through drought and desolation in order to preserve its meaning. The eel is not a part of this desolation, but is like a rainbow come to disperse its clouds. In this way, the light brought by the eel is like that of the human eye itself, "twin of that other iris shining between your lashes," which in a similar way can draw beauty even from outwardly forlorn circumstances. Because of this similarity, the eel is not a foreign creature to humans. In fact, at the end of the poem, the reader is urged to recognize her as a sister.

Forms and Devices

Eugenio Montale wrote this poem in such a cunning way that he almost seems to be playing a trick on the reader. For most of the poem, he seems to be telling the story of the eel in a very straightforward manner. Even after the journey is ended and the more philosophical burst of praise for the eel begins, one thinks one is listening to a story from which one is far removed. In the last line of the poem, however, the poet suddenly poses a question to the reader, asking "can you deny a sister?"

It is revealed that, far from passively or impersonally describing an eel, the poet has is fact been talking to the reader all the time. The force of this address is multiplied many times by the way it is suspended until the end. Montale anticipates this revelation when, by his praise of the eel in the middle of the poem, he shows that the creature has a spiritual as well as a material dimension. The full impact is delayed until the conclusion, however; because of this delay, the nature of the poem bursts upon the reader with the same surprise and intensity with which the eel bursts upon the Italian landscape.

By packing the very complex theme and story of the poem into one relatively short stanza, the poet creates a density through which the reader has to struggle, much as the eel does through the mountains. One's appreciation of this density is heightened when one realizes that the entire poem is contained not only in one stanza but also in one long sentence, which is divided into several clauses by commas, colons, and semicolons. Its energy rolls magnificently through these obstacles, but the fact that there are obstacles is important. The comma is particularly effective in this regard. By placing a comma after nearly every action or gesture of the eel, the poet wraps up these actions and gestures in the mantle of his own language. This language, rife with vivid natural images, charges the meaning even as it impedes it. The energy and beauty represented by the eel must be delayed in order to break out so brilliantly at the end. The poem's organization enables the ending to stun the reader metaphorically into awareness and exhilaration.

Montale's difficulty and density of texture has led to his being labeled a "hermetic" poet, one who does not easily surrender his meanings to the reader. "The Eel," however, shows that the prime effect of the density is to give the poem an almost overwhelming rhetorical and emotional force.

Themes and Meanings

This poem is full of compressed meaning and resonance. One expects a poem about an eel to concern the rawness and strife in nature, but the role of the eel seems far more elevated than this. The eel is on the verge of being a symbol of fertility, of the ongoing cycle of life and death. The poet is careful to prevent the reader from seeing the eel as simply a part of nature. This is emphasized as soon as the arduous portion of the eel's journey begins, when the eel is poised against the brute reality of nature just as a human voyager would be.

The geographical course of the eel's voyage from north to south is no accident. The eel makes the journey from the Baltic to northern Italy that, practically, cannot be made by water in order to suggest a subterranean, intuitive route of transit that can be found underneath those of surface reality. Since Montale was writing this poem shortly after the end of World War II, it is not too far-fetched to suppose that the eel's successful migration symbolizes the hope of resurrecting a Europe divided and devastated by war. Montale, a committed anti-Fascist, experienced the horrors of the war personally. The significance of the eel managing to tunnel through barriers thought impassable would thus have all the more appeal for him.

Yet the full meaning of the eel is only revealed after she has reached her goal. Breaching the territorial and geographical obstacles is not her only task. She also has to confront the despair that afflicts the human spirit. Once the eel is in Italy, within the poet's sight, she becomes a highly charged emblem of an experience very close to salvation. The transformation of one of the lowliest, the least romantic, of the creatures of the earth into a beacon of redemption is all the more dramatic for its unlikelihood. This redemption seems at first to be universal in scope. As a principle of the life force itself, it can change the entire desolate landscape by illuminating it.

Though the poet wishes the reader to accept this universal significance, in the close of the poem he offers a more personal meaning. The eel has gone from the impersonal to the personal and has been identified throughout as distinctly feminine. This has been underscored by the association with the cycle of fertility and by the image of the eel, in being like a rainbow, resembling "that other iris shining between your lashes," presumably the eye of a beloved woman. The eel, like a shining human glance, permeates the order of nature with a power that is all the more forceful because it seems to be of nature, not something primarily spiritual. Montale avoids triteness and conventionality by picking an unexpected symbol for redemption. The eel's creatureliness also indicates that the transcendence that will save us is hidden in a source near or even under the earth. The poem finds that the natural is really supernatural; one translator of "The Eel," William Arrowsmith, is astute when he describes it as "a cosmic love-poem."

Nicholas Birns

EFFORT AT SPEECH BETWEEN TWO PEOPLE

Author: Muriel Rukeyser (1913-1980)
Type of poem: Lyric
First published: 1935, in *Theory of Flight*

The Poem

"Effort at Speech Between Two People" appeared in Muriel Rukeyser's first book of poetry, *Theory of Flight*, which was awarded the prestigious Yale Younger Poets Prize when Rukeyser was twenty-one years old. The poem is a lyric meditation on the difficulty of communication. Its thirty-six lines are divided into seven unrhymed stanzas; four stanzas of six lines each alternate with three stanzas of four lines each. The colons that appear at the beginning of each stanza give an illusion of alternating speakers, but the content of the stanzas does not seem to follow this interpretation. The fact that the poet does not make it clear that more than one person is speaking suggests instead an internal monologue with one person sorrowfully considering the impossibility of truly knowing someone else and of being known in return. The opening words show that the speaker is eager, even desperate, to learn and to know: "Speak to me." That taut, imperative sentence is repeated twice in the poem. The speaker also repeats the promise "I will be open," implying a willingness to tell the deepest truths and to listen to others and truly hear what they have to say.

The gender of the speaker is not given, but the lyric poem traditionally reflects the voice of the author. The illustrative memories of childhood also suggest a female speaker. She reveals chronological stages of her life in tiny vignettes: She remembers her third birthday when she was read a sad story about a pink rabbit who died, burned her finger on the flame of a birthday candle, and was told to be happy. She recalls, at nine years old, crying at the sad beauty of Frédéric Chopin's music, which her widowed aunt played on a piano. At the age of fourteen, she says, she had thoughts of suicide and was saved only by the beauty of a sunset.

Another problematic issue emerges as she reviews who she is now. She lost someone she loved, and, thinking about their past together, she concludes, "I think he never loved me." The object of her love is unspecified. It could be a friend, a lover, or her father. He liked to sail, and the thought of waves and seagulls reminds her of him and his love for the sea. Though he told her blithely that he loved her, he is no longer there (he is presumably dead, for she speculates on "what a tragedy his life was, really"). The true tragedy, however, seems to be that he was unable to be emotionally close to her. Throughout the poem, the speaker calls out to be known. It could be a cry to other people to take the time and to have the openness to share themselves with her, or, just as relevant, it could be herself whom she addresses and whom she wants to know. Without self-understanding and acceptance, she cannot be open enough to give herself to knowing another. However, even if she is open enough, the chances of finding another person equally self-aware and willing to share personal truths are not high. It takes effort and trust, and those qualities seem limited in an alienated society where, even in a crowded street, people do not speak to each another.

Forms and Devices

Rukeyser uses several rhetorical devices to slow the pace of the poem and to suggest pauses, as though the speaker is thinking carefully about what is being said. These devices include colons that are combined with spaces within a line, spaces between sentences, and ellipses in two lines of the final stanza. These spaces and punctuation marks provide visual breaks that slow the reading and imply that speaking openly to another person about one's feelings is difficult and that the words of self-revelation do not flow easily or casually.

The poem is written in free verse without rhyme or a definite metrical pattern. It relies instead on imagery, the repetition of key words and phrases, and the juxtaposition of those images and phrases. The speaker states that she is "not happy," and she reinforces that sentiment throughout the poem with the words "unhappy," "lonely," and a second use of "not happy." There are many images of sadness in her life—being read the story of a rabbit that died, burning her finger, weeping, thinking of leaping out a window, and being deserted by someone she loved. However, she also has memories of moments of sheer joy and beauty—the "white sails against a sky like music," the piano music composed by Chopin, and the sunset with light that "melted clouds and plains to beauty."

Just as short sentences and phrases are repeated, though in no predictable pattern, so too are specific words and concepts repeated. Some of these are state-of-being adjectives ("open," "happy," and "close"), while others are action verbs ("speak," "tell," "link," "love," "take my hand," and "grow to know"). These all function as possibilities of action and conditions of existence. They also function as metaphors for the giving of life, for ideals of what human beings could be and what changes there would be in social interaction if individuals could learn to break through to genuine communication with themselves and others. The juxtaposition of these phrases and images is vital in creating the tone and meaning of the poem. The speaker not only thinks of her aunt playing the piano but also remembers that her aunt is a widow; the music thus stirs the speaker both to sadness and to a rather pleasing melancholy and self-awareness ("I was fruitily sentimental,/ fluid"). The sea that carries haunting memories of a lost love also brings the beautiful image of "little lips of foam/ that ride small waves." Even in the crowded street where no one speaks to each other, "the morning shone."

Themes and Meanings

The basic theme of the poem is asserted in the title: an effort at speech as opposed to clear and meaningful speech that is heard and understood. The poem expresses the need to share and communicate, and it implies the difficulty of achieving this with others or even with oneself. Critic Louise Kertesz, in *The Poetic Vision of Muriel Rukeyser* (1980), refers to "Effort at Speech Between Two People" as a classic dialogue, but whether the poem is seen as a dialogue or a monologue, the message is the same: It is difficult to know oneself and to know others, and it is difficult to reveal oneself in a world where people move in crowds and do not speak. The world is a lonely place where strangers ache with the need for intimacy. This theme is made explicit in the rhythmic refrains "Grow to know me" and "Speak to me," which express the human need to communicate and the difficulty of achieving true communication.

This need to know people applies to knowing oneself, as shown by the speaker's memories of earlier eras of her life and her attempts to understand what she is now. It also refers to the basic human longing to be understood (as in the phrase "First my mind in your hand"), which, for the speaker, should precede touch and make possible the linking of the minutes of the day with each other or make "separate entities" come together like pieces of a puzzle. Further, this need to know refers to knowing other people. To know other people is to learn what humans share in common and thus reduce the sense of individual isolation. To know and learn about others is to create a sense of human community to which people can feel they belong. "Speak to me," repeats the speaker, reassuring the other person (or another part of herself) that she will be open and receptive rather than judgmental and separate. In a larger sense, the poem speaks clearly not only to the need for a change in consciousness and openness in the individual or between two individuals but also to the imperative need for increased communication and openness among all people, groups, and nations.

"Breathe-in experience, breathe-out poetry" is the opening line of the first poem in Rukeyser's first volume of verse ("Poem out of Childhood," in *Theory of Flight*). Rukeyser thus announced her desire to communicate and share with others. She believed that poetry was a way "to share something of our experience by turning it into something and giving it to somebody." Poetry itself, then, is an effort at speech between two people, between writer and receptive reader. Rukeyser wrote repeatedly on behalf of liberal political causes, speaking out for freedom and justice at all levels. All her poetry, including "Effort at Speech Between Two People," reaches out to touch, to teach, and to communicate, always with the central theme that human beings could and must share themselves with others. That emotional intimacy has the power to transform society.

Lois A. Marchino

THE EISENHOWER YEARS

Author: Paul Zimmer (1934-   )
Type of poem: Narrative
First published: 1983, in *Family Reunion: Selected and New Poems*

The Poem

Paul Zimmer's "The Eisenhower Years" consists of four stanzas of varying length, unrhymed and of irregular meter, that offer a socially representative picture of the author's poetic persona, Zimmer, over the course of a typical day in his young adult life during the 1950's. Although this period, mostly under the presidency of Dwight D. Eisenhower, was a halcyon time of national prosperity in the United States, in the view of many it was also a period of cultural blandness and conformity, and of ignorance and complacency with regard to such continuing social ills as racism and misuse of U.S. power abroad. In this light, Zimmer instills the poem with a cautionary tenor—one that it introduces as early as the opening line, if only on the personal level of its protagonist—as Zimmer, "Flunked out and laid-off," puts in a seemingly typical day working at his father's shoe store, "Zimmer's Shoes for Women."

The inherent if unacknowledged pain of the speaker's directionless and dependent life is underscored by the substance of his work: "the feet of old women," which "groan and rub/ Their hacked up corns together." The women come "in agony" to the speaker, who in the *reductio ad absurdum* of his life, "talks to the feet,/ Reassures and fits them."

The sense of the speaker's aimlessness mounts in the second stanza as he returns home from work habitually to check the mail for the ironic "greetings from his draft board"—the wait for the draft notice and the military service itself composing one long rite of passage for the era's young men, one that threatened easy or directionless lives, not with the sacrifices of war but with the imposition of greater social obligations, beyond their easy comfort. The speaker idles away the time after supper listening to music, drinking cheap wine, smoking cigarettes, and reading a best-selling novel. This spiritual indolence continues into the third stanza's evening, when the speaker simply "goes" to bars to do, apparently, no more than drink large quantities of beer. He ends up, "in the wee hours," alone, braced against a lamppost, a little disheveled, with a cigarette "stuck to his lips," the stuck cigarette seemingly emblematic of the stuck nature of his behaviors and life.

In the final stanza, the poet finally comments explicitly on the speaker and the routine, vacuous world he inhabits. As he leans against the lamppost, "All of complacent America/ Spreads around him in the night." The night and America are a "void" in which for Zimmer all that moves are "the feet of old women,/ Twitching and shuffling in pain." His response to finding himself in this void is to sigh and drag on his cigarette, exhaling "through his nostrils" in an almost dismissive posture of hopeless deflation. The poet offers his deepest insight into the speaker, and the strongest commentary on him, in the poem's closing lines:

He knows nothing and feels little.
He has never been anywhere
And fears where he is going.

Forms and Devices

The personal immediacy of Paul Zimmer's poems, particularly "The Eisenhower Years" and the other "Zimmer" poems, serves largely to make the poet himself the subject of his poetry. In characteristic twentieth century fashion, however, "The Eisenhower Years," as do the other "Zimmer" poems, plays with such narrative and poetic elements as voice, persona, narrator identity, and uncertain distinctions between poet and the poetic voice in a poem. Through the poetic persona of "Zimmer," the poet draws direct attention to these issues, when they are otherwise, often, only implicit considerations. "Zimmer" may be a purely fictitious character, but the persona's name and the seemingly biographical continuities with non-"Zimmer" poems cloud that understanding. In another "Zimmer" poem, "Zimmer in Grade School" (1983), the poet, or his persona, states, "Even now/ When I hide behind elaborate mask/ It is always known that I am Zimmer." The poet purposely obscures the fictional nature of the "Zimmer" persona, which can lead the reader to understand the "Zimmer" poems as being simply autobiographical.

An analysis of narrative voice in "The Eisenhower Years" leads to a different understanding. It is only in the final stanza that the voice analytically distances itself from Zimmer. The judgment of U.S., and by inclusion, Zimmer's, complacency, and of the poet's ignorance and emotional numbness, might exhibit no more than an impersonal, though editorializing, omniscient narrator; however, the "Zimmer" poems, in toto, reveal a very close identity between the poet and the narrative voice of his poems. Indeed, some of the "Zimmer" poems, as in "Zimmer in Grade School," are written in the first person. Consequently, one might understand the voice of the narrator in "The Eisenhower Years" as that of an older Zimmer reflecting on his younger self and making characteristically harsh judgments.

The title of the poem places its retrospective character in a broader social context, as do further strains in the poem: the use of plain, even vernacular, diction, and reference to popular culture. The plain language and prosaic syntactical structures provide narrative accessibility. That "Zimmer" is, in the vernacular, "Flunked out and laid-off" signals his membership in an ever-expanding middle class during "The Eisenhower Years," one in which his father might yet own a shoe store to provide a safety net of aimless employment.

The popular culture and popular images of the era easily evoke the texture of the times. The speaker waits for his draft notice during an affluent period of peace. He listens to Dave Brubeck, a white jazz musician whose popularity helped increase the acceptance of jazz among the white middle class. Zimmer drinks Thunderbird, a cheap wine commonly chosen by barely employed young people with little experience or sophistication. He drinks Stroh's as well, a popular middle-American beer, in multiple pitchers, refined pleasure not being the object. He also smokes Chesterfields, a famous brand of cigarette during the era. Still, unlike young men of later eras, the speaker dresses properly, wearing a tie and an emblematic fedora hat.

Before going out for the evening, the speaker casually "lays out" with James Jones's *From Here to Eternity* (1951), a powerful novel of the time about a, perhaps, complacent United States in the days before World War II. *From Here to Eternity* portrays often-petty and rudderless lives as they are subsumed in a great national drama. No such immediate national drama awaits Zimmer and his United States, but history reveals that multiple national dramas—the Civil Rights movement, the Vietnam War, and the rise of the 1960's counterculture—would ultimately challenge the complacency of "The Eisenhower Years." In the meantime, however, the speaker leans against a lamppost, his tie "loosened" and his hat "pushed back on his head," dragging from his cigarette and exhaling from his nose with a sigh. The image suggests much of the era, including images from almost any *film noir*, a popular film genre of the 1950's in which directionless young men with no great understanding of their lives are often led astray, to their own destruction.

Themes and Meanings

Paul Zimmer's early and midlife poems are often comical narratives recounting the mundane escapades of someone, as the poet explains in "Zimmer the Drugstore Cowboy" (1983), who was "stunned by a concrete tit at birth,/ Dull as a penny bouncing off a cinder block." He is, in "The Sweet Night Bleeds for Zimmer" (1983), a "sorry man/ Remembering each cruelty under the stars;/ Someone wagging submission forever." In this light, Zimmer is in the long tradition of the comic and foolish Everyman, an individual who represents the frail, even buffoonish, nature and aspirations of all humankind. The poet's apparently severe judgments upon him must thus be leavened with a universal compassion.

The Zimmer of "The Eisenhower Years," though the life he leads is purposeless, is a kind young man. While the old women of the poem live in a United States in which their only "agony" may reside in feet "twitching and shuffling in pain" for new shoes, still the speaker "talks to the feet" and "reassures" them. If he drinks cheap wine and too much beer, he also listens to good and sophisticated music, music that has its roots in a culture and world other than his own very limited one. The novel he reads, by choice, is serious fiction, literature that exposes him to deeper issues in life, however immune to that exposure he may be at the time. Even the strikingly askew pose he assumes in the end suggests his emotional and spiritual desolation, and desolation is a conscious state. There are signs of hope for the speaker, though he must heed the signs.

Frozen in the image against the lamppost, the pettiness of the image in Zimmer's own mind haunts him in the final stanza: "the feet of old women" are all that move for him in the "void" of "complacent America." Life must be more than this, for Zimmer and for America. He is ignorant and almost emotionless, and he is without real experience of life. What is crucial for him is that he "fears where he is going." This fear, like his numb unhappiness, signals that he is conscious of his condition, however inchoate that consciousness may be. The speaker's fate may not be identical to that of America, but in "The Eisenhower Years," Paul Zimmer chooses to link the condition of his Everyman poetic persona with that of the country in which he lives. Voids are inevitably filled. The lesson of history is that the void some saw in the United States during the Eisenhower years was ultimately filled by a greater but tumultuous self-consciousness. In the poem "The Eisenhower Years," what will fill the void in Zimmer is left uncertain.

A. Jay Adler

EL DESDICHADO

Author: Gérard de Nerval (Gérard Labrunie, 1808-1855)
Type of poem: Sonnet
First published: 1853; in *Les Chimères*, 1854; English translation collected in *An Anthology of French Poetry from Nerval to Valéry in English Translation with French Originals*, 1958

The Poem

Originally, this French sonnet was entitled "Le Destin" (the destiny), but its published title even in translation is "El Desdichado," the Spanish words for "the unhappy one." It is one of a series of twelve sonnets that Gérard de Nerval wrote while confined in an asylum in a state of delirium. The poem is written in the first person, and it is a part of the poet's anguished effort to escape from the horrors of insanity into a state of comfort, represented by women, and to evaluate his poetic talent.

Nerval's blending of mysticism and personal experience in a traditional literary form is original. Many poets have expressed their personal feelings in sonnets—for example, William Shakespeare in Sonnet 29 and John Milton in "On His Blindness"—but Nerval is perhaps unique in clothing his feelings in mysticism.

El Desdichado is a name found in Sir Walter Scott's *Ivanhoe* (1819), where it is the motto of a mysterious knight in black armor who turns out to be Ivanhoe in disguise. He is unhappy because he has lost his estate and has been forbidden to court the lady he loves. Nerval says that, like the black knight, he is desperately unhappy. He has lost his inheritance, and his "only star" is dead. He may be referring to Adrienne, a childhood sweetheart, and also to Jenny Colon, an actress whom he had loved. Both are dead. The star may also represent pure love and spiritual faith. His consolation may refer to Octavia, an English girl whom Nerval met in Italy in 1834 and whom he credits with saving his life on Mount Posilippo when he was contemplating suicide. In addition, he may be thinking of his love for his mother, buried in Italy, whose memory he cherishes despite the fact that he was only two years old when she died.

Seeking to understand himself, he asks whether he is Love—that is, Eros, the nocturnal lover—or Phoebus, the Greek god of light and poetry. Is he Biron or Lusignan? Biron is a French hero immortalized in song. According to legend, Lusignan was a lord who had married the fairy Melusina. Melusina had a human form every day except Saturday and had forbidden her lover to come to see her on that day. Lusignan disobeyed, and she left him, to his despair. The poet is asking: Am I truly a poet or a lover? If I am a lover, am I a happy lover like Biron or an unhappy lover of fairies like Lusignan? He concludes that he is Love, not Phoebus, and is Lusignan, not Biron.

The kiss of the queen may be one he received as a child from Adrienne, or it may be a reference to the biblical Queen of Sheba, who seemed to haunt Nerval. His two crossings of the Acheron, the river between life and death, almost surely represent his two worst spells of madness. As Orpheus returned from the underworld playing the lyre, so Nerval found again his poetic talent in his delirium. Both triumphs, however, were short-lived.

Forms and Devices

The French original of this sonnet is completely traditional in form: fourteen lines of twelve syllables each, arranged in two quatrains followed by two tercets. The rhyme scheme is also traditional, and each line, with two exceptions, is complete in itself. This rigidity presents a tremendous problem to the translator.

Nerval is considered a precursor of the Symbolists because he bound his images chiefly by the dreamlike quality of his musical fancy, and because, like them, he avoided concreteness and clarity, relying instead on imagination and suggestion.

The density of his expression allows him to tell his life story in fourteen lines. Almost every line is, in a sense, a complete poem; each follows the preceding, not logically, but in the way a vision follows another vision. Everything mentioned carries at least two meanings. There is nothing as simple as a simile: Nerval does not say that one thing or person is like another. He leaves the reader to decipher the hidden meanings. A determined reader needs knowledge of Nerval's life, Greek mythology, the Bible, Oriental mysticism, and tarot cards to understand this poem; even eminent scholars cannot agree on the significance of numerous words.

The poem is not a sort of exorcism that is read solely for its incantatory power; it is a poem of expression, a kind of meditation that is meant to be a striving for the essential, the eternal, the absolute. The frequent use of the definite article reinforces the universal nature of the emotions so succinctly expressed.

Nerval makes frequent use of contrasts: While the first quatrain is filled with despair, the second quatrain recalls his days of happiness. He turns from the blackened sun to the radiant light of Italy. Similarly, in the first tercet he is doubtful, questioning his role in life, but the last tercet is triumphant with decision. Allied to this use of contrast is Nerval's use of juxtaposition. From the midnight of the grave, he invokes the sunny sea, a flower that once pleased him, and thoughts of love and wine.

Alliteration cannot be noted in translation, but it is markedly evident in the original, where in the first eight lines there are thirteen prominent *t* sounds. It is not by chance that each quatrain contains five pronounced *s* sounds, and each tercet contains four. This is like the repetition of a note in music, and the repetition helps to unify the independent lines. It is a tremendous feat to condense the story of one's life and emotions by means of metaphors involving several religions and civilizations, and to weigh one's possibilities and arrive at an answer, all in fourteen evocative, musical lines.

Themes and Meanings

Scholars have explained this poem at length biographically, metaphysically, and astrologically. The simplest way to read the poem is as a beautiful, condensed biography. Such an oversimplification, however, gives no idea of the great knowledge that Gérard de Nerval possessed of Oriental mysticism, Greek mythology, alchemy, and astronomy.

In a time of great depression, Nerval examines his life lucidly, reflecting on his past and his present misery and trying to evaluate his talent. By means of mysterious symbols in a hauntingly musical form, he offers this brief poetic account of his years of anguish, his dreams and plans. It is the essence of his life.

In the first quatrain, Nerval tells the reader that he is the incarnation of everything dark and gloomy, widowed, alone, disconsolate. He likens himself to a legendary hero, the Prince of Aquitaine, whose castle tower was destroyed. Although Nerval's family was not of the nobility, he invented some noble ancestors for himself, along with a coat of arms that contained three silver towers. When he unexpectedly acquired a rather large sum of money, he lost it almost immediately.

His "only star" probably refers primarily to Jenny Colon, whom he had truly loved and who seems to represent a feminine ideal that he cherished all his life. She broke off their liaison after about a year, married a musician, and died four years later. His ill-fated lute, his poetic talent, bears the black sun that is supposed to herald the end of the world; it is a reference to a famous engraving by Albrecht Dürer called *Melancholia*. The star and the black sun are symbols of the poet's deep despair.

While the first quatrain contains symbols only of darkness, the second quatrain offers symbols of light. The poet asks for the restoration of the happiness he had known in Italy. The flower he wants represents all flowers, and the union of the rose and the vine is a reference to Venus and Bacchus—love and wine.

The first tercet indicates his identity crisis: Is he primarily a lover or a poet? Is he happy, like Biron, or unhappy, like Lusignan? There is much disagreement on the identity of the queen whom Nerval mentions. She may be Adrienne, the Queen of Sheba, or a combination of several mystical figures found in Nerval's poetry. More likely, she represents his "only star," and the grotto where the Siren swims may be a reference to his childhood dreams. In the original, this line ends with suspension points, indicating the end of the reverie.

The final tercet identifies the poet with Orpheus returning from the underworld playing his lyre. It sounds a triumphant note. His terrible fits of madness have made him a seer, and he has transformed his sufferings into poetry.

Dorothy B. Aspinwall

ELEGY FOR A DEAD SOLDIER

Author: Karl Shapiro (1913-2000)
Type of poem: Elegy
First published: 1944, in *V-Letter and Other Poems*

The Poem

Karl Shapiro's "Elegy for a Dead Soldier" is a long poem consisting of eleven twelve-line stanzas and a six-line envoi, which Shapiro calls the "epitaph." As part of Shapiro's *V-Letter* collection, which won the Pulitzer Prize in 1944, the poem chronicles one of the poet's experiences in the battle zones of Australia and New Zealand during World War II. In *V-Letter*'s introduction, Shapiro noted that he guarded "against becoming a 'war poet,'" yet clearly his work as a wartime medic shaped much of his early work. "Elegy for a Dead Soldier" is one of the best of these poems.

One might argue that so-called war poets either romanticize or condemn war; however, Shapiro places himself in the more objective middle ground of his subject. He neither elevates the fallen soldier to heroism nor glorifies his war activities any more than he idealizes war's significance. Conversely, Shapiro does not blame the dead for their war involvement, nor does he condemn war as pointless. Interestingly enough, the middle ground of the poet as outsider or voyeur, despite his direct involvement in the war, may result in part from Shapiro's own position as a World War II conscientious objector. While he did not carry a gun, his status as an army medic put him in the same proximity and peril as those who did. His Jewish faith forbade him to wage war; it did not, however, forbid him to assist his countrymen.

The first stanza of the poem opens almost journalistically: "A white sheet on the tail-gate of a truck/ Becomes an altar"; two candlesticks "sputter at each side of the crucifix"; "The chaplain chats, the palmtrees swirl their hair,/ The columns come together through the mud." In these lines, Shapiro is careful not to evoke any particular emotion or attitude. The effect of this initial distancing from the dead soldier and from his funeral is to make the event less personal, more matter-of-fact. Thus, as the soldiers separate themselves from the dead man, they can also separate themselves from the horrors of war that could just as easily have put them in the man's position.

The flowers "laid round" are "brighter than the blood,/ Red as the red of our apocalypse," and the "great morning-glories [are] pale as lips/ That shall no longer taste or kiss or swear." However, the uninflected lines create a flat, conversational tone that evokes neither sorrow nor repugnance. When Shapiro juxtaposes the flowers and their inherent beauty with images of death, he creates an interesting paradox in which contrariety fuses the two extremes into something simultaneously beautiful and sorrowful. The sum of the two extremes negates, and the zero emotion ensues.

In subsequent stanzas, Shapiro turns his attentions to what he knows or speculates about the dead soldier. While Shapiro sees the man as heroic, he does not exaggerate or romanticize the man's common heroism in unreasonable platitudes. Rather, the man Shapiro says he "by chance" saw die, "stretched on the ground,/ A tattooed arm lifted . . . had never questioned the idea of gain"; "his laugh was real, his manners were homemade," and "he paid his bill" and "belonged to church." The soldier who would have been a truck driver had there been no war, or had the war delivered him home unharmed, is entirely unpretentious. "He and the world had winked," and his "end was sudden, like a foolish play,/ A stupid fool slamming a foolish door." Death by war, Shapiro writes, is "the absurd catastrophe, half-prearranged." Yet since the man pretended to be nothing other than what he was, the poet does not pretend to glorify him beyond that simple humanity.

Ultimately, Shapiro and the other soldiers identify with the commonness of their fallen comrade. After all, they are like him, followers that the "leaders could not seek/ Beyond." Shapiro writes, "We ask for no statistic of the killed,/ For nothing political impinges on/ This single casualty, or all those gone." He continues, "However others calculate the cost,/ To us the final aggregate is *one*." His death is their death, his number theirs. There is no preselection, just selection.

At the poem's end, in the envoi, the poet writes,

> You who read,
> Remember that this stranger died in pain;
> And passing here, if you can lift your eyes
> Upon a peace kept by human creed,
> Know that one soldier has not died in vain.

The greatest sorrow, then, is that the fallen man is often the forgotten man. The common soldier dies a common, painful death on the battlefield; consequently, because he is not glorified unless he holds rank, his sacrifice will go unremembered except by one reading about him. The peace in the aftermath of war was provided in part by the man about whom Shapiro writes. If readers remember that, then his death, and his anonymity, are not in vain.

Forms and Devices

Shapiro claimed in *V-Letter and Other Poems* that he had not "written these poems to accord with any doctrine or system of thought or even a theory of composition." Furthermore, he stated, "I have nothing to offer in the way of beliefs or challenges or prosody." This poetic self-effacement aside, Shapiro clearly understood poetic conventions and, eventually, would become one of the postmodern champions of form and prosody.

In a broad context, Shapiro's elegy functions much the way all elegies function. It is a poem to commemorate the dead. However, Shapiro shapes his elegy into what might be termed a *nonce canzone*. Typically, a *canzone* is an old Italian form of varying lengths and patterns. Most often, it comprises five twelve-line stanzas and a five-line envoi that turns on repeated words. In Shapiro's *nonce* or "irregular" form of the *canzone*, he gives us eleven twelve-line stanzas and a six-line envoi that does not use repetition. Additionally, Shapiro's twelve-line stanzas operate upon a specific, consistent rhyme pattern of *abbcdaedfefc*, while the envoi follows a joined tercet pattern of *abcabc*.

Another interesting convention Shapiro employs in "Elegy for a Dead Soldier" is his personification of certain abstracts. So much of what people place value upon in modern society is idealistic or ideological. In Shapiro's poem, loss, for example, "seems to point at nothing," and doubt "flirts." However, what, tangibly speaking, is loss or doubt? War gives "Freedom of self and peace to wander free," and "poverty pursued him least" because the dead soldier did not understand lack.

Comparatively, when Shapiro writes of tangibles, such as people and objects, he creates metaphors that evoke the hard, dissolvable reality beyond ideas: "palmtrees swirl their hair," "blue morning-glories [are] pale as lips," the soldiers "are ashes," the "bullet found its aim," and "the red flag" of blood "marked the sewer main." The contrariety of Shapiro's use of personification and metaphor illustrates how people attempt to make war a lofty, idealistic concern while, realistically, war makes refuse of the world.

Themes and Meanings

Shapiro never intended to be a "war poet" because it was not his design either to celebrate war or to disparage it. Rather, he wrote about what he was exposed to during his service in the South Pacific. World War II, it might be suggested, was the last war in which a popular sentiment supported extensive military involvement; Vietnam, certainly, ruined public support of war. Thus, because this poem comes from a collection written about a war that carried much public support, it is perhaps too easy to see it as a testament celebrating those common people who fought in the war. However, Shapiro chooses to show us the commonness of war and its common destruction. Where war is glorious, it is glorious primarily at its completion and in the aftermath, peace. Glory is not, as Shapiro deliberately illustrates, found in the jungle, in the foxhole, or among the carnage.

What seems important, thematically, is that Shapiro leads the way for the antiwar sensibilities that would proliferate across the United States in the 1960's and 1970's. Granted, he does not condemn the war, but his objections to man's inhumanity to man, for the sake of ideology, seem clear enough. "Elegy for a Dead Soldier," like the other poems in *V-Letter and Other Poems*, is a song about common men who are misplaced in battle. For in the natural, peaceful world, one's place is the preferred mundaneness of home or occupation.

Mark Sanders

ELEGY FOR JANE

Author: Theodore Roethke (1908-1963)
Type of poem: Elegy
First published: 1953, in *The Waking: Poems, 1933-1953*

The Poem

"Elegy for Jane," subtitled "My Student, Thrown by a Horse," is a poem in free verse whose twenty-two lines are divided into four stanzas. The poem follows the elegiac tradition insofar as it mourns the death of a loved one. The first nine lines follow the custom of honoring the deceased by describing Jane's delicacy and youthful exuberance. Roethke describes Jane as a light, quick animal, the epitome of the lovely in nature. Her neck curls are damp as plant tendrils, trailing, winding, and new. Quick and nervous in her movements, Jane's smile was nonetheless wide as a fish's ("pickerel"). Jane was also shy, for she had to be startled into talking. Once she started talking, however, she showed that she delighted in her thoughts. These lines may be alluding to Roethke's calling on her in class and her corresponding pleasure in answering.

When she was happy, Jane was like a bird with its tail in the wind; her song was so energetic that small branches trembled. The courage and adventurousness that cause a tail to be immersed in wind imply a daring that might have resulted in Jane's being thrown to her death by a horse. Jane's vitality was so inspiring that all nature rejoiced in her exuberance, even gloomy natural items such as shade and mold. Jane's happiness was so beneficent that the leaves turned to kissing.

The following stanza states that when Jane was sad, she plunged from a joy that even shade and mold reflected into an abyss of sadness so deep that "even a father could not find her" (line 11). The soaring bird suddenly fell to the rough earth and stirred its fundamental element, water. Jane, usually a joyous wren flying into the wind, sometimes dove into such unhappiness that her cheek scraped dried grass and stirred water.

The third stanza continues the bird metaphor, only this time Jane is a sparrow who is forever gone. The speaker also identifies himself with nature, not as a soaring or plunging bird but as a passive plant that can only wait, rooted in the earth. He is a fern whose thin leaves make thin shadows, implying that the speaker is grief-stricken to the point of being skeletal himself. The speaker's grief parallels Jane's deep sadness, for now that Jane is gone the speaker is no longer consoled by nature's beauties, its wet stones and moss lit by twilight.

The last stanza again refers to Jane's active but shy personality in birdlike terms; she moves from being described as a joyful wren to a lost sparrow to a skittery pigeon. Roethke longs to bring Jane back from death, but in addition to his powerlessness in the face of death, Roethke feels impotent in that his feelings are not legitimized because, being only her teacher and not a father or lover, he has no socially sanctioned right to grieve her loss publicly. Roethke mourns not only for the loss of Jane to himself and to all nature but also for his sense that no one will recognize his loss or console him.

Forms and Devices

Roethke is famous for inventing a new form, a long poem in parts, which seems borrowed from drama. In the relatively short poem "Elegy for Jane," as in his other works, the parts are "fluid," allowing him to swing back and forth through time. The first two stanzas are nostalgic, the third brings the speaker into the sorrowful present of Jane's death, while the last combines a wish for Jane's resurrection with the grim realizations that Jane is gone forever and that Roethke's own grief has no socially approved existence.

Roethke interlaces his dramatic stanzas with long, leisurely lines followed by energetic short lines that punctuate his lengthy descriptions with cogent, staccatoed points (as line 7, "The shade sang with her," and line 22, "Neither father nor lover"). "Elegy for Jane" uses Roethke's typical juxtaposition of opposing elements. The metaphor of Jane as a bird joyfully darting into the sky, then thudding to earth in sadness and in death, also symbolizes a soul's ascent and descent. Images of energy and life contrast with those of stasis and death. Jane darts, skitters, startles, casts herself down, even scrapes her cheek when she is sad, all active images that contrast powerfully with those of immobility: "waiting like a fern," "sleep," and "damp grave."

Another juxtaposition of opposites is the contrast between water images and those of land and sky. Water also symbolizes flux, perhaps beyond or undergirding life and death. Jane's smile is like a pickerel, presumably swimming in water, and her grave is damp. Water is the element in which Jane swims and lives, and it is the element in which she is buried. Dampness itself is not ominous, and the speaker implies that ordinarily he would be consoled by "wetness on stones." The use of water as the ground of both life and death evokes Walt Whitman's "Out of the Cradle, Endlessly Rocking," in which the sea is the "old mother." Roethke's images of stasis—waiting, stones, moss, sleep—are not portrayed as undesirable but as a backdrop for movement, vitality, and light. Roethke suggests that were it not for Jane's death, even the light fleeting on moss would delight him. Her death has not only robbed him of herself and all pleasure but also turned him into a shadow, not a being of light. Light in this and other Roethke poems symbolizes life. Jane's syllables were light, her thoughts were delightful to her, and her pickerel smile evokes a fish whose scales glimmer in water.

Roethke uses iambic, trochaic, anapestic, and sprung rhythms in "Elegy for Jane." He mixes these varied metrics with lists of varied images, marked by three elements. Stanza 1 is marked by images of rapid movement, and stanza 2 by images of stasis. The concluding stanza is shaped by the vitality of fantasy juxtaposed with a moribund actuality—vital fantasy and deathly reality are balanced. The long lines and repetition of water and movement images control the poem's pacing, giving it the deliberateness of a dirge. The short, terrible last line is as final in its loneliness as the lowering of a casket into a grave.

Themes and Meanings

Although Roethke can usually find transcendent happiness even in melancholy images, such as mold or stones or moss in the last light of day, Jane's death has silenced the speaker's joy in any of nature's light or dark aspects. That society does not sanction his right to grieve in front of others forces him to mourn only to the elements over Jane's "damp grave." His sense of abandonment and loneliness finally diminishes him to a shadow. Both Jane's physical death and society's prohibition against his open expression of grief leave the speaker alienated from nature and humans. Although "Elegy for Jane" gives the impression of being a classical elegy, it is not. The standard celebration of the vegetative god, Adonis, contains regeneration. "Elegy for Jane" contains no regeneration, unless it is in a mysterious diffusion of Jane's darting energy into the windy, scattered movements of nature.

"Elegy for Jane" can be seen as Roethke's comment on the finality of nature's cycle. Jane is presented as one of life's small, treasured creatures, whose death is a violation of the natural order in that she died before flowering. Although Roethke's lengthy, cadenced lines with his layered images are reminiscent of Whitman's long lines, they are different. Whitman simply cataloged images of all kinds. Roethke's detailed, meticulously described small things imply value—the tiny things of this world are at least as significant as the large. That Roethke acknowledged death as part of nature's cycle is seen in his juxtaposition of damp neck hair that sprawls like young plants with the "damp grave." This interruption of the natural cycle by the demise of a girl who made the leaves kiss violates the cosmic order of birth, growth, aging, and death. Jane's death is also terrible on a personal level. It has disrupted the speaker's connection with a creation that he found exhilarating in all its aspects, in its mold as well as in its birds, in its stones as well as in its trees. Jane's ups and downs reflected the light and shadows of nature in which the speaker once reveled. Her premature death and the lack of social ritual available to the speaker result not only in grief but also in a hopeless acceptance of a devastated outer and inner landscape.

Mary Hanford Bruce

ELEGY FOR JOHN DONNE

Author: Joseph Brodsky (1940-1996)
Type of poem: Elegy
First published: 1965, as "Bolshaya elegiya Dzhonu Donnu," in *Stikhotvoreniya i poemy*; English translation collected in *Selected Poems*, 1973

The Poem

As the title "Elegy for John Donne" indicates, the poem is an elegy, a formal and sustained lament in verse form mourning the death of a particular person—in this case, the death of John Donne, the seventeenth century Metaphysical poet. The Russian title includes the word *bolshaya* ("big"), which connotes the importance and depth of this tribute to Donne. This adjective is omitted in the translation by George L. Kline used here. In the original and in translation, the poem is written in pentameter (ten syllables per poetic line), the metrical line used in Donne's Holy Sonnets. The Russian version uses a precise rhyme scheme (*ababcdcd*); this English version does not.

The poem can be divided into four parts. In part 1 (lines 1-95), the absolute silence that Donne's death has caused is felt throughout the world. Likening death to sleep—a celebrated Donnean metaphor—Joseph Brodsky gives the reader a catalog remarkable for its inclusiveness. Images of simple, everyday household items (beds, walls, carpets, pots, pans, doors) sleep next to a greater sleeping cosmos: St. Paul's Cathedral, London, the sea, "this Island," angels, even God.

In the second part (lines 96-127), this silence is broken by the sound of weeping: "But hark! Do you not hear in the chill night/ a sound of sobs, the whispered voice of fear?" There is a change in perspective. The speaker in this section addresses several questions, trying to discover who is crying, asking in succession his angel, the cherubim, Saint Paul, God, and Gabriel. Only silence answers back.

In the third section (lines 128-184), Donne's soul identifies itself as the one grieving and credits Donne with the power of soaring above the "dark sins and passions" of which his poetry speaks so eloquently. Again, the reader is given a catalog of some of the varied subjects of Donne's poetic voice: Hell, Heaven, love, life, lust, the Last Judgment. This section ends with the soul claiming that it is Donne himself who weeps: "It is not I who sob. Tis thou, John Donne:/ thou liest alone."

By the last section (lines 129-213), dawn, the image of regeneration and rebirth, starts to break. Brodsky likens Donne to a wild bird who will wake at dawn so that he can finish his final lines, uniting body and soul. Throughout the poem, the images of sleep and silence are intensified by the snow falling and swirling in, on, and between the poetic lines.

Forms and Devices

The power of "Elegy for John Donne" is developed through Brodsky's use of images, metaphors, and specific allusions to Donne's work. The strongest image is that of the silence that pervades the entire poem, a silence so deep that the reader can hear his or her own breath. The snow gently falling and blanketing all things sleeping adds to the intensity of silence and darkness. The images range from the smallest, most insignificant items to the cosmic order of the universe: "Dark Hell-fires sleep, and glorious Paradise." Brodsky's lists are reminiscent of the staccato lists in Donne's poems. In lines 7 and 8, Brodsky strings together sleeping images: "fresh linen, nightlamp, chests of drawers, a clock,/ a mirror, stairways, doors." Donne, in Holy Sonnet 7, enumerates the causes of sleep/death: "War, dearth, age, agues, tyrannies,/ Despair, law, chance."

The poem, as a whole, turns on the metaphor of death as sleep. Donne, too, employs this metaphor in several of his poems. Brodsky's sleep image permeates the poem, especially in the first part where, because Donne is dead, "All these things have sunk in sleep./ Yes, all things." This is strongly reminiscent of the dead world that Donne experienced after the early death of his wife: "The world's whole sap is sunk . . . Life is shrunk,/ Dead and interred" ("A Nocturnal upon St. Lucy's Day, Being the Shortest Day"). In Holy Sonnet 6, Donne writes, "And gluttonous death will instantly unjoint/ My body and soul, and I shall sleep a space." "Elegy for John Donne" moves from deep night toward a physical waking from sleep as dawn breaks at the end of the poem and toward a spiritual waking from death: "But see, there from the clouds will shine/ that star which made thy world endure till now." This echoes Donne's own conviction that "One short sleep past, we wake eternally" (Holy Sonnet 10).

Specific allusions to Donne's poetry, prose, and life abound and give the poem added depth and significance. Some knowledge of Donne's poetic voice enriches the reader's experience and enhances the power of Brodsky's poem. The juxtaposition of anxiety and sin in line 73 evokes many of Donne's Holy Sonnets. In line 42 ("This Island sleeps, embraced by lonely dreams"), the key words "Island" and "lonely" echo and deny Donne's assertion that "No man is an island, entire of itself; every man is a piece of the continent, a part of the main" ("Meditation XVII" from *Devotions upon Emergent Occasions*, 1624). Both the sound of weeping and the image of tears permeate Donne's poetry. Other images shared by both poets include shadows, mirrors, the crucifix, windows, and the sea.

A crucial echoing image is Brodsky's tolling bell, now silent: "No din of baying hound/ or tolling bell disturbs the silent air," resounding in its silence Donne's bell that called him toward death when he was seriously ill: "never send to know for whom the bells toll; it tolls for thee" ("Meditation XVII"). Donne implies that, when a member of the community dies, those involved in that community participate in that death, just as Brodsky implies that Donne's death has diminished the world and its inhabitants.

Themes and Meanings

"Elegy for John Donne" embodies several important themes. Brodsky posits that, when a poet dies, the world he or she has created also dies, as Donne testifies in "The Will": "I'll undo/ The world by dying." Brodsky intensifies the totality of this dead world by including the world as he knows it in the sleep that settles upon the universe. Simultaneously, however, Brodsky asserts the immortality of the world created by the genius of the poet. Donne's England comes vibrantly alive because of Brodsky's power of evocation.

Another crucial theme is the affinity between Brodsky and Donne. They share a strong spiritual bond: Both of them are Metaphysical poets deeply concerned with realities, beyond the merely physical, of love, death, solitude, sin, salvation, and regeneration; both are poets who are lone islands isolated from the greater sea of humanity, Donne because of his thwarted political ambitions and his self-imposed exile from a world that did not understand him and Brodsky because of political powers that accused him of scorning useful work that would contribute to the good of Communism. Eventually, Brodsky was tried for "social parasitism" and exiled to five years of forced labor at a state farm in Arkhangel'sk; he left his homeland for good in 1972 when he emigrated to the United States. This shared loneliness resounds throughout "Elegy for John Donne."

Brodsky's poem moves toward regeneration, especially near the end of the poem, where images of falling rain and wet earth signal rebirth. The star, mentioned twice in the latter part, illuminates the final moment of spiritual awakening. At first, the star is hidden, yet felt, as Brodsky imagines Donne "himself entrusting to that steady star/ which now is closed in clouds." This star soars into full view at the close of the poem, where it clearly evokes the stars with which Dante Alighieri (another exiled poet) ends each of the three parts to his *La divina commedia* (c.1320; *The Divine Comedy*, 1472), especially at the end of *Inferno*, when Dante physically and spiritually has conquered death: "we emerged to see—once more—the stars." Using the image of the star pointing to a transcendent reality of a possible reunion with the Creator, Brodsky ends his poem, "But see, there from the clouds will shine/ that star which made thy world endure till now."

The poem, as a whole, is held together by Brodsky's brilliant intertwining metaphor of weaving, using such ephemeral material as snowflake needles to thread together the web of images and allusions, healing the torn body and stitching together body to soul, night to dawn, and earth to heaven. Early in the poem, the needle is threadless, as the soul of Donne is shown as "needle-thin,/ yet without thread." By the end of the poem, the snow closes the gap between Donne's body and soul, "its needles flying back and forth, back, forth!" This metaphor is complemented by the conventional metaphor of the body as a garment for the soul. In death, it is torn, full of holes, and in shreds. The metaphors combine in the symbolic and transcendent image of the star "bringing the healing needle home."

Koos Daley

ELEGY FOR N. N.

Author: Czesław Miłosz (1911-   )
Type of poem: Meditation/elegy
First published: 1974, as "Elegia dla N. N.," in *Gdzie wschodzi słońce i kędy zapada*;
English translation collected in *The Collected Poems, 1931-1987*, 1988

The Poem

Written in free verse, this elegy by Nobel laureate Czesław Miłosz consists of seven irregular verse-paragraphs that form an extended meditation on human love, remorse, and memory. It is addressed to "N. N.," a woman who is not so much the subject of the poem as its audience and who shares with the poet certain memories of youth in Lithuania. Elegies are traditionally occasioned by a death, but here it is not a person but the poet's sense of connection to his past that has been lost. The poem is composed in the first person, and the reader seems to be overhearing one side of a conversation between Miłosz and his friend on the subject of loss.

The poem begins with a considerate request regarding a journey: "Tell me if it is too far for you." Immediately, the themes of distance and human limitation are presented. The poem will attempt to bridge a widening gap between the poet and his addressee, an effort which, as Miłosz's hesitant, polite tone indicates, may prove insufficient. Miłosz proceeds to escort the reader on a flight of poetic imagination halfway around the globe, beginning at the Baltic Sea and swooping over Denmark, the Atlantic Ocean, Labrador, and the Sierra Mountains to arrive in California, where he waits in a eucalyptus grove. In his mind, Miłosz helps his listeners to make the same great journey that, in the course of his life, he had made himself. He had traversed whole continents on his path from Vilnius, Lithuania, his birthplace, to Berkeley, California, where he lived at the time of the composition of this poem.

In the second section, finding the distance enormous, Miłosz reverses direction, traveling "reluctantly" back through memory to the Lithuanian countryside where he knew "N. N." Yet, the reality of that landscape, including its particular smells, contours, and features, has "changed forever into abstract crystal," oddly purified and idealized in the poet's mind.

He longs in the third section for such lost things "as they are in themselves" rather than for idealized images, but he finds that he "really can't say" how daily life there went on. He has lost touch with significant details, his "knowledge of fiery years"—perhaps the years of the Prussian and German occupations and the subsequent Soviet takeover—having scorched the elements of his pastoral and left him exiled and homeless.

The fourth and fifth sections recall images and events of World War II, with suggestions of Holocaust atrocities and of anti-German violence. Miłosz reflects on the impermanence of what he once believed to be immutable, on how "what could not be taken away/ is taken." He echoes the pre-Socratic philosopher Heraclitus, whose famous maxim that "one cannot step twice into the same river" is a depiction of restless change and eternal mutability.

In the last two sections, Miłosz comes to terms with the failure of his sense of connection to his homeland through memory. He is cut off not because of physical distance, which he demonstrates can be bridged imaginatively in memory, but sadly because of his growing indifference to the world and to life around him.

Forms and Devices

At times, the poem uses a private vocabulary which contains certain personal "secrets." Clearly, the elegy is addressed to a close friend with whom alone Miłosz shares some of his memories. Experiences and feelings are described to which an impersonal reader could not possibly have access, even if Miłosz were to supply notes or commentaries. The reader is given no exact idea, for that matter, of the identity of "N. N." The features of the Lithuanian landscape and of Vilnius are given only in flashes—the bath cabin, the scent of leather, horses at the forge—without any overall picture emerging. This technique suggests fragmentation and discontinuity in the poet's mind, as well as discrepancies in the reader's ability to read that mind. Some of those flashes use Germanic names, such as "Mama Fliegeltaub" and "Sachenhausen," names foreign to the Lithuanian landscape and language that make no sense either to the reader or to natives of Vilnius without an explanation, although Miłosz offers none. Consequently, the reader must piece together his or her own (necessarily flawed) sense of person and place. Some important figures in the poem, such as "the German owner," are unnamed, increasing their strangeness. Miłosz writes privately and exclusively in order to make the reader sense the opacity of distance and understand both his sense of separation from the past and the growing impenetrability and sterility of his memories.

In Polish, from which Miłosz himself translated this poem along with Lawrence Davis, the tone of the poem is more aggressive and personal than in English, and the opening imperative is much more direct and informal: "Powiedz czy to dla siebie za daleko." Generally, Miłosz's Polish has a more concise, direct, and condensed effect than can be captured in English. "Skręcić na ocean," for example, must be rendered as "could have turned toward the ocean," a much more unwieldy phrase. Generally, however, the translation captures the imagistic fervor and sensuality of the original.

Miłosz verges at times on surrealism, juxtaposing unexpected images in a kind of cinematic jump-cutting or montage. He sees a bath cabin, for example, transformed into "abstract crystal," a metamorphosis which is difficult to imagine if one is limited by common sense. His peculiar vision and sensual counterpoint only increase the reader's sense of being a stranger in his world, helplessly dislocated and unable to make clear sense of what is seen and heard. Like Miłosz, the reader seems to be cut off from the comforts of stable knowledge and fulfilled expectations.

Themes and Meanings

The poet laments not the death of "N. N."—which, if judged only from the content of the poem, may not even have occurred—but the loss of vitality in his imagination and memory. He mourns the failure of his spiritual connections both to an idyllic image of the past and to "things as they are in themselves," the self-sufficient world of creation around him. Miłosz's elegy, like many of his poems, deals with the loss of spiritual energy in the modern world and with his growing inability, as a poet and a human being, to remake the link between the spiritual and the physical in order to restore some sense of belonging and meaning to life. In the poem, Miłosz sees himself as indifferent and increasingly unwilling to make the effort to bridge the distances between the actual and the ideal through the medium of poetry.

Miłosz tries to come to terms with the insufficiency of poetic "greatness" and with the failure of his imagination to transcend the often trivial aspects of ordinary life. He finds, upon reconsideration and self-examination, that he has no "great secrets" to reveal. Indeed, this failure—which finds a correlative in the scorched, arid postwar landscape of his faraway homeland—becomes for Miłosz inevitable, fated, like a cancer growing within him from year to year "until it takes hold."

Miłosz is clearly pessimistic about the fate of humanity, and he condemns himself to gradual decline in the face of an inability to make sense of what he once thought were immutable values that "could not be taken away." Yet, Miłosz's thought has been characterized—by various readers and critics as well as by himself—as an "ecstatic pessimism"; that is, in the midst of tribulation and decline, the poet is able to discover some ecstatic core, some essentially vital, energetic center upon which he can draw for poetic inspiration. In this elegy, despite his apparent failure to connect to his homeland through memories, Miłosz can still imagine a sensuously dense landscape, rife with surprising juxtapositions and aesthetic promise. Though reluctant to face the possibility of failure again, Miłosz nevertheless undertakes his poetic work and, out of the scorched ashes of his memory, is able to make, if nothing else, a poignant tribute to his loss.

Kevin McNeilly

ELEGY OF FORTINBRAS

Author: Zbigniew Herbert (1924-1998)
Type of poem: Elegy
First published: 1961, as "Tren Fortynbrasa," in *Studium przedmiotu*; English transla-
tion collected in *Selected Poems*, 1968

The Poem

At the end of William Shakespeare's *Hamlet* (c. 1600-1601), Fortinbras, the prince
of Norway, arrives in Denmark just in time to witness the aftermath of the tragedy.
The bodies of Hamlet, Laertes, Gertrude, and Claudius litter the stage; the sight,
as Fortinbras says, may become the battlefield, "but here shows much amiss." Fortinbras's role in the play is small. The audience occasionally hears of him but only
briefly sees him as he brings his army through Denmark to reclaim territories elsewhere. Hamlet, who glimpses Fortinbras as he traverses Denmark, immediately begins to chastise himself for being unlike Fortinbras, who goes to battle "even for an
eggshell." Hamlet has more cause for action and yet has done nothing.

It is this Fortinbras, this minor star in a stellar cast, that Zbigniew Herbert selects to
deliver a final tribute to Hamlet. Given that Fortinbras's perspective and character are
so slightly developed in the play, it is somewhat surprising that Herbert elects this
nondescript personage to lament the hero's death. Why not Horatio, Hamlet's dearest
friend? Perhaps the audience knows Horatio so well that it can imagine what he would
say. The relatively empty character of Fortinbras gives Herbert more imaginative freedom. Also, Fortinbras will assume the rather major task of cleaning up after Hamlet.
If critics are right about Shakespeare's tragedies ending with intimations of order,
Fortinbras is the person who will order a disordered kingdom. It is this cipher, rather
than the stars in the cast, that Herbert chooses to give a voice.

Herbert's Fortinbras delivers an elegy which brings Hamlet's life into bold and simple relief. The intensity with which Hamlet experienced life was, Fortinbras reveals,
incompatible with the living of life. Hamlet was "always twitching as if asleep," preoccupied by "chimeras." A too-pure vision of life can cause life to wither—such is
Hamlet's vision. As Fortinbras portrays him, Hamlet was made to live in a different
element, one more ethereal, less sullied by the trivia, plodding, and patience that life
requires. Fortinbras accepts, unlike Hamlet's personal advocates, Horatio and Ophelia,
that Hamlet could not live: "Anyhow you had to perish Hamlet you were not for life/
you believed in crystal notions not in human clay . . . wolfishly you crunched the air
only to vomit/ you knew no human thing you did not know even how to/ breathe."
Even the air seemed to make Hamlet ill. He was too inquisitorial and too impatient for
life, and thus he could not find a way to live it.

Fortinbras's elegy expresses both admiration for Hamlet and a subtle envy. It also
expresses some little contempt and perhaps a great love. Fortinbras realizes that, in
comparison to Hamlet, he himself appears thoroughly banal. He is soldierly and inele-

gant, whereas Hamlet is a fashionable melancholiac. Fortinbras is very much aware as he speaks his elegy that the martial funeral rites that he will provide for Hamlet will be gauche, inappropriate to one who was a scholar, courtier, and glass of fashion.

While Fortinbras believes that what he leaves "will not be worth a tragedy" and that the "star named Hamlet" will always outshine him by magnitudes, he also believes that Hamlet took the easy way out: "you chose the easier part an elegant thrust/ but what is heroic death compared with eternal watching." Fortinbras has the less glamorous job, the almost janitorial task of cleaning up a bloody stage and a bad government, but he takes some pride in his drudgery: "Adieu prince I have tasks a sewer project and a decree on prostitutes and beggars/ I must also elaborate a better system of prisons/ since as you justly said Denmark is a prison."

Forms and Devices

The version of "Elegy of Fortinbras" described above is a translation of Herbert's poem by Czesław Miłosz, who, like Herbert, is a Polish poet. Miłosz has translated his own Polish poems into English, often in consultation with the poet Robert Hass. In translating Herbert's poems, Miłosz collaborated with Peter Dale Scott, a Canadian who worked in an embassy in Warsaw and appreciated Herbert when his poems were first published in 1956. Herbert lived through both the Nazi occupation and the Stalinist repression, and he had to wait until the thaw to see his poems published.

The elegy is presented as a direct address to Hamlet alone. Everyone has left the stage; only Fortinbras and the dead Hamlet remain. This direct address or apostrophe gives the poem great intimacy. Readers feel as though they are overhearing words meant for Hamlet alone, or that Fortinbras's soliloquy is really meant for himself. This intimate tone is in very stark contrast to the cool, highly formalized public speech that Fortinbras delivers at the end of Shakespeare's play.

Fortinbras speaks his elegy in six verse paragraphs. These paragraphs contain no punctuation either between or within them. The weightiness and balance of the language, however, suggest very clearly when and where the reading voice should pause. Song and sense are so powerful in the poem that the notation of punctuation is unnecessary.

The tone and language of the poem are stately, respectful, somber, and even awed, not only by the death of an exceptional creature but also by the raw fact of death. Fortinbras speaks of death with an awareness of both its generic and its particular force: "I could never think of your hands without smiling/ and now that they lie on the stone like fallen nests/ they are as defenceless as before The end is exactly this/ The hands lie apart The sword lies apart The head apart/ and the knight's feet in soft slippers." The figurative language of the poem is genuinely remarkable. That Hamlet's hands remind Fortinbras of "fallen nests" suggests their vulnerability, a vulnerability which was once concealed by their activeness. The comparison to fallen nests also suggests lost fruitfulness, abbreviated youth, and the actual physical curvature of reposing hands. Fortinbras also remarks that Hamlet's feet now appear to be in "soft slippers"—so unlike the strutting buskins of tragedy.

Fortinbras's description of himself is perhaps even more remarkable. Contrasting himself to Hamlet, who left the world by "an elegant thrust," Fortinbras predicts that he himself will have a longer, harder, lonelier life. The dull but durable ruler is one who eternally watches "with a cold apple in one's hand on a narrow chair/ with a view of the ant-hill and the clock's dial." Indeed, Fortinbras seems to be unaware of his own eloquence.

The last figure of the poem is equally evocative. As Fortinbras completes his elegy, he says that he and Hamlet will never meet—neither in reality nor in the words that Fortinbras tries to send to Hamlet. They live on different islands, and neither water nor words can unite them: "It is not for us to greet each other or bid farewell we live on/ archipelagos/ and that water these words what can they do what can they/ do prince." With these words, Fortinbras concludes his elegy, realizing that even to say "good-bye" to Hamlet is impossible.

Themes and Meanings

These last lines are a powerful summation of the poem's emotional core, which is Herbert's lament that Fortinbras's way of being and Hamlet's are forever irreconcilable. The idealist and the pragmatist are two different species: One admires the former and never hears of the latter. As Fortinbras knows, it will be he who does the work, who makes the filthy world that Hamlet rants about more clean. He will build sewers, and he will deal (one fears, harshly) with society's problems—the prostitutes, beggars, and criminals—but he will be neither remembered nor admired.

Herbert lived much of his life in a time of political tumult and human agony: The Nazi occupation killed one of every five Polish people, a catastrophe which makes the catastrophe of *Hamlet* seem very small indeed. Having lived through a succession of idealisms turned awry and made brutal, Herbert may have acquired a real admiration for the literal-minded and modest medicines of a Fortinbras, who will "elaborate," as he says, "a better system of prisons."

Hamlet fascinates everyone, but those who help the world keep turning may very well be undistinguished or have, like Fortinbras, a quiet poetry of their own.

Anne Shifrer

ELEGY TO THE MEMORY OF AN UNFORTUNATE LADY

Author: Alexander Pope (1688-1744)
Type of poem: Elegy
First published: 1717, in *The Works of Mr. Alexander Pope*

The Poem

"Elegy to the Memory of an Unfortunate Lady" is a melancholy, emotion-charged poem of eighty-two lines, involving a poet's celebration of his lady, who committed suicide because her guardian thwarted their love. As an elegy, the poem follows the conventions of the genre in its effusive praise of a young, prematurely deceased person whose foreshortened life serves as an inspiration to present and future generations.

The elegy opens with a male poet who beholds his beloved's ghost with a sword piercing her bleeding heart. He addresses her, until line 74, questioning her fate as a thwarted lover and a suicide: "Is it, in heav'n, a crime to love too well?" Why has she been treated so shabbily by her family? Will she be remembered for the wonderful woman that she was? Is she now in heaven, now in possession of some kind of peace, despite her Christian sin of suicide? Her ambition destined her for the heavens, and her departure from this earth has deprived her family below of all "virtue (to redeem her race)" (lines 11-28).

The poem proceeds next to a diatribe against her uncle and guardian. The poet-lover actually compounds the guardian's failings in Christian charity toward his female ward by heaping curses for the early death of the uncle's entire family to an overwrought, even surrealistic degree ("And frequent hearses shall beseige your gates/ . . . While the long fun'rals blacken all the way").

There are suggestions that the lady died tended by strangers—that strangers buried her in an unhallowed grave, without Christian burial rights because of her suicide—but that nature restored beauty and sacredness to her unmarked grave site, where angels "o'ershade/ The ground, now sacred by thy reliques made." The next lines add that she is now mere dust, "as all the proud shall be."

The poem concludes with a *memento mori* (a reminder to be prepared for death) in which the lover laments that he too will die and will no longer be able to mourn his beloved (lines 75-82): "Life's idle business at one gasp be o'er,/ The Muse forgot, and thou beloved no more."

Many critics have found the poem to be somewhat unsatisfactory and problematic. The circumstances of the lady's life and death, for example, are not clearly portrayed; the feeling sometimes seems forced, the rhetoric artificial. Samuel Johnson, in his *Life of Pope* (1781), although he "allowed" that parts were written with "vigorous animation" or "a gentle tenderness," stated that "the tale is not skilfully told," noting that it was difficult to determine the character of either the lady or her guardian.

Forms and Devices

Alexander Pope's "Elegy to the Memory of an Unfortunate Lady," like his equally melancholy *Epistle from Eloisa to Abelard* (1717), is usually associated with an atypical impulse toward Romanticism in his canon because of an indulgence in sentiment that is uncommon in his longer poetry. The fact that both poems are monologues, treating women in a similar grandiose vein of thwarted love and loss, emphasizes their kinship, especially in relation to contemporary conventions of excessive passion in the sentimental tragedies of a playwright such as Nicholas Rowe.

The elegy's opening lines are stagey; they seem an echo of Hamlet's meeting with his father's ghost. Pope makes use of a supernatural Gothic situation and a declamatory style of address often seen and heard on the eighteenth century stage. Pulling out all the stops in the presence of the gory ghost, the grieving lover stresses the pathos of his lady's tragedy.

The heightened sentimentality of the poem stems from its being packed with elaborate rhetoric. There is the pounding symmetry of Pope's masterful heroic couplets (or closed pentameter couplets) to lend order to the emotionally discordant subject matter of lost love. As part of his declamatory mode, the poet-lover's couplets can employ rhetorical repetition, replete with parallel phrases, echoing sounds, and modulated meaning that climaxes in a summary closing line possessing internal balance:

> By foreign hands thy dying eyes were clos'd,
> By foreign hands thy decent limbs compos'd,
> By foreign hands thy humble grave adorn'd,
> By strangers honour'd, and by strangers mourn'd!

By the same token, the poet-lover makes repeated use of rhetorical questions, which bid defiance to any answers other than what he already assumes: that his lady was wronged and should be glorified.

Pope's heroic couplets give his poetry an aphoristic quality, as in the following observation on human mortality: "A heap of dust alone remains of thee;/ 'Tis all thou art, and all the proud shall be." Poetic diction—elevated poetic statement—comes into play when black funeral clothes are termed "sable weeds." There is pathetic fallacy when nature is said to cooperate in mourning at her gravesite: "There shall the morn her earliest tears bestow."

Finally, in keeping with the rhetorical quality of "Elegy to the Memory of an Unfortunate Lady," a simile appears in the explicit comparison between dull ordinary mortals with no "ambition," and lazy oriental monarchs devoid of the dead lady's godlike ambition (aspiration) in life: "Like Eastern kings a lazy state [sedateness] they keep."

Themes and Meanings

The poem is, as an elegy should be, about death in the romantic context of thwarted love at a time when European women of the upper classes could fall under the almost absolute power of a guardian or parent until the age of maturity. Despite references to the dead lady's soul's flight to heaven—"its congenial place"—or her body in the grave (lines 63-70), her premature death inspires a concentration on the mortality of the human race, including that of the poet and the cruel uncle. The theme is only slightly less nihilistic than the related meaning of Pope's satiric last judgment on the benighted human race in Book IV of *The Dunciad* (1742): "And Universal Darkness buries All."

When, around 1717, Pope was contemplating a collected edition of his poems, he possibly regretted that certain kinds of Roman poems were not represented among them. Like Vergil, he had produced pastorals and an epic (a mock epic); he had also composed a Horatian *Ars Poetica* in his "Essay on Criticism" (1711). Missing from his canon was any imitation of Ovid's *Heroides* (before 8 C.E.) or elegiac passages of the *Metamorphoses* (c. 8 C.E.). This poem and *Epistle from Eloisa to Abelard* filled this gap with amatory and self-consciously melancholy poetry. There are similarities between Pope's two love poems in tone and rhetorical devices, in basic motifs, and in the vagueness of the narratives.

Heroic love in the Ovidian tradition is not a private affair, but rather a drama that is played on the stage of history and that is supposedly well known to readers. In "Elegy to the Memory of an Unfortunate Lady," Pope was trying to write an Ovidian poem of heroic love, but about a private—even obscure—affair. His own note on the poem's title suggests that the lady was a woman intending monastic retirement, as memorialized in verses by "the Duke of Buckingham." There have been conjectures about the reality of the unfortunate lady; many commentators, however, doubt that she existed anywhere outside of the author's imagination.

The poem, emulating Renaissance aesthetics, contains a mixture of Christian and pagan classical sentiments; this mixture, sometimes confusing, is especially important because the poem deals with an issue that Christianity views as a sin—suicide. Pope wants his readers to overlook this aspect (a difficult task, especially given the era in which he wrote), so he stresses the classical noble or heroic view of the suicide of a true lover or an ancient Roman hero. The opening question about the lady's eligibility for a "bright reversion" to a Christian heaven is therefore answered by assertions that her death had a pagan nobility (a "lover's or a Roman's part") or had the flawed grandeur of rebellious "Angels and of gods." The mixture of pagan and Christian sentiments may also have led to the poet-lover's vengeful (and contradictory) cursing of the "false guardian" because of the guardian's lack of Christian charity toward the ward: "So perish all, whose breast ne'er learned to glow/ For others' good, or melt at others' woe."

Thomas M. Curley

ELEVEN ADDRESSES TO THE LORD

Author: John Berryman (1914-1972)
Type of poem: Poetic sequence
First published: 1970, in *Love and Fame*

The Poem

The title of "Eleven Addresses to the Lord" suggests its basic structure and intent. Eleven short poems, each capable of standing alone but enhanced by association with the others, compose the whole. Each poem is written in quatrains of varying line length; rhyme is often, though not consistently, used.

In the first address, Berryman (there is no perceivable distance between the persona-narrator and the author) praises God as the "Master of beauty" and the fashioner of things exquisitely small and lovely (the snowflake) and grandly inspiring (the earth). These are common ways of looking at God, but soon Berryman's focus becomes more personal: God has come to his rescue "again and again" over the years. Had he not, the implication is quite clear, the narrator would have destroyed himself as so many of his friends have done. Both the praise of God's creation and gratitude for his sustaining blessing are traditional poetic gestures. What is less traditional, however, is the open doubt expressed by the poet: "I have no idea whether we live again."

The first address sets the pattern that the succeeding ten will follow in whole or in part: praise of God and his creation, gratitude for his assistance, and a strain of doubt that is sometimes subtle but elsewhere blatant enough to border on cynicism or sarcasm. Address 2 finds Berryman once again praising God the Creator and especially for his "certain goodness to me." By the end of address 2, however, doubt once more encroaches: "'I say Thy kingdom come,' it means nothing to me."

Addresses 3 and 4 are closely related. Three is perhaps the most conventional of the eleven poems. Here, Berryman prays that God will protect him from his sinful nature, which in the past, it is obvious from the allusions, has caused the author to hurt others as well as himself. Having called for God's aid in the third address, in the fourth Berryman wonders whether God is there to hear his request and prays for strength and faith.

The fifth address narrows the focus to one specific question: What follows life? Probably the damned will suffer no pains of hell; the faithful will likely receive no heavenly reward, either. "Rest may be your ultimate gift," Berryman surmises. The sixth address locates the source of Berryman's conflicts with God and his fellow man. Until he was twelve, he served at Mass six days a week; then his father committed suicide, and thereafter, "Confusions & afflictions/ followed my days."

The seventh address advises a desolate young woman to look to Justin Martyr's words of wisdom. The eighth ("A Prayer for the Self"), ninth, and tenth addresses find Berryman asking for God's blessing, as God blessed him before. In the eleventh address, Berryman cites martyrs who died for their faith and ends this moving poetic sequence by praying for the strength to bear up under whatever "Thou wilt award."

Forms and Devices

Berryman has long been considered one of the twentieth century's great innovators, a master manipulator of poetic conventions. These manipulations are most fully developed in *The Dream Songs* (1969) and are, to a degree at least, more muted in "Eleven Addresses to the Lord." Nevertheless, Berryman provocatively utilizes many poetic devices to enhance the sequence's complex interplay of sincerity and irony. Indeed, just as the poem thematically wavers between faith and doubt, its form varies from the almost anachronistically traditional to innovations that, especially in a context of conventional devices, are deliberately jarring.

At first glance the conventional elements seem to predominate. The title predisposes the reader to expect something traditional, "Eleven Addresses to the Lord" being as appropriate for the twelfth century as the twentieth. Moreover, the individual poems seem very close to Horation odes—that is, discourses on a single subject employing an unvarying stanzaic pattern. As with this centuries-old form, the language, initially at least, seems appropriately lofty and dignified.

Even if the reader did not recognize the Horatian ode form, however, one glance at the page would seem to promise poetic conventionality: All sections are written in apparently standard quatrains. This promise seems confirmed at the beginning of the poem, where God is described as "Master of beauty, craftsman of the snowflake"— imagery so traditional as to border on the trite. Proceeding through the poem, the reader encounters rhyme both internal and end, placing this sequence once more, apparently, in the conventional category.

Save for the quatrain, however, which is maintained throughout, these early impressions of stylistic conventionality are soon shattered. Line lengths vary with no apparent pattern. Predictably, the meter also varies, from as many as seven accented syllables per line to as few as two. This poem, which at first glance appears to be "old-fashioned" is, therefore, written in free verse. Similarly, although Berryman writes beautifully and rhythmically, the rhythm is less than conventional. Indeed, there is hardly a single line in the entire sequence that has a consistent rhythm (that is, entirely iambic or entirely trochaic).

When the reader turns to other apparently conventional features of the poem, a similar undermining of tradition is found. Berryman uses rhyme, for instance, but in no discernible pattern. Some of the addresses have no rhymes, others one or two or several. Moreover, the rhymes are rarely strong rhymes but are almost invariably slant rhymes ("begins" and "eloquence"; "done" and "come") or combinations that barely hint of rhyme and can hardly be classified even as slant rhymes ("Paul" and "chair"; "man" and "doom").

The diction and imagery are also deliberately inconsistent in tone and effect. "Through" is anachronistically and unnecessarily spelled "thro'," while "and" is sometimes written using the modern stenographer's ampersand ("&"). The syntax is sometimes so determinedly poetic as to be stilted ("cross am I sometimes"), while elsewhere Berryman throws in a slangy colloquialism: "Uh-huh." And Berryman's God may be "craftsman of the snowflake"—an image poets centuries ago would have been very comfortable with—but what medieval poet would dare describe part of God's creation as the "boring Moon"? All of these deliberate inconsistencies serve to jar the reader out of complacency and underscore a thematic development that is equally ambiguous.

Themes and Meanings

"Eleven Addresses to the Lord" was originally collected as part 4 of *Love and Fame* (1970), a volume that explores with often shocking frankness John Berryman's relationship with women and his public life. In "Eleven Addresses to the Lord," however, Berryman's public life for the most part disappears as a subject, and love becomes his love for God.

Critical reaction to the collection as a whole and to "Eleven Addresses to the Lord" specifically has been mixed, with a number of critics taking at face value Berryman's self-congratulatory bombast in the earlier sections of the collection and concluding that his expressions of faith in "Eleven Addresses to the Lord" are uniformly sincere. Examination of the poem's forms and devices, however, should warn the reader against assuming that anything in the poem is free from ambiguity and irony.

Berryman's ambivalence toward God is evident from the very beginning of the sequence. In the first quatrain of the first address, God is praised in conventional terms as "craftsman of the snowflake," but that craftsman also created "the boring Moon." This ambiguity leads directly to that quatrain's final line, in which the author thanks God for "such as it is my gift." Is his gift analogous to the "Earth so gorgeous" or the "boring Moon"? If the latter, should such a gift truly elicit gratitude to God? Two stanzas later Berryman praises God in apparently unequivocal terms for repeatedly rescuing him. This, however, is immediately followed by "You have allowed my brilliant friends to destroy themselves," the "allowed" being troubling in reference to a supposedly merciful, loving God.

Is God truly loving or indifferent? The next quatrain concludes that there is no clear answer. Rather, God is "unknowable, as I am unknowable to my guinea pigs." This doubt is stated in the clearest possible terms in the next stanza in reference to the possibility of an afterlife: "I have no idea whether we live again." Still, Berryman insists that he believes in Christ's resurrection as firmly as he believes he sits "in this blue chair." The reader might well wonder what color chair Berryman was sitting in when he penned that line.

The first address ends in an apparently unequivocal expression of faith, but given what has gone before, readers cannot with confidence know whether this ending is sincere or ironic bordering on the sarcastic. The following ten sections of the sequence address varying specific aspects of the question of faith. Everywhere apparently sincere avowals are undercut with at least subtle irony and often open doubt. Berryman clearly defines the problem: in questions of religious faith, he states in the last line of address 6, "I identify with everybody, even the heresiarchs."

Dennis Vannatta

ELLEN WEST

Author: Frank Bidart (1939-   )
Type of poem: Dramatic monologue
First published: 1977, in *The Book of the Body*

The Poem

"Ellen West" is a long dramatic monologue written from the point of view of a woman battling her body. The tone is conversational, but interspersed in the monologue are four prose passages written from a physician's clinical perspective. In fact, Frank Bidart's poem centers on the dilemma of mind and body, inner and outer. The chatty, introspective, philosophical tone of Ellen West contrasts with the detached observations of her doctor, who documents her decline. From multiple perspectives, the reader comes to know the struggles of this woman trying to come to terms with her "true self."

The poem is divided into eleven unnumbered parts, each separated informally by a set of three centered typographic bullets. In the first section, Ellen expresses her wish to be thin, "the sort of blond/ elegant girl whose/ body is the image of her soul." She recognizes that her own love of sweets is in direct opposition to this ideal. She also finds herself in conflict with her doctor's and her husband's images of who she should be. In a short space, part 1 documents an emotionally turbulent person, one who moves rapidly among humor, desire, determination, and anger.

Part 2 opens with "Why am I a girl?" The doctors cannot tell her why. They say "that it is just 'given.'" Her preoccupation with her identity eludes the doctor, who is keenly interested in Ellen's physical symptoms. In part 3, the first prose passage, the reader sees how the doctor sees her: "Now, at the beginning of Ellen's thirty-second year, her physical condition has deteriorated still further. Her use of laxatives increases beyond measure." He goes on to describe her self-induced vomiting and loss of weight. Ellen's condition, as the reader may have suspected, is critical.

Part 4 is a flashback, told as a story by Ellen about one time, before she was married, when she ate alone in a restaurant. She was "sitting there alone/ with a book, both in the book/ and out of it, waited on, idly/ watching people,—" when a very attractive couple entered. Ellen always seems to be both "in" her experience and "out of it," watching the world. As with her paradoxical obsession to eat whatever she wants and to be thin, she is both attracted and repelled by the couple. Food becomes associated with desire: "Then . . . I noticed the way/ each held his fork out for the other/ to taste what he had ordered . . ./ . . . I knew what they were. I knew they slept together." Ellen recognizes that she can never have that kind of intimacy. To be with another, "to become a wife," she "would have to give up [her] ideal."

In the next section, Ellen vows: "I shall *defeat* 'Nature.'" She is stunned both by her mother's natural aging and by her own terrible attraction and repulsion to food: "In the hospital, when they/ weigh me, I wear weights secretly sewn into my belt." If her ideal is to be loved or to be thin, she will not let herself have either. Part 5 is a series of journal entries written by Ellen's doctor in prose. Ellen is "the patient." Her condition is described by its physical signs, "Salivary glands are markedly enlarged on both sides," and in quick notations: "Agitation, quickly subsided again." Through the doctor's report, the reader discovers that, because Ellen has felt degraded by her attraction to food, she has "stopped writing poetry." The reader is given a sample of Ellen's poetics through the doctor's quotation of her diary: "art is the 'mutual permeation' of the 'world of the body' and the 'world of the spirit.' "

Ellen's physical obsession extends to a section on the opera singer Maria Callas, her favorite. When the artist is at her peak, she is fat and her voice is "healthy; robust; subtle; but capable of/ crude effects, even vulgar,/ almost out of/ high spirits, too much health." When Callas loses weight, Ellen notices, her voice deteriorates. It is as if she swallowed a tapeworm and "the *tapeworm*/ was her *soul*." Deteriorating both mentally and physically, but still deeply perceptive, Ellen speculates: "Perhaps her spirit/ loathed the unending struggle/ to *embody* itself, to *manifest* itself, on a stage whose/ mechanics, and suffocating customs,/ seemed expressly designed to annihilate the spirit . . . " Ellen projects her own battle of spirit and body onto Callas and concludes that perhaps "*the only way/ to escape/ the History of Styles/ is not to have a body.*"

Part 7 is the emotional climax of the poem. Here, Ellen examines her destructive, compulsive behavior. She debates within herself the wish to be thin—"the ideal/ *not* to have a body"—and the problem that "without a body, who can/ *know* himself at all?" For a moment, she knows who she is—"Only by/ acting; choosing; rejecting; have I/ made myself—/ discovered who and what *Ellen* can be . . . "—but then she immediately denies it. The third prose passage reveals that the doctors have decided to discharge the patient. They doubt that they can help her: "All three of us are agreed that it is not a case of obsessional neurosis and not one of manic-depressive psychosis, and that no definitely reliable therapy is possible."

In part 9, describing a train ride with her husband, presumably to go home after her discharge, Ellen again cuts herself off as she observes the strangers around her. While these strangers have "ordinary bodies," she feels "surrounded by creatures/ with the pathetic, desperate/ desire to be *not* what they were." Her attention moves to a piece of orange a child drops on the dirty floor. As she stares longingly at the food and back at her husband, she feels his "disappointment." She has trapped herself in the desire to have—or to be—what she tells herself she cannot.

Part 10, the final prose passage in the doctor's voice, begins in elation. Ellen "is as if transformed." She is satisfied with food for the first time in thirteen years. She appears happy, she writes letters—and then, suddenly, she is dead. After taking a "lethal dose of poison . . . she looked as she had never looked in life—calm and happy and peaceful."

The final part is a letter, written in verse, from Ellen to a friend and fellow patient. She acknowledges that this friend and Ellen's husband "have by degrees drawn me within the circle," the circle of friends and other people, "But," she says, "something in me *refuses* it." Ultimately, she feels that she cannot compromise, she cannot "poison an ideal." She ends, sadly, knowing that she disappoints her friend but unable to help herself.

Forms and Devices

Bidart's poem has the look and sound of prose. Some parts actually are prose, as when the poem switches to the doctor's clinical perspective, but in the rest of the poem as well there is never a predictable line length or stanza. Instead, words stretch across the page. Lines begin at the left margin or are indented to capture a rhythm of speech or a subtle manipulation of suspense. For example, a typical passage can be seen in the fourth part, when Ellen is alone in a restaurant watching a man and woman:

> —Were they married?
>> were *they* lovers?
>
> They didn't wear wedding rings.
>
> Their behavior was circumspect. They discussed
> politics. They didn't touch.

Bidart uses typography to emphasize his words. Dashes and semicolons abound, sometimes one unexpectedly beside the other. Words are italicized or capitalized for dramatic emphasis. It is not uncommon for a line to begin with a dash or to end with ellipses. Because "Ellen West" is an interior monologue, thoughts interrupt themselves and trail off. A line may appear by itself to emphasize an isolated thought. The words are orchestrated on the page with spacing, line breaks, punctuation, and capitalization. The effect is as though the reader were inside the speaker's mind, shifting with her mental scrutiny and quick-changing emotions.

The plainness of the diction also creates the sound of prose. Bidart's poetry does not include much imagery and metaphor; rather, it follows the dynamics of speech. In some ways, this kind of poetry has to be even more controlled. While it is clearly intentional, it also has the look and sound of natural, unrehearsed speech, which fits with the form of a monologue, especially one by a person undergoing severe physical and psychological change.

Along with its prose rhythms, "Ellen West" has the development of character and plot one might expect in a short story. Parts of the poem, in fact, are stories describing episodes from the main character's life, such as the scenes in the restaurant or on the train. At other points, Bidart switches to a more abstract diction:

> "Art has *repaid* me LIKE THIS?"
>> I felt I was watching
> autobiography—
>> an art; skill;
> virtuosity
> miles distant from the usual soprano's
> athleticism,—
>> the usual musician's dream
> of virtuosity *without* content . . .

With the technique of a short-story writer, but with a much more musical line, Bidart moves comfortably from a concrete scene to a philosophical speculation. His form allows him to be speculative. It is not at all out of place for the woman with eating disorders to raise serious questions of being or of art. Here, the "virtuosity" Ellen respects in Callas is the same principle that drives Bidart's poetry—not the "usual musician's dream/ of virtuosity *without* content," but virtuosity of language with content. Bidart's style allows him to capture voice and thought in a way that would not be possible in conventional verse.

Themes and Meanings

On the surface, this poem is about a woman with serious eating disorders who has a breakdown and ultimately commits suicide. There is a story here with drama, suspense, and a strong point of view. In its examination of Ellen's relationship to the world, though, the poem raises deeper questions about identity. The poem begins simply and prosaically: "I love sweets." Within four lines, however, the speaker asserts: "But my true self/ is thin, all profile/ and effortless gestures, the sort of blond/ elegant girl whose/ body is the image of her soul." For the rest of the poem, the speaker is pulled in opposite directions to follow her impulses to eat or to try to become her "ideal" self. "Art," she is quoted as saying in her diary, "is the 'mutual permeation' of the 'world of the body' and the 'world of the spirit.' " Her obsession to control her body, to control "Nature," is an effort to embody her spirit. It is a struggle to gain control of herself. She has "the ideal/ *not* to have a body," but "without a body, who can/ *know* himself at all?"

Ellen confounds her doctors by asking questions of being such as "Why am I a girl?" Ultimately, they discharge her because "no definitely reliable therapy is possible." The doctors in the poem are easy to criticize for missing the true issues that were battling inside the speaker, but the doctors are less important for their understanding than for providing an outside, pseudoscientific perspective on her "case." The doctor's voice, in prose, is a musical counterpoint to the highly charged, highly emotional, and introverted voice of Ellen. The multiple perspectives, reinforced by the varied diction and style of the poem, create a persona who is always separating herself from the world and observing her own behavior. She is "both in the book/ and out of it." Her vision is always questioning, never stable. In the final letter to her friend before her death, she is clearly aware of the kindness of others and of her own inability to combine body and spirit in a healthy way.

Jeffrey Schwartz

ELM

Author: Sylvia Plath (1932-1963)
Type of poem: Dramatic monologue
First published: 1962, as "The Elm Speaks"; collected in *Ariel*, 1965

The Poem

"Elm," a poem in free verse, has fourteen stanzas of three lines each. The title under which it was first published, "The Elm Speaks," indicates that it is a dramatic monologue. Yet "Elm" seems to be a more suitable title for the poem, because Sylvia Plath uses three pronouns—"she," "I," and "you"—which can be read as the divided selves of one identity as well as three separate roles. "She" not only engenders the elm tree but also signifies an artistic detachment of the poet from both "I" and "you." "I"—the elm—both distances herself from and merges with "you" to create the double voices inside the poet's psyche. What weaves the poem together is the powerful image of an elm tree with a protean identity.

The poem starts with the image of the elm as a woman who knows "the bottom"— the essential nature of truth—through personal experience. Inside her, this knowledge boils like a sea of dissatisfaction. The phrase "the voice of nothing" reminds the reader of one of William Shakespeare's most famous lines from *Macbeth* (1606): "sound and fury,/ Signifying nothing." The poet successfully creates an atmosphere of maddened sound and fury for unfolding a bitter experience.

The tree speaker, assuming the role of a woman, tries to impart the truth she knows about love to the innocent "you." She declares love "a shadow" and depicts its irretrievability as the sound of the hooves of a horse running away. She also acts as the agent of sexual seduction. The "sound of poisons," "rain," and "hush" are sexual allusions, but this love bears only a fruit "tin-white, like arsenic."

In stanza 6, the elm takes over the role of "you" and suffers the loss of love ("sunsets"); her lifeblood ("red filaments") is reduced to broken nerves ("a hand of wires"). Then, the elm, a tree battered in a violent storm, assumes the part of a revengeful woman. Yet she is horrified by her own capacity for violence.

Stanzas 8 and 9 shift to the moon, an image of the barren female. The moon is portrayed as an external power that can harm the female tree, as well as its internal alien force. The female tree removes its barrenness symbolized by the moon and becomes pregnant with the dreams of the victimized woman, merging with her spirit. What she carries in her womb, however, is not a physical child but an artistic cry for love as well as a phobia about the ephemeral nature of love.

The final two stanzas, the first of which begins with the declaration "I am incapable of more knowledge," correspond to the beginning of the poem ("I know the bottom"). These stanzas carry this finality of truth to a climactic intensity. Now, the image of a contorted elm tree mirrors the ugly face of love, which is murderous because it truncates a woman's growth (in its stranglehold of branches), turns a woman's will into stone, and kills a woman by penetrating her female body, causing fissures as faults do in the body of a rock or wearing her away as acid does. The phrases "snaky acids kiss" and "the isolate, slow faults/ That kill" represent more grim allusions to sexual love. Nevertheless, comparing the beginning and the ending of the poem carefully reveals that the poet affirms love instead of rejecting it: The slow killing by love is the way to tap the bottom, to gain ultimate knowledge.

Forms and Devices

"Elm" shows the influence of Theodore Roethke. In the poem, Plath develops the Roethkean system of correspondence between nature and humankind. She makes the elm, in reality an enormous tree that stood by her house in Devon, England, speak in a human voice, and she follows the shifting images of the tree through different circumstances to portray the mental turmoil of a suffering woman.

The poem demonstrates Plath's accurate observation of natural objects. Even if the reader were to read the poem superficially, without thinking about any deep interpretation, "Elm" could still be enjoyed as a portrait of a tree from root to branches, from day to night, and in all weather. Onomatopoeic expressions, such as the galloping sound of the tree's leaves in the wind, the hissing sound of poisons at the time of pesticide spraying, and the shrieking of the tree in storms, combined with precise physical pictures such as "a hand of wires," flying "clubs," and "tin-white" fruit, animate the tree throughout while catching and maintaining the peculiar features of an elm.

Apart from the controlling image of the elm, other images, both bold and subtle, are abundant in the poem. The sea represents the inner world of disturbance, conflict, and distress. The moon, as in Plath's other poems, represents hateful barrenness. For all of its purity and radiance, it "scathes" the elm and scours the sea. The moon can be an imposing authority, such as the speaker's mother, or an alien force inside herself. Plath uses the phrase "radical surgery" to suggest her resolute separation from the moon's influence either on her or inside her. The image of the snake is developed with the phrases "sound of poisons" and "snaky acids kiss," which also strongly evoke the image of the Gorgon. The poet's experience of pregnancy is implied in "this dark thing/ That sleeps in me;/ All day I feel its soft, feathery turnings. . . . " No matter what images Plath employs, she molds each one into a precise association with the elm tree to present a female's experience of the loss of love.

Although its psychological landscape is fragmented, the structure of the poem is highly coherent. Its movements are chain reactions of imagery or verbal associations: "Horse" in stanza 3 can be paired with "gallop" in stanza 4; "sound of poisons" and "arsenic" are both found in stanza 5; "atrocity of sunsets," "scorched," and "red filaments" are all together in stanza 6; "sunsets" in stanza 6 can be paired with "moon" in stanza 8; and "shriek" in stanza 7 can be linked with "cry" in stanza 10.

As an adolescent, Plath wrote, "I write only because/ There is a voice within me/ That will not be still." That voice, in "Elm" as in her later poems, became a scream of consciousness, with painful and outrageous passions.

Themes and Meanings

"Elm" is one of the great poems dealing with the loss of love. Unlike Emily Dickinson, who went through painful ambivalence and eventually rejected love to preserve her independence as a woman, Plath accepted love as an anchor for a woman's feelings and as a prerequisite for her personal and artistic integrity. To her, loss of love was the most horrible figure of torture and deprivation, which could fragment a woman and leave her a helpless victim of cruel abandonment. The elm tree, nature's witness to such atrocity, shrieks and cries for the inarticulate woman.

Although "Elm" does not link a woman's suffering with a particular historical atrocity of political and social impact, as Plath's "Daddy" and "Lady Lazarus" do, it transcends the agony of the female sex to reflect an acute sense of fragmentation and depersonalization.

"Elm" is also one of Plath's best philosophical poems. Her philosophical vision of the interconnection among love, death, and truth is achieved not by traditional meditation in solitude but by a brainstorm of hallucinations. Both the elm speaker and the trapped victim have experienced love and the loss of love. At first disillusionment, the poet defines love as a shadow. With the emotional torture of abandonment, the poet further realizes its fluctuation. "The faces of love" are in fact the changing phases of love. Instead of lamenting the irretrievability of those phases, the poet sees through the disguised hideous face of love, which suffocates a woman, deadens her sensitivity, and fragments her body. The redefinition of love enables one to regain the strength to survive in the loveless world.

"Elm" was written in April, 1962, a time when Plath's first surge of fury, self-pity, and despair at her husband's infidelity had abated. She turned to examine the roots of her pain with an involved passion but a detached eye. The first seven stanzas depict how deceitful love and loss of love can turn a woman into a violent and revengeful angel. In the last seven stanzas, however, Plath turns to scrutinize her own psyche. Part of her rejects the lovelessness associated with barrenness; part of her still clings to the desire to love. Part of her seeks malignant revenge, and part of her is agitated by the irretrievability of love.

In the end, however, it is not loss of love that kills, but the fissures in the woman's psyche. With the final line's cathartic shriek ("That kill, that kill, that kill"), the poet seems to have achieved an emotional transformation, if only momentarily. If the poem starts with a protest against male atrocity in abandoning the female, it ends in self-mockery. Like Robert Lowell, Plath turns external and internal chaos into artistic irony.

Qingyun Wu

ELOISA TO ABELARD

Author: Alexander Pope (1688-1744)
Type of poem: Epistle/letter in verse
First published: 1717, in *The Works of Mr. Alexander Pope*

The Poem

Alexander Pope's "Eloisa to Abelard" is a 366-line verse epistle written in heroic couplets (pairs of rhymed lines in iambic pentameter), which explores a woman's struggle to reconcile her desires for physical passion and spiritual contentment. Based largely on John Hughes's English translation of Heloise and Abelard's correspondence (1713), the poem retells a tragic story of love and separation. Peter Abelard, a twelfth century theologian, was hired to tutor Heloise, who was then sixteen or seventeen years old. The two fell in love and secretly married after Heloise gave birth to a child. Heloise's uncle, who had originally hired Abelard to tutor his niece and who did not know of the marriage, arranged to have Abelard castrated as retribution for his seduction of Heloise. Separated from each other forever, Heloise became a Benedictine nun, and Abelard became a Benedictine monk. Their subsequent correspondence has been translated and published many times and has inspired generations of writers.

Pope's poem begins as Eloisa, an English variation of Heloise, reads a letter from Abelard recounting their past. The letter awakens passion in Eloisa, who is unsatisfied with her life in the convent. Although she is a devout Christian, Eloisa realizes that religion cannot calm her heart: "In vain lost *Eloisa* weeps and prays,/ Her heart still dictates, and her hand obeys." The convent has become "cold . . . unmov'd, and silent," and Eloisa longs for the warmth and passion she once knew. Grateful that she has "not yet forgot [her]self to stone," Eloisa recounts the story of her love.

Before they became lovers, Eloisa saw in Abelard "some emanation of th' all-beauteous Mind" and conflated his image with that of God. "Heav'n listen'd" as Abelard shared "truths divine" with his "Guiltless" student. Once their relationship became physical, Eloisa accepted his humanity and discovered happiness: "Back thro' the paths of pleasing sense I ran,/ Nor wish'd an Angel whom I lov'd a Man."

Their joy was short-lived. After Abelard's assault, Eloisa was forced to trade human love for spiritual love, but she could never forget Abelard. Even as she took the holy vows, her eyes were fixed not on the cross, but on her earthly lover, whose remembrance now draws her away from God. Her memory of Abelard casts a "Black Melancholy" over her spiritual meditations, and she confesses that his image "steals between my God and me." Knowing that only death will bring her peace, Eloisa hopes she and Abelard will be reunited in a single grave. The poem ends with Eloisa imagining that their tomb will not only warn young lovers to love more wisely but also add warmth and humanity to the "dreadful sacrifice" of religious ritual, and inspire a poet who will sooth Eloisa's soul by retelling her tragic story.

Forms and Devices

Although Pope's subject is medieval, the form of "Eloisa to Abelard" is classical. Pope's model is Ovid's *Heroides* (before 8 C.E.; Eng. trans, 1567), which contains a series of verse epistles in which fictionalized representations of historical women address their lovers. Pope was by no means the first English writer to borrow Ovid's form. During the renaissance, Samuel Daniel, Samuel Brandon, and John Donne each wrote verse epistles, sometimes called heroic epistles, modeled on the *Heroides*. The most important Renaissance collection of heroic epistles is Michael Drayton's *Englands Heroicall Epistles* (1597), which was revised and expanded in John Oldmixon's *Amores Britannici* (1703).

Like Oldmixon's work, Pope's "Eloisa to Abelard" is very much the product of the eighteenth century. The poem, in fact, contains many of the characteristics of neoclassical literature, which flourished in late seventeenth and early eighteenth century England. In addition to basing his work on a classical model, Pope follows neoclassical practices by writing in heroic couplets, a verse form well suited to conveying the symmetry and balance central to neoclassical art. Describing the conflict within her own heart, for example, Eloisa states: "Ev'n here, where frozen chastity retires,/ Love finds an alter for forbidden fires." In this couplet, the cold sterility of monastic life is balanced by the heat of passion, a juxtaposition that Pope repeats throughout the poem. Hoping, as he wrote in *An Essay on Criticism* (1711) to make the "*Sound . . .* an *Eccho* to the *Sense*," Pope slows the pace of the first line with a pause after the word "here" and with the long vowel sounds in "frozen" and "retires." In contrast, the second line of the couplet re-creates Eloisa's passion as it accelerates with Pope's use of alliteration and the repetition of the stopped *t* and *d* sounds.

A consummate artist, Pope creates similar effects and balances throughout the poem. The virgin's "visions of eternal day," for example, are contrasted with Eloisa's "horrors of all-conscious night." Pope achieves a sense of symmetry for the entire poem by dividing it into three roughly equal parts: the first third of the poem explores the love that existed in the past, the middle third Eloisa's present conflict, and the last third her hope for future reconciliation.

Neoclassical art also celebrates verisimilitude, the appearance of being true or real. In *An Essay on Criticism*, Pope instructs poets to "First follow NATURE, and your Judgment frame/ By her just Standard." On occasion, Pope appears to violate this principle. Eloisa, for instance, seems to attribute human emotions to inanimate objects, a poetic trope common in romantic poetry and sometimes referred to as the pathetic fallacy. Pope is careful, however, to preserve the verisimilitude of even the most imaginative passages. Eloisa reports, for instance, that while she was taking her sacred vows, "The shrines all trembled, and the lamps grew pale." On first reading, the shrines and lamps appear to respond sympathetically to Eloisa's plight, which would be an unmistakable violation of verisimilitude. The reader must remember, however, that the line records Eloisa's impressions at a time when her eyes were filled with tears. The visual distortion caused by the tears could cause objects appear to tremble and the lamps to appear less bright. Although Pope's speaker explores emotions that overwhelm her, the poet remains entirely in control. Using his carefully crafted couplets and respecting the bounds of realism, Pope remains true to the neoclassical aesthetic of his time.

Themes and Meanings

While some of Pope's contemporaries, such as Lady Mary Wortley Montague, used the verse epistle as a vehicle for satire, Pope used the form to explore the conflicting desires and psychological torment of his heroine. Eloisa longs for the love and passion she and Abelard once shared. Her desire for Abelard prevents her from finding solace within her present life of quiet celibacy. At times Eloisa regrets her love for Abelard, which she associates with both the flames of passion and damnation: "In seas of flame my plunging soul is drowned." Eloisa recognizes, however, that without the memory of their love, she would be less alive, even less human. She understands that her religious vows, a final rejection of earthly love, represent a death as well as a rebirth. The warmth and vitality of her youth died when she "with cold lips . . . kiss'd the sacred veil."

Eloisa cherishes the memory of her time with Abelard even as she acknowledges their sins: "I ought to grieve, but cannot what I ought;/ I mourn the lover, not lament the fault;/ I view my crime, but kindle at the view,/ Repent old pleasures, and sollicit new." She further expresses the ambivalence of her feelings through oxymoron; Abelard's memory is a "delicious poison" that causes her "dear horrors."

Earlier poets such as Edmund Spenser, William Shakespeare, and John Donne explored the relationship between human and divine love, often repeating the Neoplatonic idea that human love can ultimately bring an individual closer to God. Eloisa's experience, however, is more complicated, and Pope refuses to reduce her story to a salvation narrative. Eloisa's love for Abelard prevents her from finding spiritual bliss, yet spirituality, or at least the poem's medieval Christianity, is cold, barren, and lifeless. When Eloisa reports that her love causes her to shed "too soft a tear," the reader recognizes that without human love she would be not only less passionate but also, perhaps, less compassionate, more like cold "pale-ey'd virgins" of the convent. Through love and suffering, Eloisa has grown spiritually, but her reward is unceasing torment.

Far from a simple poem about lost love, "Eloisa to Abelard" explores the sometimes agonizing complexity and irreconcilability of physical and spiritual longing. Equally important, it does so through the voice of a heroine who is intelligent, articulate, and sophisticated. While many eighteenth century writers, including Pope, satirized women and ridiculed feminine passion, Eloisa is presented sympathetically, even heroically. She is, perhaps, the most complex female character in early eighteenth century British literature, and she anticipates the heroines of later literature, including those of Henry Fielding's *Amelia* (1751), Samuel Richardson's *Clarissa* (1747-1748), and Emily Brontë's *Wuthering Heights* (1847).

Christopher D. Johnson

EMMETT TILL

Author: Wanda Coleman (1946-   )
Type of poem: Elegy
First published: 1986; collected in *African Sleeping Sickness: Stories and Poems,* 1990

The Poem

"Emmett Till" is an elegy in four parts that shows American racism at its ugliest in the pre-Civil Rights era. Wanda Coleman's title is the name of a fourteen-year-old black boy who was murdered and has since become a popular historical figure in fiction and poetry. The facts surrounding his death have been recorded by journalists and historians: Till was visiting a great-uncle in Money, Mississippi, in 1955. According to testimony, he whistled at the wife of a local store owner. She was white. One of the biggest taboos in the pre-Civil Rights South was a black male showing interest in a white female. The fact that Till was a boy did not matter; this kind of behavior required that white men teach "a lesson" to the youthful offender. This lesson evokes several stereotypes that were the crux of considerable racial tension. One was that black people were always thinking about sex; the other was that white women, who were more virtuous than anyone else, had to be protected at any cost. Hearing about the incident secondhand, the white woman's husband and brother-in-law took Till away from his great-uncle's residence. Three days later, a local fisherman saw feet sticking up from the Tallahatchie River. Those feet were attached to the mutilated body of Till. His murder and the subsequent trial were widely publicized, and some historians have credited his murder with inducing the birth struggles of the Civil Rights movement. Because of the brutality of his death, especially for such a minor offense, African American writers tell and retell Till's story as a symbol for the tragic stories of many nameless African American males.

In the first of the four parts, the third-person narrator provides the setting and atmosphere that permeated the "hate-inspired" Jim Crow South. The narrator also describes the natural movement of the river and its part in Till's transcendence. Because of their role, the waters of the river are "sanctified" for the final journey, as the bloated body of the dead child is carried home. The narrator charges the water with a sacred duty even as it erodes stone and Till's flesh, a testament to its dual nature as nurturer and destroyer. The second part of the poem relates Till's transgression: the whistle at the store owner's wife. The narrator even speculates about his motivation: She was desirable, and, as any red-blooded, all-American boy would, Till reacted. This "rape by eye" was enough to make two white men angry enough to kill, while the black community, impotent with rage and ineffective slogans, watched. Part 3 gives the details of the men taking Emmett away from his great-uncle's home and to the water. The narrator does not describe the murder but refers to it as "the deed." In part 4, a black preacher eulogizes Till by recapping the time, place, and events of his murder.

"Weighted down" but "too light," Till's body rises, Christlike, on the third day.

The refrains in parts 1 through 3, alphabetical lists of rivers in the United States, exemplify the pastoral elegy's use of nature. The absence of a river refrain in part 4 makes the narrator's mention of "the tallahatchie," the river that held Till's body in its "mulky arm," even more emphatic. This part focuses on "murder" and Till's resurrection to a higher existence.

Forms and Devices

Coleman's masterful use of imagery creates the powerful effect of this poem. The most visible images involve water and religion. The poem begins with the "river jordan," which functioned in the Bible as, among other things, a safe passageway for the Israelites to get to the Promised Land; many African Americans also saw such a spiritual crossing as better than their material existence. This is followed by the haunting refrains of the rivers in alphabetical order, beginning with "*the alabama*" and ending with "*the yellowstone.*" The river's destruction of Till's flesh is attributed to the men who dragged him from home and are thus responsible for "blood river born." As nurturer, the river "come[s] forth to carry the dead child home." The narrator invests the river with maternal instincts: "river mother carries him" and "from the mulky arm of the tallahatchie." Even mythology is utilized, as Till's body becomes "waftage" in "that grotesque swim up the styx." Finally, just as the Israelites were carried by the Jordan, Till "was carried forth to that promised land" by the river. Though the overwhelming use of water is positive in its ability to cleanse, nourish, and nurture, two references evoke negative images. These occur in part 2, as the narrator relates that Till's offense makes a white man "pass water mad/ make a whole tributary of intolerance."

Coleman's religious imagery is also powerful. In addition to the narrator's reference to the Jordan, Till's mother, a modern-day Mary, is "the black madonna/ bereft of babe." Like Christ, Till was also "crucified" and "crown[ed]" before he "crossed over into campground." Finally, Till is "baptized" and "*on that third day/ he rose*" to complete the Christian cycle of sin, redemption, and resurrection. Thus, another martyr is created from the "nidus" (breeding ground) of racism.

Claiming not to see herself in "terms of a tradition," Coleman admits, in a 1990 interview in *Black American Literature Forum* (*BALF*), that she draws from the black tradition and the culture of the black church. In part 4, for example, the voice of the black community emerges in the traditional verbal pattern of "call-response," which is most often found between a preacher and the congregation. All of the preacher's statements (calls) are punctuated by the congregation's responses: "lord!" or "lord! lord!" Also, Coleman acknowledges the African American church as the race's strongest institution, which often nurtured its members in times of racial conflict.

Also worth noting is Coleman's use of multiple voices. The primary narrator is objective, describing the scenes from a distance, but the poem also contains the voice of a bulletin/commentator that reveals the impact of the murder: "killing of 14-year-old/ stirs nation. there will be a public wake." Moreover, consistent with conventions of the pastoral elegy, the rage of the black community comes through in the language of the people: "but she be a white woman. but he be/ a black boy," and "cuz she was white woman virtue and he/ be a black boy lust." The second quotation differs from the first in that individuals are no longer involved; they have become symbols of racial conflict.

Themes and Meanings

"As a writer I feel I best serve my readership when I rehumanize the dehumanized, when I illuminate what is in darkness, when I give blood and bone to statistics that are too easily dismissed," says Coleman in *BALF*. The world's final view of Till was his grotesquely disfigured face and bloated body, so the narrator reminds readers that "(once it was human)" as she tells Till's story and illuminates racism "from the deep dank murk of consciousness." According to Stephen Henderson in *Understanding the New Black Poetry* (1973), much black poetry deals with the theme of liberation from either physical or political bondage. This poem is a variation on a historically popular theme: the preference for death over slavery. Here, set free by death, Till is "sovereign at last." Thus, Coleman's theme emphasizes the liberated spirit and the enduring legacy of Till, which can be seen in her dominant images.

Coleman's irreverent parodies of "America, the Beautiful" and "The Star-Spangled Banner" reveal the brutality of a Jim Crow system in a democratic society and the hypocrisy of America, which fostered this hostile climate for African Americans. Coleman juxtaposes the ideal with the reality. For example, the beauty of America is revealed by the "purple mountain" majesties and the "amber" waves of grain, but the ugliness is revealed by the narrator's insistent questioning of what people can see: "oh say do you see the men off/ the bank dredging in that/ strange jetsam," and "oh say Emmett Till can you see Emmett Till/ crossed over into campground." This ugliness, this dehumanization "in a supposedly great nation like this one" is what Coleman, in the *BALF* interview, refers to as "gangrenous," as "cancer" in need of excising.

First, however, someone must "talk seriously" about American racism, "the only major untouched area" in literature, Coleman concludes. Thus, "spirit uplifted," Till represents the collective spirit of African Americans in this country. His rising symbolizes the race's refusal to stay down. The Tallahatchie, for example, could be any river, as evidenced by the alphabetical listing of American rivers, and Emmett Till could be any black person who has died violently at the hands of whites for some perceived offense and without due process. In this poem, his death becomes a symbol of the lack of both democracy and Christianity in a supposedly democratic and Christian society.

Loretta McBride

THE EMPEROR OF ICE-CREAM

Author: Wallace Stevens (1879-1955)
Type of poem: Lyric
First published: 1923, in *Harmonium*

The Poem

"The Emperor of Ice-Cream" is a short but intensely compacted poem of sixteen lines, divided into two stanzas. The title reflects the irony and complexity of the poem as a whole, perhaps suggesting that humans are no more resistant to death than ice cream is to the sun. The poem is filled with the visual imagery, wordplay, humor, and thematic tension common to Wallace Stevens's poetry.

The poem is written in the third person, seemingly by someone who is assembling a group of people both to create and to attend a wake (it is common in some cultures to have a celebration of the life of the person who has died, with food and drink, after a time of mourning) for a poor woman. In stanza 1 there is a call for a person muscular enough to whip up desserts by hand; evidently there is not enough money for an electric mixer, let alone someone who would be paid to cater the food. The desserts will have to be served in kitchen cups; there is no fine china or crystal. The common people who will attend will come in their everyday clothes, rather than formal attire; the flowers will be brought in last month's newspapers, rather than in vases, or as wreaths or other floral arrangements. All these details suggest that there is nothing fancy or special about death and its aftermath; indeed, in this poem, death is so ordinary as to be shocking and unusual rather than trite, because Stevens avoids the euphemisms and denials that often accompany the details and descriptions of death.

Stanza 2 continues with the preparations, except that now someone is being asked to take a sheet from the top of a cheap and broken dresser to cover the deceased person's face, even if that means that her ugly feet protrude. Instead of soft lights or candlelight, the lamp should be turned to glare on her body, to show that she is now cold and silent in death. Stevens is insisting that one must look directly at death, in all its matter-of-factness, and see it not as a stage of some mystical or spiritual transformation, but rather as actual fact to be faced and dealt with.

Two facts—that the wake takes place in the woman's own home, rather than in a church or mortuary, and that preparations are inexpensive and minimal, including making the food in her own kitchen—reflect Stevens's insistence that death not be romanticized, idealized, or sentimentalized. Perhaps if death indeed will melt everyone away to nothing, no matter how tasty or delicious they may be while alive, then in the classic tradition of *carpe diem*, they should seize the day while they are able.

Forms and Devices

Language play is an important feature of this poem, as it is in many of Stevens's poems. Given the associations many readers will have with curds (for example, curdled milk, which is spoiled, or Miss Muffett being scared by the spider), "concupiscent curds" (line 3) may seem like a poetic oxymoron (a conjunction of incongruous or contradictory terms). In fact, however, Stevens is pointing to the fact that something as ordinary and bland as milk may, if whipped properly, be turned into ice cream, a dessert that is to many people so luscious, sweet, and desirable that it is the object of a food-lust.

Other words are used as puns (words with multiple and often contradictory meanings, which may be serious as well as humorous); one example is "dumb" (line 14), which suggests both that the dead woman is no longer intelligent and that she is as mute and silent as the grave. Stevens also uses the sound devices of assonance and alliteration to emphasize the musical quality of the poem. In line 3, for example, "cups concupiscent curds" uses the alliterative device of four hard *c* sounds in only three words; "dresser of deal" in line 9 is alliterative in a similar fashion.

Another device common in the poem is the use of ordinary images to create an extraordinary scene. One such image is that of the person making the ice cream; he has strong enough hands, wrists, and forearms to do it because he makes hand-rolled cigars, a special art in Stevens's time. A second image of those who will be attending the wake is the "wenches," or serving girls; a wench is not only a serving girl but also, by connotation, a "loose woman." The central image of the poem, however, is certainly "the emperor of ice-cream." This metaphor is complex and ambiguous enough, in fact, to be a literary symbol rather than simply a metaphor.

Themes and Meanings

Two lines in Stevens's poem have often caused readers to wonder in puzzlement at what they might mean. The first is the title itself, "the emperor of ice-cream," a phrase which is repeated in the last lines of both the first and second stanzas. Indeed, as part of the closing lines of each stanza, its importance is underscored and re-emphasized: In these lines, the emperor of ice-cream is in fact the *only* emperor. In order to understand this image and its symbolic aspects as fully as possible, one need also understand its corollary, the line which precedes it in the first stanza: "Let be be finale of seem."

Emily Dickinson, in "I could not see to see," the last line of her well-known poem "I heard a Fly buzz—when I died" (poem 465), makes a pun out of a simple verb. Since her eyes cannot see, she cannot understand. Just as Dickinson uses "see" on two quite different levels, the literal and the figurative, Stevens does here with "be."

When Stevens writes "Let be be finale of seem," he is using the first "be" as a noun (being) and the second as a verb. His line might be translated as "let being be the end of appearance," or—to paraphrase Kurt Vonnegut, Jr., in his introduction to *Mother Night* (1961)—be careful who you pretend to be, because who you pretend to be is who you are. Stevens is suggesting that there is, or at least ought to be, a close connection between one's actions and who one is; the way one is in one's existence in the world should reflect one's inner essences (or perhaps, at another level, it already does, whether one wishes to acknowledge it or not). In one of his letters, Stevens commented on this line, suggesting that being should become the denouement or conclusion of appearing to be; in other words, what one sees is what one gets, and how one acts becomes in fact who one is.

Another way to put this would be to say that one should abandon one's search for idealized or romanticized possibilities in one's life and accept what is already there for what it is. Stevens went on to comment in his letter that ice cream is an absolute good. If one is aware of how transitory ice cream is, how filled with fat and sugar, how unimportant (if not negative) it is to one's nutrition and health, one will not be able to appreciate it for what it is: a dessert that is cold, sweet, and delicious, and immensely satisfying on its own terms.

Stevens is suggesting far more than that one should indulge oneself in richly satisfying desserts, however; he is using ice cream as a symbol of life itself. While ironically reminding readers that they, too, will end up poor and cold and dumb, like the woman in the poem who has died, he is more positively asserting that life can be fun—that one should enjoy one's life as fully as possible while one is able. To do this, one must experience and enjoy those things which please the body as well as those which please the heart, mind, and spirit. In other poems, Stevens writes at length about and advocates the pleasures of the mind engaged in art; here, he advocates the pleasures of the senses. One may choose to live most significantly in one's mind, heart, or spirit, Stevens knows, yet one can also enjoy one's physical life lustily, enjoying it like the pleasure-filled process of eating "concupiscent curds," or erotic ice cream.

Clark Mayo

END OF THE SEERS' CONVENTION

Author: Kenneth Fearing (1902-1961)
Type of poem: Narrative
First published: 1943, in *Afternoon of a Pawnbroker, and Other Poems*

The Poem

"End of the Seers' Convention" is a narrative poem in blank verse which is essentially a conversation or series of statements delivered by various delegates at an imaginary conference of mystics and other representatives of the occult. After the narrator, or central consciousness of the poem, sets the scene, one of the practitioners of parapsychological phenomena offers prophetic observations on the future of humankind to which the others respond with derision or dismissal.

The incredible is casually established when the narrator remarks that he and his fellow seers were "walking and talking on the roof of the world." The focus of the meeting is described as a potential unification of all the realms that rule and influence life in the universe. The body of the poem consists of prophetic utterances from members of specific disciplines, followed by qualifications, challenges, or rebuttals by members of different ones.

The first stanza contains a prediction by an astrologer of a world which is much like the mid-twentieth century, when the poem was written, but is set in a distant era. A Gypsy, who represents the humane aspects of life in opposition to the scientifically analytic or mechanical, denigrates the technical marvels as less significant than the question of who will control the forces created by technology. The astrologer appears uninterested in this question and returns to his initial vision of great global trends, remarking indifferently that a cycle of war and "victory" will follow, perhaps endlessly.

The debate among the participants seems to develop into a dichotomy between massive historical movements and their effects on individual human lives. When a crystal gazer calls the astrologer's predictions "trite" and asserts that a more crucial question is "how to seize power" from an indifferent, self-preserving government, the astrologer expands the terms of the discussion by forecasting a time when people will pursue frivolous goals ("live on top of flag-poles") in an era akin to the 1920's. His interest in the whimsical and the mechanical is met with derision by a numerologist and an illusionist, who are less concerned with human welfare than with their own specialities. The astrologer, however, remains as unaffected by personal concerns as he was by social ones.

In the longest stanza of the poem, the astrologer finally becomes involved in his visions. He shouts, and his proclamations seem to displace the cosmos itself. His final prediction is a confluence of the power of the state and the instinctual basis of human desire, a vision of a society unlike any previous one on earth, which is a reversal of the lessons of most human experience. This fantastic revelation has little effect on the other delegates, who remain trapped in their own narrow styles of seeing. The positions that they propose are an implicit refutation of the astrologer's dreams.

The final stanza is a mordant comment on the conditions that have called the seers to the convention. In spite of their (unproven) abilities, they have accomplished nothing in concert. As the poem concludes, they hold umbrellas to protect themselves from what may be as innocent as rain or as ominous as "dragon's blood."

Forms and Devices

In the 1930's, Kenneth Fearing examined ordinary situations, using powerful language, rhetorical techniques, and unusual rhythms. As Kenneth Rexroth pointed out, Fearing's voice developed from an immersion "in the lingo of the mass culture." By the mid-1940's, however, he began to work in a vein which might be called visionary. In dealing with the extraordinary, the metaphysical, and the fantastic, Fearing realized that understatement was crucial and that a very careful control of tone was necessary to maintain the spell of the poem. Therefore, "End of the Seers' Convention" begins in an extremely low-key fashion, the narrator remarking as if in recollection of a thoroughly ordinary event. The supernatural is abruptly, but almost offhandedly, introduced when the location is revealed and the narrator observes that the subject of the discussion is the key to life itself.

In an extended figure designed to emphasize the importance of the theme, Fearing repeats the word "seven" (with all its mystical associations) three times, using it to modify Great, True, and Ultimate, and heightens the setting by referring to "leagues" and "spheres." After this declaration of magnitude, Fearing returns to his initial tone, humanizing the participants with descriptive touches: The astrologer is from Idaho, the Gypsy is a self-described "simple reader of tea-leaves," the crystal gazer is from Miami, and the illusionist is from Bombay. Furthermore, Fearing mixes prophetic commentary with the mundane, as the "bored numerologist" reaches for his hat during a disagreement and a "puzzled mesmerist" is seen "groping for the door." The effect is to undercut the mystery but not to destroy it completely.

The poem is written in a straightforward narrative voice, with occasional flourishes to generate emotion or emphasis. There is no use of metaphor, no rhyme, and little dependence on sound. When a memorable section is reached, however, Fearing shapes an image to guide the thought and, when he wants the reader to consider a serious statement, it is presented with enough force to separate it from the whining quibbles of the less important observations. The Gypsy's terse challenge to the first forecast is direct and unavoidable: "How does this combat the widespread and growing evil of the police?" The crystal gazer's question is reinforced by the repetition "damn fool . . . damn time." The astrologer's rambling flight into fancy in the sixth stanza is couched in the humor of the ludicrous, and his full-scale forecast of an absurd but appealing future is carried by three of the longest lines of the poem, each beginning with an assertive "I" and each containing a surrealistic image which defies ironic objectivity.

Fearing reserves traditional figurative language for three occasions in the poem. The astrologer's primary legitimate power is suggested when he shrugs and a meteor falls from his robes "and smolder[s] on the floor," a manifestation of the physical amid much verbiage. When he is in a frenzy of prophecy in the crucial eighth stanza, the astrologer has "comets and halfmoons dropping from his pockets and his agitated sleeves." In the chilling concluding stanza, the cosmic rain descending on the delegates is compared to "dragon's blood" and then to "cinders." The final image is of tiny, insignificant figures amid the vast powers of the cosmos, their "small, black umbrellas" a symbol of their helplessness before the great, mysterious forces of the universe.

Themes and Meanings

Throughout the 1930's, Fearing wrote angry poetry that satirized the excesses and failures of a society. By the end of World War II, he had not changed his mind about the social system, but he had developed a degree of perspective. Therefore, the visionary strain that runs through his later poems is a kind of speculative transcendence. These poems suggest that the "normal" is haunted by the nonnormal, the abnormal, or the supernormal; the rationalistic position of the social critic gradually gives way to the mystical imagination of the prophet or seer.

"End of the Seers' Convention" joins Fearing's critique of society with the stirring of a millennial vision. The idea of a merger of occult approaches is unlikely, and therefore humorous, but the whimsical nature of the proceedings is darkened by the bizarre explanations of human motives. The polarity established between those who believe that humanity's redemption is spiritual (the mesmerist, the illusionist, and the card reader) and those who take a more political perspective (the Gypsy and the crystal gazer) seems permanent. Fearing chides both sides, criticizing the apparent "spiritualists" for losing their spirituality in the practical and the political realists for losing their faith while pursuing the narrowly tactical. When the Gypsy asks how to "combat the widespread and growing evil of the police" and the crystal gazer asks how "to seize power from entrenched and organized men of Common Sense," Fearing is voicing his own immediate concerns. The "organized men of Common Sense" stand for the entire apparatus of the modern state, the focus of Fearing's wrath, but the poem's mood of semicomic resignation deflects the anger. The final vision of the astrologer, which portrays an absurdist society in which authorities pursue those who follow the conventional models for success and social norms encourage "laziness and sleep, and dreams of utter peace" is a cartoon idyll. The concept has an amusing appeal, but Fearing remained too much the hard-boiled realist to argue for this vision.

Leon Lewis

ENTRANCE TO WOOD

Author: Pablo Neruda (Neftalí Ricardo Reyes Basoalto, 1904-1973)
Type of poem: Lyric
First published: 1935, as "Entrada a la madera," in *Residencia en la tierra*; English
translation collected in *Residence on Earth*, 1973

The Poem
"Entrance to Wood" is a lyric poem of seven stanzas written in free verse. It is the
first and best known of Pablo Neruda's *Tres cantos materiales*, which were included
in book 2 of his Residencia series, *Residencia en la tierra* (1935). The poem that immediately precedes "Entrance to Wood" is "Agua sexual" ("Sexual Water"), which
ends with a vision beyond the grave. "Entrance to Wood" can be viewed as a response
to that particular experience.

That response begins with the poem's title, which not only reveals a symbolic shift
from water to the more substantial wood but also makes a revealing pun. The Spanish
"Entrada a la madera" (entrance to wood) echoes the phrase *entrar en materia*, which
means to get into a subject or to get down to business. This poem becomes the first
"material" of the "Three Material Cantos" (the other two cantos are entitled "Hymn to
Celery" and "Statute of Wine.")

As in "Hymn to Celery," the action of the poem begins with a fall. Somewhat like
Alice in Wonderland, the "I" or speaker in the first two stanzas of the poem falls into
an enchanted forest, toward a physical union with earthly things that is initially ominous. The speaker does not fall intellectually but bodily, with his senses, into the "forgotten decayed room" of the forest. The forest of "secret inconclusive woods," however, becomes gradually familiar, as the speaker wanders in his new surroundings.

As the topic of the apostrophe (a manner of speech in which someone, some abstract quality, or a nonexistent person is directly addressed as though present) in the
first line of the third stanza, "matter" comes to replace the "wood" of the title. The
speaker addresses matter directly, saying, "Sweet matter, oh rose of dry wings." The
image of inversion (sinking upward) is of the speaker eagerly climbing up the rose's
vertical branches (the "rose," however, is composed of "dry wings," that is, wood).
The references to fatigue, tired feet, and kneeling inside the "hard cathedral" of the
wood—as if enacting a ritual within a sacred sanctuary—and the bumping of his lips
against the wooden statue of an angel, combine to stress the corporeal quality, if not
the uncontrolled nature of this hurtling fall toward materiality, this physical "entrance
to wood," that is the real subject of the poem.

In the fifth stanza, the speaker also alludes to his journey or quest, his "funeral journey" among the "yellow scars" of the tree. He is alone on this journey to the source of
"mysterious matter," toward death (he feels "leaves dying inwards") or toward life in
the sense of a rebirth, a return to the womb.

This new setting provides a dramatic context for the long final stanza. In the final stanza, the opposing elements of the physical and the spiritual are fused together as though in a dream to create a strange atmosphere of a bodily union with the cosmos. The speaker becomes one with the "matter" in which he lies. He becomes part of the "pores, veins, circles of sweetness,/ weight, silent temperature" of the wood. He goes on to describe his union with wood as if he were uniting with a physical body, referring to the "mouth, power of sweet consumed pulp" of the wood. In a liturgical invocation to matter midway through the stanza, the speaker says "come to me, to my limitless dream,/ fall into my bedroom." In his role of mystic or magician, the speaker evokes a sexual union and then proceeds to describe in realistic terms the desired act as though it were actually occurring.

The speaker compares the falling night in his bedroom to water "breaking" (as in a woman about to give birth). The night continues its falling motion, and the speaker asks to be bound not only to its life but also to its death and its "subdued materials." In the final lines of the poem, the speaker addresses the wood, saying, "let's make fire, and silence, and sound,/ and let's flame up, and be silent, and bells." The act of rebirth, dying in the material world in order to be reborn in the spirit, rising up out of the wood's ashes, is complete at the poem's end.

Forms and Devices

While the "entrance to wood" both materially and spiritually is the central image of the poem, the poet's language accomplishes this physical and spiritual "entrance" as clearly as the poem's imagery. The summons in the poem's final stanza constitutes the first of three interconnected series that provide the poem with a highly structured conclusion. The first of these series is the sequence "fall into my bedroom in which the night falls." The structuring clause in the second series is the conjunctive phrase "and to your subdued materials," except for one line that balances the earlier addition of the conjunction by clearly omitting it. The symmetrical balance of the two sequences conditions the reader to expect a similar order in the third and final series in the last two lines, a formal pattern that implies that integration (with matter, mother, or object) can take place only under highly structured conditions.

In the last two lines, the conjunctive clauses increase in number and, in contrast with the vertical arrangement of the previous four lines, their horizontal sweep suggests a mirror inversion. Both the new format and the steadier rhythm indicate a new stage in which subject and object are gradually drawn closer together, as conveyed first by the shift of address from plural "you" to "we," as well as the switch from verbal phrases to verbs. The latter, especially, set up a semantic correspondence that enhances the symmetry of the parallel lines.

Yet, no sooner is the new order introduced than it is jolted by the grammatical disjunction of the last word, which replaces the verb ("to sound") with a noun ("bells"). The bells range in symbolic meaning from death to marriage, but the context suggests that their meaning derives mainly from the grammatical difference that is interposed within the series. The change from verb to noun, or from action to substance, signals the union between subject and object. In deriving the final symbol from sound, however, the sequence points to a specifically aural origin that the "Three Material Cantos" consistently identifies with poetic presence. Moreover, the final sequence articulates that presence as the end result of a three-stage process beginning with a purifying journey, a quiet death in stillness, and finally, a rising from the ashes as "sound" and "bells." Thus, what at first seems to be restricted to a material identification is actually the attainment of poetic experience, of presence, even if the cost of attaining that experience is a disintegration of language and the speaker's ultimate dissolution.

Themes and Meanings

"Entrance to Wood" is essentially a mystical poem. In spite of its simple subject— wood (celery and wine are the subjects of the other two of the "Three Material Cantos")—"Entrance to Wood" is a poem written in the manner of the best religious poetry of the Spanish golden age. In this poetry, the speaker, through a total renunciation of the senses, usually rises to a new intellectual level and, ultimately, to spiritual communion with God. In Neruda's poem, through a structured reversal of this procedure, the spiritual aspect is minimized and sensory perceptions are maximized as the speaker bodily falls down toward a physical union with earthly things. What at first appears to be a fall toward death is actually a fall toward life. Neruda uses familiar religious symbols to represent the vital union, not with God, but with matter, "sweet matter."

The mystical theme is underscored by the speaker's material/spiritual journey. The poem's rhythms move forward ritually. The speaker's sinking through time and space creates the potential for soaring above them. Having reached the dark core of the wood (an inverted dark night of the soul), having exposed himself to matter at this depth, the speaker (and the poet) can join in its essential dialectic of death and life.

At the end of the poem, the speaker asks the wood to act along with him. Linking his "fallen soul" to his own night falling like "broken" water, he makes the wood's life and death his own. More precisely, it is he who breathes life into the wood by bringing his own spirit to its "crushed materials." It is the poet and the wood, human and non-human, that unite, ignite, and burn with pure passion at the poem's end. In the act of writing, the poet and his "matter," his poetry, are one.

Genevieve Slomski

THE ENVOY OF MR. COGITO

Author: Zbigniew Herbert (1924-1998)
Type of poem: Meditation
First published: 1974, as "Przestanie Pana Cogito," in *Pan Cogito*; English translation
collected in *Selected Poems*, 1977

The Poem

"The Envoy of Mr. Cogito" is a medium-length poem in free verse, divided into fifteen short stanzas. The title contains a pun, for Mr. Cogito is an envoy, a kind of messenger, and the poem is also an envoy (or envoi), summarizing the poet's message in
the closing lines of his collection *Pan Cogito*. Envoys, however, are usually diplo-
mats, conveying carefully worded messages from their governments; they are the
bearers of political, not poetic, statements. Yet the language of both diplomacy and
poetry is simultaneously precise and ambiguous, providing room for multiple and
even contradictory interpretations. Herbert's poetry is political—if only by implication—since it addresses itself to the fate of the messenger, the poet, Mr. Cogito, who
must refuse to be an executioner, informer, or coward and must, instead, abide by his
sense of what is true and good.

There are at least two ways of interpreting who is speaking in the poem. Someone is
addressing Mr. Cogito, providing him with a set of instructions, or Mr. Cogito is
speaking to himself, directing himself to "go upright" among those who are on their
knees or fallen in the dust—the defeated, in other words—and among "those with
their backs turned," the ones who will not acknowledge reality. Although Mr. Cogito
must deliver his message, he is told (or he is telling himself) that he will not be a survivor, that his "last prize" is the "golden fleece of nothingness"—an allusion to the
Greek myth of Jason and the Argonauts who embark on a heroic journey to recover
the golden fleece. If Mr. Cogito is to exhibit heroism, it will be of a moral nature that
scorns those who have capitulated, and yet of a modest kind, for he is enjoined (or en-
joins himself) not to be proud of his independence but rather to recognize his own ri-
diculousness and to shun bitterness ("dryness of heart"). He must be alive to nature, to
all that he cannot define, such as "the bird with an unknown name."

If there is a reward for Mr. Cogito's journey, it will be in his repeating the old
"fables and legends" of humanity. He will fail, like the heroes of old—such as the legendary Babylonian hero, Gilgamesh, who battles but succumbs to his fear of death,
the noble Hector, who dies gloriously defending his native city of Troy, and Roland,
the mythic French hero, who dies outnumbered but unbowed by the attacking Sara-
cens. At his best, Mr. Cogito is told, he will die mocked by his murderers, and yet he
should remain "faithful" to the idea of the "good" which, in fact, he will not be able to
attain.

The short stanzas of the poem shift between stating what will happen to Mr. Cogito
and how he ought to act. The sense of what is right is tempered by a resigned recogni-

tion that moral values do not prevail in reality, although they endure in literature, in the poem or in the envoy himself.

Forms and Devices

One of Zbigniew Herbert's most effective devices is his use of literary allusion. Although Mr. Cogito's mission could be regarded as unheroic, since he accomplishes nothing, the recognition of this nothingness is itself heroic—as Herbert suggests in his ironic phrase "the golden fleece of nothingness your last prize." By looking without illusion on the hopelessness of his situation, Mr. Cogito can, in fact, bear comparison with the heroes of old.

The literary allusions also reflect Herbert's sense of history, which he treats as a source of universals, moral laws men must obey no matter what the consequences may be to themselves. Thus Mr. Cogito must "go where those others went." Where they went is not made clear, because the specific location and events are not important; rather, it is the going itself, making the journey for truth, that is important.

Irony is a key feature of this poem. Sometimes, within a single line the poem seems to contradict itself: "you were saved not in order to live." Literally speaking, to be saved is to live, but here a positive statement is turned into a negative one. Yet the line implies a sense of purpose in history, which is strengthened by the next line that tells him, "you must give testimony."

The poet's use of metaphor and imagery is also striking. He adapts an allusion to the golden fleece, the wool covering of a sheep, to express futility: Mr. Cogito will find that his quest contains or covers nothing. He is told that he will go to the "dark boundary," without any specification of where that boundary might be. At his funeral, he will be disposed of with "relief" and commemorated in the "smoothed-over biography" of the "wood-borer," which suggests a dull, dishonest, account which will drill the life right out of him.

Just as Mr. Cogito must go to the "dark boundary," the poem later suggests he is guided by his "dark star," which is the blood pulsing in his own breast, linking him to the humanity of an earlier age and to the defenders of the "kingdom without limit and the city of ashes," a line which may be taken as a reference to the world of the imagination ("without limit") and the world of reality ("of ashes"). These images of the darkness within human beings and of the mass destruction of civilization are also, paradoxically, images of renewal, of the sights Mr. Cogito must be "faithful to," if he is to express the endurance of human suffering.

The grim images are meant to suggest that there can be no facile optimism but only the long view of humankind which builds upon and destroys itself. It is important in the first and last lines that Mr. Cogito "go"—resist the inertia of the defeated and actively express this somber view of human continuity.

Themes and Meanings

Mr. Cogito is a figure Herbert uses in many of his poems. While not exactly an autobiographical character, Mr. Cogito is clearly emblematic of the poet's calling. The poet speaks to the world, carries his message, but he does not expect to change reality, to be victorious, to be heeded by his readers. The very name Herbert has chosen for his alter ego implies cogitation, thinking, imagination—all the qualities that distinguish civilization. Mr. Cogito is the poet who must go forward—must go at any cost to his own life—because this is what humankind has always done in spite of the long record of defeats.

By cogitating, so to speak, the poet maintains a humanly imagined world. He is also speaking to himself, carrying on a dialogue, urging himself on—as Mr. Cogito is urged (or urges himself) on in the poem—because "you have little time," the span of a single life is short. The poet also carries on a dialogue with himself within and between his poems. As the last poem in the collection *Pan Cogito*, "The Envoy of Mr. Cogito" states the poet's imperative to his own book of poems: It must go on to whatever "dark boundary" awaits it, for the poet can only imagine how he will be received, although he has a good idea of what his reception will be by his reading of history. He knows the dire fate of other Cogitos.

In the largest sense, the theme of the poem is human expression itself. It does not seem to change things, yet the possibility of change—or, at least, of standing "upright"—is articulated, and the poem itself becomes its own envoy, standing up for itself. It is faithful to its own perceptions, which are not a matter of pride, for the poet can be as foolish as anyone else in his "clown's face," and he is certainly not better than others. It is rather a vehicle of expression, repeating "great words . . . stubbornly."

Mr. Cogito, then, is suggestive of humanity which must, in the poet's view, be ruthlessly honest with itself precisely because so much of the truth has been buried and "smoothed-over" by those in power. Self-critical, ironic, and disciplined—these are the values of Herbert's historically conscious verse. It is self-reflexive writing, aware that it must reflect and surmount in its own form, in its address to itself, a precarious and perishable world.

Carl Rollyson

THE EOLIAN HARP

Author: Samuel Taylor Coleridge (1772-1834)
Type of poem: Lyric
First published: 1796, in *Poems on Various Subjects*; revised in *Sibylline Leaves*,
1817

The Poem
"The Eolian Harp" is a lyric poem written in blank verse paragraphs of varying
lengths. The title refers to a stringed instrument which produces music when placed in
an open window so that the breeze may pass over it. The eolian harp was commonly
used by poets in the Romantic period as a metaphor for the creative process.

The poem begins with the persona, who is clearly Samuel Taylor Coleridge himself, addressing his wife, Sara. They are sitting affectionately together outside their
cottage in Clevedon, in the English county of Somersetshire. It is a quiet and peaceful
evening scene. They look up at the evening star and the passing clouds; they can smell
the pleasing scent from the nearby bean field, and they listen to the distant murmur of
the sea.

In the second verse paragraph, the poet turns his attention to the eolian harp placed
in the window of the cottage. Touched by the intermittent breeze, it is sending its music into the air. Coleridge compares the harp first to a girl "half yielding" as she is ca-
ressed by her lover; then, as the music grows stronger, he compares the harp to en-
trancing sounds coming from fairyland. The combination of silence and soft sound
leads the poet into an intellectual reverie. He celebrates "The one Life within us and
abroad," a single spirit infusing everything in creation with joy. He feels that in such a
world, in which the very air seems to be filled with music, it is impossible not to be
filled with love for all things.

Stimulated by this thought, he remembers an incident when he was climbing a hill
at midday and had watched, through half-closed eyes, the sunbeams dancing on the
sea. The tranquil scene had stimulated his mind, and the present scene is having the
same effect on him: A stream of thoughts rushes spontaneously through his "indolent
and passive brain." Another intellectual meditation follows, which develops the ideas
implicit in the previous reverie. The poet speculates that perhaps everything in nature
is like an eolian harp, brought into being as one vast "intellectual breeze" sweeps over
it, a breeze which is at once the soul of each individual thing and the God of the whole
creation.

In the final verse paragraph, the poet catches sight of his wife, Sara, who is chastis-
ing him for indulging in fanciful ideas. She tells him to "walk humbly with [his] God."
The poet praises her as a "Meek Daughter in the family of Christ!" and accepts her re-
buke. He dismisses his thoughts as nothing more than the "shapings of the unregener-
ate mind" and concludes the poem with a more orthodox Christian position. He remembers that God is beyond understanding, except to the eye of deeply felt faith, and

he accepts that it is only through God's grace that he has been saved from his sins and granted the peace and happiness he now enjoys with his wife.

Forms and Devices

"The Eolian Harp" is one of Coleridge's first achievements in a new lyric form he developed, which is known as the conversation poem, or greater Romantic lyric. The form was later used by almost all the major English romantic poets, including Coleridge's close friend William Wordsworth in "Lines Composed a Few Miles Above Tintern Abbey" (1798).

The conversation poem, so called because it embodies the relaxed and informal tones of the speaking voice, is usually addressed to a silent listener, in this case Coleridge's wife Sara. It usually begins with a description of a quiet scene in nature, then turns inward, to the workings of the poet's own mind. Typically, the poet will reflect on an emotional or intellectual problem and work his way to some kind of resolution before the poem rounds back to where it began, in the calm of the natural scene. The rhythm is one of systole and diastole.

"The Eolian Harp" underwent many revisions before it reached its final form. Lines 26-33 did not appear until 1817; however, it clearly follows the pattern of the typical conversation poem. From the scene outside the cottage, the poem moves progressively away from the everyday world to more refined levels of the poet's mind and imagination. The movement begins with the music from the harp prompting a simile (the harp is "like some coy Maid"); another simile follows, when the music is compared to the sounds that "twilight Elfins make" and the poet evokes the world of fairyland. Finally, the poet drifts into an inspired consideration of the fundamental structure of the universe. Notable is the synesthesia contained in the line, "A light in sound, a sound-like power in light."

This structure repeats itself in the next verse paragraph. This time the external scene, which like the earlier one is described in terms of quiet tranquillity, is one that the poet remembers (his climb up the hill). The memory prompts another inward turn of the mind, which culminates in another of the poet's stabs at the ultimate nature of life, in lines 44-47. Finally the poem returns to its starting point, and the poet realizes, with more than a little encouragement from Sara, that his metaphysical speculations are of little use to him.

The dominant image is that of the eolian harp, whose spontaneous music feeds the poet's loftier speculations. The harp also provides the poet with an image of himself and his own craft: Like the harp, the poet waits passively for inspiration to come to him. He must "tranquil muse upon tranquillity" until the external scene, received through "half-clos'd eyelids," stimulates his "indolent and passive brain" to deep thoughts. Linked to this interaction between active and passive modes of being is another prominent group of images, in which silence coexists with soft sound, as in the line, "The stilly murmur of the distant Sea/ Tells us of Silence," and in all the passages that describe the harp's music.

Themes and Meanings

"The Eolian Harp" expresses Coleridge's belief in a natural philosophy that emphasizes the connectedness of all things, both inner and outer: "O! the one Life within us and abroad," as he puts it in this poem. Coleridge believed that any separation between subject and object, the knower and the known, was ultimately false, and he was always searching for the ways in which the laws that govern the operation of the human mind could also be discerned in the workings of the external world. Like Wordsworth, he thought this could best be achieved when the mind was quiet—hence the emphasis in the poem on his own "indolence." (Wordsworth called such a state "wise passiveness.") Settling down into its own silence, the mind could then perceive the underlying principle of joy and harmony which runs through the whole of creation, the "Rhythm in all thought, and joyance every where" suggested to the poet by the music of the harp.

Later in Coleridge's career he became dissatisfied with the image of the eolian harp because it suggested that the mind was passive in perception, merely waiting to receive input from the sensory world. Coleridge rejected this view, which is associated with the English philosopher John Locke, replacing it with the idea of the mind as a fountain or a radiating light which actively projects life into all that it perceives. This view finds clear expression in Coleridge's poem *Dejection: An Ode* (1802).

Throughout Coleridge's life, as he sought to create an organic philosophy to replace the prevailing mechanistic worldview, he was acutely aware of the tension between this dynamic, quasi-mystical philosophy and orthodox Christian belief. The poet and mystic inside him was often at war with the rationalist theologian and Christian minister. (Shortly after he wrote "The Eolian Harp," Coleridge temporarily became a Unitarian preacher.) This tension is clearly discernible in the poem. For many readers the final verse paragraph, in which Coleridge, prompted by the disapproving eye of his wife, rejects the speculative philosophy that his reveries have produced, is an unsatisfactory and awkward conclusion. The poet and thinker are hobbled by the intrusion of religious dogma. This may be a valid point, but perhaps Coleridge (and Sara, who in this poem symbolizes an aspect of his own mind), have been too harshly judged. The poet's metaphysical speculations may have struck him as being unbalanced, in the sense that they were too much the product of the intellect, divorced from truths that could be directly known through the heart. The point is made emphatically in the assertion that God can only be praised "with Faith that inly *feels*," the italicization clearly pointing to the perceived deficiencies of "vain Philosophy." Coleridge once remarked in this connection that "deep thinking is attainable only by a man of deep feeling . . . a metaphysical solution that does not tell you something in the heart is grieviously to be suspected as apocryphal."

Bryan Aubrey

EPIPSYCHIDION

Author: Percy Bysshe Shelley (1792-1822)
Type of poem: Lyric
First published: 1821

The Poem

    Epipsychidion is a love lyric of 604 lines, written for Emilia Viviani, whom Percy Bysshe Shelley met while she was "imprisoned" by her family in a convent near Pisa, Italy, in 1820. The title is Greek for "concerning a little soul."

    Epipsychidion opens with an invocation to Emilia as a spiritual sister of the speaker. He addresses her as a "captive bird," for whose nest his poem will be soft rose petals. He calls her an angel of light, the light of the moon seen through mortal clouds, a star beyond all storms, and a mirror like the sun itself, making everything shine in its light. He wishes she were his twin sister, or the sister of his wife. They could blend their separate beams of light together into one.

    The poet calls her the lamp into whose light his muse flies like a moth. He is annihilated by her love and beauty, as if he were drowned by water flowing from the well of her being. He strives to express her essence, but he cannot find the right comparison.

    Then the poet addresses the reader, a "Stranger," to explain how he met Emilia. She lured him from night and winter into day and spring. The sound of her voice was a "liquid murmur" of sweet music from heaven. The warmth of her love enlivens the cold air, and her very fingertips glow. Her hair emits a sweet fragrance that fills the wind. She is like the power of the moon's gravitational pull on the tides of his earthly love. Finally, the poet admits again how desperately he searches for the adequate phrase, for she is the metaphors themselves.

    Transported by his song of ecstasy, the poet asserts the equalizing power of love; the lowly worm is made one with God Himself by love. Thus he laments his failure to have met Emilia earlier in his life, when her love might have made him feel as one with divinity. Now he must accept a different relationship with her, even though he knows that they were made for each other, the way musical notes make sweet concord.

    He says that he should be a warning, as a lighthouse which stands on dangerous rocks. Here Shelley begins a spiritual autobiography, with a creed of free love. He has never accepted the "code of modern morals" that confines one person for life to another in marriage. Instead, he asserts, love does not diminish when it is shared with many others. It is not like gold or clay; it will not become smaller when it is divided. Instead, it is like the mind itself, which grows stronger the more it is applied to understand the truth; it is like the light of imagination, which fills the universe and destroys dragons of ignorance.

    When he was young, he wandered far and often, until he was met by a "Being" that spoke to him through the harmony of nature's beauty. He flitted about like a moth, looking for her, calling for her to remain with him. She passed by him and disappeared; in his frenzy to find her perfect form, he missed her altogether. He tried magical charms and rituals to force her to reveal herself, but to no avail. He continued his wanderings, more lost than ever, looking for "one form resembling hers." Then he was seduced by a woman sitting beside a well in a forest, but she was false and filled with poison. She nearly killed him with her foul loving, turning him into an old man, worn out in youth.

Still looking for an ideal form, he suddenly turned on his own thoughts, the way a deer will turn on chasing dogs. In that moment, a bright Being appeared; she reminded him of the Spirit he sought, though she was the Moon to that Spirit's Sun. This new Being came to him the way the Moon came to Endymion, making love to him in the night when he was near death. She made him tranquil. Suddenly a great storm rocked him, blotting out the light of that Moon, as another Being, a "Planet," disappeared and left him frozen, a lake of ice.

Then Emilia entered his life as "the Vision" he had been seeking. She came upon him like the dawn that slowly radiates, surely warms, and enlivens the universe. Music and fragrance came to him with her light, and she sent her beams into the cave of his desolation. She was the Sun beckoning him into a new life. He is the Earth, governed by the Being of the Moon and the Vision of the Sun. They are his "married lights," who move him from Winter death through three seasons of vitality. He calls for yet another heavenly being, a "Comet beautiful and fierce," who had once attracted him as well; she had been nearly wrecked before she "went astray." Now he calls for her to return and make complete the universe of his new-found being.

In such a state of cosmic harmony, the poet suddenly turns to address Emilia directly again. He asks her to accept these verses as flowers from his heart; they will produce the fruit of Paradise. The day and the hour have arrived when she will be liberated from her prison; love will break down the barriers that divide her from the poet, and they will fly together. She will be his "vestal sister," but also, paradoxically, united with him "even as a bride."

The poet calls to Emilia to sail away with him. Their ship will become a bird to fly them to Eden, on "an isle under Ionian skies." It is beautiful, with woods, fresh water, caves, and waterfalls to protect them from the outside world. They will feel as if they were in "an antenatal dream"—a time before birth; there are no wars, famines, or diseases in that place. Deep in its protective forests is a lonely dwelling: a "pleasure house" carved out of mountains. From its high terraces they can look down upon the beaches, where "Earth and Ocean seem/ To sleep in one another's arms."

The poet has prepared that place to receive them with simple pleasures: nature's beauty, a few books, and music. Birds and deer will entertain them, as they explore the island's secret delights. In some cool cavern they can kiss and talk, love one another completely, until they become "one Spirit within two frames," "one passion in twin-hearts." They will be like flaming meteors mixing their fiery lights until they become one transfigured, unconsumed energy of delight. Their separate beings will be annihilated.

On this thought, the poet expires beneath the weight of inexpressible desire: His very words, before winged with love, turn into "chains of lead," and he falls into silence. Rather, he almost falls silent. Though the poem proper has ended with the speaker's collapse, there is an envoi, a farewell by the poet to his poem. He bids his "weak Verses" to tell his Lady that he will serve her every desire. He tells his poem to prophesy that his love for Emilia will be fulfilled in another life, if not in this one. She and all his friends may join him as guests of Love, even beyond the grave.

Forms and Devices

Epipsychidion is an erotic poem of pentameter couplets. There is a pattern of highly sensuous imagery which climaxes in sexual intensity. Since Shelley himself cites Dante's *Il convivio* (c. 1307, *The Banquet*, 1909), he draws attention to his poem's kinship with that one, a spiritual feast of life's pleasures. Also, as in the biblical "Song of Solomon," Shelley's poem is an epithalamion, a marriage song (as illustrated by Edmund Spenser's *Epithalamion* in 1595, and *Prothalamion* in 1596).

The form of the marriage song is generally followed in "Epipsychidion," which begins with a salute to the beloved, then presents a lamentation for her virginal imprisonment, a catalog of her beauties and virtues, a history of their meeting, and an invitation for her to join the bridegroom in the marital bliss of Eden.

The rhetorical devices which establish the tone of the poem are the apostrophe, or address of salutation, and the invocation, or calling, to the beloved. To develop his relationships, Shelley relies upon similes and metaphors, primarily using images of moon, sun, earth, and comet. The result is to imagine a harmony of love in the human community which is a restoration of the heavenly harmony that prevailed before the Fall of Man, when the cosmic spheres moved together to make celestial music.

Shelley rapidly takes up one image after another in his urgent attempts to capture essential, though evanescent, qualities. He moves forcefully and excitedly, from the comparison with a "poor captive bird," through "Seraph of Heaven," to the light of the moon, the sun, and the pole star that guides mariners. One of the interesting qualities of the poem is that its speaker is very conscious of his limitations—of the fundamental limit of language—in attempting to reach the kind of truth that he is anxious to describe. Therefore, he rises in frantic explorations of metaphors and similes until he runs out of energy, reaches the limits of referentiality, and then falls exhausted into despairing frustration.

Themes and Meanings

Epipsychidion is an obviously autobiographical poem, despite the transparently self-effacing "Advertisement," a disclaimer with which Shelley began the poem. Emilia Viviani is named in the poem several times, and three of Shelley's companions in Italy are alluded to in the envoi: "Marina, Vanna, and Primus" are masked names for Mary Shelley, Jane Williams, and Edward Williams. Given such clues, most readers can piece together the story of Shelley's love affairs to which the poem alludes, including Claire Clairmont as the Comet and Harriet Westbrook (Shelley's first wife) as "the Planet of that hour" when the poet's "Earth" was shaken by a Tempest (this refers to Harriet's suicide).

The autobiographical level of the poem, however, is not its only meaning; its title is a clue to another theme. *Epipsychidion* is an attempt to capture in poetry the experience of self-discovery, of a "soul within the soul." This occurs through the power of love, or desire, as it makes one aware of a void in one's being. To realize that one is not sufficient unto one's self is to drive one to search for the sufficiency of fulfillment in another. There is a profound truth in this experience, a truth which is elusive, constantly changing, and seductive. It requires constant pursuit and active commitment to something or someone outside the self. The poem is therefore an essay on love as the power of imagination to find truth, lose it, and search again for it. The "little soul" is the "soul within the soul," the sweetly painful voice of desire which echoes the being of another, of the Other, who promises completeness.

Finally, the poem is also about making poetry itself. The art of language is frustratingly insufficient to realize all that it aims for, including the release of the imprisoned Emilia, the captive spirit, either from the convent or from the flesh (of the woman or of the poet). It is, however, the most effective medium of art available to imagination for mediation between mind and body, body and body, spirit and spirit. The frustration is that the poet desires an absolute, unmediated union with his beloved, with no differences; he can only barely reach the possibility of that kind of union, because it always eludes him. The poet is as much a prisoner of language as Emilia is a prisoner in her convent.

Richard D. McGhee

AN EPISTLE CONTAINING THE STRANGE MEDICAL EXPERIENCE OF KARSHISH, THE ARAB PHYSICIAN

Author: Robert Browning (1812-1889)
Type of poem: Epistle/letter in verse
First published: 1855, in *Men and Women*

The Poem

"An Epistle Containing the Strange Medical Experience of Karshish, the Arab Physician" is presented in the form of a letter from a garrulous physician to his mentor. Correspondence in the first century C.E. was an uncertain affair: Karshish is entrusting his letter to a Syrian vagabond who promises to deliver it in return for medical treatment.

The document at first has the appearance of a mere historical curiosity, a scrap preserved by chance for nearly two thousand years. Then it becomes apparent that this eccentric "absent-minded professor" had accidentally encountered Lazarus, the man who had reportedly been brought back from the dead by Jesus of Nazareth, hailed by many Jews as their Messiah and executed like a criminal by crucifixion. Karshish's unworldliness lends credibility to his report; he is too guileless to be able to invent such a story. Robert Browning has made his speaker an Arab, an outsider, so that he has no ulterior motive in helping to extend the reputation of Jesus as a prophet and miracle worker.

The story of Lazarus being raised from the dead is told most fully in the Gospel of Saint John in the New Testament. The biblical account does not tell what happened to Lazarus after he emerged from the tomb or how his experience of being dead for several days had changed him. These are questions on which many creative writers have speculated. In recent times, there has been considerable scientific and quasi-scientific interest in persons who have apparently died and then returned to life. Many such subjects have reported wonderful experiences. Browning uses his powerful imagination to try to imagine what it must have been like for Lazarus.

The reference to Vespasian and the later statement that Jesus died "many years ago" indicate that the date is approximately C.E. 66, when the Jewish revolt against Roman rule began. This would mean that Lazarus would have to be older than fifty, as Karshish states, although he could look younger. The Bible does not give Lazarus's age, but does call him a man and not a boy at the time of his return from the dead, which occurred shortly before Jesus was crucified in approximately C.E. 30. Lazarus seems both wise and childlike. He presents the appearance of a man who has undergone such a profound experience that it has changed his whole view of life. Having experienced death, he realizes that mortality is just one stage of existence and that a much more marvelous stage awaits beyond the grave. He sees the cares and conflicts of mortal men as having no real importance. Karshish, who possesses some of the skepticism of a good scientist, tries to find a physical explanation for Lazarus's apparent death, his subsequent revival, and the transformation in his character; however, the truth-seeking Arab physician cannot help but wonder if the stories of this man having been raised from the dead by the Son of God might actually be true.

Karshish then goes on to speculate about the implications of such an event. He wonders if it is possible that God could have assumed a human form and, even more important, if the God most people regarded as a vengeful and demanding deity could be capable of the same kind of love for humanity that human beings feel for one another.

Forms and Devices

Although this poem is presented as a letter, it is only a variant of the dramatic monologue, a form in which Browning created his greatest poems, including the well-known "My Last Duchess," "Fra Lippo Lippi," "Andrea del Sarto" (called "The Faultless Painter"), and "The Bishop Orders His Tomb at Saint Praxed's Church." All these poems are a little difficult to understand at first reading because their speakers are addressing not the reader but a contemporary who understands their many hints and allusions. The poems are worth studying, however, because they are so well executed, because they make history come alive, and because they were so influential in the development of modern poetry.

As can be seen in "An Epistle of Karshish," Browning achieves his effects by two principal means: his vivid depiction of human character, and the inclusion of specific concrete details that reveal the depth of his studies in history, art, and many other fields. Every aspiring creative writer needs to learn that concrete details always enhance verisimilitude: They make the poem, drama, short story, or novel more convincing and consequently more effective. Karshish's references to such things as powdered snakestone show the primitive state of science in his time—suggesting by implication that the scientists of Browning's own day, who were bringing traditional Christianity more and more into question, might be equally benighted though equally confident of their scientific methodology.

Browning had to struggle for many years to achieve the recognition he deserved. Critics claimed that his poems were not "poetic": They were not euphonious and romantic like the poems of the popular Alfred, Lord Tennyson, who was named poet laureate in 1850. Many of the things the critics complained about can be seen in "An Epistle Containing the Strange Medical Experience of Karshish, the Arab Physician." The lines do not rhyme. The poem is in iambic pentameter, but the rhythm is continually and perversely interrupted, so that the whole piece seems jerky and discordant. A line of more or less straight iambic pentameter, such as "The vagrant Scholar to his sage at home," is rare. The poem is difficult to follow; it is full of cryptic remarks and obscure allusions.

These features are like those of modern poetry, but many modern poets have taken the further step of abandoning meter as well as rhyme. Browning's elaborate use of a speaker or "dramatic persona" in many of his poems is another example of his modernist spirit. It gives the poems a multidimensional, relativistic quality that prefigures the Einsteinian view of the universe. Browning's technical experimentation represents a more important contribution to the development of poetry than his conventional ideas about religion and morality. He had difficulty achieving recognition because he was ahead of his time. His influence as an artistic innovator can be seen in the works of many of his successors, including T. S. Eliot's landmark modern poem *The Waste Land* (1922) and Ezra Pound's highly influential *Cantos* (1917-1970).

Themes and Meanings

What is admirable about this poem from an artistic standpoint, as it is about most of Browning's dramatic monologues, is that it makes the past come alive—in this case, the past of nearly two thousand years ago. The closest parallel to Browning's unrhymed iambic pentameter in his dramatic monologues is to be found in Shakespeare's historical dramas. Shakespeare was never greatly concerned about historical accuracy, however, and his historical plays are full of anachronisms and other glaring errors. Browning could not rival Shakespeare as a dramatist, but he excelled at being able to give the reader the feeling of having been swept backward in time.

Browning's purpose in persuading the reader that the story of Lazarus was literally true was to persuade the reader of the truth of a religion founded on the belief that the Son of God had appeared on earth and had brought salvation to humankind. Browning lived at a time when scientific discoveries were undermining the authority of the Bible. For example, it had been estimated that the universe, instead of having been created some 6,000 years ago, as recorded in the Old Testament, was actually billions of years old. The most telling blow against established Western religion was to come in 1859 with the publication of Charles Darwin's *On the Origin of Species*, which argued convincingly that life had existed on earth for billions of years and had been gradually evolving since its spontaneous generation in the form of single-celled organisms. Darwin later theorized that man himself was only an animal descended from apelike ancestors. Evidently, the story of Adam and Eve was only a myth. God did not create man; life originated in blind chemical reactions and gradually evolved into more complex forms until the genus Homo appeared around two or three million years ago.

Browning was always a staunch defender of Christianity. Some have called him a reactionary; others have called him an escapist. Much of his poetry can be viewed as symptomatic of a yearning for an earlier time when life was simpler and man's belief in a divinely ordered universe was unthreatened by the dispassionate probing of science. Like many concerned thinkers of the Victorian era, Browning believed that civilization itself was in jeopardy, that the mass of men obeyed the Ten Commandments because they were afraid of being sent to hell. If their faith in a judgmental God were shattered, they might feel free to murder, steal, rape, and commit all the other sins forbidden by traditional Judeo-Christian religion. It could be argued that Browning's forebodings were not entirely alarmist: The rise of immoral behavior and serious crime in the Western world has been paralleled by a dramatic decline in church attendance.

Bill Delaney

EPISTLE TO DR. ARBUTHNOT

Author: Alexander Pope (1688-1744)
Type of poem: Epistle/letter in verse
First published: 1735

The Poem

Alexander Pope's *An Epistle from Mr. Pope, to Dr. Arbuthnot* (better known simply as *Epistle to Dr. Arbuthnot*) is a poetic "letter" (epistle) of 420 lines written in heroic couplets. In his epistle, addressed to his close friend, the writer and physician John Arbuthnot, who died just before the poem was published, Pope discusses the current state of artistic and political affairs in England while examining his own long career as England's foremost poet—and most feared satirist.

As was his habit in verse satire, Pope writes in the first person, speaking directly to Arbuthnot (who occasionally interrupts Pope to caution him or to offer a different point of view). Pope's voice is his own and is fittingly "conversational"; his tone is alternately indignant, comical, bitter, ironic—a rich "orchestration" of moods and attitudes. Throughout much of the poem, readers get a keen sense of Pope's playfulness: He charms readers with his theatrical posturings (as in the opening vignette, in which a horde of bad writers storms the door of Pope's retreat at Twickenham), while reminding them with a wink—that they are, after all, only posturings.

The poetic tradition of which Pope was the acknowledged master prized control, and in *Epistle to Dr. Arbuthnot* Pope is always in control. When he indulges in self-dramatization, or seems to skirt the edges of self-pity ("how wretched I!"), he does so knowingly, with a greater purpose in mind.

Though he tried his hand at virtually every traditional poetic form (and even produced an English translation of Homer's *Iliad* that is still highly esteemed), Pope found satire to be most congenial to his talents. The reasons for this reach to the very core of his personality—and can be glimpsed in *Epistle to Dr. Arbuthnot*, which is in part a classic apologia of his satiric career.

Pope's need to defend himself is easy to understand. Through his writing, a satirist "attacks" people and their institutions. Sometimes the attack is light-hearted and comic; sometimes it is dark and scornful. In any case, people stand to be hurt by such attacks, and the satirist, if he or she is at all sensitive to such things (and Pope *was* sensitive), must be aware that his or her art carries with it an undeniable moral responsibility. With this in mind, Pope defends himself in several ways: by showing himself to have been the undeserving victim of satiric attack earlier in his own life; by depicting his targets as either comically inept or morally despicable; by underscoring the social benefits of satire; and by suggesting that respected writers urged him to respond to his enemies in kind.

Pope's defense of his satiric career is itself a supremely effective satire. (Together with John Dryden's "Mac Flecknoe," it is perhaps the finest short poetic satire in the language.) Many of Pope's old enemies appear, only to be heaped once again with satiric scorn. In a series of brilliant satiric portraits, Pope attacks not only individuals but "types." His portrait of Lord John Hervey (the "Sporus" of lines 305-333) is both a devastating attack on Hervey personally and an unforgettable indictment of the political, sexual, and moral "double-dealer." (With an irony Pope surely would appreciate, Hervey is now remembered principally as the target of this acerbic satire.)

Forms and Devices

Effective satire of the kind Pope favored works not so much in calling a fool a fool as in creating a world in which fools show themselves to be fools. Pope is able to create such a world largely through his use of Arbuthnot. As a writer of some talent, but more important as a man of great personal honor and integrity, Arbuthnot provides a firm moral standard against which Pope can implicitly measure both himself and his enemies. Arbuthnot's background presence is always felt. Readers align themselves with him; when he speaks, they listen. Readers (like Pope) know the moderation he advises to be wise; yet when he lashes out against Sporus, readers know without being told that there are times when even the mildest of men are obliged to strike out against moral and political corruption. The world for which Arbuthnot is the apt moral representative is the reader's world before it is Pope's, though soon they share it with him willingly.

In addition to being a great satirist, Pope was a great poet—"If Pope be not a poet," wrote Samuel Johnson in 1779, "where is poetry to be found?"—and *Epistle to Dr. Arbuthnot* is packed with the stuff of great poetry. Pope uses imagery, for example, in particularly effective ways. From the beginning, he initiates a running cluster of images based on animals, insects, dirt, and disease that culminates powerfully in the portrait of Sporus as "This painted Child of Dirt that stinks and stings" in line 310. Hence, imagery reinforces meaning on several levels: Sporus has not only the existential status of a "Bug," but he is a carrier of diseases, both physical and moral. As a brilliantly concise metaphor, Sporus sums up all that is wrong with the England of the 1730's: corrupt politics, corrupt personal morality—what amounts to a blinding obsession with self-interest that infects the entire social spectrum. To attack such a creature, Pope implies, even to grind it beneath one's foot, is no more than a good man's duty.

Few morally "serious" satires pack quite so much life into their lines as does *Epistle to Dr. Arbuthnot*. This is attributable in part to Pope's ability to manipulate language within the formal constraints of the heroic couplet. Though in some ways a highly "artificial" form, in the hands of Pope the heroic couplet resonates with vitality and immediacy. The voice readers hear opening the poem ("Shut, shut the door, good John") strikes their ears as a real voice, a human voice, and they respond to it with sympathy and interest.

Pope's talents allow for other effects as well. Whether he is describing a "mad" writer scribbling on the walls of a lunatic asylum or an awful poet named Codrus whose moronic self-absorption makes him deaf to the "Peals of Laughter" inspired by his work, Pope opens up a world of vivid sensory impressions. The sights, the sounds, even the smells of this strange world surround readers as we read.

Themes and Meanings

Epistle to Dr. Arbuthnot shares the theme common to satirists since the days of the Roman poets Horace and Juvenal: the constant struggle of "good" writers to maintain their standards of artistic achievement and integrity in a world dominated by "bad" writers and their corrupt patrons and sycophants. Pope imaginatively realizes this struggle by guiding readers through a kind of "rogue's gallery": Codrus is a supremely bad writer, Sporus a monster of duplicity and deceit, and Bufo a "patron of the arts" with absolutely no genuine interest in art and artists beyond his own self-aggrandizement.

For Pope, however, more lies at stake than art. For art, though a supremely important means of expressing human value and meaning, is merely one aspect of civilization as a whole. Its "diseased" condition is only a symptom, an indicator of a problem that runs much deeper. This problem (Pope refers to it as a "Plague") is not so much "bad writing" as it is "bad thinking" and, by extension, "bad living." What has created this problem? For Pope, nothing more or less than a fundamental distortion in human values. A world, after all, in which creatures such as Bufo and Sporus can prosper is a world whose values have been turned topsy-turvy. It is a "sick" world badly in need of a doctor's curative abilities.

Arbuthnot is that doctor, and Pope is his assistant. Just as Arbuthnot's medicinal skills had helped Pope survive one disease after another in his "long disease, my life," so now Arbuthnot's moral goodness can prove therapeutic for society. Why? In part, because goodness is still possible; good men and women, though perhaps in the minority, still exist. In the concluding lines of the poem, having spent his passion excoriating Sporus and his kind, and having claimed for his own poetry the task of seeking "Virtue's better end," Pope turns quietly and reverently to his parents, whose "spotless" lives exist as proof that something of real human value yet remains for the poet to celebrate—and to protect.

Epistle to Dr. Arbuthnot thus "means" what all great poetry will always mean: that what is truly human is redeemable and is well worth the cost of redemption.

Michael Stuprich

EPISTLE II. TO A LADY

Author: Alexander Pope (1688-1744)
Type of poem: Epistle/letter in verse; satire
First published: 1735, as *Of the Characters of Women: An Epistle to a Lady*; collected in *The Works of Alexander Pope*, 1735

The Poem

    Epistle II. To a Lady is a long poem of 292 lines, written in heroic couplets in the form of a pseudo-Horatian epistle, or verse letter, that is a satire against women. It is one of four poems that Alexander Pope grouped together under the title *Moral Essays* (1731-1735), which were supposed to be an integral part of an ambitious and never-completed "ethic work," inaugurated by his philosophic manifesto *An Essay on Man* (1733-1734) two years before the publication of *Epistle II. To a Lady*. The first of these four epistles illustrating the ideas of *An Essay on Man* concentrates on the characters of men; the third and fourth deal with the use of riches; and the second contains a brilliantly wrought series of female portraits exemplifying the thesis "Women's at best a Contradiction still."

    Although the poem ranks as a masterpiece of satire, its stereotypical view of women as exemplars of inconsistencies, whose proper sphere is in domestic life, offends modern sensibilities and repeats stale criticisms of women reaching back to the antifeminist literature of Geoffrey Chaucer's "Wife of Bath's Tale" and diatribes of certain church fathers. Yet Pope is not a misogynist. Dedicated and addressed to his beloved female friend Martha Blount, *Epistle II. To a Lady* does not really indulge in hatred of women, but ends on a note of praise for the sex, with a presentation of a feminine ideal of goodness to be respected by male and female alike. Morality may be ultimately gender-neutral; a good woman, like a good man, is ultimately a sensible, well-rounded, and self-possessed human being. As Maynard Mack noted in his authoritative *Alexander Pope: A Life* (1985), women evoked Pope's deepest fascination and sympathy, especially "with the lot society had assigned them as pawns in the chess game of family aggrandizement that did not blind him to the alacrity with which they sometimes embraced their own destruction." In a fundamental sense, *Epistle II. To a Lady* is especially directed at female readers: for their moral instruction, to prevent their destruction, and to promote their well-being.

    The poem opens with the poet in the guise of a painter taking readers on a tour through a gallery of portraits of women who demonstrate that the entire sex is more incredibly inconsistent than males are. The survey begins with a procession of foolish females. Pseudo-intellectual Rufa illustrates affectation, with a sarcastic Swiftian comparison with Mary Wortley Montagu as "Sappho." Soft-spoken Silia next appears, in a sudden rage over a pimple; impossible Papillia wants shade but hates trees; unattractive Calypso attracts by cunning; whimsical Narcissa lacks mental or moral stability; lively Flavia plays the fashionable wit prone to melancholy and radical ideas, and, following a brief study of silly triflers, violent Atossa—alias the Duchess of Buckinghamshire—and heartless Cloe close the ranks of the female fools.

This negative portraiture gives way, in the final third of the poem, to positive glimpses of the good woman, as personified by an overly glorified Queen Caroline and an understated Duchess of Queensbury. The poem concludes on an upbeat if extremely chauvinistic note, insisting that women's delicately complex personality suits them for domesticity rather than for a public life, driven as they are by two ruling passions: "The Love of Pleasure, and the Love of Sway" (lines 207-248). Let women, therefore, emulate the life of Martha Blount, being addressed throughout the poem. Let them cultivate good sense and good humor in order to transform the contradictions of their divided nature into an integrated personality ("a softer Man") that is an ideal synthesis of male and female traits.

Forms and Devices

The outstanding example of Pope the caricaturist at work is *Epistle II. To a Lady*, a poem that the great critic Samuel Johnson praised despite reservations about its unwarranted psychological generalizations: "That his excellence may be properly estimated, I recommend a comparison of his *Characters of Women* with Boileau's Satire; it will then be seen with how much perspicacity female nature is investigated and female excellence selected; and he surely is no mean writer to whom Boileau shall be found inferior."

The painting metaphor, a recurrent one in Pope's poetry, is introduced at the outset, when the painter-poet invites the reader around an art gallery of painted beauties that exhibit one consistency—namely, that they are all inconsistent: " 'Most Women have no Characters at all.' " This infamous maxim drips with the irony of dubious double or triple meaning: Women are infinitely various, fickle, and/or unprincipled. The primary concern is with the infinitely various female personality. The painter-poet captures the inconsistencies through taut and witty couplets loaded everywhere with paradox, rhetorically and thematically—much as a caricaturist such as Annibale Carraci would delineate his grotesque subjects with a few quick and clever strokes of the brush.

The painting metaphor is kept up in various ways, especially through the poet's role as painter, but also by small hints of pictorial quality in visual imagery and by the use of technical terms from painting. The variegated colors, tools, and skills of the artist's trade are necessary to paint the inconsistencies behind the glittering surface beauty of the portraits: "For how should equal Colours do the knack?/ Chameleons who can paint in white and black?"

Allied to the painting metaphor is another visual metaphor, the imagery of light, which appears in references to women as changeable as the moon (lines 19-20); as fairest in domestic shade, far from the glare of the male-dominated public arena (lines 199-206); as temperate moonlight (lines 249-256); as sunshine cheering home and hearth (lines 257-268); and as capable of the radiance of a Martha Blount, nurtured under the influence of Phoebus, the sun god (lines 283-292).

Paradox—an apparent contradiction that is somehow true—is at the heart of the poem's meaning and rhetorical fireworks. Pope was the inimitable master of the closed pentameter couplet (also called the heroic couplet), and his verse repeatedly lapses into the rhetorical harmony of antithesis to capture a transcendent order and divinely guided purpose behind the mortal contradictions of the female lot. Paradox, for example, captures female frailties, such as Calypso's mediocrity ("Less Wit than Mimic, more a Wit than Wise") and Narcissa's infidelity ("Chaste to her Husband, frank to all beside,/ A teeming Mistress, but a barren Bride"). In the end, paradox expresses ultimate female virtue and the ultimate human being, "a softer Man," who unites contrary traits of femininity and maleness into a serene oneness of being:

> Reserve with Frankness, Art with Truth ally'd,
> Courage with Softness, Modesty with Pride,
> Fix'd Principles, with Fancy ever new;
> Shakes all together, and produces—You.

Themes and Meanings

Epistle II. To a Lady is a poem about the need for women to cultivate a rounded and rational perspective on life in order to overcome the contradictory shortcomings of their nature that, unrestrained by reason, true love, and common sense, can lead to emotional and immoral excesses. As a satire modeled on the casual Horatian verse letter, or epistle, the poem inculcates this theme through ridicule of excessive female types and through closing praise of female norms of right conduct for the edification of female readers. In meaning and movement, the poem is very much like Pope's famous *The Rape of the Lock* (1712, 1714), but without the epic machinery or the focus on a single and more innocent beauty such as Belinda. The poem's gallery of portraits and casual elegance also bear comparison with the technique and tone of *Epistle to Dr. Arbuthnot* (1735).

The greatest artists share an underlying vision of reality as a contradiction, a duality of oppositions, a paradox. Many authors envisage the end of life and the aim of art to be the synthesizing of contradiction, the integration of dualities, and the harmonizing of paradox. Pope is no exception, in either philosophical vision or moral-artistic goals. Of all the poems in his canon, *An Essay on Man* offers the underlying optimistic vision for *Epistle II. To a Lady* and expounds a psychology and philosophy of paradox, at the crux of his satire against women. In *An Essay on Man*, humanity is defined as a paradox, "A being darkly wise, and rudely great," made imperfect by pride but capable of pursuing perfection under the guidance of reason and good instincts, both of which help to transform innate self-love and distinctive ruling passions into virtuous conduct and a higher love of others and of God. Such a process of internal transformation causes the harmonizing of human paradox and the transmutation of human ills into goodness and meaning. If one submits to the process and the divine scheme of things, Pope insists, then the contradictory chaos of reality is only an appearance, whereas the serene oneness of reality asserts itself to prove "Whatever IS is RIGHT."

These assumptions buttress the theme of *Epistle II. To a Lady*. All foolish beauties, from Rufa to Cloe, are creatures of contradiction misled by pride, weak in reason, and, therefore, unrestrained in their self-love or their female ruling passion for pleasure and domination. By the same token, even good women such as Martha Blount are "at best a Contradiction"; however, they find integration through reason and common sense ("Sense, Good-humour"), generating useful and selfless service to others and becoming models of an ideal humanity ("a softer Man") to be admired by all.

Thomas M. Curley

EPITHALAMION

Author: Edmund Spenser (c. 1552-1599)
Type of poem: Lyric
First published: 1595, in *Amoretti and Epithalamion*

The Poem

Epithalamion is a poem of 433 iambic lines of varying lengths, divided into twenty-three stanzas and an envoi—twenty-four sections in all. The title means, literally, "at the nuptial chamber," from the Greek (*epi* and *thalanos*); the poem celebrates the twenty-four hours of the poet's wedding day. The poem is written in the first person, and much of it is addressed to the Muses, nymphs, other bridal attendants, and wedding guests. The twenty-four sections do not correspond precisely to the twenty-four hours of the wedding day, yet the poem moves chronologically through the entire day.

In the first stanza, the poet speaks to the Muses, who have often inspired him in the past, asking that they "Helpe me mine owne loves prayses to resound." Edmund Spenser quite often begins his works this way, with the poet/narrator requesting divine assistance as he undertakes a task that is beyond his mortal skills. His bride is so magnificent, it is implied, that he cannot find words to describe her. The next three stanzas anticipate the awakening of the bride on her wedding day. The poet beckons the Muses to wake her, and to summon nymphs from land and sea to bring garlands and flowers to adorn the bride and her chamber. In stanzas 5 and 6, she awakens and is dressed for the wedding.

"Now is my love all ready forth to come," the poet announces, and he is ready, too. He then invokes the sun, praying that its lifegiving rays will brighten this joyful day without burning his bride's bright "sunshyny face." The wedding musicians play, boys run through the streets shouting, and the wedding guests clamor until finally, in stanza 9 (nearly 150 lines into the poem), the bride appears. She is "like Phoebe," like "some angell," like "some mayden Queene." Addressing the women around the bride, the poet declares that, much as they admire her physical beauty, they would stand amazed at the "inward beauty" of her spirit. "Open the temple gates," the poet demands, and the marriage ceremony actually takes place, in stanzas 12 and 13—the center of the poem.

During the ceremony, the bride blushes in purity and modesty, impressing even the angels. When the ceremony is over, the groom's thoughts turn to celebration, to wine and dancing—but only for one stanza. By stanza 15 he is impatient for the wedding day to end and the wedding night to begin. "Ah when will this long weary day have end,/ And lende me leave to come unto my love?" he asks. Again he turns his attention to the Muses and nymphs, asking them now to stop celebrating and to help the bride prepare for bed. Repeatedly he complains that the day has been long and tiring.

In stanzas 18 through 20 he asks the night to provide a mantle of privacy for the couple and cautions various creatures to remain quiet so as not to disturb them as they enjoy "sweet snatches of delight." When the moon rises, in stanza 21, the poet asks her and other goddesses and gods to bless the couple with happiness and fertility.

Forms and Devices

Epithalamion is a nuptial song, and references to singing are everywhere in the poem. At the end of the first stanza, the poet declares that he will sing his love's praises, and "The woods shall to me answer and my Eccho ring." Each of the twenty-three stanzas ends with some variation of this refrain. For example, in stanza 8 the wedding guests sing to greet the bride, "That al the woods them answer and theyr eccho ring"; in stanza 19, the groom asks for quiet, begging the night creatures not to sing, "Ne let the woods them answer, nor theyr eccho ring." This refrain helps mark the passing of each stanza. The repetition also reinforces the unity among the stanzas, which are not strictly regular in length or in rhyme scheme.

Based on the Italian canzone, the stanzas are not uniform in structure, but they all use similar devices to enhance their musical qualities. The simple rhyme scheme, for example, is reminiscent of the ballad form, easily remembered and sung (unlike the complicated Spenserian stanza of *The Faerie Queene* (1590, 1596). Each stanza contains three lines of iambic trimeter, which appear abruptly after four or five lines of iambic pentameter. The effect is of three short verses of a song within each stanza. Because nearly all the lines are end-stopped, the rhythm is even sharper, and the refrain, in iambic hexameter, makes unambiguous the notion that this is a song.

A wedding is a joyful occasion for everyone involved, and here that joy is expressed through singing. The bride is awakened by the birds singing carols in praise of love, and the three Graces sing to her as they dress her for the wedding. Out in the streets, minstrels are playing, while damsels are singing and dancing. As the marriage ceremony begins, the tone of the poem is for a brief time solemn. The bride comes into the holy temple "with trembling steps and humble reverence" to take part in the "sacred ceremonies." Even here, the music is not solemn, but joyful: "the roring Organs loudly play/ The praises of the Lord in lively notes," while the choir sings a "joyous Antheme."

The message is clear; marriage is a holy sacrament, to be taken seriously and reverently. Yet it is also a wondrous miracle, and celebration and joy are entirely appropriate as well. The connection between holiness and joyful music is made most clear in stanza 15, as the wedding celebration begins to wind down: "Ring ye the bels, ye yong men of the towne,/ And leave your wonted labors for this day:/ This day is holy."

From this point on, although the refrain continues to appear at each stanza, the poet/ narrator refers to music only to wish aloud that it would cease. Although the musicality of the poem itself continues, with the strong rhythm, the long and short lines, and the complex rhyme schemes, the time for celebrating the wedding day with song ends when darkness falls.

Themes and Meanings

The idea of the epithalamion, or wedding song, was not new with Spenser. Poets as early as Sappho, the Greek woman who wrote in the early sixth century B.C.E., composed such poems, as did many others, such as Pindar and Catallus, in Greek and Latin, in the intervening years. Although each poet naturally brought her or his own vision and style to the wedding song, the "epithalamia" share many images and themes. Spenser was well aware of this tradition and intentionally followed many of its conventions in this poem. One of the most complicated matters for the Renaissance poet who wrote in traditional forms was the balancing of conventional devices with contemporary demands. More specifically, Spenser had to find a way to utilize the conventional gods and goddesses of mythology in a poem about Christian marriage. He could well expect his contemporary readers to be familiar with mythology, especially with the stories recounted in Ovid's *Metamorphoses* (c. 8 C.E.), and he uses allusions to these stories as a sort of shorthand. In the first stanza, the poet/ narrator announces that he will sing his love's praises, and he points out that this is what "Orpheus did for his owne bride."

Spenser's readers would know that Orpheus had the power to charm animals and trees with his music and that he almost won his wife back from the underworld with his music. These readers would probably also relate this myth to Spenser's courtship of his own bride through the powers of his music, by writing the sonnet sequence *Amoretti* for her.

In effect, the poet tells both those stories simply by using the one word "Orpheus." This use of mythological allusion, along with the references to Muses and Graces, Hymen and Juno, reinforces the theme of repetition and tradition that is so important to this poem. Women and men have been marrying—and poets have been celebrating marriage—for thousands of years. The emphasis on tradition, and on the wedding guests and attendants, makes clear that marriage is important, not only to the couple, but to all of heaven and earth.

By marrying, and by bringing forth the "fruitfull progeny," the couple will increase the number of "blessed Saints." This reference to the saints at the end of the poem culminates a thread of Christianity which has continued through the whole poem. This is clearly a Christian marriage and a Christian ceremony.

When the bride enters into the sacred temple, the "pagan" and Christian are solidified as one. Although the term "temple gates" is not reminiscent of Christian churches, once past the gates the poet describes the roaring organs, the choristers, the holy priest, and the angels flying above the service and singing "Alleluya." This is inarguably a Christian church.

This fusion of Christian and non-Christian elements was common for Spenser and for poets of the Renaissance. They saw the opportunity to borrow elements of the rich Greek and Roman traditions and to use them to show the continuity and universality of the Christian world.

Cynthia A. Bily

THE EQUILIBRISTS

Author: John Crowe Ransom (1888-1974)
Type of poem: Meditation
First published: 1925; collected in *Two Gentlemen in Bonds*, 1927

The Poem

"The Equilibrists" consists of fourteen quatrains of end-rhymed couplets, with four of the couplets exhibiting slant rhyme. The title states the condition of the man and woman in the poem. Emotional and philosophical acrobats, they balance opposites: passion and intellect, carnal lust and spiritual purity, heaven and hell, life and death.

The first stanza begins in the third person as the man recalls the physical attractions of the woman. He imagines her "long, white arms," and "milky skin," conjuring up an image that blocks his external perceptions; he is "alone in the press of people." The images hint at courtly love: the man journeying apart from his beloved, worshiping an elevated image of femininity.

In the second stanza, the ambiguities of the couple surface. They kissed, and then abruptly she rejected him—also a courtly love convention. Her body responded to his passion, but her intellect was an "officious tower" that would not permit consummation. In the third stanza, he compares her body to "a white field" where "lilies grew, beseeching him to take." The destructiveness of physical love is indicated; the purity he desires would be destroyed if he should possess her, yet it is her unspoiled beauty that attracts him. The fourth stanza continues his impressions of her physical beauty; in her eyes, he saw her desire for him, while she continued to deny it aloud. Knowing that her words alone could not prevent the consummation of this desire as long as they were together, she ordered him from her side, never again to approach close enough to endanger her honor.

The sixth stanza illustrates their stalemate. They acknowledge their love, yet will permit the "little word . . . Honor" to separate them. John Crowe Ransom gives no overt reason why they cannot find an honorable path to love (such as marriage), preferring instead to romanticize the abstraction of honor. Courtly love and the honor of chivalric days are reinforced in the invocation of the Tristram and Isolde legend by the words "between them cold as steel." The image adds another strand to the tapestry of medieval allusion; it conforms to the conventions of courtly love in that the woman is desirable but unattainable.

Stanzas 7 and 8 switch point of view to an outside narrator who comments upon the balance that the pair has struck. They have "Dreadfully . . . forsworn each other" yet cannot escape social contact. The "clustered night" filled with other people is their "prison world" where they must constantly, painfully, experience simultaneous deep attraction and self-imposed repulsion. Their situation has not gone unobserved, however, as the narrator goes on (in stanza 9) to comment upon the couple's situation, then slips into a moralizing speech about the choice they have between heaven and hell.

In stanza 13, the narrator continues to observe the pair, noting that no matter what roles they play, whether pretense of anger or cool civility, their love continues to be a "radiant" force between them. The narrator expects no change in this balance, and, since neither heaven nor hell offers the lovers an alternative, death itself can only continue their present state. The narrator devotes the last stanza to an epitaph for the lovers that grants them this finely wrought balance that they have achieved, lying side by side but untouching in the absolute separation of death.

Forms and Devices

Ransom's liberal use of metaphor contributes to the poem's mood of courtly love and chivalric intentions. He chooses to compare the woman in the poem to objects that summon up feudal days. Her head is "the officious tower" from which "words . . . spiral" as "grey doves." Her body is a "field ready for love," a fertility image linked to the agrarian way of life, in which the peasants lived close to the earth while those of the aristocratic class or those involved in intellectual pursuits dwelt above in a "gaunt tower" or castle. The addition of the lilies completes the appeal of a pastoral image: The shepherd calls the shepherdess to lie among the flowers in harmony with nature. Yet the flowers will "bruise and break"; ironic reality intrudes as the woman's purity, likened to the fleshy but delicate flowers, would be ruined by the encounter. Her words are compared to swords, another evocation of chivalric trappings. They can separate the two lovers as the sword between them kept apart the sleeping lovers Tristram and Isolde.

Having established this scene, the poet switches to a metaphysical comparison in stanza 8. The lovers are called two "painful stars" orbiting each other. They "burned with fierce love" as stars burn with fierce heat. In stanza 13, they are "radiant" with "flames" as well as with "ice"; an icy object can shine quite brightly with reflected sunlight. As they move about each other, there is balance, precision, and control; the narrator, however, cannot help but see their passion burning.

After using the metaphysical star images, Ransom crafts the couple's epitaph plainly with images of the grave. He employs synecdoche, or the use of a part to represent the whole, with "mouldered . . . lips" and "ashy . . . skull" standing for the dead bodies of the two lovers.

Although most of the couplets are perfectly end rhymed, the poet has used occasional slant rhyme (or near rhyme) to emphasize moments of disappointment in the poem. In stanza 4, the rhyming of "words" and "swords" mirrors the frustration of the man, who receives mixed signals from the woman's eyes and her words. In stanza 9, "brave" and "have" add awkwardness to the narrator's turn of speech as he begins his "descant" on morality. Stanza 11 rhymes "marriage is" with "lecheries," emphasizing the opposition of those states concerning physical love, as well as the disappointment for lovers of a heaven without physical pleasures. The last slant rhyme, in stanza 12 on hell, rhymes "ones" with "bones," adding unease to the horrible image of the destructive power of physical love.

Juxtaposition is another important element of the poem. In diction, Ransom con-

trasts a common word such as "mouth" with the latinate and more suggestive "orifice." In stanza 9, the narrator "cried in anger," an intense emotional state, then immediately is "devising" and "descanting," describing controlled, rational ability. The
juxtaposition of images runs throughout the poem. The woman is a field of flowers
"ready for love," and she is an "officious tower" ordering him away lest he "bruise and
break" her. As the lovers are compared to orbiting stars, they exhibit both "flames"
and "ice." They "dreadfully" forswear each other, yet are "bound each to each." Especially graphic is the linking of physical pleasure with physical torment in stanza 12.
The tension between these opposites necessitates the equilibrists' delicate balancing,
which they have come to exhibit exquisitely in pain and pleasure.

Themes and Meanings

Ransom states the major theme by his choice of title: equilibrium, or balance. *Webster's New Collegiate Dictionary* defines "equilibrist" as "one who balances . . . in unnatural positions and hazardous movements." Intimations of the calm and serenity of
balance are replaced by awareness of awkwardness and imminent imbalance; there is
implicit threat in this position. The would-be lovers do not display grace and ease, but
rather tension and discomfort. Equilibrium is "torture" for them; they are "rigid" and
"painful."

Ransom has become something of an equilibrist himself in creating this poem. His
choice of diction at times seems awkward—words such as "orifice," "importunate,"
"saeculum," and "infatuate." Ransom was a disciplined stylist who worked with difficult forms, not sparing himself. Here, form mirrors meaning. He treads precariously
in places. It may be a difficult, tortured form, but the result is admirable. This is not a
poem of simple choices; the poet refuses to advocate either the romantic vision of pursuing the heart's passion or the closing off of all feeling and desire through intellect.
There is a bitter irony displayed: In attempting to serve honor and deny lust, the lovers
lose all. They do not give in to carnal desire, yet the desire remains.

In the first three stanzas Ransom creates a romantic, sensual image: the beautiful
woman desired by the man. He uses images of nature, such as doves, lilies, fields, and
flowers, which might have been employed by the Romantic poets in an expansive
psalm on love and sensual delights. Yet nature abruptly turns against the lovers. The
doves fly at the man as words of denial; they clamber awkwardly upon his shoulders.

The images of nature quickly move from the sun-drenched, flower-strewn earth to
the coldness of outer space. The lovers are compared to "painful stars" orbiting each
other as in a binary system. Such stars can be hazardous to each other, as in the usual
pairing of red giant and white dwarf. The red giant can eject a volume of hot matter
large enough to rip away part of the white dwarf, exposing its core and hastening its
end.

If nature is no refuge, neither is the intellectual posturing of the narrator. His "descanting" is awkwardly executed and furnishes only uncomfortable images. The tone
softens in stanzas 13 and 14 as the language returns to images of the earth, although it
serves as a "tomb." The epitaph, stanza 14, again creates a romantic image of the lov-

ers as "perilous and beautiful." They have passed beyond the choice of heaven or hell, now finding neither acceptable. Clearly they have gained something. In his essay, "Observations on the Understanding of Poetry," Ransom says that "without the horror we should never focus the beauty; without death there would be no relish for life; without danger, no courage . . . without the background of our frequent ignominy, no human dignity and pride." Through this painful experience, the lovers have gained a moral advantage and a greater understanding of their own limitations.

Patricia Alkema

EROS TURANNOS

Author: Edwin Arlington Robinson (1869-1935)
Type of poem: Lyric
First published: 1916, in *The Man Against the Sky*

The Poem

"Eros Turannos" ("tyrannic love") is an incisive verse portrait of forty-eight lines, depicting an aging wife willing to lead a life of self-deception to hold onto her marriage with a worthless husband. The noteworthy twentieth century poet and critic Yvor Winters, in *Edwin Arlington Robinson* (1946), considers this poem to be not only one of the best in the Robinson canon but also "one of the greatest short poems in the language." It first appeared in the same 1913 issue of *Poetry* that published the first group of Carl Sandburg's award-winning *Chicago Poems* (1916). While critics' estimates of Sandburg's work subsequently have declined, critical esteem of Robinson's work, for "Eros Turannos" especially, has increased gradually.

Reared in Gardiner, Maine, Robinson often used a small-town New England scene as the setting for verse portraits of lonely people, such as the wife in "Eros Turannos," who lead wasted, blighted, or impoverished lives. Robinson's poetry reflected the realism of much European literature of the late nineteenth century, and this poem is almost a realistic short story in verse. The "plot" of the poem involves inertia, regret, and illusory love worsened by the passing of time and middle age.

The title "Eros Turannos" is an echo of Sophocles' tragedy *Oedipus Tyrannos* (which has been translated as meaning "Oedipus the king" or "Oedipus the tyrant," although "tyrant" would not necessarily have the same implications the word has today). Robinson intends irony by contrasting the ancient play with his own pathetic story, a bourgeois domestic drama in which the woman is a self-deceived slave to her husband—her *eros* (a Greek word meaning love in the form of passionate desire).

The first stanza indicates that the wife sees through her husband's false front ("engaging mask") but, although she may even fear him, she is more afraid of losing him as she ages and loses her attractiveness ("the foamless weirs" are water traps too far above the water level to capture fish).

The second stanza enumerates the psychological factors behind her self-delusion that the husband recognizes and complacently exploits her "blurred sagacity," or an original wisdom about his real self that she has allowed to fade from her mind. The survival of her love for him prevents her from writing him off as the Judas she knows he really is (she discovered his betrayal of her in the past). Her husband exploits her vanity, which makes her keep up appearances and preserve a marriage that she had chosen long ago, however wrongly.

The third and fourth stanzas depict the couple's coastal New England surroundings. The husband complacently enjoys "tradition"—including his domestic arrangement of long standing, especially if the community is ignorant of the actual nonexistence of romance in their relationship, and even though the wife knows their love is a delusion. The wife retreats to her house as the community buzzes with suspicions; she lives in an autumnal mental state of distraction from recognizing the death of their once ignited love.

The fifth stanza is an intrusive statement by the poem's narrator who, aligning himself to literary realism, claims to tell a greater truth about this bleak relationship than the wife admits to herself. Yet even the narrator must acknowledge, in fitting humility, that nobody knows the full truth about human lives, including the lives of the subjects of the poem.

The sixth stanza ends where the poem began: The couple's doomed marriage is like a losing battle with the false god Eros, and it seems headed for the death and destruction suggested by a crashing wave, a tree losing its leaves, or a suicidal walk by a blind person into the sea.

Forms and Devices

"Eros Turannos" is a lyric poem consisting of six stanzas whose prevailing meter of iambic tetrameter (with variations) is as tightly controlled as the wife's self-deluding hold on her failed romance in marriage ("She fears him, and will always ask").

Of particular interest in each eight-line stanza is the unusual and intricate rhyme scheme (*ababcccb*), which, in the first three stanzas, places the stress on "him"—the worthless husband—to an increasingly ominous degree. The only feminine or weak end rhyme in the entire poem is in the last stanza ("striven," "given," and "driven") to capture the futile, evanescent quality of the blighted marriage through climactic sound effect.

The typical irony of a Robinson poem is here less blatant and more subtle, for the principal irony is the wife's pitiful self-delusion: She, as well as the reader, sees through the discrepancy between what her marriage was and what it has come to be.

There are two major allusions, one to Eros (the god of passionate love, worshiped by the wife) and the other to Judas (the apostle who betrayed Jesus Christ as this husband betrays his wife).

Unifying the poem are recurrent images of declining or destructive forces of nature on sea and land in downward motion: in the first stanza ("downward years,/ Drawn slowly to the foamless weirs"), the third stanza ("A sense of ocean and old trees/ Envelops and allures him"), the fourth stanza ("The falling leaf . . . The pounding wave"), and final stanza:

> Though like waves breaking it may be,
> Or like a changed familiar tree,
> Or like a stairway to the sea
> Where down the blind are driven.

The poem combines Robinson's distinctive techniques of blending character portrayal, implicit narrative, and abstract, generalized statement, a sparing but careful employment of allusion, an indirect manner of providing the overall meaning, a conscientious use of a regular and restrictive verse form, and a unified pattern of images that make the entire poem cohere.

Themes and Meanings

"Eros Turannos" is about a doomed marriage in which an aging wife living in a coastal New England town holds onto the bleak relationship, even though she knows that her husband has betrayed her and that her love for him and his love for her are largely a self-created illusion.

The wife tries desperately, from pride and need, and in defiance of community gossip, to maintain a positive image of her husband, an image she knows is not true. Her husband, aware of her conflict, plays a deceptive role both with her and with himself. Intertwined images run through the poem suggesting the themes of deception, age, struggle, and decline, all of which are brought together at the end of the poem.

"Eros Turannos" is a peerless example, among many poems in Robinson's literary canon, that demonstrates the truth of the critical verdict of Robert Frost, another excellent New England poet, who, in the introduction of *King Jasper* (1935), commented that "Robinson was a prince of heartachers amid countless achers of another part. . . . He asserted the sacred right of poetry to lean its breast to a thorn and sing its dolefullest."

Thomas M. Curley

THE ETERNAL DICE

Author: César Vallejo (1892-1938)
Type of poem: Meditation
First published: 1918, as "Los dados eternos," in *Los heraldos negros*; collected in *The Black Heralds*, 1990

The Poem

"The Eternal Dice" is a poem of four stanzas, the first and third having lines of alternating rhyme in the original Spanish, and the second and fourth relying on internal rhyme and assonance. It is the eighteenth poem in the fifth section, entitled "Thunderclaps," of César Vallejo's first published book of poems. The title is suggestive of Stéphane Mallarmé's classic poem *Un Coup de dés jamais n'abolira le hasard* (1897; *Dice Thrown Never Will Annul Chance*, 1965; also translated as *A Dice-Throw*), in which the poet explores the connection between the elements of chance and the mysteries of the universe.

Vallejo's poem, however, begins with a dedication to Manuel González Prada, who was a prominent intellectual in Peru and was the director of the National Library. González Prada was highly political, even revolutionary, and Vallejo's dedication to this man, in conjunction with the allusion of the title to the Mallarmé poem, gives a hint of the duality, the combination of earthly and unearthly concerns, that pervades and characterizes Vallejo's poetry.

The poem proceeds with a direct address to God. The persona, the "I" of the poem, laments his life. Then, by indirect reference to the Holy Communion—"it grieves me to have taken your bread from you"—the persona laments and rejects his belief system. Vallejo acknowledges man's vulnerability by recalling the biblical "clay" of his creation and exhibiting his anger at the powerlessness of both man and woman by broadly alluding to the traditional Adam and Eve story: "this poor, pensive piece of clay/ isn't a scab fermented in your side:/ you don't have Marys who leave you!"

By the second stanza, Vallejo has completely obviated the distance usually maintained between a supplicant and his God, and he turns the traditional relationship on its ear: Man is the superior figure. It is man who, through his suffering, knows and feels the burden of being God, and it is the traditional figure of God, who was "always fine," who can take a lesson from man.

By the third stanza of the poem, one can hear the voice of the poet through that of the persona. It is the man/poet with the "fire" in his demon eyes, the fire of creation that is both God's and the poet's, who is condemned. He is condemned by fate to write and thus to challenge God to the eternal game of chance whose end is survival or destruction. The game is to be played with the old toys—the earth and the universe. When this ultimate challenge is made to tradition and to its elements, it is the poet who decides that God "can't play any more."

The Earth is God's dice, and from the poet's point of view, it is already worn. God has toyed with the Earth, and with man, for too long, and the Earth "by chance" has been rolled endlessly, so that it has rolled itself round. If the traditional God continues the game, the poet says, the end will find the Earth in its grave, and the implied result is the ultimate and all-encompassing void.

Forms and Devices

The critic Jean Franco, in her book *César Vallejo: The Dialectics of Poetry and Silence* (1976), says that the poetic education of Vallejo began in 1915 when he and a group of his fellow students in Trujillo, Peru, began to meet and to read their own poems and the poems of Walt Whitman and the modernist poets. In addition, he read an anthology of French poetry that included selections by many great Symbolist poets translated into Spanish. He also read, in translation, Mallarmé's *A Dice-Throw*, which, as noted earlier, provided an inspiration for "The Eternal Dice."

When one looks at Vallejo's poem, then, one sees evidence of the Symbolists' attempt to create a correspondence between heaven and earth. While the French poets tried to reproduce or re-create the intangible quality of an otherworldly experience, however, Vallejo interpreted this linking of the beyond with the here and now as a confrontation between man and God or, more precisely, between the poet and God. For the Symbolists, the poet was God, the supreme creator, and indeed, Vallejo alludes to the powerlessness of the old God playing the old games in the old ways. By implication, he demonstrates that when the earth is rolled to eternal oblivion, the record made by humanity, by the poet, will remain.

In addition, Vallejo succeeds in creating an unusual and ephemeral effect in a potentially prosaic context by his use of the Symbolist device of evocation. The Symbolists discovered that one power of language exists in its ability to be evocative, to cause new sensations and impressions by the unusual juxtapositions of incompatible ideas or realities, by the linking of opposites, or (as in this case) by the use of old forms in an allusively new way, catching the reader or listener off guard. Thus, by turning the relationship of man/poet and God around, by inverting the hierarchy and making the man/ poet all-powerful, by referring to the suffering of the man/artist as more divine than God, the result is evocative and startling. Using this traditional relationship in an unanticipated way, Vallejo creates an entirely unexpected effect.

Further, when the host of Communion is diminished by becoming "your bread from you," Vallejo's use of small rather than capital letters further diminishes the traditional relationships and causes a more powerful expression to occur because of that diminution.

Themes and Meanings

"The Eternal Dice" is layered with meanings. On the surface, one sees a man confronting God. The man is dissatisfied, discontent. He has suffered, has lived his life humbly and with deprivation. There is something special here, however; this is no ordinary man confronting his God. This man is a poet, and as a poet, he has the right and the power to create, to create a new relationship in the universe, one in which he wields the power. Thus, the poet creates, and among his creations is God.

The Symbolist poets were irreverent. They rejected institutionalized religion as they rejected all systems which inhibited their free expression. Old forms were to be destroyed, and the new was sought. When interpreters of the poem caution the reader against being too literal-minded in the reading of "The Eternal Dice," they ignore the poetic history in which Vallejo was immersed at the time of writing *Los heraldos negros*. Vallejo, as did his predecessors, sought the Absolute. He was willing, as were they, to gamble, to risk everything in the effort to find some essential reality.

In "The Eternal Dice," he sought to shock, to use the "God is dead" idea of the modernists, and to use, in the manner of the Surrealists and the Dadaists (with whose aesthetic theory Vallejo was familiar), the unusual: that which was orthographically, ideationally, and aesthetically illogical, disorienting, and disquieting.

Vallejo, in a volume entitled *Contra el secreto profesional* (1973), in the chapter "del Carnet de 1929 (20 set.) y 1930," explains. He seeks a new poetics, a style in literature not unlike Pablo Picasso's style of art, where for reasons of harmony or balance of line, a box, or a stairway, or a vase, or an orange would be placed where a nose should be. Poetry was to be concerned, therefore, with only what was poetically beautiful, and it was to be without logic, coherence, or reason.

Heather Rosario-Sievert

ETHICS

Author: Linda Pastan (1932-   )
Type of poem: Lyric
First published: 1979; collected in *Waiting for My Life*, 1981

The Poem

"Ethics" raises a number of significant philosophical issues, and it does so in language that is clear and direct and in a voice that immediately elicits an emotional and intellectual response from readers. The poem's title, like its subject, is rather abstract, but Linda Pastan immediately and consistently grounds the poem in her unique narrative voice.

As a student in a philosophy course years ago, the speaker says in the poem's opening lines, she was given one of those difficult questions that ethics teachers like to pose—what are often called "values clarification" questions—and asked to choose between saving a great work of art (a Rembrandt painting) or an old woman from a fire in a museum. There is never a "correct" answer to such questions; rather, the process of thinking the question through often exposes the student's own value system in clearer outline. The first part of the poem makes the students' values clear and reveals that the question is hardly relevant to them: "Restless," "caring little for pictures or old age," the students can only answer "half-heartedly."

This classroom exercise in the first part of the poem is interrupted, at least in the speaker's own mind, when she recalls that sometimes the woman in the ethics question "borrowed my grandmother's face." The abstract philosophical question, in other words, has been personalized, made human by the speaker's own real-life experiences, by the memory of her grandmother. This recollection is a hint of what is to come in the poem's closing lines.

In the last section of what is essentially the longer first half of the poem, the speaker—still imagining herself as the student in that philosophy class—tells readers about the year when she answered her teacher's question with one of her own: "why not let the woman decide herself?" She gave, in short, a clever response, and one that offered autonomy to the imaginary character in this ethics exercise. The point is important, because Pastan the poet is, in a sense, doing the same thing in her own poem—she is personalizing an abstract ethics issue, giving it human dimensions. The teacher, using the academic jargon of the profession, notes that Linda "eschews" (avoids or shuns) "the burdens of responsibility." The teacher, in short, like all good teachers, tries to bring the discussion back to the subject and to the classroom exercise.

Although there is no stanza break at this point, the poem clearly shifts focus after line 16. The first two-thirds of the poem recall a school experience; in the last third, the poem shifts to the immediate present ("This fall"). Past tense becomes present tense, and the ethical conundrum of the first part of the poem is tentatively answered.

The speaker is now standing in a "real museum" looking at an actual painting; the abstract example of the academic exercise has become "a real Rembrandt," and the speaker herself an "old woman,/ or nearly so, myself."

With this new perspective, which only time could give her, the speaker now is able to look closely at both choices in the ethical problem. The colors of the painting—Pastan is describing what Rembrandt does in his most famous works—are "darker than autumn,/ darker even than winter—the browns of earth." She recognizes how Rembrandt has captured something natural, even mystical, in his paintings, for she observes further the ways in which "earth's most radiant elements burn/ through the canvas."

Her conclusion from this intimate knowledge of both subjects? She still cannot answer the ethical challenge. Rather, she goes beyond the question—as she first did in lines 13-14 with her clever answer—to the realization "that woman/ and painting and season are almost one/ and all beyond saving by children." She overthrows the very terms of the ethical choice of the first part of the poem, in other words. The ethics problem implied that human life can be reduced to categories; now, as an older woman, she knows truths which transcend any such limitations.

What started as an ethics exercise, then, has become something much more important: the recognition of the power of art, an understanding of the seasons of human life, and the realization of how she herself, the speaker, shares so much with both the last seasonal stages of autumn and winter and the Rembrandt painting, where one can also sense something beyond those seasons ("darker than autumn,/ darker even than winter"). The speaker thus comes to see how Rembrandt has captured nature and yet has also rendered something mystically beyond, that "burns through the canvas."

Finally, the speaker knows, in a poignant recognition, that "woman/ and painting and season"—are "beyond saving by children." The restless students in the ethics class at the start of the poem can know nothing about old age, or about art, or even about natural life cycles—and they certainly cannot save one or the other from the death or destruction that awaits them all.

Forms and Devices

For a poem that deals with some rather abstract philosophical issues, "Ethics" is remarkably accessible. Pastan accomplishes this feat by using language that is clear and direct and metaphors that tie the experiences of the poem together for the reader. The language in the poem is almost monosyllabic: fire, chairs, life. The most difficult vocabulary (eschews, responsibility) appears mainly in the philosophy teacher's language. Likewise, the experiences of the poem are rendered as physical images: restless students on hard chairs, the speaker's grandmother in her kitchen and then wandering in a museum, the speaker herself as an older woman standing in "a real museum." The abstract nature of the poem's subject, in short, is softened somewhat in the concrete ways that Pastan renders it. Only the last few lines, when the speaker describes an essentially mystical experience, cause any difficulty in understanding.

The language is also made approachable through alliteration and assonance—

through poetic devices, in other words, that lead readers to move from word to word more easily: "real Rembrandt" (line 18), for example, or "autumn," "brown," "burn," (lines 20-22). The devices Pastan employs help to bring the complex ideas in the poem down to earth.

The central metaphor of the poem is the poem's very subject and idea. The old woman and the Rembrandt painting, which are posed as ethical opposites in the first lines of the poem, have become, by the end of the poem, the same thing, and they are joined by the seasons as well. One element comes to stand—as in any metaphorical comparison—for the other. Old age, the seasons, and the dark colors and "radiant elements" in Rembrandt's paintings have so much in common: fullness, value, and beauty.

Themes and Meanings

For such a short poem, Pastan has packed into "Ethics" a great deal of meaning. Some commentators see the poem as containing a *carpe diem*, or, "seize the day," theme, as in a number of famous older poems (such as Robert Herrick's "To the Virgins, to Make Much of Time" and A. E. Housman's "Loveliest of Trees, the Cherry Now"), but the focus in Pastan's poem is quite different from the typical *carpe diem* theme. The poem seems both more accepting and more critical. Restless young people sitting on hard chairs, the speaker contends, cannot appreciate the fullness of life or its complex cycles. They cannot see the significance of the ethics question, nor are they capable of understanding either the full force of old age, with its proximity to death, or the true beauty of great art.

Rather than being depressed by her own approaching death, the speaker seems to be accepting it. In fact, the comparison with the Rembrandt painting carries an affirmation of life. Only as an old woman ("or nearly so") has the speaker been able to appreciate the power of the painting and the mystical ways in which human life, art, and nature are linked. The poem seems to be chiding youth for its shallowness; better not waste great paintings, or old age, on them, the speaker implies, since they cannot appreciate either. By the end of the poem, readers have been led to see that the academic exercise poses a false choice and that the real opposition is between spring and fall, between the shallowness of youth and the depth of old age, when one can finally experience life's more powerful truths.

David Peck

EVENING MEAL

Author: Rainer Maria Rilke (1875-1926)
Type of poem: Lyric
First published: 1908, as "Abendmahl," in *Der neuen Gedichte anderer Teil*; collected in *New Poems: The Other Part [1908]*, 1987

The Poem

"Evening Meal" is a brief lyric consisting of sixteen lines broken down into four quatrains. The rhyme scheme in German follows the pattern *abba, cdcd, efef, gghh*. The lines average ten syllables in length. The German title "Abendmahl" may be translated both as "evening meal" and "last supper," and the translator of this version, Edward Snow, employs both meanings in his translation. As Snow notes, in a letter Rainer Maria Rilke wrote to his wife in 1907, he described walking in Paris in the evening and seeing families seated at dinner in the back rooms of their shops. The families seated in the evening light behind the glass window reminded him, Rilke explained, of depictions of the biblical Last Supper.

Indeed, the opening lines of the poem refer the reader to this possible religious dimension, but with a characteristically Rilkean reversal. Whereas one typically thinks of religious feeling as an aspiration toward the transcendent, Rilke states baldly that "Things eternal want to join us," that somehow eternal things might aspire to be part of a human reality.

Rather than attempting to explain this mysterious statement, the poet immediately draws the reader's attention to the scene at hand, to the family seated at the table for their evening meal (it is here that the translator has chosen to translate "abendmahl" as "last supper"). The actual scene of the family at dinner is rendered with a minimum of descriptive detail. One can imagine the poet glancing in the shop window through the "twilight of the shops" now closed and darkened, and seeing the family seated at the table as though in a framed tableau. It is worth noting too that the poet can only see the family from a distance, that he has no personal knowledge of the people he describes but sees them as representative of all families.

In the second, stanza, the poet describes the gestures of the family and affirms that such gestures have symbolic significance, that they are in fact "signs," even though the participants in the meal do not realize this. Only the poet (and by extension the reader), as one who stands outside the scene and looks on, is capable of recognizing the significance of these simple, everyday acts. While these might be as simple and ordinary as passing plates of food, in the third stanza the poet states that each gesture nevertheless "establishes . . . what one shares." In other words, with each participant's gesture the bonds between the members of the family are renewed. Yet simultaneously, with each renewal of the family bonds, there is also the threat of a family member "secretly departing," secretly breaking the bond that joins the family together.

In the concluding stanza, the threat to the family bond becomes clear. One of the children at the table, the poet imagines, has already "cast off" his parents, even though the parents themselves are unable to recognize this. At this point, the poet reasserts the "last supper" allusion with an ironic twist: The child's need to "give away" his parents resembles Judas's betrayal of Christ, yet the child need not "sell" his parents as Judas, after the Last Supper, sold Christ.

Forms and Devices

In the course of its sixteen lines, "Evening Meal" articulates an astonishing array of thematic variations, yet all of these arise from the basic figural situation of the speaker in the poem. While Rilke does not render this situation explicitly, one might imagine the poet standing in the city street, looking in on the family through a store window. The window frames the scene the way a painting would (consider, for example, Vincent van Gogh's 1885 painting *The Potato Eaters*, in which van Gogh renders a scene of peasants eating with a simple clarity and grace). Rilke further emphasizes the tableau quality of the scene in line 3 when the poet asks "Can't you see?" as though he were urgently pointing the scene out to the reader.

Thus, from the opening of the poem, the poet draws a distinct line between those (the poet and reader) who are outside the scene depicted and those (the family) who are inside it. The poet and reader on the outside are able to recognize the signs conveyed by the meal, while the family seems oblivious to the signs they enact. Yet by the end of the third stanza, Rilke gives this inside/outside division an ironic twist when he suggests that even those seated at the table might be divided within themselves. In the third stanza, this is conveyed in general, even universal terms when the poet suggests that "there is no one anyplace who isn't/ secretly departing, even as he stays."

In the concluding stanza, Rilke reinserts this figure of division into the scene at hand. It is possible that a child sitting at the table has already figuratively gone away from his parents, "given them away," while the parents continue in the rituals of everyday life, oblivious to the child's "departure." By this point in the poem, poet, reader, and child now share a common alienation from the everyday ritual; all three, in one sense, look in on the scene through the glass.

When Rilke closes by alluding to the child as a Judas figure, one probably ought to take this with tongue in cheek, since such "betrayal" is only part of the natural course of things. Yet if one returns to the opening statement of the poem, it would seem that the poet considers the division he finds in this scene emblematic of a greater division marking all things—a division between "things eternal" and the things of this world. Turning back to the poem's title, one sees that this same division is also present in the two meanings of "abendmahl."

Themes and Meanings

Perhaps, in the most general sense, "Evening Meal" is a poem about alienation—the alienation of the poet as an outsider looking in on the family scene, the alienation of the child from his parents, the alienation of "things eternal" from the realm of everyday life. Yet Rilke also seems to suggest that it is precisely because of this alienation that the poet is able to read the signs of the scene he witnesses. Paradoxically, one can only understand the true value of something by looking at it from the point of view of an outsider (and Rilke is careful to put the reader into this outsider's role).

The poem also touches on the almost infinite subtle forms that alienation can take. The poet is only a few yards away from the scene, yet he might as well be a thousand miles away, so impossible would it be for him to cross the boundary between himself and the scene he observes. Even more ironic is the situation of the child, who, while seated at the table with his oblivious parents, also senses an impenetrable boundary between himself and them. When the poet universalizes this sense of alienation in the third stanza, he suggests that such boundaries are not merely physical, but are psychological and spiritual as well.

In short, Rilke seems to be describing a world in which all things are simultaneously at home and lost. The religious allusion present in "last supper" and in "things eternal" suggests that the alienation the poet describes might have theological significance also. After all, the story of Christ is that of God's attempt to "join" human beings by becoming human, and the biblical Last Supper is one of the central emblems of this attempt. By breaking bread with the disciples, Christ shows himself to be a human being subject to ordinary human needs.

This theological motif is definitely present in the poem, yet Rilke is a poet, not a theologian, and he might be concerned primarily with showing that division and a subsequent longing to be a part of something pervade every level of existence. "Things eternal" want to be part of humanity; meanwhile, the poet looks in on the meal, perhaps longing to be part of the family, and ironically sees a youth who (perhaps like the poet at an earlier time) only wants to escape. There is no way to resolve the dilemma, Rilke seems to be saying, between the need to stay at home and the need to go away.

Vance Crummett

EVENING SONG

Author: Georg Trakl (1887-1914)
Type of poem: Lyric
First published: 1913, as "Abendlied," in *Gedichte*; collected in *Autumn Sonata: Selected Poems of Georg Trakl*, 1989

The Poem

"Evening Song" is a short lyric poem written in a symmetrical structure that contributes to the poem's cyclical effect. The poem is only fourteen lines long, the same length as a sonnet, although Georg Trakl's poem does not function quite like a sonnet. Trakl creates his structure by repeating the pattern of a three-line stanza enclosed by two-line stanzas. In German, stanzas 3 and 4 contain the same number of syllables, which reinforces the poem's symmetrical nature as well as acting as an echo. All of these elements lend a feeling of closure to the poem.

Although "Evening Song" is technically written in free verse, some of the couplets form end rhymes, which extends the symmetry of the poem. This technique and the intricate rhythms of the language are lost in translation, but the overall rhythms of Trakl's poem come through in English, combining with the poem's motion to create a circular, unified result.

Trakl begins "Evening Song" in the same way that he begins many of his poems: The speaker is somewhere unknown, walking on a dark path. Even in English, Trakl's language reinforces the idea of walking. The rhythm of the language is steady and methodical, but occasionally pauses, reminding one of walking.

Despite the fact that Trakl goes to some effort to construct a sensation of motion for the reader, he is most concerned with what happens on the walk. Between stanzas 3 and 4, the fulcrum of the poem, a shift occurs, which, in effect, divides the poem in half. In the first part (stanzas 1-3), the functions of the speaker are those of observation and narration, but in the second part (stanzas 4-6), the function of the speaker is introspection.

In the first three verses, the speaker employs the first-person-plural "we" and speaks in the present tense only of activities: "When we are thirsty,/ We drink the white waters of the pool." These three stanzas depict a landscape experienced equally by both parties. In the final three stanzas though, the speaker shifts from "we" to "I" and from present to past tense: "When I took your slender hands/ You opened your soft round eyes." This deviation signals the end of the outward journey and the beginning of an inward one.

From here, the poem shifts its visionary plane back to the present, and the speaker experiences a moment of insight—what James Joyce might have called an "epiphany." These two final lines give significance to the speaker's "walk" and to his introspection, because the "you" he speaks to appears "white" "when a darker melody visits the soul." Traditionally, and in this poem, white serves as a symbol of purity.

Therefore, the walk leads the speaker to the realization of his friend's purity when the soul is at its most impure. Furthermore, the use of "dark" and "appear" in the final couplet echoes their appearance in the opening couplet. The circular motion of the poem is realized, and, in effect, the end becomes the beginning.

Forms and Devices

Because "Evening Song" is such a short poem, there is not much room for weighty or repetitive poetic techniques, such as one might find in Rainer Maria Rilke's "Duino Elegies" or Vicente Huidobro's *Altazor*. Trakl does, however, infuse the lines of his poem with a mysterious force that derives from his use of adjectives and concrete nouns.

Almost no noun in the entire poem appears without an adjective, yet many of the adjectives are not particularly precise. In "Spring clouds rise over the dark city," spring does not really describe the clouds, nor dark the city, because the function of these adjectives is not one of description but one of evocation. The images of spring clouds and of a dark city do not so much characterize the objects as create a mood. The images in a Trakl poem express auras and possess tonality and ambience, like the colors in a painting by the Russian Wassily Kandinsky.

"Spring clouds" rising above a "dark city" suggests that life or rebirth (something archetypally associated with spring) is commandeering the dark city, which seems to represent death or decay. The whiteness of the clouds contrasts with the darkness of the city, just as, in the final couplet, the "white" of the friend contrasts with the "darker melody" of the soul.

Trakl's images may appear arbitrary and disjointed because they do not work progressively in the poem. The images seem to be linked mysteriously, like arms reaching through a fog, and it seems that the images contain the weight of myth, but only within the world of the poem. In "Evening Song," such a phenomenon helps to reinforce the circular connections that are already at work in the poem.

Another interesting poetic device that Trakl employs in almost every one of his poems is silence. No sounds occur in the poem at all. There is a "melody" in the final couplet, but it makes no noise; it simply "visits." Not even the "gray gulls" make noise; the speaker and his friend watch them without hearing them.

Trakl is also fond of silencing objects that cannot speak anyway. In stanza 4, the dark city is "Silenced by the monks of nobler times." Often Trakl silences birds, trees, stones, even God, but in "Evening Song," Trakl the poet does not do the silencing; instead, it is the monks who silence. Because they hail from nobler and no doubt purer times, the monks are imbued with more power of voice than the dark city.

All these silences affect the tone of the poem. Because there are no sounds, the poem seems to exist within a void, unable to reach beyond itself. Perhaps this is why Trakl's images operate internally and why they do not reflect his voice, but speak so powerfully for themselves.

Themes and Meanings

Virtually all Trakl's poems possess the same thematic concerns. Throughout his canon, Trakl perpetually laments the fallen state of humanity and humanity's inability to return to a state that is not laden with corruption. "Evening Song" is no exception.

In stanza 2, Trakl first makes reference to something white: "We drink the white waters of the pool,/ The sweetness of our mournful childhood." Here, the water clearly becomes a symbol of purity, not only because of the word "white," but also because of the implication of "white water." White water implies a purity of cleansing or baptism—something truly pure. In this verse, Trakl associates the "sweetness" of his childhood with the white water, suggesting that Trakl perceives childhood as a state of innocence to be envied.

This preoccupation of Trakl is reaffirmed in the following stanza when he says, "Dead, we rest beneath the elder bushes." Because Trakl and his friend have moved out of childhood, they have fallen from innocence. For Trakl, this is a lethal fall; he aligns the fall from innocence with the inescapable fall into death. Trakl's fall from innocence is strikingly similar to William Blake's fall in his *Songs of Innocence and of Experience* (1794), though Trakl's fall into knowledge is the fall into the knowledge of decay.

The only unsoiled beings in "Evening Song" are the monks. As was stated earlier, because they are from a purer, "nobler" time, they alone can silence the moans of the dying city. It is plausible to argue that Trakl believes the world would be much better if only it were possible to return to those noble times. Interestingly, Trakl appears to equate childhood and the noble times of the monks. Perhaps he synthesizes them because of their irretrievability in the past.

Trakl's nostalgia for the past appears in stanza 5: "You opened your soft round eyes./ That was a long time ago." The past tense suggests the distance of the event. The speaker, musing "That was a long time ago," almost echoes "The sweetness of our mournful childhood," found in stanza 2. Again, the reciprocity of action between the first and second halves of the poem is rooted in a shared perspective and shared experience.

What is happening in the poem, then, is the realization of the poet's desire to return to the past. The actions of the figures almost mirror each other, the two halves of the poem seem to join, and the final couplet is a revision of the first couplet in which the poet's companion is actually able to appear "white," symbolizing her purity. All these factors combine to achieve the desired effect of past becoming present, and present past.

Throughout this cyclical poetic evolution, Trakl is able to restore, if not himself, then his friend, to the state of innocence for which he desperately longs, and for which his entire body of poetry ceaselessly yearns.

Dean Rader

EVERYONE IS A WORLD

Author: Gunnar Ekelöf (1907-1968)
Type of poem: Lyric
First published: 1941, as "En värld är varje människa," in *Färjesång*; collected in *Songs of Something Else: Selected Poems of Gunnar Ekelöf,* 1982

The Poem

"Everyone Is a World" is a short poem in free verse, its twenty-four lines divided into three stanzas. The title is formed from the first line of the poem; the original poem has no title. In the original collection, it is grouped together with some other poems under the musical subheading "Etydes" (études). The first line captures the main theme of the poem: The mind of each human being is plural, formed by many voices, most of them hidden or silenced.

The poem is written in a collective plural voice, underlining the general tone of the poem, which describes what the poet believes is true of all human beings. Meditating on Sigmund Freud's three-part description of the human unconscious as id, ego, and superego, the poet illuminates his sense of the inner world of the mind. His vision emphasizes both humankind's ultimate power and an individual's powerlessness over him or herself. First, the poet meditates on the suppressed "masses" of the mind, the trapped impulses of desire in constant rebellion against "the rulers" of the ego. Second, he describes the dilemma of the ego as that of a king or a prince who can rule the masses but who in turn is ruled by a higher power. The first stanza closes on a more intimate tone as it brings the reader back to his or her own feelings and to how those feelings change with the power struggle within.

The second stanza further illustrates the struggle between the oppressed and the rulers of the mind. Using the extended image of a ship on the sea, the poet envisions the waves created by the boat. The people on the beach do not know that a ship has passed, but they hear and see the waves that the movement of the ship has stirred up. These waves eventually die down and leave things as they were before; yet, the poet maintains, everything is different. When the poet paints the image of "a mighty steamship," he emphasizes the curious relationship between power and powerlessness within the world of the mind. The ship itself is a powerful engine, but the individual mind has no control over its direction or speed. It brings forth what waves it must, and the human mind must change according to the strength of these waves.

In the last and shortest stanza, there is a shift back to the meditative, general tone of the opening of the poem. The last three lines describe the reaction of mighty wonder, magical worry, enchanting terror that human beings may feel when inner waves signal great movements in the unconscious. The lines capture our sense of wonder and fear when confronted with the possibility of freedom and liberation.

Even though the poem describes powerlessness, it ends on an optimistic tone: Some of a person's possible and fettered selves may break free and move ahead.

Forms and Devices

The striking force of Gunnar Ekelöf's poetry often stems from the simplicity of the techniques and metaphors he uses to illustrate very complex issues. "Everyone Is a World" provides two clear examples of this in the overall design of the poem and in the central image of the steamship.

"Everyone Is a World" is divided into three stanzas, and the relationship between the three is an important key to the meaning of the poem. The first stanza looks much like a sonnet of fourteen lines; in Swedish, most of the lines scan like iambic pentameter. The lines do not rhyme; yet this tight-knit, sonnet-like stanza aptly illustrates the lack of freedom in the world that it describes, the inner lives of human beings as Ekelöf captures them. In contrast, the second and third stanzas grow increasingly shorter (stanza 2 is seven lines; stanza 3 is three lines) and more impressionistic. These stanzas break away from the need to evoke established poetic forms in free verse, and thus they emphasize the possible liberation of thoughts and feelings that they describe.

The poem moves from a general statement to an image and back to a general statement. In the third stanza, however, the poet's voice has achieved a tone of intimacy and shared experience that the abstract depiction of stanza 1 lacks, and that may not convincingly come across in the English translation. The Swedish Ekelöf scholar Anders Olsson maintains that "this combination of abstraction and intimacy is one of the most characteristic traits of Ekelöf's poetry" (in *Ekelöf's No*, 1983).

The central image of a "mighty steamship" on the horizon also illustrates Ekelöf's captivating ability to express complex thoughts with very simple means. The steamship image ties Ekelöf to many other poets of the great modernist tradition, poets who, like Ekelöf or, for example, the Swedish poet Artur Lundkvist, were fascinated by the power and liberating possibilities of machines and who saw in the machine an emblem of a new kind of poetry that would liberate the human soul much as machines liberated human bodies. As machines grow increasingly powerful and dangerous, humans might become increasingly wary of them; Ekelöf captures the ambivalent quality of the machine and presents it as both attractive and abhorrent at the same time. The steamship is beautiful at a distance, and it appears beautiful because it is distant. Its power and direction are beyond individual human control. The image draws a parallel between the changes provoked by the machine and those that take place in the human unconscious: Powerful and uncontrollable, predictable yet chaotic, these changes severely limit the autonomy of the human mind.

In one simple image, and without a trace of nostalgia, Ekelöf expresses his ambivalent attitude toward the abdication of the once supreme and, in his or her own mind, central human being, and presents the frustrating position of modern humankind: having lost control not only over its own inventions but over the inner territories as well.

Themes and Meanings

"Everyone Is a World" is a paradoxical poem, setting up an impossible coexistence of the singular and the plural individual, of imprisonment and freedom, and of powerlessness and power. Its paradoxical statement well represents Ekelöf's poetry. A modernist rebel poet who believed in the individual and who feared the dehumanization of an increasingly mechanized and bureaucratic society, Ekelöf wrote many poems with a similar message. With the title of the 1945 collection *Non serviam* and in poems such as "I believe in the solitary human being" (the Swedish original appears in *Färjesång*), Ekelöf fiercely placed himself as an outsider and a rebel. He also believed that it was exactly by finding and capturing in poetry what was unique within himself that he might express a universal human soul and be able to share experiences with other human beings. As a poet, he did so again and again. Thus, paradoxically, the outsider and rebel becomes the true insider, the speaker for humankind.

In "Everyone Is a World," Ekelöf writes that human beings are plural. Equally often, in other poems, he maintains the opposite: that to be human is to be nobody. In the poetry sequence "Write It Down," Ekelöf writes, for example: "You say 'I' and 'it concerns me'/ but it concerns a what:/ In reality you are no one." One could argue that Ekelöf is inconsistent, but in his view, the plural and the nonexistent self are not incompatible. The notions of self may be paradoxical, but then, in Ekelöf's poetry, all truth is paradoxical.

Ekelöf developed a unique poetic style to enhance these contrasting meanings. He describes poetry writing as a quest for the hidden meaning, "a kind of *Alchemie du verbe* . . . poetry is this very tension-filled relationship between the worlds, between the lines, between the meanings." "Everyone Is a World" has one central image, the meaning of which can be seen between the parts that the image includes. The mighty steamship violates the natural, undisturbed world, the sea and the evening. The reader grasps the unnaturalness of the machine only through a contrast between it and the natural scene.

Using fragments and uncertain poetic locations, Ekelöf often frustrates his readers. His view that meaning is created in between elements rather than within separate entities can assist the reader in approaching his poems.

Gunilla Theander Kester

EWIGEN MELODIEN

Author: William Heyen (1940-   )
Type of poem: Lyric
First published: 1977, in *The Swastika Poems*; volume expanded and reissued as *Erika: Poems of the Holocaust*, 1984

The Poem

"Ewigen Melodien" is a free-verse lyric poem of fifteen lines, organized in five stanzas of three lines each. The title is German and means "Everything Melody." According to William Heyen, he took the title from a letter of the British Victorian era philosopher and man of letters Thomas Carlyle, who, responding to Ralph Waldo Emerson's *Nature* (1836), wrote to the American philosopher: "You have written the ewigen melodien." The title also clearly suggests that the poem itself is a kind of song.

The poem is meant to embody the combined voice of all the victims of the Holocaust (the intentional murder by the Nazis of approximately six million European Jews during World War II). It is a questioning voice, reaching toward some new kind of knowledge after the horrors that have been endured. In the first stanza, the representative speaker, while acknowledging that "we are all dead," nevertheless hears what might be the "whispers" of dead friends and the sounds of small bells and chimes—the beginning of a kind of music. In the second stanza, the sound is specifically called music, and the speaker says that the victims' screaming throats have relaxed in death. Yet, though dead, they are quickening with a new awareness. Their ears now can "hear" the smallest natural sound. In the third stanza, the speaker says that the fingers and lungs of the brutalized victims are softened in death, and that these dead can hear (and almost see) the grain rustling in the fields.

The fourth stanza develops the idea of music further: The dead now hear the "windsong" in the trees, and it becomes a "deep cello timbre." Their jaws, necks, and tongues are added to the list of physical organs that have found a relaxation, or softening, in death. The final stanza identifies the strange, faintly heard music that has run throughout the poem with the once-vital organs of the victims—"brain hymn, bodiless heartbeat"—as if to give a name to what seems to have survived death. The next-to-last line contains the odd confession that "we should have known this," and the poem ends with a tentative but definite sense of something more—some larger music—beginning to be heard.

Forms and Devices

"Ewigen Melodien" is a highly rhetorical poem. The first line begins with an initial capital ("Something"), and the last ends with an ellipse. In effect, the poem has the form of a single sentence containing seven separate questions (two each in the first and fourth stanzas). This complex sentence is full of repetition, juxtaposition, and paradox. These rhetorical devices are employed to control an evocative, multilayered imagery. The poem is structured by its punctuation to a degree that is unusual among contemporary poets—somewhat suggestive of the experimental work with grammar and syntax (in a much lighter vein) of the modernist E. E. Cummings. Each line begins with the pronoun "something" followed by a colon. Seven of the colons are followed by questions, eight by declarative sentences. This slight imbalance seems very deliberate, as if to indicate that assertion ultimately outweighs doubt. Ten of the lines end with "but" and three with "and," running the thought into the next line (this technique is known as enjambment). The final two lines move in a new direction, breaking the pattern by ending with "this" and "begin," respectively. Yet the brief final assertion, "the melodies begin," is made even more tentative by being framed within a double ellipse, as if it is not a conclusion at all, but only a fragment pointing to what comes after the poem.

The imagery is simple but emotionally charged. Images of faint sounds beginning with "dead friends' welcoming whispers" convey the precise perception of a natural "music." These subtle but very sensuous sound images ("rustle-of-grain-sound somehow yellow" employs synesthesia, the mixing of senses) are juxtaposed with the physical imagery of the once-tormented bodies becoming transformed in death ("our lungs that burst with blood are soft now. . . ."). This vividly allusive imagery not only evokes the horrors of the Holocaust but also juxtaposes life and death in a way that is highly paradoxical—as if some impossible state of consciousness is being described, at once vague and absolute. The compressed imagery becomes suggestive, at almost the same moment, of both human music, or art, and manmade destruction by fire ("deep cello timbre, low resinous hum?"). The final images are nearly surreal, suggesting that the unnamed "something" has, if only by repetition, become possible: "something: brain hymn, bodiless heartbeat? but/ something." The physical has become music, the music physical. A final paradox is that the poem ends with the word "begin."

With its careful repetitions and controlled syntax, the poem is a peculiar "song" of its own. It makes effective use of alliteration (beginning words with the same sound) and assonance (internally rhyming vowels). The dominant pattern is one of sibilants working against short and long *o* sounds, but distinctive "musical variations" mark each stanza, ranging from the *w* sounds in the first ("wooden wind-bells"), to the *d* in the second "(dew drying from grassblades"), to *b* in the third ("burst with blood"), to the deployment of the short *i* and *u* in the fourth stanza. The final stanza seems to "open" its sound pattern as it also reaches for a larger meaning.

Themes and Meanings

"Ewigen Melodien" is a mystical poem, a poem of transfiguration. It speaks of violent death and natural life—and of the eternal life that may transcend both. It tries to offer hope in the face of the most enormous and horrible suffering offered by the violent history of the twentieth century. It does not turn away from the reality of torture and physical decay but portrays death as something more than dissolution—an entry into a new state of consciousness, or bodiless being, which somehow offers a promise of something more.

The vagueness of this state of being, the tentativeness of this promise, is at the center of the poem. Reading this poem to audiences (in synagogues and elsewhere), Heyen has remarked that he is not certain exactly what status Judaism affords to personal immortality, but that he wanted to imagine that the dead are not finally dead. The poem, he says, represents their very first moment of awakening beyond death. It does not presume to theology, only to the hint of faith.

"Ewigen Melodien" is perhaps best understood in context. It is the next-to-last poem in *The Swastika Poems*, an intense, introspective account of the Holocaust from the perspective of a German American poet whose relatives fought (and died) on both sides during World War II. Visiting several of the death camps years later, the poet comes face to face with the destructiveness of which humankind is capable—and with his own sense of implication in these awful events. In this light, the poem may be seen to have been written to offer the poet himself some solace in the face of the unspeakable. (The fact that Heyen published an expanded version of *The Swastika Poems*, retitled *Erika* after the name of a wild plant that has grown up on the mass graves at one of the camps, and containing some dozen new, more positive poems, seems to confirm this.)

Moreover, the poet seems to be testing the limits of his art. In a well-known remark, the social theorist Theodor Adorno once stated that "to write poetry after Auschwitz is a barbarism." Yet poets have continued to write. Heyen here seems determined to wrest a "melody" from anguish—yet in a way that will not offend. The struggle between an often brutal history and the claims of poetry is an old one (dating back at least to Aristotle); Heyen's highly contrived poem is in the modern tradition of art offering solace where religion may fail.

There is further thematic resonance in the poem's placement within its original volume. It is to be found in the third section of *The Swastika Poems*, entitled "The Numinous," an ancient philosophical term referring to the spiritual level of reality. Heyen, long identified with the American Transcendentalist vision, seems to want to see nature, even in its decay, as pointing to a larger unity, a higher state of being in which earthly paradoxes are reconciled. Thus the poem's title works doubly: It points to a transcendent realm and also indicates this poem's presumed role in helping the reader become aware of it.

Stan Sanvel Rubin

EX-BASKETBALL PLAYER

Author: John Updike (1932-   )
Type of poem: Lyric
First published: 1958, in *The Carpentered Hen, and Other Tame Creatures*

The Poem

John Updike's "Ex-Basketball Player," a poem of five stanzas each containing six lines and written in blank verse, describes the life of Flick Webb, once a high-school basketball star but now, his glorious past several years behind him, a gas-station attendant whose life appears to have reached a dead end. The first stanza begins with brief geographical detail of Flick's hometown, a town never named in the poem but presumably somewhere fairly small and rural (possibly like Updike's own hometown of Shillington, Pennsylvania). The reader learns that Flick spends his days helping out "Berth," who runs a garage located on the west-facing corner of Colonel McComsky Plaza.

The second stanza is a snapshot of Flick at Berth's Garage, standing "tall among the idiot pumps." The "bubble-head style" of gas pump, old-fashioned even at the time the poem was written in 1954, features a glass globe on top: In earlier decades of the twentieth century, gasoline was often sold at stations that might sell more than one brand, the brand identified by the globe. One of the pumps at Berth's dispenses Esso brand gasoline, and the narrator of the poem sees it and the other pumps as athletes, the hoses "rubber elbows hanging loose and low" like a basketball player. Another squat pump, with no head, is "more of a football type."

In stanzas 3 and 4, the narrator's camera lens widens, and the reader begins to learn more about Flick's story. The narrator reveals the fact that Flick was a fine high-school basketball player, having scored 390 points in 1946, still a county record. The narrator also, in the third stanza, refers to himself directly for the first time in the poem, noting that he had once seen Flick score "thirty-eight or forty" points during a home game, a detail implying that Flick and the narrator attended the same high school. However, as the reader learns in the fourth stanza, Flick's successes were all in the past. Having never learned a trade, he just works at Berth's now, selling gasoline, checking oil, and changing flat tires. Once in a while "he dribbles an inner tube" for the amusement of friends, most of whom would not need the reminder of Flick's past.

If Flick has seemed until this point in the poem a slightly comic figure, cheerfully dribbling his inner tubes, he begins to appear more pathetic, perhaps even sinister, in the fifth stanza. The picture of him here, "Grease-gray and kind of coiled," playing pinball, smoking cigars, and drinking lemon phosphates (a kind of soft drink) at Mae's Luncheonette, where he hangs out when he is off work, is disturbing, as is the fact that he seldom speaks to Mae, but rather nods "Beyond her face toward bright applauding tiers/ Of Necco Wafers, Nibs, and Juju Beads." The audience that loved him in high school when he was scoring points for the basketball team has moved forward.

Yet still wanting the applause, Flick turns toward junk food and candy for sale at the small-town diner for the emotional sustenance he still craves.

Forms and Devices

Although "Ex-Basketball Player" was written after the heyday of literary modernism, and Updike would have had the examples of radical poetic experimentation from which to draw, this poem, like many of Updike's, is fairly traditional in form. Each stanza has the same number of lines, each line begins with a capital letter, and the grammar and syntax are standard. In short, "Ex-Basketball Player" looks the way many readers expect a poem to look.

Although Updike occasionally varies the rhythm of the lines, and a few contain eleven rather than ten syllables, most are written in iambic pentameter, the most common line of poetry written in English. Two syllables form an iamb when the first syllable is stressed and the second is unstressed, and a line is written in pentameter when it contains five feet, or syllabic units. Thus, "Their rubber elbows hanging loose and low" is a line of perfect iambic pentameter. "Ex-Basketball Player" is written in blank verse, or lines of unrhymed iambic pentameter. Since blank verse's introduction in the mid-sixteenth century, poets have prized it because it closely approximates everyday speech: Updike's choice of blank verse for this poem describing Flick, a former sports hero slowly going to seed, an all too familiar figure in small town America, seems appropriate.

To say that the poem is not especially experimental, however, is hardly to say that it is not skillfully constructed. The poem's images and the interesting ways that Updike presents them merit consideration. The poet chooses to open the poem not, as one might expect, with a picture of Flick, but with a picture of the streets leading to Berth's garage:

> Pearl Avenue runs past the high-school lot,
> Bends with the trolley tracks, and stops, cut off
> Before it has a chance to go two blocks,
> At Colonel McComsky Plaza. Berth's Garage
> Is on the corner facing west. . . .

Updike leaves it to the reader to draw the comparison: Flick, like Pearl Avenue, is cut off "Before it has a chance." One might wonder who Colonel McComsky was. Some war hero, now forgotten? Such obscurity sounds like Flick's own destiny, probably not many years in the future. Another implied metaphor is that comparing Flick and the "old bubble-head style" gasoline pumps. Flick, a stereotypical student-athlete hero whose identity was so entangled with basketball that he surely never bothered to study much in school or learn a trade, seems quite at home where the narrator consigns him, "among the idiot pumps."

Updike's use of sound devices is also interesting. There is no real rhyme scheme in this poem, but the lines have a way of almost rhyming, of subtly echoing, that is worthy of mention. Most of the stanzas use half or slant rhyme to some degree. Consider for instance the end words of each line in the second stanza: "pumps," "style," "low," "eyes," "without," "type." None of these words rhymes, but the second, fourth, and sixth words do echo one another through the use of assonance, or repeated vowel sounds: the long *i* sound, in each case employing a *y*. It is not a rhyme scheme, but it does provide a kind of balance. Several of the stanzas have this quality of almost, but not quite, containing a rhyme scheme. Perhaps Updike is using this "almost, but not quite" quality to suggest something about Flick, a former high-school basketball star, now a marginally employed young man—not even really a mechanic—who might have made it, should have made it, but will not, quite, ever make it.

Themes and Meanings

Updike was a young man, just twenty-two, when he wrote "Ex-Basketball Player," but he has returned to the figure of a high-school basketball star and his anticlimactic adulthood throughout his career. Updike's "Rabbit" novels, *Rabbit, Run* (1960), *Rabbit Redux* (1971), *Rabbit Is Rich* (1981), and *Rabbit At Rest* (1990), considered by many to be the author's masterpieces and arguably milestones in twentieth century American fiction, trace the life of their hero, Harry "Rabbit" Angstrom, through his late twenties until his death in his mid-fifties. Flick Webb is surely a prototype for Updike's much more famous literary creation.

Like Rabbit, Flick was a high-school basketball record holder whose early successes and, within a provincial context, fame, have dire consequences. Readers might ask themselves who is to blame for what appears to be Flick's certain future demise. Is the problem that Flick allowed adoration to get to his head and never bothered to prepare a better future for himself, or is the problem that Flick lives in a society that confers such status on exceptionally talented high-school athletes that their future failings are almost preordained? The casual reader who reads the poem as a simple indictment of Flick or simply as a portrait of a pathetic former high-school basketball star rapidly approaching a disappointing middle age might consider a few of the poem's details.

There is Pearl Avenue, "cut off/ Before it has a chance." If the comparison is with Flick, then he too is "cut off," perhaps not by his personal failings so much as by the town itself. One might want to consider the names of the places Flick works and frequents as well, "Berth's Garage" and "Mae's Luncheonette." Updike might be employing puns here on the words "birth" and "may." Both words imply possibility, forward movement, but both are transformed by the poem into images of stultification: the garage where Flick can never hope to make much money and the luncheonette where nothing nourishing is offered to sustain either body or soul.

Flick's essential goodness is suggested by his good humor dribbling inner tubes, and his spiritual capacity is suggested by the name of his high-school team (Wizards), his hands "like wild birds," and the fact that "The ball loved Flick." Perhaps he has been transformed into a pitiable man/boy who, smoking "those thin cigars, nurs[ing] lemon phosphates" cannot leave his past behind because his society idolized him in a way that would eventually leave him emotionally, intellectually, and economically unprepared to meet the demands of adulthood. The narrator is a fellow townsman who sees gas pumps in athletic terms (as basketball and football "types"), who cheered Flick at basketball games, and who needs no reminder of Flick's glory days because the worship of sports heroes is as much a part of his own worldview as everyone else's. The narrator implicates himself in Flick's tragedy more than he implicates Flick himself.

Douglas Branch

EXEAT

Author: Stevie Smith (Florence Margaret Smith, 1902-1971)
Type of poem: Lyric
First published: 1966, in *The Frog Prince and Other Poems*

The Poem

"Exeat" is a highly personal and disturbing poem that moves from a remembered history lesson to direct confrontation with the desirability and morality of committing suicide. The twenty-one lines of the poem are free verse, divided into four unequal sections. The first and last sections are the longest (seven and eight lines, respectively); the second is two lines; and the third, four lines. The title is a Latin word meaning "let him/her go out," and leads directly to the opening idea of the "Roman Emperor."

In the first five lines of the poem, the first-person speaker tells of "one of the cruellest" of the Roman emperors visiting his captives. Nero, who tormented captives in a wide variety of ways, is probably the model for the unnamed tyrant. These miserable "prisoners cramped in dungeons" wanted to be released from their suffering through death, and "would beg" the emperor for that release. He, however, would refuse, saying, "We are not yet friends enough." The speaker herself interprets this statement, noting that "He meant they were not yet friends enough for him to give them death." In the last two lines of the section, the speaker returns to the present and describes her own situation as analogous to that of the prisoners, for her "Muse," when she wants death, says to her, "We are not yet friends enough."

The short second section parallels the end of the first section, as "Virtue," like the "Muse," refuses the speaker's desire to die, again with the statement, "We are not yet friends enough." The third section, one rhetorical question in four lines, explicitly raises the issue of suicide and suggests that "a poet" or a "lover of Virtue" cannot kill himself or herself as long as he or she is not fully attuned to the demands of the "Muse" or is "always putting [Virtue] off until tomorrow."

The concluding section sets out the conditions under which a person "may commit suicide." "A poet or any person" might have lived a long, full life but may be unable to care for himself or herself, and may realize that the power of deciding may itself be lost soon to old age. Then, the speaker asserts, "Life" may "come to him with love" saying, "We are friends enough now for me to give you death." The last line translates the title another way, as "He may go."

Forms and Devices

Without regular meter, rhyme, or stanza forms, Stevie Smith in this poem relies upon personification, repetitions, and analogies to present her views of life and death. The abstractions of poetic inspiration and duty, or the "Muse," and goodness, or "Virtue," have an almost animate existence. The poet may or may not listen "properly" to the Muse, and the "lover of Virtue" may treat his beloved as discourteously as any human, "always putting her off until tomorrow." The last abstraction, "Life," has total power over the speaker and may choose to give or withhold the gift of death.

The names "Muse" and "Virtue" each appear twice in the poem, and the phrase "friends enough" appears five times. These repetitions establish the key terms of the poem by insisting that—at least for the poet-speaker in this work—art and goodness are the two most important entities in life, and the goal is to become wholly attuned to them, as "friends." With each appearance, these words and phrases become charged with further significance. "Muse" and "Virtue" become more than flat abstractions, and being "friends" enough to die becomes a deeply paradoxical comment on both life and death.

The analogical relationship most important to the poem is that between the speaker and the Roman emperor's prisoners. Like those captives wanting whoever is in control to give them death, the speaker longs for the same gift. Life seems to be a prison, one which must be endured until art and virtue are satisfied; then the personified "Life" can, like the emperor, grant the gift most desired and permit the speaker to die and escape his or her suffering. The position of "Life" in this scheme of things is the same as the position of "one of the cruellest" Roman tyrants, forcing prisoners to continue their agony.

Themes and Meanings

According to her biographer, Smith first thought of suicide at the age of eight when she was confined to a hospital, and the power consciously to choose death over life is a common theme in her poetry. "Exeat" explicitly confronts two elements of this theme: First, the desirability of death, and second, the conditions under which suicide can be a rational and moral choice.

The conditions of life that might lead a poet, or anyone else, to desire death appear both directly and implicitly in this poem. The opening story of the Roman emperor and his prisoners invites one to see the speaker of the poem and oneself as captives of a cruel ruler, forced to remain in dungeons because that ruler will not permit dying. The speaker, like the prisoners, might "beg" for death as the one thing most desired. The "prison" most feared by the speaker of this poem, however, is not a literal dungeon but rather the prospect of being "feeble now and expensive to his country/ And on the point of no longer being able to make a decision."

To earn the chance to escape the prison (whether literal or metaphorical), the speaker asserts, one must live virtuously and produce good work; to commit suicide without meeting those conditions is impossible. Thus, the human being must keep working and keep trying to be good, even though he or she is at best a chained captive longing for death as a release.

Having met the conditions of "Having a long life behind him," however, and realizing also the social as well as the personal dimensions of old age and decrepitude, the poem asserts a freedom for the modern person unavailable to the emperor's prisoners: "he may commit suicide," the poem declares explicitly. Smith herself, in an introduction to this poem, said that she felt "haunted by . . . the fear of being an old helpless person in an Even-tide home. . . . I would rather be dead. . . . But by the time you get into a Home, you have lost the power of decision." Thus, ultimately, the decision for suicide asserts autonomy and celebrates individual decision-making. In fact, it affirms life in this poem, for at the proper moment "Life," like a Roman emperor, may show its power by "com[ing] . . . with love" and saying, "We are friends enough now for me to give you death."

This poem, then, unflinchingly confronts issues that most people prefer not to think about, and it reaches conclusions different from those usually accepted. Smith does not necessarily hold that life is always pleasant or precious, and she does not see suicide as wrong. Instead, she invites her readers to imagine a world-weariness so profound as to make life itself seem a dungeon, and then to realize that every person risks exactly that feeling, especially given old age and physical and mental debility. For her, historical figures and stories (such as the Roman emperor) are important in providing the metaphors and analogies that enable one to come to terms with these difficult problems.

Julia Whitsitt

AN EXECRATION UPON VULCAN

Author: Ben Jonson (1573-1637)
Type of poem: Meditation
First published: 1640, part of *Underwoods*, in *The Works of Benjamin Jonson*

The Poem

This 216-line poem of heroic couplets was written on the occasion of a fire that destroyed Ben Jonson's house and—most important—his books, in November of 1623. It derives its form from an attack on the Roman god Vulcan (Hephaestus in Greek myth), the god of fire and metalworking. A denigrated and crippled god, rejected by his mother, Juno, thrown from heaven by his father, Jupiter, Vulcan was married to, and cuckolded by, Venus, the goddess of love.

The poem starts with Jonson protesting his innocence. He has never ridiculed Vulcan or courted his wife. It was Jupiter who threw him from the heavens and denied him his first choice of a wife, Minerva, the goddess of wisdom. Jonson speculates that it was the failure of this courtship that has made Vulcan inimical to intellectual pursuits.

Jonson declares that he has not been writing seditious or scurrilous materials that deserved to be burned. Neither has he been indulging in the literary fashions of the day: compilations from romances, or word games like acrostics and palindromes. The only Jonson papers worth burning were some lesser writings and part of a play, but these should have been judged by the public before being condemned to the flames. If Vulcan wanted to emulate public judgment, he should have drawn out the torture and condemned Jonson bit by bit.

Had Jonson known beforehand of the coming fire, he could have provided "many a ream/ To redeem mine." Likely substitutes include non-Christian holy books, medieval compilations, romances, Rosicrucian and alchemical books and devices, popular pamphlets, and newspapers. Instead, Vulcan ate what Jonson had, and here Jonson provides a list of his works in progress, works that, it is implied by the juxtaposition with the ephemera just mentioned, were of lasting value.

The remembrance of what was lost launches Jonson into an ad hominem attack on Vulcan. The pairing with Minerva could never have taken place, Jonson claims, as Vulcan is a god fit only for clowns and alchemists. Jonson takes delight in the Thames river pilots who call their torches "Vulcans" and so burn the god in effigy.

The river and reeds remind Jonson of the fire that burned down the Globe theater in 1613. He recounts the popular stories, transmitted in pamphlets, that sprang up around that event and lists other London fires: the Fortune theater, which burned down in 1621, and the banquet hall Whitehall, which burned in 1618.

These disasters lead Jonson to speculate on the history of Vulcan and his influence. Vulcan burned Troy even though his wife supported the Trojans, but his victory was short-lived, for the Trojan Aeneas went on to found Rome. Vulcan burned down a

London records house, called Six Clerks, in 1621. For this, a law should have been passed condemning Vulcan to inglorious confinement in a shop, kiln, or tavern fire.

The poem winds to an end with a "civil curse." If Vulcan has been as fatal to everyone else as he has been to Jonson and such famous structures as St. Paul's (partially burned in 1561), the Temple of Diana (burned in 350 B.C.E.), and the library at Alexandria (burned in 640 C.E.), then Jonson wishes him confined back to the forge to make swords and guns for the ongoing war with Spain over the Netherlands.

Jonson concludes by wishing Vulcan's absence from peace-loving England and calling a pox upon the god: all the evils of Pandora's box (which Vulcan himself crafted) and the plagues and venereal diseases of both Venus and London's famous courtesan Bess Broughtan.

Forms and Devices

A typical example of Jonson's plain style, this poem contains little in the way of poetic devices. It derives the bulk of its poetic power through the sustained metaphor of Vulcan, through allusion, and through the list.

Vulcan is a symbol not just of fire but of destruction in general. In particular, he is those forces marshaled against the endeavors of the human mind, especially art. Jonson specifically aligns him with war and public opinion but also alludes to a malevolent, capricious fate. The burning of Jonson's house, then, becomes a symbol of all thwarted human activities and a reminder of the necessity for perseverance.

Jonson emphasizes the universality of Vulcan's destructiveness through allusion. The poem is centered on a classical allusion—to the Roman myths surrounding the story of Vulcan—but there is also reference to the Trojan War and the Greek and Roman empires. This pattern of learned reference is not mere pedantry or antiquarian nostalgia. Rather, Jonson is suggesting that throughout history there have been forces of destruction and peace, and that culture worth saving has transcended its physical embodiment to remain intellectually vital.

Mixed with the classical allusions are allusions to English history, contemporary London, and Jonson's own life and works. This makes the forces of destruction more immediate and relevant. At the same time, the classical and the contemporary blend, often through direct juxtaposition, to suggest a timeless web of culture constantly under threat from Vulcan.

Another device is the list. The most obvious lists in the poem are those of places destroyed by fire. These are, for the most part, edifices of culture: theaters, libraries, temples. The combined force of these lists, and their regular placement throughout the poem, emphasizes Vulcan's ubiquity. Two other types of list are important: lists of the literary and cultural ephemera of Jonson's age, and a list of his own literary output. Jonson is underscoring the irony of Vulcan's choice: He chose to burn Jonson's work, which is learned and classical, while allowing the faddish and inane to flourish.

Themes and Meanings

The poem explores the contrast between the ideal world of intellectual and artistic pursuit, and the contingent world of human history and objects. This dichotomy is clear from the nature of Jonson's regrets about the fire. The only personal losses he details are manuscripts and books, the physical embodiment of intellectual endeavor. Such endeavor survives the destruction of the physical. This poem itself is a phoenix of the fire, a Rome to replace the Troy that Vulcan has destroyed. It is also, with its dense allusion, a small library of history and culture to replace the one burnt in the house.

On a less elevated level, the dichotomy between the ideal and the actual is present in the distance between Jonson's own literary output and the fashionable writings that seem to dominate his culture. Certain works deserve destruction because they are outdated, derivative, or faddish. Jonson's work is classical (this poem is dependent upon a knowledge of Roman mythology), and therefore timeless. It, like Troy and Rome, will be remembered even after physical destruction. Jonson's juxtaposition of the faddish with his own works gives the poem the feeling of a poetic manifesto; writers who do not follow his plain style and classicism are doomed to be forgotten.

While other writers may be pursuing insignificant forms, they have garnered a substantial audience. Jonson is quick to point out that this is proof of another insidious, and torturously slow, form of destruction at work against art: ignorant public opinion. Jonson aligns Vulcan with this process, and his desire to ban Vulcan from England is, therefore, also a cry for greater artistic appreciation from his audience.

Destruction and public opinion are also yoked together in the burning of the Globe theater, the historical event that receives the longest meditation in the poem. The Globe theater was important to Jonson's career as a playwright and was the theatrical home of Jonson's friend William Shakespeare. Jonson puns on the word "globe" to see the destroyed theater as "the world's ruins," and he condemns the vulgar accounts of the fire that sprang up in its wake. The public, it seems, often takes a mindless delight in Vulcan's destructive ways.

Finally, the historical perspective of the poem, which sweeps from the fall of Troy to the destruction of Jonson's house, presents a vision of destruction and contingency that stands in contrast to the poem itself and, by implication, to all great art.

Paul Budra

THE EXEQUY

Author: Henry King (1592-1669)
Type of poem: Elegy
First published: 1657, in *Poems, Elegies, Paradoxes, and Sonnets*

The Poem

"The Exequy" is an elegy of 120 lines of iambic tetrameter couplets, a verse form popular in a wide variety of early seventeenth century English lyrics. The second line fittingly designates the poem a "complaint" (or lament), and it appropriately sustains a tone of grief over a personal loss throughout. Henry King wrote the elegy on the death of his wife Anne, who died seven years after they were married, having borne him five children. Although first-person speakers are never identical with the authors, the speaker of "The Exequy" reflects, with reasonable accuracy, King's personal grief over the loss of his wife. He originally gave his elegy the subtitle "To His Matchlesse Never To Be Forgotten Freind."

The text is divided into eleven verse paragraphs of varying lengths, ranging from two to eighteen lines. Essentially, the speaker expresses his grief, develops a meditation on time, and looks to the future. In the opening paragraph, the poet establishes an elegiac tone through an address to the burial site, the "Shrine," offering poetry instead of flowers as a fitting adornment for his "Dear Loss." In the second paragraph, the address turns to the dead wife as the object of the speaker's meditation and emotion. She has become his book or library, and his only business, which he peruses though blinded by tears. Paragraph 3 introduces images and metaphors related to the cosmos. Grief reminds him that she died before reaching the normal midpoint of life, and the effect on the speaker has been that of an eclipse, as earth has interposed between himself and his beloved, metaphorically depicted as his sun. The poem's metaphors in this section become increasingly complex, as if to suggest that meditation allays the speaker's grief.

In the fourth paragraph, the speaker expresses an especially poignant, yet normal, reaction to bereavement, an effort to strike a bargain with fate. He could willingly give her up for a period, a year or even ten years, if he knew she would return. However, the subsequent paragraph brings the realization that he cannot hope to see her again until Judgment Day, when all the resurrected are assembled. Whatever consolation the speaker can wring from this event derives from the hope of a reunion in the remote future.

In a long paragraph continuing the section on grief, the poet invokes the earth to keep what he can no longer possess but to restore its charge fully on Judgment Day. The section concludes with a single, two-line paragraph, as if the grave were being closed: "So close the ground, and 'bout her shade/ Black curtains draw, my *Bride* is laid." In the remaining paragraphs, the speaker turns to his own future and looks forward to death, when his body will join hers in the earth. The images and figures of speech emphasize both the transience of life and the inevitable march of time. The speaker views himself as moving inexorably toward death, as a ship on a long voyage or an army unit ready to join a battle already under way. By viewing his own existence as tending toward her and rejoining her in death, he finds some consolation for his loss and a kind of subdued acceptance of the future. The poem concludes on a note of personal reconciliation and hope for reunion: "I am content to live/ Divided, with but half a heart,/ Till we shall meet and never part."

Forms and Devices

The elegy's most prominent figure of speech is apostrophe, an address to an inanimate object or abstraction as if it were alive or to a person absent or dead as if present or alive. In its application, apostrophe is thus related to personification. It establishes a dignified, somewhat elevated tone and is often hortative and ecstatic. However, King's apostrophes are restrained, decorous, and appropriately subdued in tone. Initially, the apostrophe is to the grave, metaphorically the "Shrine of my dead Saint." Imperceptibly, however, the dead Saint becomes the object of the speaker's address as he develops the theme of mourning. Shifting the subject of the apostrophe usually marks a transition in the tone or movement of the poem. The change from his wife to earth signals the speaker's intent to close the section on grieving. He admonishes earth to hold her body but to yield it in its entirety on Doomsday. The poem's final apostrophe, beginning "Sleep on my *Love* in thy cold bed/ Never to be disquieted," once more treats the dead person as if alive; it establishes a meditative tone, allowing the speaker to make a transition to his own journey toward death. The apostrophes do more than establish a serious tone; they also focus attention on the dead wife and her resting place. They have the effect of increasing the immediacy of the speaker's expressed emotions of loss and grief.

"The Exequy" is often included in anthologies of Metaphysical poetry, the poetic tradition founded by English poet John Donne. The primary reasons for its place in the Donne tradition are its meditative content, its reasoned analysis, and its striking and complex metaphors and similes. The dead wife becomes a "book," then, hyperbolically, the speaker's "library," which occupies all of his attention. Her dying has been like the setting sun that will not rise again. First, she is his day, then a falling star, and finally her death becomes a never-ending eclipse as earth is placed between her and the speaker. While some figures are brief and striking, others are more ingenious, intricate, and complex. The remote comparison of her burial to an eclipse, a never-ending one at that, represents a bold metaphysical conceit.

In the section looking forward to his own death, the speaker employs more conventional figures. He metaphorically equates his own journey toward death with that of a ship sailing inexorably toward its destination. In a further comparison, he portrays himself as a military unit joining a battle that has already consumed his love. The passage introduces a memorable simile: "My pulse like a soft Drum/ Beats my approch, tells *Thee* I come." The figures that indicate his own passage of time are designed to convey a sense of steady, constant movement, whereas those applied to her suggest more rapid and overwhelming movement.

Themes and Meanings

In its thematic development, "The Exequy" follows the overall pattern of an elegy. The poem begins with a statement of mourning and loss (lines 1-80), followed by passages of acceptance and reconciliation in which the speaker comes to terms with his grief (lines 81-114). The concluding section (lines 115-120) looks to the future in the spirit of hope and acceptance, although the hopeful tone in King's poem is remarkably moderate. Unlike many elegies written about subjects whom the poet scarcely knew or perhaps had never met, King's poem includes a genuine sense of personal loss and grief. The speaker refers to the youth of his bride, suggesting that death overtook her before she had reached the halfway point of life. In another passage, the speaker refers to himself as older and, therefore, reasonably expects that he would be first to die. While it does not give the specific cause of her death, the poem suggests that she died of a fever. Although the tone remains restrained and dignified, the speaker goes beyond the conventional, formulaic expressions often found in elegies. The resolution to look toward the future is achieved only through the poignant theme stressing that the speaker will join his wife in death.

At a deeper level, the poem develops a meditation on time. The first and more distant form is the time of Judgment Day, when the speaker asserts that his wife will be resurrected entirely. Until then, she sleeps in the earth, which the poem invokes to fully render her back. The vision of Judgment Day is consistent with the literal belief in bodily resurrection, a belief widely held in the seventeenth century. This idea was often accompanied by another somewhat contradictory one: that the soul of the deceased had gone to heaven and would rejoin the body at a later time. King expresses a simpler version, making no reference to a separate existence of the soul. Rather, the speaker derives comfort from the hope of a final and permanent reunion in the distant future.

More vividly expressed is the speaker's contemplation of his death, when he will join her in the grave. Picturing the inexorable movement of his own allotted time, he designates each passing minute and hour as moving him measurably toward his goal. Even a night's sleep brings him eight hours closer to his destination, a westward journey toward death. Each pulse beat marks his movement toward the end of life, the final battlefield. The prospect of his own death becomes not a subject for grief but a welcome assurance and a means of reconciling the speaker to his wife.

Stanley Archer

EXILE

Author: Julia Alvarez (1950-   )
Type of poem: Narrative
First published: 1995, in *The Other Side = El Otro Lado*

The Poem

Julia Alvarez's "Exile" consists of seventeen four-line stanzas that convey a sense of shared recollection between the poem's persona and her father. As she reflects upon the family's abrupt departure from their Dominican homeland and their subsequent cultural adjustment to New York City, she reveals that, as the poem's title suggests, this uprooting creates a sense of exile: a lamentation for those places and things left behind and a confused uncertainty about the new. The chronological sequencing of events gives the poem an autobiographical tone, but, placed as it is in a chapter in *The Other Side = El Otro Lado* entitled "Making up the Past," one must acknowledge that this exile narrative encompasses the universal experiences of many immigrants, powerfully demonstrated via the memories of the poem's persona.

Because the poem relies on an innocent, almost childlike, voice, memories of the family's departure and arrival are shrouded in a child's observations and interpretation of the adult intrigue necessary for a clandestine flight from their homeland. Alvarez alludes to Papi's "worried whispers," uncle's "phony chuckles," and Mami's consoling promise that "there was a better surprise" in store for the children at the end of their journey. The persona reveals that she was "young" at the time of the family's flight and thus "didn't think adult things could go wrong"; this sense of expectation versus reality haunts the entire poem.

The first glimpse of the disappointment that awaits the family occurs in the pivotal middle stanza, which opens with a quick reversal of Mami's promise through the persona's revelation that she (the persona) has "already swum ahead." Her childish instincts have seen through the parental subterfuge surrounding their exodus to the inevitable loss and danger inherent in their situation. These elements of complication and conflict are more fully developed in the stanzas that follow: the persona's "fitful sleep" at the "dark, deserted airport" and her intuitive knowledge that Papi's final glance at the horizon signals a severing of the familiar moorings that have held the family fast. This notion of being "set adrift" permeates the remainder of the poem as the persona continues to recall, in this one-sided conversation with Papi, her initial experiences in the family's "new city."

Alvarez provides a catalog of big-city images and the persona's father's explanations of these strange, new phenomena: "escalators/ as moving belts; elevators: pulleys and ropes;/ blond hair and blue eyes: a genetic code." It is not, however, the technological wonders that dominate the poem's final stanzas but rather the image of a "summery display" in Macy's store window. Here, the American ideal, the handsome mannequin father, "slim and sure of himself," is dramatically contrasted to the persona's father, with his "thick mustache," too-formal three-piece suit, fedora hat, and telling accent. The persona recalls how she and her father stood in front of the window marveling at the implements of ease and leisure displayed there: "beach pails, the shovels, the sandcastles/ no wave would ever topple, the red and blue boats" or the storybook girl who "waded in colored plastic."

As the persona and her father back away, almost recoiling from the unreal specter of the store display, their own reflections, superimposed upon the glass, reveal a stark contrast. They stand apart as "visitors to this country," exiles whose uncertain future in a land of plastic and ease haunts their "big-eyed" faces, like those of the island swimmers in the home they have left behind, whose faces, "right before plunging in," are "eager, afraid."

Forms and Devices

The poem's italicized epigram consists of two place names, Ciudad Trujillo (now known as Santo Domingo, a port city in the Dominican Republic) and New York City, along with the date 1960. This important information sets the stage for the exile experience in terms of time and place. It becomes apparent, then, that the poem will consist of adult recollections of childhood memories, and the use of direct address to the persona's father, who never speaks, reveals the close relationship that the two share. His name, Papi, is repeated six times in the poem, reinforcing his importance in the persona's life as well as his preeminence in the family, thus evoking a great sense of loss as the poem develops to reveal his metamorphosis into an uncertain outsider in his chosen land of exile.

Dramatic contrasts such as the images of the family's homeland compared with New York City, the father's fall from knowledge to uncertainty, and the expectation of the vacation at the beach that is promised compared with the false beach scene that awaits the persona and her father in the reality of New York all demonstrate the conflicting nature of culture shock and its unnerving effects on newly arrived immigrants. The inner conflicts faced by those in exile from their homelands are further developed by the repeated use of water imagery to reinforce the struggle of the immigrants to resist submersion in their new culture. They must adapt and learn to navigate the deep, unknown, treacherous waters like the persona's imagined vision of the struggling swimmer whom Papi "frantically" tries to wave back to safety. The act of exile, by its very nature, is a risky plunge into an uncharted pool, leaving behind the safe harbor of that which is known for the unfamiliar surroundings that frequently reject those who are somehow different.

This sense of being the outsider, full of wonder and fear, is heightened by the language Alvarez employs. Her simple, everyday vocabulary convincingly conveys a tone of childish recollection filtered through adult experience and draws the reader into a sympathetic identification with the persona. Her misty memories of the family's journey, arrival, and reaction to New York depict a scene universal and familiar; the reader, too, experiences the rushed departure from a curfew-bound place, the disappointing artificiality of the new culture, and the loss of personal dignity inherent in the exile experience. The use of direct address, the constant use of "you" in reference to Papi, also has the effect of pulling readers into the story, making them participants who are also reflected in the glass of Macy's store window.

Themes and Meanings

"Exile," rich with watery images of beaches and divers, is about learning how to swim; simultaneously, and more important, the poem threads the liquid images throughout the narrative of the persona's immigration memories to create a natural comparison of the immigrant experience with that of swimmers learning to brave the deep pools of their new environment. Swimming is the perfect metaphor for the hastily departed immigrants who dive into an idealized America to discover, with some surprise, their own vulnerability and a keen sense of loss.

This juxtaposition of dramatically different expectation and reality heightens the poem's sense of unease. The beachwear-clad family in the department store window marks a sharp line between the privileged, successful upper-class American (who can afford to shop at Macy's) and the almost mirror inversion of the out-of-place persona and her Papi. (They are never named; they represent universal immigrant experiences of exile.) Readers sense that they are swimming against the current, but the persona has been told by her uncles, *"What a good time she'll have learning to swim!"* This prediction, and her own admission that she "had already swum ahead," seems to foreshadow the rapid assimilation of the persona, like most children, into a new culture; but the portrayal of the artificial pursuits of the window people leads to the conclusion that her old culture offered a more tranquil, a more natural immersion. The exile experience of the persona, as for many immigrant children, thus represents a tremendous loss of culture.

This idea of loss is reinforced by the final images of the poem, which convey an implicit juxtaposition of the persona and her father to the "two swimmers looking down" into the quiet waters surrounding their homeland, ready to plunge, "eager, afraid." This current of longing, plus the comment that the swimmers' faces reveal that they are "not yet sure of the outcome," reflects the precarious position that the persona and her father, and many immigrants before and since, have faced.

Julia Alvarez's poem "Exile" leaves one feeling submerged, like the newly arrived family, through the many water images she employs. Stanza 5's almost baptismal description of the persona's dreamy descent into the "deep waters," arms out "like Jesus' on His cross," also contains the mysterious, supernatural realism of magical levitation that occurs on "that night," the night of the family's departure. The poem provides a powerful picture of an inevitable clash of cultures, from the sustaining values of the old ways to the shallow capitalistic pursuits of the new, and the reader may come away feeling plunged into this uncertain pool of adjustment.

Kathleen M. Bartlett

THE EXPLOSION

Author: Philip Larkin (1922-1985)
Type of poem: Pastoral
First published: 1974, in *High Windows*

The Poem

"The Explosion" is a short poem of twenty-five lines made up of eight unrhymed tercets and a final, isolated one-line stanza. It is written in trochaic tetrameter with a number of metrical variations and substitutions. The speaker of the poem is an observer and commentator on the crucial event of the poem, an explosion at a mine. The language is clearly that of a speaker who is more highly educated than the working-class people that the poem represents. He is not involved in their lives but attempts to render their nature and experience as fully and truthfully as possible. The title of the poem announces the event and suggests its significance: It is "the" explosion rather than "an" explosion. The poem also begins with a description of the world surrounding the event. In the first tercet, the speaker describes how "On the day of the explosion/ Shadows pointed towards the pithead." These "shadows" are an omen of the terrible event that is to follow, but they are balanced, to some degree, by the sun in which "the slagheap slept." Both the sun and sleeping suggest the continuation of a peaceful world.

The next three tercets deal with the mine workers. They are defined as a group rather than singled out as individuals. Their "oath-edged talk and pipe-smoke" define them as men of the working class at ease with one another. One of them is more adventurous and active as he hunts some rabbits. The rabbits escape, but he finds a nest with a lark's eggs in it. He does not destroy or harm this nest but shows it to the others and returns them to their place in the grass. The fourth tercet sums the miners up as types: "So they passed in beards and moleskins,/ Fathers, brothers, nicknames, laughter." Significantly, they pass through the "tall gates standing open." The scene is normal and benign; they pass to their usual work and all is "open" and apparent.

It is significant that poet Philip Larkin does not describe the actual explosion but rather its effects on the outer world. With the tremor, cows stop chewing and the sun is "dimmed." Readers do not see its effect on the miners who are dying under the earth. That horror and suffering is hidden from view; clearly, it is not what Larkin is interested in about the event. The sixth tercet is in italics and announces a change in speaker and language. It is now the language of church, formal and stately and attempting to provide consolation: "*The dead go on before us, they/ Are sitting in God's house in comfort,/ We shall see them face to face.*" The next two tercets return to the ordinary language of the speaker and that of the miners' wives; it also alters the comforting religious view of the church speaker. The wives of the dead miners see their men in a new way, "Larger than in life they managed." After this transformation, the final line of the poem recalls the miners as they were and as they are: "One showing the eggs unbroken." Their lives and their deaths were a harmonious, unbroken whole.

Forms and Devices

"The Explosion" is written in trochaic tetrameter without rhyme, both of which are very unusual in the poetry of Larkin, who used the iambic meter, usually pentameter and hexameter, and brilliant rhyme. There must have been something in the event and his treatment of it that insisted on this meter. Perhaps it was the transformation of very ordinary workers into people on a higher plane that demanded he abandon his usual metrical practice. Trochaic tetrameter does have a parallel in American literature: It is the meter that Henry Wadsworth Longfellow used in *The Song of Hiawatha* (1855). Larkin does not fall into the monotone chant that Longfellow did, but the meter does have a propulsive effect as it moves from the announcement of the event to its occurrence and consequences. Larkin does use the traditional sound patterns such as alliteration: "In the sun the slagheap slept." The miners are also portrayed predominantly through the use of verbs: "One chased after rabbits; lost them;/ Came back with a nest of lark's eggs;/ Showed them; lodged them in the grasses."

There is also some significant imagery in the poem. For example, the first tercet contrasts the shadows that "pointed" to the pithead with the sun that "slept" on the slagheap. The slagheap is also an indicator of the world with which the poem deals: a mining community with its own special landscape. The workers are also defined with a few class-specific images: They wear "pitboots," their talk is "oath-edged," and they cough "pipe-smoke." The men, unaccustomed to talk, are described as "Shouldering off the freshened silence." It is a gesture that says more than words about the type of people these workers are. They speak with their bodies to relieve the silence.

There is an interesting shift in diction, tense, and speaker in the sixth tercet, which is presented in the formal and resounding language of the preacher in a church or, more likely, a chapel. The preacher uses the future tense, while the wives use a past tense that reunites them with their men. This formal language is also contrasted with the simpler words ascribed to the wives of the dead men, and the passage uses a significant metaphor. The dead miners are "Gold as on a coin, or walking/ Somehow from the sun" toward their wives. The metaphor defines the transformation of the miners from ordinary working men to men of value and even greatness as the figure on a gold coin suggests. Furthermore, the sun image also returns at this point of the poem. The sun is no longer sleeping at the slagheap; rather, it is behind the men as they are walking to their spouses.

The description of one of the workers finding a lark's eggs is an image that develops into a metaphor and, finally, a symbol. The worker does not destroy these eggs or displace them; he shows them to his fellow workers and then returns them to the grass. In the last, isolated line in the poem, the worker is evoked once more. He is "showing the eggs unbroken." The unbroken eggs are a symbol of the world and lives of the miners. Even in death, their world remains as it was, or perhaps it is even enhanced; it is unbroken.

Themes and Meanings

"The Explosion" is about the lives of British working-class people. Larkin portrays them in all of their ordinariness in the first part of the poem. He describes their walk to work, their dress, and, above all, their interaction with one another. A few words and significant gestures define the closeness of the men to each other and to their world of work. The origins of the poem can be found in a British Broadcasting Corporation (BBC) television program that Larkin saw in 1969; the natural lives of these people gave him a subject on which he had not often written.

The theme of the poem is made clear by the symbol of the unbroken eggs. The lives and deaths of the miners form an unbroken whole, a harmonious and organic life that seems almost to come from another century. A possible influence for Larkin's theme is the early novels and stories of D. H. Lawrence, who portrayed the lives of miners as harsh but in touch with the primal earth. Larkin softens the romanticism of Lawrence, but his attitude is similar in many ways. Another important theme is that of transformation. After the miners' deaths, the survivors are given the usual comfort of the church. They are told that their men are not suffering but "*sitting in God's house in comfort*" and that they will one day see them "*face to face.*" However, Larkin then offers a very different and more convincing transformation and consolation by having these wives see their men as larger than they were in life but still rooted to that organic world they inhabited. They are "walking/ Somehow from the sun" toward their wives and now exist on a different plane, "Gold as on a coin." They are not in a Christian heaven but remain closely connected to the living.

"The Explosion" is the last poem in *High Windows* (1974), even though it was written earlier than a number of other poems in the collection. The poem gives a very different view of death than nearly all of the poems in the book. Larkin's view of his inevitable death was filled with terror and horror. The union of the dead and the living seen in the conclusion of "The Explosion" gives a more hopeful and human perspective. There have been relatively few poems written about the working class, since poetry seems to be written and supported by people of a more educated class. However, Larkin provides both an insight into that world and a sympathetic and realistic view of its wholeness.

James Sullivan

EXPOSURE

Author: Wilfred Owen (1893-1918)
Type of poem: Meditation
First published: 1920, in *Poems by Wilfred Owen*

The Poem

"Exposure" examines the sensations of soldiers slowly freezing to death in the trenches of World War I in a poem of forty lines divided into eight stanzas. The persona of the poem adopts the identity of all the soldiers as they huddle against the wind and snow on the war front waiting for something to happen. As the cold sets in, sentries and ordinary soldiers watch confusing flares in the frontline fortification from which they have withdrawn for the night. Gusts of wind moan on the barbed wire of no-man's-land like dying men, while guns rumble in the distance, apocalyptic portents of other possible wars. The numb soldiers ask, "What are we doing here?" but nothing happens.

Dawn itself, traditionally a symbol of hope, is ominous as "clouds sag stormy," the men grow colder and wetter, and the new day marshals its cloudy troops to usher in a new day of fighting for the soldiers. Suddenly, bullets fly but are tossed about by the wind, which appears to be a more powerful instrument of death than the artillery.

In the fifth stanza, the snow and cold send the soldiers into a numbed reverie about home. The bemused soldiers ask of their freezing selves, "Is it that we are dying?" In stanza 6, their disembodied ghosts visit the banked, early-morning fires of home and observe crickets on the hearth and mice playing while the household sleeps; however, the ghosts feel shut out of this domestic scene and must turn back to their own slow deaths on the front. Faith in the comforts and certainties of home clashes with the conviction that God intended for these men to die in cold misery. The love of God itself is remote and seems to be dying.

The last stanza observes that God's frost will freeze the mud in which the soldiers find themselves, and it will freeze their hands, foreheads, and, finally, their eyes in their final act of dying. The next morning, burial parties with "shovels in their shaking grasp" will half recognize their comrades, who died of exposure while nothing in particular was happening in the war. They were felled by wind, snow, mud, and the seeming indifference of God rather than by wounds caused by bullets and bayonets.

Forms and Devices

"Exposure" exemplifies one of Wilfred Owen's most noted techniques: the use of slant rhymes, such as wire/war, grow/gray, and us/ice. Emily Dickinson and Gerard Manley Hopkins also used this type of rhyme, as does Welsh poetry, but Owen seems not to have been familiar with any of these traditions. Slant rhyme and assonance bring out the jarring sensations of war and move "Exposure" and Owen's other poems away from more refined poetic forms of earlier centuries.

Owen also eschews elegant language, preferring to record more stark images such as "mad gusts," "twitching agonies," and "flickering gunnery." The only images that are nurturing and warm are the ones that depict the fires of home in stanzas 6 and 7, and they stand in ironic contrast to the freezing soldiers. Indeed, the warmth of home seems to mock the realities of war, since civilians "believe not otherwise can kind fires burn;/ Nor ever suns smile true on child, or field, or fruit." This clash of home-front experience and battlefield reality is also echoed in Owen's poem "Futility" in its vain hope that "the kind old sun" of childhood will know how to rouse a dead comrade.

The stillness of slowly freezing to death becomes a counterpoint to the progressive verbs in the poem: "watching," "twitching," "massing," "shivering," "wandering," "fingering," "shrivelling," "puckering," and, finally, "dying." As in other Owen poems such as "Greater Love" and "Arms and the Boy," the occasional attractive word such as "nonchalance" is used ironically to depict the carelessness of the wind as it tosses snowflakes around and "knives" the soldiers.

The heroic "war music" of Homer's *Iliad* (c. 800 B.C.E.; English translation, 1616), Vergil's *Aeneid* (c. 29-19 B.C.E.; English translation, 1553), or William Shakespeare's *Henry IV* (c. 1597-1598) and *Henry V* (c. 1598-1599) is absent from Owen's war poems. Instead, an eerie keening of wind on wire in "Exposure" and "the shrill demented choirs of wailing shells" in "Anthem for Doomed Youth" are in evidence, a cacophony of dissonance and loss. The English composer Benjamin Britten recognized these musical possibilities in Owen's poetry in his choral masterpiece *War Requiem*, an elegy to the dead of both world wars first performed in 1962.

"Exposure" depicts a gray landscape broken only by the dull brown of dawn and the white snowflakes and ice. The "pale flakes" are personified as they "with fingering stealth come feeling for our faces," as blind as the "snow-dazed" soldiers and the dead with their eyes frozen. This bleak landscape is highlighted by the streaks of unnaturally colored phosphorescent flares. Again, the warm colors of home are contrasted with the moonscape of no-man's-land. At home, fires are "glozed/ With crusted dark-red jewels," and a kind sun shines on all. The soldier is only permitted a glimpse of home and must soon turn back to his task of dying in a strange landscape bereft of family and the love of God.

Themes and Meanings

To understand the meaning of "Exposure," and indeed of all of Owen's poetry, it is necessary to turn to his own words: "Above all I am not concerned with Poetry. My subject is War, and the pity of War. The Poetry is the pity." Owen's desire to convey the pity of war led him to the antipoetic devices that make his work so powerful. The particular pity conveyed in "Exposure" is the irony of dying of exposure to the elements rather than "the monstrous anger of the guns." Thoughtful students of World War I may realize that many died of cold and disease, but Owen is correct in supposing that these mundane, though no less tragic, ways to die are lost in the heroic jingoism of most wars. Bullets are hot and searing, while cold is dehumanizing. The aching brains of the dying cannot understand why nothing is happening, why they are where they are, and why God seems present only in "His frost," not his love; the befuddled questioning of the fifth lines of each stanza mirrors the confusion of a brain slowly freezing to death.

Unlike English poets Sir Philip Sidney or Percy Bysshe Shelley, Owen does not see poets as teachers or "unacknowledged legislators." He says, "all a poet can do today is warn; that is why the True Poets must be truthful." Owen strives for the aching cold of truthfulness in "Exposure" as the poem exposes the reader to the cold indifference of nature and nature's God.

Stanzas 7 and 8 deal specifically with Owen's view of God's role in death by exposure. Owen came to mistrust the dogmas of national churches, finding solace only in the role of Christ, a passive emblem of love who gives his life for his friends just as soldiers often die for their comrades. Owen's poem "At a Calvary near the Ancre" explores the role of Christ in the war, but "Exposure" appears loveless and Christless. Owen's poetic mentor, Siegfried Sassoon, also reflects skepticism toward the warlike nature of the church's God and his indifference to the plight of the soldier. Sassoon encouraged Owen to tell the truth of the pitiless nature of the nationalistic God in poetry such as "Exposure," which frankly blasphemes conventional pieties.

"Exposure" is not one of Owen's best-known poems, but it is surely one of his bleakest. The unrelieved cold and misery of the freezing soldiers are contrasted with the warmth of the home front, a home front that cannot imagine and chooses not to see their pain, offering instead a platitudinous God for comfort; the soldiers' real God "will fasten on this mud and [them],/ Shrivelling . . . puckering," and ultimately killing with no pity. The pity of "Exposure" is the pity of indifference: the indifference of nature, of the home front, of God, and of the soldiers themselves, who are "not loath" to freeze into the icy destiny to which they were born. At the end of the poem, the staring eyes of the dead convey the icy indifference of men for whom the world knew no pity. In "Exposure," Wilfred Owen's dead-eyed soldiers lie frozen as a warning to an indifferent world of the horror of war.

Isabel B. Stanley

EYES OF NIGHT-TIME

Author: Muriel Rukeyser (1913-1980)
Type of poem: Lyric
First published: 1948, in *The Green Wave*

The Poem

"Eyes of Night-Time" is a full-throated song about the beauty of night and darkness. This short poem in free verse expresses the poet's awe over nature's beauty at night. The first stanza describes with passionate wonder the creatures that see in the dark. In the second stanza, the poet considers what human beings may see in the darkness, or what the darkness may reveal to them.

For Muriel Rukeyser, "night-time" has strong metaphorical connections to the human spirit's darkness or hidden truths. The poem, while offering minute observations on nature at night, also deals with self-examination and attempts to comment on human nature in general. Speaking in the first person, as if recalling a recent experience, the poet describes in the first stanza what she saw "On the roads at night." Nighttime, traditionally a time of openness and reflection, allowed her to see "the glitter of eyes." Eyes are often thought of as windows to the soul or entryways into the inner life of another being. Much communication occurs through the eyes alone. Thus these eyes of nighttime creatures are potentially the bearers of important messages. Each might be an entrance point for understanding some mystery of nature or its beauty.

The poet enters a nighttime temperament, one of free-ranging thought and expression. She confides that "my dark around me let shine one ray." This ray could be interpreted as her inner light, which is responding to the "spangles" and "eye shine" of the creatures whose eyes she sees. She is attempting to connect somehow with nature, and the intensity of her descriptions indicates how urgently she is doing so.

The sight of the "horned toad sitting and its tear of blood" (a horned toad does actually squirt blood from its eyes to cleanse them), however, causes her thoughts to turn to people: the "fighters and prisoners in the forest." This image alludes to the violence in human nature, which is often wanton, unlike nature's violence of necessity. The image "tear of blood" is a riveting evocation of suffering.

She ends her reverie in this stanza with a hint of irony. Like the forest's animals, people are "aware in this almost total dark." That is, they have the capacity to see and feel harmony as they look into the blackness. What makes humans different, however, is "the one broad fact of light." This light is human intelligence, or more precisely, self-awareness, a faculty that animals lack. Nature's creatures do not analyze themselves, and they are supposedly emotionless, with "eyes that never weep," but they have a sort of advantage: They live in a natural state of grace, while intelligent humans are often "fighters and prisoners" by choice—battling themselves and one another. The poet observes that self-consciousness does not necessarily provide human beings with happiness or harmony.

The second stanza continues to describe the creature- and shadow-filled forest at night, expanding to include sky and water: "the illumined shadow sea" and "eyes of the brittle stars." The fifth line shifts in setting and perspective: The poet is now addressing another person, someone close to her. This person's eyes shine in a "shadowy red room" that nature suddenly floods—so freely and seductively that the room seems not to have walls or ceiling:

> scent of the forest entering, various time
> calling and the light of wood along the ceiling
> and over us birds calling and their circuit eyes.

The two seem immersed in a natural world—it practically inhabits them. In fact, in the last two lines, the poet reveals that they *are* inhabited: They have in their "bodies the eyes of the dead and the living." These spirits offer gifts, like knowledge handed down from generation to generation.

This wisdom from the ancestors (like nature's wisdom) comes to those who are receptive. The poet's receptivity has been heightened by her awareness of the harmonic natural world, her courage to explore her own spiritual night, and her apparently loving relationship with another human being. The poem is actually a travelogue of self-examination prompted by a meditation on nature.

Forms and Devices

In many of her poems, Rukeyser relies on a fabric woven of imagery and rhythm to provide formal unity. *The Green Wave* (1948), in which "Eyes of Night-Time" first appeared, contains other poems in which she experimented with her powers of observation and concentrated on new rhythms. Rukeyser preferred not to use traditional forms or patterns of fixed rhyme and meter. She wanted a poetry in which the material would generate its own form. Therefore, rhythm—the cadence, pace, and momentum of the line—was important to her. The music of the poem ought to allow it to echo and suggest—perhaps reproduce—the natural rhythms of the world she was attempting to describe.

The rhythm of stanza 1, for example, in which she describes the nighttime forest lit up by shining eyes as she passes by, is quick-paced as she recites her vision. The stanza is one sentence, which runs headlong, almost hurtling, toward a complete and sudden stop. Except for two pronounced pauses (suggesting uncertainty) near the beginning, the phrases cascade along as the rich physical details pile up. The rhythm conveys her excitement.

This technique is repeated in stanza 2, but the rhythm is different: The first four lines, in the ebb and flow of the accent and intonation of the words, create the sound of waves lapping the seashore. The rhythm suggests nature's rich flow, the perpetual outpouring in which the poet lets herself plunge.

The long exhalation of images in "the shadowy red room" creates the sound of ecstatic release. In addition, the rushing phrases linked with "and" four times might suggest the sound of animals darting through the brush, or the rhythm of the eye lights blinking randomly like fireflies. The repetition of "eyes" here and earlier in the poem adds to that effect.

In the poem, images of light and dark intertwine; points of light continually pierce the darkness. These emerging lights represent, as images of light often do in poetry, possible revelations of truth. The play between dark and light, shadow and eye shine, gives the poem both tension and balance. Dark things bear light: "the illumined shadow sea" and "the light of wood" are two examples.

Themes and Meanings

Images of darkness inhabit every corner of "Eyes of Night-Time." The poet has studied night, and nighttime is this poem's territory. The earth's night and the human spirit's darkness, metaphorical counterparts in the poem, are fertile places the poet considers with full respect. The soul's darkest, most threatening realizations, she knows, will reveal the light (self-knowledge) that is needed to free the "prisoners in the forest . . . in the almost total dark."

Rukeyser's poem offers her ecstatic awareness of the healing power of darkness: If one goes deeply enough into one's own darkness, one finds, paradoxically, the light of truth that heals dark sufferings and misgivings. This light is the "glitter" she recognizes in the last line as "gifts" given, really, by all those people who have gone before her and all those who are alive now.

The poem is about examining oneself and one's spirit. It is also a statement on the need for human unity. "And in our bodies the eyes of the dead and the living" is a powerful way of saying that human beings inhabit not only the earth, but also one another. Like the creatures of nighttime—the cat, moth, fly, beetle, and toad—humans are interdependent and must rely on one another to survive.

JoAnn Balingit

THE FACE IN THE MIRROR

Author: Robert Graves (1895-1985)
Type of poem: Lyric
First published: 1957; collected in *Five Pens in Hand*, 1958

The Poem

"The Face in the Mirror," an autobiographical lyric poem, presents a definitive image of the poet's aging face. Simultaneously, it includes reflections upon central moments and concepts in his life, which carved that face so graphically. Weaving physical description with allusions to significant memories, Robert Graves creates poetic tension in stanzas 1 and 2 and resolves it in stanza 3.

The tension in stanza 1 develops as the poet describes his eyes and brows. The eyes are "Grey" and "haunted." The softened spelling of "gray," juxtaposed with two hard syllables in "haunted," achieves poetic tension, while the multisyllablic, hyphenated adverb "absent-mindedly" softens the sense of "glaring," the verb it modifies, to such a degree that it seems to modify "eyes." Readers, then, see haunted, hollow eyes staring vacantly from the mirror. This image heightens tension and holds readers hostage, although they may wish, desperately, to look away. With readers' eyes pinned to grotesquely mirrored eyes, Graves makes the first autobiographical allusion of the poem: a reference to the most grotesque event of his life, World War I.

Grotesquerie continues in stanza 2. The poet expands the mirrored image to include an array of broken and lined facial features, from crown ("coarse . . . hair, flying frenetic") to "Jowls." Again juxtaposing marred, bigger-than-life features, he makes them more grotesque against the image of few teeth between full, glowingly red lips, drawn together in judgmental fashion. In this stanza, however, the poet's allusion to significant memories is woven throughout the lines ("low tackling" in line 1; "pugilistic" in line 4), while in stanza 1 he reserved it for the end. These allusions emphasize, physically, Graves's participation in sports, which he reveals also left him marked and ugly.

The final stanza, less prosaic and more lyrical for all its pathos, has a lighter air than do the other stanzas. Graves's ending resolves tension, allowing readers to experience an epiphany, akin to his own, when he confronts the mirrored reality of his aging face behind which he continually forgets that he is no longer young. Here, the poem confirms an old Hebrew notion that people look in a mirror and walk away, promptly forgetting their own images. In lines 3-5, Graves indicates that such looking and forgetting is not a new experience for him when he "once more" asks "the mirrored man" why "He still stands ready, with a boy's presumption,/ To court the queen in her high silk pavilion." This "moment of truth" reminds him of his two selves—one external and aging, visible to himself only in a mirror, the other internal and perpetually young, the perceived self. Graves manages to catch both selves in the pause of an uplifted hand with "razor poised." As readers grasp the poem's truth, theirs becomes the face in the mirror.

Forms and Devices

Graves, a noted lyric poet, uses an array of poetic devices to achieve his ends. He uses the poem, an extended metaphor, to explore distinctions between his "face in the mirror" and his inner face. As an extended metaphor, the work becomes a metaphysical conceit. Indeed, Graves's canon is filled with metaphysical leanings, for he considered all true poetry a thing of inspiration. He called it "muse poetry."

Within the poem, Graves uses poetic tension and sprung rhythm. Poetic tension relies on juxtaposition of sounds and of sensory images and meanings, devices that Graves uses repeatedly in this work. Sprung rhythm, however, breaks the familiar patterns of rhyme, displacing melodious sounds often expected from lyric poetry. Here, Graves uses unnecessary functional words ("Somewhat," "Because of"), prosaic syntax, and prolific semicolons to distort rhythm and melody; however, the third line of each stanza rhymes, and lines 1, 2, 4, and 5 have the same ending sounds within each separate stanza.

By definition, lyrics are brief, subjective poems marked by the individual and personal emotion of the poet; their rhythms vary, they can be unrhymed, and, ideally, they are pensive and melancholy enlargements of the poem's theme. "The Face in the Mirror" fulfills these requirements in the use of poetic devices and in terms of melancholic theme. It is Graves's use of assonance and alliteration that brings the sounds of melody to the poem's prosaic lines: the *a*, *i*, and *o* sounds; the alliterative *d*'s, *t*'s, *f*'s, and *p*'s; and the vowel alliteration in lines such as "I pause with razor poised, scowling derision." Arguably, Graves breaks the textbook definition of assonance and alliteration, but the sounds of assonance and alliteration cohere throughout this poem, providing a reader's ear with the sense of rhyme and melody associated with lyric forms.

Themes and Meanings

"The Face in the Mirror" is autobiographical. It presents a definitive image of the poet's face, and its allusions to "old-world fighting" (World War I), "low tackling" and pugilism (fighting through life), and "a boy's presumption,/ To court the queen in her high silk pavilion" (the muse) reference influencing factors in the poet's life. Stanza 1 presents the poet's literal face. Shrapnel, embedded since the war forty years before, makes the face look grotesque ("one brow drooping/ . . . over the eye"), but the allusion indicates that the primary grotesquerie was World War I itself, which marked the man with internal aberrations. In that war, bright young poets, friends of the teenage Graves, died. Worse, soldiers died from "friendly fire" due to disorganization among commanders. Once, Graves, mangled by enemy fire, was left for dead in the field. These aberrations appear as sprung rhythms in the poem, causing it, like his life, to fall short of melody. Yet as Graves's long, renowned, prolific life as a poet was dotted with accolades, the poem is dotted with assonance and alliteration. That neither his life nor his poetry represent the song he meant to sing is clear when Graves explains, in the foreword to his 1958 *Collected Works*, that only the first poem in the collection (written before he entered the war) represented the poetry he might have written had he not been "caught up" in the war, which, he said, "permanently changed my outlook on life."

Stanza 2 juxtaposes nonmelodic phrases and broken, etched images descriptive of the poet's photographed face. Again, grotesquerie marks the mirrored image but, on a deeper level, refers to his serious participation in sports and possibly to verbal "fights" with critics, publishers, and fellow poets over what defines poetry as poetry. Most of these fights concerned Graves's contention that only "muse poetry" was true poetry. Those who disagreed, Graves said, wrote "Apollonian poetry"—poetry of the intellect that, he argued, fell short of presenting pure truth.

Stanza 3 also uses grotesquerie, but the tone of it becomes bemused self-perception. Graves mocks himself with old familiarity: He has been in this posture before. Nevertheless, the emotional impact on readers, looking over his shoulder into the mirror, remains arresting. The autobiographical allusion is to the poet's overweening interest in the muse, "the queen in her high silk pavilion," a reference to Graves's belief that all true poetry is inspired by the muse. In time, he believed in the "White Goddess" (the muse of truth) and the "Black Goddess" (the wisdom of darkness or pain). Graves believed that the dual nature of the goddess brought both poetry and pain to humankind, and that, as poets, humankind inevitably embraced both. Nevertheless, Graves also argued that a poem always says what it means. Ultimately, disputes over these beliefs in his professional life marked him as greatly as did World War I.

Graves expands the grotesquerie of images in the poem to the grotesquerie of life itself. He puzzles over universal questions, pausing in his shaving ritual to ask the ugly face in the mirror why he, who had no pleasing physical feature, who had become ugly because of marks life placed upon him, who had learned that muses have little mercy upon man, still dreamed that dream of idealistic youth: His queen would deign to be courted by him. In that moment of the poet's mocking awareness of the ridiculous, the poem achieves its greatest power: It is an awareness that, no matter what marks life etches upon people's faces, something within them keeps its biggest dream. In that "pause," readers enter the poet's truth.

Published in 1957, during a time that many literary theorists identify as the cusp between the end of modernism and the advent of postmodernism, "The Face in the Mirror" has marks of postmodern texts: It is self-reflexive—Graves peers at his face in a mirror, reading it as a text written upon by events he could no more control than a blank sheet of paper controls a poet's pen; it reflects the belief of both postmodernists and Graves that pure poetry lives in blank sheets, visible only to the muse who, in her time, reveals it to poets as truth; and it poses unanswered questions, leaving readers to find answers, since truth comes from the muse within the poem rather than from the poet, and her answer is always universal truth. This poem asks: How can it be that, within an old, battered man, a youth survives, expectant dreams intact? Universally, readers know that such a youth lives in them, but they cannot say why.

Jo Culbertson Davis

FACING IT

Author: Komunyakaa (1947-   )
Type of poem: Lyric
First published: 1988, in *Dien Cai Dau*

The Poem

"Facing It" has been widely anthologized in textbooks, in part because it deals so powerfully with the Vietnam War. The poem provides few answers to the complex questions the war has raised in the United States, but it approaches the subject in ways that can help heal the multiple scars the war has left.

The poem describes a visit to the Vietnam Veterans Memorial in Washington, D.C., by an African American veteran who plainly saw action in the war, but its lines hardly provide the kind of psychological closure readers might expect from such a visit. The first-person narrator sees his "black face" fading, "hiding inside the black granite" of the Memorial, and a series of crucial oppositions is established at the opening which will work throughout the poem: outside/inside the wall, now/then, reality/illusion, life/death. This first visit to the Memorial is clearly an emotional experience for the narrator, and he has promised himself he will not cry; however, and in another binary opposition, he is "flesh," he reminds himself, not "stone." Everything is distorted in the surface of the black granite: his own reflection "eyes [him]/ like a bird of prey," like the opposition of night to morning. When he looks away, he is freed ("the stone lets me go"), but when he looks at his reflection, "I'm inside/ the Vietnam Veterans Memorial/ again, depending on the light/ to make a difference." This last line suggests that the visit is a little less fearful in the day, perhaps, for the "light" reminds him that he is outside the black granite, not trapped inside it as in a tomb, or, symbolically, inside the darkness which is Vietnam, in both the American experience and its collective memory of that war.

These first thirteen lines act as a kind of prelude to the subject, mood, and manner of the whole poem; at line 14, the narrator starts reading through the names on the Memorial, "half-expecting to find/ my own in letters like smoke." The war was so awful, that on one level he did die, or went through warfare so violent that it was as if he had. This visit thus represents his attempt to move beyond his own history. He finds and touches "the name Andrew Johnson" and immediately sees the "white flash" of the exploding booby trap that killed his comrade. The central opposition between inside and outside continues, however, for he sees the names of the dead reflected in a woman's blouse, "but when she walks away/ the names stay on the wall."

The narrator notes other differences between the images in the granite and reality: what look like "brushstrokes" on the granite wall turn out to be "a red bird's/ wings cutting across my stare." He sees the reflection of a white veteran, but the man is looking "through" the narrator's eyes, seeing through the narrator's reflection in the wall to the names beneath. This confusion prompts the narrator to recognize he's "a window," in other words, a clear and transparent perspective into the Memorial. He is right in another sense as well, for readers are experiencing the Memorial through his eyes. The white veteran has "lost his right arm/ inside the stone"—and perhaps in the war. The two have become interchangeable for the speaker.

In the final striking image, however, a woman appears to be "trying to erase names" in "the black mirror" of the Memorial, but the narrator realizes that instead she is only "brushing a boy's hair" on this side of the stone. This last image captures a trivial, everyday gesture, but it takes reader out of the deadly grip of the Memorial to a restorative action being played out among the living.

Forms and Devices

"Facing It" describes a particular experience, but it is neither a narrative nor dramatic poem because it relates only a few particulars of the visit and instead focuses on the images that come out of that experience. The poem is deceptively simple in both denotative and figurative language, and this is undoubtedly part of its power. Many lines are monosyllabic in their vocabulary, which adds to the directness of the poem. Even the images—tears, stone, flesh, a bird of prey, a red bird's wings, a plane in the sky, a window—are almost elemental in meaning. Yet beneath this simple surface of word and picture is the complex idea of what the Memorial celebrates: the soldiers who were killed in one of the most controversial conflicts in American history.

As in many of Yusef Komunyakaa's poems, sound is important here, and he works the sense of his lines through both alliteration and assonance, such as in line 1, "My black face fades." He also varies the rhythm of the poem by employing both caesuras, on one hand (lines 4 and 5), and enjambment or run-on lines (lines 6, 7, and 8), on the other.

Those who have visited it in Washington, D.C., can testify to the power of the Vietnam Veterans Memorial itself: The black granite is sunk in several acres of ground in a large *V* shape. There is something awesome about the Memorial, like a cathedral or some other religious site. The simplicity of the structure allows visitors to experience its power immediately; there is no ornate or stylized structure to work through to the experience itself. One walks up to the wall, and the names of the dead are there. Form, in short, frees function. The poem resembles its subject in style as well as content.

At the same time, the poem, like the Memorial it describes, captures the complexity of the experience and conveys it through its imagery as well. The central opposition in the poem—the confusion between inside and outside the black walls—represents perfectly the contradictory feelings veterans may experience visiting the site: wondering why they are alive while their comrades are dead. Komunyakaa works that opposition from the opening lines of the poem, when his "black face fades" into the black granite, to the closing lines, when he realizes the woman is not erasing names but brushing a boy's hair. The tension between opposites in the poem leads the reader to identify with the speaker in the poem and to realize that the simplistic notions that often operate when people talk about the dead in war will not work in the experience here: The Memorial is both a mirror that gives back the viewer's reflection, even the confusion about the Vietnam War, and a window that allows the viewer to glimpse again the violence of the war. Language and metaphor thus function in the poem to challenge the reader's assumptions about that war and to work toward resolution.

Themes and Meanings

There are at least two levels of meaning to "Facing It," as there are several levels of experience on which its action takes place. On the simplest level, the poem is a meditation by a soldier returning to the Memorial of the Vietnam War, in which he has served. On that level, he fights back tears, finds the name of a fallen comrade (among the 58,022 names of the dead), and observes others standing at the black granite wall. On another level, the poem sets up an opposition between what happens "here," in the light of day, and what happens "there," inside the Memorial, which is dark and threatening. The opposition on this level is between death and history inside the wall, and life and reality outside it.

"Facing It" is thus a complex and challenging meditation on the experience of war—and the memory of it. For the veteran in particular, the black granite brings the war back or, in the central metaphor of the poem, draws him or her back into its violence and horror. In certain ways, however, the poem challenges readers as well to contemplate that experience for themselves, for people can become trapped inside the Memorial (as inside the past, or inside history), or can escape to the present, to life, to the plane and the red bird that are flying free in the sky above the black wall. The choice, Komunyakaa implies, must be made.

The narrator's reflection on the wall is "like a bird of prey," but outside the wall "a red bird's/ wings" fly free. The very title of the poem carries the notion that readers can "face" or confront the experience the Memorial represents and move beyond it, or they can remain trapped like the names of the dead on the wall. The speaker touches the name of his comrade, but the last image describes a mother touching her son: Death has given way to life. The narrator experiences his own catharsis in the poem's brief thirty-one lines, in his figurative choice to focus finally not on the death the Memorial represents, but on the life that is still being lived outside its black walls.

David Peck

FACING THE SNOW

Author: Du Fu (712-770)
Type of poem: Lyric
First published: wr. 756, as *"Dui xue"*; collected in *Zhuan Tang Shi*, early eighteenth
century; English translation collected in *The Selected Poems of Tu Fu*, 1989

The Poem

Two of Du Fu's poems bear the title "Facing the Snow." One was written in late 756; the other, two years before his death in 770. The later poem essentially deals with the arrival of the northern snow, the inclement weather it brings, and the fact that although the poet is penniless, his reputation allows him to buy on credit as much wine as he pleases. The earlier poem, however, to be discussed below, has been translated more frequently and is better known. Full of anxiety and tension, it is also a much more engaging poem.

"Facing the Snow" was written in late 756 in the capital, Ch'ang-an. Rebels of the An-Lu Rebellion had been occupying the capital for several months, and Du Fu had been detained there, unable to take office or return home. Although the new Emperor Su-tsung mounted an attack against the rebels, his ineffective commanders lost thousands of men in several engagements in the early winter of 756.

The first line of the poem, "Battle-wailing, numerous are the new ghosts," refers to this military disaster. The poet's response to the situation was simply to grieve about it in his poetry: "Sorrow-singing, solitary is one old man" (line 2). As can be seen, the poem begins with a couplet that highlights the revolt rather than the snow. This suggests what the major concern of the poem is. The snow itself is mentioned in the next couplet: "Chaotic clouds descending upon the dimming dusk,/ Impetuous snow ruffling in the whirling wind." The weather, described with great precision, is not only inclement but also ominous. The fact that the poem begins with two couplets, one about war and the other about the snowstorm, implies that there is an analogical relationship between the two. In fact, the analogy seems to be enlarged into an extended conceit in the next couplet: "The ladle is laid aside, the jar contains no green wine;/ The stove remains, the fire appears to be red still." Although drinking wine and drawing warmth are mundane practices in winter, this couplet seems to be stating more than the obvious. As A. R. Davis points out in *Tu Fu* (1971), there "could be a symbol of the distress of a nation" in the poem. If this is so, then the idling ladle and the empty jar may refer to the lost government and the ravaged country, whereas the stove and the fire may imply that the new emperor still holds the country together with the moral leadership required for containing the rebellion. This extended conceit is made the more apparent by the conclusion of the poem, in which the poet states that because news has been cut off from several prefectures as a result of the occupation of the capital, he sits in sorrow "writing to the air" (a difficult phrase, which may mean he is at a loss about what to write in a letter, or about how to send or where to receive one).

Forms and Devices

"Facing The Snow" is written in the "recent style", which came to full flower in the T'ang dynasty. Poems written in the recent style (so named to differentiate it from the "ancient style") follow regular tonal patterns, and their couplets adhere to the rule of semantic and syntactic parallelism. The two types of recent-style poems are the *lü-shih*, or "regulated verse," and the *chüeh-chü*, or "truncated verse." The *lü-shih* has eight lines, the middle four of which are usually couplets, whereas the *chüeh-chü* has four lines and almost appears to be half of a *lü-shih*. All recent-style poems, whether "regulated" or "truncated," have either five or seven characters per line.

"Facing the Snow" is a regulated-verse poem with five characters per line. Although most regulated poems have two couplets in the middle, "Facing the Snow" has three, which occur in succession beginning from line 1. It is unusual to begin a poem with a couplet. By doing so in "Facing the Snow," Du Fu immediately directs the reader's attention to the devastation of the current war and the effect it has on the poet. This couplet seems to be setting a pattern of macrocosmic-microcosmic correspondence for the next two, because the two situations described here (the outside world and the personal predicament) are dealt with in the second (the snowstorm) and the third couplets (a person running out of wine in winter), respectively.

The second couplet is characterized by the dramatic tension created by the antagonism of the elements. In each line there is some sort of battle going on. The "chaotic clouds" seem to threaten the "dimming dusk" (line 3), and the "impetuous snow" seems to be in conflict with the "whirling wind" (line 4). This impression is reinforced by the syntax of each line, which in the original has the following structure: Adjective + Noun → Verb → Adjective + Noun.

> Chaotic clouds → descend → dimming dusk;
> Impetuous snow → ruffle → whirling wind.

Since the storm is still developing, the outcome is uncertain. This storm could very well be a thinly disguised trope for the current unrest.

While the second couplet deals with the macrocosmic dimension, the third couplet shifts back to the microcosmic. Here are two series of objects (the ladle, the jar, and the green wine in line 5, and the stove and the red fire in line 6) that suggest the interdependent bond between lord and subject, the governing and the governed. Despite the parallelism, however, the two halves of the couplet are antithetical because the first half stresses the negative (the ladle is abandoned and the jar is empty), whereas the second hints at the positive (the stove remains and the fire is red). Because the ladle, the jar, the wine, the stove, and the fire can very well be metaphors for the political conditions of the state, the negative half of the couplet thus alludes to the social upheaval and political disjunction of the time, whereas the positive half, which suggests a sense of connectedness, suggests that there is hope for the continuation of the T'ang regime.

Taken together, the second and third couplets constitute an extended conceit about the relationship between the political and the personal. This conceit is clarified by the last two lines. Because the conclusion is not in the form of a couplet, in effect it disrupts the prosodic regularity built up by the previous series of lines. Nevertheless, the conclusion does follow the same rhetorical pattern established earlier, because line 7 deals with the outside world (news from several prefectures has been cut off), whereas line 8 deals with a personal predicament (the poet sits in sorrow writing to the air). In a sense, thanks to this pattern, the conclusion draws the reader's attention back to the beginning of the poem, thus creating a circular closure.

Themes and Meanings

"Facing the Snow" is a war poem that employs meteorological rhetoric to great advantage. The winter snowstorm is especially suitable as the theme of the poem because the war raging in the background was a cataclysm of cosmic proportions in the T'ang dynasty.

China has a long tradition of war poetry that focuses on the suffering of the people and the devastation of the country. Unlike Greek poetry, Chinese poetry generally does not glorify the heroism of military prowess, and an awareness of this humanistic vision is crucial to an appreciation of the poem. "Facing the Snow" dramatizes the traumatic upheaval of a nation by underscoring the anxiety and stress experienced by a citizen who also happens to be an official, a writer, and a victim of the war.

A political theme is also embedded in the war theme of the poem. To understand this, one has to make a distinction between the frontier war and the civil war. Although the T'ang dynasty—one of the greatest ages of China—was successful in many of its frontier wars against the "barbarians," T'ang poets were inspired not by war's triumph, but by death, desolation, and devastation. Frontier wars, in other words, generally carry negative connotations in T'ang war poetry. In contrast, civil wars, which official historians describe in terms of "chaos," "rebellion," and "bandit uprising," are usually treated with a double awareness. On the one hand, civil wars are horrifying because they are just as destructive as any frontier war can be; on the other, since the livelihood of poets—many of whom are government officials—will be jeopardized if the government loses, the rebelling party often carries a disproportionate share of the blame in the eyes of poets. Seen from this perspective, "Facing the Snow," written in the context of the An-Shih Rebellion, can be described as a poem typifying the "civil war complex." This complex is further complicated by the facts that the rebel leader An Lu-shan has an ethnic ("barbarian") background, that his rise to power is a result of the incompetence of court ministers, and that the emperor has been blind to the ill effects of the nepotistic intrigues that have been wreaking havoc in the political system. Although "Facing the Snow" is not designed—like Po Chü-yi's "Song of Eternal Sorrow"—to treat these complicated issues, Du Fu's position is that of a patriot.

Balance Chow

FALLING

Author: James Dickey (1923-1997)
Type of poem: Narrative
First published: 1967, in *Poems, 1957-1967*

The Poem

"Falling" is a long poem that uses the "split line"—a technique innovated by James Dickey—in a block format; its title suggests the poem's dramatic situation, a flight attendant falling out of an airliner, as well as a metaphor for the human condition. The flight attendant's fall from the airplane serves as an analogy for an individual's descent through life, where every moment brings one closer to the time when one will not exist. This process is depicted as an unavoidable progression over which a person has little or no control. The question the poem poses implicitly is: Since death is an inescapable part of the human condition, and there is no certainty of an afterlife, how does one make existence meaningful?

To create the poem, Dickey draws on a newspaper account of a twenty-nine-year-old flight attendant who fell to her death when the emergency door of an airplane accidentally opened. Through a third-person narrator, Dickey imagines her thoughts and sensations as she is swept out of the plane and plunges to her death.

The poem begins by describing the plane flying at night and the flight attendant pinning a blanket over an emergency door that is emitting air. Suddenly, the door blasts open and the flight attendant is sucked out into the night sky. The narrator emphasizes that, at this point, the flight attendant is "Still neat lipsticked stockinged girdled by regulation." In other words, she is still bound by the conventions of the everyday role she performs. Though she is frightened, she also comes to realize that she has the opportunity "to be something/ That no one has ever been." As she discovers that she can maneuver her body in ways she had never previously imagined, she becomes increasingly immersed in air, which she has always depended on for life but which now completely encompasses her, making her, paradoxically, feel more alive ("There is time to live/ In superhuman health") as she hurls toward death.

As she falls, the flight attendant engages in various gymnastic tricks and attempts to control her fall by arranging her skirt "Like the diagram of a bat." She also evokes media images—television sky divers as well as Coca-Cola commercials of someone diving into a pool, emerging, and being handed a soft drink—to help her comprehend and react to her situation. These images from American popular culture provide her with an illusion of control, and she determines that she will "hold out/ for water," into which she can dive and survive.

When the flight attendant realizes there is no water below, she panics momentarily but then determines she "still has time to die/ Beyond explanation" and begins to perform a midair striptease. As she sheds her clothes, she takes on a new identity—a sacrificial virgin who will be "desired by every sleeper in his dream"—and begins to caress herself in a masturbatory fantasy. The narrator suggests that the flight attendant's actions result in her transformation into a goddess who will resurrect feelings of sensuality and enhance the procreativity of the people who live below.

As she is about to hit the ground, however, the narrator interrupts the description of her plunge to emphasize that the flight attendant's thoughts of survival and transformation are illusions, though she maintains them to the end by picturing herself as a "Girl in a bathing-suit ad" who finds water and "comes out smiling."

Forms and Devices

"Falling" is one of Dickey's most ambitious experiments with the split line, a technique with which he began to experiment in *Buckdancer's Choice* (1965). The split line captures a poetic stream of consciousness by breaking up a poem into rhythmic clusters of words. Through the split line, Dickey desires to explore "the characteristics of thought when it associates rapidly, and in detail, in regard to a specific subject, an action, an event, a theme."

In "Falling," the block format Dickey uses in conjunction with the split line makes the poem's appearance on the page look much like that of prose, except that each cluster is separated by a distinct space ("with the delaying dumbfounding ease Of a dream of being drawn like endless moonlight to the harvest soil/ Of a central state of one's country with a great gradual warmth coming"). Though that makes the poem read much like a short story, each unit of words is highlighted in order to capture various effects. The form of each cluster is often determined by the sound of the words that are grouped together, but Dickey also uses them to isolate particularly vivid images, key ideas, or moments of realization. These rhythmic clusters build upon each other, making the verse gradually pick up speed, until at the poem's conclusion, there is the effect of frenzied desperation. In essence, Dickey patterns the verse to reflect the continually increasing speed with which the flight attendant experiences her descent, as the earth, and death, loom closer and closer.

"Falling" also employs point of view in a manner usually associated with novels and short stories. Though "Falling" primarily uses a third-person narrator, at certain crucial moments the poem is written from the perspective of the flight attendant. This switch in narrative point of view is essential because the poem comments on how the flight attendant's thoughts reflect and are limited by her cultural milieu. The third-person narrator enables Dickey to provide an assessment of the flight attendant's thoughts, while his ventures into her perspective enable him to dramatize those thoughts.

Themes and Meanings

"Falling" dramatizes the existential predicament every person faces: Since life inevitably leads to death, how does one infuse existence with meaning so that one's plight on earth seems significant? The flight attendant's fall from the airplane is symbolic of an individual's journey through life, which inevitably culminates in death. In the poem, the flight attendant tries to comprehend her situation by engaging in a variety of acts that she feels will allow her to exercise a degree of control; her actions, however, ultimately are illusions, though perhaps necessary ones.

The dramatic situation in which Dickey initially places the flight attendant stresses an individual's lack of control over his or her own destiny. Instantaneously, the flight attendant goes from a situation of security and certainty, as she performs her socially sanctioned role in the safety of a modern-day airliner, to a state in which she is on her own and facing certain obliteration. This situation is portrayed as simultaneously horrifying and exhilarating, as the flight attendant discovers she is in the "void falling living beginning to be something/ that no one has ever been."

During her fall, she attempts to deal with her plight by interpreting it through images from American and Western culture, which constitute her reality and represent her only means of understanding existence. Dickey draws on images ranging from popular culture to Western mythology to show how immersion in a tradition endows one with a means to comprehend an otherwise meaningless existence in which the only certainty is death. These images allow the flight attendant to experience a degree of control. Her recollections of a television show in which one sky diver passes a parachute to another and a soft-drink commercial in which a woman dives into a swimming pool and emerges smiling make her feel that she can manipulate her fall, discover water, and save herself by plunging into it. She thinks that, by opening up her "jacket/ By Don Loper," she can form wings and glide toward water. Finally, she indulges in the belief that the experience is transforming her into a fertility goddess who will awaken the slumbering libidos of persons below. Though she feels she is shedding societal constraints when she peels off her clothing and imagines herself a goddess, this role is yet another conception emanating from the very culture she feels she is eschewing. Indeed, to emphasize this fact, the moment is described with a phrase out of Barnum & Bailey: "the greatest thing that ever came to Kansas." As the narrator informs the reader, the flight attendant is still passing through "all levels of American breath."

Though her effort to wrench meaning from an ultimately meaningless and incomprehensible dilemma is pictured as heroic, it is ultimately a futile illusion. As she is about to hit the ground, the narrator asserts that "the whole earth . . . told her how to lie." In other words, the means for interpreting reality with which society equips people are lies or illusions: No sky diver will come to her rescue; her death will not result in any supernatural transformation. Yet such illusions are vital because without them the will to exist and to continue to exert control over life is extinguished. The flight attendant is able to live out her life more fully and intensely because she is able to create significance. Up to the moment when she hits the ground, the flight attendant "tries tries" to cling to her illusions. Her final two words, "AH, GOD," are deliberately ambiguous. They are a plea for rescue, but the poem abruptly ends, suggesting the uncertainty of existence after death.

Ernest Suarez

THE FAR FIELD

Author: Theodore Roethke (1908-1963)
Type of poem: Meditation/ode
First published: 1964, in *The Far Field*

The Poem

"The Far Field" is the title poem of Theodore Roethke's posthumously published 1964 collection. Like the other five poems in his "North American sequence," "The Far Field" is a visionary poem about how meditation itself can help individuals transcend their fears about mortality. "The Far Field" is written in free verse, which is undulating lines of various lengths with no set regular metrical or rhyme patterns; it is divided into four unequal sections.

Part 1 starts with an archetypal dream sequence about journeys toward death. This bleak car journey begins in a nocturnal snowstorm on a deserted, snow-laden road and ends with the car stalled in a snowdrift until its lights and batteries give out; it presents a scene of desolation and human isolation in an implacable and cold universe. The cold fear of death is a kind of "problem" the narrator confronts starkly. In the remaining three sections of the poem, the narrator "solves" his problem by meditating until his fear disappears and he reaches a peaceful state of mind.

He begins his "solution" in part 2. First, he remembers the childhood encounters with death he experienced in the "far field" behind the greenhouse his father, Otto, owned in Saginaw, Michigan. There he first saw "the shrunken face of a dead rat" and the blasted "entrails" of a shot "tom-cat." As a child, he had mourned dead animals but says, "My grief was not excessive." Grief was balanced by his memories of swarms of "warblers in early May" whose flights and twittering created images of a living, pulsating nature world that was so beautiful he temporarily forgot "time and death."

Further, he remembers other hypnotic natural scenes of beauty and feelings of unity with the natural world such as lying "naked in sand" while "Fingering a shell" and, significantly, "Thinking" that he himself might in one reincarnation be "mindless" like the shell. Through these memories of beauties experienced in the past, he "learned not to fear infinity" nor to fear his future death. Here his "vision" begins as he edges into a meditative trance that affords him some psychic distance from his fears of death.

Part 3 reflects on the process of meditation; Roethke creates analogies between the actions of natural water imagery (rivers, streams, ocean waves) and mental changes that happen during meditations. Using images of water flowing from mountain to valley to "alluvial plain" to estuary to ocean, Roethke demonstrates how the mind within the process of meditation gradually comes to "a still, but not deep center" as his "mind moves in more than one place." At this intermediate stage of meditation, Roethke is reaching a tranquil state where his earlier fear of death is replaced by a feeling of being "renewed by death, thought of my death." He transcends his fear and reaches for a more profound peaceful visionary unity that is "near at hand."

His profound peace involves loss of the ego. In his vision, he "sees" himself as a timeless, wise, old man "in garments of adieu." His fears of death and of being limited both vanish—he now is able to face "his own immensity." He feels a compelling unity, a psychic oneness with the waters and waves of the earth.

His newfound sense of freedom permeates the waters of the world as he contemplates the world in quasi-godlike vision; now his "spirit moves like monumental wind" and he feels he is the "final man" who is past life and past death. Now, in this timeless vision, "All finite things" of the natural and material world reveal "infinitude." The poet, as a finite person recounting his own memories, can create profound unities so his words seem to ripple "around the waters" of the entire world, a world without end or dimensions. Through an intense meditative vision, poets and readers both can become united in a vision that is transpersonal and timeless.

Forms and Devices

Like the nineteenth century poet Walt Whitman, Roethke uses free verse and poetic catalogues to express his images and feelings. Poetic catalogues are lists of details and images that both activate the senses and try to capture psychological states; often the images and details are drawn from very different spheres of human experiences. Roethke uses a poetic catalogue, appealing to various senses, in part 1 to draw the reader into his state of cold fear; he notes small details from within a car to give visual images (such as "The road lined with snow-laden second growth" or "no lights behind"), auditory images (such as "dry snow ticking the windshield" or the car "churning" while stalled), and kinetic or motion images (such as "The road changing from glazed tarface" to the bumpy "rubble of stone").

In addition, he repeatedly uses present-tense participles to create timelessness in this passage; action happens now, continues, and never ends—the verbs "flying," "driving," "ticking," "changing," and "ending" are examples. Combining a catalogue of sensory images with the present-tense, continuous-action verbs, he draws readers into opening scene of cold fear of death as if they are co-passengers in that automobile stuck out on a "peninsula" far from help.

Roethke's catalogues can also be simple lists, such as the several names of different birds mentioned in part 2: "warblers," "Cape May, Blackburnian, Cerulean." Lists work by citing different species so that if readers do not know one bird, they might know another. Roethke also clusters images, rather than using single images, to help readers visualize the "dump" behind his father's greenhouse. In the dump, he lists "tin cans, tires, rusted pipes, broken machinery" to show a humanmade graveyard that introduced him to varieties of death when he was a child.

The point of such lists is to get the reader to see as the poet sees. Since Roethke is a "visionary poet," his strategy is to get his audience first to see visions with which they may be familiar, found in the material world early in the poem (such as the dump), as a kind of preparation for the more abstract "visionary" world outside the physical senses, which is presented later in the poem. Catalogues first hook the audience in the material world as a means of moving them to a more immaterial world within a meditation.

Themes and Meanings

Roethke uses images of flowing water to help create his sense of unity with nature and to portray states of mind during various stages in his meditation. Waters start in mountain creeks (headwaters), then flow into wider rivers, which end at the seashore in a fusion of inland (mentally, individual thought) and more universal oceanic waters. Roethke's diverse forms of water imagery create an analogy between flowing water in the natural world and a similar but psychological movement in the mental world during an intense meditation. His watery landscapes are both physical and mental, but he seeks to merge the two different levels.

On a physical level, Roethke's waters follow a downward flow toward larger and larger bodies of water to represent the natural unity of all waters in the world. The mental dimensions of aquatic flow involve a quest for unity in the mind by moving through stages of meditation. Roethke shows how in meditation emerging thoughts from the unconscious, such as fear of death in this poem, can flow outward toward some kind of transpersonal mental realm to create a kind of temporary mental unity. This transcendental unity is a peak experience for humans and is shared by the poet if the poet can get his or her audience into the "flow" of physical objects, such as bodies of water, and then move them to a mental plane and "flow" into a desirable psychological state of unity with the natural world. Creating moments of great psychological unity in a constantly changing world is a goal of Roethke and a goal of most visionary poets. Creation of such timeless moments is one possible goal of all art, and Roethke tries to forge one such moment in "The Far Field."

Roethke also is one of the post-World War II founders of the confessionalist poetry movement in the United States. Confessionalist poets are openly autobiographical; they use personal experiences in most of their poems and use the first-person tense to refer to versions of themselves. Confessionalists believe that if they dive deeply enough into their own psyches and expose their own fears, desires, and taboos, they will find a more universal level of experience shared by all peoples in all times. In his poetry, Roethke shares moments of depression and despair—such as part 1 of "The Far Field"—and even his struggles with manic depression and madness, in other poems.

Yet Roethke also celebrates his loves and desires for wholeness and turns to the natural world's beauty as an antidote to the ugliness of much of modern existence. His confessionalist poems are affirmations of being. He sees the creation of hope and of alternate visions of the world as being a responsibility of the post-World War II poet. He was a teacher-poet all his life and felt that modern education was too analytical. He sought to teach ways of synthesizing, speaking of metaphor as being "a synthesis, a building up, a creation of a new world." The creation of a new mental world is what he envisioned in "The Far Field."

David J. Amante

A FAREWELL TO LI YUN IN THE XIE TIAO PAVILION

Author: Li Bo (701-762)
Type of poem: Lyric/elegy
First published: wr. c. 753, as "*Xuanzhou xietiaolou jianbei jiaoshu shuyun*"; in *Chüan Tang Shi*, early eighteenth century; English translation collected in *Poetry and Prose of the Tang and Song*, 1984

The Poem

The poem has also been translated as "At Hsieh T'iao's High Mansion in Hsüan-chou: A Parting Banquet for the Collator Shy-yün." Either version of the title contains important information. Li Bo (Li Po) held a farewell banquet in honor of Li Yün (endeared as "Shu," or "uncle"), who was leaving for the capital to work in the imperial library. The banquet took place at a tower built by the poet Hsieh T'iao (464-499) of the Southern Ch'i dynasty when he was governor of Hsüan-chou.

The poem opens with an unusually long couplet that establishes an elegiac tone by focusing on the passage of time and its psychological impact. Musing upon the migration of wild geese riding on auspicious winds, the poet observes to the collator that it is a good time for drinking, and he begins to discuss matters of a scholastic nature by alluding to three important moments in the history of Chinese literature.

The first moment, mentioned in the phrase "splendid writings of Peng-lai," is the assimilation of Taoist philosophy into Chinese literature. (Peng-lai is believed to be inhabited by immortals who have achieved eternal life through Taoist studies and practices.) Although Taoist elements have been pervasive in Chinese literature, the classics, as defined in the early years of the Han dynasty, have been Confucianist texts. Finding its way into the canon during the unstable years of the Han dynasty, Taoism nourished poets by giving them a suitable rhetoric and repertoire to explore nonconformist modes of expression.

The "substantial style of the Chien-an Era" refers to a crucial stage in the development of Chinese poetry. During the reign of Emperor Hsien-ti of the Eastern Han dynasty (the Chien-an era of 196-219), a group of innovative poets known as the "Seven Talents of Chien-an" demonstrated the vitality of the relatively new genre of poetry based on the five-character line. Incorporating subject matter derived from folk lyrics and treating it with an eye for refinement, these poets established a literary style, *Chien-an feng-ku*, characterized by the balance between substance and elegance. This "substantial style" laid the foundation for the future of Chinese poetry.

The third moment is represented by Hsieh T'iao. The phrase "little Hsieh" is also intended to remind the reader of the "great Hsieh," or Hsieh Ling-yün (385-433) of the Southern Sung dynasty. Whereas the "great Hsieh" inaugurated and established landscape in itself as a legitimate subject for poetry, the "little Hsieh" further endowed the landscape with a more profound meaning by joining it to the human condition. Specifically, Hsieh T'iao's poetry harmonizes his public life as an official and his aspirations toward a private life of withdrawal and seclusion. What Li Bo admired in him must have been his ability to stay in touch with the larger contexts of human existence, of which the functionary's career is merely a transitory part.

These three allusions are not pedantic exhibits of scholarship. On the surface, they are used as a rhetoric of courtesy, apropos of the farewell banquet, to show admiration for the collator's talent and achievement. Beyond this rhetoric, however, they also constitute an ode to poets of philosophical, literary, and political significance to Li Bo. Intoxicated by his own discussion, it seems, he begins to envision poets soaring into the azure sky to embrace the moon. This image could be interpreted as a desire to achieve transcendental liberation from a banal world.

The climactic flight, however, is subverted by a plunge into the emotionally depressive couplet that follows: "Draw a sword to cut up the water—the water flows on as usual;/ Raise a cup to get rid of sorrow—the sorrow continues to be sorrow." This symptomatic couplet underscores the anticlimactic emotions to which Li Bo was susceptible in many of his drunken frolics.

Disenchanted, the poet reaches the bitter resolution that, if "Human life in the world is not gratifying;/ Tomorrow morning, with dishevelled hair, [one might as well] relax in a tiny boat." As officials are supposed to be groomed and dressed according to appropriate protocols, the "dishevelled hair" stands for an aversion to public life. Although the two lines seem to be resentful and sarcastic, behind the "sour grapes" disappointment there is also an affirmation of reunion with nature.

Forms and Devices

T'ang poetry can be written either in the "recent style" or the "ancient style." All the lines in a recent-style poem are required to follow a set pattern of tonal contrasts and harmonies. An ancient-style poem, however, does not have a predetermined number of lines, nor is there a rigid tonal requirement. Because the format is tailored to the needs of the poem itself, the freedom from prosodic constraints makes the ancient-style format an ideal vehicle for narration and cursive expression.

"At Hsieh T'iao's High Mansion in Hsüan-chou" is basically an ancient-style poem having twelve lines. The majority of lines have seven characters, but both of the first two lines have four characters added to the beginning of the seven-character line structure:

> That which abandons me, yesterday's a day not here to stay;
> That which troubles my heart, today's a day full of dismay.

These two lines also form a couplet. The irregularity turns what could have been a cliché about time into a psychological truth that is haunting and disturbing. Such an effective beginning testifies to Li Bo's innovative spirit.

The poem employs at least two *topoi*, or rhetorical commonplaces. The first *topos*, the wild geese migrating in the autumn, implies that Li Yün's departure is only temporary. The ascension of the high mansion constitutes another *topos*. On a tower, the sense of one's solitary existence is heightened, and the mood is that of dejection. One should also remember that drinking wine is one of the hallmarks of Li Bo and that, in his drinking sprees, he frequently plunges from joyfulness to sorrow.

Another device is historical allusion. Because Chinese poems are usually brief, allusions to well-known historical figures or events help to compress the largest amount of information possible within a limited space, thus enriching the implications and intensifying the textual complexity of the poem. Li Bo's use of allusions in this case concentrates on significant events in literary history. These allusions are also relevant to the occasion of the poem and the location of the banquet.

Other important devices include the symbol of the bright moon to be embraced in the blue sky and the implied simile that drinking to dispel sorrow is analogous to drawing a sword to sever the river. Finally, the "dishevelled hair" as an image objectifies antiestablishment sentiments resulting from deprivation or abandonment.

Themes and Meanings

In spite of his talents, Li Bo was treated as a courtier during his brief career in the capital of Ch'ang-an, from 742 to 744. Disillusioned, he resigned his post and resumed his earlier interest in travel. In 753, he reached Hsüan-chou, where the poet Hsieh T'iao wrote a substantial part of his poetry while serving as the governor. Hsieh T'iao himself died in jail as a result of political intrigue. The name "Hsieh T'iao's High Mansion" thus points to the historical, literary, and political dimensions of Li Bo's poem.

The first main theme of the poem is that of human existence in relation to history and time. The poem begins with a couplet which focuses on the problematic nature of time. The abandonment of yesterday and the intrusion of today, however, are but different stages in the passage of time that will be continued, as the concluding line suggests, with the promise of a pacifying tomorrow. Despite its transient nature, time is seen as a larger framework within which the human drama is enacted. Its devastating effects, Li Bo's Taoist vision seems to suggest, will be compensated for if one is ready to "relax in a tiny boat" and drift along with the currents of nature without imposing one's will on it.

Self-definition in relation to literary history is the second main theme. As the allusions to Peng-lai, Chien-an, and Hsieh T'iao indicate, there had been important moments in the development of Chinese poetry, one significant aspect of which was the Taoist aesthetic. Li Bo seems to take pride in being an esoteric member of the literary tradition. Judging by his jubilant fantasy of flying to the moon, it can be perceived that he feels particularly at home with the Taoist sensibilities that have provided him with the appropriate means of self-expression.

The third main theme is the preservation of self-integrity in the political world. Since the "dismay," "sorrow," and dissatisfaction lead up to the image of "dishevelled hair," it is clear that the negative emotions of the poem are the culmination of frustrations with the uncongenial nature of politics.

The three themes are intertwined. They coalesce into the overall theme of how an individual might come to terms with human existence in the body politic, in history, and in the cosmic order of things.

Balance Chow

FAREWELL WITHOUT A GUITAR

Author: Wallace Stevens (1879-1955)
Type of poem: Lyric
First published: 1954; collected in *Opus Posthumous*, 1957

The Poem

"Farewell Without a Guitar"—in which a lover accepts and laments the end of an affair—is a short lyric in five variable-meter, three-line stanzas. In typical Wallace Stevens fashion, it works essentially by indirection; that is, Stevens lets metaphors and images represent the feelings involved in the situation. The poem is nevertheless eloquent and evocative, and every nuance of feeling is shaped with subtlety.

The title begins the articulation of mood. "Farewell Without a Guitar" is an inversion of a popular title for Romantic lyric piano pieces, "Songs Without Words." These are "Words Without Music"—the unaccompanied lyric poem. Stevens implies that solitary words can reflect and induce moods as well as music. The title also indicates that the poem is a statement of parting, final but wistful: The persona wishes that it had not come to this, but he accepts it with a sigh.

The first stanza documents the loss. This marks the end of "spring's bright paradise"—of all the hopes and expectations caught up in the onset of the romance, of all the fantasies triply multiplied by the three terms, each of which separately connotes hope, growth, flowering, and fruition. The tree planted in that soil comes to this end: The "thousand-leaved green" reaches the end of despair and comes fluttering down. The persona bids farewell, significantly to "his days." The suggestion is that he now has nothing left but nights.

In the second stanza, the green has changed to red: Leaves change color in fall, but the hopes have also been killed. The color is spectacular, brilliant, a "thunder of light"—as much a crescendo of color and sight as thunder is a crescendo of sound. It occurs at the "autumnal terminal," again a multiple connotation: Autumn is the season of fall and endings, and terminal is an end-stop, not a point of departure.

The next two stanzas transfer to a parallel scene: a landscape depicting the aftermath of a sudden storm in Aragon, a region in Spain. The countryside is still, shocked into submission. All that moves is a single horse, hanging its head, saddled but riderless. The sequence of images, like a transposition of keys in music, makes this scene the emotional equivalent of the departing lover's feelings. The details can only be suggested here. Some include the sense of survival, the lack of direction, the stunned absence of feeling, and the desperate search for shelter by one left at the limit of his strength. Light echoes and eddies across the landscape, which lies bruised and battered, not ready to recuperate.

At the end, Stevens focuses on the final sense of this severance. The horse leads to it: The fact that he lacks a rider symbolizes the quintessential male feeling about this situation. The lover has lost control, which largely means losing his maleness. That reveals only his partial perception, however, for he was not the only one involved. "The rider that was" is one pole ("male reality"), but there remains that of "that other and her desire."

Forms and Devices

It is frequently difficult to name Stevens's figures and techniques, because he often does not conform to conventional means. His predecessors are difficult to identify; his methods seem idiosyncratic and of his own devising. His poetry is an art of indirection, implication, and suggestion. The reader new to Stevens often wonders why he does not simply say what he means. The answer is that he does. It is simply that what he means is complex and not statable in conventional ways. Perhaps the easiest way to approach his work is through the observations that he likes to play with words, ideas, and sounds and that he proceeds largely by suggestion. This kind of playfulness and allusiveness has already been noted in the poem's title: This is a sad little song, like a minor-key Spanish guitar piece about parting, except that this lacks the sonority of accompaniment.

"Farewell Without a Guitar" begins by establishing the end of "spring's bright paradise" and everything promised by spring: the advent of light, growth, flowering, love. Spring is the season of love; its bright paradise is the ecstasy of falling in love, a time when all the senses become tuned to expectation, when one's entire being is caught up in hope. All of this has come to ruin: "the thousand-leaved green falls to the ground." Literally, this is the falling of the leaves; metaphorically, it is the desolation of all hope. The tree of promise, "leaved" in spring, is now bare; the thousand leaves are no more, and the green has departed. In taking leave of his days, the persona metaphorically asserts that his life is over.

The green turns red before the fall: It both comes to a stop and flames up in sacrifice. Stevens continues by arranging evocative words, drawing out connotations in sequence. "Thunder of light" is at first paradoxical, but then resolves by way of crossing senses: The sacrificial blaze of fall colors is equivalent to a peal of thunder, and the leaves are so many light-reflecting facets. The thunder of light also operates on other levels. The fall of a thousand leaves collectively makes a thunderous sound, and the light released through the new bare tree strikes like a clap of thunder.

The thunder bridges into the image of the "Spanish storm," which centers on a riderless horse walking home. The riderless horse appears in formal military funerals, and even if that specific association is not intended, it aptly sums up the feeling of loss and lack of direction, especially when joined with the reference to "the rider that was." Together these reinforce a feeling of remorse, which leads to the next phrase, "the reflections and repetitions." This primarily refers to the way the survivor endlessly replays the relationship in his mind, trying to determine what went wrong. This merely reproduces the pain, "the blows and buffets of fresh senses." Together these form a "final construction"—a composition in the imagination, which alone contains all these ingredients. In this case, it is a combination of "male reality" (the sense of desolation) and "that other and her desire" (the woman who continues to attract him, but does not desire him).

Themes and Meanings

Like many of Stevens's poems, "Farewell Without a Guitar" does not yield its secrets easily and does not resolve readily into neat thematic packages. Stevens's approach to poetry was complex and subtle. He viewed the creation of poetry as humankind's supreme imaginative act, a necessary response to and reaction against the prosaic routine of daily life. He believed people had to escape into the world of supreme fiction, where alone their higher functions could realize themselves.

"Farewell Without a Guitar" is one of those fictions, a verbal construction built from experience but far transcending it, if only because it is devoid of personal emotional pettiness. Because it is one of those fictions, it is a song that needs no music; it occupies a region above and beyond the material, hence beyond music. Stevens considered his "song" a pure composition, in which an emotional impasse will never be resolved but will pass into the timeless level of the imagination. This is what it means to create beauty, to preserve a moment in eternity.

This is exactly what this poem accomplishes. It presents four different polarized images reflecting and capturing identical emotional tensions. Stevens shows four versions of the same opposed feelings, those of the departing male and the rejecting female, although the situation primarily focuses on the male's perceptions and feelings.

The first image is spring and fall, presented counterpoised: Spring finds its natural end in fall, and fall resolves the promise of spring. Joined in this paired image, they are raised beyond time, caught in a warp that leaves them eternally reflecting each other. The second image is the Aragonese storm scene, with the head-hanging riderless horse and the reminiscence of the rider. Like the previous image, this resolves past and present in a timeless equipoise. Imagining the horse, the reader recalls the rider. Thinking of the rider, the reader projects ahead to the time when the saddle will be empty. Each pole of the image reflects and contains the other; past and present exist simultaneously in the image.

The third image depicts the process directly, thus reinforcing the practice with the concept. Stevens introduces the "reflections and repetitions" that "are a final construction/ Like glass and sun." In this disclosure, Stevens explains the technical basis of the poem. By abstracting these polar sequences from the order of time, he presents them as mirror images, each projecting and receiving the other. These images are true reciprocals: glass and sun reverberate, echo, pulse, vibrate, regenerate each other. They translate a temporal sequence into permanence.

The final image recapitulates and encapsulates the series. It is the opposition-resolution of "male reality/ And of that other and her desire." This polarity is basic; it underlies all the rest. Like them, it is a reflective and reflexive pairing. Like them, it is wrought out of time into the timelessness of the imagination.

James Livingston

THE FARMER'S BRIDE

Author: Charlotte Mew (1869-1928)
Type of poem: Dramatic monologue
First published: 1912; collected in *The Farmer's Bride*, 1916

The Poem

"The Farmer's Bride" is a description of a wife, narrated by her husband. The first two stanzas of the poem are written in the past tense, and the last four shift to the present tense to describe the present situation. He first states that he married her three years ago, when she was very young. The proposal and subsequent marriage were rushed; he decided in the summer and married her soon after without spending much time with her, because he was busy with the fall harvest.

As soon as they were married, she became unhappy and afraid of him. The implication is that she was afraid of his sexual advances; he matter-of-factly characterizes her as being afraid of "love and me and all things human." Since he associates womanliness with sexuality and welcoming smiles, she became more like a "fay," or fairy, to him, something spiritual and intangible rather than physically present.

Her fear of him and repugnance at her life reached an apex when she fled from home soon after their marriage; they were married "at harvest-time," and she ran away in the fall. The other farmers presumed that she was merely tending the sheep, though it was night and she should have been in bed. When they found her gone, she led them on a long chase. She was swift as a hare, but they captured her and locked her in her house.

Now, three years later, she makes a place for herself at the farm, doing her housework adequately and communing with small animals. The only thing that brings out her original fear is the presence of men. Her fear is evident in her eyes; she does not voice it, but the husband knows that she does not want him near. The woman remains uncommunicative, except to call the animals, who are very responsive to her. The farmer hears this from the other women on the farm, who see her with the animals but do not seem to speak with her themselves.

The fourth stanza changes tone. Rather than continue his objective description, the speaker begins to characterize his wife sympathetically as shy and slight, sweet and wild. He regrets that these qualities are not available to him and are reserved for herself. There is another turn in the fifth stanza, as the speaker wistfully notes the passing of fall into winter. Looking to Christmas, he laments that this is a family time and they have no children: "What's Christmas-time without there be/ Some other in the house than we!"

The final stanza brings the buried emotion and repressed sexuality to the fore. He begins with a description of her sleeping alone, a stairway above him, again implying that they are not sexually intimate. All of his love and longing for her surface in the final four lines as he imaginatively grasps at her soft, youthful image.

Forms and Devices

"The Farmer's Bride" is a skillful rendering of the dramatic monologue. The farmer, who describes his wife's actions, reveals more and more of his own feelings and failings until readers know his character and understand the reason for his wife's behavior. The poem is as understated and evocative as its speaker, a fact that makes his revelations of love and strong sexual feelings, which are unrequited and unconsummated, truly poignant.

The unfolding revelation of the man and woman's relationship during the monologue complicates what could be seen as a straightforward story of male oppression. Throughout, the husband reveals his inability to recognize his wife's reaction to his patriarchal power, seen in his choice of her, his capturing and locking her in his house, and his defining her in terms of his own needs ("But what to me?") and projecting his feelings onto her ("poor maid").

However, his perceptive understanding of her fears and his refusal to force himself on her, together with his outburst of emotion at the end, make him sympathetic. The tensions in the poem between his obtuse conventionality and his unexpected tender patience and respect for her person create a multilayered, sympathetic character. Much of the power of the poem stems from his feelings of anger and frustration at being denied his wife's affection and his realization of his part in it.

Imagery and similes are used as part of the dramatic irony. The farmer describes his wife in natural similes: "like a hare," "like a mouse," "as a leveret," "as a young larch tree," "as the first wild violets." These similes idealize, diminish, and feminize the wife rather than individualize and humanize her. He never speaks her name. The similes show the reader that the farmer sees human beings and their emotions as part of the natural world. He sees love and sexuality as "natural" rather than as socially constructed, so it does not occur to him to cultivate these feelings in his wife.

Further irony is seen in the wife's escape into nature in order to eschew social expectations. By communing only with animals, she is shunning "all things human." The statement "*I've* hardly heard her speak at all" emphasizes the farmer's bitterness at her decision not to communicate with him. She is asserting her own right to choose by positioning herself in nature in order to flee the society of men, and she is strong in this environment. She has authority with the animals; they look to her as children look to adults for assurance and care.

The overall seasonal structure of the poem also shows the speaker's view of essential human nature. The events are ordered by seasonal chronology: He chooses her in summer and marries her at harvest time. She runs away in the fall, and the distance between them grows as winter passes and they are alone in the house together. In the world in which he lives, it is as "natural" that women submit to being wives as it is that autumn brings the harvest and winter brings Christmas joy for children.

The melodic lines and beautiful natural images belie the uneducated diction and expected roughness of the taciturn, working-class, male farmer. They humanize and underscore the fears and frustrations and unhappiness he relates.

Themes and Meanings

"The Farmer's Bride" is about innocence and ignorance. The bride is too young to marry and to have sex with a man she hardly knows. The imagery of the first stanza is of a smiling, attractive, competent girl whom the farmer has chosen because she will make a good farm wife. Unfortunately, her youthful innocence is matched by the farmer's insensitivity toward the young, sexually naïve, frightened girl and his ignorance of a woman's needs and humanity. He chooses her as he would his cattle, seeing no need to woo her. Having no concern for her feelings, he expects her simply to step into the role of his wife.

To him, as a farmer, human nature is not much more complicated than animal nature. The pairing of two people is not guided by more than the natural urge to procreate, the social roles of man and wife, and the man's need for someone to keep house for him.

Mew also indicates that the man is not cruel, only conventional, in her description of the townspeople's (probably the men) chasing her and locking her up. They seem to think the same way the farmer does: A wife, even a young, frightened wife, belongs at home with her husband. Even the women make little attempt to help her; they are perhaps busy with their chores or have forgotten their own transition into married life.

Their expectations and actions are based on what "should properly" be done. Although they run after her and bring her home forcibly, they are acting, in their minds, according to what is socially, and even naturally, prescribed. What the poem depicts as a somewhat frightening scene—the townspeople chasing a young woman as hounds chase a hare—most likely seems protective to them, since she is cold and afraid and "belongs" home in her bed.

By the end of his monologue, the speaker has revealed his love and his bewilderment that it is not returned. By the last two stanzas, when readers see his desire for children and his longing for his wife, their sympathy is with the farmer's unrequited love. Readers fully understand what he dimly understands: His wife has again fled from him (this time emotionally), and he has been complicit in alienating her.

Critics have found this poem unrealistic, saying that a farmer would have forced himself on his new bride without qualms. Yet the brilliance of the poem comes from the characterization of a man, a common hardworking farmer, with a sensuous appreciation of the life around him and with respect and gentleness toward his wife. Thus, what could have been a clichéd poem about an oppressive brute or a failed marriage becomes instead an insightful study of human misunderstanding that explores problems of class and gender

Sandra J. Holstein

FATHER AND SON

Author: Stanley Kunitz (1905-   )
Type of poem: Lyric
First published: 1944, in *Passport to the War: A Selection of Poems*

The Poem

"Father and Son" is a dramatic lyric in four stanzas, inclining not quite decisively to blank verse. The neutrality of the "and" in the title understates the poem's tenor, suggesting neither the son's anxiety in coming to terms with his father nor the inevitable one-sidedness of their relationship. The speaker of the poem need not be understood as Stanley Kunitz; references to time and place are not indubitably autobiographical. The son speaks in a direct, if elliptical, manner. He recounts a journey from the "suburbs," through the "sleeping country where [he] was young," and thence to the edge of a forested pond, where his father may have died.

The opening line implies the urban origin of this journey, however, and suggests that just as the son moved toward the forest from the suburbs, so had he recently exited the city. The first stanza also makes clear that the son is pursuing his father through time. The speaker's narrative begins with dusk, but implies in the opening word, "Now," a preceding day. As the first twelve lines of his narrative conclude, he has fully entered the night, thus giving the sense of a complete day.

In the second stanza, the son asks how he shall convey to his father his "fable" and "fears." His life is troubled by a "chasm," representing not only the distance between the dead father and himself, but also a sundered family, which "lost" the house the father had built. A perhaps nomadic sister who "went from home" sends "nothing" back from "where she goes." The feeling of annihilation derived from the chasm, the lost house, and the gift of nothing have rendered the son's existence disconnected and dispassionate: "I am alone and never shed a tear." Without the father, he has had adequate "light" but insufficient "warmth," words suggesting awareness and affection, respectively.

In the third stanza, the speaker recounts his arrival at the "water's edge," intimated in the first stanza when the father is "steeped in the odor of ponds." All urgency and need, he implores the father to return, yearning for his knowledge, not of the intellect but of the heart. Placing himself "between two wars," the son would learn the father's "gentleness" so that he might be a child for "those who mourn," the parents of the dead; for the surviving children, he would be a "brother." To "innocence" he would become a "friend." Having referred to his father's "indomitable love" and to his own need for warmth, he finally asks his father to "keep me kind."

The two-line stanza that concludes the poem reveals the fruit of the son's entreaties— a vision of the father's skull. Nothing remains to be conveyed. The brevity of this climax and denouement is arresting. The son's yearning and his belief in his father's love make "the white ignorant hollow of his face" an unexpected and shocking final image.

Forms and Devices

The poem's details are integrated by several patterns of diction. The "pond" in the first stanza and the "water's edge" in the third envelop the poem. By being "whiter than bone dust," the "road" of the first line prefigures its dead end in the skeletal "white ignorant hollow" of the father's face, the poem's terminal image. This whiteness, connected to bone in both cases, stands against the diction of darkness or insufficient light rendered in lines 1, 12, 19, and 20.

The language in which Kunitz wraps the son's desire belongs to education. Of the father, the son says, "You know/ The way." Positioned at the end of the line, "know" has a universal status, but enjambed with "The way," it belongs precisely to the moral domain which orders the third stanza. Line 26 ends in "Instruct." Standing alone, it is any sort of pedagogical directive, but run on ("Instruct/ Your son . . ./ In . . . gentleness"), it bespeaks the need for affectional learning. The last line of the third stanza begins with "O teach me," referring to proper work and kindness. In the concluding couplet, "ignorant" paradoxically gives ironic fulfillment to this body of words. Finishing the poem, the reader may re-evaluate "master" (line 7). Its immediate context ("chains") implies dominance and servitude, but the whole poem enlivens its suggestion of a perfect mentor as well.

The poem is, however, more mystifying than such a semantic characterization suggests. The son's travel is curious, as is the coalescence of past and present and of time and space. Such merging renders the poem's narrative and atmosphere strange. One senses the texture of a dream. Kunitz works surrealistically, realizing a son's psychological, not literal, quest for the father. The method is controlled principally by words joined so as to confuse time and by imagery that blends temporal and geographical realities.

The surreal conjunction of time and territory is achieved largely through imagery. The son says that he followed the "master of [his] blood" not briefly, but "Mile after mile," and not plausibly, on foot, but "with skimming feet," as though afloat. Those miles, at one level the recollected places of the son's and father's common past, become time. Thus the son says suddenly of his pursuit and those skimming feet that he "Strode years." The "skimming" turns to flight as the son metamorphoses, "stretched into bird." On the wing, he "Raced" not through a strictly recollected countryside (though its vegetation, as the forest's later, is well delineated), but through "sleeping country," a phrase suggesting a dream. Such country, when recalled, represents not only where he passed his youth but also the youth itself, time long out of mind but fluently resurrected in a dream.

Themes and Meanings

"Father and Son" is about the desire for a source of psychological and spiritual certitude. It is also about the acute frustration in the individual prematurely deprived of one who could have provided it. Yet the poem is not for the fatherless or orphaned alone. In the ordinary course of life, everyone loses his or her parents. Later, one may yearn, consciously or not, for a bygone security that they represent. Such feeling does not require that security to have existed in fact. It is fueled by loss and by the alienation and dissolution which often follow from it. Moreover, the one lost may or may not have possessed the love requisite to this need. By its nature, desire requires no such guarantee.

Does the concluding couplet, then, cynically denigrate this yearning? Probably not, because this desire and its gratification are imagined as in a dream, suggesting their unconscious nature. The voice of the poem is not engaged in a realistic social exchange. What the son finally realizes is not the sort of rebuff one gets from an impatient realist. It is more like the half-conscious, desultory insight that follows a dream embodying some personal unhappiness. Such an insight could be as salutary in the long run as it is disquieting for the moment.

Maturity finally requires one to acknowledge that a dead source of surety cannot be otherwise. In addition, an absolute and dead guarantor of one's well-being, by its magical, unconscious empowerment, enslaves one. (The dead father's "indomitable love" has kept the son in "chains.") One may esteem that love, real or not, but one wishes the person who seeks it free of bondage as well. Thus, the terrible experience of the "white ignorant hollow" is ultimately liberating. Learning to live independently of perfect guidance is often a painful experience, but it vitalizes one's autonomy and self-reliance. The son is finally free to be a real moral agent, to act through his own judgment, even ignorance, there being no morally omniscient guide anyway, as the innocently "ignorant . . . face" makes clear.

David M. Heaton

THE FATHER OF MY COUNTRY

Author: Diane Wakoski (1937-   )
Type of poem: Lyric
First published: 1966; collected in *Inside the Blood Factory*, 1968

The Poem

"The Father of My Country" is a long poem of more than 170 lines in which an adult woman looks back and tries to come to terms with what she feels was her father's desertion. The poem is in the confessional mode—it deals with a private subject (in this case, family problems) in a public way. There is a feeling of taboo about the subject, and though the poem is not necessarily true in a literal sense, it does give the impression of being drawn from life.

Although the poem is quite long, many of the lines are short, some of them consisting of a single word. The others are of irregular length, in free verse, and give the poem a free-swinging emotional feeling. The length of the poem allows space for Diane Wakoski to weave variations on her subject and to build to a climactic ending in which her feelings are somewhat resolved.

The poem deals with memories of the speaker's father evoked in objects associated with him, such as telegrams and presents from faraway places. George Washington appears throughout the poem as a symbolic father figure the poet can use to talk about her own father and his frequent absences in her childhood. When she tells the reader that her father was an officer in the Navy and that fatherhood has "a military origin" (related to being authoritarian), the reader sees the connection she is making between General George Washington, first president and symbolic father of the United States, and her own father. When she says that George Washington "won the hearts/ of his country," it becomes a reflection of her love for her father. This love is necessarily remote, since its object is rarely there.

Many of the statements in the poem are simple and direct. The speaker says about her father, "I'm not used to talking/ about him"; however, she also uses dreamlike surrealist images to depict intense emotional states. When she says that a woodpecker is pecking at her mouth, she is showing how wooden—that is, how unemotional—she has become in denying her feelings. The "bloody crest" of the woodpecker helps the reader feel how painful it is for her to break her silence.

Memories of her father seem to be evoked when she discovers a variety of objects associated with him in a trunk: "the trunk yielding treasures of/ a green fountain pen, heart shaped mirror,/ amber beads, old letters with brown ink." She remembers, "You came, to me, and I at least six." The number six, her age at the remembered time, inspires a catalog of sixes, everything from doilies to beer bottles, from baby teeth to hats. Perhaps the remembered visit from her father when she was six was so important that it multiplied itself in her memory. The effect of such multiplication is dreamlike, and the passage ends with a memory of a frightening dream with erotic overtones.

As she continues to trace memories and influences of her father, she concludes that by not being there for her, he gave her a lack of confidence in men, the men she wants and loves: "Father who makes me know all men will leave me/ if I love them." Presumably by the sensitizing effect of his desertion, however, he also made her a "maverick,/ a writer,/ a namer"—in short, a poet.

With that realization, Wakoski reels off a catalog of longings and absences as if in an attempt to purge herself of bad feeling. Having worked through these memories, she turns to a substitute father, symbolized by George Washington, and says, " 'George, you have become my father.' " In a cry full of disbelief, longing, and joy, she asks "Father,/ Father,/ Father,/ have you really come home?"

Forms and Devices

Wakoski is frequently referred to as a confessional poet. Taboo material can be used for powerful effect, and Wakoski is one of the outstanding practitioners of the confessional mode. By violating the reader's sense of decorum and boundaries, she taps into deep feelings both in herself and in her reader.

The confessional aspects of her poem intensify the feeling that the poem is important because the writer feels strongly enough about the material to break taboos. Using and shaping personal material, she develops a personal mythology that is both a re-creation of the self in a new identity and a coherent interpretation of the chaotic old self. Like other mythologies, the personal mythology is a story of origins peopled by heroes and villains and dealing with elemental emotions.

The mythic world of Wakoski's imagination is inhabited by many created or adapted characters, such as George Washington in this poem; in fact, Washington appears in a whole series of her poems. Sometimes her characters seem to be masks for real people in her life, while at other times they seem to be simply types filling some symbolic role. That is, George Washington may be a name she uses to depict a real person who has filled the need for a father figure in her life, or he may be a symbol used to express and resolve conflicts in her own psyche. In either case, this personal mythology becomes a means of interpreting and re-creating the self.

Wakoski's poems are typically long, in the tradition of Whitman and many examples of American free verse. The loose, expansive structure allows her to develop complex themes and variations that remind readers of improvisational music. Within her long poems, such as "The Father of My Country," she finds room for extensive catalogs or lists that give her poetry an incantatory quality. The use of the catalog or list in poetry is one way that modern poets have given form and music to free verse, and Wakoski makes particularly dramatic use of the device. In this poem, there are several such lists, including the list of objects found in a trunk, the list of things her father has left her, and the list of the ways in which she felt abandoned.

Finally, Wakoski uses surrealistic images in her poetry to evoke strong feeling and to write about emotions that are hard to describe in any other way. Sometimes these images are dreamlike in mood, and other times she actually places them in dreams. One such image in the poem is the diamond shaped like a dog that leaves her and runs away with her father. Although it is possible to make logical associations, such as seeing the diamond as a symbol of marriage, the image really works in a more emotional way, like something in a dream that gives one peculiarly intense emotions whether it makes sense or not. Frustration, desertion, possession, value, and anger are all evoked by this image. Surrealistic images can work as symbols and also give a strange, interesting mood to the writing.

Themes and Meanings

As she does in some of her other poems, in "The Father of My Country," Wakoski is writing about the failure of a human relationship. She deals with this failure on the one hand by venting emotion in expressions of anger, grief, and longing, and, on the other hand, in a contrasting stoicism by which she takes all responsibility onto herself and re-creates herself in her poetry.

Men have powerful roles in Wakoski's poetry. In this poem, the father is much more powerful than the mother because of his power to come and go, to control the choices in the family, and to affect others more than they apparently affect him. Because she is a "maverick," Wakoski is bound to identify with and envy that masculine power more than she identifies with the mother who is left behind. The speaker in the poem, however, is also left behind, and this is the source of much of the sadness and anger in the poem.

Wakoski's themes sometimes parallel or incorporate the metaphors of psychoanalysis, and the situation she explores here suggests the Electra complex. Though there is little about the mother in this poem except by inference, it is still an example of the theme of longing for the father while rejecting the mother, which appears in other examples of her work. She is also writing about the pain of breaking through silences surrounding taboo subjects. She uncovers negative aspects of childhood that prevent the adult from living an emotionally healthy life, then faces and purges them.

In the last stanza, the speaker addresses George Washington—symbolic father, surrogate, and possibly even a living person to whom she has assigned this mask. She says, "I need your/ love," and although the poem ends with a question ("have you really come home?"), that question is charged with feelings of relief and resolution.

Barbara Drake

FEAR AND TREMBLING

Author: Robert Penn Warren (1905-1989)
Type of poem: Lyric
First published: 1981, in *Rumor Verified: Poems, 1979-1980*

The Poem

"Fear and Trembling" is a poem of twenty-one lines expressing a poet's questions about his ability to commune with nature in old age when he seeks to understand nature's lessons and feels a burst of energy for poetic creation.

As its title implies, "Fear and Trembling" is a dark meditation about the limits of the ability of the human mind and the poetic imagination to bridge the gap between the subjective and objective realms of reality and to apprehend intimations of immortality in nature. The title may also express the awe-filled emotions inspired by the possibility of communing with nature. Emphasizing the poem's dark side are the many questions posed by the speaker; questions far outnumber declarative statements in the poem.

The first stanza presents the setting, which the rest of the poem explores for meaning. There are no questions here, only a simple description of a completely quiet forest in high summer during sunset. Despite the simple narration, however, phrases such as "that is" (suggesting intensity of being) and "final fulfillment" (suggesting totality of being) hint at a transcendent experience or vision springing from this preternaturally silent scene. The aged speaker will meditate on the meaning of the natural scene in the remaining lines of the poem.

The second stanza inaugurates a series of disturbing questions that cast doubt on the power of words (as in the case of poetry) to create a vital communication of nature. Are words trapped within the poet's psyche (mere "wind through the tube of the throat"), without a direct and meaningful relationship to the objective reality of nature? Are words merely arbitrary symbols of human fashioning that do not necessarily correspond to the external world of nature? Can words tell the truth of nature, capture its moods rightly, and convey its lessons correctly?

The third stanza seems to provide an answer to these questions and exhorts readers to commune with the silent and sunlit forest and to experience a transcendent early spring in high summer, abstracted from evil. This upbeat stanza, like the first, avoids the questions found everywhere else in the poem.

The rest of the poem resumes the disturbing questioning of the second stanza and expresses doubts about the ability of human beings to plumb nature's meaning and moods ("is it in joy or pain and madness?"). It would be wonderful for the speaker to know certainly that he could pierce the veil of nature in his old age when creative energy surges from his unconscious in a manner reminiscent of the Socratic illumination of the cave-dwelling souls in Plato's *Republic* (fourth century B.C.E.). Ripe for poetic creation, the speaker wants to commune with nature for the wisdom that could further abstract him from the ambitions of youth and the concerns of the world, but in the end he can only pose questions, wait for surer answers, and hope for intimations of immortality from nature.

Forms and Devices

"Fear and Trembling" is a lyric poem written in free verse that consists of five quatrains (rhyming *abab*) and an additional final line. Robert Penn Warren's earlier poetry had been strongly influenced by the formal control and the elegant, well-mannered rationality of John Crowe Ransom's verse, but beginning with the volume *Promises* (1957) and revealing itself fully in the major book-length poem *Audubon: A Vision* (1969), his poetic line became more free-flowing and energetic in the modernist mode. A distinguishing mark of his poetry, including "Fear and Trembling," is a passion directed toward the physical world and toward a knowledge of truth. He was a writer who yearned for more than life normally discloses yet was full of appreciation of the world that instigated that yearning.

Assonance and consonance abound ("The sun now angles downward, and southward"). Paradox, an apparent contradiction that is somehow true, appears in the affirmation that early spring can coexist with high summer for anyone who is in communion with nature (lines 11-12). The language of the poem veers toward a colloquial informality, but there is an occasional ornate phrase with a shocking suggestiveness of spiritual meaning (for example, "final fulfillment" and "vernal translucence"). Line 20 has a monosyllabic tendency and a generative sound system in the principal vowels that bear comparison with the experimental poetics of Father Gerard Manley Hopkins.

There is an allusion (in lines 17 and 21) to Socrates' tale of cave-dwelling souls in Plato's *Republic* (one of Warren's novels, published in 1959, was entitled *The Cave*). The sunset and high summer are symbols, respectively, of the poet's old age and poetic ripeness for communion with nature (such a communion is symbolized by the merging of "the lost spring" with the "summer, that is").

Themes and Meanings

"Fear and Trembling" is about an old poet's desire to commune with nature and his doubts about his ability and poetry's power to do so at a time in his life when an inner energy makes him ripe for poetic creation and communion with nature.

The poem is a modern American Romantic poem, following a well-established literary tradition of searching in nature for meaning in life and worrying about the possibility and authenticity of a poetic communion with nature. William Wordsworth and Samuel Taylor Coleridge spearheaded this doubt-ridden Romantic quest for the truths of nature in English poetry; others, such as Thomas Hardy, renewed it in the later nineteenth century, and Robert Frost transported it starkly and darkly to the twentieth century New England scene. Warren continued the Romantic quest, vacillating between affirmation and questioning.

Cleanth Brooks, in *Modern Poetry and the Tradition* (1965), remarked on Warren's preoccupation (as early as 1939) with the theme of knowledge and noted those flashes of pessimism that elucidate the limits of human knowledge in poems of his later years: "A number of Warren's poems . . . concern themselves with explorations of the problem of knowledge. . . . The absolutes are gone—are dissolved, indeed, by our consciousness of a plurality of histories and meanings."

Thomas M. Curley

THE FEELINGS

Author: Sharon Olds (1942-   )
Type of poem: Elegy
First published: 1991; collected in *The Father,* 1992

The Poem

"The Feelings" is a forty-one-line poem in free verse, artistically recounting the poet's feelings immediately following her father's death. It is highly personal and familial, as are many of Sharon Olds's poems. Written in the first person and past tense, the experience seems fixed, inevitable, available to retrospective analysis. The poem begins in a hospital room, the poet watching as an intern "listened" to her father's stopped heart, and concludes with the poet contemplating the meaning of life the following morning as her husband lies atop her. The "feelings" include physical sensations—such as her father's "faintly moist" face and hair "like a wolf's"—and emotional and philosophical reactions to the father's death.

Inasmuch as it recounts her reaction to her father's death and moves her beyond that death, "The Feelings" may be considered an elegy. However, unlike traditional elegies such as John Milton's "Lycidas," Percy Bysshe Shelley's "Adonais," or Matthew Arnold's "Rugby Chapel," there is no recounting of the wonderful qualities of the deceased or sorrow at the loss of this positive force in the world. Olds's father apparently deserved no such praise (a conclusion bolstered by references to him in other Olds poems). Nor was he a figure to arouse intense hatred, as is found, for instance, in Sylvia Plath's "Daddy." He was more of a nonentity, whose claim to attention is that he was the poet's father.

The poem moves through a series of relationships. In the first six lines, Olds's intimate relationship to her father contrasts with the alien presence of the intern. The poet, realizing her father is dead, stares at the intern "as if he or I/ were wild, were from some other world." The loss of her father seems to threaten the poet's identity and makes her unnaturally wary of others. The alienation of poet and intern broadens in lines 7 to 17 to include "everyone else in the room," presumably other hospital personnel, who mistakenly—according to the poem—believe in the Christian God and who believe that the body on the bed is only a "shell" from which the spirit has departed; the poet alone knows her father is "entirely gone."

In lines 18 to 21, Olds imagines herself, in the Eskimo tradition, letting her father float away in the "death canoe"; in lines 29 to 34, she imagines herself accompanying him to the crematorium and touching his ashes to her tongue, but in reality she walks out of the hospital room and does not attend him. Lines 34 to 41 add an interesting postscript, in which Olds returns to a living relationship. The poet is under her husband's body the next morning, which crushes her "sweetly," holding her "hard to this world." This sensual image is likened to a fruit, with tears coming out "like juice and sugar." This image is then tied back to the death of her father as the fruit's "skin thins and breaks and rips." The last two lines suggest recognition, if not acceptance, of this immutable mortal destiny: "there are/ laws on this earth and we live by them."

Forms and Devices

In a strong juxtaposition of contrasts, this poem is at once sensual and philosophical, concrete and abstract. The father's silent heart, the poet's wet face, their dry lips, and the weight of the husband's body all locate the poem firmly in the physical world. The dissonance between the poet's atheism and the Christian beliefs of other people in the "death chamber," as well as the conclusion—"there are/ laws on this earth and we live by them"—make this poem a philosophical disquisition.

Another forceful contrast is the relationship between death, with her father, and life, with her husband (the latter also associated with procreation). The paradox of juxtaposed life and death appears succinctly in the image of the fruit, which is crushed "sweetly," where tears are like juice and sugar, and where they come out to be tasted only as "the skin thins and breaks and rips." In some ways, this "contrarieties of life" paradox is similar to the paradox in John Keats's "Ode on Melancholy," where "in the very temple of Delight/ Veil'd Melancholy has her sovran shrine."

In another contrasting juxtaposition, Olds shares a physical intimacy with both dead father and living husband. She "held hard" to her father's foot, "felt the dryness of his lips under/ [her] lips," and "felt his hair rush through [her] fingers." She imagines herself at the crematorium, touching "his ashes in their warmth" and bringing her "finger to [her] tongue." This intimacy with the dead father provides continuity and contrast with the image of her "husband's body on [her]/ crushing [her] sweetly." Ironically, the live husband does not demonstrate any more life than the dead father: In this poem, he is just a sweet, crushing weight. However, these two bodies are not the focus of the poem; as springboards for the poet's ruminations, they serve their purpose silently.

All these paradoxes enhance the sense of mystery about death and its meaning, which in turn illustrates the paradox of life itself: It is a sweet fruit and a fragile container that, at some moment, will inevitably burst into death ("tears" and "sugar"). The extensive use of paradox appropriately conveys the wide, even irreconcilable, range of the feelings expressed in the poem.

Themes and Meanings

The many faces of Olds's relationship to her father are represented in over fifty poems in *The Father* and in many other poems by Olds published before and after. One of her fortes is poetry about relationships—she has written numerous poems about, for instance, her son, her daughter, her husband, and her elder sister. Curiously, although Olds's mother is occasionally mentioned in her poetry, her father seems to be, by far, her most animating subject. This must be due, in part, to Olds's implied model of conception, in which personhood originates in a single sperm (with the father) while the mother presumably serves as a sort of incubator. Thus, Olds the author/poet is authored by her father, making her connection to him uniquely significant.

Putting dozens of poems in a nutshell, Olds appears to be entranced with the idea of "the father" but rather disappointed with the actual model allotted her. The moments of tenderness between them primarily take place without mutual conscious intention—as in the many poems in which Olds treats her dying and unconscious father with tenderness. He is matter, revered for having cast her into the world, connected by the mystery of biology, and valued as such despite failing by the usual measures of fatherhood: According to other poems, for instance, he was an alcoholic, thrown out of the house by Olds's mother to a chorus of cheers from the children. Olds's treatment of her father as more matter than person achieves succinct expression in "The Dead Body," where she refers to him as "this man who had so little consciousness, who was/ 90% his body."

In "The Feelings," the idealized concept of "the father" supersedes the actual relationship to the dead man in the room. That he has stopped breathing seems to make it easier for Olds to treat him as more of a concept than a person of mostly unpleasant traits. Furthermore, the father's absence of personhood as defined by an interesting set of conscious characteristics—"personality"—makes him interesting in only two ways: as a piece of matter and as Olds's father. In that sense, Olds is similar to Gerard Manley Hopkins's character Margaret ("Spring and Fall"), who, while lamenting "goldengrove unleaving" (the leaves falling in autumn), is unconsciously lamenting her own mortality. Olds does not describe a person worth caring for because of positive attributes; therefore, her father is worth caring about only in the way that any death is significant or in the sense that this death strikes home as a reminder of Olds's own mortality—the death of her "author" foreshadows her own death.

The poem ends on a note of heroic stoicism. The author has stared death in the face—her father's and, vicariously, her own—has admitted the laws of this earth, and continues on. At first, "The Feelings" seems to be about a unique and intimate relationship between Olds and her father. Their closeness contrasts with the alien presence of the hospital personnel. Since Olds's father lacks a necessary personhood to qualify as "other," however, this poem takes on a more solipsistic note. In the end, it is Olds alone who faces the bittersweet world. Her only intimate connection to the rest of humanity is that everyone lives under the same law of mortality.

Scott E. Moncrieff

FELIX RANDAL

Author: Gerard Manley Hopkins (1844-1889)
Type of poem: Sonnet
First published: 1918, in *Poems of Gerard Manley Hopkins, Now First Published, with Notes by Robert Bridges*

The Poem

"Felix Randal" is a sonnet with an Italian or Petrarchan rhyme scheme (*abba, abba, ccd, ccd*); although not published until 1918, it was written in 1880. The title character is known from extrinsic evidence to have been a thirty-one-year-old blacksmith named Felix Spencer, who died of pulmonary tuberculosis; Father Gerard Manley Hopkins, while a curate in a slum parish in Liverpool, visited him often, administered the last sacraments, and officiated at his funeral.

Hence the poem is largely romantic self-expression. There is little or no ironic separation between the "I" (the speaker within the poem) and the author (the historical Hopkins outside the poem), so the "I" may be taken as a Roman Catholic priest reflecting on the news of Randal's death.

His reflections begin with an objective recollection of the facts of the sad case, but after the apparently laconic generalization of line 9, the poem breaks into a gripping personal cry of loss. Then the poem offers a lovely image of the dead friend enjoying the prime of his short life.

The first four lines react to the news that the blacksmith has died. Lines 2 to 9 are interior monologue, spoken by the speaker to himself. The speaker realizes that Felix Randal's death means the end of dutiful visiting, the end of watching the man's decline from outstanding vigor into bodily debility and periods of insanity as four ailments (tuberculosis and three attendant "complications," among them a fever that makes his mind wander) fight it out to see which disorder can kill this prize victim.

The next quatrain casts further back in the history of the illness as the speaker recalls the patient's initial impatience and denial. The anointing in line 5 was the church sacrament now called the Sacrament of the Sick, then known as Extreme Unction. Months before that, after Randal's initial stage of cursing and denial, the priest had first administered the other two of the three "last sacraments," Penance (confession) and the Eucharist. The priest's impromptu prayer recapitulates the reprieve granted in confession.

After eight lines of speaking objectively about Felix Randal in the third-person-singular "he," the ninth line is a generalization about the bond of affection that grows between the patient and a priest who comes regularly to visit. At this point a sedate, well-behaved, almost dull poem leaps to life. The little phrase "child, Felix, poor Felix Randal" is the emotional center and high point of the sonnet.

The final three lines raise an enduring image over the farrier's grave: Felix at the height of his physical vigor, the human correlative of the huge draft-horses which he shoes so effortlessly.

Forms and Devices

The sentence structure follows the sonnet's Italian or Petrarchan rhyme scheme (*abba, abba, ccd, ccd*), forming four self-contained statements. The rhythm is accentual hexameter (modeled on Anglo-Saxon and Middle-English prototypes); only the accented syllables count in the scansion, and there may be any number of unaccented syllables. Hopkins believed that the English iambic pentameter line of ten relatively short syllables was too "narrow," too light and short, relative to its Italian model in which each line had eleven relatively long syllables, so he experimented with many different formal adjustments to try to bring the English sonnet into conformity with the Italian model.

The first image that needs special comment is "mould" (line 2). In Hopkins's poetry, the word sometimes refers to shape, sometimes to earth and burial. Here, "mould" comprises both Felix Randal's shape of body and the vulnerability of that body to disease, death, and burial. The four fatal "disorders, fleshed" in Felix's body may therefore be taken as symbols of the sinful, mortal, fleshly, earthly aspect of Felix (and of Everyman and Everywoman).

Next, grace impacts the world of the poem, that of traditional Roman Catholic belief and practice, through the sacraments—three of which appear explicitly. As the old name suggests, Extreme Unction was not given until death was imminent. A deeper flashback then recalls the "reprieve and ransom" Father Hopkins had "tendered" to Felix; these are the sacraments of Penance (confession), by which the penitent is reprieved from the judgment he faced, and the Eucharist (Communion), where the communicant receives the very Body of Christ, the ransom given on the cross in the passion and on the altar at Mass: "the Man Christ Jesus, who gives Himself as ransom for all" (1 Timothy 2:5-6; see also Mark 10:45). Hence the "tongue" and "touch" of line 10 refer less to comforting talk and handshakes and more to the sacramental form (the ritual formula of words) and matter (the action of anointing with oil, the blessing hand of the priest absolving the penitent in confession, the tendering of the consecrated host of bread)—the three sacraments Father Hopkins administered to the dying Felix Randal.

Also in line 10, however, the two uses of the auxiliary verb "had" imply that Hopkins believed that he failed to comfort Felix Randal as much as he wished: Hopkins bestowed the sacraments, but he did not possess the right "bedside manner" for a bluff working man such as Felix and never effectively communicated how dear Felix was to him. Yet in the same line 10, one notes the emergence of the intimate second-person singular; the reader is reminded that in the context of the poem's casual dialect, "thou" expresses intimacy and informality.

The word "boisterous" in line 12 suggests much about the farrier's earlier life. Boisterousness denotes great energy and connotes noise and lack of restraint, a kind of unbridled excess of animal vitality neither wicked nor quite human; in other poems, Hopkins calls a river "boisterously beautiful" and describes the wind on a sunny day as a "bright wind boisterous." The word may provide a clue to the poet's choice of "Randal" as the dead man's last name. Three words in the poem echo it. "Ransom" (line 7) names the cure the blacksmith found in Christ. By contrast, "ramble" (line 3) and "random" (line 13) might suggest the farrier's faults of character. He is errant and unshaped, astray and haphazard; "random" can even name a disorderly life. Further, the British "randy," or guilty of excess, might echo in the surname Randal.

Themes and Meanings

In the Liverpool slums, the classics scholar Hopkins was as far removed from his natural habitat (the university and the seminary) as Felix Randal was from his (the forge) when he lay in his sickbed. The two dislocations brought the two men together in a totally unpredictable friendship—"How far from then forethought of"—and a deep religious relationship of father and child, of tiny Father Hopkins, barely five feet tall and scarcely a hundred pounds, and "child, Felix, poor Felix Randal," the giant blacksmith dwindling to death.

The two were bound together by the three sacraments of Penance, Eucharist, and Extreme Unction, known collectively as "the Last Sacraments," since their reception accompanies life's end. Since three is traditionally the number of the heaven archetype and four the number of the earth archetype, the three sacraments and the "fatal four disorders" of the poem may suggest the underlying theme of the poem: As the "mould of man" pines and dies, the graced spirit mends, finds holy friendship, and comes more to life. This poem suggests no Puritan, platonic, or Oriental rejection of materiality, for the sacraments to which Hopkins mainly attributes the transformation are insistently material, and one's last glimpse of Felix Randal shows him totally involved with the material world. Felix is depicted in the prime of his energy, nearly innocent even in his sins, physically preeminent in a crowd of other muscular laboring men, easily managing the huge gray Shire horses of the English midlands—the largest horses in the world, larger than the Clydesdales of the north, the Suffolks of the east, the Belgians, Percherons, and other breeds of the continent—as conspicuous among ordinary carriage and saddle horses as Felix is among ordinary workmen. Since the horse symbolizes masculine libido, the poem celebrates both Felix Randal's final achievement of self-possession and (as a horse trots noisily on new steel sandals down the cobblestone street of the reader's imagination) the ultimate felicity which verified his given name, Felix.

Thomas J. Steele

FELLOW DINERS

Author: Yannis Ritsos (1909-1990)
Type of poem: Lyric
First published: 1972, in *Muted Poems*; English translation collected in *Exile and Return: Selected Poems, 1967-1974*, 1985

The Poem

"Fellow Diners" is a short lyric of eight lines in free verse. The title refers to the thirteen places set for Christ and his disciples at the Last Supper.

The poem begins on a bracingly contemporary note of the modern commuter's frustration with public transit. "Endless transfers" suggests that the journey to the communal meal, which seems to have been taken by train or bus, has been arduous, fraught with delays and detours. These transfers were "unwanted," at least by the traveler, but perhaps both wanted and "willed" by those running the system.

In the face of so much systematic frustration, "suddenly" time itself "delays, holds back." The merely logistical inconvenience of transit delays has now become a metaphysical delay, halting all forward progress. The oppressive authority behind "willed" transfers is echoed in the will that "holds back" the traveler's advance.

During this hiatus, "the dead disappear," and those still present, the living, are actually "absent." This phenomenon is expressed with almost telegraphic economy: "those present: absent." The colon acts as an equal sign, showing that there is no difference between the present and the absent, the living and the dead—or what difference there is, is minimal.

In a way, then, the traveler has crossed over a boundary, from the everyday world of buses, transfers, and time schedules, into a world where these systems of order do not prevail. When he arrives at his destination, he notes that "the table is set." Everything seems to be in order. A voice invites him in, with a troubling note of superfluous reassurance: "Nothing's wrong. Come in." Yet it is this very assurance that signals that something may be very wrong indeed.

There are twelve glasses on the table. "And one more," presumably for the guest who has just entered. (The unlucky number thirteen is tactfully not mentioned.) The identity of the voice, like that of the guest, is unknown. Again the voice interrupts, this time in a tone of warning: "Still, be careful."

The reason for the warning becomes apparent in the next line: "don't step on the floor—there is no floor. Here. . . ." The line break suggests that there may be a floor elsewhere. Yet what sort of place is this, without a floor? The warning seems almost like a joke, and yet there is a surreal ring of truth to the warning. In a world of "Endless transfers" where "time delays, hold back," and "the dead disappear," anything may happen. Yet if there is no floor, what of the voice's assurance that nothing is wrong?

The next line is tautological in its structure: "those who can sit comfortably are only those." Taken by itself, this equation is a self-evident truth: Those who sit comfortably are those who sit comfortably. Like the scene itself, however, this assertion cannot be taken at face value, for what appears to be true here is not necessarily true. The final line completes the sentence by qualifying the second term of the equation. Those who sit comfortably are only those "who have eaten both of their wings and are no longer hungry." What this means exactly is left for the traveler, and the reader, to decide.

Forms and Devices

"Fellow Diners" appears in a volume entitled *Muted Poems* (1972), the tone of which, as Edmund Keeley writes in *Modern Greek Poetry: Voice and Vision* (1983), is "muted in its terror." The dramatic situation, a Last Supper, is that of imminent betrayal. The false note of reassurance—"Nothing's wrong"—in the center of the poem arouses one's suspicion, which is heightened by the disembodied voice of the host informing the guest, quite calmly, that there is no floor. That suspicion is confirmed when he just as calmly instructs the guest about what one must do to dine comfortably there. His matter-of-factness is the source of the poem's muted terror.

Perhaps the most striking aspect of "Fellow Diners" is the effortless juxtaposition of the miraculous with the everyday. Transfers and table settings give way to a room without a floor and diners who eat their own wings. Yannis Ritsos is a master of this surrealist technique. What distinguishes him from other more strident surrealists is the quiet way he goes about his work. His language is simple and direct. He dispenses with metaphor, simile, and other devices of poetic embellishment, opting instead for poetic economy. The clipped, fragmented sentences of the first six lines—expressing the hurried chaos of transfers and delays, as well as the fragmented society the poem addresses—finally roll out in the fluid, if perplexing, image in the last lines.

The perplexing image of the diners eating their own wings is stated as factually as the number of glasses on the table. This tone is appropriate, since in the surrealist view there is no clear distinction between the rational and the irrational or between reality as one commonly thinks of it and that super-reality that is grasped through imaginative apperception.

Themes and Meanings

Muted Poems appeared in 1972, one of seven volumes Ritsos published that year. Ritsos had always been a prolific poet, but that year's output had a special cause. Since 1967, his work had been banned in Greece by the Georgios Papadopoulos dictatorship, and he was imprisoned or living in exile under house arrest on the island of Samos until 1972, when the official policy of censorship eased, allowing his poetry to be published again.

"Fellow Diners" is one of the poems written in exile. Its meaning is political rather than religious, in spite of the biblical situation. As a Marxist committed to political comment, Ritsos was not interested in religion itself but in redefining the cultural heritage of Greece, both pagan and Christian, in a way that would be useful and significant for the common man of modern Greece. The story of the Last Supper would be a familiar drama of betrayal, to which Ritsos could draw certain political parallels in his own time. If anything, the poem criticizes the church by suggesting that it has its own brand of hypocrisy and corruption not unlike that of the Papadopoulos dictatorship.

By giving the poem a contemporary setting, Ritsos is granting the story of Christ's betrayal, foretold at the Last Supper, a decidedly secular interpretation. Only the number of glasses invites the reader to make the parallel. The diners are unidentified, so who is supposed to be Christ and who Judas? For a religious reading of the poem, that would be a vital question. For a political reading, it hardly matters. The diners' anonymity, indeed, is a functional ambiguity, since the political situation in Greece during the late 1960's was so confused as to make it difficult to identify friend from foe, betrayer from betrayed.

The political reading, however, clarifies much in the poem that at first appears enigmatic. The systematic transfers of a dictatorship bogged down in "willed" bureaucracy is symptomatic of the halted advance of the society. The inconvenience with individuals, such as Ritsos's own imprisonment, is minor in comparison with the social standstill of an entire nation. More serious is the political persecution in which the dead literally "disappear," and those who are still visible are "absent"—if not physically then morally—in the climate of repression.

Still, there will always be those who claim that "Nothing's wrong," that there is always room for "one more" at the table of the ruling party, as long as one is willing to ignore the fact that fellow diners have no floor to stand on. As long as one is willing to give up freedom, he or she will be well fed, or at least "no longer hungry," for the price of admission is to eat one's own wings.

Ritsos was unwilling to engage in such self-destructive hypocrisy and paid for it with his physical freedom. In exile, he was not allowed to sit at the table of the ruling party because he refused to stop publishing or renounce his own writings; in other words, he refused to eat his own words, which were his wings, the essence of his freedom. "Fellow Diners" is a testament to the fact that he refused to imitate those who had willingly "eaten both of their wings." There are more important liberties than the freedom of the body or the freedom from hunger, such as the freedom of the spirit, which must sometimes suffer exile in order to speak the truth.

Richard Collins

FERN HILL

Author: Dylan Thomas (1914-1953)
Type of poem: Lyric
First published: 1945; collected in *Deaths and Entrances*, 1946

The Poem

The speaking voice belongs to a male adult recalling his childhood and its inevitable end. "Fern Hill" re-creates and communicates the experience of a child who (for the first part of the poem) has not yet grown into historical awareness and who consequently lives in an eternal present in the Garden of Eden ("it was Adam and maiden" and "the sun grew round that very day," lines 30 and 32).

The boy's life is composed of repetitions of the cycles of nature, so to him there seems to be no passage of time; from his adult vantage point, however, he realizes that time was toying with him ("time let me," he says in lines 4 and 13) until, inevitably, it exiled him from the privileged land of childhood.

In a casual, conversational tone, the poem begins by introducing the innocent boy in the context of a "middle landscape" composed of nature, the cultivation of domesticated plants and animals, and the art of song (the "lilting house") in a small Welsh valley with wooded sides (a "dingle"). Because he still lives in the innocent world of the fairy tale ("once below a time"), he has the power of a lord to command the trees and leaves, to have them do his will. This time of life, as the poet idealizes it, is a windfall—an undeserved and unexpected boon, like a ripe apple that has blown off a tree on a stranger's property and that the hungry passerby has a right to take and eat.

The second stanza reinforces the picture of the first with different images. The boy lives in happy unison with the domesticated calves and the wild foxes; time passes musically, like the eternal Sabbath, as the instrument the boy plays consorts in a single hymn with the voices of the singing animals.

Stanza 3 presents a capsule summary of the days in the boy's life and of his experience of falling asleep every night. The owls and nightjars, two sorts of nocturnal birds, seem to carry the farm off (the "ricks" are well-built haystacks), and the horses seem to escape from him.

The next stanza, appropriately, presents the experience of awakening. The farm returns, with the crowing rooster on "his" shoulder, like a sailor coming home with a parrot he has trained to talk. This new day is, as always, the first day in a brand-new world in which God has created the animals afresh.

The next stanza begins the breakdown of the illusory world of the eternal present. The boy's "heedless ways" have kept him ignorant of a central fact of human life—that because time is like the Pied Piper, childhood innocence is ephemeral, and the experience of graceless adulthood is inevitable. The final stanza offers a brief account of the end of childhood, a sort of rising in space or falling asleep in which the child dies to his childhood and the farm departs forever; yet both survive in the form of poetry.

Forms and Devices

The poem is composed of six nine-line stanzas that rhyme (mostly with slant rhymes) *abcddabcd*. The lines have a very flexible accentual rhythm. Lines 1, 2, 6, and 7 have six accents each; lines 3, 4, 8, and 9 have three accents; and line 5 usually has four accents.

Dylan Thomas ties the poem together effectively with strong verbal formulas. The "I" is described as "young and easy," "green and carefree," "green and golden," and finally "green and dying." Furthermore, he is "happy as the grass was green," "singing as the farm was home," and "happy as the heart was long"; he is "honoured among wagons," "famous among the barns," "blessed among stables," and "honoured among foxes and pheasants." His adversary, time, is also accorded verbal formulas: "Time let me hail and climb/ Golden in the heydays of his eyes"; "Time let me play and be/ Golden in the mercy of his means"; "time allows/ . . . so few and such morning songs." There are other formulaic systems to charm the ear, such as the conversational "Now as I was," "And as I was," and "Oh as I was"; the spatial "About the lilting house" and "About the happy yard"; and the temporal "All the sun long" and "All the moon long."

The color scheme is pervasive and insistent. Implied or explicit, it portrays the Edenic color scheme of nature and its growing things: green, golden, yellow, white, and blue. Even fire is "green as grass." Green is the most pervasive color, with gold second, as is appropriate for a poem about childhood ripening into adulthood.

There are delightful images, such as the half-concealed list of the four elements in lines 20-22 ("fields," "air," "watery," and "fire"). The eternal day of creation (Genesis 1:3-4, 16-18) is elegantly described as a time and place in the passage "So it must have been after the birth of the first simple light/ In the first spinning place." God sets the sun spinning in a place called "day"; God the Creator spins the cosmos out of chaos as a woman spins a strong, even thread from a random mass of raw cotton or wool or flax, then to weave it into the fabric of the material world.

Themes and Meanings

The "I" of the poem begins in innocence, the young Adam of the new world. As he experiences it, his correlative is as innocent as he, whether that be the farm or the princess, who is "maiden" rather than "Eve" because (as Genesis 3:20 states) the latter name means "giver of life" or "mother of all the living." Saint Augustine of Hippo said that history began only after the Original Sin, so the child's world seems timeless, a new world freshly created at each dawn.

As in many Renaissance poems (William Shakespeare's Sonnets 18, 55, 65, and 116, for example), time is the enemy, but for the Renaissance reader, Father Time was Cronos (Saturn), who in Greek myth devoured all of his own children. In Thomas's poem, time is a temporarily benevolent despot, "allowing" and "permitting" the child a time of perfect happiness before he sacrifices his own progeny to the demands of his cannibalistic nature.

At the beginning of the final stanza, Thomas uses a very private and obscure symbol: The lamblike child ascends to the loft of the barn at moonrise and sleeps to awaken no longer innocent, no longer childlike, alienated from the farm and from nature—expelled from Eden. Thus far, the reader may choose to understand this as a symbol of sexual experience of some sort. The episode involves bird symbols as well, however, and these the reader may well interpret as symbols of poetry—swallows, the implied owls and nightjars from the earlier episode of literal sleep (lines 23-27), and the moon herself as mistress of the creative imagination (like the fairy queen, Titania, in Shakespeare's *A Midsummer Night's Dream*, c. 1595-1596). A child does not compose the songs of childhood. Only an adult can do so, for only the adult is thematically possessed of his own past history. Under the influence of the moon of imagination, the sea rises and falls; although a repressive king-figure (Father Time, the god Cronos, the Persian despot Xerxes, or the Danish King Canute of Britain) can attempt to chain the sea, he will not succeed. Hence, the perennial human symbol of expulsion from the limited Eden of newly created innocence also symbolizes the initiation into the more fully human and creative world of mature experience.

When the sea "sing[s] in its chains," therefore, it does not sing only the green, white, and golden world of Fern Hill, it also sings the green and dying world of the mortal adult. Like a ritual incantation, the poem "Fern Hill" re-creates for the reader the Eden of boyhood, its loss, and its retrieval. Whenever the poem is read and for as long as it takes to read it, the paradise of Fern Hill exists again, is lost again, and is regained.

Thomas J. Steele

A FEW THINGS EXPLAINED

Author: Pablo Neruda (Neftalí Ricardo Reyes Basoalto, 1904-1973)
Type of poem: Lyric
First published: 1937, as "Explico algunas cosas," in *España en el corazón*; English translation collected in *Selected Poems of Pablo Neruda*, 1961

The Poem

"A Few Things Explained" is a lyric poem written in free verse in which the poet directly addresses the reader in an attempt both to explain why his poetry has become more sociopolitical and to denounce the Nationalist side of the Spanish Civil War.

The seventy-nine-line, twelve-stanza poem can be divided into four sections. The first section consists of the first two stanzas. In the first of these, the poet anticipates questions his reader might have concerning the rather sudden and radical change his poetry has undergone. "You will ask," he writes, "And where are the lilacs?" The five-line stanza of questions is followed by a one-line stanza that introduces the poet's answer to his reader, as he writes, "I'll tell you how matters stand with me."

The second section, consisting of four long stanzas, tells how things were when the poet lived for a time in Spain, on the outskirts of Madrid. He speaks of how his house was called " 'the house with the flowers,'" a happy house, he implies, frequented by small children, as well as some of Spain's most famous poets, among them Federico García Lorca. He goes on to tell about his neighborhood and its teeming marketplace, characterized by "all the avid/ quintessence of living." Virtually every image in this section suggests life, the day-to-day activities of living, happiness and plenitude.

This positive atmosphere is in sharp contrast with that presented in the third section of the poem, a section of five stanzas that tell of the bloody civil war that interrupted the happiness of the previous scene. This section begins with one of the strongest poetic fulcrums to be found in Pablo Neruda's poetry. Immediately following the section of positive images, the poet begins a stanza that reads: "Till one morning everything blazed:/ one morning bonfires/ sprang out of earth/ and devoured all the living." This fire, and "the blood and the gunpowder," the poet implies, are all Spain has experienced since civil war broke out.

The poet goes on to describe those he blames for the war, those, he says, who have come "out of the clouds to a slaughter of innocents." The perpetrators of this slaughter are, he implies, the Nationalist troops and their supporters; "jackals abhorred by the jackal!" he calls them. In the fourth and fifth stanzas of this section, he actually turns his attention from the reader and directly addresses the Nationalists, telling them at one point, "see the death of my house,/ look well at the havoc of Spain." He follows this with a promise that although the Nationalists may win in the short run, they will pay for their treatment of Spain and its people in the long run ("out of your turpitude, bullets are born/ that one day will strike for the mark/ of your hearts").

The fourth and final section of the poem functions as a coda. The first of the two stanzas that make up this section returns the poet's address to the reader and repeats the essence of the content of the first stanza of the poem, as in it the poet anticipates the reader's questions about the change in his poetry. The final stanza provides an answer in miniature to that question, as the poet simply states three times, "Come see the blood in the streets."

Forms and Devices

Given its political subject matter, its declarative intent, and, in particular, its strong and unmitigated political message, "A Few Things Explained" is a poem that could have fallen easily into the category of literature that sacrifices art for message. Neruda, however, has not allowed that to happen, for while the poem's message is indeed clear, the poem is as artful as its message is strong.

One of the things that Neruda does to lift his poem above the potentially prosaic reality of its subject matter is to rely heavily on telling nouns and equally telling adjectives while almost eliminating (or at least making only very limited use of) verbs. This makes the poem read more like a list than a fully detailed description of people, places, and events. The reader still receives the information, but the vehicle that conveys the information is both more poetic and more subtle than outright and direct description. For example, when the poet describes his neighborhood before the war, virtually all his description is in the form of a series of nouns and adjectives that suggest normal, day-to-day life, happiness and plenitude: "a wild pandemonium/ of fingers and feet overflowing the streets,/ meters and liters, all the avid/ quintessence of living." The poet continues, "fish packed in the stands,/ a contexture of roofs in the chill of the sun/ where the arrowpoints faltered;/ potatoes, inflamed and fastidious ivory,/ tomatoes again and again to the sea." This series of images not only paints a vivid picture of the marketplace in question, but also does so in a more poetic and perhaps even more vivid fashion than standard prose description might have been able to do.

The above images contrast strongly (and contrast is another of the poet's devices in this poem) with those that follow, which describe the situation after war breaks out. Once again, Neruda resorts to suggestive images rather than straightforward description, at first limiting his description of the war to three essential images: fire, blood, and gunpowder. Even when he discusses the Nationalist troops and their supporters, he does not name names or groups, for the most part, but instead alludes to them by means of images that suggest their identities: "Bandits in airplanes," he writes, suggesting the help of Adolf Hitler's Germany in the war; "marauders with seal rings and duchesses," alluding to the monarchy; and "black friars and brigands signed with the cross," suggesting the Catholic church.

The poet's reliance on image is evident as well in the stanza in which he promises that the victims shall be avenged in the future. "Out of dead houses," he writes, "it is metal that blazes/ in place of the flowers." He warns the Nationalists that from their actions "bullets are born/ that one day will strike for the mark/ of your hearts."

Finally, one of the most poetic passages of Neruda's poem is also probably its most famous. The final stanza, as stated above, provides a compact answer to the question

"Why has Neruda's poetry changed?" The answer is, simply, "Come see the blood in the streets," but Neruda repeats it three times, each time dividing the sentence (with respect to lines) differently from the time (or times) before. The repetition emphasizes the answer, and the variations suggest movement, perhaps much like that of the blood itself. This suggestion, through repetition and line division, not only makes the final stanza more poetic, but also takes the poem and its reader one step closer to the horrible reality the poet seeks to describe.

Themes and Meanings

As stated above, in "A Few Things Explained" Neruda attempts both to explain why his poetry has become more sociopolitical and to denounce the Nationalist side of the Spanish Civil War.

Neruda's poetry in the late 1930's, and particularly in *España en el corazón* (1937, "Spain in the heart"), of which "A Few Things Explained" forms a part, was indeed different from the poetry for which the poet was known until that time. The vast majority of his earlier poetry was very personal, interior, concerned often with metaphysical issues, such as the question of existence in the modern, chaotic world. It was largely hermetic, aloof poetry, in both expression and theme. The poet's experience in Spain at the beginning of the Civil War, however, radically changed his life and, consequently, his poetry. Rather suddenly he was less interested, for example, in metaphysical questions and far more concerned with issues of social and political justice, and this was reflected in his poetry. "A Few Things Explained" explains the reasons for this change.

The poet does not miss the opportunity, while explaining the reasons for the change in his poetry, to cast blame for the Civil War, and his attitude toward the Nationalists could not be clearer. He does not simply paint them as the ones at fault, but instead goes a step further, portraying them as "bandits," "jackals," and "turncoats" who slaughter innocent children. This poem and the volume of which it is a part (*España en el corazón*) were so well thought of by the Republican side of the conflict that the Republican Army had the book reprinted in 1938, complete with a dedicatory note from the army.

In spite of the potentially prosaic subject matter and the blatant political purpose of Neruda's poem, "A Few Things Explained" is every bit as poetic a work as it is a work of political statement. It stands as a major poem in Neruda's vast repertoire because of these elements and because of the turning point it marks in the poet's life and career.

Keith H. Brower

FIELD WORK

Author: Seamus Heaney (1939-   )
Type of poem: Lyric
First published: 1979, in *Field Work*

The Poem

"Field Work" is a love poem in four parts. It begins with a reasonably traditional joining of nature poetry and love poetry, seems to call itself into question, then resolves in an act of human contact and an assertion of the "perfection" of the beloved. The beloved is unidentified. So, too, is the landscape, although most of the details—"sally" or willow trees, furze, wildflowers, and currant shrubs—fit the Wicklow countryside often evoked in the book from which the poem comes (and to which the poem gives its title). Seamus Heaney often writes about the work on the Derry farm of his childhood, so the title of the poem at first suggests another evocation of farming; the "field work" here, however, amounts to a kind of peeling away of mistaken vision and literary allusion in order to find the actuality of the beloved.

Part 1 of the poem seems to be an observation of an idealized landscape of green ferns, breeze-rustled trees, and "perfect" nesting birds. The poet's vision is sharp enough to focus on a particular and apparently unromantic, unpastoral detail: a vaccination mark on the upper arm of an as-yet-undefined "you." A train comes by to interrupt the poet's vision—indeed, to block his line of sight—and to intrude a harsh "coal smell" into the bucolic scene. The poet's eye is echoed by the "perfect eye" of "nesting blackbirds" and the "big" eye of cattle on the passing train.

Part 2 begins with a surprise: The vaccination mark so carefully seen in part 1 now seems to be an error; the beloved's vaccination is not on her upper arm but on her thigh. The possibility that vision has been distorted by a kind of literary learning arises when the poet seems almost to argue with himself as to whether the woman he watches is woman or dryad, human or a mythological wood-nymph. The smells that seemed such an intrusion in part 1 return more pleasantly, as a "mothering smell"—but, troublingly, one that arises apparently from a pile of old and rotting wood.

The poet's eye or mind shifts to the moon, sadly to be seen only at a distance and in fact only remembered, not seen (the rest of the poem occurs in daylight, as far as one can tell). There is another suggestion of distortion, as well, in the image of the round coin nailed to the mast of the *Pequod* by Herman Melville's Captain Ahab in *Moby Dick* (1851)—a prize for whoever first sights the great white whale. The ship's officers look upon the coin and "interpret" it very differently, each according to his disposition and background. But the coin here seems to represent not the variousness of human understanding, but constancy; it remains "brilliant" despite the ship's long voyage "across Atlantic and Pacific waters."

Interestingly, when Heaney decided whether to include the poem in the substantial collection *Selected Poems, 1966-1987* (1990), he omitted this part of the poem and reprinted only parts 1, 3, and 4. Perhaps the denial of the first two lines of the section made the first part seem too opaque; or perhaps, given its invocation of dryads and Captain Ahab, the whole section seemed too literary and allusive.

Part 3 makes another sudden jump, from the imagined world of the *Pequod* into the messy reality of nature, in the form of mud slicks, weedy water, and leaves. Yet the poem insists that these are "not" what the poet and the poem wish to draw our attention to. After nine lines of negatives—a prolonged and insistent effort to direct and focus the reader's and the poet's unreliable vision—the poem turns the reader's eyes toward what it *does* want its audience to see: a single flower, a sunflower "braced" to a wall to support its great height. It is "all mouth and eye"—the O which is the center of its blossom dominates the petals of the flower; puzzlingly, it is "dreaming umber"—a word that will reappear more comprehensibly at the poem's end. Unlike the mess of mud, reminiscent of the ring-wormed chestnuts in part 2, in the section's opening lines, the flower stands apparently alone and aloof, suggesting a love that can withstand and indeed deny the muddy actualities of life. Yet the wall it stands against is "pebble-dashed" and thus like the water full of "pock-marked" leaves in the first stanza of the section, suggesting that such beauty and certainty must be seen within a context of disorder.

In part 4, the poem consists of three sentences spread out over twenty lines of poetry. The poem, as if to prepare its audience by contrast for the assertion of the final lines, reaches a low point of unpleasantness: a smell again, this time the "cat-piss smell" of the blossom of a currant shrub, unlike the sunflower of part 3 in that it is pink. Now the poet no longer relies upon the dubious and often distorted eye; he makes physical contact, touching the beloved for the first time in the poem, to place a moldy thumbprint on her hand, another O-shape, now not like a vaccination mark but like a birthmark, umber like the dream of the sunflower. The final lines are a clear and direct assertion of love:

> you are stained, stained
> to perfection.

The image both contains and conquers much of the poem's unpleasantness; the mark is a stain but also a sign of love. It may just be that the stain is necessary; it is what makes the perfection. Perhaps love requires such acts of possession.

Forms and Devices

The poem operates mostly as plain speech, avoiding decorative language and only occasionally (in the allusiveness of the dryad and the doubloon, for example) demanding some learning on the part of the reader. What is more relevant to the poem's working its way toward the final assertion is some firsthand knowledge of nature; perhaps that is the "field work" (the work of the naturalist) to which the title refers. The four sections do not follow any fixed stanza pattern and eschew all rhyme; parts 1 and 3 employ free-verse tercets but differ in line length (part 1 employs a line of ten to twelve syllables, while part 3 varies much more, from four to ten syllables). Part 2 is arranged in unrhymed couplets, ranging from six to ten syllables per line. Part 4 is one continuous stanza, unrhymed and with short free-verse lines (three to six syllables). Offsetting this apparent randomness are recurrent metaphoric and actual instances of the shape of an O, which appears variously as a vaccination mark, a bird's eye, a distant moon, a doubloon, a sunflower, and finally a thumbprint on the beloved's hand. There are as well recurrent smells, not always pleasant by any means, but all likely to be encountered in a country landscape.

Yet the poem often seems at odds with itself, not only when it harps on the word "not" in part 3 but also in the apparent denial, in part 2, of the central image in part 1. In a very small space, the poem engenders a kind of tense dialogue, although the lovers do not speak to each other, and only at the very end do they touch. The poem is more enigmatic than most Heaney poems, although he is often a love poet and even more often a poet of nature—even of unpleasant and rather frightening nature, as in his famous "Death of a Naturalist."

Themes and Meanings

The poem establishes a rather puzzling context, like the "dashed" wall against which the beauty of the sunflower can be seen, in which the final lines carry, by their very clarity, comprehensibility, and directness, a force of truth and relief. The poem is also about vision and its problems, about the difficulty of seeing the beloved clearly. The eyes of the blackbirds in part 1 may be perfect, but the eye which sees the poem is clearly not. The umber mark which the poet puts on his beloved's hand is a sign and token of love, yet it is also a stain, as if he were undeserving or unworthy. The poem as a whole remains mysterious, almost as if its real subject somehow cannot quite be discussed directly.

John Hildebidle

FIGHT

Author: Federico García Lorca (1898-1936)
Type of poem: Ballad
First published: 1928, as "Reyerta," in *Romancero gitano* (1924-1927); English translation collected in *Gypsy Ballads*, 1990

The Poem

Federico García Lorca's "Fight," in Robert Havard's translation, is a short ballad narrating a fatal encounter between rival gypsies in the mountains of southern Spain. As in an ancient Greek tragedy, the story opens *in medias res*—in the middle of things—in this case, both spatially and temporally, as knives already flash half-way down a ravine. Horses rear in fury, a man named Juan Antonio of Montilla tumbles, his brow pomegranate-red with blood. A magistrate then arrives, accompanied by rural police, called "Civil Guards," and sums up the event with: "it's the same old thing again./ Four Romans have died/ and five Carthage men." The reader has witnessed, it seems, the reenactment of a centuries-old quarrel in which the identities of victims change over time while the plot remains the same.

The ballad is traditionally a sparse, dramatized narrative. Sometimes long, as in the case of epic ballads, the narrative is nevertheless sparse in the sense of providing few descriptive details and little or no commentary. In "Fight," García Lorca barely sketches in the events, and one's initial perspective on them is distant, as if one is in the mountains and suddenly, across a distance, catches the bright flash of metal, hears the scream of horses, sees a man fall, and instantly knows what has happened. The perspective shifts somewhat as the ballad names the dead man and transports the reader to the site of the encounter. These shifts add little to the reader's knowledge of the actual fight, however, while other information leads the reader to explore the meaning of this "same old story."

Knives of Albacete, the Spanish city famous for its curved blades, flash as if acting independently. Old women cry atop a tree (*lechuza*—owl—figuratively means "hag" in Spanish). A bull symbolizes fury as he clambers walls. Angels, in black robes of death, bring ice water and kerchiefs, as if they know in advance that there will be wounded. A burning cross bears away the dead man, and the afternoon itself swoons as if wounded. All the while, it seems, black angels trailing long tresses are flying about.

The spiritual, natural, and historical worlds have symbolically joined forces, each providing its share of participants. Even blood, rather than congealing as silent evidence, takes up the ancient song of the snake, which is feared by so many. The *way* in which the fight becomes a story and the poetry that makes it meaningful thus take center stage in this narrative.

Forms and Devices

Western ballads have been transmitted orally, often as songs, since the Middle Ages, when they became known in Spain as "romances," poems composed in the vernacular, romance tongue. The Spanish ballad, composed in verses eight syllables long, rhymes the same final vowels in every other line. Like most ballads, it incorporates dialogue and refrain. García Lorca adheres closely to this familiar form. "Fight" is also a rich example, however, of the kind of complex imagery that is often thought of as differentiating "high" from popular poetry and lyric from narrative. Fusing these genres was a goal García Lorca set for himself in composing *Gypsy Ballads*.

This poem tells its tale in a rapid sequence of largely visual images. Much of this poem's charm in the original is in the complex awareness produced as the regular cadence carries the body along, while unusual images hold the mind's eye in suspense. Rolfe Humphries' 1953 translation sensitively recasts lyrical mood and cadence, while Robert Havard's 1990 translation is more faithful to narrative elements such as verb tense. Two images illustrate the poem's generally complex manipulation of cultural material and its interweaving of poetic device and narrative.

The fifth verse sets the stage, bathing it in a "hard" light of playing cards. The brightness of sunlight in southern Spain can make it appear hard, while light emanating from a deck of cards might also appear hard, since its source is stiff, its outlines are crisp, and the snap of cards is as sharp as that of knives crossed in anger. In addition, the Spanish deck of cards consists of four suits: gold coins, goblets, swords and clubs. Each contains, among others, the figure of a rider on horseback; therefore, the reference to these cards leads the reader to superimpose on the figures of mounted gypsies those of the riders on the cards.

The gypsy belief that one's fate has already been written in the cards allows for isolation, through synecdoche, of the abstract concept of destiny that is inherent in the cards. Thus their light may also be "hard" because it is immutable, flooding a now tragic stage for the sake of a story that has already been told.

The twenty-fifth verse, literally "Trickled blood moans/ a mute serpent's song," is rendered by Havard as "The silent song of a snake/ in trickling blood groans." A comparison of this translation with the original reveals significant devices at work in the latter which Havard has unfortunately obscured. It is the blood, not the song, that is personified as groaning: Metonymy has transferred to his trickling blood the groans of the wounded man nearby. When this device is lost in translation, so too is the recollection of the man whose blood provides the song.

In addition, "mute" is not necessarily "silent." A groan might well be audible yet mute, in the sense of a person being unable to speak in words. Might not the song also be mute because it is a "signing" rather than a "singing"? Ancient legend has it that snakes may sing, and as the blood trickles in curves down the ravine, visually evoking a slithering snake, the mind's ear may recall that legendary serpent's song. Humphries' English version—"The slippery blood gives tongue,/ A dumb and snaky song"—is more satisfactory in this case than Havard's.

Themes and Meanings

In the same way that the ballad is brief yet dense with symbolic exchanges, the historical events of "Fight," which last only an instant, raise questions of great historical scope. A quarrel that might be no more than an anecdote soon forgotten—"the gypsies again, the same old story"—is rendered as a reenactment of centuries of violence stretching back to the first wars in Europe. This particular fight thus becomes like a refrain in a much longer ballad. One might dismiss it wearily, as the judge seems to do. He sees that this story could be rewritten, but he can only read back in time, always arriving late.

The balladeer, however, always arrives in time; the story is yet to be sung to an audience that is waiting to learn it. As this story takes shape, one is invited to repeat and learn, and also to pause and wonder: Do human beings determine their own actions, or are those actions only the repetition of historical rivalries? Would a keener attention to the refrains that human beings learn so effortlessly provide a fundamental knowledge of what drives them, as well as their stories, forward?

The force of weapons carefully crafted to kill, of myth, superstition, ubiquitous images of death upon a cross, popular belief in angels of death, a history of war after war, and rumors in the air, ever present as incitements, all play roles in the story. The perspective of the balladeer seems limited indeed on such a crowded stage. Yet that perspective has written all those actors into a form—the ballad—that is the stuff of popular song in the balladeer's culture, while saturating that form with complex imagery.

Among the worlds that come together in this ballad, therefore, are those of high poetry and of the songs that people sing without pausing to reflect upon their imagery and symbolism. "Calling . . . a sweetmeat 'bacon from heaven' or 'nun's sighs,'" said García Lorca, is a charming, clever, everyday use of Spanish. He considered popular imagery in general to be "extremely refined and marvellously sensitive."

Everyday English also makes frequent, if generally unremarked, use of poetic devices, as in "raging river," "crows' feet," "the apple of my eye." An important theme of this ballad, carried by its language, is that one may mean more than one realizes in one's everyday speech, structuring thought and the world with symbolic associations that are anything but natural.

Like most ballads, this one presents a story as if it "speaks for itself," as is often said of everyday language. Poetry, however, is not assumed to "speak for itself" in this culture. Responding to an unfamiliar convention, one discovers other stories—implied in images, symbols, legends, or traditions—that give rise and lend meaning to both fight and ballad. Poets can imply and help one to read those stories within stories. García Lorca has done so here, and as a result, a song of blood that was "mute"—but all too comprehensible to an unconscious mind—is given a voice and a body that one can consciously read, and choose to rewrite.

Julia A. Urla

FILLING STATION

Author: Elizabeth Bishop (1911-1979)
Type of poem: Lyric
First published: 1965, collected in *Questions of Travel*

The Poem

Elizabeth Bishop's "Filling Station" leads the reader in six exacting stanzas through a series of observable details to a revelation that is simultaneously gratifying and enigmatic: "Somebody loves us all." Set in the small world of an ESSO gas station, now Exxon, the poem poses the largest of theological questions, here recontextualized in the domestic terms of home and family, a preoccupation in much of Bishop's work. The speaker's initial exclamation "Oh, but it is dirty!" accurately describes the station as the details, particularly in stanzas one and two, insist. The father and his several "greasy" sons run this "family" station and, like it, they are "all quite thoroughly dirty," a state that also describes the family dog. In contrast with the family's apparent contentment, the speaker declares such dirtiness is "disturbing" if not dangerous: "Be careful with that match!" she cautions, exaggerating a wholesale conflagration.

Stanza three begins "Do they live in the station?" thus initiating a line of inquiry that will eventually bridge the distance between the speaker and the family. In this transitional stanza the location shifts to the "cement porch// behind the pumps," sufficiently domestic with its wicker sofa, dirty dog, comic books, doily, and begonia, but still open to public view. These details engage the reader's powers of deduction about the family: The wickerwork is "crushed and grease-/ impregnated" because the father and sons lounge on it, probably to thumb through the comic books on the taboret. Furthermore, the dog is allowed to settle in on the sofa. This comfortable sloppiness stands in contrast with the station's fussier details, such as the doily and the begonia, a fussiness that extends to the speaker, who wonders at these disparities but fails to reach a conclusion. The porch, neither inside nor out, neither wholly public nor wholly private, is where the poem's description must end. The uninvited eye stalls and the speaker, either traveler or passerby, concludes her ruminations.

The poem's final third begins by itemizing the speaker's questions before indulging in one last irresistible fling with description, this time of the stitches used to embroider the doily. Although parenthetical, the pause is an important one because it permits both the speaker and the reader to call up the absent "somebody," the wife and mother most likely, who is never directly mentioned. Her hand, however, is evident in the embroidered doily, the living plant, and in the neatly arranged cans of oil that whisper their reassuring "SO—SO—SO" to passing cars as well as to the speaker, who also must move on.

Forms and Devices

An accomplished painter, Bishop produced the watercolors that grace the covers of several of her books. Description, a staple in these sister arts, is both her subject and her process in the first two-thirds of the poem. Even for a casual reader of "Filling Station," Bishop's language, once filtered through her writer's eye, renders a verbal portrait so precise that the station emerges detail by detail as it is painted on the canvas of the reader's imagination. The resulting poem-as-painting is a still life in a palette of blacks and grays with "the only note of color" provided by the comic books. Ultimately, however, the poem is animated by its shifting emotional trajectory as the speaker assesses and reassesses her stance, thus giving rise to a richly ambiguous tone that draws the reader into a world of meaning far more complex than this seemingly simple encounter with the ordinary suggests.

It is the poem's perspective that permits the speaker's detachment from the family she views from a safe vantage, as if sequestered behind a two-way mirror. The initial judgments and jokes at the family's expense are sustained as late as stanza four when the taboret is referred to as "(part of the set)." Although the taboret is part of the wickerwork set, the term also suggests a facade occupied by characters rather than by real people who host an array of messy emotions. Given Bishop's typically evocative word choice, associations quickly multiply: the father and his like-minded sons are themselves a set, garbed, perhaps, in matching monkey suits, clarifying that for this speaker they are not individuals; they are, in fact, only partly human. About this her mind is set.

Even if the act of description in and of itself suggests a degree of receptivity, engagement begins when the speaker first turns to inquiry. Only a few lines later she chooses the colloquially intimate "comfy" to describe the dog, a term that would easily fit the mouths of the father and sons. This is one of several surprising tonal shifts from a speaker whose vocabulary is skewed toward formality in words such as "translucency," "impregnated," "hirsute," and "extraneous." When the questions proliferate in stanza five, they are clipped, breathy, an effect that quickens the pace as the poem prepares to rush toward its startling revelation. The three questions, a number that suggests the infinite, conclude with the exasperated "Why, oh why" that doubles back on itself to document the speaker's involvement. Since questions elicit answers, the reader also ventures a speculation or two, thus earning admittance into the extended family.

Only in the parenthetical description of the doily, however, does the speaker draw close enough to her subject, both literally and psychically, to speculate about the doily's patterns, its "daisy stitch" and "marguerites." Her conjecture calls up the hand that worked the needle, a necessary step toward de-objectifying the family. This pivotal detail catapults the speaker into the revelation in the final stanza, again proving the power of observation. Finally, both speaker and reader join the family in the inclusive and accommodating pronoun in the poem's last line, "Somebody loves us all." Thus, the speaker's journey toward engagement has also become the reader's, both finding solace in the proof of a loving hand, previously unarticulated but always hoped for.

The three two-stanza sections in "Filling Station" use an array of devices characteristic of Bishop's work, including multiple questions and exclamations, parenthetical expressions, self-corrections and qualifications, and repetitions, all of which shape a voice that is recognizably hers. These are among the techniques of the self in conversation with the self, a dialogue that convinces the speaker to abandon her own dark view and celebrate her integration into the drama of daily life.

Themes and Meanings

Famously reticent about her personal life both on and off the page, Bishop's speaker in "Filling Station" watches the father, the sons, and the family dog, although she herself remains unseen. Voyeurism, however, is not only the province of the speaker. By the poem's close the reader turns an eye on the speaker, who has revealed something of herself through her choice of recorded detail. In a rich, multilayered exploration of this theme, the watcher becomes the watched, and Bishop's readers are encouraged to step outside the poem and consider whose eye is fixed on them.

Meticulously spatial and deductive, the poem repeatedly posits the order that is the poet's process against the disorder in the messy, "oil-soaked" world of the family that, the speaker jokes, perhaps even oils the begonia instead of watering it. The theme of order allows this "little" filling station to function as a microcosm of the created world. An ordering hand, unseen but capable and beneficent, embroidered the doily, waters the plant, and arranges the rows of cans, as the poem notes, but also presumably nurtures—or fills—the father, the "saucy" sons, and even the family dog. Reasoning backwards from fact, there is evidence that the hand is a mother's; however, she is identified only as a "somebody." Her tasks, ordering and beautifying, are the tasks of creation ascribed to God, but Bishop was a confirmed atheist whose private theology would be unlikely to admit this interpretation. Clearly, though, the mother is a creative force the reader comes to know through her handiwork and who, in the penultimate line, directs her message outward to the larger world. The reader knows far more about this absent figure than about the father and sons, even though the latter appear in the poem.

The idea of a home and mother carries emotional resonance, particularly for Bishop, who at the age of five saw her mother for the last time. When Bishop was eight months old, her father died, and her mother suffered subsequent breakdowns that ultimately required her institutionalization. Perhaps the vagaries of her itinerant childhood prompted Bishop's focus on her themes of travel and home. At the close of the title poem in *Questions of Travel*, in which "Filling Station" was first collected, the traveler queries, "*Should we have stayed at home,// wherever that may be?*" Bishop pondered this question in both her life and in her art.

In a letter to John Frederick Nims dated October 6, 1979, the day she died, Bishop addressed his suggestions about footnotes for "Filling Station" in an anthology he was editing. She replied that she would like her readers to know "SO-SO-SO" was at one time a phrase commonly used to soothe horses. With Bishop's flair for the music of repetition, she insists on the "so," embedding it in "softly," "Esso," and the oft-repeated "somebody," as well as in the implicit "soothe" until its hypnotic echo also calms the reader, who likewise delights in the premise that "Somebody loves us all." This epiphany fills the speaker and the reader, both of whom savor its consolation.

Paulette Roeske

FIR TREES

Author: Guillaume Apollinaire (Guillaume Albert Wladimir Alexandre Apollinaire de Kostrowitzky, 1880-1918)
Type of poem: Lyric
First published: 1909, as "Les Sapins"; in *Alcools*, 1913; English translation collected in *Alcools*, 1964

The Poem
    First appearing in the French publication *Le Voile de Pourpre* (1909), "Fir Trees" was later published in Guillaume Apollinaire's *Alcools* (1913) as one of nine short poems that make up the Rhenish suite. The poems were written during his stay on the Rhine in Germany from August, 1901, to August, 1902, as a tutor in the household of Vicomtesse de Milhau. In its original French, "Fir Trees" is composed of six stanzas of five eight-syllable lines, with six-syllable middle lines and a rhyme scheme of *aabab*.
    "Fir Trees" is a purely descriptive poem, focusing on the picturesque appearance of the trees as seen through the changing seasons. Apollinaire essentially creates a fantasy by whimsically toying with a German tradition of attributing benevolent magical powers to trees.
    In the first stanza, Apollinaire draws on his visual imagination, seeing the pine trees as wearing "peaked bonnets" and "trailing robes." These are the firs of spring or summer. The robes, those of "astrologers," personify the trees as enchanted entities. From the beginning of the poem, they are cloaked in awe-inspiring mystery. Whimsical lines follow in which the trees view the wooden boats on the Rhine as "felled brothers."
    The poem then establishes almost a mythology as the reader learns that young firs are apprentices to their wise "elders," who instruct them in the magical "seven arts"; seven is a significant number in the folklore of the supernatural. Notice the self-referential line that the old and wise trees are "great poets." Apollinaire associates poetic vision with the supernatural: Like the great fir trees, poets are in touch with the secrets of life, knowledge that is beyond that of the common man. The fir trees are eternal, omnipotent in their connection with the cosmos; they are "fated/ To outshine the planets."
    In the next three stanzas, the reader is treated to a beautiful vision of fir trees going through various transformations in the changing seasons. In winter, they become "stars," gleaming in the snow, but they are quiet in trancelike dreams, perhaps storing their magical powers for spring's enchantments. In stanza 5, Apollinaire envisions the snow-covered trees swaying in the wind as "white cherubim/ Rocking their wings."
    The rustling noise of autumn's winds whirling through the fir trees' branches is heard as "ancient carols" sung by the "fair musicians." The use of "ancient" associates the trees with the primeval forests of aged Earth; their experience and knowledge significantly precede the advent of man. Yet, suddenly, autumn transforms them into

ominous "magicians," conjuring incantations to "hurl" at "thunder." The visual source for this image may be lightning bolts striking the tops of trees during a thunderstorm.

Summer offers a more whimsical change as the trees are seen as "tall rabbis" or "aged spinsters." The inspiration for these metaphors belongs entirely to the fantastic and often puzzling imagination of Apollinaire. As "rabbis," the trees may be seen as spiritual guides; in the next stanza, their healing qualities are introduced as "traveling doctors" whose "pungent salves," strong aromas of tree sap, remedy the mountain's ailments.

Forms and Devices

The poem follows regular verse form, with one important exception: There is no punctuation. Apollinaire reportedly chose to remove all punctuation at the last minute, when he read the proofs for *Alcools* right before publication. He later claimed that the rhythm and division of the lines are the only punctuation that is needed. In essence he is correct. "Fir Trees" is a very accessible poem, and the lack of punctuation provides a fluidity of language that enables the transformation of images without sacrificing understanding. In this poem, punctuation would seem redundant. The combination of conventional form and lack of punctuation shows an adherence to traditional poetry while looking forward to the much more modern free verse of Apollinaire's later poetry.

The essence of the poem is infused by metaphor. Often, however, the poem does not reveal the identity of the metaphor's source; that is left up to the reader. A metaphor seeks identification between the known and the unusual. If the metaphor were to reveal its source, the poem might contain a line such as: "The very tops of fir trees are peaked bonnets." "Fir Trees," however, does not provide the reader with the element on which the metaphor is based; thus the poem simply reads: "Fir trees in peaked bonnets." A metaphor with an indefinite source allows more freedom in interpretation. It appeals to the individuality of a reader's perception. The reader may decide for himself or herself a source that best allows the reader to identify with the metaphor.

Many of the poem's metaphors are based on unusual associations between normally incongruous images. For example, the full bases of the trees are "trailing robes," and their lush snow-covered boughs blown by the winter wind are like "rocking wings" of "cherubim." Such descriptive and, in many ways, poignant images are essential to the effectiveness of this poem.

The metaphors are not limited, however, to visual associations. The trees' associations with "tall rabbis," "aged spinsters," or "traveling doctors" are based on qualities that the poet attributes to the fir trees. Like religious leaders, they are spiritual guides. Like spinsters, they grow old, lonely, and unappreciated. Like doctors, their ointments "heal." Like magicians, they possess the mysterious and charmed powers of nature.

Above all, the fir trees are extensively personified, or given qualities usually attributed to human beings. They display pride as they "hail their felled brothers." They raise their young and teach them the "seven arts." They dream, sleep, sing, and "hurl spells" in anger. The trees are envisioned as sentient beings conscious of their own existence and of their profound fate.

Themes and Meanings

The dominant theme in "Fir Trees" is nature. The poem offers a conception of nature that smacks of folklore or fairy tale in that the natural world is given supernatural powers. The fantasy Apollinaire has created suggests that fir trees, representatives of nature, embody all the various qualities and mysteries of the universe, both natural and supernatural. They have in common with man the joys, sorrows, and pains of experience. Unlike man, however, they are in touch with planes of existence beyond the reach and knowledge of human beings.

The "humanity" of nature pervades the entire poem. Seeing trees and men as brothers in the world delightfully enriches and expands one's experience of life. By offering visions of trees saluting their fallen brothers or singing carols, the poem helps expand one's focus from a narrow preoccupation with the trivialities of the human world to include the broader concerns of nature in general. This expanded vision offers a new perspective to otherwise human-centered priorities. The poem's personification of the trees also offers a new perspective on the way humans see themselves. The absurdity of envisioning trees as "aged spinsters" or as old men whose bones (branches) creak in the rain adds whimsy to the way one views one's own aging body and mind.

In one sense, the trees seem to share the concerns of the human world, but in another sense, they belong to a mysterious world beyond human experience. They possess magical powers and "know themselves fated/ To outshine the planets." Poets throughout the ages have attributed profound knowledge to nature. Nature has been seen to embody a spiritual consciousness of which humankind has little or no awareness. The trees, with their "grave spells" and "trailing robes/ Of astrologers," have contact with a divine realm that dictates all existence.

In addition to the theme of nature, "Fir Trees," like many poems in *Alcools*, seems to celebrate the passing of time. The poem traces the trees through the changing seasons, from youthfully singing carols to sinking "down to slumber," boughs creaking of old age. The tone of this celebration seems ambivalent. Seeing the trees as "aged spinsters" suggests a melancholy attitude toward the fleeing years. Passing time means little, however, to beings that will "outshine the planets." That suggests a mood of exaltation as the trees live out their corporeal years to take their rightful place in the eternal sphere, "subtly changed into stars."

Yet one should not forget that the poem is essentially a description of a real place and real trees. "Fir Trees" offers impressions of Germany's Rhineland seen through the eyes of the twenty-year-old Apollinaire. The poem reveals much about the subjective quality of human perception. Apollinaire seems to project the hopes and fears of his own life upon the natural world, the trees. His suggestion that the trees are "great poets" destined "to outshine the planets" is probably a speculation upon his own purpose and fate as a poet. Apollinaire's poem of animated trees thus can be seen as a projection of his inner state.

Heidi Kelchner

FIRE ON THE HILLS

Author: Robinson Jeffers (1887-1962)
Type of poem: Meditation
First published: 1932, in *Thurso's Landing and Other Poems*

The Poem

"Fire on the Hills" is a short description and meditation in a sonnetlike form—that is, it is in fourteen lines of free verse. It depicts a brushfire along the mountainous coast of the Monterey Peninsula, contemplates the animals caught up in it, and suggests the cosmic indifference of the context in which this takes place. Ultimately, Robinson Jeffers considers the intellectual attitude that humankind must cultivate to adapt to the universe.

The poem begins by establishing the scene of the brushfire, as observed by the speaker. Those animals that can escape range ahead of the raging blaze, which pursues them as if it were an incarnate being; yet it is all part of a mechanical process. The observer considers the myriad other animals and birds that could not escape.

The simple cinematic opening establishes the initial perspective, much like a wide panning shot at the beginning of a film. The reader is caught by the energy of the event, admiring the movement and the color—especially since the first note struck is of exhilaration at the escape of the deer fleeing the advancing flames. Then, however, the reflection that less fortunate animals are trapped brings the reader up short. In this way, Jeffers catches the readers in his ideological net, seducing them into perceiving beauty in an event of death and destruction.

Jeffers forces that recognition by injecting the reflective note that "beauty is not always lovely" into the poem. The scene is beautiful even in its terror and loss. He goes on to describe an eagle later drawn to the burned area by the prospect of carrion, implying that even this act participates in the beauty. The horror of the little deaths is rectified somehow in the splendor of the eagle. The eagle is magnificent, "cloaked in the folded storms of his shoulders," despite gorging on offal.

Jeffers goes on to suggest that all of this is part of a coherent system: What is bad for the small game animals is good for the eagle. This natural cycle is objective, indifferent, and impartial—"merciless," in Jeffers's terminology. He is borrowing an idea and a phrase from the fourteenth century English poet Geoffrey Chaucer, who composed a poem entitled "Merciless Beauty."

The final focus is not on this cosmic system itself but on man and his awareness and acceptance of it. Jeffers suggests that man needs to develop the tough-mindedness necessary to confront this reality, a reality that most would call hostile. This vision of the world has appeared in poetry beginning in the mid-nineteenth century; Alfred, Lord Tennyson, for example, described a "nature red in tooth and claw." Jeffers's sense of the antagonistic post-Darwinian universe was intensified by his extensive studies in biology and medicine. In so uncompromising a universe, man must develop an equivalent cold-bloodedness in order to survive, but Jeffers believed that this would not exclude beauty.

Forms and Devices

Jeffers became famous in the first half of the twentieth century for writing an unusually accessible poetry; he was one of the two best-selling poets of his time. One reason for this was that he was primarily a narrative poet, but another was the simplicity of his verse. Unlike most poets, Jeffers is not conspicuous for the elaboration of particular technical devices. His religious upbringing, however, had familiarized him with the rhythms and imagery of the King James Bible, and his education in the classics taught him the metrical patterns of the Romans and Greeks. He also learned from the free verse of Walt Whitman, the most innovative American poet of the nineteenth century, who developed the long lines that Jeffers favored in his own poetry.

"Fire on the Hills" uses devices from those sources to support its theme. The rhythms that ripple beneath its lines are not the regular meter of conventional poetry but the driven pulse of organic forms, like those of waves breaking on a beach. They give the lines in this poem a distinctive animation, supplementing the imagery. The first line illustrates this: "The deer were bounding like blown leaves." The underlying rhythms advance fitfully, reinforcing both the image of deer darting ahead of the flames and the doubling simile of leaves being driven fitfully by the wind. Similarly, the final line, "The destruction that brings an eagle from heaven is better than mercy," is simultaneously biblical, classical, and Whitmanesque in its straightforward declamation and its sinewy rhythms.

In other respects, too, Jeffers uses simple means to force his readers to look at things they would customarily overlook. This appears most clearly in his presentation of the eagle. It is hard for most people to dissociate this animal from its conventional trappings; as the American national bird, it symbolizes aspiration, freedom, independence, and strength—a multitude of superlatives. Not so for Jeffers. The bird is "perched on the jag of a burnt pine," the overlord of the wasteland, "insolent and gorged." This bird is not a national pretense but a predator and master scavenger; it impresses only because it succeeds and dominates, "sleepily merciless" in its reduction of its domain. Yet to Jeffers, this is still an "eagle from heaven." It is not necessarily good, and certainly not benevolent, but it is extraordinarily successful at what it does.

In one other respect Jeffers's work developed from his readings. He tends to phrase his conclusions as paradoxes, thus paralleling both the Proverbs of the Old Testament and the oracles of classical literature. Two lines already cited show this: "Beauty is not always lovely," and "The destruction that brings an eagle from heaven is better than mercy."

Themes and Meanings

Because Robinson Jeffers's poetry is marked by unusual economy of phrasing, his themes are relatively easy to perceive. Still, his uncompromising positions and the starkness of his visions sometimes have made readers balk. He is never unwilling to look hard truths in the eye. He does that here; moreover, he forces the reader to do it.

His tactics are simple. He begins by presenting the scene on which he will comment. Once the reader is committed to the scene—by the basic process of projecting imaginatively into it—the reader finds it difficult to withdraw from the conclusion. The energy of the brush fire compels one to remain mesmerized by its power. The fleeing deer, fragile and vulnerable in the face of the inferno, attract the reader with the automatic sympathy offered to underdogs. All of this rivets one's attention, as beauty always does; but then one is reminded that other animals are not as fortunate as the deer. Yet one still stares, entranced; the scene is still beautiful. Thus Jeffers slips in the theme: "Beauty is not always lovely."

His larger theme is communicated as much by what he does not do as by what he does. He depends on the reader's reaction to his announcement. If beauty is not lovely, the reader wonders, what is it? Another question follows immediately: If this is beautiful, what constitutes its beauty?

As if to provide the answer, Jeffers moves to the scene of the eagle perched brooding over the burnt-over area. He implies that this, too, is beautiful; this scene recapitulates the first, catching the eye and the mind at once as that one did. As before, the reality underlying the surface seems to contradict it. The eagle may be striking, but it is glutting itself on carrion that has been laid waste by the cruelty of the fire. That is not something that one likes to recognize, let alone stare at. Cultivated human feelings do not permit it. Jeffers suggests that this is one of the lies of civilization.

He makes this suggestion by a progression in which he uses the term "merciless" three times, on each count changing the focus. First the sky is "merciless blue"—blue skies are attractive, hence beautiful; yet the blue is blank and indifferent. Then the hills are "merciless black"—attractive as a swatch of color against the sky, an "effective" composition, but the expanse attracts only so long as one does not look too closely. In the third repetition, the gorged eagle is merciless, beautiful like the other two scenes though battening on cruel death.

By confronting one with these situations and helping one to recognize the elements they have in common, Jeffers forces a redefinition of beauty. This redefinition divorces beauty from sentiment and sentimentality. If beauty animates these scenes, then beauty must be simply an exhilaration at recognizing the efficiency of the natural order in subordinating individual lives to the order of the total physical machine of the universe, however heartless it may be.

James Livingston

THE FIREBOMBING

Author: James Dickey (1923-1997)
Type of poem: Elegy
First published: 1965, in *Buckdancer's Choice*

The Poem

"The Firebombing" is a musing in almost three hundred lines of free verse, some twenty years after the event, on the horror of incinerating the Japanese city of Beppu with "300-gallon drop-tanks/ Filled with napalm and gasoline." The vagaries of fate are announced in the first line, a peremptory "Homeowners unite," but the bitter truth is that though "All families lie together, . . . some are burned alive." The account is impressionistic and roughly follows a sequence of events beginning with the airman's nighttime trudge to his plane ("A booted crackling of snailshells and coral sticks") and culminating in his safe return "To where Okinawa burns,/ Pure gold, on the radar screen." As the speaker coolly recalls the destruction he viewed from the safety of his "glass treasure-hole of blue light" with his "Bourbon frighteningly mixed/ With GI pineapple juice," he keeps reflecting on his comfortable middle-class suburban life. The bombing mission, Okinawa to Beppu and back, becomes the narrative line along which are strung the speaker's ironic comparisons of the deaths he caused and the life he enjoys.

The speaker's story of his flight begins with lovely passages describing the flights through banks of cumulus clouds, emerging into a vision of the landscape beneath, with its "Rice-water calm at all levels/ Of the terraced hill." The rivers below guide the death-ship through the sky, where five thousand people lie sleeping below, and as the airman in memory maneuvers his deadly freight into position he thinks of his own house, "Where the lawn mower rests on its laurels" and "Where the diet exists/ For my own good." His catalog of his homeowner's bounty is extensive, but it modulates into guilt:

> I still have charge—secret charge—
> Of the fire developed to cling
> To everything: to golf carts and fingernail
> Scissors as yet unborn   tennis shoes
> Grocery baskets   toy fire engines
> New Buicks stalled by the half-moon

The carnage that the airman finally unleashes is unspeakable, turning "the bathhouse upside down," "kicking/ The small cattle off their feet," and "Flinging jelly over the walls." Leaving "a town burning with all/ American fire," the airman follows "the huge moon-washed steppingstones/ Of the Ryukyus south."

The narrator concludes by confessing that after all this reliving of the event he is "still hungry,/ Still twenty years overweight" and unable to imagine just what agony he inflicted on the sleepers below. Yet despite it all, he doubts that he could "say to any/ Who lived there, deep in [his] flames," "Come in, my house is yours." The truth is he has lived with Beppu for twenty years and remains American "and proud of it." His final judgment is "Absolution? Sentence? No matter;/ The thing itself is in that." Years later, James Dickey confessed to "guilt at the inability to feel guilty" and of how "The detachment one senses when dropping the bombs is the worst evil of all—yet it doesn't seem so at the time."

Forms and Devices

Long lines and short lines come and go in no pattern, with single lines interspersed among stanzas as long as twenty-one lines, as short as two. Most lines are enjambed to imitate an uninterrupted flow of images in the mind, and words are often separated by several spaces for rhetorical effect in reading. Dickey is a master of the imaginative conceit, as in the "undeodorized arms" of the underside of the plane wings where the deadly fluids bide their time. The plane disappears into the marvelously oxymoronic "white dark" of the cumulus, and "Rice-water calm" and engines that "ponder their sound" exploit the pathetic fallacy. Frequent alliteration ("dark dream") and, especially, sibilance ("silver side," "sea/ Slants," "sleep-smelling") combine with occasional assonance ("Come up," "dark arms," "eight blades") and repetition ("Think of this think of this/ I did not think of my house/ But think of my house now") to complement sense with sound.

Other subtle patterns can be seen in the preponderance of gerund forms that structure so many of the passages recounting the mission: "Coming out," "passing over," "Sliding off," "coming slowly," "going forward," "Going: going," "dogs trembling," "Rivers circling," "sleeping off," "racking slowly," and "flying inside." This structural device disappears in the "suburban" passages dense with details of domestic life but reappears in the second round of the bombing horror ("clutching the toggle," "fulfilling/ An 'anti-morale' raid," "Singing and twisting," "kicking," "Flinging jelly," "Holding onto"). Only reading "The Firebombing" aloud, obeying Dickey's spacings and enjambments, will do full justice to the rhetorical fullness of the poem. What at first glance seems a scattering of words in random lines emerges finally as the product of considerable self-conscious artistry.

A sort of perverse romantic menace pervades the cockpit imagery: "One is cool and enthralled in the cockpit,/ Turned blue by the power of beauty,/ In a pale treasure-hole of soft light,/ Deep in aesthetic contemplation." Many of the images startle at first reading. To speak of being "twenty years overweight" is witty and striking; "Oriental fish" with eyes that reveal "one tiny seed/ Of deranged, Old Testament light" are creatures that challenge the explicator; and a hammock that "folds its erotic daydreams" executes an imaginative transference from the hammocker to the hammock; "Japan/ Dilates around [the aircraft] like a thought"; in a cruel vision "another/ Bomb finds a home/ And clings to it like a child."

Themes and Meanings

"The Firebombing" became one of the most controversial poems by this controversial poet. The first issue is Dickey's war record, a matter extrinsic to consideration of the poem's merits but important in the larger context of the poet's persona. Dickey's biographer, Henry Hart, relentless in his debunking of the Dickey myth, claimed that Dickey "assumed the role of a battle-scarred pilot who had flown one hundred combat missions over the Philippines and Japan." The truth is that Dickey washed out of flight school at Camden, South Carolina, and trained as a radar observer, a period in his life drawn on in his novel *Alnilam* (1987). Hart tells the whole story of Dickey's war, both the reality and the self-aggrandizement, but Dickey was flying combat missions from Okinawa by July, 1945. Another poem, "The Eye of the Fire," treats the same subject of firebombing, as does Dickey's last novel, *To the White Sea* (1993). The vital critical concerns about the poem lie elsewhere, however, primarily in the intense attack on it—and by implication, on Dickey—mounted by Dickey's fellow poet and critic Robert Bly.

Bly's 1967 essay "The Collapse of James Dickey"—perhaps brought on by Bly's anger at Dickey's failure to unite with liberals against the Vietnam War—called Dickey's volume *Buckdancer's Choice* "repulsive," citing a tone of "gloating about power over others." "Slave Quarters" was called "a *Saturday Evening Post* cover, retouched by the Marquis de Sade," and it is just a short step to "The Firebombing," where, "As objects of sadism, the Negro women have been replaced by the civilian population of Asia."

Bly's assault on Dickey's humanity overshoots the mark. Given Dickey's position in the war, certainly any feelings of power that bombing nurtured were not unique to him; in having the power of words to express what he felt, he laid himself open to unfair charges. The airman reports

> It is this detachment,
> The honored aesthetic evil,
> The greatest sense of power in one's life,
> That must be shed in bars, or by whatever
> Means, by starvation
> Visions in well-stocked pantries:

Throughout his work, Dickey is aware of the cruelty that power can foster, as he sees it reflected in the "deranged, Old Testament light." The two epigraphs to "The Firebombing," one from the German poet Günter Eich, the other from the Book of Job, warn the reader of themes of destruction and forgiveness, and it is quite possible to identify in the poem more moral courage than Dickey's critics allowed him.

Frank Day

FIRST COMMUNIONS

Author: Arthur Rimbaud (1854-1891)
Type of poem: Narrative
First published: 1886, as "Les Premières Communions"; in *Reliquaire,* 1891; English translation collected in *Complete Works, Selected Letters,* 1966

The Poem

"First Communions" is a long poem which is cut into nine sections of one to seven stanzas. The first two sections are composed of six-line stanzas and the last seven sections of quatrains, but the rhyme scheme remains a consistent alternation of rhymes. The poem is dated July, 1871, and Arthur Rimbaud included it among the poems sent to Paul Verlaine before their first meeting in September, 1871. Like other early poems of Rimbaud, including "Seven Year Old Poets," "The Poor in Church," and "The Drunken Boat," it is written in Alexandrine verse, a formal verse line of twelve syllables, which is traditionally reserved for serious subjects. The poem is centered on the preparation for first Holy Communion and its effects on a girl from a country town, a theme treated with heavy irony and hostility by the young poet.

The first two sections set the context and present the Priest and the Child. The tone is set by the first phrase, "Really, they're stupid, these village churches." The Priest is presented as a grotesque black figure in fermenting shoes, surrounded by ugly children who befoul the pillars they lean against. The church, built of native stones, is part of the countryside; it is a "barn" and attracts flies that smell of stables. The patron saint is stuffed with straw. The parents pay the Priest so that he will leave their children free to work in the sun.

The sun and nature are presented positively; life vibrates in the countryside. Families are dedicated naïvely to "good, mind-destroying work." Children retain a few sweet memories of the "Great Day" of First Communion, then go on to banal lives, forgetting the contagion of the touch of Christ's Priest. The Priest chooses one sickly, sad little girl for distinction, and this child is the center of the next six sections.

In section 3, the child is on the eve of her Communion, sick in bed and counting visions compounded of bits and snippets of ecclesiastic imagery and "Latin endings." She seeks remission of her "virginities, present and future," but the pardons of the "Queen of Zion" are icy. In section 4, the vision recedes, becomes a "book virgin," and is succeeded by immodest curiosity about the nudity of Jesus. Leaving the abstract vision, the poem focuses on the child's physical and emotional condition. Her head is buried in her pillow, and she thrashes about and drools as she tries to regain her vision, finally opening the curtain to let night air cool her belly and chest.

In the fourth and fifth sections, the child wakes at midnight and goes outside after a "red dream" and a nosebleed. She seeks the night as a locus of both exaltation and degradation, a Virgin Mother who bathes her children in silence and indifference. The child plays the roles of victim and bride, spending her holy vigil night in the latrine.

The seventh section, a single stanza, apostrophizes the "dirty madmen" whose divine work deforms worlds and infects the child with leprosy.

The eighth section presents a woman whose lover dreams of "the white million Marys" after a night of love. She confesses that her love is death and disease and that Christ soiled her breath when she was young. Even the most loving woman feels herself thus prostituted and suffering. Her first Holy Communion was also carnal: She cannot feel her lover's kisses because her whole heart and body swarm with the putrid kiss of Jesus.

The final two-stanza section is an apostrophe to Christ, the "eternal thief of energy." It is an accusation that his curses separate man and woman because, for two thousand years, his deathly paleness has nailed suffering woman to Earth with shame and headache.

Forms and Devices

"First Communions" is not devoted primarily to formal beauty, because its energy is turned toward polemic. Yet, Rimbaud chose a formal verse structure, frequent in his early works, which is tied closely to beauty and elevated thought. Technical mastery of the Alexandrine lends dignity to the material expressed in it, yet its inevitable ties with classic forms and idealistic themes contrast with the strongly sacrilegious, antiestablishment "First Communions." There is ironic weight in the juxtaposition of rhyming Alexandrines and the debunking of First Holy Communion and Christianity.

Throughout "First Communions," the reader encounters expressions that are chosen for their incongruousness or shock value. In the first stanza, for example, the churches are "stupid," the children are "ugly brats" who soil the pillars of the church, and the Priest is "grotesque" with fermenting shoes. Moreover, his speech is broad, "babbling," and badly pronounced. The description is enhanced in the seventh stanza: It is the priest's feet that define him again as his toes tap along to music against his "heavenly prohibitions." His prestige disappears and his power, mentioned in stanza 4, becomes a contagion which makes the skin crawl.

Churches are "barns," and their relics "grotesque mysticities." The girls are called "sluts" by the boys, and the boys "howl out frightful songs," far-away music is heard as nasal twanging, the child drools, the paving stones stink of wash water, the woman has internalized "knots of hysteria," and her flesh "swarms with the putrid kiss of Jesus." The use of vigorous, unexpected, and negative descriptions determines the tone of the poem and contaminates its individual elements. There is no ideal or admirable figure.

"First Communions" is built on a system of polar oppositions. Most are implicit, produced by the juxtaposition of two terms, as in the contrast of the "stupid" church of the first stanza with the countryside of the second, where everything is "in heat," fertile, and trembling with life and color. The opposition of natural vigor and ecclesiastical futility, once established, recurs in the third stanza, in which the white-washed barn of a church, with its relics and straw stuffed images, is contrasted with flies gorging in the sunshine and smelling like inns and stables. "But" and "however" emphasize the opposition in other cases, such as the sunlight shining through church windows opposed to the grotesque priest and his followers, or the nocturnal plots of the Priest set in contrast with the thoughtless banality of young men and girls.

There are many other opposed pairs in the poem. The mystic images of the child's vision are compared to the "book virgin" and "immodest curiosities" of the fourth section. The heart is exalted and degraded in the night. The white specter of the drying blouse is related to the black specters of the roofs. There is a holy night in the latrines, and there are sorrows of happiness. A woman is the most loving and the most prostituted, and the soul is rotten and desolate. The spirit of opposition and rebellion is knit into the very fabric of the poem.

There is a certain awkwardness in the change from the six-line stanzas of the first two sections to the four-line stanzas of the body of the poem. The change to quatrains changes the tempo, however, and the power of the contrast compensates for the awkwardness. In the first, longer stanzas, the opposition between the Priest and the natural world predominates. In the shorter, quicker stanzas, the more dramatic scenes of the young girl and the woman that she becomes are dramatized.

Themes and Meanings

In "First Communions," Rimbaud developed two themes found in other poems of 1870 and 1871: his anticlericalism ("The Poor in Church") and his glorification of the powers of nature, the sun in particular ("Sun and Flesh"). It has been suggested that the poem was written in reaction to the first Holy Communion of the poet's sister in May, 1871. Whatever the specific inspiration of the piece, it falls within his universal rejection of the structures of society. Through the institution of the church and its priest, however, he also attacks Christ as a god of death who is opposed to the life force and is responsible for maiming women.

The poem does not actually present the girl's first communion in the church or her first communion of the flesh with her lover: The reader is presented with the eve of the former and the morning after the latter. Instead, there is the first communion of the child with the religious vision of angels, Jesus figures, and Marys. In the ninth stanza, "her soul drank all her conqueror," and in the tenth, "she bites into the coolness of your Remission." With the disillusionment of section 4 comes a carnal first communion, as the child imagines the nudity of Jesus and thrashes in physical distress. These communions prefigure those yet to come. The figure of the girl is inextricably linked with the Mary image (thus her lover dreams of Marys) and frigid virginity, yet her body and soul are irremediably polluted by her reception of Jesus, the dead god.

Throughout "First Communions," with its vigorous use of language and the overwhelming strength of its images, the energy of the young poet can be sensed. Rimbaud was yet to enter fully into his great experiment of poetic madness, and his most daring formal ventures lay ahead. Yet, his rage at the structures of his world and his joy in verbal pyrotechnics are already in full motion in this contentious and troubling piece written before his seventeenth birthday.

Anne W. Sienkewicz

FIRST CONFESSION

Author: X. J. Kennedy (Joseph Charles Kennedy, 1929-   )
Type of poem: Lyric
First published: 1961, in *Nude Descending a Staircase*

The Poem

"First Confession" is the opening poem in X. J. Kennedy's first collection of poems, *Nude Descending a Staircase*. This twenty-four-line lyric depicts the emotions of a young man as he experiences his first confession, a ritual in the Catholic religion. The poem's placement in the collection is significant, for it serves as Kennedy's first poetic "confession" and basis of his art.

The poet's attitude toward traditional form in this poem sets the tone of Kennedy's entire poetic career, irreverent, impatient with authority, yet obedient to it. Traditional form is clearly evident in the poem's six quatrains, all of whose lines rhyme and contain a basic four-foot regularity. This ballad structure allows Kennedy to address the restrictions of poetic ritual in a dramatic presentation of a young man's struggle with religious authority. While the drama of this first confession unfolds, another kind of initiation is taking place as well, that of the poet, who balances the authority of poetic form with a spirited and personal desire for freedom of expression and emotional release. This dual character of the poem enhances the emotional tension arising from the young man's fear of punishment and his impulse to defy it.

Although the poem's young speaker is recalling his first confession, the recollection is made immediate and highly dramatic. The speaker's emotional state is emphatically expressed from the outset: His blood is thudding in his ears as he approaches the confessional booth, knowing that on the other side of the curtain sits the person who will judge him. Aware of the gravity of his guilt, the young man senses that the universe itself hovers close to hear his confession. Inside the booth, he confesses his sins, and their insignificance seems ludicrous at first: a stolen sip of his father's beer, his withholding a dime from the offering plate, and a small sexual episode with his girlfriend. These minor confessions are immediately followed by a litany of larger sins, however—"sloth pride envy lechery"—whose gravity imbues his sinfulness with that universal importance he feared at the outset.

By the end of the third stanza, his sins have been laid before the priest and, in the next quatrain, his fate is weighed. Appropriately, Kennedy chooses the scales of justice, "Hovering scale-pans," to represent the young man's suspended state as he awaits judgment. His sentence is rendered in a quick line in the seventh stanza: "Seven Our Fathers and a Hail," which he performs at the altar before leaving the church. The poem ends with an emphatic demonstration of his untamed spirit—he sticks his tongue out at the priest—yet he is aware of what this defiance is likely to cost him, the continued close scrutiny by authority in the form of the Holy Ghost hovering over him. The poem's emotional intensity peaks in the final line, when the young man acknowledges that he shall continue to pay for his defiance, and the tension is relieved by readers' sympathy for him.

Forms and Devices

The poem's language and structures are well suited to the emotional state of a young man facing the ordeal of confession. The lines are short, each having four stresses, and most of the words in the poem are single-syllable. Twenty-one of the poem's twenty-four lines end on a word of one syllable, and all of the rhymes are stressed—that is, all are masculine rhymes. These structural features suggest fleeting impressions, impatience, rapid movement, even hurried breath. Sometimes, too, vividly expressive language, such as scuffing steps and a slat shooting back, contrasts with language that conveys an ironically indistinct formality, such as "The robed repositor of truth."

Sound, too, plays a major role in the poem. Both consonance and assonance are used liberally to convey the young man's agitation, as in the opening lines: "Blood thudded in my ears. I scuffed,/ Steps stubborn, to the telltale booth." The repeated vowel sounds in "blood," "thudded," "scuffed" and, in the second line, "stubborn" mimic the thumping of the young man's heartbeat; the resistant shuffle of his feet is echoed in the alliteration of "scuffed," "steps," and "stubborn." Even the word "telltale" suggests that the young man may be somewhat tongue-tied before his confessor.

Although the lines are relatively and uniformly short, Kennedy varies the length of his sentences to express dramatic shifts. In the confessional booth, the young man's abrupt confrontation with Church authority is described abruptly: "The slat shot back." This sharp report is followed by a sentence that runs through seven and a half lines, the unbroken flow suggesting the outpouring of the young man's sins.

This structural feature, contrasting long and short lines, reflects a similar contrast in the poem's overall meaning, in which both the physical universe and Church authority stand in ironic contrast to the insignificance of the young man's sins and his common humanity. These realms, the universal, religious, and the human, are constantly played off against one another. In the third stanza, for example, the list of mortal sins—"sloth pride envy lechery"—is contrasted to the young man's withholding a dime from a charity box. He confesses that he used the dime to bribe his girl "to pee/ That I might spy her instruments." The word "instruments" in this line refers to the formal documents of Church business, and the phrase "spy her instruments" refers both to astronomical observation of the heavens and to the young man's very human desire to catch a glimpse of a more human realm. Those three words, "spy her instruments," fuse into a single phrase the authority of the Church, the physical universe, and the human realm of the young man.

Themes and Meanings

One can see how Kennedy explores the poem as a confession booth in "First Confession" and how his play on sound is an important feature in the way in which he sees the world, a nexus of ritual and authority, of opposition and fusion. Here, Kennedy reaches beyond the individual poem to offer a view of the nature of the poet and art and how both relate to that other spiritual authority, the Church. As the young man is confronted by the imposing authority of his religion, so the poet confronts ritualistic poetic forms, using them to express conflict. In doing so, the poet brings them together and, paradoxically, makes an artistic whole out of opposing realms. If art is a spiritual experience, then the poem unifies human experience despite, or because of, religion.

The poem's display of technical skill underscores the idea that art plays a major role in the spiritual life. Poetic technique is inseparable from spiritual expression and fulfillment. Kennedy's witty handling of language is both a quest and a demonstration. It fulfills his desire to be a poet, free to construct witty poems, but his poetry is also a serious quest for meaning and guidance. He makes and explores at the same time. Poetry makes the two acts inseparable, as religion and humanity are inseparable, when rightly aligned. Kennedy reveals in this poem some ambivalence on this point. On one hand, confession is a voluntary submission to authority, as is writing in a traditional poetic form. On the other hand, the untamed, irreverent part of nature also wants expression. This ambivalence is reflected in the way in which Kennedy uses rhyme. Off-rhymes such as "scuffed/coughed," "doled/soul," and "light/priest" mingle with exact rimes—"most/Ghost," for example—drawing attention to the idea that in this world, as in art, absolute alignment is rare. Humans are imperfect, and so is rhyme. Traditional authority is a framework that allows this kind of meaning to be expressed. Without the ritual, one would have no poetry.

Inasmuch as the young confessor is speaking for Kennedy himself, the poem is saying—and showing—that religious ritual is too rigid, too impersonal, and too narrow in its view or acceptance of human nature. By using a traditional rhyme, meter, and stanzaic pattern to express his view of Church authority, Kennedy suggests that his loyalty lies with secular, not religious, ritual. Poetic authority is more humane, adaptable, and personal than Church ritual. Yet Kennedy knew that it is no easy matter to dismiss Church authority or elude its judgment, and the poem suggests that heavenly authority and human impulse may not be absolutely separate. The image of "the restless dark" suggests an ominous universe surrounding the young man, who is compared to a heavenly body as he burns "Bright as a brimstone" with guilt. The word "brimstone" has biblical overtones, and the image it completes places the young man in the heavens. In the second stanza, another image gives the universe a human form, perhaps that of a monk, who "Bowed down his cratered dome . . . ." By elevating the sinful youth and humanizing an overpowering authority, these images bring the two closer together and render the universe more forgiving, the human less depraved.

Bernard E. Morris

FIRST DREAM

Author: Sor Juana Inés de la Cruz (Juana Inés de Asbaje y Ramírez de Santillana, 1648-1695)
Type of poem: Meditation
First published: 1692, as "Primero sueño," in *Segundo volumen de las obras*; English translation collected in *A Sor Juana Anthology*, 1988

The Poem

"First Dream" (it has also been translated as "Primero Sueño," its original title) is a long narrative poem about knowledge and the act of knowing. It is written in the classical style known as the dream poem. The poem is actually the narrative of a dream, in which fantastical images are described as if from within the subconscious. The device of the dream allows the poet certain license with controversial ideas, because dreams are not expected to be "correct."

Although Sor Juana Inés de la Cruz was born in Mexico, her writing is influenced by Spanish literary conventions. "First Dream" is, according to Sor Juana herself, the only thing she ever wrote for her own pleasure. "First Dream" consists of 975 lines. It has been translated into roughly thirty-five irregular stanzas. As the title suggests, the poem is the "first dream" of the narrator, who falls asleep and has a dream in which the "soul" is the main character. The soul then explores the nature of knowledge from its lofty position above the world.

Presumably this is the first of many dreams to come in the life of the poet. Although it was composed during the colonial period in Mexican literature, it was first published in Spain. Sor Juana lived in the New World in an age when knowledge was expanding, and the source and purpose of knowledge were readily debated among theologians and intellectuals. In this "dream," Sor Juana tries to reconcile the world of the theologian (she was a nun) with the world of the intellectual (she was also an intellectual); she tries to reconcile the concept of faith with its supposed contrary, knowledge.

The main irony of the poem is expressed in a metaphor. The overly confident "ship of the soul" suffers on the beach of knowledge but has no choice but to advance further. Thus, the soul cannot possibly understand the cosmos and all of nature, but it nevertheless feels compelled to examine the hierarchy of being.

Most of "First Dream" is written in the omniscient first person, as if the "objective" narrator were recalling a powerful dream that was full of allusions to diverse classical myths and mythic heroes. The narrator occasionally reminds the reader of her presence by inserting "I say" or "I mean." Halfway through the poem, the narrator addresses the reader directly because what she declares is of the utmost thematic importance: "In short, I speak of man, the greatest wonder/ the human mind can ponder."

It is conventional for meditative and highly intellectual poetry to make use of the metaphor of the dream. The dreaming state is an altered state of consciousness with which every one is familiar. Sor Juana believes that she is free to dream only when the mind is "loosed/ from the bodily chain" in sleep. She likens the sleeping body to "a corpse with soul"; it is the soul that propels the dreaming state. The body inevitably wakens, however, and the soul cannot complete its task. If there is a weakness in the poem's logic, it is in the relation between the soul and the mind, a relation which is not clear.

When the mind is "loosed," says the poet, it wants to understand nature; yet, in spite of its worthiness, the mind is hampered by its own limitations, its inability to comprehend all, or to comprehend at different levels simultaneously. The mind must proceed "step by step" through "a graduated form of reasoning."

Sor Juana then details what she perceives to be four discerning "operations." These operations begin with the "basest level of being—the inanimate" and ascend to the most animate—human beings. Human beings are "the greatest wonder/ the human mind can ponder." They constitute a "complete compendium/ resembling angel, plant, and beast alike," and this is what makes them extraordinary.

Forms and Devices

"First Dream" begins with an inscription: "So entitled and so composed by Mother Juana Inés de la Cruz, in imitation of Góngora." The reader gets two messages in this brief inscription. First, Sor Juana (*Sor* meaning "Sister") is a nun (she joined the order of Saint Jerome in 1669). Second, Sor Juana knows something about Spanish literature. She considers one of the great euphuistic poets of Spain, Luis de Góngora y Argote (1561-1627), worthy of imitating in some aspect of her own work. Like Góngora, she employs an affected style of writing, one that relies on two main literary devices: numerous allusions to classical mythology, and hyperbole, or exaggeration.

The euphuistic poem is not straightforward in its meaning. It is characterized by alliteration, simile, and long series of antitheses. Some of the alliteration in "First Dream" (alliteration refers to the repetition of the same sound or syllable in two or more words of a line) has been resurrected in translation. Examples abound in the first stanza: "towering tips," "scaling stars," "forever free, aglow forever." The simile, a comparison of one thing with another, announced by the word "like" or "as," is more difficult to reproduce in modern English. Probably the translator's task is easiest when it comes to the series of antitheses.

The antithesis is the most significant literary device used in "First Dream." An antithesis is a rhetorical term meaning "opposition." Thus ideas are opposed, or contrasted, by using words of opposite meaning in contiguous clauses or phrases. A series of antitheses is, when read aloud, a mouthful, as in the first stanza of the poem. Here, with numerous phrases and clauses, the poet refers to the change from daylight to night as a "shadowy war" waged in "gaseous blackness" by the sun before it reaches "the convex side" of the "fair goddess' orb" known as the moon.

The point is that, as simple as night may seem, the heavens must overturn in order for night to appear. The poet wants to give philosophical complexity to a phenomenon of nature; she wants the reader to think deeply about what is involved when the sun and the moon trade places, so she uses a series of antitheses, or opposites, within the same line.

The poet has chosen a very loose verse form. The *silva* is a Spanish form consisting of seven-or eleven-syllable lines. These lines are of unequal length, and the rhymes are not placed in any set pattern. On first reading, the *silva* structure may seem ponderous.

Themes and Meanings

"First Dream" has both a philosophical component and a personal component. It is about the apprehension of knowledge and about the nature of knowledge itself, but it is also an experiment with the poet's own dream vision. The dream vision makes up the "story" of the narrative. This story is simple: As night falls, the poet sleeps in order to dream, in order to release her "soul" from her body. Only then is she free to investigate her subject—knowledge—in a sustained way.

The story illustrates the philosophical problem—the opposition between faith and knowledge, and the consequences for humankind. Sor Juana presents the church doctrine that condemns the pursuit of knowledge: The wish for knowledge is the hubris of humankind. Like Icarus, humans may fly too close to the sun, be blinded by its light, and then fall to the earth. This, in fact, is what happens to the mind. The mind's ascent to God is pyramidal in shape; by the time it reaches the top of the pyramid, it is unable to distill further what it has apprehended. It falls back down into chaos, at which point the soul retreats. It is because of this fall that the Church condemns the pursuit of knowledge. Yet at the same time as Sor Juana teaches this doctrine in the poem, she presents an opposing view of the pursuit of knowledge.

There is a paradox between faith and knowledge, but that does not mean they cannot coexist. In other words, it may be, according to Church doctrine, folly to covet knowledge; but it is also courageous to crave knowledge, especially because full knowledge is never attainable. Unable to know fully, the narrator herself is finally wakened by daylight. Ironically, every "outer sense" has been restored to "full functioning." The dream, then, has come to an end, and the poem has ended with the same (paradoxical) antithesis with which it began: faith versus knowledge.

"First Dream" is a significant poem for two reasons: It is probably the most sustained philosophical poem of the Baroque era (c. 1600-1700), and it was written by a woman. Although Sor Juana's feminism is muted in this poem, her anger at the inferior role imposed upon women by men and, in particular, by the church is revealed elsewhere in her work, especially in the *Respuesta de la poetisa a la muy ilustre Sor Filotea de la Cruz* (1700; reply of the poetess to the illustrious Sister Filotea de la Cruz).

Marlene Kadar

FIRST FIGHT. THEN FIDDLE

Author: Gwendolyn Brooks (1917-2000)
Type of poem: Sonnet
First published: 1949 in *Annie Allen*, 1949

The Poem

Gwendolyn Brooks's "First Fight. Then Fiddle" is a sonnet that advocates the use of militancy to make the environment safe for art to flourish. The poem is the fourth sonnet in the sequence "children of the poor" in the "The Womanhood" section of *Annie Allen (1949)* and uses the persona of a black mother whose meditations on her fears, concerns, and hopes about her children lead to, in the poet's own words, "preachments" to negotiate the pitfalls and dead ends they would face. "First Fight. Then Fiddle" can be better understood when discussed in the context of sonnets that precede it. The second sonnet of the sequence raises a question, "What shall I give my children? who are poor" and is followed by "And shall I prime my children, pray, to pray?" Finding solace in religion or faith, thus, is one possible alternative for the children. "First Fight. Then Fiddle," the fourth sonnet, then presents another option, a resorting to violence for self-preservation.

"First Fight. Then Fiddle" begins with the speaker commanding aspiring musicians, ostensibly her children, to prepare to fight before turning to their fiddle. The fiddle is, in fact, the metaphor for all art, and the poem is an expression of the speaker's proffered solution to the dangers faced by African Americans during the period of rigid segregation. The lines that follow the two short imperative statements "First fight. Then fiddle" depict what the aspiring artists can expect —a life of working incessantly, muzzling their hurt, and playing the masterpieces. Softened with silky effects and sweetened with honey, music would have to be an integral part of their disciplined lives. In a life devoted to music, according to the speaker, there is no room for unpleasantness—"no salt, no hempen thing." They would need to rise above the malice of their surroundings and quell the repeated temptation to avenge themselves.

However, the next stanza shifts its focus away from the portrayal of a life of industry and tranquility required of an artist. Art cannot serve as an escape from reality. The speaker announces that before such a life of dedication and devotion to art can be pursued, the aspirants would have to arm themselves, thus reverting to the idea of fighting presented in the first line. The reality of the world would demand that in order to win the war, they use "hate" as their armor and make themselves oblivious to the infinite beauty of the world of art. Understandably, they would be bloodied by the confrontation but, according to the speaker, it is imperative that they tame the world into accepting them. Only a civilized world would provide them an opportunity to play their violin "with grace."

"First Fight. Then Fiddle," in short, dwells on the need for total devotion to art and at the same time the necessity of fighting for a just world.

Forms and Devices

In "First Fight. Then Fiddle" Brooks takes liberties with the traditional sonnet form. The rhyme scheme of the poem reflects the influence of the Shakespearean sonnet—three quatrains, abba, abba, cddc, followed by a rhyming couplet, ee. However, in the development of thought, it follows the Petrarchan model of structuring the poem in an octave—an eight line stanza—followed by a sestet—a six-line stanza. The first eight lines, after the initial imperatives, picture the lives of artists, and the next six lines advocate fighting the war against discrimination or tyranny in order to create an environment safe enough for nurturing art.

Formal devices, such as meter, diction, and imagery create a distinctive mood in the poem. The superb control of rhythm and language makes the sonnet tremendously appealing. Here again, Brooks departs frequently from the customarily used iambic meter to create the desired effect. For instance, she uses two accented syllables "First Fight" and then again in line twelve, "Win war" for emphasis "First fight. Then fiddle" is followed by a soft "then" leading to a string of alliteration— "slipping string"— and repetition of vowel sounds "feathery sorcery." "Bewitch, bewilder" follow next. The repeated use of alliteration and assonance underlines the musicality of the poem—almost like playing of the violin. In addition, Brooks also uses frequent enjambments—ending sentences in mid-line—to further emphasize words. The second line with its four stresses moves emphatically through a progression of verbs, such as "Bewitch, bewilder," "Qualify," "Devise," "Devote," "Be remote," "Carry. . . ." The capitalization of these verbs lends added force to the exhortations of the speaker.

Brooks's intricate word play further enhances the complexity of the poem. Phrases such as "feathery sorcery," "hurting love," and "Bewitch, bewilder," have connotations that deepen the meaning of her words. For instance, feathery suggests the airiness, the lightness, but is juxtaposed with sorcery, thus bringing in a magical quality to the plying of strings. Seemingly opaque phrases as "Qualify to sing/ Threadwise. Devise no salt, no hempen thing/ For the dear instrument to bear" tease the reader into discovering the intent of the poet. The listeners are being asked to weave music in the fabric of their lives "threadwise," and the admonition to "Devise no salt, no hempen thing" offers an effective contrast to the "silks and honey" imagery in line 7. The advice to suppress hurt and "be remote from malice" is later substituted by a reminder to use hate as a protective sheath. War allows no time to reflect on art or beauty: winning is the ultimate goal. Finally, the metamorphosis of the fiddle in the first line into a violin in the last line is accomplished artfully. The fiddle with its rustic suggestiveness is appropriate for the beginner; the violin with its aura of sophistication is naturally apt for a civilized world.

Themes and Meanings

"First Fight. Then Fiddle," was written by Gwendolyn Brooks during her initial stage of creativity, which she names "express myself" phase. Her first book, *A Street in Bronzeville* (1945) brought her recognition, and the critical acclaim for her next book, *Annie Allen* (1949), won her the honor of becoming the first African American to be awarded a Pulitzer Prize in literature in 1950. The book is about Annie brooding over her pre-War dreams and post-War realities. Annie is an individual in her own right but is fairly representative of most other black women. In her poems of this period, Brooks portrays with sensitivity the lives of men and women around her and captures their lives not just in the moments of despair but also during their little victories in the face of adversities. She never forgets the world of segregation that overshadows the lives of her racial world, but, in general, her early poems are devoid of racial polemic and focus mostly on black experience from a woman's perspective.

"First Fight. Then Fiddle" foreshadows the next phase of Gwendolyn Brooks's poetry, which reflects her growing commitment to the political function of the arts. Written after the end of the Second World War, the poem seems to be addressed to African American youth, caught between the desire to pursue their artistic inclinations and the resistance offered by the white society that refused to acknowledge their humanity. When the end of the War brought no relief to the black community, even though it had offered more than its fair share of young lives to fight for freedom, Brooks and other creative artists began to question the wisdom of giving inordinate importance to art in such perilous times. In this poem, the speaker clearly argues for fighting for a world where artistic creativity can flourish.

Yet, to limit the call for militancy in "First Fight. Then Fiddle" to just African Americans would not offer a complete interpretation of the poem. The poem could also be read as a commentary on the process of creating art which requires a certain nurturing environment to bring forth its fruit. However, examined against the backdrop of World War II, the poem could also be read as a protest against all violence and hatred that deters the artist. The savagery of the Second World War was certainly not conducive to the creation of artistic works, and in this context, the call to arms may be seen as addressed to all the citizens to help preserve a civilized world where art can be created and valued. The poem also reminds us that all art requires unfettered devotion, and suffering and hurt are often the fate of the artist. Creation of art demands sacrifice in the face of resistance and indifference.

"First Fight. Then Fiddle," often anthologized, remains one of the most popular poems of Gwendolyn Brooks. Its use of traditional form and techniques to treat contemporary themes continues to delight readers of all ages.

Leela Kapai

FIRST SNOW IN ALSACE

Author: Richard Wilbur (1921   )
Type of poem: Lyric
First published: 1947 in *The Beautiful Changes and Other Poems*

The Poem

Richard Wilbur's "First Snow in Alsace" consists of eight three-line stanzas and a final line that completes the rhyme scheme. The poem describes the first snowfall of winter in Alsace, as the title indicates. Alsace is a region of eastern France frequently the subject of border disputes between France and Germany. Alsace was ceded to Germany as a result of the Franco-Prussian War but restored to France after World War I. The area was occupied by Germany during most of World War II until French and U.S. troops recovered the territory for France in 1945. The references to "shell-bursts," gutted homes, and an ammunition pile make the time as clear as the place: This snowfall occurs in the midst of the hostilities of World War II. Wilbur served in Europe in the war, and he credits his war experiences with stimulating his career as a poet. Wilbur felt that only when one was faced with chaos did one discover the need for the ordering forces of art.

The first four stanzas vividly describe the beauty of the nighttime snowy scene, in which the evidence of war is transfigured by the delicacy of the snowfall. Stanza five places the reader in the poem, opening with "You think," and speculating that the snow falls on the eyes of recently deceased soldiers still lying in fields. The next two stanzas describe "persons and persons in disguise" encountering the transformed landscape. Then the final stanza identifies a night guard returning from his post who cheerfully brags that "He was the first to see the snow." His youthful innocence contrasts with the grave images of warfare as it reminds the reader that war is indeed fought by the young.

Forms and Devices

The first part of this poem is highly descriptive and metaphorical. Wilbur uses a variety of figures of speech to evoke the snowy landscape. The falling snow is compared not simply to moths but to the unearthly image of "moths/ Burned on the moon." The snow cover is evoked with the metaphorical "simple cloths," a figure that is carried on with the adjective "rumpled." A rich use of metaphor is appropriate for Wilbur's emphasis on transformation: Just as metaphor expresses something in terms of what it is not, the snow transforms a grim, inhuman landscape into a vision of peaceful loveliness. Thus "the ration stacks are milky domes," and the snow-bedecked ammunition pile appears as "sparkling combs."

Wilbur personifies the snow to heighten the sense of it as an agent of transformation. Winter is personified as "benign," and the frost is depicted as an artisan capable of delighting children. But the most complex personification occurs in stanza three, where the snow blankets the roofs of houses "as if it did not know they'd changed." The change Wilbur refers to here is not the transformation of the snowfall but the change from peacetime to war which has left the homes "fear-gutted, trustless and estranged." "Fear-gutted" suggests, but does not literally denote, houses gutted by bombardment. More generally, it suggests a humanity transformed by the terror of war into a state of estrangement and suspicion. Wilbur's figurative language heightens a simple contrast between the world wrenched by the agonies of war and the natural events, like a first winter snowfall, that proceed unchecked, oblivious to the tortures humans inflict upon themselves.

Wilbur is a masterful versifier, using in his poetry a wide variety of traditional forms. Here he writes with a brisk iambic tetrameter and uses the *terza rima* made famous by Dante in *The Divine Comedy*. In this rhyme scheme, the first and last lines of each three-line stanza rhyme, while the second line initiates the rhyme of the next stanza: aba bcb and so on. This rhyme scheme creates a forward motion or march in which the energy of the next stanza grows out of the unresolved rhyme of the middle line of the preceding stanza. This motion may be appropriate to Wilbur's voyage or march through a transformed military landscape. The dramatic last line, rhyming "snow" with "slow," brings this forward progress to a halt.

Wilbur's use of assonance and alliteration is subtle but noticeable. Repetition of "s" and "r" sounds combined with a medial slant rhyme leads to a particularly vivid presentation of the chaos of warfare: "What shellbursts scattered and deranged,/ Entangled railings, crevassed lawn." The latter section of the poem is less figurative but denser in terms of sound. The serial rhyme words seem to echo one another as "mile" and "while" yield to "eyes," "disguise," and "surprise," to be succeeded by "fine," "benign," and "designs" (which in turn are echoed by "shines" in mid-line). Following this mellifluous series of long "i" rhymes, Wilbur slows down the prosody with the walking guard. The first two lines of the last stanza begin with metrical variations, clustering stresses on "night guard" and "ten first-snows" and ending with the alliteration of "boyish boast."

Wilbur uses strict poetic forms at a time when the dominant energies of modernist poetry tended toward free verse. While many poets felt that traditional forms did not fit the rhythms of modern life, Wilbur, throughout his poetic career, has used formal devices precisely to impose artistic order upon chaotic and fragmentary experiences. Dante's *terza rima* was widely interpreted as a unifying poetic device, symbolically invoking the Holy Trinity. Wilbur's more secular adaptation of the form still seeks to unify disparate and disturbing experiences in a sympathetic poetic vision.

Themes and Meanings

Understanding "First Snow in Alsace" begins by appreciating it as a war poem. The physical reminders of the war are few but vivid: shellbursts, fear-gutted homes, "soldiers dead a little while." Wilbur seeks to illuminate the horror of war by focusing on a brief respite from those horrors, the simple peacefulness of an evening snowfall. He describes the snow with a puzzling abstraction as "absolute snow." This phrase suggests the blanketing ubiquitousness of snow, the way it covers everything, even erases borders. It is as if the snow heals or covers over a wounded landscape.

Such symbolic readings imply a judging observer, and Wilbur's poem, which begins as an unpopulated natural scene, is peopled in interesting ways. The sudden "You think" of stanza five announces a move from physical description to human imagination. The dead soldiers introduced next are not literally within the range of the poet's description; they are annexed by an act of thought, by the unifying force of the snow which falls on the dead and the living alike. Against this eerie image of the eyes of the recently dead, comes a sudden peopling of the scene with "Persons and persons in disguise." While their disguise may suggest military camouflage, the context implies that it is the snow itself that transforms them within an altered landscape. That landscape and the fresh, white air stimulate the "shared surprise."

Now among the living, the reader is reminded that first snows hold special significance for children, children still innocent enough to read the frosted windowpanes as the work of a sprightly Jack Frost. It is in this context that Wilbur introduces the night guard. This boyish guard has his memory stimulated by the snow and thinks "ten first-snows back" to when he was, perhaps, a boy of eight or ten encountering the season's first snow fall with uncomplicated joy. His pride in being the first to see the snow actually warms him in the chilly landscape. The poem has moved from a wide-ranging descriptive vision to a focus on an individual character; its increasing warmth reflects that increasing intimacy.

Wilbur has subtly introduced familiar wartime themes in a fresh way. The gap between human pettiness and natural beauty, the youthful innocence of the combatants, the preciousness of a moment's joy in a time of fear and despair—all these themes emerge from the precise but emotionally loaded description of "First Snow in Alsace."

The poem traces the border between natural description and emotional tract, mingling the two in phrases such as "fear-gutted." Wilbur uses attentive and detailed description to ground the poem and eschew the clichéd and sentimental. The vividness of the description of the snow and the deftly created character of the youthful guard reveal a landscape in which time and place are especially poignant: occupied France in World War II.

Christopher Ames

THE FISH

Author: Elizabeth Bishop (1911-1979)
Type of poem: Meditation
First published: 1946 in *North and South*

The Poem

Elizabeth Bishop's "The Fish" is a highly compact meditative lyric of seventy-six free verse lines, relaying a first person narrator's experience of catching a "tremendous" fish, coming to an empathetic understanding and appreciation of it, and subsequently letting it go. The narrator's unspoken and self-transforming reaction to this fish, conveyed largely through imagery, contains the poem's theme and underlies the narrator's external actions. The poem begins significantly with the fish already caught and the speaker's awareness that the fish had really not fought her. She holds the fish "half out of water" so that he exists briefly in a liminal area half in and half out of his natural environment. In this place the narrator can examine him closely. Her initial observations are scrupulously objective. Any thoughts that the speaker may have are carefully masked by descriptive imagery which largely targets negative aspects. The fish which is "battered and venerable/ and homely" is also "infested/ with tiny white sea-lice."

While the verb "I caught" precedes this objective description of the fish, the narrator uses the verb "I thought of" to depart from objective appraisal in favor of interpolating aspects of the fish which she cannot see but which she knows must be present. Here she envisions the flesh that must lie beneath the fish's skin as well as its bones, entrails, and swim bladder. Her evaluation is not yet complete even after this thorough examination, for she then looks closely into his eyes, contrasting them minutely with her own. Though the speaker has been trying to comprehend the fish, it refuses to return her stare, remaining completely indifferent to her.

At this point the speaker utters for the first time an emotion brought about by her encounter with the fish: admiration for "his sullen face." It is with this expression of admiration that the narrator is enabled to notice details that her previous painstaking examination failed to uncover, details that will increase her admiration and intensify her experience. Embedded in the fish's mouth are five additional hooks, trailing broken fishing lines of various weights. After realizing the fish's earlier successful battles, she "stared and stared." Her thought process remains unrevealed, but in it there occurs a moment of epiphany, realization, comprehension. It is for the narrator a moment of breakthrough, of seeing something clearly and holistically that was previously unapprehended and which will slip away as the moment fades. For that moment, however, "victory filled up/ the little rented boat." Even nature cooperates with the inner dynamic of the speaker as oil and bilge water within the boat combine with sunlight "until everything/ was rainbow, rainbow, rainbow!" It is at this point that she, almost automatically, without the need for thought, releases the fish.

Forms and Devices

The narrator's empathy with the fish arises from her concentrated examination of him. Bishop conveys this empathy to the reader through dense and exacting descriptive phrases replete with similes and metaphors. Every single word serves to convey what the fish is like and indirectly communicates the narrator's thoughts and feelings. In her initial examination, the speaker compares his skin to strips of "ancient wallpaper," a homely image that belies her apparent objectivity by depicting the fish in terms of something familiar. As she extends her wallpaper imagery, she stresses the age of the fish, for, appearing on the wallpaper/fish are "shapes like full-blown roses/ stained and lost through age." While the fish has not fought her, he has not given up for his gills continued to struggle to strain the "terrible oxygen" of the air. The narrator refers to them as "frightening gills" and hints at past experiences in which she discovered that gills "can cut so badly." The description of the fish is exhaustively thorough; nothing is neglected, not the banal, the possibly disgusting, or the frightening. Though objective, the description alludes to thoughts and feelings and prepares the reader for the narrator's response.

As the narrator relates those parts of the fish that she cannot see, her desire to do so and her choice of imagery again reveals her growing empathy. She envisions "white flesh/ packed in like feathers," "the dramatic reds and blacks/ of his shiny entrails," and even his swim bladder which she compares to a "big peony." Nothing about the fish disgusts her as she concentrates on what is before her. The narrator devotes more imagery to the eyes than to any other part of the fish. Traditionally it is the eye that conveys much about person or creature. Here too, for the first time, the comparison is not with an outside object, but initially, at least, with her own eyes. Noting that the fish's eyes are "larger than mine/ but shallower, and yellowed," she strains for an exact representation, describing the irises as "backed and packed/ with tarnished tinfoil/ seen through the lenses/ of old scratched isinglass."

When the narrator notices the hooks, she notes that they are hanging from a lip that is "grim, wet, and weapon-like." She describes the hooks and trailing lines as "medals with their ribbons" and a "five-haired beard of wisdom." Obviously the fish has become a kind of symbol for the human qualities the narrator and Bishop admire: courage, strength, perseverance, shrewdness. Yet it never becomes abstract for these very qualities are inherent in the actual, living fish. Neither is the personification of victory an abstraction as it fills the boat, but it is the very real result of the narrator's concentration on the unique individuality of the fish. The rainbow at the end of the poem literally takes over everything, making all the faulty and ordinary artifacts of the boat, the "rusted engine," the "bailer rusted orange," the "sun-cracked thwarts," into itself "until everything/ was rainbow, rainbow, rainbow!" This final image speaks of the transformation taking place within the narrator through an encounter with what appears ordinary to the outward eye. Yet the rainbow, too, preserves its own reality as oil in bilge water. The ordinary reveals the uncommon when penetrated by perceptual imagination.

Themes and Meanings

This poem contains three significant themes: the integration of subjective and objective observation, an almost feminist definition of victory, and the active involvement of the reader in the experience recreated in the poem. These themes also appear in much of Bishop's other works. Bishop felt strongly that to discover the truth or reality of anything, one must become self-forgetful, totally caught up in the apprehension of what one is concentrating on. She illustrates this poetic tenet in many of her poems, like "The Fish," which is essentially a lyric meditation. It is the combination of her close objective examination of the fish and her richly speculative subjective interpolation from what she sees that enable her to grasp intuitively the qualities inherent in the fish she has caught. For a brief, but intense moment, she is at one with nature as represented by the fish and at one with the values he embodies.

As she stares and takes in the reality of the fish, "victory filled up/ the little rented boat." The adjective "rented" indicates her own fragility. Just as the fish is being held partly out of the water, its natural home, so she is in a sense equally out of place on the water in a boat she does not own. The victory filling up the boat is not her victory over the fish she has caught, but victory over the tenuousness and precarious mystery of the human situation brought to her in her interaction with the fish, transformed in her imagination into a veteran fighter. It is a victory brought about by and belonging to both combatants. She turns the tables on those who believe that victory entails a winner and a loser.

The perceptive reader is also included in this victory. For Bishop, the poet who conceives a certain truth through a real or imagined experienced must convey this truth to the reader. Bishop does so here by making the reader participate in the narrator's discovery by working through the imagery. It bears in upon the reader's consciousness just as the actual observation of details works on the consciousness of the narrator, allowing her to see the fish in a new light. Though the narrator carefully suppresses any emotion until the last lines of the poem where they burst out in ineffable triumph, the reader is impelled through a series of emotions through the power and vividness of the imagery. The last line, "And I let the fish go," appears almost anticlimactic for the narrator, who cannot do anything else, but the action signals a release of emotion for the reader. "The Fish," firmly places Bishop in the tradition of Wallace Stevens and Marianne Moore in her insistence on the need for acute observation of the ordinary, strict rhetorical control over imagery and description, and the poetical authority to convey the truth of an experience to perceptive readers.

Christine R. Catron

THE FISH

Author: Marianne Moore (1887-1972)
Type of poem: Lyric
First published: 1918; collected in *Poems*, 1921

The Poem

"The Fish" is a short poem in rhymed syllabic verse; its forty lines are divided into eight stanzas. In this poem, Marianne Moore utilizes elegant imagery and a highly visual structure. Many readers have found "The Fish" obscure, since its primary subject seems not to be fish but the defiant independence of a seaside cliff. Actually, the poem is about the sea, the cliff, and the relationship between them.

Moore often uses the first line of a poem as its title, as she does with "The Fish." This technique sometimes makes the title less a summing up of the poem than a point of departure. Such titles may also be misleading. "The Fish" starts with a reference to fish, moves through a rich descriptive array of aquatic life, and finally makes a point about a cliff buffeted by the sea. Like the fecund ocean it describes, the poem moves inexorably toward the cliff, but there is more description of beautiful sea life than there is of the "dead" cliff.

The poem begins with an image of fish swimming "through black jade," which suggests dark, viscous water. Moore goes on immediately to describe mussels, focusing on one mussel in particular, which is stirring the sand ("adjusting the ash-heaps") by opening and closing itself. The intensely visual description of sea life suggests the force and fecundity of the ocean.

To the observant speaker, barnacles "encrust" a wave of water as they would the hull of a ship. The barnacles "cannot hide," however, because sunlight refracted ("split like spun glass") through water appears to move with the undulant motion of the waves, and illuminates "the turquoise sea of bodies."

As the waves strike the shore, "The water drives a wedge/ of iron through the iron edge/ of the cliff," pushing flotsam into the wall of earth, which is already rusty from iron deposits or the waves' earlier leavings. The action of the waves also washes starfish, small shellfish like "pink rice grains," jellyfish, crabs, and "submarine toadstools" against the shore, where they "slide each on the other" with the motion of the water.

The last three stanzas further describe the cliff as a "defiant edifice," covered with scars from the action of the sea, "all the physical features of/ ac-/ cident," and human activity, "dynamite grooves, burns, and/ hatchet strokes." The cliff is one side of the "chasm" the ocean occupies. "The sea grows old" in this huge space, for without it there would be no sea.

The poem's penultimate sentence, "Repeated/ evidence has proved that it can live/ on what can not revive/ its youth," is ambiguous. "It" refers to the cliff, but "its" may refer to both the cliff and the sea. The "dead" land "lives" on what the sea deposits, creating a fossil record of "what cannot revive its youth"; as time brings constant change, the sea's leavings make more land. Neither land nor sea can "revive its youth." At the end of the poem, the inanimate cliff, a "defiant edifice," endures all the sea's changes, but the sea endures too.

Forms and Devices

Moore said in an interview that what she wrote "could only be called poetry because there is no other category in which to put it," but her writing uses the forms and devices of poetry to produce interesting effects. Visual description and careful attention to a formal structure of syllables and rhymes devised by the poet for the particular poem are poetic devices Moore uses in "The Fish."

In metrical verse, the poet pays attention to which syllables are stressed and which are unstressed. In syllabic verse, the poet creates a pattern by simply counting the number of syllables in a line. In "The Fish," the syllabic pattern is one syllable in the first line of each stanza, three syllables in the second line, nine in the third, six in the fourth, and eight in the fifth. The rhyme scheme of each stanza is *aabbc*. In the version of "The Fish" published in *Observations* (1924), the stanzas were six lines long. Moore moved words to create five-line stanzas for the version in *Collected Poems* (1951) and subsequent editions of her work.

The description in "The Fish" is more visual than auditory, and the appearance of the poem is as important as its sound. Fish are not usually described as "wading," which suggests shallow water, as does the solitary word "wade." The phrase "split like spun," appearing between "sun" and "glass," mimics the split the lines describe. With "ac-," Moore uses the accident her syllabic verse produces by requiring her to have a one-syllable line where she needs a three-syllable word.

"The Fish" contains considerable consonance and alliteration. For example, as the second stanza carries over to the third, and the third to the fourth, *s* sounds dominate the lines, suggesting the rush of the sea. Perhaps the frequent recurrence of the letter *s* visually suggests the ripples and waves of the water.

By carrying over the words "an/ injured fan" from the first stanza to the second, Moore makes her poem visually suggest something broken and fanned out. In the seventh stanza, *k* sounds in "ac-," "lack," "cornice," "strokes," and "chasm" give the poem a hacked and chopped sound as well as a choppy appearance. "The Fish" abounds in similar consonance, relying on emphatic sounds to suggest the violence of the processes it describes.

Counting syllables and relying on rhyme allowed Moore to produce work with the formal appearance of poetry but with some of the virtues of prose as well. "The Fish" beautifully accommodates an ebb and flow of sensuous images and the linear drive of abstract prose. Moore takes pains to interpret her images. Just as the poem moves from describing living fish to describing the "dead" chasm-side, the elegant flow of images washes up on a final stanza that uses less concrete language to reveal the emotional focus of the poem.

Themes and Meanings

The accumulation of precise detail in "The Fish" at first suggests that the poem is about delicate marine life. By the last stanza, it has become clear that the poem is not merely about fish. Some readers, however, have found the conclusion difficult to paraphrase. In his book on Moore's poetry, Donald Hall, for example, has said, "The last lines . . . are moving without being entirely penetrable."

Moore sometimes creates confusion and deliberate obscurity in order to work out subtle interrelationships. Part of the difficulty of the poem's ending is that it seems to offer a moral without explicitly stating one. The emphatic conclusion, "The sea grows old in it," is hardly a moral in the traditional sense. Instead, as Hall's word "moving" suggests, "The Fish" conveys a sense of mounting emotion as Moore pursues her subject. Though abstract and evasive, the penultimate sentence of "The Fish" is obviously assertive. No living thing can "revive its youth," but the word "what" in Moore's circumlocution "what cannot revive its youth," is deliberately vague and inclusive.

The sea is a tremendous power, threatening not only the marine life that it can fling against the shore, but also the land that surrounds it. In the fourth stanza, Moore repeats the word "iron" within a single line. Whatever the literal significance of the poem's iron, it certainly stands for that which is hard and unyielding. Moore admires "this defiant edifice," but she also appreciates the beauty of marine life.

Although none of the living things in the poem is personified with the difficult intensity Moore devotes to the cliff, the life in the sea is described in careful detail. In addition, although the qualities she finds in the cliff are obviously qualities she admires in humans, Moore personifies the cliff without making it less of a cliff. Like the cliff, the form of the poem is an example of the strength of idiosyncratic individuality; like the sea, the poem is full of delicate beauty.

"The Fish" is a poem about opposing forces—the sea and the land—and about change and stasis. Moore describes the "external marks of abuse" on the cliff, and though it is "defiant," the "chasm-side" cliff is also "dead." What lives internally in the sea is the ever-changing marine life with which the poem began. Finally, it is the relationship between the cliff and the sea that gives the poem its strength and its beauty.

Describing the space that an ocean fills as a "chasm" causes one to see major geological forms in an interesting way. The sea is usually portrayed as inexorable, relentlessly wearing away the land. By seeing the land as a space the sea occupies, Moore reminds the reader that only the surface of the earth is mostly water. Under the water, the land endures both the effects of oceans and the depredations of humankind. "The Fish" is an ecological poem that is not about either ocean or cliff alone but about the way in which a poem can beautifully accommodate the relationship between them.

Thomas Lisk

FLATIRONS

Author: Lorna Dee Cervantes (1954-   )
Type of poem: Meditation, ode
First published: 1991, in *From the Cables of Genocide: Poems on Love and Hunger*

The Poem

Lorna Dee Cervantes' "Flatirons" is an evocative rendering of the mountain range situated to the southwest of Boulder, Colorado. It is dedicated to "the Ute and Arapaho," tribal communities who lived in this region for centuries, and the images that Cervantes assembles in a series of surrealistic vignettes convey aspects of the communal life that has vanished as a result of the advance of the European social order. In the opening lines, Cervantes depicts the mountains as "ghosts/ of slaughtered mules," establishing the ethos of loss that is one of the dominant modes of the poem, and then personalizes the image by declaring that "the whites of my/ ancestors rest on the glaciers," extending the concept of a haunted landscape. She develops the image further as she envisions the remains of a prior culture "veiled/ and haloed with the desire of electrical/ storms," a surreal portrayal that joins the terrain to the psychological inclinations of its inhabitants.

As the poem proceeds, Cervantes moves toward the present, noting how the vivid features of the geologic strata ("a chimney of shedding sundown") attract visitors to the region. A kind of dual perspective emerges as the ancestral connections Cervantes evokes are, in a sense, assaulted by more recent arrivals. Calling herself—and by implication, her cultural heritage—"Statuesque/ and exquisitely barren," she asserts that her "seed shines/ in the dying rays" but that the "rich earth of the wealthy" distorts the memory and meaning of the mountain range. Cervantes labels the deprivations "Monstrous/ and sullen" and likens newer constructions to "slabs of death."

Recalling her history in elemental terms—"My harmony/ of blood and ash"—she condemns the intruders with words designed to indicate their inability to appreciate the dynamics of the landscape, seeing them as "shuffling," "vague," and "derelict," and in a version of historical judgment tells how they have blighted "a dream where the bison and mammoths unite" in "The/ winter of their genocide."

The somber mood of the central section of the poem is altered as Cervantes moves back toward the fundamental elements of the land to suggest that there is a possibility that the deeper aspects of the landscape will endure, "the story of their streams is as long/ as the sabers of northern ice." To reinforce this point, she focuses on a primal union of earth and water, which created the mountains, as "conquests of the sea." The remainder of the poem is a powerful paean to the grandeur of the Flatiron range, which "stands royal in/ her invisible captivity," both "elemental and efficient." The conclusion of the poem continues the sense of a terrestrial goddess whose eminence remains in spite of destructive forces and misguided humans, most significantly "in the memory of a native" who can still see and experience the living spirit of the culture that has been reduced to the "silent baying" of a ghostly survivor of a massacre.

Forms and Devices

"Flatirons" is a tightly constructed poem that unfolds with the unrelenting intensity of a dream-vison, its language designed to maintain the kinetic force of a high-energy field. The appearance of the Flatiron range is developed in a series of surreal images that retain a degree of ambiguity that prevents an easy understanding of the power latent in each provocative description. From the start, when Cervantes declares that "The mountains are there like ghosts/ of slaughtered mules," the unusual comparison of the physical presence of the landscape to an ephemeral entity, which is likened to the destroyed carcass of a mundane beast of burden, eludes any kind of simple metaphorical equivalent. Cervantes is interested in unhinging the kind of asssured response to familiar imagery that makes some successful poems comfortable to read, and her continuing employment of radically disconcerting descriptions reflects her own uneasiness with the recent history of the locality.

The concept of the landscape itself as a kind of sentient creature is conveyed by the detailed image of her ancestor's spirit, called "white" (to suggest both its ghostly nature and a literal deposit of bleached bones) as a parallel to the glacial remnants, portrayed as "veiled and haloed" to deepen its etherial and angelic aspects and given an emotional component in its manifestation of "the desire of electrical storms." The ambiguity inherent in ascribing desire to a meteorological phenomenon contributes to the original and unexpected ambience of the world that the poem imagines. Similarly, images that join apparently irreconcilable elements, as in "my harmony/ of blood and ash," or images that consist of strikingly distinctive modifications, as in "vague ahems," carry this strategy through the poem, while the line that has these "vague ahems" operating as an agent of union with "the sucking fish in a derelict river" is a means of creating a startling juxtaposition that defies a literal explanation as it advances the poem's presentation of strangeness.

The last section of the poem is constructed as an appreciative tribute to the aspects of the mountains, which for Cervantes are emblems of the special qualities she treasures and would like to see preserved. In accordance with the inventive imagery of the previous lines, Cervantes introduces the concluding part of "Flatirons" with a group of compact depictions, stating initially that "The mountains/ are the conquest of the sea" to establish the massive forces involved. Then, the fusion of a personalized identification and the personification of the subject deepens as the mountains are explicitly refered to as "She" and are given attributes that blend psychological perceptions with geophysical attributes, as "she stands royal" with a "belly of gems," "fossil stays," and "solicitudes." The permanence of this place, its capacity to exist "after massacre," is celebrated in the poet's insistence that it remains "elemental and efficient" in spite of "genocide."

Themes and Meanings

In one of her most frequently anthologized pieces, the "Poem for the Young White Man Who Asked Me How I, an Intelligent, Well-Read Person Could Believe in the War Between Races" (from her first collection, *Emplumada*, 1981), Cervantes says,

"Every day I am deluged with reminders/ that this is not/ my land," and then ripostes, "and this is my land." "Flatirons" is designed as an explanation of just how the land belongs to the communities whose heritage and residence there stretches back across historical epochs—the "Ute and Arapaho," who are the dedicatees of the poem, and others whose experiences there are the substance from which Cervantes has fashioned the vivid images that invest the mountains with a complex personality.

Cervantes is trying to diminish the conventional European-American separation of humans from their surroundings and to introduce to the reader unfamiliar with this concept a different kind of understanding, another method for seeing and knowing. Although some of her images, such as the evocative "dripping pursuance of thawing babies," may tend to resist an immediate comprehension, the clustering of these images contributes to the development of an alternate reality in which human vision has been expanded to include the possibility of a life-spirit inhabiting nonhuman elements of the world.

The specifically capitalized "Ghost Dances" near the center of the poem functions as a register of these forces and as testament to the rituals of the communities that lived on the land prior to the arrival of inhabitants who ignored any evidence of earlier civilizations. Cervantes' continual employment of unusual syntactical constructions corresponds to the poem's suggestions that there are means of comprehension other than customary styles of description might suggest. Cervantes feels that the land contains the psychic imprint of a long historical record (as in "a dream where the bisons and mammoth unite"), and the entire poem is directed toward a condition of perception that encourages a grasp of this concept. The words "genocide" and "massacre" imply that certain powers have worked to obliterate the history she values, an idea further substantiated by the title of the collection in which the poem appeared, *From the Cables of Genocide: Poems on Love and Hunger.*

Cervantes is concerned about what might be a program to eradicate the evidence of any variant from a controlled contemporary version of events, a program initiated by those responsible for the "monstrous and sullen" constructions she identifies as "slabs of death." "Flatirons" stands as an eloquent, impassioned rebuttal to this pernicious tendency, and as a demonstration of the powers of language to reinvigorate a suppressed or hidden cultural presence. The poem is a kind of introduction to a new (but actually ancient) world for the literate but differently experienced reader who may not have thought about these issues before. Cervantes' ability to invest them with a vitality that brings them to the foreground of consciousness is her tribute to ancestors to whom she feels a direct connection, and whose lives continue to provide her with the energy of creation.

Leon Lewis

THE FLEA

Author: John Donne (1572-1631)
Type of poem: Lyric
First published: 1633

The Poem

In the lyric poem "The Flea," by John Donne, a clearly-individualized speaker attempts to persuade a lady to make love with him. He does this through a clever, well-constructed, tongue-in-cheek argument. Presented as a conversation between two people in which the man does all of the talking, the speaker pleads for the love of the woman. The silent woman responds with an unequivocal action; she squashes the flea and, in effect, his argument. The plea takes the form of three patterned stanzas of rhymed, generally iambic pentameter verse. This strict form belies the familiar manner the speaker assumes as he, apparently spontaneously, develops an analogy about himself and the lady and a flea. In the analogy, he compares what he would like to see happen, their intimate union, with what they can observe and assume about their blood mingling within the body of the flea.

The speaker begins speaking as if he and his longed-for mistress were already in a conversation. He seems to be pursuing yet another direction in his attempt to effect the woman's acquiescence when he tries this: "Mark but [look at] this flea." In pointing out the flea which has jumped into sight, the man begins an extended analogy that demands witty explanation and elaboration in order that it become a rationale for his position. He says that because the flea has sucked the blood of both of them, they are intimately connected, yet as all, his lady in particular, know there has been no sin, "nor shame, nor loss of maidenhead." The speaker then goes on to complain that this flea did not even have to "woo" her as he must do.

The second stanza draws his beloved into the poem as he begs her not to kill the flea. "Stay," he pleads. The flea, he contends, has become an icon of their love, embodying them, at least their blood, literally. In so doing the flea brings them together and is their "marriage bed" or even, he declares, their "marriage temple." As temple, the flea acquires a sacred quality, able to cloister, or hold safely, these two potential lovers as a church protects two refugees. In the "walls of jet," that is the body of the flea, these two are kept safe from the enemy, her protective parents.

To dissuade her from killing the flea, he alleges that in killing the flea she will kill herself, a sacrilegious act, as well as kill the flea and him. The line, "Though use make you apt to kill me" refers to the seventeenth century belief that each instance of sexual intercourse shortened the length of one's life and weakened the participants.

The lady does kill the flea, "Purpled thy nail in blood of innocence." The ingenious speaker seizes one last strategy when she apparently concedes, at least partially, to the analogy, when she says that neither of them is "the weaker now." He points out that seeing that this fear is groundless provides evidence that other fears are as well: "Just so much honor, when thou yield'st to me/Will waste, as this flea's death took life from thee." Her quick response with her nail in the face of this man's elaborate plea suggests her response to his final assertion as well.

Forms and Devices

The poem presents a dramatic exchange between two people that has the feel of spontaneity and witty repartee. The drama, wit, and immediacy are parts of its device. As a seventeenth century poem, a metaphysical poem, the work manifests certain qualities characteristic of the age and of this type of poetry. The metaphysical poets, of whom John Donne is the chief exemplar, wrote in a style reactive to the earlier generation of poets, chiefly the Elizabethan sonneteers writing love poems in the manner of the Italian, Petrarch. While Donne, does, at times, reflect Petrachian themes and forms, more often, he revolts against the conventional, artificial, and restrictive qualities of these poems, preferring to draw analogies from the concrete world and explore heretofore unmentionable aspects of love. He reflects not only a new approach to poetry but a new orientation of mind in that he, as well as other seventeenth century thinkers, was drawn away from philosophic concerns of why to scientific concerns of how. Thus he looks not to the traditional metaphors of love poems but, instead, looks to the everyday world for effective correlatives of experience. He prefers the mundane, contemporary analogies to the lofty and other worldly—thus, the flea. Further, he couches his poetic figures in diction and syntax that sound like conversation.

The extended analogy is also characteristic of this poetry. "The Flea" presents an example of a metaphysical conceit, a type of analogy that requires more elaboration and explanation than other more obvious analogies. Metaphysical poets saw their world in terms of comparisons. Still, even when the similarities between what the flea does with what the couple could do and then the way the flea symbolizes their love can finally be granted, it still remains a strange, if not bizarre comparison. Its outrageousness is part of the effect of the playful pose the poet creates for the speaker. In later and more serious poems, Donne uses the conceit as a way of analyzing his love and his experience of it. Here the conceit makes the poem entertaining and amusing.

Intellect and logical reasoning shape the poems. Here, the flea presents itself as an ideal comparison enabling this clever lover to demonstrate his ingenuity in creating a logical, albeit specious, argument. However a specious argument is not the nor for Donne or the metaphysical poets. The norm is logic, a movement from premise to conclusion. Here, as always, Donne uses and demands intellectual acuity.

Themes and Meanings

"The Flea" is a love poem with a difference. It reflects a new approach toward poetry. Its unconventional analogy, it extensive exploration of the subject to serve as a logical argument, and it playful intellectual tone give it fresh, even revolutionary qualities that made it appealing in its day. Donne exerted a strong influence on his contemporaries, was studied by Dr. Samuel Johnson in the eighteenth century, admired by Samuel Taylor Coleridge in the nineteenth century, and became an important influence on twentieth century poets, especially the poet and critic, T. S. Eliot. John Donne has always had an important place in the canon of English literature.

"The Flea" was written by a man who was not a professional poet but a man who initially wrote poems as a small part of a full and busy life, circulating them in manuscript to his social circle—a group of sophisticated, intellectual friends, and to his patronesses. His poems like this one explore the many moods and experiences of love—the hopeful, the philandering, the angry, the thwarted love. Later they explore secure and happily married love and, even later, religious love. This work in many ways typifies Donne's poems. It has the colloquial or conversational tone. It, like many of his poems, addresses his current love. It clearly delights in it own paradox and wit. It is structured and formal but explodes that form, here with direct address and exclamation. The poem, like others, proceeds with logic challenging the reader to follow his reasoning which reflects scientific, political, and religious themes or ideas of the day.

Like poets before and after him, Donne employs analogy, but like other intellectuals of the seventeenth century, he is imbued with the significance of the everyday world within one's perceptions in contrast to his predecessors imbued with the spiritual world or the classical world outside of immediate perception. Thus he creates analogies from objects of daily use or observation: the flea, or in other poems, a mandrake root, angels, a compass, a globe, fighting armies. Yet, despite his interest in the concrete and the contemporary, his poems reflect the conflicting claims of both the flesh and the spirit. His analogies so often strikingly unusual show his attempts to understand and express the conflicted nature of humankind. The content of the poem may, as in this poem, become the explanation of the analogy. The analogy may, at other times, be employed to reflect a state of mind. The poems are purposeful.

The poem points out the many purposes, tones, and methods of poetry. It acquaints us with a clear, individualized voice, the poetic possibility of a facetious tone, a dramatic, playful love situation. It demonstrates the use of logic, subtle, perceptive observation of the world and a colloquial style—all elements that have been influential to poets over the years but especially to Donne's contemporaries and to the poets of the twentieth century.

Bernadette Flynn Low

FLEEING

Author: Nelly Sachs (1891-1970)
Type of poem: Lyric
First published: 1959, as "In der Flucht," in *Flucht und Verwandlung*; English translation collected in *O the Chimneys*, 1967

The Poem

A brief free-verse poem of sixteen lines divided into four stanzas, "Fleeing" was written originally in German. The present progressive form of the title suggests flight as an incessant reality, intensified by the poet's unblinking scrutiny.

The poem opens with a curious observation, voiced with more wonder than irony. The poet marvels about the "great reception" one encounters "on the way" while fleeing. She reveals herself as immersed in the process, rather than focused on the point either of departure or of arrival.

This reception involves the participation of the natural world, represented by the elements and by animate life. The world is in constant motion, caught in the currents of change: wind, sand, and evolving beings. As such, it invites no comment; there is no "amen" to the prayer recited in its sanctuary. Existence is "compelled," the poet concludes in the second stanza, in its eternal metamorphosis.

The imperative of transformation is embodied by the butterfly, which the poet presents in the third stanza—presumably as an image of the self. It is "sick," and transformation can serve as a kind of healing. Metamorphosis is not without continuity; the butterfly will "learn again of the sea"—that is, be reconciled with its origins.

Every living being leaves an impression; comprehension of life's hieroglyphics is available to the imagination, as nature even in its storm of change becomes meaningful in relationship to consciousness: A stone "with the fly's inscription" gives itself into the poet's hand. The poet's borderless dwelling in the universe is conveyed by her description of it as an environment of worship: "Wrapped/ in the wind's shawl"—that is, the tallith, or prayer shawl—with feet "in the prayer of sand."

In the final stanza, the poet locates herself in a moment of time rather than a demarcation of geography (a "homeland"), and this moment is fleeting. That is, time and space are conspiring to flee with her; the entire world is gathering itself for transformation.

Forms and Devices

Recurring throughout Nelly Sachs's poetry are the images of dust, or sand, and the butterfly, both symbols of metamorphosis. Representing both the animate and inanimate worlds, these images indicate a creation that is in flux. Sachs also evokes the idea of creation as a work in progress, rather than as a finished product, in her allusion to the workings of evolution: from "fin to wing/ and further."

The imagery in "Fleeing," as in other Sachs poems, acts sacramentally; that is, natural objects become agents of spiritual awareness: The wind becomes a prayer shawl, the sand a prayer. Language itself is a vehicle for the sacred, through prayer as well as through inscription that contains revelation.

Meanings and significances of words themselves undergo metamorphosis in the course of the poem: Fleeing turns into a reception; a stone becomes something impressionable and communicative. The very alchemy of which poetry is capable is thus suggested. The poem acts like a hymn as a vehicle for transformative experience. The critic J. P. Bauke has written that Sachs's poetry "reaches the hymnic pathos of prophecy"; poet Stephen Spender has described her verse as "apocalyptic hymns."

The shortness of the lines, along with the use of the dash at the end of each stanza, helps communicate rhythmically the urgency and incompleteness, the thrust into the unsayable, conveyed by the poem's transmutable imagery and language.

With its emphasis on imagery—on metaphor, juxtaposition, ellipses—rather than on complex rhythmic texture or intricate rhyme scheme, Sachs's poetry can be readily appreciated in translation.

Themes and Meanings

"Fleeing" is, paradoxically, a poem of discovery. The poet locates home in the very becoming of the world, seeing herself in its evolving face. Life finds its reality in the act of metamorphosis; this genius for transformation is life's justification—and its only redemption.

Nelly Sachs, a Jewish poet, alludes to Jewish ritual and mystical tradition in her work. The word is sacred in Judaism; the spoken word—prayer—and the written word—scripture—culminate in a revelation of the nature of creation—that is, of its transformative power. Flight, then, in the ultimate sense, is part of the re-creation that vitalizes the world.

Sachs herself was a refugee from Nazi Germany. As cowinner of the Nobel Prize in Literature in 1966, with Shmuel Yosef Agnon, a Jewish fiction writer, Sachs commented, "Agnon represents the State of Israel. I represent the tragedy of the Jewish people." In 1940, Sachs emigrated to Sweden, and during and after World War II, she wrote the poetry upon which her reputation largely came to be based. Like other Jewish writers, such as Elie Wiesel, who survived the Holocaust, she assumed the role of witness. As such, she neither rationalizes nor moralizes.

Rather, as a mystic, she gives voice to the questions, and articulates the visions, experienced by her people, Israel, in pangs of suffering. Individuals may have disappeared, but not without a trace. Sachs's poems serve as inscriptions of their lives on the soul, and these inscriptions can be illuminated to read the meaning of the world.

Amy Adelstein

FLESH AND BLOOD

Author: C. K. Williams (1936-   )
Type of poem: Book of poems
First published: 1987

The Poems

One hundred thirty poems make up *Flesh and Blood*, C. K. Williams's fifth book of poetry and winner of the National Book Critics Circle Award. There are three parts to the book; it would not be far from the mark to say that the first ninety-six poems represent chaos, the next thirty-three order, and the final long poem harmony. The long first part contains individually titled stanzas, and except for a few pairs (back-to-back "Alzheimer," "Snow," and "Drought" poems), little at first suggests an arranged sequence. Instead, the themes are disparate and the poems stand alone.

The thirty-three poems of part 2 are also titled stanzas, but thematic keys are given as well. The first half of each title gives one of five themes: "Reading," "Suicide," "Love," "Good Mother," and "Vehicle." The second part of the title, following a colon, renders the poem more specific, as in "Reading: The Gym" or "Suicide: Anne." Of the five thematic groupings, there are six poems in the first, three in the second, ten in the third, and seven each in the fourth and fifth. With these themes in mind, the reader can identify poems in part 1 that correspond to themes in part 2. "Girl Meets Boy" and "Experience" are "Love" poems, while "Easter" extends the Good Mother theme to include a father. The "Vehicle" poems are speculative, and many poems in part 1 are also of this type. In "Herakles" and "Cowboys," for example, Williams speculates on the nature of heroism in myth and movie. In part 2, "Suicide: Anne," he explores the psychological ground of poet Anne Sexton.

Part 3 is a single poem of 144 lines, "La Petit Salvié" (the small redemption). It is an elegy to scholar and poet Paul Zweig, Williams's friend who lived in France as a semi-exile, dead at age forty-eight. These final stanzas, less than a seventh of the book, rise to a high pitch both as a speculative instrument and as a "flesh and blood" record. (*Flesh and Blood* is dedicated to another Paul—Paul B. Williams, the poet's father.)

One of the two most notable formal aspects of the poems is the fact that each poem in the book is eight lines long. *Flesh and Blood* therefore consists of 147 stanzas that appear very similar to one another and are usually presented 2 to a page. The other is Williams's use of a very long poetic line—so long that it virtually always wraps around onto the next line on the page. Without a flexible line of great length, 147 eight-line stanzas could easily induce ennui, sinking the project. Williams, whose lines vary from 18 to 30 syllables and whose stanzas vary from 174 to 215 syllables (as an analysis of 15 stanzas shows), uses diverse kinds of language, varied themes, and a plethora of tones and moods to strike the emotional and intellectual quality of his verse. A typical stanza from *Flesh and Blood* (190 syllables) is one-third longer that a typical sonnet, and the extra room often gives the stanza-poems a wider and deeper reach.

The materials for the poems come via the poet's eye as an observer of the human species. The best poems are the nonspeculative ones that show humans in situations with well-defined character motivation in postmodern settings. Linda Gregerson, writing in *Poetry*, sees the poems as "an impassioned essay on the moral life of urban humanity." This characterization certainly holds true regarding the Good Mother series in part 2. Williams is able to show, with use of fine detail, the treatment children receive from unwitting parents. "Good Mother: The Plane" is an example; a mother is waiting for a flight, hours late, with a child in tow, and she "finally loses patience."

Forms and Devices

Just before Williams's first book (*Lies*, 1969) came out, Anne Sexton was asked to write something for the cover. Her words on the inside front flap describe the writer as "a demon" and a "master of metaphor." One of Williams's masterful metaphors is in "Suicide: Anne," in which he uses the phrase "a badly started nail" to stand for Sexton's emotionally aberrant life. This ingenious metaphor contains two braided truths as well as an impersonal exactness. An unstraight nail is incorrigible, an obdurate life unyielding. In "Regret," the metaphor "in its cold coils" works at a similar level.

A metaphor sometimes waits awhile before it is completed in *Flesh and Blood*. The first poem, "Elms," for example, becomes a metaphor for the last. The trees of the avenue are chain-sawed down until "naked facing buildings stare." One at a time "the winds of time" destroy all living things. Zweig's death, like the loss of the elms, exposes Williams to his unprotected thoughts. In stanza 15 of "La Petit Salvié," he writes about "Clearing clumps of shrubs" from Zweig's small, crumbling estate in the Dordogne at a time when Zweig is weak with fever. He tells of "sawing down a storm-split plum" and of "malevolently armoured maguey:/ their roots are as frail as flesh." "The winds of time" become in stanza 2 "a perfect breeze" that washes across Zweig's bed.

In "Sixteen: Tuscany" Williams likens young men drawn to his teenage daughter to bees. There are, among others, "two vacationing Sicilian bees." The last line, "The air is filled with promises of pollen," translates as possible romance, sexuality, and fecundity. Williams often prefaces a metaphor with the two-word device "the way . . . ," as in "Hooks." Here bus riders look at a pretty girl's artificial hand "[t]he way someone would glance at [an] unruly, apparently ferocious but really quite friendly dog."

Flesh and Blood is the third of Williams's books to use the long line, which has developed a characteristic quality and has become his trademark. With his third book conversational and his fourth book narrational, his long line came to display a language that challenges the traditional view that poetry is concise, tight-knit, and economical. Particularly interesting is the use Williams makes of polysyllabic abstract words and long adjectival clusters. The result is a prosody heavy with unstressed syllables, capable of cadence and incantation, not far from natural speech (although natural speakers never show such lexical wealth), charged semantically to a degree usually found only in compressed verse forms.

In "Guatemala: 1964" phrases such as "implacable, picturesque aloofness" and "disconcertingly beyond suspicion" conjure more than they define. Williams seems to enjoy sewing strings of conjecture into sentence fabrics. In "Herakles" he wonders if the hero's "feats and deeds be not exemplary but cautionary." A prose writer might find the assonance unsuitable, whereas a traditional lyricist might complain of prosy, abstract diction. Williams is plainly exploring the limits and challenging norms.

"First Desires" contains such turns of phrase as "ardent arpeggios" and "chromatic dissonance." An indigent person who traces texts in a public library, in "The Critic," has "blood-rimmed eyes as rapt as David's doing psalms." The words "inconceivable capitulation," in "Repression," beg more questions than they pin down. "Reading: The Cop" describes an armed guard's weapon as "a large-caliber, dull-black stockless machine gun," and "Souls" says that carnival teddy bears are "unrelentingly filthy, matted with the sticky, sickly, ghastly, dark gray sheen/ you see on bums."

Besides adjectival phrases and abstract diction, the poems include foreign words and phrases (usually French), European place names, musical terms (as in "Junior High School Concert: Salle Rosini"), and mythological names. The effect is that Williams takes his poetry in directions that seem to defy such traditional descriptions as narrative and lyric. Gregerson probably misses as many descriptive terms as she includes in her list of Williams's genres: "didactic fables, documentaries, confessions, indictments, portraits, billet-doux." The poems' speculation, satire, sketches, and situations contain a broad spectrum of humanity: lover, child, parent, cleric, professional, laborer, aged person, invalid, criminal, politician, cultural leader, artist, and hero.

Themes and Meanings

Williams is notable for his psychological insights and character studies as well as for his strong, expressive manner. Bruce Bauer, writing about *Tar* (1983) in *Poetry*, noted that "one has the feeling, unusual when reading today's poets, that [Williams] is truly interested in the lives around him." If anything, his interest in humanity is more pronounced in *Flesh and Blood*.

Williams adopts five different stances in the poems: He observes others; he participates in events; he seeks to explicate psychological states; given a situation, he imagines a scenario; and, least frequently, he is a watcher of nature.

Williams acts something like a sociological psychologist in many of his poems, presenting vignettes charged with human energy. He explains in "American Native" why the Henry Wadsworth Longfellow poetry his father once read to him will no longer serve: "A teacher attempted to make us understand that our vision of exotics and minorities was so contaminated/ that we not only had corrupted ideas of history but didn't know what went on under our noses." Williams's poems represent his personal struggle to find out. In "Crime" a robber is shot by police, and neighborhood children rush in to grab the dropped change; in "Pregnant" an unwed teen pushes the fetus in with her hands; in "Men" a garbage man viciously mocks a fellow worker who is in pain.

The meaning of Williams's work is seldom in question. None of the difficulty that supposedly makes poems avant-garde is here, yet he never talks down. His art is concerned with revealed clarity. As an observer he is keen of eye and discerning of detail, discriminatingly weighing without seeming to do so. In "Love: Loss" he portrays an exact motivation in terms of the Orpheus-Eurydice tale. The "pretty post-teen princess gone to the grim gutter" approaches "the half-respectful wino" in pretense of wanting a smoke, but when "their solitudes emerge" her heart fails, and she turns, leaves, and "picks herself back to the silver path . . . to the boiling whispers."

Sometimes Williams as participant compares himself to mythological figures, as in "Medusa." While in a Rotterdam "hookers' bar" at the age of twenty, he watches a prostitute flaunt her wares, beg him, and, when he refuses, maul herself "My virginity,/ that dread I fought so hard to lose," he says, "stone by stone was rising back inside me." In "Peace," another poem in which Williams is a participant, the opposite effect occurs. His wife and he go to bed, angry. Their bodies during the long, cold night are back to back, not touching. Then "toward dawn, . . . though justice won't I know be served, I pull her to me."

Some poems are about the aged. "Love: The Dance" describes a septuagenarian couple performing "old-time ballroom swirls, deft romantic dips." The poet sees them in archetypal terms, dancing "the waltz of life, the waltz of death," and concludes, "and still the heart-work left undone." It is children, parents, and lovers, however, that dominate the poems. For example, "Good Mother: The Street" shows the theme of a mother's commitment and a child's helplessness in terms both gentle and horrible. "Vehicle: Absence" and "Vehicle: Violence" use Williams's "the way . . . " device discussed earlier to compare carnal love with the loss of a loved one and violence with the "anger, pride, the primal passion to prevail" of boxers.

In "Bishop Tutu's Visit to the White House: 1984" Williams imagines something he cannot see. Because of the bishop's humanity and the president's indifference, he presumes that the man of God "will be wounded . . . humiliated . . . mortified." Another cultural exchange poem, "USOCA" (United States out of Central America), sounds a similar key. "Andean musicians . . . embarrassed" by so few rally attendees, show "smiles . . . like precious doves of hope" when their music meets with mild applause.

"The Mistress," "The Lover," and "Twins" are about adultery. In the first, the public telephone upon which a man depends for a liaison has "been savaged"—the receiver "wires thrust back up the coin slot." Desire and disappointment leave him "breathing like a bloody beast." In the second, a wife is surprised to learn that her affair with her husband's employee is common knowledge. While in a lady's room stall she overhears the two men called "the blind pig" and "that sanctimonious, lying bastard," and herself called "the horny bitch." In "Twins," unknown to everyone, a woman is carrying two fetuses. When the second is born she lets it die, believing that one is the husband's, the other her lover's. This poem and "Normality" appear in quotation marks, as though they are in the words of speakers other than the poet.

The strongest poem in *Flesh and Blood* is the final poem, "La Petit Salvié." This poem should be read in whole stanzas so that the speculative argument that Williams presents regarding time and mortality can be apprised. Parts of stanza 14 show the bonding of artist to artist. Williams and Zweig read poems to each other, "out behind the house in canvas chairs . . . in your apartment, a park in Paris—anywhere: sidewalk, restaurant, museum." Envy ("you are unimaginably insecure") and creative commerce ensue. Most important, kinship develops between them, with "envy sublimated into warmth and brothership." Stanza 10, referring to Zweig after his death, ends in italics, quotes, and monosyllables: " *and I have a ghost I love and who loves me.*"

John Young

THE FLY

Author: Miroslav Holub (1923-1998)
Type of poem: Lyric
First published: 1961, as "Moucha," in *Slabikář*; English translation collected in *Selected Poems*, 1967

The Poem

"The Fly" is a short poem in free verse, in thirty-three lines, divided into eight stanzas. The title reflects Miroslav Holub's practice, as a distinguished scientist, of frequently drawing on biology, with its life-forms and life processes, for his imagery. The fly serves as an observer of the Battle of Crécy, the fly's demeanor and behavior being apposed to the human drama being enacted on the battlefield. Behind the fly is a second observer, the poet. The poem is a meditation on a historic event. The poem is also divided into what Holub calls units of attention, some of them long to achieve effects of suspense, others short for emphases, often one-word or one-image lines.

In the first line, the fly sits at a distance on the trunk of a willow tree. Then Holub uses one of his one-word lines, the word "watching," to focus on the demeanor of the fly. It is watching the historic Battle of Crécy. Then, with four one-image lines, Holub quickly develops the drama on the battlefield: the battle cries, the surprise, the moans of the wounded, and, finally, the panic as the soldiers fall over each other in their frantic flight.

Holub now skips to the last of the fourteen futile charges by the French cavalry, concentrating the tragedy in two powerful images: a disemboweled horse and the blue tongue of a duke. He interpolates an image of the fly mating with a brown-eyed male fly from the neighboring village of Vadincourt (Wadicourt) during the charge and then descending to sit upon the disemboweled horse and rubbing her legs together, meditating. Here Holub again uses a one-word line, "meditating," for emphasis. The fly is meditating on the immortality, not of itself, but of all flies. Here Holub is paraphrasing an old German folk saying, "Er grübbelt über die Unsterblichkeit der Maikäfer" (He meditates upon the immortality of the junebug), a saying well-known to Czechs. The subject is ironically juxtaposed with the death scene, the immortality of a lower life form against the deaths of human beings.

Then the poem uses a slow, ten-line, four-stanza sentence that begins with three sobering images: a silence settling upon the battlefield and the faint odor of decay and bodies—followed by a pause between stanzas—and then the picture of a few arms and legs still twitching jerkily under living trees, and, finally, these images climaxing with the fly, against the backdrop of death, as it lays its eggs on the dead eye of the Royal Armorer.

In the final short stanza, the fly quickly meets her own death, devoured by a swift from the neighboring village of Estrées, that in another one-word line, is itself "fleeing"—fleeing, one learns in the ominous last line, from the fires of Estrées.

Forms and Devices

The poetic technique of Holub has had two major influences: his involvement with the *Květen* movement, the generation of young poets that emerged in Czechoslovakia after the death of Joseph Stalin, and his profession as a scientist.

The *Květen* advocated a return to reality, even to the dark side of situations. The poet, Holub said, should turn to "facts" and should use words at the level of the common man. For this reason, Holub's poems are relatively easy to translate. Holub's interest in facts frequently led him to probe the meanings in historical events, as in "Fall of Troy," "Discobolus," "Achilles and the Tortoise," and "The Fly."

As a research scientist, he carried over into his poetry what A. Alvarez described in his introduction to *Selected Poems* (1967) as a "probing below the surface of received, everyday experience to reveal new meaning . . . as though his poems and his researcher's microscope worked in the same way," isolating details for analysis and reflection. This technique is similar to that of the abstract painter when he reduces a situation to its bare elements, or like that of Holub's one-time collaborator and photographer, Jan Pařík, who specialized in subjects found in hospital wards, except that Holub proceeds behind the scenes to meditate on their meanings.

In "The Fly," Holub probes beneath the surface of facts about the Battle of Crécy: the rout of the Genoese, the massacre of the mounted knights, the surprise to the French army by the introduction of a new weapon and a new military strategy, and the massive shower of arrows from longbows that pierced the previously impenetrable medieval armor. The significant details are condensed into a few simple images: the initial enthusiasm, with "shouts"; the shock, with "gasps"; the pain, with "groans"; the panic, with "the tramping and the tumbling." The slaughter of the mounted knights is conveyed by two images: the "disembowelled horse" and the "blue tongue" of the duke. The aftermath is suggested by "silence," "the whisper of decay" over bodies, and "a few arms and legs" that "twitched jerkily."

Holub's images are sometimes grotesque, with hints of surrealism. Some of these images derive from his interest as a biologist in lower life-forms and life processes, often in startling juxtapositions. In "Suffering," microorganisms "graze in the greenish-blue pool of the chromatogram," while the "ugly animal" watches them through a microscope. In "The Fly," the fly mates during the charge of the French cavalry, alights upon a disemboweled horse, and lays her eggs on a dead eye.

After isolating the details of a situation, Holub proceeds to reassemble them into meaningful patterns. In "The Fly," these patterns are the juxtapositions, the ironic reversal of fortunes from unsuspecting innocence and arrogant pride to death and destruction, for both the French army and the fly, and the interpolated meditation on immortality and the laying of eggs within the context of death.

Themes and Meanings

A major purpose of the *Květen* poets was to reject the synthetic optimism of the Socialist Positive Hero and of Stalinist Personality Cults. They turned to deglamorization of previously glorified heroes and historical events.

For Holub, who had lived through the Nazi invasion and the subsequent occupation of Czechoslovakia by the Russians, that deglamorization extended to war as a human experience, at first, war in his own time, as in "Casualty" and "Five Minutes After the Air Raid," and later to war in general, as in "A History Lesson," where a small boy after the teacher's lecture on "two victorious wars" asks, "And did it hurt in those days too?" This deglamorization can also be seen in "Soldier," where "the black shadow of oncoming eternity ooz[es] underneath." Finally, Holub turned to particular wars in the past, as in "Fall of Troy" and "The Fly." Sometimes he reduced historic generals to sorry figures: Charlemagne, Napoleon, Achilles.

The Battle of Crécy was an opportune subject for such deglamorization. It was instrumental in destroying the medieval system of warfare, and it helped bring about the decline of the Age of Chivalry. It was also one of the bloodiest of battles, destroying much of France's nobility. The tragedy of war is conveyed through the use of vivid images: the groans of the dying, the mad panic of the foot soldiers, the disemboweled horse, the dead duke, the bodies reduced to arms and legs, the dead silence, and the whisper of decay.

Holub, however, does more than deglamorize war: He moves into war scenes with an ironic compassion. In "Five Minutes After the Air Raid" a woman climbs a stairs and reaches the top, where a door opens only to the sky, and she gapes over the edge before descending to wait "for the house to rise again/ and for her husband to rise from the ashes/ and for her children's hands and feet to be stuck/ back in place." In "Fall of Troy" a pitiful old Anchises leaves burning Troy, "teeth in a glass," finally stopping to sleep on the ground, "rags wrapped" him, "just like home."

"The Fly" opens with a reference to a willow tree, traditionally the symbol for grief and lamentation, and then proceeds to enter into the emotions of the Genoese soldiers—their "shouts," their "gasps," their "groans," their "tramping" and "tumbling." There is a sobering and sad, caring tenderness in the image of "silence" and "whisper of decay" that "softly" encircle the dead bodies. The poem ends on a sad, thought-provoking picture that shocks the reader with the realization of the fate that befalls proud men, social systems—and flies—as the unsuspecting fly is caught and devoured by the swift.

Throughout the poem, the life force asserts itself in elemental life-forms—the willow tree and the trees over bodies, the flies, the swift—and in elemental life forces—mating and laying of eggs, even in the dying throes of the arms and legs.

Thomas Amherst Perry

THE FLYING CHANGE

Author: Henry Taylor (1942-   )
Type of poem: Lyric
First published: 1974; collected in *The Flying Change*, 1985

The Poem

"The Flying Change" is a short poem; in its two distinct parts the speaker establishes a metaphor comparing a maneuver that is taught to a cantering horse to a stance the speaker has adopted for his own life. The poem's two parts are numbered, as if to underscore their distinctive characters, and they look quite different on the page and exhibit very different voices.

Part 1 is a prose poem, set out on the page like a standard paragraph. It sounds rather like a textbook on horsemanship in its explanation of the flying change maneuver. It describes the nature of a horse's canter, a gait in which the animal's "leading foreleg is the last to touch the ground before the moment of suspension" as the horse moves forward. The horse can canter by leading with either the right or the left foreleg, but as it rounds a curve, it usually leads with the inside foreleg. If the horse must change leads to put the inside foreleg first (the "flying change"), it can do so easily when it is running free. If the horse is being ridden, however, the rider's added weight makes the shift more difficult, and the rider must teach the horse to compensate in order to carry out the change. Part 1 of the poem explains these matters in a matter-of-fact, third-person voice and without editorial comment except for the last sentence: "The aim of teaching a horse to move beneath you is to remind him how he moved when he was free."

In part 2 Taylor changes form and voice to create a short (three five-line stanzas) series of statements in which a first-person speaker indirectly compares himself to the horse that must learn to do what once it did naturally. The images of this part recall the diagonal motion of the flying change made by the horse; they also suggest the idea of suspended motion (the moment of the change) and the idea of the tensions between one's innate abilities and what one learns to do. Thus the first image is of a leaf turned "sideways in the wind," which somehow moves the speaker "like a whipcrack" into a past where, rather like a horse in training, he once studied moves on a "barbered stretch of ground." Later, he says, he taught himself to move away from those past skills, skills which he still possesses but "must outlive," as if they are no longer useful to him. The act of cupping water in his hands reminds him of how age must affect him, making his hands "a sieve" instead of a cup. Time can never stand still, but—like the horse shifting its leading hoof and thus suspended for a moment in air—the speaker briefly feels "sustained in time."

Forms and Devices

The division of this short poem into two parts strongly suggests its two voices, the "textbook" voice, which explains the riding maneuver, and the personal voice of one who finds himself also making a "flying change" and cherishing the brief moment of suspension above the earth. In the second part, Taylor uses five-line stanzas in iambic pentameter for the development of his speaker's understanding of how the flying change applies to him. In each stanza, the first and fourth lines demonstrate slant rhyme, as do the second and fifth. The slant rhyme mutes the poem's rhyme to such a degree that the reader may not notice the rhyme at first reading, but the *nd* sound of "wind" in the first line of part 2 echoes the *nd* of "ground" at the end of the fourth line, while "day" and "away" in lines 2 and 5 create true rhyme. Similar effects apply to the rhyme in the other stanzas.

The poem's lines are also heavily enjambed so that their sense runs on from one line to the next. That effect is particularly noticeable between the three stanzas of part 2. In each case, Taylor withholds an important element of a sentence's grammar until the first line of the following stanza. The effect is to make the reader see two layers of meaning in the lines. At the end of the first stanza, the speaker suggests that he taught himself to "drift away"; only in the first line of the following stanza does the reader understand that he drifted away not from the world in general but from something specific—skills which he still has.

The poem's central metaphor lies in the description of the flying change itself, and in part 1 Taylor concentrates specifically two elements of that change. One is the moment of suspension as the horse shifts its lead foot; the other is the commentary included in the last sentence of that part. The whole point of teaching a horse to carry a rider is to teach it to maintain some of its natural movement under the "unnatural" burden of its rider, "to remind him how he moved when he was free." In the second part, that metaphor is expanded to apply to the speaker, who also finds himself executing a flying change.

The poem's form can now be seen to echo its content in that the second part, with its careful stanza organization, its rhyme and iambic pentameter, seems to suggest the schooling of both horses and humans to make artful things seem natural, things such as running while carrying a rider or writing a line of iambics. Indeed, the suspension of a line to balance its meaning between two stanzas seems to suggest the horse's task of balancing the rider while shifting its weight in the canter.

In the thirteenth line of part 2, Taylor refers to "works and days," an allusion to the Greek poet Hesiod (eighth century B.C.E.), who wrote a poem called "Works and Days" about the proper conduct of agricultural life—another instance of Taylor's submerging elements of art in a poem which is partly about art and nature. In fact, much of the *Flying Change* collection deals with agricultural life.

Themes and Meanings

"The art which conceals art" is a phrase that has often been used to indicate the artist's task. Ideally, a poet (or any other artist) wants the created work to seem natural and inevitable rather than artificial and labored. On one level, that is the concern of "The Flying Change." The horse's art is its running, and, as the impersonal voice of part 1 points out, when it successfully carries a rider, it moves as if it were unburdened. (It is notable that in the course of concealing his art, Taylor has created the bookish tone of that discussion, just as he created the three metered stanzas which follow it.) Like the horse that must appear free while performing a task, so the poet's task is to manage carefully ordered steps without appearing to carry a burden. The speaker of part 2 suggests that this feat is possible and that it may even allow the artist moments when he seems completely free of earth-bound concerns, however illusory that freedom, like the horse's freedom, may be.

On another level, the poem seems to address the more general tension between the speaker's desire for freedom and the constraints of time and age and obligation. Like the horse, the speaker has taught himself to cease the practice of skills he still has, skills he says he must outlive, as if age has brought him to the necessity of moving beyond the skills of his earlier years. This is a recognition that many people come to—that growth (which suggests maturity and adulthood) may require one to abandon some of the colt's pleasures in freedom. Yet the poem suggests that, like a well-schooled horse, one can somehow retain the memory of what free movement was like.

Because it is time which brings one to these contradictions, time is a significant issue in the second section. The act of cupping water in his hands reminds the speaker that advancing age will make his hands no better than a sieve for holding water in this very natural way. In fact, the whole world seems to be moving in a "mindless plunge" as it races through time. There is no stopping this process—except, the poem suggests, that the art of the flying change, the moment in which time seems to be held in suspension, may allow one to experience for a moment the brilliant sensation being free of the pull of earth and time, an illusion created by the flying change.

Ann D. Garbett

FOG TOWNSHIP

Author: Brendan Galvin (1938-   )
Type of poem: Meditation
First published: 1986, in *Seals in the Inner Harbor*

The Poem

Brendan Galvin's "Fog Township," a stichic, forty-three-line poem, meditates on contending forces in the world—hot and cold, moist and dry, human and inanimate, to name a few—yet at the same time recognizes the interconnectedness of things. "Fog Township" observes the subtle interplay of what is often called the Apollonian (human-made) and the Dionysian (natural) worlds and discovers a tension vibrating always within the "delicate time" of the first line.

The poem is in three movements of almost identical length. The first is an objective description of the natural world, winter turning to spring, and the uncertainty of those days as hot and cold collide and fog is the real and figurative result. It obscures the knowledge of where people will go next. "Cathedral/ and Round Hills" stand out, not only because they rise above the fog to become "high islands" but also because they are human-named places in this otherwise Dionysian world. Humans tend to gravitate toward what they have made, according to Galvin.

Part 2, which begins after the caesura in line 14, introduces the "I" persona, who seeks to read the "message/ tapped on twigs out there." The "out there" is very important, ultimately, because it represents "the other," the Dionysian world. As are so many things in this poem, the term is repeated in line 40, reinforcing the separation of the human-made and the natural.

Part 3 begins after the caesura in line 29. Here the reader is introduced to the very Romantic notion that concludes the poem. A personified Nature, gendered feminine, is introduced as the speaker "imagine[s] her." Imagination is the key idea that drove Romanticism and is here revitalized in a woman who, "crouched on/ a stump" and "hair wet," has been, one realizes, knitting "April back together" throughout the entire poem. More important, readers learn that the persona has participated in this scene in his mind, has resisted nature's invitation to come out into the fog, and has chosen, because of "lethargy," to remain apart, to avoid the otherness of "out there." Humans have, he hints, separated themselves from the natural world forever.

Forms and Devices

Subtlety is a hallmark of Galvin's work. Whether it is form, language, or theme, the "how" of his poems is always much more difficult to discern than the "what." He prefers a plainspoken, direct approach to his meanings while deftly using poetic and linguistic devices to shape and manipulate sounds and meanings. Among the many devices at work here, the use of vowels, alliteration, and rhyme are some of the most useful for understanding the inner workings of the poem.

Part 1, the objective description of the fog and its effect on the landscape, is dominated by round, open vowels that seem to suggest the grand openness of nature itself. The letters *o*, *a*, and *u* predominate. There is nothing pinched or thinly pitched in this world where "fog/ rides into the hollows," and "Brooks/ . . . [churn] back/ into their beds." One irony here—irony often occurs in Galvin's poems because of clashes between what is said and how it is said—is that while visability is diminished by fog and "cloud shadows," the open vowels open the world even as it is being compressed and limited. When the senses are challenged, the poem reminds us, the imagination takes over.

As part 1 draws to a close, the alliteration of part two is hinted at in line 13. "Landscape's lightest" echoes the numerous alliterations of the next fourteen lines. The letters *t*, *c*, *s*, and *d* are all closely and distantly repeated. One suspects that the "message/ tapped on twigs" would sound like this, a seductive collection of noises hinting at words that can never quite be interpreted, like the clicks and squeals of dolphins or an alien tongue. Humans listen but are finally frustrated.

Part 3 combines the open vowels of part 1 and the alliteration of part 2. It brings the "out there" and the "I" together, even as it makes it abundantly clear that "out there" and "I" are not, have not been for a long time, and never will be together. Even as people long for communication with "the other" in the "out there," the poem reminds readers that they have been responsible for creating even greater distances among humans and the rest of the creatures of the world. With an imagination, people can live vicariously without having to overcome "lethargy" and actually engage the world. Ironies abound. As humans reach out to a receding world, attempt to offer their own round, open vowels to it and tap out their own alliterative love letter to nature, they are constantly and clumsily moving farther away from one another.

There is no rhyme scheme here, but like the other two devices discussed, there are hints and echoes at work. Just as the poem uses knitting as a metaphor for nature "pulling/ April back together," so the rhymes loosely stitch the three parts together. Galvin's touch is light; he never uses devices, poetic or linguistic, to bludgeon the reader. More often than not, devices must be sought out to be seen at all. In the end, they are there to whisper and gently guide the reader through complexities of language and thought. Not to be dismissed, they are a way to play with language.

In part 1 these three half rhymes appear: "spill" in line 2; "Cathedral" in line 5; and "trickle" in line 9. These do not form a pattern, but they are close enough to each other to qualify as rhymes. The poem waits thirteen lines for the sound to repeat, as it does in "simple" in line 22. By then it is a mere echo, recalling faintly the earlier *l* sounds and pulling part 2 gently back toward part 1. Then, just as part 3 begins, the rhyme appears again in "needles"; part 3 also contains a rhyming sound from earlier in the poem. Thus, just like vowels and alliteration, rhyme assists in the "knitting up/ cable and chain to bind/ the acres."

Themes and Meanings

Galvin's theme is an ancient one. From Ovid's three ages of humanity, to Gerard

Manley Hopkins's ". . . nor can foot feel, being shod" in "God's Grandeur," to Robert Frost's constant turning from nature's invitation to "Come In," poets have struggled with the distances humankind has put between itself and the natural world. Though perhaps just beyond the window, "out there" is worlds away. It is a seductive world that "click[s] like sparks fired/ across a gap," enticing the reader to enter, to listen to the "message/ tapped on twigs," to be part of it. Yet people have grown to fear it, ignoring or shunning it. Although it calls with its fog-shrouded voices from water and wood, humans often turn instead to the nature in imagination, the idealized place.

Galvin tells the reader: "I might walk around/ out there until I meet her,/ or scare off the jay." The speaker might enter the "out there," where it is uncertain whether he will encounter the significant—"her"—or the insignificant—the "jay" feeding. Rather than take a chance, he decides to "imagine her," a wet-haired, knitting woman who is domestic and nonthreatening. As with many things humans do not understand, and hence fear, they reduce them to cartoons that no longer threaten them. The woman is, after all, the "spring genius," that which has the power to pull seasons together, that which clashes hot and cold, moist and dry, to make fog and obscure the world.

"Fog Township" sits comfortably in Galvin's canon. From his earliest books he played with language with abandon, a maker of myths, fables, and superstitions. He has the ability to bring into the present time old beliefs and make them gleam as if brand new. More than anything, Galvin is a keen observer of the natural world. His poems abound with birds, animals, and fish. He is no lurker behind windows. Galvin is not likely to abandon himself to nature, but his eye falls keenly and honestly on the "out there," and what he reports back is to be trusted.

H. A. Maxson

FOGGY STREET

Author: Andrei Voznesensky (1933-   )
Type of poem: Lyric
First published: 1960, as "Tumannaya ulitsa," in *Mozaika*; English translation collected in *Antiworlds, and the Fifth Ace,* 1967

The Poem

Andrei Voznesensky's "Foggy Street" is a thirty-line rhymed poem reflecting the poet's concern with loss of identity and his fascination with ambiguity. In "Foggy Street" time, space, and identity have blurred to the point of disintegration, but the poet's treatment is occasionally light and humorous so that the overall effect is paradoxical.

In the opening lines, Voznesensky establishes the atmosphere, a foggy street on which the only discernible figures are police officers. The fog, both literal and figurative, so disorients the narrator that he is unable to determine even the period he is living in: "What century is it? What era? I forget." The poet's attempts to describe this oblique world take up the body of the poem. The poetic landscape, presented through a mosaic of images and comparisons, is by turns nightmarish and amusing, romantic and absurd.

The second stanza introduces images of general disintegration: "everything is crumbling," and "nothing's intact." The people whom the poet encounters are undifferentiated, but at the same time unconnected. This series of vague but unsettling images breaks off to be replaced by a more precise and less unpleasant one of the poet "flounder[ing] in cotton wool." Although the poet continues to stumble through the fog and his vision remains blurred, the language with which he describes the scene in the third stanza becomes more concrete; he begins to pick out a few details, and a specific although unidentified voice calls out a mild warning, "Your hat check, sir?/ Mustn't walk off with the wrong head, you know." Perhaps the poet is merely talking to himself, reminding himself not to panic—to keep his head—and to remember who he is: a poet.

It is his skill with language that he must use to find his way in this world, and in the next stanza, he attempts to define his situation by introducing a romantic simile, but he soon loses heart. By the third line the diction has grown melodramatic, "widowed by your love's eclipse," and the stanza ends without completing the idea. Subsequent attempts to match name to person, word to reality, fail as well. In the fifth stanza Venus turns out to be a street vendor; friend is indistinguishable from foe; and in the sixth stanza, the poet mistakes a strange man for his lover. By the penultimate stanza, the poet's perseverance has taken him so deeply into the fog that he can no longer see; his fears return, and he calls out in vain, for "One's voice won't carry in this heavy air." Again, the poet does not complete his thought, and in the closing line the reader is left with the impression of a world that glistens all the more for having been obscured.

Forms and Devices

Voznesensky is a highly innovative poet whose verse eschews classical metric patterns and who often startles the reader with abrupt shifts and unusual rhymes and juxtapositions. "Foggy Street" typifies Voznesensky's early style, combining traditional alternating rhyme with a metric pattern suggesting, but not corresponding to, classical Greek forms.

The form of the poem is cleverly matched to its content; just as figures emerge, but dissolve or fragment before they can be clearly identified, the poem's structure varies slightly from stanza to stanza, so that a pattern appears to form, only to disappear as the reader moves further into the verse. The theme of fragmented self is reinforced by a structural sense of fragmentation developed through frequent use of dashes, ellipses, and caesuras or internal pauses, such as those created by the question marks in the final line of the first stanza.

Indentation of the second line in most stanzas, followed by a very short third line, contributes to the sense of disjuncture, as do sudden shifts in register and tonality. Consider, for example, the third stanza, which begins "Noses. Parking lights. Badges." This line, with its staccato beats, contrasts with the smoother rhythms of the previous verses. The playfulness of the combination of images lightens the tone, as does the shift in voice as the poem seems suddenly to address the poet in the stanza's closing lines.

Voznesensky plays with voice throughout the poem. The more traditional voice narrates with standard convention as it attempts to identify through simile and metaphor, as in the second and fourth stanzas. A less formal and seemingly more authentic voice inserts itself, taking control in stanzas 5 and 6. This second voice, perhaps representing the poet's interior monologue, is more conversational than the first, and it is the voice with which the poet is able to designate individual people and discrete objects, but his identifications are always wrong. In the end, the second voice seems no more successful than the first.

In 1963 Voznesensky's experimental style was denounced by Nikita S. Khrushchev, then premier of the Soviet Union. Yet, despite his inventiveness, Voznesensky is not rebelling against tradition. The allusions in "Foggy Street" connect the poem with both Russian tradition and the classical culture from which much Russian poetry is derived. The questions that end the first stanza are a reference to the famed Russian poet Alexander Pushkin, and in the original Russian version, Baba Yaga, a witch in Slavic folklore, makes an appearance. Baba Yaga is changed in the English translation to "Iago," the villain of William Shakespeare's *Othello, the Moor of Venice* (1604), a change that preserves the sense of connection to literary tradition. Similarly, the appearance of Venus, goddess of love, in the fifth stanza reflects the influence of ancient Greek and Latin mythology. Even the situation in which the poet is immersed suggests Homer, the poet of ancient Greece.

Themes and Meanings

Written during the "Russian thaw," the period following the death in 1953 of the brutal Soviet dictator Joseph Stalin, "Foggy Street" invites a political interpretation.

Voznesensky himself has referred to the Stalin years as "a fog," and the positive image of clarity and brilliance on which the poem ends seems an apt description of the flowering of Russian culture in the latter part of the 1950's. However, interpreting the poem simply as a commentary on life in the Soviet Union during Stalinism is too narrow a reading to encompass the entire poem. Like the others with which it was originally published, "Foggy Street" takes the human condition as its subject. The poet who walks down Voznesensky's "foggy street" could be walking down any street at any point in time. As the title of his first collection, *Mozaika* ("mosaic"), indicates, Voznesensky intends his poems to be read in groups, and the meaning of an individual poem contributes to the meaning of the collection; the pattern that emerges, in turn, informs the meaning of each separate piece. To understand "Foggy Street" more fully, it is useful to examine the worldview reflected in the larger body of the poet's work.

Voznesensky believes that humans are part of a universal life force and that human nature is essentially good; however, society and technology have distanced humans from their connection with the natural world, and it is this distancing that permits evil to thrive. He holds technology responsible for the sort of fragmentation and disorientation described in "Foggy Street." Technology alienates through categorization, specialization, and mechanization. Instead of increasing knowledge of the world, science distorts it, producing chaos and confusion.

Negotiating his way through this world of contradiction is the task of the poet in "Foggy Street." The magnificent irony at the heart of the poem is that to succeed he must fail; in an unstable universe, any sense of permanent stability is false. Yet by articulating the paradoxical nature of reality, the poet can achieve equilibrium. With its fragmented lines, separate voices, unique juxtapositions, and irregular rhythms, the poem balances contradictory impulses, allowing them to coexist. The police who "bob up like corks" in the second line are simultaneously sinister and innocuous. Similarly, the "unsoldered" figures of the following stanza suggest opposing images, one in keeping with the nightmarish scene, the other reminiscent of the dreamily floating figures in the paintings of Marc Chagall, a Russian artist greatly admired by Voznesensky. The poet's inability to distinguish friends from enemies and male from female compromise his ability to survive and procreate, yet these failings are rendered in a humorous tone that undercuts their seriousness. Abrupt shifts in tone and voice and other stylistic innovations that startle the reader are an essential part of the balancing act in a constantly changing world.

The ultimate paradox is that the very fog that prevents the poet from seeing or being heard generates a highly visual and delightfully resonant poem, a point that the poet realizes, perhaps, in the closing line, "When the fog lifts, how brilliant it is, how rare!" This line is itself ambiguous, however, for the term "when" does not assure that the fog has lifted, only that on rare occasions it does.

K Edgington

FOR A FRESHMAN READER

Author: Donald Justice (1925-   )
Type of poem: Lyric
First published: 1966; collected in *Night Light*, 1967

The Poem

"For a Freshman Reader" is a poem of twenty-two lines divided into eleven un-rhymed couplets. The poem is exemplary of syllabic structure; each line is precisely seven syllables long. While the syllabic form may seem restrictive, each line achieves the naturalness and fluidity of speech. This poem creates a particular tone and cast to the speech of its narrator. In the first person, the speaker directs comments to those present—listeners, readers, disciples, pupils—as in a dramatic monologue. One does not hear the responses to the poem. The voice, however, is seamless and provides a miniature but complete portrait of the speaker.

The epigram's reference is to the German poet Hans Magnus Enzensberger who, writing in the decades immediately after the World War II, rebuked any inward turning as a sign of the conditions that led to the rise of Nazism and the persistence of the underlying prewar conditions after the war. Donald Justice adopts the severe tone of Enzensberger's poetry to warn of history's lessons.

The title suggests a proposal for a textbook, course of study, curricula, or anthology to introduce a beginning reader into something beyond literature, as the ominous opening couplet suggests: "Don't bother with odes, my son./ Timetables are more precise." This opening couplet establishes an ironic tone that implicitly condemns those who believe in timetables rather than odes or those who put more value in precision than what may be discovered in odes or poetry. The poem is composed as a list of warnings and bits of advice administered with a certain amount of ironic self-appraisal: "Learn to be anonymous,/ Learn more than I did: to change/ Your identification." The enjambment of these lines suggests a self-directed sarcasm, for it is not simply the ability "to change" that is advised, but more specifically "identification" is suspect. The speaker suggests that change might be politically convenient or self-serving, and he sarcastically provides advice on how to survive in times of political crisis. The speaker ironically recommends that anonymity is best, that timetables and not odes are more suitable since they are more precise, encyclicals are good tinder, and manifestoes are "handy/ For wrapping up the butter/ And salt given to victims." All this is offered as a condemnation of the listener or reader who has compromised himself or herself morally or ethically.

In the poem's final three couplets, the speaker warns that it will require more than anger to destroy the authority that has required such a circumscribed way of life. Patience is called for, but it is a "fine deadly powder/ Ground by those with the know-how." The poem concludes with the speaker stating that those with the "know-how" are the "precisionists, like you." The closing word, "you," draws the reader into the drama, assuring that he or she be listeners—or pupils—of the narrator. The narrator's descriptive terms, "precisionists" and "those with the know-how," complete the poem's ironic and condemnatory position. As "precisionists," readers are returned to the beginning of the poem, with its phrase "Timetables are more precise," and are fully exposed as morally corrupted.

Forms and Devices

The two most significant aspects of "For a Freshman Reader," as well as for many of Justice's poems, are the voice and the formal structure of the poem. In "For a Freshman Reader," the two are inseparable. This achievement suggests how complete the poem is, how it refutes critical or interpretive interventions because the poem is a thing unto itself, an entity whose elegance allows for nothing extraneous. Indeed, to be elegant, by definition, demands choice and selection; there is no place for the extraneous. This consideration is very much part of the poem's demands of its form and voice.

The syllabic demands create a spare, balanced, and direct voice. The formal limits of syllabic composition provide, but do not necessitate, the sense of restraint in the voice. The voice commands and assumes a paternal air in such lines as the opening line or "Watch it, don't sing." The measured pace of the syllabic form suggests the speaker's character is methodological and circumspect, yet also angry. The voice also carries within it a historical knowledge that allows the speaker to foresee the future's possibilities: "The day will come when once more/ Lists will be nailed to the door." The employment of syllabics conjoined with Justice's ability to conceive of a dramatically whole voice gives the poem the quality of the inevitable. While syllabic composition can be used extravagantly, as in the poetry of Marianne Moore, Justice usually uses such formal demands to focus and contain the poem—to give each poem an invariable shape and presence.

The syllabic form also can compress and invoke an austerity in the use of language. This is certainly true of "For a Freshman Reader," yet again it is also contingent upon the character of the speaker. In the imperative line "Learn to be anonymous," the speaker's character and the line's syllabic form are seamless. Justice's comments about the poetry of Weldon Kees pertain to Justice's own work: "Kees is original in one of the few ways that matter: he speaks to us in a voice, or, rather, in a particular tone of voice which we have never heard before" (from Justice's introduction to *The Collected Poems of Weldon Kees*, 1960).

"For a Freshman Reader" avoids metaphor, allowing only the statement "Currents are changing" to generate, with grim humor, "Unroll/ The sea charts." The penultimate couplet shifts to the allegorical with the fusion of abstraction with a physical object: "It will take patience to force/ The lungs of authority." These are difficult lines, for they are not only imagistic but also establish the speaker's position and his condemnation of the "you." They also implicitly pose the question of the value of anger and expression in contrast to the precisionists' patience. These lines are the only departure from the prosaic and concrete language used by the narrator. Their use of the trope prepares the reader for the poem's closure that acts to name and include the reader.

Themes and Meanings

"For a Freshman Reader" offers a warning that political and social upheavals recur. The twentieth century is replete with nightmarish histories. The poem suggests that everyone must understand that no one is immune to the possibility of the return or the arising of authoritarian regimes. Certainly, this is the primary concern of the poet Enzensberger, and it is also Justice's concern here. By adopting Enzensberger's poetic stance, Justice positions the reader to recognize a particular history, Nazi Germany, and to consider the possibility that such conditions could occur again. The speaker says to remember that "numbers [will be] stamped on the chest/ Of anyone who says No." The poem also suggests George Santayana's warning that history repeats itself for those who are unaware is an issue anyone embarking on a program of study—to read in a freshman reader, to begin college, to commence an intellectual life—should know. By knowing this, the reader or the "you" will have the power to confront authority.

The poem was written in the mid-1960's and reflects that political period. It is important to read "For a Freshman Reader" in its original relationship to the poems preceding and following it in *Night Light*, for questions of political and social action, change, and vision were ever present. "Memo from the Desk of X" critically parodies bureaucratic language which soullessly passes judgment: "I therefore must recommend," the speaker concludes, "Though not without some regret,/ The extinction of poems." Immediately following "For a Freshman Reader" is the poem "To the Hawks," which has as its epigram and ironic dedication "*McNamara, Rusk, Bundy,*" who were involved with the escalation of the Vietnam War and proliferation of nuclear weapons. The poem sounds an alarm and a farewell—like William Blake's poetry—to innocence.

"For a Freshman Reader" works to establish the poet's uneasiness with the political conditions shared with these other poems. None of the poems is declamatory or sensational but works through the integrity of the language and the voice of each poem's speaker. A closer examination of the poem reveals that the poem's political and historical concerns point to a sensibility that is captive. The poem's voice verges on fatigue; it is the voice of experience and witness, yet also one that has recognized thoroughly the failures of this century. As in the work of W. H. Auden, also an ironist and political poet, there is a minor affirmation in the right measure, in the precision of language. This is not to say, however, that Justice is a "precisionist," for, as the opening and closing couplets suggest, expression is essential. There is an element of longing or nostalgia in the poem, insofar as the speaker addresses neophytes or the next generation. By the use of sarcasm, the speaker hopes to warn the reader away from political expediency. Despite the reticence of Justice, there is a generosity, for words must be exact and true to be authentically shared.

James McCorkle

FOR A SISTER

Author: Adrienne Rich (1929-   )
Type of poem: Lyric
First published: 1972; collected in *Diving into the Wreck*, 1973

The Poem

"For a Sister" is a short poem in free verse; its twenty-four lines are divided into six stanzas. It is dedicated to Natalya Gorbanevskaya, who was imprisoned in a mental asylum for her political activism. By referring to this Soviet dissident as a "sister," the title puts the struggle of a distant and unknown woman into close relationship with the speaker. Another woman's struggle for empowerment, the title suggests, no matter how far away she is or how little is known of her, sufficiently resembles an American feminist's struggle that she might be called "sister." The poem's use of the first person expresses the personal viewpoint and experience of the poet. While often in lyric poetry the poet addresses the reader directly, in this poem the poet speaks to herself and to the absent Natalya Gorbanevskaya, while the reader overhears.

"For a Sister" begins with the poet imagining her own existence as a towchain. Like a chain, the poet feels herself twisted and pulled by various outside forces. A chain never initiates a motion; it pulls or twists only in response to being maneuvered. Even the connections, the links in the chain, are made by some external force: chance. Though it does not specify the object of the poet's distrust, the first stanza links the poet's caution with her experience of powerlessness. Perhaps the poet does not trust "them" because "they" are the causes of her disempowerment.

In the second and third stanzas, one learns that Adrienne Rich has read a few paragraphs about Natalya's imprisonment. The poet does not trust the information she gathers from the media, knowing that newspaper articles are full of intentional omissions and errors. Rather than accepting the portrait painted by a journalist, she imagines her own version of the story of Natalya's arrest. This is how Rich, though she does not trust the male agents in Natalya's story—police officers, doctors, journalists, printers—is "learning how to use them." From the information she collects from the newspaper, Rich imagines the arrest from Natalya's perspective. Rather than entering her house with the police, readers see themselves as its inhabitants. They witness the police bursting in the door and Natalya glancing homeward while being carried away. They even remain in the house when Natalya is away, becoming privy to the domestic signs of her absence: the dusty floor, the milk souring in the pantry.

The fourth stanza conjoins the story of the arrest with the towchain metaphor. The towchain is a metaphor not only for the poet's sense of herself as an instrument but also for her rescue of the actual events from the muddy waters of the newspapers. Natalya's face is compared to the sunken marble that is "cranked up from underwater." Not until one recognizes that the newspaper's "facts" are merely partial truths can one engage in the more honest—and more poetic—pursuits of conjecture and imagination.

Rich's poetic conjectures continue with Natalya being searched; her behavior and possessions are recorded in notebooks. Like the poet, who learns how to use male-dominated language by imagining beyond the paragraphs in the newspaper, Natalya uses the patriarchal system in order to reduce her sentence from twenty years to two. Rather than revealing her intelligence to the officials, she pretends to be insane, tracing circles in the air with her fingers and smiling vacantly. The officials willingly dismiss her political activism as madness, and she is given two years in a mental asylum rather than twenty in a prison.

Natalya returns home in the final stanza to set her story right. When she returns to her kitchen and lights her stove, she also takes out her typewriter to tell the stories that the newspapers omitted. Rich's poem has already begun to imagine the story that Natalya might write, giving her what the male agents so vehemently withheld from her: the power to tell her own story.

Forms and Devices

An "apostrophe" is an address to an absent person or thing; as the speaker of "For a Sister" addresses the absent Natalya as though she were present, she brings her, in effect, into being. If one were to read the same newspaper article that Rich read, one might feel Natalya's absence as she did. After reading Rich's "For a Sister," however, one feels as though one has met Natalya personally, peeped into her pantry, found dust on her floor, and witnessed her arrest. By addressing her directly, Rich humanizes that which the newspapers treated as an object, and the result is that Natalya becomes alive and present.

Another important device in "For a Sister" is the use of water imagery. In "Diving into the Wreck," the title poem of the volume in which "For a Sister" appears, the image of a scuba diver exploring the underwater wreckage symbolizes the exploration of the past. In "For a Sister," water is also reminiscent of a past event, but the movement has changed from a descent into the water to a drawing out from the water.

The image in "For a Sister" of the submerged marble statue as it gradually emerges from the water is a metaphor for the poet trying to peel away layers of storytelling in order to get to the truth about Natalya: "the wreck and not the story of the wreck/ the thing itself and not the myth" ("Diving into the Wreck"). Just as a towchain extracts from the river the sunken marble statue, the poet extracts Natalya's story from the murky waters of the newspapers. As the water conceals the particular features on the marble face, so do newspaper articles omit most of Natalya's story and even misrepresent the facts.

Themes and Meanings

The central theme of "For a Sister" concerns a poet's confinement within traditional language. The double bind of the feminist poet is that though she cannot trust traditional language, she cannot do without it. Nevertheless, she struggles to transform the "objective" language of the journalist, rendering Natalya's story with humanity and compassion. Even in the first three stanzas, when the poet reflects on the misinformation of the newspaper articles, she begins her corrections, adding to the story what the reporter left out: Natalya's kitchen and her backward glance. The second half of the poem continues in this direction, constructing the truth from half-truths. That is what Rich means when she declares at the middle of the poem: "I don't trust them, but I'm learning how to use them." What she uncovers in her linguistic archaeology is not—as was probably implied, if not explicitly stated, in the newspapers—the face of an insane woman, but rather that of a woman who is wise enough to know that being completely rational would bring her twenty years in prison, while feigning madness would let her off after two.

The extended metaphor of the poem, which compares revealing the truth of Natalya's arrest and imprisonment to the cranking up of her marble face from underwater, implies the equation of the poet to the towchain. Just as a towchain cranks up a statue from under the water, the poet reads a newspaper article, sees through its lies and half-truths, and imagines beyond them. The poet thus becomes the instrument whereby the truth is revealed.

The poem ends with the poet reflecting on how poetic image-making might further the interests of truth and justice. Readers see the same domestic scene that introduced Natalya to them but from which she was taken: her kitchen. When, after two years in a mental asylum, she returns to her kitchen, her first act, lighting the stove, affirms her femininity. When she takes out her typewriter, however, she frees herself from the prison of journalistic reports and assumes control of her own language. Rather than allowing her story to be misrepresented by the journalists, Natalya will tell it herself—or, perhaps Rich's poem, dedicated to telling Natalya's story from Natalya's viewpoint, will give her voice.

In the final stanza, the poet's goal of using language in the service of women is realized. Each image in "For a Sister" is imagined as becoming the property of Natalya. The sight of a geranium from a distance might be seen, as Rich sees it in line 22, as fire pouring from a green cloth. Though scientifically named by its genus *Pelargonium*, characterized by red flowers and smooth, peltate leaves, the geranium Rich sees in line 22 resists the name and description given to it by scientists. That name, like "the trained violence of doctors," originates in patriarchal oppression. Rich frees herself from the confines of male-dominated language by transforming the geranium into a poetic image: "flames on a green cloth."

In these final lines, Rich ceremonially gives this image and the others that constitute the poem—the souring milk, the towchain, the emerging marble statue—to Natalya. That is suggested by the first and last two words of the final stanza: "My images" and "Your story." What the poem depicts is the process by which the poet derives power from her own images: the power to transform male-dominated language into a feminist story, a power that she shares with Natalya. The result is Rich's gift of her poem, given not only to Natalya but also to all women involved in the struggle for a voice and for the power to make themselves heard.

Nancy D. Goldfarb

FOR PLANTS

Author: Gary Snyder (1930-   )
Type of poem: Meditation
First published: 1967, in *The Back Country*

The Poem

"For Plants" is a meditation on the mythical and magical properties of certain psychoactive plants. The poem is written in free verse consisting of forty-two lines in roughly seven sections. Poets sometimes make lists of persons or places or things in poems. Gary Snyder uses this catalog form in "For Plants" to present several plants known since ancient times to possess medicinal or hallucinogenic properties. The effect of the rhythmic repetition of strange or exotic plant names in Snyder's catalog is often like an incantation.

The poem begins with a four-line stanza that describes the gathering of psychedelic mushrooms. The stanza simply and effectively conveys the sense of mystery and power that surrounds the fungus. The image of an "ancient virgin" (perhaps a goddess or priestess) gathering magic mushrooms in a dark forest casts a meditative spell and draws the reader into the poem.

The next stanza is about peyote. In this stanza, there is no human involvement other than via the poet's observation. The poet instead focuses on the cactus plant, which, like some natural gift or "dream-child bud," is found "glowing in hollow desert." The image of the peyote as childlike confers the qualities of innocence, purity, and even holiness upon this hallucinogenic substance. In fact, the poet refers to the peyote as "the holy baby."

The following stanza addresses the thorn apple or datura in four short lines. Legend has it that the priests of Apollo at Delphi valued the plant highly and used the leaves to give inspiration for prophecies. The poet's mention of "datura highsmoke" refers to the fact that the leaves were often smoked for narcotic effect. The poem also alludes to the belief that the thorn apple was used as a drug by the early settlers at Jamestown.

In continuing the catalog, the next section offers a glimpse of hashish being handed by sailors from supply boat to ship in some unnamed harbor. Hashish is a powerful derivative of marijuana.

In the following scattered lines, there are references to cascara, or the buckthorn shrub, and calamus, often found growing wild and also known as sweet rush. Cascara is native to Northwestern North America, and its dried bark is used as a stimulant and cathartic. Calamus historically was employed as a flavoring for wine spirits. The poet offers homage to calamus, with its strong cinnamon scent, whose "cut bark is vapor/ of paradise odor."

The final stanza presents an image of the goddess Artemis, the Greek virgin goddess of the hunt and moon and the twin sister of Apollo. Here Artemis is seen in nonhuman form as a naked sprout, the first plant to emerge from the world's first seed. Artemis may refer to the "ancient virgin" in the first stanza and thus serves to unify the poem and give it a sense of closure.

Forms and Devices

"For Plants" was published in *Back Country* (1967), a collection of poems that dealt with nature and the wilderness. Gary Snyder's poetry has often been compared to that of Robinson Jeffers and Kenneth Rexroth, two poets who wrote poems inspired by what has been called a "Western literary imagination." Such poetry takes the wilderness as its main subject and stresses a reverence for its personal and social value. The poet (who is usually alone in this type of poem) is barely present. The poet's voice is that of an impersonal, solitary observer in meditation. It is a voice that speaks for the vitalizing and essential sacredness of nature.

Though Snyder had read and absorbed much from Henry David Thoreau and Jeffers, it was Rexroth and Asian Buddhist nature poetry that influenced him the most. In the 1920's, Rexroth began to write poems about his backpacking trips into the wild and unspoiled far West. He rejected traditional Romantic nature poetry and instead embraced a direct, nonintellectual approach to his subject.

Therefore, the form of "For Plants" is derived from both Asian nature poetry (specifically Buddhist) and sensibilities explored by Rexroth in his mountain poetry. The poem has, first, a wilderness setting, though in this case the exact location is unspecified. This lack of a definite sense of place results from the fact that each of the plants described is physically rooted to a different landscape in nature. The mushroom of the first stanza grows on the soft, decaying floor of a dark forest. In contrast, the second plant described, peyote, is found in the arid terrain of the Southwestern desert.

Like Rexroth, Snyder writes in concrete language, avoiding abstraction. In "For Plants," his choice of words is plain and sparse as in "sky is solid rainbow/ squash maiden/ corn girl." Such brevity adds to the effect of understatement and objectivity. The lyrical flow of such language as "ear, eye, belly/ cascara calamus" is evidence of Snyder's concern for the sound of poetry as well.

Snyder uses imagery in "For Plants" to convey the immediacy of direct observation. Abstraction is avoided, as in the direct statement, "gum of hashish/ passt through the porthole" Similarly, the poet describes the peyote plant in language simple but imaginative enough to give a mental representation that captures the essence of its "faceted jewel bush" appearance. This use of imagery is reminiscent of the qualities found in the poetry of Ezra Pound and in haiku, the Japanese short-form poem.

The most important organizing device in "For Plants" is the list or catalog. This cataloging of plants gives the poem its vertical nature. As the poem is read, it seems to unroll from beginning to end much like a scroll. The final image of the seed paradoxically becomes both the end of the poem and a beginning.

Themes and Meanings

As a meditation on the religious nature of plants, "For Plants" is an example of Gary Snyder's belief in the sacredness of all life. His fascination for primitive sources of knowledge is also evident in his references to the Native American use of peyote in religious rituals. Snyder even describes the peyote cactus as a blessed infant, a "holy baby." Marijuana (hashish) and other psychoactive substances derived from plants have been used for centuries by people in Asia, the Middle East, and Africa to alter consciousness or to facilitate the religious experience.

Snyder's interest in the mythology of other cultures has taken him on journeys to India, Japan, and other countries in the Far East. He spent several years as a merchant seaman, and it was during this time that he discovered lands which were distant both physically and psychologically from the west coast of North America where he was born and reared.

Living in the Pacific Northwest, Snyder looked to China and the East for inspiration rather than to Europe. *Six Sections from Mountains and Rivers Without End* (1965) displayed evidence of an extensive Asian influence. In fact, Snyder studied both Chinese and Japanese and has translated poems from both languages. As a graduate student at Reed College, he became interested in Zen Buddhism and later, in Japan, attended lectures at the First Zen Institute. He has been a practicing Zen Buddhist ever since.

The Zen belief that everything, in a sense, is alive is conveyed in "For Plants." By referring to various plants as children, even goddesses, Snyder is trying to show that plants not only have a lifeforce but possess a kind of sacred energy as well. By being aware of the healing and consciousness-altering properties of plants, humans may better understand the connection between themselves and nonhuman life forms.

This sense of interrelatedness, in a very basic way, embraces the ecological concept that all life forms are dependent on one another. By citing primitive myths regarding the healing and religious uses of plants, Snyder finds support for this view. Snyder is also mythmaker in "For Plants." He reminds and instructs the reader to "see" and revere objects in nature not merely as inanimate or nonhuman things, but more deeply and more significantly as part of the vast web of spirituality that unites the universe.

Francis Poole

FOR SAPPHO: AFTER SAPPHO

Author: Carolyn Kizer (1925-   )
Type of poem: narrative
First published: 1973, in *Kayak*

The Poem

Carolyn Kizer's "For Sappho: After Sappho" is a remarkable free-verse narrative that addresses the parallel relationships of a poet and her muse and the similarly creative bond between a mother and her daughter. The speaker, "Aphrodite," mourns the death of the poet, "Sappho," whose works celebrated the goddess both as an inspirational "mother" and as a loved muse. Like several of Kizer's earlier poems, "For Sappho: After Sappho" uses the reader's familiarity with the mythological goddess of love and the historically obscure poetess to address societal problems with female sexual creativity (both physical and literary).

As if starting her verse from the middle of her thoughts, the goddess details the beginning of her bond with Sappho in a paean to the poetess. She speaks intimately to her worshiper, addressing her directly from the first section where "[she] sang eloquently/ for my pleasure/ before I knew/ [if she were] girl or boy." The lesbian poet "sang" her verse (which celebrated love and Aphrodite) no differently than would a male poet, but her loving poetic tributes to the goddess drew attention to her different gender: "not sister not lover." The relationship, that of woman to woman, promised to be a difficult one fraught with the uncertainties of either the mother/daughter or the homosexual love-bond.

As a poet, Sappho drew her inspiration from the love-goddess initially as an infant daughter "blindly seeking the breast." This blind seeking awoke an equally blind protectiveness in the goddess borne of the sympathy of shared female experiences: "what to do but hold you/ lost innocent." Like her male colleagues, Sappho also sought to make her muse into an idealized, beloved figure, but, unlike her male compatriots, the goddess discourages such dependence for a woman who does not have the same kind of societal enjoyed by male poets whose mother-love can become the societally accepted heterosexuality. Half-heartedly, for Aphrodite feels intensely for her "daughter," the goddess must act to the young poetess as a mother weaning a baby from the breast: "you the green shoot/ I the ripe earth/ not yours to possess/ alas not yours."

The second section moves the poem from the poet's infantile need for a motherly muse to a description of the poet's adolescent-like struggles with her sexual identity. Like a teenager at a party, the poet's different sexuality draws her away from her heterosexual associates—"the company laughed at your desperation"—back to the object of her unconventional love: "you screamed after me/ Aphrodite! not giving/ as with a sweep of my cloak/ I fled skyward." Both mother and beloved, Aphrodite acknowledges Sappho's determinedly individual love from amongst her sea of male admirers: "Aphrodite thick-armed and middle-aged/ loving the love of men/ yet mourns you."

But Sappho's self-perceived difference as a poet and woman breeds only despair. The infant poet whose verses "broke my heart with pity" grows more and more alienated throughout the poem and, finally, commits suicide in section three: "and the unwritten poems lept with you/ over the cliff-side." Her praise of the love-goddess in verse, "thirstily" sought by Aphrodite, ceases, but the goddess's maternal anguish continues throughout the fourth and final section of the poem—"yet I hold you in mid-air/ androgynous child of dream" while she herself dreams of the eternal poetic connection between artist and muse defying the death that is "separating us/ for this moment only."

Forms and Devices

"For Sappho: After Sappho" depends strongly on the use of symbolism and parallel imagery. Kizer's work, as noted by numerous critics, has progressed slowly from an early reliance on traditional (Chinese or Latinate) forms with often-harsh imagery to a freer, more thoughtful and "confessional" style. Throughout all of her poetry, however, Kizer's ironic voice, both tersely emotional and heavily controlled, reveals a desire to perfect a range of forms both traditional and free. "For Sappho: After Sappho" is a poem which straddles the conventions of both Kizer's eras. Similarly to early works, "For Sappho: After Sappho" uses shocking, sometimes sensational imagery and extended metaphors to describe and evaluate the consequences of personal, often internal conflicts that individuals create; the conflicted young poetess, laying "on the grass/ retching then spewed [her] love/ over the bed of crocus buds," the detritus of her heavy night of drinking reflective of the troubled, emotive poetry which spews identically from her mind: "some drops/ some essence/ has been distilled." Just as in earlier writings, Kizer refuses to hide the ugliness of life behind artistic phrasing, choosing the birth and raising of a troubled daughter as a metaphor for the evolution of a reluctant poetess in the hands of a sometimes overly encouraging mother. However, the poem's casual style is more suggestive of her later works, where free verse and everyday idiom replace her early tendency toward traditional forms and formal verse. "For Sappho: After Sappho," collected in *Yin*, a volume of feminist-leaning verse, is replete with more sensual imagery. Kizer's depiction of both Sappho and Aphrodite understates the bitter nature of female sacrifice to patriarchal society: Sappho's "desperation" is mocked by her peers and Aphrodite, even though "loving the love of men," "mourns" her grievously: "this mouth drinks thirstily/ as it chokes on the dust of your death."

In all of Kizer's poetry, but particularly in "For Sappho: After Sappho," a nimble use of language, frequently tending toward the epigrammatic, is forefront in defining Kizer's style. The narrative form employed in this poem constructs with magnificent brevity not only a story line but also characters and setting. The feelings evinced in the work are both personal and social, portraying the attitudes and manners of a whole community. Sappho and Aphrodite both become figures, rather than individuals, emblems rather than people, so that what one learns by reading Kizer is a lesson larger than life—a grand feminist and womanist ideology—though composed of punchbowls, crocuses, and grass-stains as the details one normally relates to in "smaller than life" anecdotal narratives. As in Kizer's earlier use of mythological figures in her poetry, Sappho and Aphrodite are clever emblems of womanhood rather than women per se and, as usual in mythology, there is always a certain acrid recognition of the traditional limits to identity: Sappho pausing on the ledge of her downward fall into death, "hyacinth hair rising/ in the rush of wind"; Aphrodite's "thought holds you/ straight-browed and piercing-eyed"—mythological life, whether a reflection of historical fact or simply human nature, usually turns out tragically.

Themes and Meanings

Carolyn Kizer has been frequently described by critics as a poet heavily influenced by her own, personal, background; when her writing demands a paradigm, she assembles it from the details of her own life. Then, deftly, the structured personal narratives are exaggerated and expanded into situations that can be described only as commonly experienced and, even, universal. In "For Sappho: After Sappho," Kizer depicts her own discomfort with her somewhat overbearing mother's insistence on her daughter's creative development in the face of her evolving individuality: Kizer becomes Sappho herself and her mother the ubiquitous Aphrodite whose demands for "a speaking instrument" forces her daughter's dedication to the writer's craft, which, eventually, became her only emotional outlet: "breath immortal/ the words nothing/ articulate poems/ not pertinent the breath/ everything." These images, although striking in their personal relation to Kizer's life, interact and merge into a larger perception of the power of a somewhat Freudian, devouring maternity over an emergent filial rebelliousness. Every daughter can see the essence of female rebellion from maternal, or societal, domination. Hence, Kizer's personal becomes a female universal; sexual exile and humiliation, loneliness, and renunciation of all pleasures as the punishment for a creative writer's life. *Yin*, the volume in which "For Sappho: After Sappho" was originally collected after its first publication in *Kayak*, is titled in Chinese, literally, as "the female principle." Most of the poems, not surprisingly, then, deal with female thoughts, perceptions, instincts, and creativity in the face of sometimes-brutal repression. Sappho, like the adolescent girls depicted in the companion poem "Running Away from Home," is caught up in a society whose stifling restrictions preclude deviation from the norm, and her very lack of "yin," or passivity, is what dooms her. Kizer herself, often described by critics as not writing like other women, tenuously seeks a balance between what may be termed her female consciousness and her frank, "masculine" style—that is, its very lack of sentimentality or (as one may observe in Plath or Sexton) neuroticism. Sappho's poems, which somehow survive her even if only as "the fragments," demonstrate her creativity and will—prominent themes in the books as a whole. Its variety of female utterances (by mothers and daughters, muses and goddesses) consolidate into a single, mature, female voice that refuses to be either passive or bleak: "you dart through the future/ which is memory/ —words heard a thousand times." Carolyn Kizer, throughout all of her works, but particularly through this poem, has found a voice for the female condition in life, as well as the human condition overall.

Julia M. Meyers

FOR THE GRAVE OF DANIEL BOONE

Author: William Stafford (1914-1993)
Type of poem: Lyric
First published: 1957; collected in *The Rescued Year,* 1966

The Poem

William Stafford's "For the Grave of Daniel Boone" is composed of twenty-five lines, in four unrhymed stanzas of six lines each and a final one-line stanza. A speaker, perhaps Stafford himself, recalls the Kentucky pioneer who explored the American frontier westward even to the Yellowstone country, broadening the borders of a fledgling nation. The poem addresses not so much a personal memory of the man but rather the heritage of his image and his relentless perseverance, his "going on." It likewise honors him as one of the country's spiritual forefathers, a man who embodied the desire to explore and embrace the land.

In the first stanza, "he" clearly refers to Boone, the frontiersman who makes a new wilderness his home. The farther west he travels, "the farther home grew," but his home does not grow more distant *from* him as much as it grows *with* him, enlarging. As Boone journeys beyond the Mississippi River and enters a different landscape, one carpeted with flowers, Kentucky becomes merely a single room of his expanding home, this nation.

Then, "[l]eaving the snakeskin of place after place," just as a snake sheds and abandons its old skin, Boone presses on through forests, grasslands, and the world of nature. His vision is so steady, his marksmanship so true, that his image is preserved into the present, a model or "story-picture" from which children can learn and be inspired. The third stanza shifts into the metaphor of a velvet tapestry, describing how the children smoothly enter Boone's natural world as heirs to the landscape, able to recognize his world as their own. "It is like [the coming of] evening" is an intuitive explanation for the gradual intensity of discovery, as the children learn of his world and are drawn to it like quail "coming in for the kill"—that is, quail coming in close enough to be killed by the hunter if he so desires. (A hunter himself, Stafford has recalled elsewhere how quail would be attracted to his campfire, walking innocently right into the range of his gun.)

The speaker then addresses the reader in a grandfatherly fashion, remarking, "Children, we live in a barbwire time." Theirs is a modern world where the land is quite literally divided by fences of barbed wire, but perhaps the line also alludes to the political and emotional uncertainty of postwar, mid-twentieth century life. Informed by the figure of Daniel Boone, those in the present are likewise "hunting [their] own kind of deepening home," seeking their place in the natural world. The speaker then lifts a rock from the Kentucky earth and, following the old custom, places it on the frontiersman's grave. One should note that the poem's title is not "At the Grave of Daniel Boone" but "For the Grave of Daniel Boone." The poem, like the rock, is an offering that is placed there, a token of respect.

Forms and Devices

Stafford is basically an intuitive poet who denied using any conscious literary technique, choosing instead to come at his poetry by means of sound and emotion. Witness the power of the poem's last two lines, which consist only of plain, one-syllable words. He seldom employs strict form, writing here in a loose, accentual meter, using four (or occasionally three) stressed syllables in each line but varying the number of unstressed syllables per line from three to seven. These lines are essentially breath lines, shaped by the natural rhythm of respiration. Mistrusting rigid intellectual patterns or formulas, Stafford prefers to be guided by impulse. In a 1984 interview he admitted, "I like syncopated rhythms . . . broken rhythms, things that start and stop, vagrant impulses, rather than marching rhythms." Perhaps this mistrust is one reason why he seldom uses traditional rhyme. He declared, famously, "For me, all sounds rhyme, sort of."

In "For the Grave of Daniel Boone" Stafford does employ slant or near rhyme in stanzas 3 and 4: "quail" and "kill"; "time," "palm," and "home." Still, the primacy of sound remains, for he strongly relies on the repetition of words ("The farther . . . the farther" in line 1, "deepening home" in the first and fifth stanzas) or repeated vowel and consonant sounds ("snakeskin. . . place"). All the sounds within a poem, he believes, depend on and influence each other.

Stafford seems to agree with the English Romantic poet William Wordsworth that the language of poetry should be the informal language of ordinary, sometimes even colloquial, speech. While this poem captures the nuance and flavor of everyday language ("I heft this rock"), it also depends heavily on the richness of connotation and the subtle ambiguity of simple words. For instance, the phrase "his picture freezes" creates an image of stasis, a lack of motion like action caught in a photograph, but it also suggests the chill of death. When the children "go over the velvet falls" into Boone's world, the word "falls" connotes the drape and folds of velvet, as well as the waterfall that may appear in this tapestried landscape.

As these examples demonstrate, Stafford is largely a poet of vivid image and metaphor: Boone's world as a mansion, history as a tapestry, quail-children that tread "sacred sand," modern life as "a barbwire time." The speaker and those whom he addresses "like to follow the old hands back," that is, follow the wise old ones like Boone, represented by their ringed and knuckled hands, who can lead them back into nature and the past to instruct them. The poem is characterized by a quiet intensity, simplicity of language, and acceptance of whatever truth will come.

Themes and Meanings

Even this relatively early poem of Stafford's foreshadows themes that are characteristic of his work. Noteworthy here is his typical concern with external nature and Boone's intimate association with it. The crucial connection between human experience and the earth itself is an integral part of Stafford's writing, as it was in his own life. Like Wordsworth before him, he seemed to believe that in many ways nature is a beneficent and moral teacher. As a Westerner and environmentalist, he was thus concerned with the modern dissociation of human beings from the natural world. Like many poets from the American West, Stafford wrote with a sense of place, which here is the landscape familiar to Boone. (Other poems may be set on a Kansas farm, in the small towns of Stafford's boyhood, or even in an Oregon blackberry patch.)

Those critics who charge that he is a Western (and therefore regional) poet tend to minimize the significance of his work, for what is regional must necessarily be specific and particular, and as Stafford noted, "All particulars reflect something. . . . The job in writing is the repeated encounter with particulars." While Boone's search for a "deepening home" may indeed have regional overtones, it embodies a universal desire. What is regional is also universal. A corollary theme is his sense of the past, of an earlier time and world not too different from now. In Stafford's poetry the past is always real, yet often transfigured (flowers spread all over the floor) and with a hint of nostalgia.

Obviously, this lyric poem is a personal response to a visit to Boone's grave. Stafford believes, with Wordsworth, that art is born out of emotion and that he must trust in emotion to lead him through the creation of a poem. As he indicated in another interview, "For me, writing . . . is a process of relying on immediate pervasive feelings, not an escape from them." "For the Grave of Daniel Boone" emphasizes not so much the man's life or death as his effect on the lives of those who come after him. Stafford's poem honors Boone, who enlarged American experience as well as the frontier and who now continues as a sort of spiritual guide to the young. The children and the pathfinder remain connected to each other and to the natural world. Boone's legacy is their love of and familiarity with nature. The poem demonstrates an awareness that the world changes while there is still continuity. The past informs the present, and nature informs humanity.

Joanne McCarthy

FOR THE HILLMOTHER

Author: John Montague (1929-   )
Type of poem: Lyric
First published: 1975, in *A Slow Dance*

The Poem

"For the Hillmother" is a thirty-two-line invocation of nature and paean to fertile sexuality consisting of sixteen pairs of short lines. The first line in each pair calls upon an aspect of nature, and the second asks it to perform a particular beneficent action. The poem is a secular version of a litany, a traditional form of group prayer in which a leader and a congregation recite alternating lines. Standing immediately behind this poem is the Litany of the Blessed Virgin Mary, sometimes called the Litany of Loreto, a prayer in use in the Roman Catholic church since the sixteenth century.

In the Litany of the Blessed Virgin, the priest addresses Mary forty-nine times, using names descriptive or symbolic of her virtues or her religious significance. Forty-nine times the congregation responds, "pray for us." A number of the names are metaphorical, some colorfully so: "Mirror of justice," "Vessel of honor," "Mystical rose," "Tower of David," "Tower of ivory," "House of gold," "Ark of the covenant," "Gate of Heaven," "Morning star."

It is these "poetical" names, which draw upon Old Testament prophetic imagery, that John Montague's invocations to "the Hillmother" especially call to mind, but in the poem each of the responses is different:

> Hinge of silence
>   creak for us
>
> . . . .
>
> Leaves of delight
>   murmur for us
>
> . . . .
>
> Freshet of ease
>   flow for us

Only a few lines of the poem closely echo the litany on which it is based. "Gate of birth" recalls "Gate of Heaven"; "Rose of darkness" may suggest "Mystical rose"; and "sway for us" is playfully close to "pray for us." The poem's main resemblance to the prayer is in its overall format.

"Hillmother" in the title is a suggestive term. It calls to mind the phrase "Hail, Mary" and the prayer of that name, reinforcing a reader's sense of how this poem plays off another prayer for Mary. At one level, the hill should be understood literally: One can see and feel the flora ("Wood anemone," "Blue harebell," "Moist fern," "Springy moss"), smell the "Odorous wood," hear the "Secret waterfall" and the wind rustling "Leaves of delight." At another level, however, the landscape is clearly ana-

tomical (as in "Hidden cleft" and "Portal of delight"). The poem principally celebrates female anatomy, though "Branch of pleasure" seems undeniably male in its implications. The hillmother is mother Earth—or, perhaps more accurately, mother/
lover Earth. The hill is evocative of the Venusberg in German legend and Richard
Wagner's opera *Tannhäuser* (1845); it is most certainly the *mons veneris*.

Forms and Devices

The poem is unrhymed (though the repeated "us" has an incantatory effect); but it is
rich in sound effects, including alliteration: "unfold for," "Blue harebell/ bend," "fern/
unfurl for," "Freshet . . ./ flow for." (Notice in particular the accumulation of *f* and *r*
sounds.)

The poem's vocabulary is unusual. There are no articles or conjunctions. Of the
poem's eighty-six words, twenty-four are nouns, sixteen are verbs, and only eight are
adjectives. This is a heady mixture, dense with strong nouns and verbs.

The poem also has a wealth of mouth-filling one-syllable words: "Hinge," "creak,"
"Branch," "breathe," "pearl," "cleft," "birth"—including an abundance of words with
expansive *s* and *z* sounds: "Rose," "moist," "moss," "Leaves," "dews," "ease." On the
tongue, the poem is profoundly sensuous: It is a pungently tactile experience.

"For the Hillmother" is completely without punctuation (which is unusual but not
unprecedented among Montague's poems). The poem illustrates what its author has
called "the circular aesthetic" of Irish art. It begins with the "Hinge of silence"—
silent because motionless; it ends up calling upon the "Gate of birth" to (swing) "open
for us." As with James Joyce's *Finnegans Wake* (1939), which begins and ends in mid-
sentence (the same sentence), the ending of "For the Hillmother" leads back to its beginning. The "Gate of birth" turns on the "Hinge," not of silence but creaking. If the
poem were printed on a Möbius strip, it would be seamless; without beginning or end.
The absence of punctuation, of termination points, underscores its seamlessness.

The mention of James Joyce is not arbitrary. In *A Portrait of the Artist as a Young
Man* (1916), the young Stephen Dedalus wonders, "How could a woman be a tower of
ivory or a house of gold?" Memory provides empirical evidence to answer half of this
question: He remembers the cold, white hands of Eileen Vance and thinks, "That was
ivory: a cold white thing. That was the meaning of *Tower of Ivory*." Montague, in his
essay "The Figure in the Cave" (1989), recalls the "cathartic effect" that his first reading of Joyce's *A Portrait of the Artist as a Young Man* had on him: "it was like a case
study of my own little psyche." Like that book's Stephen Dedalus, but as a mature
man and poet, he has translated the litany into secular, physical, and erotic terms.

In imitating and adapting the religious litany for secular use, Montague implies no
disrespect for the sacred form. On the contrary, it enables him to reinforce the sense of
reverence which his poem expresses for nature, for sexuality, and for procreation.
There is even a kind of aptness to his secularization of the form, which bears a general
resemblance to certain pagan invocations and which, according to *The Catholic Encyclopedia* (1910), derives primarily "from popular medieval Latin poetry." Montague's
adaptation of the litany for secular, poetic use, then, has brought it full circle.

Themes and Meanings

When "For the Hillmother" appeared in *A Slow Dance*, it was the sixth of seven poems in the opening section of that book. A number of images and themes in the poem are repeated, and sometimes clarified, elsewhere in the section. The opening lines of the first poem ("Back")—"Darkness, cave/ drip, earth womb/ we move slowly/ back to our origins"—introduce darkness and wetness (which recur in "For the Hillmother") and evoke both primordial and prenatal shelter (prehistoric in two senses). Most important, these lines begin the motion "back to our origins" which is characteristic of Montague's work in general.

The third poem in the section (a prose poem, "The Dance") concludes with a sentence in which wetness and darkness are again associated and in which the human figure, the dancer, has grown as close to the earth as a deeply-rooted tree: "In wet and darkness you are reborn, the rain falling on your face as it would on a mossy tree trunk, wet hair clinging to your skull like bark, your breath mingling with the exhalations of the earth, that eternal smell of humus and mould."

"For the Hillmother" celebrates the "pull/ of the earth," embraces the "move . . ./ back to our origins"; in doing so, it links up with what is probably the major theme in Montague's poetry: exile and return. For reasons traceable to disruptions in Ireland and in his own life (born in Brooklyn, New York; sent at age four to County Tyrone, Ireland; reared apart from his parents and brothers), he has written often about displacement, dispossession, and separation—but also about coming back, circling back, and going home. Exile and return, or at least the desire to return, define the dynamic of Montague's poetry.

In "For the Hillmother," the desire to return is couched in terms, not of geography or politics or society, but of local landscape (in an introduction to *A Slow Dance*, Montague recalls "the wet lushness which excited me so much when I returned to Ireland, after a decade in exile")—and landscape is metaphor for anatomy. Montague has said that the first impetus for the poem came from viewing an exhibition of Pablo Picasso's graphically sexual engravings, an homage to female genitalia. Montague's later, much earthier, poem, "Sheela na Gig" (*Mount Eagle*, 1988), sees birth as "banishment" from "the first home" and "our whole life" as an effort "to return to that first darkness." "For the Hillmother" transposes that effort and the (male) desire for return to "the first home" into images of nature and the general shape of the litany.

Richard Bizot

FOR THE MARRIAGE OF FAUSTUS AND HELEN

Author: Hart Crane (1899-1932)
Type of poem: Narrative
First published: 1923; collected in *White Buildings*, 1926

The Poem

Hart Crane's "For the Marriage of Faustus and Helen" is in three parts, with a total of 139 lines. Like much of Crane's poetry, it gives the appearance of a rigid, formal structure on the page. Yet, the blank verse lines that he most often employs are seldom perfect pentameters; furthermore, Crane does not hesitate to yield to the pleasures of a rhymed couplet as the spirit moves him, and stanzas in the highly evocative middle section are clearly influenced by free-verse styles typical of the time in which Crane wrote.

The poem is typical of the literary modernism flourishing in the post-World War I era, when innovative young poets and novelists felt free to pick and choose and to mix and match styles from a rich literary tradition that seemed somehow to have failed them. Thus, Crane's poem combines both the lyric and the narrative mode, telling a boy-meets-girl tale in a distinctly contemporary setting overlaid with a lyric vision that seeks to heal the wounds of warfare by combining myth and legend in modern moment.

It is also, then, as the title confirms, an epithalamium, or poem in honor of a marriage. The happy couple in this case are Faustus, the legendary Renaissance doctor who supposedly made a pact with the devil, and Helen, the mythical beauty and daughter of Zeus for whose alienated affections a ten-year war was fought and a fabulous city, Troy, utterly destroyed.

Crane adds a unique twist by setting the couple in a typical contemporary American city. Indeed, after an epigraph from Ben Jonson's *The Alchemist* (1610), which, in its parody of alchemical spells, reminds the reader that magic always happens in the strangest ways and often in the strangest places; part 1 opens to find Faustus working as a stock clerk. It may be stocks and bonds; it may be socks and bonnets. In any case, Faustus recounts his story: He is bored—not, like his legendary namesake, with a surfeit of all human knowledge but with all the trivial details and data modern means of communication can dish out, like "Smutty wings flash[ing] out equivocations."

The mind is also "brushed by sparrow wings," however, for humans can day-dream, and so as he leaves the office or shop one evening and gets on the streetcar for home, Faustus imagines what might happen if "I forgot/ The fare and transfer" and, stuck on the wrong line as it were, "might find [Helen's] eyes across an aisle/ . . . uncontested now." Part 1 ends with Faustus promising that if such a thing were to happen he would be both up to and willing to make himself worthy of the task.

In part 2, the chance meeting has already occurred, for Faustus is taking Helen out for a night on the town. They dance together in a penthouse jazz club, where amid "snarling hails of melody,/ White shadows slip across the floor/ Splayed like cards from a loose hand." There, "Among slim skaters of the gardened skies," he woos and apparently wins her. Yet there have already been hints that the course of true love will not be an easy one. In part 1, Faustus had to remind himself that Helen has known and been known to countless males, "their million brittle, bloodshot eyes," many of whom died on her behalf. Also, in the middle of their good time in part 2, the semblance of a war memory merges with the music in "the deft catastrophe of drums" and "the groans of death."

In this context, the sudden shift to the potential for violence as part 3 opens is not merely understandable but also necessary: Faustus must be willing to accept the destructive quality of Helen's beauty. The "capped arbiter of beauty in this street" may be some thief lurking in the shadows, a rival who thinks that he can win Helen for himself, or simply someone who intends to do them both harm. This ambiguous figure may be Helen herself, who has seen "intricate slain numbers" both in her bed and on the plains beyond Troy's walls.

Whoever the "religious gunman" is, Faustus asserts that he is a match for the man. Indeed, Faustus is fresh from the war, in which as an aviator he "drove speediest destruction." "We did not ask for that," he reminds both himself and her, "but have survived." In Faustus, Helen has met her match, her male equivalent at last, and so: "Let us unbind our throats of fear and pity," that is, end any remorse about death and destruction, which is all behind them now.

Those "Who dare not share with us the breath released," who dare not rejoice in what is, rather than despair over what has been lost, can "Laugh out the meager penance of their days," but as for Faustus, a modern, Industrial Age man, and his newfound love, Helen, the eternal female, they will "praise the years." For "The imagination spans beyond despair."

Forms and Devices

Detractors still speak of Crane's density and obscurities, but he is very much, and quite intentionally, a poet of the word. To say that his poems are mere "word paintings," however, cheapens both the concept and the execution. Rather, Crane seeks verbal equivalents for experience, and these equivalents transcend words' descriptive powers by reaching instead for their incantatory and onomatopoeic qualities. The task of the poet is to manipulate words into images that lend a dimensionality to poetic language that cannot be approximated in any other mode of discourse.

Speaking of "For the Marriage of Faustus and Helen," Crane in his essay "General Aims and Theories" proposed an "absolute" poetry free from his personality and from what he called "any chance evaluation on the reader's part. . . . as though a poem gave the reader as he left it a single new *word*, never before spoken and impossible to actually enunciate."

Crane's attempts at achieving an absolute control over both the denotative and connotative aspects of language account for his apparent obfuscations. The image "corymbulous formations of mechanics" in part 3 offers a convenient example. In this phrase, Crane is describing airborne formations of fighter aircraft. "Corymbulous" is a botanical term describing groupings of flowers that have clustered on the same horizontal plane. Very few readers would be familiar with this word, but it might remind a reader of or be confused with the words "cumulous" and "cumulus," which refer to cloud formations. Connecting the destructiveness of deadly flying machines with objects as indicative of life and fruition as flowers and clouds is a wholly intentional aim on Crane's part at a subliminal language effect. Careful scrutiny, with an unabridged dictionary nearby, will reveal that "Faustus and Helen" is a wellspring of such carefully wrought verbal formulations.

Themes and Meanings

"For the Marriage of Faustus and Helen" is the literary equivalent of Art Deco design and architecture. As such, and from the vantage point of time, the poem exemplifies the exuberance and optimism, as well as many of the fears and doubts, of the 1920's, a decade associated with the spirit of modernism and with the cultural angst that followed swift on the heels of World War I.

Separated from the era that engendered it, however, "For the Marriage of Faustus and Helen" has deeper and more lasting significance. Crane is neither retelling nor redefining the two archetypal figures upon whom his hero and heroine are based; rather, he is interpreting them as representatives of individuals at odds either with themselves or with the world. From this angle, the poem is best summed up in these words from the poem: "There is the world dimensional for those untwisted by the love of things irreconcilable."

Ultimately, the love affair the poem describes is not between a man and a woman but between the individual and his hope that there is a meaningful, purposeful universe somewhere just beyond the reach of his senses—but not beyond the grasp of his imagination.

"For the Marriage of Faustus and Helen" is a quest poem, then, and the quest is for sympathy and understanding. That Crane uses two timeless figures who are associated primarily with tragedy and destruction, in one case of a city, in the other of one's immortal soul, to dramatize the quest is his way of asserting that love and forgiveness are the key to achieving the goal. For his Faustus and his Helen do indeed find their peace in each other through the catharsis of accepting themselves, their past deeds, and their present place in "the world dimensional."

Russell Elliott Murphy

FOR THE UNION DEAD

Author: Robert Lowell (1917-1977)
Type of poem: Lyric
First published: 1960; collected in *For the Union Dead*, 1964

The Poem

The ironies of Robert Lowell's "For the Union Dead" begin with its title. "Union" and "dead" are each adjective and noun. The obvious reference is to the dead of the Union forces in the American Civil War; in a sense, however, the very concept of union is dead in the poem, which depicts a society fragmented by the results of its devotion to the machine and divided by persisting racism.

"For the Union Dead" begins as a very local and topical poem in its evocation of a series of scenes in Boston about the year 1960, with a focus on the construction of a huge garage beneath the Boston Common. The poem alludes briefly to a televised news story about African American schoolchildren in the South who were then undergoing the rigors of forced desegregation, and it alludes at greater length to a Civil War monument imperiled by the excavation beneath. The significance of the poem, however, is much broader than the temporary dislocations it describes.

In the first of its sixty-eight lines, the poem takes a nostalgic look at an aquarium, now abandoned, that the speaker visited as a youth. (There is no reason for supposing that this speaker is anyone but Lowell himself.) He is reminded of a much more recent sight: steamshovels carving out a parking garage beneath Boston's ancient central meeting place. Among the things braced against the shocks of this project is the statehouse across the street; another is one of sculptor Augustus Saint-Gaudens's finest works, a bronze relief of white Colonel Robert Gould Shaw leading his black infantry regiment to the conflict in which most of them perished. Lowell's beautifully metaphorical description of the monument, of Shaw's face and figure and those of his infantrymen, contrasts vividly with the city's indifference to this commemoration of the men who had to endure the scorn of the local citizenry even while marching forth to duty with the Union forces.

After expressing admiration for the monument, Lowell contemplates the "thousand small town New England greens" populated by "stone statues of the abstract Union Soldier," while this particular one quakes from the "underworld" activity. Lowell recalls the officer's fate: his body thrown contemptuously into a ditch with his " 'niggers' " by Confederate soldiers.

Then Lowell remembers an advertisement for a safe that he has recently seen in a window on a nearby street. The advertisement boasts that this safe had survived the atomic attack on Hiroshima during World War II—a war that he notes is uncommemorated on the Common. He thinks of the African American children, still victims of racism a century after the Civil War, then muses again about Colonel Shaw.

The Boston of his youth is gone. In its place has risen a "savage" society that is dedicated to the automobile and indifferent to the amenities of the past, to dislocated landmarks, and even to sobering reminders of injustice. Meanwhile, destruction and racial injustice continue in the larger world around Boston.

Forms and Devices

This poem of seventeen irregular four-line stanzas is pervaded by images of reptiles and fish. Lowell remembers the South Boston Aquarium, his own nose pressed snail-like to the glass as he contemplated the "downward" creatures there on display. Now he watches mechanical creatures at work, "dinosaur steamshovels" digging an "underworld garage."

The Shaw monument is like a fishbone stuck in Boston's throat. In keeping with the "downward" tendency of fish and reptiles, he thinks of the ditch into which Shaw and his men were thrown and then of the physical and moral contemporary ditch. In place of the aquarium, automobiles of the time with their exaggerated tail fins loom like weird, mechanical versions of fish. Lowell generalizes this imagery as the "savage servility" of a society devoted to the proliferation and storage of motor vehicles.

Bubbles, evanescent things associated in this poem with fragile and easily neglected values, also recur. There are the bubbles that drift from the noses of the fish in the aquarium, the faces of African American schoolchildren that rise like balloons on the television newscast, and the "bubble" on which Shaw rides in Saint-Gaudens's monument. In contrast, the solid artifacts of the poem—the steamshovels, the girders that brace the statehouse, the Mosler safe (which, unlike thousands of people in Hiroshima, "survived" the atomic blast that leveled the city), the garage, the innumerable automobiles—symbolize a materialistic society that contemns frail spiritual values.

Another feature of Lowell's poem is paradox. American philosopher William James's reaction to the Shaw monument—that he could almost hear the soldiers breathe—attests the paradoxical tendency of an inert work of art to radiate life. It also brings to mind the fact that those men, caught in the act of marching, perished soon thereafter. The likeness of Shaw himself is both "angry" and "gentle"; he has chosen "life" and therefore must die.

The state of the monument is also paradoxical. Whereas the lesser memorials on sleepier New England commons continue in uninterrupted repose, the integrity of this masterpiece is threatened by the restless urban forces. Lowell notes that Shaw's father wanted no monument for his son. Perhaps he thought that any monument would be likely to ignore Colonel Shaw's subordinates—as a matter of fact, the inscription on the monument, *Omnia Reliquit Servare Rem Publicam* ("He gave up everything to serve the Republic"), does ignore them. In using the inscription as an epigraph for his poem, Lowell changed the verb to *Relinquunt*, making it plural and present tense: "They give up everything."

Paradoxically, the Boston Common contains no statues honoring World War II heroes. Instead, Lowell finds nearby a commemoration of the intact Mosler Safe, a mere box for possessions. The final paradox concerns the aspirations of the modern city. In the name of progress, human ingenuity produces an overall effect of savagery, as if humans themselves are reverting to a fishlike or reptilian stage of the evolution-ary process.

Themes and Meanings

These paradoxes point to several interrelated themes in "For the Union Dead." One is the decline in urban civility. The disruption on the Boston Common was only tem-porary, but scenes similar to it are a constant feature of American city life in the sec-ond half of the twentieth century. Art, landscape, and people themselves must all yield to the demands of the automobile. Good buildings are demolished to provide parking lots; neighborhoods are sliced by expressways; pedestrian access to places of leisure is rendered bewilderingly difficult. The new city offers a new savagery in the name of technological progress.

Officialdom does not formally repudiate the civilities created by past generations, but the continued existence of officialdom depends on its accommodating itself to the changing scene. The Shaw Monument is an embarrassment; it "sticks like a fishbone/ in the city's throat." People can still walk on portions of the Boston Common but must expect to be jolted by an "earthquake" every so often. The aquarium, boarded up and decaying, has become part of a "Sahara."

The most important artifact in Lowell's poem, the bronze relief of the Caucasian colonel and his brave African American regiment, stands for a fact of American life that a terrible war and the passage of a century have not succeeded in correcting: racial division, strife, and inequality. Lowell's reference to Hiroshima reminds one of the ease with which racial hatred persists in modern warfare. The "drained faces" of the African American schoolchildren being conducted to formerly all-Caucasian schools furnishes a bitter commentary on the failures of a society too preoccupied with auto-mobiles and parking spaces to notice that after a hundred years, the promise for which Shaw and his men died has still not been fulfilled.

These two themes, imagistically related in the poem, finally blend into one. What America was belatedly trying to accomplish was integration; what it was achieving might better be termed disintegration. Well-intentioned people were trying to bring citizens together in some kind of equality, but in a setting of disintegrating cities. Those who neglect truly creative achievements such as the Shaw Monument in favor of what Lowell calls "civic sandpiles" by this very act neglect the values that Saint-Gaudens was capturing in bronze, and thereby condemn themselves to more genera-tions of bigotry and turmoil. The failures of democracy and of civility turn out to be two sides of the same coin.

Lowell's poem does not say that union is dead. Someone has thought to prop up the monument with a plank, and people are still risking their own safety to help the op-pressed fulfill the rights of citizenship. As long as a work such as the Shaw Monument remains (as Lowell puts it) "out of bounds," however, those who are thoughtful will wonder whether the heroes have died in vain, and union will remain a dream deferred.

Robert P. Ellis

THE FORCE THAT THROUGH THE GREEN
FUSE DRIVES THE FLOWER

Author: Dylan Thomas (1914-1953)
Type of poem: Lyric
First published: 1933; collected in *Eighteen Poems*, 1934

The Poem

"The Force That Through the Green Fuse Drives the Flower" is a carefully sculptured poem of four stanzas and a coda, its twenty-two lines scrupulously crafted for maximum power and, to some extent, maximum puzzlement.

The poem, as the title echoing the first line suggests, is about a mysterious force, which the poet proceeds to define, qualify, and examine in a variety of ways. This force, presumably the force behind all nature and reality—maybe even a divine force—paradoxically combines life and death and links the poet—the "I" of the poem—to the universe.

Each stanza identifies the force in a slightly different way, defining a different aspect of its operation. The effect of the stanzas is cumulative and progressive; each definition qualifies and amplifies the last. Each stanza ends by establishing the poet's relation to the force.

In the first stanza, the force is the "life" force or growth force that drives flowers through the soil into bloom. Death, however, is also a part of natural growth, and this same force destroys the roots of trees. After all, photosynthesis (one natural process) enables flowers to increase in size and bloom; worms, wind, or disease (other natural processes) can dramatically eat away at the roots of trees and cause them to topple suddenly. Simultaneously, the poet has linked the force of life/death to himself, for it both drives his youth and will eventually lead to his death. Nevertheless, the poet is unable to communicate with nature ("the crooked rose") and express or articulate his kinship with growing things in life and death.

The second stanza sees the same generative/destructive power in the force but now extends it to an inanimate, though powerful, natural element: water. Again, the poet states that the force both produces flow and activity and dries up streams. Gravity "pulls" water down from mountains, creating rivers; when all the water (for the time being) has been "pulled," the streams disappear. As before, the poet sees the same force at work in himself, for the blood in the human body is itself a form of sustaining water—and biohistorically was once sea water. As a stream may dry up, so may a human being die and the blood cease to flow. Yet Dylan Thomas cannot mouth this truth to his own veins, to his own body.

The third stanza defines the force in the anthropomorphic metaphor of an unseen hand, suggesting a quasi-divine or at least a mystical being. Such a force sets life-giving water in motion but also creates quicksand, usually associated with death. Similarly, like a human hand that pulls in a line on a sailboat to control the wind and make the boat go faster, the trimmed sail simply pushes the boat farther toward its ultimate destination—which is the "shroud sail" associated with death and often seen as an allusion to the lover's death in *Tristan and Isolde* (twelfth century). The intertwining of all life and death is imaginatively startling but incommunicable because the poet cannot explain this universal kinship of all human beings to one another. Though the decaying flesh of the poet may turn into quicklime, used by a hangman to speed the decomposition of a hanged man, Thomas cannot articulate this spiritual-chemical unity to the person hanging from the rope.

The fourth stanza suggests a countermovement to the ultimate destructive power of the force with images of time, love, and heaven. Here the destructive process, seen as fallen blood and time itself, appears to lead to healing, resolution, renewal, and hope. In the final coda, the poet, echoing the recently announced theme of love, reminds the reader that although he cannot communicate with dead lovers, his living body shares the full panoply of love's experiences.

Forms and Devices

The key devices in the poem are paradoxical metaphor, oxymoron, and pun—all interwoven. The central metaphor is that life and death are interlinked, inextricable, part and parcel of the same force. Thomas keeps this striking paradox constantly before the reader in a number of ways. For example, "fuse" and "flower" both appear in the poem's first line, though the destructive fuse of military ordnance seems completely opposed to the beauty of nature's flower. Yet, the "green fuse" is the stem of the plant through which, in Thomas's image, the flower bursts into bloom. The paradoxical image is carried further in the verb "blasts," for the destructive energy implicit in a fuse gives way to the demise of trees.

One form of paradox is oxymoron, a strategy Dylan Thomas employs repeatedly, yoking seemingly unlike qualities together in a single phrase that seems at first self-contradictory; "green" is young and growing, and "age" is old. Thus the phrase "green age" echoes the "green fuse" of the earlier line and suggests that though Thomas may be young, he is also aging: The force that is working in him to make his youthful exuberance (he was eighteen when he wrote this poem) is also the force that keeps adding years and experience that bring him ultimately to death.

A similar pattern to the paradox and oxymoron is that of punning, which occurs in a variety of forms. The near-rhymes characteristic of poetry are also puns that play on the similarities in words, suggesting the unity of the all-encompassing force that creates both life and death. Thus the verb "drives" of the first seven lines, with its suggestions of force, power, energy, and life, is transformed into "dries" in the seventh line: Life and death are virtually the same, almost contained in the same word. The driving force has now become the drying force, the one that eliminates water, the source of life.

There is a powerful triple pun in the words "sheet" and "worm" of the poem's final line: "How at my sheet goes the same crooked worm." In the most immediate sense, the worm is the slightly sinister, snakelike creature that eats decaying flesh in the grave, that has eaten the flesh of previous lovers in tombs, and that will eat the poet's flesh when he dies and is ensconced in a winding sheet. The worm, however, is also a penis on a bedsheet, reminding one of the life-giving sexual force of love—this is also a force and a body part the poet has in common with previous lovers. Finally, the "crooked worm" going at the sheet is Thomas's finger writing this poem on a sheet of paper, as previous lovers have, though dead, immortalized their feelings about love in literature—giving the force a kind of immortality that transcends the decay of death.

Themes and Meanings

The primary theme of this poem is the mysterious paradoxical "force," puzzling in its unity of nature, life, and humans. It is a unity between nature and humans, between the individual poet and all other human beings. It is a unity that ties together all things living and dead and that culminates in love. The unity is also that of creation and destruction, however, and in that sense, it is sobering and painful. In addition, the unity is incommunicable. Growth and death, creation and destruction, the blooming of the merest flower, the tumbling of large trees, the law-abiding citizen, the hanging man, and the man who hangs him—all are bound into one by the poem with its complex pattern of interlocking paradoxes, oxymorons, and puns.

Thomas reiterates his comment of incommunicability at the end of each stanza and in the poem's two-line coda: "And I am dumb to tell." He is "dumb" because, in slang occasionally characteristic of Thomas's love of play with language, it is stupid for him to talk to roses or to the veins in his own body or to the hanged man. He knows and the readers know these cannot hear and do not understand. He is also dumb in the literal sense, unable to speak, as a poet is constantly frustrated by words in trying to articulate feelings. So the deep, painful irony of the poem is that, though he is bound to the total physical universe, he is unable to express this unity, except by writing this poem, placing the "crooked worm" of his finger on the sheet of paper on his desk.

The "crooked worm" of the last line ironically unites with the paradoxical echo of the line from the first stanza, the "crooked rose," a traditional image of beauty and romance from medieval and romantic poetry. Roses and worms thus go together; they are part of the same unity, even though one is usually identified with beauty and love, and the other with ugliness and death. The rose is literally crooked, bent by the same force (life-death) as the poet: Roses grow in spurts, and each spurt tends to bend the stem slightly. The worm is also crooked because it is alive: It is wriggling to move. Therefore, though "crooked" also suggests cheating and something amiss, it is finally a sign of life and vitality, as is the poem that the poet's crooked finger writes.

Jonathan L. Price

FORCED MARCH

Author: Miklós Radnóti (Miklós Glatter, 1909-1944)
Type of poem: Lyric
First published: 1970, as "Erőltetett menet," in *Bori notesz*; English translation collected in *The Complete Poetry*, 1980

The Poem

"Forced March," by the Hungarian poet Miklós Radnóti, is a poem of twenty loosely rhymed lines describing a war prisoner's physical and emotional anguish in the midst of being forced to march toward an unnamed destination. The man imagines his home and his wife in an attempt to keep hope, despite the fact that it seems otherwise clear that he will never reach home.

The opening lines of the poem describe this man who, immediately after collapsing, makes the effort to rise again, overcoming the pain in his ankle and knee and the fact that it would be easier to remain prone and simply die. However, even though "the ditch will call him," he will continue to rise and walk "as if wings were to lift him high." Rhetorically, the poet asks, "why not?" Why should he not continue to rise? If this man were to answer, the poet says, he might explain that his wife is waiting at home, and it is at this home that he can anticipate a different death, one that is "beautiful, wiser."

Against the backdrop of these images, the poet labels the prisoner a "wretch" and a "fool," for in truth there is nothing left of his home where only "singed winds have been known to whirl." The walls of the house have been knocked flat, and his plum tree has been "broken clear." Worse than this physical razing is that "all the nights back home horripilate with fear," describing the bristling of hair from terror.

The poem then shifts its point of view as the speaker becomes the man on the march, despairing over the thought that he may be uselessly hoping for the existence of what remains at home, that he has not "merely borne/ what is worthwhile, in my heart." "Tell me it's all still there," he exclaims, as he lists the pleasant aspects of an early autumn in his home: "the cool verandah, bees/ of peaceful silence buzzing" and freshly canned plum jam cooling. In his imagination, "summer-end peace" sunbathes "over sleepy gardens," and "fruits [sway] naked" in the fruit trees. In the center of this scene stands his wife,

> blonde, my Fanni . . .
> with morning slowly tracing its shadowed reticence.

This imagined recollection of his former life is brought into sharp contrast as the poet returns to the present scene with his assertion, almost against hope, that "all that *could* still be," an idea that may be suggested by the round moon, the one object that this landscape seems to have in common with the paradise of his former home. In the poem's final line, the poet calls to a comrade to wait for and encourage him: "shout!

and I'll come around!" The poet seems to have all reason to lose hope, for he has likely lost his home, his wife, and his former life, yet he uses this image of his former existence to goad himself to rise one more time and continue his march.

Forms and Devices

In Emery George's translation, Radnóti's poem is built on paired rhymes, both conventional ("insane" and "pain," "clear" and "fear") or slant ("high" and "stay," "answer" and "wiser"). The rhymed couplets give the poem a marching regularity, and the partial rhymes create a forced structure that suggests the compulsory march that is the subject of the poem. Yet more remarkable are the imposed breaks in the middle of each line. These caesuras give a halting quality to the reading of poem, like the halting pause of the man who tries to march, despite his limping and the occasional fall: "The man who, having collapsed,   rises, takes steps, is insane." When reading this poem, one is struck by how difficult it must be for the man to complete a step, to complete a phrase, and even to complete a breath.

Halfway through the poem, the point of view changes. In the first ten lines, the narrator speaks of "the man" in third person. Even the reader is addressed in second person directly ("should you ask, why not?") and implicitly through commands ("But see . . ."). However, in the tenth line, that point of view shifts to first person; the poet and the man on the march become the same as he calls out in anguish, "Oh, if I could believe   that I haven't merely borne/ what is worthwhile, in my heart." The effect is to make the object of suffering more personal, as the reader more easily sympathizes and identifies with the speaker as he dreams of his former home and what he hopes still remains. As the poet (the man on the march) addresses "my friend," one may assume that this comrade is a fellow marcher. However, because the second-person pronoun has been used before to address the reader, Radnóti creates the effect of the reader being addressed as "my friend"; thus, as one leaves the poem and its suffering prisoner of war behind, one feels that the prisoner's survival depends on the reader's sympathies.

At the poem's end Radnóti appended the place and date of the poem's composition: "Bor [a town in former Yugoslavia], 15 September 1944." While Radnóti might not have known he had less than two months to live, the shortness of the poem and its strong visual imagery suggest the "postcard" technique that Radnóti used in other poems, especially during this final creative period of his life. As a postcard often conveys both a picture and a message, Radnóti seems to be recording this event to tell someone else what is occurring to him. Also, since postcards rarely request or require a reply, the poem's extreme circumstances are heightened by the sense that he is capturing a series of events that may be lost with the poem.

Themes and Meanings

The "forced march" of the title can be interpreted in two ways. The first is the forced march that the prisoner is a part of as he presses on, despite his physical pain, toward a destination not named in the poem. In the second sense, the poet forces himself onward, as "he simply dare not stay" in the ditch in which he has collapsed. In fact, the compulsory nature of the march may be caused more by the poet's own drive. Though he "is insane" and "a fool" for hoping that his home and wife still exist, he creates a pastoral scene. "Tell me it's still there," he commands himself; his insistent tones can be heard in lines such as "Oh, if I could believe . . ./ . . . that there *is*, to return, a home." In contrast to the way he compels himself onward are the "sleepy gardens," his waiting wife, and "morning slowly tracing   its shadowed reticence." The languorous nature of his mental destination serves as a fitting goal to the pure relentlessness of his journey. The final lines, as he calls to a comrade to rouse him back to action, end this reverie and return him to the reality of the forced march.

The poet's imagined home life also operates in the context of a biblical allusion. He imagines his wife waiting in a garden in the morning where "among bow and foliage   fruits were swaying naked." In its innocence, the scene suggests Eden before the Fall of Man. By contrast, he is in darkness (despite a full moon) and believes that the plum tree (like the Tree of Knowledge of Good and Evil) has been broken. This land of his pleasant past is gone, and with his inability to return to it he resembles the cursed Adam, who must labor to survive. The paradise of his former life exists only as a dream.

These literary meanings are made more significant when the poem is placed in its autobiographical context. Of Jewish lineage and an outspoken leftist writer, Radnóti was drafted into forced labor by his government at the outset of World War II. In 1944, during his third term of labor, he worked mining copper and constructing railroads until prisoners near the war's front line were relocated at the approach of Allied forces. This forced march ended when Radnóti and twenty other prisoners, sick and brutally treated by their fascist Hungarian captors, could not be placed in a local hospital. They were shot and buried in a mass grave. When Radnóti's body was exhumed two years later, his wife identified his body and found a small notebook, soaked with blood and stained by earth. "Forced March" was among these 144 poems that Radnóti had written during the last months of his life.

The feelings in the poem, therefore, come out of a historical as well as a personal context. The poet wanted to give witness to the atrocities committed against him and his fellow prisoners—and against his fellow citizens and even all humans. The resulting poem must be viewed in this context to receive its full impact, so that readers will listen and remember. In fact, the final line reaches out to a fellow prisoner: "Don't go past me, my friend—   shout! and I'll come around!" The camaraderie between the prisoners allowed Radnóti to survive long enough to pen these words, and that final image, however desperate, attests to the poem's message of aid and succor. This plea in the poem, which comes to the reader even across the gulf of death, reaches out to ask the reader not to pass him by but to give voice and bring his message back to life.

Brian C. Ferguson-Avery

THE FORGE

Author: Seamus Heaney (1939-   )
Type of poem: Lyric
First published: 1969, in *Door into the Dark*

The Poem

From a strictly formal point of view, "The Forge" is a sonnet. As is typical of Seamus Heaney's work, however, and reflective of this poem's unobtrusive depths, it is more interesting for the ways in which it departs from conventional sonnet forms than for its attachment to them. Thus, "The Forge" opens with a representative sonnet rhyme scheme. Once this is established, however, it is not adhered to. Similarly, the familiar internal organization of a sonnet into octet (the first eight lines) and sestet (the concluding six lines) seems promised but is not maintained.

"The Forge" presents the poet as an observer of a familiar childhood scene (the village "smithy" has a long history as a poetic subject). The poem is written in the first person, and there is little doubt that Heaney draws on material familiar to him and to which he has remained imaginatively attached. The elements of the scene are described in loving detail, so that the reader has a strong impression of immediacy and intimacy. The poet's strong visual imagination—whereby evidence of the everyday catches the reader's eye like the smith's "unpredictable fantail of sparks"—places the reader in direct sensory relation with the subject matter.

The poet remains an unobtrusive facilitator throughout. His presence enables the reader to see, rather than enjoining the reader to read. This approach suggests that experiencing is as significant as reaching conclusions, a suggestion that may be considered an example of the poet's debt to William Wordsworth. (Heaney has acknowledged this debt on a number of occasions and has edited a selection of Wordsworth's poetry.) Such a poetic objective—to return the reader by means of imaginative engagement to elements of nature, entities beyond, and prior to, the page (water, iron, air)—is in keeping with the poem's essential simplicity.

Although the poem is entitled "The Forge," it is clear that its ambition is as much to depict the man who carries out the work as it is to show the nature of the forge's dark interior and materials. The labor and what it takes come before the carefully integrated description of the smith. There is a sense in which the other images of the poem are subsidiary to that of the smith, whom the reader would expect to be the dominant presence in the poem. It is striking, however, how the poem avails itself of this normal expectation quietly to draw attention to the human image that is beyond the public point of entry and labors at the core of darkness. The gradual, self-effacing buildup to this recognition creates a number of resonances, which go well beyond the poem's apparently simple occasion and make "The Forge" a more subtle piece of work than its deceptively simple surface might lead the reader to believe.

Forms and Devices

"The Forge" is a typical Heaney poem in a number of respects. It exemplifies the poet's striking use of what he has called (borrowing a T. S. Eliot phrase) "the auditory imagination." At one level, the sense of sound works in a familiar poetic, as, for example, in the internal rhyme of "know" and "door" and the juxtaposition of "door" and "dark" in the poem's opening line. Such sonar relationships give the poem a pleasing degree of sensory interplay that engages the reader's imagination, as slowly reading "The Forge" aloud will reveal. Additionally, it is noticeable how "short-pitched," used to describe the sound of hammer on anvil, evokes in its taut sibilance the chink of metal on metal, as well as more distantly suggesting the smith's muscular stroke. Those two associations facilitate and reinforce the mention of "shape and music" in later lines—"shape" being the immediacy of the thing made and "music" an abstract consequence of the making.

Though verbally rich, "The Forge" does not rely on facile verbal fireworks. The smith "grunts and goes in" back to work, and work has its unglamorous mundanity, as the colloquialisms "slam and flick" state. Generally speaking, the poem's combination of restraint and attachment provides the reader with an attractive experience of the domestic and the vaguely exotic—"door" and "dark," "outside" and "inside." The one occasion in which an image is elaborated into simile—the sharp end of the anvil seen as "horned as a unicorn"—is arguably the weakest component of the poem, though it cannot be rejected totally since it potently underscores the poem's thematic substance.

The metaphor of the anvil as "altar/ Where he expends himself in shape and music" draws attention to the presence in "The Forge" of another typical feature of Heaney's verse. The perhaps unexpected connotations of smith as expressive celebrant reveal a sacramental undercurrent to the overall depiction; they are particularly striking in view of being in such sharp contrast to the "old axles and iron hoops rusting" encountered in the poem's second line. Such a view supports the perception of the smith as a somewhat distant and mysterious dweller in darkness. This perception is substantiated by the poem's opening declaration of a limited awareness of the smith ("All I know . . .") and, at the end of the poem, by the smith turning his back on the social scene beyond the forge to tend to his solitary exertions. The poet's adoption of a limited perception makes more of the smith by seeming to have little to convey about him. "All" is the word that signals from the outset the poem's perspective of enabling restraint.

The opening statement of "The Forge" can be read as one made in the present tense. It seems more in keeping with the poem's subtle resources, however, to consider the verb "to be" in the historic present. By that means, the poem's activity, glossed in the smith's work ("To beat real iron out"), is a deliberate act of imaginative reconstitution that also acts as a hint to the reader to iron out the full imaginative potential of this illusorily simple poem.

Themes and Meanings

Poems of notably succinct, imagistic directness about his rural life growing up on the family farm in County Derry, Northern Ireland, formed the core of Heaney's first book, *Death of a Naturalist* (1966). To a certain extent, the poems in his second book, *Door into the Dark*, are in the same vein. "Bogland," the concluding poem in this volume, indicates how comprehensive a grasp the poet has on the metaphorical resonances of landscape and origins. "The Forge" is an important illustration of the process of achieving full poetic identity, which is what gives *Door into the Dark* its wider fascination and significance. Here, as elsewhere, the poet does not merely draw on background material but also allows the occasion of doing so to substantiate the activity of doing so.

The smith, then, is more than a figure from the past. He is also an emblem of present transformative energies. The forge is more than a place by which a child was fascinated. The poem actively rehearses the recognition of there being entry to a place of making, and it welcomes the possibility. The smith's withdrawal into his vaguely Promethean cave and his invisibility within it is counteracted by the poet's refusal to look away, frustrated by what he cannot see. The poem becomes an extended metaphor for the activity of poetry.

The tendency of "The Forge" to see its material in somewhat larger-than-life terms—as in the "unicorn" simile and in the consequence of perceiving the anvil as "an altar"—clearly enhances the status and potential of what the poet's memory has unearthed. This process—which converts the incidental and the elementary to new uses—is the smith's business; it is also a metaphor for what the poet is doing on this particular occasion and for what the process of making poems requires. The commitment to go beyond "All I know," which is the point from which "The Forge" sets out, is articulated in terms of an admiration of energy and a recognition of the need to work in isolation, away from "where traffic is flashing."

Heaney's development into one of the leading Irish poets of his generation has derived from this commitment to a wide-eyed, wondering plumbing of darknesses. "The Forge," part of whose first line provides the title for the poet's second book, is a vivid example of that commitment in the making.

George O'Brien

A FORM OF WOMEN

Author: Robert Creeley (1926-   )
Type of poem: Lyric
First published: 1959, in *A Form of Women*

The Poem

The title of Robert Creeley's first collection of poetry from previously published volumes, *For Love* (1962), is an accurate summation of one of the essential concerns of many of the poems gathered there, but as critic Cid Corman points out, the second section includes "some of the unhappiest love poems of our time." While Creeley has always maintained that the possibility of love is one of the strongest restorative forces humans can bring to bear against the ruins of time, the poems in *A Form of Women* were written during the strained, difficult days when his first marriage was moving toward dissolution.

Utilizing a four-line stanza that is like a short quatrain without rhyme, Creeley has created a basic unit that can either advance or "stop anywhere" so that each stanza is both a single meditative block and a part of a larger grouping. The first section, composed of three stanzas, begins with a couplet which presents the poet's philosophical position—his belief that his previous experiences have so shaped his sense of himself and the world that they will be a dominant factor in any relationship. The next two stanzas amplify this idea, asserting that the accumulation of experience has been driven by the will to probe and question even at the risk of uncovering some disquieting or unsettling aspect of his psyche. These stanzas move toward a pause, leading to the development of a meditative mood as the poet examines his investigative impulses. Recalling how he has often journeyed in solitude through the natural world, considering phenomena while subject to the apprehension induced by the unknown, the poet establishes one of his most fundamental motives in his last observation: the desire "to know," which stands in opposition to the fear of unnerving revelation.

The next section introduces the woman to whom the poem is partially addressed, drawing her into his sphere of experience, joining her presence to the other mysteries of existence. He finds that he is inclined to reach toward the woman, to make contact, but is prevented by the same abstract fear that has troubled him before. In spite of their shared experience, he is still unable to "touch" her in the most crucial ways.

In the sixth stanza, a midpoint or balancing point, the poet frames the developing poem in the midst of its composition as a kind of gift—a presentation of the self which explains the value of what he is offering ("have care for its contents") as well as the difficulty he has in making the presentation. The intimate nature of his gift ("My face . . . My hands . . . My mouth") is expressed as an aspect of tangible physicality, but his uncertainty continues as he wonders whether those features most crucial to his being are sufficient to explain who he is.

Ostensibly addressing the moon (a figure for mystery) in the eighth stanza, the poet plaintively states that when "you leave me alone/ all the darkness is/ an utter blackness"—an expression of desperation, since he feels that he cannot make contact or live without an attempt at contact. The prospect of separation leaves a "pit of fear," and because of this "stench," he knows that he must try again, reassured by the knowledge that in spite of all difficulties, he can still say "But I love you." This remains a source of hope but not of confidence, since the poem closes with his recurring concern, "What to say/ when you see me."

Forms and Devices

The poem "A Form of Women" is concerned with understanding the self, the world, and the way in which a relationship with another person shapes this understanding. Each of these aspects of existence is a part of the uncertainty of knowing, and the poet's attempts to describe and perceive the form (that is, the essential nature) of the things of his life is concentrated in his quest for some ways to realize the self through the process of love. In order to do this, he attempts to examine the elusive forms of the woman who has been a part of this process. While he is never so direct as to establish an equivalence between the forms of a woman and such abstractions as love, life, or light, the poem moves tentatively in that direction.

The most specific metaphoric arrangement occurs in the eighth stanza, with the address "Moon, moon," which is both to the "you" (the woman) in the poem and to a lunar diety as a feminine goddess, an idea which is extended further by the idea of the woman's removal as the cause of "utter blackness." The sense of moonlight and love as intermingled is implied by the poet's plea for care when "the moon shines." The setting, a walk "to see the moonlight" within a cloak of darkness, emphasizes the intimacy of the relationship and contributes to its mystery. Images of light and dark are employed throughout the poem to render the shifting perspective of the poet toward the woman he loves and toward his sense of self.

Creeley's use of language is primarily abstract and suggestive rather than specifically descriptive in accordance with his search for universalities of form. He refers to a previous part of his life as "where," refers to "things" looking at him; and says that he fears "shapes." The tension between the vague unease of existence and the attempt to locate something specific he can hold is paralled by his desire to "touch"—that is, to measure shape or identify form. This urge is developed through the course of the poem by the initial repetition of the word "I," followed by the eventual introduction of "you"; in the final stanza, "I" shifts to "me," which is joined, tentatively, to "you." The disjunction between "I" and "My" adds additional weight to the pressures dividing the self, and dividing the self from another.

The complete reliance on a conversational vernacular, wound into tight clusters of words almost entirely of single and double syllables, is characteristic of the spare, trim language Creeley uses. The minimal use of metaphor and external reference is a part of Creeley's strategy to make the poem "exist through itself," an appropriate technique for a poem that works as an exploration of language and self-consciousness while providing an emotive context for abstraction.

Themes and Meanings

As the title *For Love* indicates, many of the poems in Creeley's first collection were written in an attempt to understand, express, or locate love in a world of confusion, threat, and loneliness. The poem "A Form of Women" is part of a larger context—not an interlocked poetic sequence, but a group of poems that cast light on one another and that move from an elliptical anger toward a more relaxed lyricism. As critic Robert Kern points out, the "quest" of the book is toward a sense of grace, which Creeley has powerfully evoked in the later poem "Oh Love" (from *Mirrors*, 1983): "Oh love,/ like nothing else on earth!" The lyrics toward the end of *For Love* are "grateful celebrations" of "love and domestic conditions," but "A Form of Women," at the center of the collection, is more of a projection of those possibilities.

The transformative power of love is conveyed by the seventh stanza, in which the poet speaks of the most personal qualities (face, hands, mouth) as no longer sufficient to define the self. Those features which are still "his own" cannot encompass the full range of consciousness, since the relationship with another has added the weight of "a thousand years" to his features. The poet's recognition of this power leads to a faith in its capacity to transcend the abstractions of existence, to make the physical presence of another an actuality as a means of fulfillment. The inability of "hands unreasonable" to touch, however, remains a source of pain. The struggle between the promise of love, already experienced to some extent, and the frustrations of the particular relationship in which the poet is involved fills the poem with a tension that is also a part of the fascination which love offers. The poet's questions, epitomized by the universal "Do you love me" of the final stanza, convey both the uncertainty and necessity bound together, inseparable and inescapable. The poet's attempts to explain to himself why he wanted "very much to/ touch you/ but could not" are at the heart of the mystery.

The exploratory nature of "The Form of Women" is evidence of the poet's realization that he must confront his own psychic uncertainty before he can expect to enrich a relationship. Because it is written entirely as a reflection of the "I" who has "thought," "watched," and "wanted" but has been unable "to touch," it is an act of love in language. It holds an optimistic conclusion—that imagination can resist the terrifying "stench" of the darkness from which the poet recoils. An underlying yearning for a more complete commitment than the poet is able to make, based on the necessity of becoming more comfortable with the self before it can be extended to another, is expressed in the paradox that the self can be really understood only through the love of another. Thus the recognition that "I love you" provides the strength for him to ask "Do you love me," mingling tentative hope with its accompanying, continuing uncertainty as the poem closes.

Leon Lewis

FORMAL ELEGY

Author: John Berryman (1914-1972)
Type of poem: Elegy
First published: 1964, in *Of Poetry and Power: Poems Occasioned by the Presidency and by the Death of John F. Kennedy*; collected in *Collected Poems, 1937-1971*, 1989

The Poem

"Formal Elegy" is written in what one would generally call free verse. It incorporates occasional rhymes but does not follow any strict form. Its ten stanzas range in length from two to twenty lines. The title suggests a closure to the confusion surrounding President John F. Kennedy's assassination; yet, characteristic of John Berryman's work, the poem indicates an inability to settle upon any conclusion. Written primarily in the first person, the poem occasionally lapses into third person and first person plural. It consists of scattered images of Kennedy; accused assassin Lee Harvey Oswald and his murderer, Jack Ruby; Dallas, Texas; Arlington Cemetery; and the poet himself. Almost all images are offered in relation to television, which the poet considers another player in the tragedy. This poem is a traditional elegy only in that it attempts to encompass all of the poet's thoughts upon the subject. It does not specifically elegize Kennedy but seems to elegize the entire sequence of events related to his presidency and assassination.

In the first stanza, "Formal Elegy" presents the reader with several images that establish the poem's tone and scope: Americans as survivors, the shocked poet, and the killers and the killed. The beginning of the second stanza—"Yes, it looks like a wilderness"—attempts to summarize this confusion, and the third stanza relates the confusion to television, which has presented these scattered images to the public. In the fourth stanza, the speaker likens himself to a car, another machine, which represents the mechanical perceptions people have acquired through television by recalling images of cars as they appeared throughout the televised drama in question. The following two stanzas relate television to people: their paralysis in front of their television sets, their perceptions of Dallas, and their perceptions of Kennedy himself, who now moves and acts only on television. The next three stanzas relate the events to the poet, a one-time Texan and an indirect participant (through television), who takes some of the shame upon himself.

The poems ends with its longest stanza, which, as any good elegy should, points the reader toward the future; yet, this future is less secure. Kennedy's youth is mourned but then dismissed in a halfhearted attempt to face facts. The end suggests that the nation should "continue," that it will, as it always has, though "stunned, survive." Yet due to television's persistence in numbing people to horrors, this ability to survive is no longer admirable but is an "insolence," a symbol that the nation is unable to move (or be moved) either physically, away from its black-and-white screens, or emotionally, toward a more natural grief.

Forms and Devices

Berryman's fragmented style represents the nation's confusion. The poem's images are many and disjointed, their only commonality existing in their having been first seen in televised reports concerning Kennedy. However, the poem's language acquires continuity through these images as it assumes the reader's familiarity with the events surrounding Kennedy's assassination. Thus, the speaker relies upon his audience's knowledge, through television, of these references. Television, therefore, is the subject of the poem; the human actors are merely the objects.

"Nobody goes anywhere," the poem asserts, "lengthened (days) into TV." From now on, but especially in this crisis, Americans are lost to the images reflected on a television screen. "Some in their places are constrained to weep," the speaker reveals, portraying the messages of television as "Black foam. A weaving snake. An invulnerable sleep." Though what has happened is real, what people see is somewhat unreal. Televised images actually become reality as "Images of Mr Kennedy blue the air,/ who is little now, with no chance to grow great."

The poem resembles a montage of Kennedy's television images, and the speaker calls the reader's specific attention to the images themselves: Kennedy's hair "kept not wholly real"; the car in the motorcade, where "Onto him climbed/ a-many and went his way"; Ruby's "mad claim/ he shot to spare the Lady's testifying"; Kennedy's casket, which "I sidled in & past"; "schoolgirls in Dallas"; and "black & white together, stunned." The language of the commentary also refers to images, to what people see rather than (necessarily) to reality: "it looks like a wilderness"; "Fat Dallas, a fit set"; "He seemed good:/ brainy in riot, daring, cool"; "We compose our faces." The speaker comments upon televised images by speaking in their own terms, leaving the reader with the postmodern sense that reality is different for each person rather than a truth known to all. Yet since national television has homogenized these images, they have become the only truth.

The poem's montage, then, creates its own reality, displaying for the reader, as it did for the viewer, a confusing sequence of events, repetitious, nonchronological, and without conclusion. The elegy must, therefore, be disjointed as well. Viewers could not draw a conclusion and neither can the elegy; it must tell the truth as it knows it: without certainty.

Therefore, Berryman's fragmented presentation and his alternately reverent and irreverent tones further emphasize the scattered nature of the poem's images. In this sense, the poem is not really an elegy at all. It offers no conclusion, no satisfaction, and no understanding. It merely reflects on a relatively new American condition—the age of television—while it literally reflects a situation that promises to become a classic example of this condition. Images are key; their meanings and order are not. People learn from their memories. As a culture, Americans remember what they see, and what they see is now fuzzy and unreliable.

Themes and Meanings

"Formal Elegy," as an elegy, attempts to point the reader toward the future following the death of someone important. Traditionally, elegies offer hope; this one offers little. In the final stanza, the speaker echoes what one now recognizes as the sentiments of a generation that watched these details unfold on television screens across the nation; yet there is much less reverence here: "Everybody should/ have his sweet boneyards. Yet let the young not go,/ our apprentice King! Alas,/ muffled, he must." There is sorrow for the youth of the president who was "ours." Yet the reference to Kennedy as king recalls the press's image of Camelot, and, in this poem, images created by the press are not necessarily to be trusted. The speaker had claimed earlier that "I would not perhaps have voted for him next time," and so the term "apprentice King" implies that this young president had much to learn and was not (yet) a hero. The tragedy is his youth; all that is known is that he "seemed good."

The next step, the speaker tells Americans, is to "abandon the scene of disorder. Drop/ them shattered bodies into tranquil places,/ where moulder as you will. We compose our faces/ . . . ready again." From the tone of the poem thus far, the reader can understand this as a shameful method of dealing with grief, yet it is the way Americans always survive. The problem now is the emphasis on image, on the effect of a disjointed televised history upon people in need of continuity. People will "abandon" this reality since their memories, constructed by others, are not real. The irreverent tone concerning the burial reflects the speaker's expectations of the American public to "moulder as you will." In understanding history only through the television, American reverence for those once considered "excellent" will steadily decay.

The speaker refers to American people as "black & white," possibly referring also to the medium through which Americans understand themselves: "All black & white together, stunned, survive/ the final insolence to the head of you;/ bow./ Overwhelmed-un, live." People of all races in America will not only "survive" this crisis, but also will survive it "All black & white together," themselves a mass of jumbled images. No longer separate entities, human and individual, they will become one audience to a mass-media show, acting, thinking, and remembering only images. Ultimately, they are not overwhelmed but merely waylaid. The poem's final suggestion then becomes a twist on the traditional elegy's hopeful tone: "The man of a wise face opened it to speak:/ Let us continue." Americans always continue, but, from now on, they will be colder and harder.

Earlier, the speaker expressed his personal wish that future "bullets swim astray/ sent to the President, and that all around/ help, and his heart keep sound." The final images draw sharp contrast between this wish and the nation's probable progress toward recovery. This poem's primary images are of images themselves, and their message asserts that empty images are now standard. In the future, people will "compose [their] faces/ . . . ready again" for more of the same, reacting each time with colder and more composed faces.

Judith Collins

THE FORSAKEN MERMAN

Author: Matthew Arnold (1822-1888)
Type of poem: Dramatic monologue
First published: 1849, in *The Strayed Reveller and Other Poems*

The Poem

Matthew Arnold's 143 line lament of a merman (a mythical being with the form of a human from the waist up and of a fish below) over the desertion by his wife, Margaret, pits the vitality of paganism against drab Victorian Christianity. The story that unfolds as the poem progresses is that Margaret, a human, had married the merman, had lived happily with him for many years beneath the sea, and had borne his children. Margaret's existence was a happy one in this enchanting world "Where the winds are all asleep;/ Where the spent lights quiver and gleam,/ . . . Where the sea-snakes coil and twine,/ . . . Where the great whales come sailing by . . . ," and where she shared the merman's throne in his palace under the sea. Then at Easter the sound of the church bells tolling from the world above awakened her sense of religious duty, as she said, "I must go, for my kinsmen pray/ In the little grey church on the shore today." She felt it imperative to go: " 'Twill be Easter-time in the world—ah me!/ And I lose my poor soul, Merman, here with thee.' " The merman granted her wish to go to the village, assuming that she was going only for a brief visit: "I said, 'Go up, dear heart, through the waves;/ Say thy prayer, and come back to the kind sea-caves!' " However, she did not return.

This is the situation as the poem opens. Exactly how much time has elapsed since Margaret's departure is unclear; the merman repeats the refrain, "Children dear, was it yesterday?" as he leads them to the village, "Through the narrow paved streets, where all was still," to the church in which they see her at prayer. The merman makes his plea, "Margaret, hist! Come quick, we are here!" but "she gave me never a look,/ For her eyes were seal'd to the holy book!" The father and children then see her in a house where she is at her spinning wheel, singing, "O joy, O joy,/ For the humming street, and the child with its toy!/ For the priest, and the bell, and the holy well. . . ." She at first appears content, but they observe her drop her work, steal to the window, and look longingly across the sand to the sea, obviously yearning to be again with the family she left behind as she emits "A long, long sigh;/ For the cold strange eyes of a little Mermaiden/ And the gleam of her golden hair."

Before leaving the land, the merman poignantly urges the children to add their voices to his in calling the woman back to their home in the sea: "Call her once and come away." Ultimately they are unsuccessful. The merman contemplates the future for Margaret: "She will start from her slumber/ When gusts shake the door;/ She will hear the winds howling,/ Will hear the waves roar," as the sounds of nature deny her sleep. Meanwhile, he and the children will be in their home beneath the waves, singing, "Here came a mortal/ But faithless was she!/ And alone dwell for ever/ The kings of the sea." He tells the children that from time to time "We will gaze, from the sand hills,/ At the white, sleeping town;/ At the church on the hillside—/ And then come back down." Clearly, Margaret will never return.

Forms and Devices

Arnold contrasts the vitality of the life of the pagan mermen and mermaids with the sterility of the world of humans through the imagery he creates. The world beneath the sea is filled with color, designating vitality. Margaret and the merman king sat on a "red gold throne in the heart of the sea," and it is, significantly, a "green sea." Margaret combed her child's "bright hair," which she later describes as "golden hair." The merman's palace has "A ceiling of amber,/ A pavement of pearl."

In contrast, the world on land lacks color. Margaret says she must go to "the little gray church on the shore," a description the merman later repeats. The church seems to have no brightly colored stained glass windows but only "small leaded panes." The narrator speaks of guiding the children to "the white-walled town" and anticipates regular visits to the shore to gaze "At the white, sleeping town." By repeating the adjectives "white" and "gray," the poet enforces the sense of lifelessness in the town. The visitors from the sea observe no activity there except prayer in the church and Margaret at her spinning wheel. Although in her song Margaret speaks of "the humming street," she may simply be deceiving herself, for the reader sees no movement. In the sea is vitality with a variety of creatures: "Now the wild white horses play,/ Champ and chafe and toss in the spray," "the sea beasts, ranged all round,/ Feed in the ooze of their pasture ground," "the sea snakes coil and twine,/ Dry their mail and bask in the brine" and "great whales come sailing by,/ Sail and sail, with unshut eye,/ Round the world for ever and aye"; the sea seems to be filled with perpetual motion.

One of the most effective scenes in the poem is the image of Margaret at her spinning wheel at the moment she is overcome with sorrow at the loss of her family: She suddenly stops singing, "the spindle drops from her hand,/ And the whizzing wheel stands still," reflecting the inactivity of the town. Although the story comes exclusively from the merman's narrative point of view, the reader can see clearly into Margaret. Nature has been disrupted by Margaret's abandonment of the merman, as "The sea grows stormy," and the sound of wind and waves will continue to trouble her. Before she left, the winds were "all asleep" in the caverns deep in the sea.

The movement from four-stressed lines at the beginning of the poem to the three-stressed lines of the conclusion creates a sense of calm resignation as the merman accepts the fact that his pagan world of nature worship and Margaret's world of orthodox religion can never be reconciled. This resignation is further enforced by the repetition of the lines, "Come, dear children, let us away;/ Down and away below!" or variations of these lines.

Themes and Meanings

The most forceful theme of the poem is the agony of the merman as he recounts the loss of his wife. The reader senses desperation as he urges his children to plead with

Margaret to return to them: "Children's voices should be dear/ (Call once more) to a mother's ear;/ Children's voices, wild with pain—/ Surely she will come again!" The merman feels that it is unnatural for her to leave her children. He is so distraught that he is even unsure of how long she has been gone: "She smiled, she went up through the surf in the bay./ Children dear, was it yesterday?" His memory of their happy times together increases the pain of his desertion, as he recalls that "Once she sate with you [the children] and me,/ On a red gold throne in the heart of the sea," but when he pled with her, "she gave me never a look."

Margaret has been forced to choose between the two worlds, but she has not done so without pain of her own. Although in her singing she tries to keep up her spirits, her mind wanders back to the family she has left behind as she turns from the spinning wheel and looks out to the sea: "And anon there drops a tear/ From a sorrow-clouded eye,/ And a heart sorrow-laden."

Another theme is the Victorian loss of faith, the result of the conflict of science and religion, which had been developing rapidly through the early part of the century and was later to culminate in Charles Darwin's *On the Origin of Species by Means of Natural Selection* in 1859. Although he desperately wanted to believe, Arnold felt that Christianity had simply run down as a religion, that it no longer had any vitality, a feeling that is created through the gray and white imagery. Arnold cleverly plays on the theme of faith with the merman's song, "Here came a mortal,/ But faithless was she," emphasizing again the fact that Margaret cannot have her conventional religion and her life with the merman as well. In going back to her former faith, she becomes unfaithful to her husband.

Margaret's song contains images that may suggest her unconscious doubts about the validity of her religion as she sings of "the child with its toy" and then in the next line refers to "the priest, and the bell, and the holy well [the font containing holy water]," implying that in her mind those items associated with the priest are also playthings. The religion makes no attempt to be inclusive: "Loud prays the priest; shut stands the door."

"The Forsaken Merman" is one of Arnold's most popular and most frequently anthologized poems because of its powerful portrait of human emotion. It serves as an almost historical document of the collapse of traditional faith in the Victorian era.

J. Don Vann

FOUR GOOD THINGS

Author: James McMichael (1939-   )
Type of poem: Narrative
First published: 1980

The Poem

Four Good Things is a book-length narrative poem by California poet James McMichael. The poem is autobiographical, and McMichael makes no distinctions between himself and the speaker of the poem. The speaker describes, comments upon, and observes his world without being judgmental. By the poem's end, he has reconciled himself to the role of the past in the present.

The poem begins in the late 1940's and covers a period into the late 1960's or early 1970's. While the speaker states his age in the poem once, he eschews traditional chronology for a more loosely constructed sense of time. Each of *Four Good Things*'s sixteen stanzas describes an episode in the speaker's life from childhood through early adulthood. The first ten stanzas depict his boyhood and college years. He writes about his care provider, Florence, his father's career as a real estate agent in Pasadena, California, his mother's cancer, and ultimately, his father's death. He also describes his father's second marriage to Lucille and his adolescence living with her and her family.

The eleventh stanza begins the second section of the poem, which describes how private lives in the nineteenth century were affected by industrialization. This section is set in rural England in the 1850's and later. Stanza 12 is the turning point in the poem's narrative. Here McMichael connects the American capitalism he knew as a boy with the industrial period in England. His intent in this stanza is to draw together his personal past with the historical events he thinks shaped it.

Stanza 13 presents McMichael and his companion, Linda, on their way to Manchester, England, the heart of the British industrial movement. Once there, he hopes to establish how the world became so commercial and so interested in defining self-worth by possessions. Restless and plagued by his inability to sleep, the speaker meditates on the issues of desire, need, forgiveness, and time. He is apparently distressed that his life is directionless and disturbed over the confusion he feels in wanting to explain everything about the relationship of the past to the present at once.

The third section of the poem, stanza 15, has McMichael encountering a mentally disturbed young man named Antony. Antony is institutionalized and cared for by his mother, who visits him and takes him out for drives. The speaker contemplates how he and Antony live lives that are quite different although they are parallel in time. Once he and Linda part from Antony, they drive into Manchester, where McMichael encounters the people of that city. He observes their possessions and their living habits and is again intrigued and disturbed by the people living lives parallel to his. He comments on how materialism has replaced thinking and interaction among families: "They steady us, these things we've made."

Back at home in California in the last stanza of the poem, McMichael considers how he has and has not changed because of his experiences. He recalls how easily he has fit back into his American life, and he tries to draw parallels between the lives of the English and his own life. The poem ends with Linda telling him a story about a ski trip she took in Europe, where she saw farmers working in the winter. The point of the story would seem to be that "life goes on" and people do what they must to survive. Those tactics are different for everyone.

Forms and Devices

Four Good Things is a free-verse poem of sixty-nine pages. While its meter alludes at times to blank verse, blank verse is employed inconsistently. Sections are not numbered, but the sixteen stanzas are separated by white space. Reviewers in the early 1980's found McMichael's use of language appropriately "inelegant" for a poem about commerce and materialism. There are "unpoetical" phrasings, some vulgarity, and some obscenities. The poem's phrasing is similar to prose, leading critic Robert van Hallberg to praise McMichael for "reclaim[ing] for poetry some of the prerogatives ceded to prose, fictional and expository" writing.

The predominant imagery in the poetry involves mapping. Secondary images are created by references to home building and driving. The poem is set in neighborhoods in Pasadena and Manchester, which are deliberately depicted as being not too different. Mapping is the metaphor that unifies the poem, and *Four Good Things* is itself a map of its speaker's experiences. Mental maps created by memory, futuristic mappings of the past in the present, street maps of Pasadena, and road maps around Manchester are all described in the poem.

The first five lines of the opening stanza depict how Florence walked to the bus stop to get a ride to the grocery store and how she walked by the houses, not the addresses, of the neighbors. McMichael's father is also connected to maps. He designed a subdivision, the Pasadena Tracts, which failed to attract buyers; he "would be somewhere within his maps at any time," says the speaker. The use of "within" indicates that his father used his maps to dream or to plan his future. In the fifth stanza, a teacher walking along an English river with her students instructs them to map the plants growing there. In the sixth stanza, the speaker takes a mental walk through old neighborhoods that are now abandoned.

The seventh stanza switches tone to describe Pasadena in the way that a group of real estate agents viewing a new development site would view it. The changes in the rugged landscape, forged over time, are quickly altered when schools, hotels, and shops replace trees, open spaces, and water sources diverted for subdivisions. With the eye of a documentary filmmaker, the speaker comments, "The balance of trade was not in Pasadena's favor." To see how this has transpired, he looks into the city's suburban past and finds that "[t]he wealth of the invisible elite went into their homes." He particularly addresses the role of the Greene brothers, whose bungalows made Pasadena famous. Charles Sumner Greene and Henry Mather Greene were the premiere architects of the California Arts and Crafts movement of the late nineteenth and early twentieth centuries. Their integration of homes into the local landscape and use of local building materials are mentioned by the speaker with appreciation. He particularly likes their houses because their mapping was evident: "Everything showed you how it went together." Many such houses were razed for the very kind of anonymous development his father was promoting.

The sereneness of urban Pasadena is troublesome to the speaker. He sees the people comfortable in their houses, trading up to buy something more prestigious, and he wonders: "What did people do all day?" As a boy, he collected stamps that, when glued into his albums, provided a map of the world for his youthful imagination. As he surveys the people around him, he finds that their preoccupations are like his but different. He maps his worry about his mother's death from cancer in the hopes of coming to terms with his instinctual impulse to worry about why he does not understand the world better. The topical, regional allusions combined with information about his father's death and stepmother's dispersal of the estate, are somewhat like pushpins stuck into an urban planner's map of suburbia.

When the tenth stanza moves the poem to England in the 1850's, mapping is used to discuss how the enclosure acts changed the landscape of agricultural Britain. Enclosure, which was initiated during the reign of King Henry VII in 1489, allowed landlords to fence and redistribute farmland. It also allowed the landlords to force their tenants to farm the land according to its owners' needs. In the eighteenth century, enclosures reduced the amount of available land for tenants to farm, and when new property boundaries were drawn many people lost their homes. Abandoned farms and towns and increased poverty were caused by rapacious enclosure. A second major wave of enclosing occurred in the nineteenth century, and the consequences were as devastating to the poor as they had been a hundred years earlier. The poet is particularly interested in how the displaced poor became the factory workers in industrial cities such as Manchester. Enclosure remapped Britain and paved the way for the need for factories in the later years of the British Empire. McMichael's descriptions of enclosures are historically accurate, and his depiction of the factories' squalor is consonant with the socialist studies done by Friedrich Engels for his book *The Conditions of the Working Class in England* (1859).

From the old maps, the poet takes the reader back to California, to the Pasadena area suburbs where the landscapers' trees provide the boundaries between one house and another. Roads built by developer Henry Huntington are linked to the highways that remapped Southern California and brought in new people to buy new homes. Relentless urban sprawl eliminated the Greene and Greene houses in large numbers, and the populations of the neighborhoods the speaker knew as a child changed terrifically.

The trip to Manchester calls for both real road maps and symbolic maps. The jet-lag-induced insomnia of stanza 13 causes McMichael to move about in his memory to try to understand why he is the way he is. He speaks of his desire to know himself better in terms of driving to get somewhere. His difficulty in such an endeavor is that he has no map and no one to direct him on his journey but his own flawed self.

Stanza 16 begins with McMichael describing himself as a tenant with a lawn he has the ability to let go to waste (a term used in enclosure documents to describe uncultivated land). He parallels himself at this point in his life with the tenants who worked for their lives in England in the past. He drives through neighborhoods he has known to construct a map connecting his past to the present. Then he remembers how he and Linda had driven around England with a map as tourists; they had the freedom to see only what they wanted to see. When he drives in Pasadena, he is mainly confronted with things he does not want to see. Shifting between past and present, between what he wants and what is inevitable, he maps out a sense of closure. He decides that he is putting too much pressure on himself to try to account for his own history in the history of the world. In the end, he seems to be on the verge of balancing the functions of history, personal responsibility, chance, and change within his life. He has mapped his world; he knows where he is and seems willing to begin to map a future.

Themes and Meanings

Published in 1980, *Four Good Things* raised questions about American life that had not been routinely considered in poetry. The poem reveals the emptiness of a life based on goods, services, and the acquisition of possessions. McMichael offers a vision in this poem of the historical conditions that produced himself, the modern person living in suburban Southern California.

Through the use of images of mapping, driving, and building homes, roads, and bridges, McMichael shows how the past determines the present. His argument in the poem is that industrialization, with its emphasis on acquisition and its definition of power as military or commercial might, forever changed the landscape of Britain and America. The poem depicts someone who has stopped taking a life of materialism for granted and has paused to ask himself if the things he has are really "good."

Four Good Things is a personal narrative in which the poet-speaker speculates on the type of life he is living and what the quality of such an existence is. It is not primarily a philosophical interpretation that he develops, but a practical one that will allow him to get on with his life. At the end of the poem, he understands how the past is carried into the present and how everyone's lives are, to a certain degree, determined by circumstances. He accepts these things as part of himself; he neither despises himself for who he is nor blames the world for being what it is.

While some evidence of an epic structure is evident, it is wrong to think of *Four Good Things* as an epic poem. The speaker does go on a quest for self-realization, descending metaphorically into the underworld of insomnia and meeting a man who, like the blind prophet Tiresias, seems to know more about the world than his physical circumstances would allow. However, *Four Good Things* lacks adventure, epic language and devices, and other perspectives within the poem to extend its range beyond the viewpoint of the speaker. That the speaker has thought of the epic similarities is suggested by his saying he has read *Madame Bovary* (1857), Gustav Flaubert's great novel of a woman's quest for knowledge of herself and *Roughing It* (1872), Mark Twain's travel narrative that takes him to Nevada and California in the nineteenth century.

Beverly Schneller

FRA LIPPO LIPPI

Author: Robert Browning (1812-1889)
Type of poem: Dramatic monologue
First published: 1855, in *Men and Women*

The Poem

"Fra Lippo Lippi" is a long poem in blank verse. It is one of Robert Browning's numerous dramatic monologues, written in phrases and segments, which assume periodic unwritten questions and responses from the listener. The speaker in this poem is a historical character, Fra Lippo Lippi, who was a monk and a painter in fifteenth century Florence. Taking his point of departure from an incident described by the Italian painter and biographer Giorgio Vasari in *The Lives of the Most Excellent Italian Architects, Painters and Sculptors* (1550, 1568), Browning imagines how Fra Lippo Lippi might have seen his own life and his art.

The setting of "Fra Lippo Lippi" is an alley in Florence. The time is midnight. The watchmen on their rounds have just stopped a suspicious character slipping through the shadows. As the poem begins, the monk identifies himself and then explains that he is staying with a member of the powerful Medici family. Giving the men some money with which to drink to his health, the monk then settles down with their leader, who obviously wants to hear the full story.

The poem is divided into three sections. In the first, Fra Lippo Lippi explains that his patron has had him shut up for three weeks, so that the monk would paint instead of drinking or carousing. On this spring night, however, the temptation was too much, and Fra Lippo Lippi sneaked out a window to have some fun. When the watch caught him, he was trying to get back to his patron's dwelling before his absence was noticed.

To his new friend, who appears sympathetic but is obviously somewhat puzzled by this monk's behavior, Fra Lippo Lippi explains that he does not feel himself bound by monastic vows, since he had no choice about becoming a monk; he had been left with the Carmelites when he was only eight years old. Later, when it was realized that the boy had artistic talent, the prior decided to make him their official painter. From the time he completed his first painting on the wall of the cloister, however, Fra Lippo Lippi has been criticized for making his works too realistic.

In the second section of the poem, the monk continues his argument for realism, insisting that instead of turning humanity's attention away from God, his creations reveal the glories of God's creation to people who might not otherwise have noticed them. He admits, however, that there are practical disadvantages to his kind of painting; one of his paintings has been defaced by the pious, who have scratched off the faces of three evil characters tormenting a saint.

In the third section, the monk fears that he has been too outspoken, and he begs the captain not to report him. Then, after describing a great painting that he will complete in six months, the monk notices that dawn is approaching, shakes hands with his listener, and hurries toward his lodging.

Forms and Devices

Browning's dramatic monologues are standard selections in interpretive reading competitions because all of them are essentially one-actor plays. The poet describes the setting of his drama, indicates the appearance of his characters, gives stage directions, including entrances and exits, and suggests the speeches of the silent actors, all through the words of his protagonist.

For example, at the beginning of the poem, while he is making his explanation to the watch, Fra Lippo Lippi mentions the time, midnight, and the setting, an alley in the red-light district. Later, he speaks of the man who was holding him as having a face like Judas; in contrast, the captain of the guard has a "twinkle" in his eye.

Browning's stage directions are also woven skillfully into the monologue. For example, again at the beginning of the poem, by telling the men what not to do, not to push their torches so close to his face, not to hold him by the neck, the monk is actually describing what they are doing. When Fra Lippo Lippi tells the captain to send his men for a drink, it is assumed that they exit. A few lines later, when the monk says, "Let's sit and set things straight now," it can be assumed that the two men do so. At the end of the poem, Fra Lippo Lippi's exit is just as clearly outlined. He shakes hands with the captain, refuses his offer of a light, and then, seeing the sky turning, exclaims and hastens offstage.

Through Fra Lippo Lippi's responses, even through his pauses, Browning makes the suppressed speeches of others as clear as if they had been spoken. For example, when the monk says, "Yes, I'm the painter, since you style me so," it is evident that the captain has said something like, "Oh, I know your name, you are the painter, aren't you?" In lines 76 and 79, a more complicated dialogue is suggested. Shaking his head in disapproval, the captain has pointed out that the painter is a monk, while still reassuring him that he will not report him to his Medici patron. It is this comment from the captain that causes Fra Lippo Lippi to relate his life story.

By using interjections and colloquialisms, parenthetical comments and incomplete sentences, even snatches of a popular song, in "Fra Lippo Lippi" Browning captures the flavor of casual speech. This effect, however, is the result of painstaking artistry, for the entire poem is constructed in the most skillfully crafted blank verse, worthy of Browning's Elizabethan predecessors in dramatic writing.

Themes and Meanings

"Fra Lippo Lippi" explains not only what Browning believed to be his subject's view of the purpose of painting, but also the poet's own beliefs about the function of poetry. Both painter and poet have the power of imagination. The question is what the relationship should be between the real world about them and the ideal worlds that they can imagine.

To the Greek artists, the human form was just a starting point, from which the ideal could be constructed. It is this attitude that is shared by the prior and his learned colleagues, who believe that Fra Lippo Lippi's figures are too lifelike, that by painting so realistically the painter will cause his viewers to pay too much attention to human bodies and therefore to become distracted from their proper concern, their souls. Bodies are perishable; souls are not.

Both Browning and Fra Lippo Lippi disagree with this point of view. The simple monks respond properly to the painter's work. They enjoy seeing people they know; unlike the prior, they take a natural joy in life. Fra Lippo Lippi argues that beauty cannot diminish piety. In lines 217 to 221, he explains that by responding to the beauty of God's creation, human beings are led to thank God and thus to be aware of the souls within themselves. At the end of the section, Fra Lippo Lippi admits that he wonders whether he or the Church is right, but when he paints, he insists, he always remembers the God of Genesis, creating Eve in the Garden of Eden. That flesh that was made by God cannot be evil.

In the second section, Fra Lippo Lippi advances a further argument. Realistic paintings actually draw the attention of human beings to real-life beauty that they might otherwise ignore, "things we have passed/ Perhaps a hundred times nor cared to see." In this way, too, the artist causes human beings to praise their creator.

Thus, even though he has thought deeply about what his clerical superiors say with such certainty, Fra Lippo Lippi is convinced that his kind of art is divinely inspired. His own certainty is summed up in the lengthy description of a forthcoming painting, in which imagined beings will appear, such as God, the Madonna and Child, and various saints, but in which there will also be a lovely young saint modeled on the prior's niece, a saint who will defend the presence of Fra Lippo Lippi in the work because, she says, he is responsible for creating all the rest.

The central theme of "Fra Lippo Lippi," then, is that the function of painting should be to capture the actual beauty of God's creation and, by doing so, to reveal the invisible spiritual beauty of his creatures. In his poetry, Browning chose to do the same thing. As Fra Lippo Lippi speaks to his sympathetic listener, he becomes more than a runaway monk in a frayed robe, trapped by the watch in an unsavory area of his city; he is revealed as a dedicated artist and as a man of spiritual grandeur.

Rosemary M. Canfield Reisman

THE FRANKLIN'S TALE

Author: Geoffrey Chaucer (c. 1343-1400)
Type of poem: Narrative
First transcribed: 1387-1400, in *The Canterbury Tales*

The Poem

"The Franklin's Tale" is one of the stories in Geoffrey Chaucer's *The Canterbury Tales*, a work in Middle English that, though unfinished, is considered one of the masterpieces of English literature. Like most of *The Canterbury Tales*, "The Franklin's Tale" is written in iambic pentameter couplets. It is 896 lines in length. Although the poet was working on *The Canterbury Tales* from the 1380's until the year of his death, this story cannot be dated with any certainty. It is also a matter of conjecture as to where Chaucer meant to place "The Franklin's Tale" within the larger narrative. However, expressing as it does Chaucer's own ideals of behavior, clearly "The Franklin's Tale" would have been a cornerstone of the completed work.

The story is told by an important, wealthy landowner, elderly but still vigorous, who delights in fine food and drink and prides himself on his hospitality. However, his tale does not focus on worldly pleasures but rather on moral issues, the demands of honor, the true definition of gentility, and the substance of an ideal marriage.

"The Franklin's Tale" is set in Brittany. It begins with the marriage of a lady, Dorigen, to Arveragus, a knight who has taken great pains to win her. Arveragus takes the unusual step of setting up the marriage as a relationship between equals, with the sole proviso that in public his wife will treat him as her sovereign. In a long digression, the Franklin explains that mutual respect is the secret of a happy marriage.

Since Dorigen is as much in love with her husband as he is with her, Arveragus's departure for a lengthy stay in England leaves her desolate. She spends much of her time looking seaward, hoping to see his ship, and worrying about the black rocks near the coast, an ever-present danger to approaching ships. When a young squire, Aurelius, declares his passion for Dorigen, she responds with a firm rejection and then tries to put him off with humor. If Aurelius could make the rocks disappear, Dorigen says, she would give herself to him. This plot element is familiar to folklorists as "a damsel's rash promise."

After Arveragus returns home, Dorigen forgets all about the conversation and the vow. However, Aurelius's despair has worsened. Fearing that he may die, the squire's brother takes him to Orléans, where there are clerks, or scholars, who are skilled in "natural" magic, that is, magic based on knowledge rather than on the black arts. One of these clerks feels certain that he can remove the rocks. Promising him a substantial fee, Aurelius and his brother take the magician with them to Brittany, where he fulfills his part of the bargain.

When Aurelius reminds her of her promise, Dorigen contemplates suicide but then decides to turn the matter over to her husband. Though deeply grieved, Arveragus tells his wife that she must keep her promise. Shamed by Arveragus's high-mindedness, the squire releases Dorigen from her vow, and the clerk then refuses his fee, declaring that even a poor man is capable of noble behavior.

Forms and Devices

In the prologue to his story, the Franklin claims that it is a retelling of a Breton lay. However, scholars have not been able to find such a source. Moreover, they point out that "The Franklin's Tale" is quite different from lays modeled on those by Marie de France, the French poet of the late twelfth century who invented or at least popularized the genre. Her stories focused on extramarital relationships; there was no "natural" explanation for the supernatural events in them; and her aristocratic characters were types, while those in "The Franklin's Tale" are highly individualized. Whatever Chaucer's reasons for having the Franklin call his story a Breton lay, it would be more accurately classified as a moral tale.

The Franklin also prefaces his story with an apology for his linguistic limitations. He is a plain man, he says, not a courtier skilled in rhetorical devices. However, in telling his tale, the Franklin does utilize a number of rhetorical devices that are identified in medieval texts. One of them is the digression, like that early in the tale when the Franklin interrupts his story for a disquisition on marriage that continues for some thirty lines. Such digressions, in which a writer moved from the particular to the general and then returned to the particular, were used to make sure that readers or listeners did not miss the point of the story. Similarly, the Franklin frequently pauses for *sententiae*, proverblike truths such as the assertion within the digression on marriage that "On every wrong a man may nat be wreken," in other words, that one cannot avenge every wrong.

In other ways, too, the Franklin demonstrates that he is more sophisticated than he pretends to be. His suffering suitors, Arveragus and Aurelius, and the lady they both adore are right out of the courtly love tradition so popular among the aristocrats of his time, and the Franklin has no difficulty reproducing the highly artificial language used by such characters. There is nothing of a country squire's bluffness in their elegant discourse.

Moreover, though sometimes he summarizes events in simple language, at other times the Franklin parades his learning or perhaps parodies those who do so, as in his flowery description of December in Brittany. His use of classical allusions in that passage is just one of many instances in which the Franklin reveals himself to be a well-read man. Others include Aurelius's long prayer to Apollo, which is filled with mythological references, and Dorigen's lengthy soliloquy about women who choose death before dishonor, which alludes to twenty-two different incidents from myth and history.

Themes and Meanings

The Franklin concludes his narrative by asking who his fellow pilgrims think was most generous—the knight, the squire, or the clerk. This question would have prompted the pilgrims to make some interesting comments, and certainly the question of merit and class is one of the major themes of the story. Before he embarks upon his tale, the Franklin bemoans the fact that unlike the Squire, his own son is a wastrel indifferent either to virtue or to the ideal of *gentilesse*, which the Franklin here associates with high social status, with behaving as aristocrats should behave, with courtesy, compassion, generosity, and a keen sense of justice. By including the clerk in his question about generosity, however, the Franklin seems to eliminate social status as a prerequisite for someone's possessing *gentilesse*. This reflects Chaucer's view, as stated in his short poem entitled "Gentillesse": that one's position in the social hierarchy has very little to do with whether or not one has *gentilesse*.

Another obvious theme in "The Franklin's Tale" is the definition of honor. In the medieval mind, a gentleman's honor was displayed in his being brave, truthful, and loyal, but for a lady, honor was defined as chastity. Therefore it would seem that Dorigen must choose to remain faithful to her husband, ignoring the promise she had rashly made to Aurelius. However, the Franklin places truthfulness, or keeping one's word, on the same level as chastity, thus suggesting that a woman who is made equal to a man must adhere to the same ethical standards as a man. Arveragus evidently adheres to that notion, for he insists that Dorigen keep her word.

It has long been assumed that at least four of the stories in *The Canterbury Tales* constitute a "marriage group," whose subject is the question of sovereignty in marriage. While in each of the other stories either the husband or the wife is dominant, "The Franklin's Tale" presents an Aristotelian *via media*, or middle way, which is Chaucer's idea of what a marriage should be. However, it can be argued that the Franklin does not necessarily speak for Chaucer. The author may wish the reader to see what the Franklin does not seem to notice, that when Dorigen has to turn to her husband for a decision, she has relinquished her equal status and assumed the role of the submissive wife. On the other hand, Chaucer may see a good marriage as one that permits an alternation of sovereignty, consisting of the natural ebb and flow of strength and weakness, foolishness and wisdom, in even the most well-meaning human beings.

In "The Franklin's Tale," as in the rest of *The Canterbury Tales*, Chaucer expresses his firm moral convictions, but at the same time he reveals his compassion for human beings, enslaved as they are by their emotions, driven as they are to foolish words and actions. As the Franklin points out, "in this world, certein, ther no wight is/ That he ne dooth or seith somtyme amis," in other words, there is no human being who never does or says something wrong. Clearly Chaucer is at one with the Franklin in suggesting that *gentilesse* is the secret of harmonious relationships among human beings.

Rosemary M. Canfield Reisman

FREE UNION

Author: André Breton (1896-1966)
Type of poem: Lyric
First published: 1931, as "L'Union libre," in *L'Union libre*; English translation collected in *Selected Poems*, 1969

The Poem

In order to appreciate André Breton's "Free Union," a basic understanding of Surrealism (or *surréalisme*) is helpful. This artistic movement, which Breton more or less founded, constituted a rebellion against the realism and naturalism dominating literature and the other arts during the late nineteenth and early twentieth centuries. In a literal sense, the word means beyond or above realism. Surrealist art, whatever the form—literature, painting, film, sculpture—does not intend to recreate the phenomena of the outward world but focuses instead on the inward state and reports how people respond to the world around them.

A poem such as "Free Union" may seem at first reading a disconnected and unrelated series of illogical images; however, when approached as an exploration of the subconscious and its mental activity, the poem takes on meaning. Granted, readers must suspend their conventional idea of meaning and be willing to accept the fantastic and often incongruous imagery. Such is the stuff of the individual's subconscious, which "Free Union" explores.

The reader of "Free Union" should also keep in mind the major Surrealistic techniques developed and propagated by Breton. For one thing, he relies on juxtapositions, placing dissimilar ideas and phenomena side by side to form unlikely and often absurd combinations. From the poem's beginning to its end, any set of images illustrates this practice. Breton also depends on what he called "automatism" to lend the poem its apprehension of the subconscious. Not to be confused with automatic writing, automatism places greater demands on the artist's state of mind, according to Breton. To avoid the clichés, repetition, and general dullness of automatic writing, the poet must in a disciplined manner make uninhibited responses to phenomena and develop free associations. While "Free Union" might seem to have been written automatically and without artistic discipline, it does possess structure. Each image depends on "My wife" to trigger a comparison, even if many of the images seem to have little relationship to a real wife. It could be said that a Surrealist poet makes a self-conscious effort to appear unconscious.

Dreams are also important to the Surrealistic literary technique. Breton noted that Sigmund Freud's theory of dreams and the unconscious heavily influenced his thinking. Not only does Breton draw from his own dreams, but he also imparts to his writing a dreamlike quality, with its discordant nature, abrupt juxtapositions, and incoherent responses. "Free Union" could be taken as a retelling of the poet's dream about an imaginary, surreal woman who emerges from the subconscious and becomes a fleeting creature endowed with qualities most peculiar, then fades away once the poet awakens and faces reality. Finally, visual aspects play a prominent role in surrealistic technique. In fact, Surrealism probably enjoyed its greatest success in painting and film. Approaching a poem such as "Free Union" from a visual standpoint—as a kind of word version of an abstract painting or the disordered frames of a film—makes it more accessible.

While Surrealism as a means of artistic expression has faded with the years, Breton's one-time revolutionary theory greatly influenced twentieth century art. Thus "Free Union" is an important poem. First, it stands as a prime example of pure Surrealism. Second, it introduces techniques that are echoed and refined throughout much of twentieth century poetry.

Forms and Devices

For the Surrealist writer, imagistic language itself is poetry, and in that "Free Union" abounds and excels. Even in translation—probably the cruelest thing to do to poetry—the richness, variation, and extravagance of the language emerge fully. The poem does not rely on the conventions of poetry, such as rhyme, meter, or stanzas; nor is there any punctuation to separate ideas.

"My wife" serves as the poem's connecting device. At first glance, it appears that Breton is following the tradition of Renaissance poets who celebrated feminine beauty by comparing the various parts of a woman—an actual person or an imaginary one, it did not matter—to the stars and moon, to flowers and the sun, to precious jewels, and so on. As the poem unfolds, however, it soon becomes apparent that it presents no ordinary celebration of a woman's physical charm. In traditional poetry, for a simile or metaphor to work it must show some logical connection with that which is being described. "Free Union" defies that rule, for its imagery goes far beyond any natural relationships. For example, the "belly" of "My wife" is said to be "like the unfolding fan of the days," then "like a giant claw." On the other hand, the image employed to describe her eyelashes is quite striking and is more appropriate than most of the others: "with eyelashes like the strokes of childish writing." Most of the imagery is drawn from nature and from animals, birds, and fish. Yet the inconsistency is heightened by a line such as "with eyes of water to drink in prison."

The poet may have intended that the poem sound automatic, as though he had focused on the words, "My wife," then through free association listed everything about her that entered his thinking. Thus in the opening three lines he can move from "woodfire hair" to "lightning thoughts" to "hourglass waist," the latter description being something of a cliché both in French and English, but Surrealism tolerated the cliché for effect. Through this uninhibited—seemingly automatic—expression of responses, the poet at one moment conjures up a lovely image such as "fingers of new-mown hay," then a few lines later says "My wife with the spindle legs." The imagery of automatism has been called "palimpsestic"; that is, it has a rubbed and erased quality, as though something else had been written before and new material was then added to the fragments left over before a complete erasure was made.

Because dreams play so important a role in Surrealistic art, the poem also carries qualities of that subconscious state when unlikely associations become the norm. Someone appearing in a dream may well possess "Hips of chandelier and arrow feathers" or may move "like clockwork and despair." Like a dream, this poem—no matter how disconnected the images may seem—succeeds as an expression of the unconscious.

Themes and Meanings

At the outset, "Free Union" appears to be a tribute of sorts to the poet's wife, even though it has been pointed out that Breton was not married at the time he wrote the poem. There is an irony in that biographical detail, but the fact does little to help understand the poem—if it indeed can be or should be "understood" in a conventional way.

Some critics have interpreted the poem in erotic terms, seeing the imagery as a collective description of female sexuality and the sexual organ in particular. It has also been described as an impressionistic record of sexual intercourse, as a sexual fantasy, and as the recounting of a sexual dream. While it is tempting to follow this path, especially considering the Freudian overtones of Surrealism, the poem itself does not altogether support such a reading. For one thing, only a small section is devoted to "My wife with sex of seaweed and stale sweets." For another, lines such as those lack eroticism.

Where, then, does the meaning lie? Because an attempt to explicate the poem would end in failure, perhaps another question ought to be asked: *How* does the meaning lie? Important in answering this question are the poem's juxtapositions: for example, from beauty to ugliness—from the throat that "is a golden dale" to "the buttocks of sandstone." The poet who views the world through a Surrealistic lens does not report on it in the ordered way a traditional poet might. Breton, at any rate, makes no attempt to organize what he sees, experiences, and feels. The materials that Breton uses, though, are not otherworldly; instead, the images he draws are quite concrete. Some are appropriate, some not—that is, if the poem were to be taken literally as a description of "My wife."

Possibly the title, "Free Union," holds a key to the abstractions, which will never form themselves into a tidy message or a universal meaning that readers often expect from poetry. If the poem was approached as a kind of sexual fantasy, then "free union" would stand for intercourse. Yet this use of the title borders on the simplistic and in a way maligns the poem. Maybe the free union takes place in the mind—both in that of the poet and the reader—and expands thinking beyond the ordinary, the commonplace, the mundane. The poem, a free union of imagery, may simply offer a feast for the imagination. Through the rhythmic rise and fall of the lines, the images stacked on one another, the incoherence, and the rich language, a poem such as "Free Union" finds its meaning in its form and its form in its meaning.

Robert L. Ross

FRENCH AND ENGLISH

Author: Leonard Cohen (1934-   )
Type of poem: Satire
First published: 1978, as "Our Government-in-Exile," in *Death of a Lady's Man*; as "French and English" in *Stranger Music: Selected Poems and Songs*, 1993

The Poem

"French and English" comprises fifty lines of mostly satirical free verse. In this poem Leonard Cohen attacks extremists in the political and linguistic dispute that began to intensify in Quebec during the early 1960's. No explicit mention is made of this most distinctive of Canadian provinces in the poem, but Cohen grew up there in the 1950's and 1960's. His primary residence is now near Los Angeles, but he still maintains a home in Montreal. His own experiences in Quebec are clearly the inspiration for this poem. It is an attempt to shock, shame, and insult fanatics on both sides, encouraging everyone involved to find a peaceful solution to the escalating conflict.

French Canadians and the language that they speak are subjected to rhetorical scorn in the first sixteen lines. For example, the extremely abstract thinking of French philosophers such as René Descartes is mocked as "inflamed ideas" and as "a theoretical approach/ to common body functions" caused by the French language. The domination of Quebec society before the 1960's by the Roman Catholic Church is burlesqued by the reference to "a tacky priesthood devoted to the salvation/ of a failed erection." Even the stereotype of poor dental care in Quebec is flung into the reader's face. Quebeçois "pepsis" are ridiculed for drinking too much soda pop, causing the "rotten teeth of French." Effective expression of the glorious goal of independence for Quebec is thus overwhelmed by bad teeth and halitosis.

The next fourteen-line segment of the poem is devoted to English, described as a "sterilized swine of a language that has no genitals." Scatological images and references proliferate, identifying English-speaking people with "peepee and kaka and nothing else." The stereotype of English culture as particularly reserved is lampooned by the implication that the English are hesitant to French kiss because they "are frightened by saliva." As a final insult to conclude the stanza, the English are castigated as being "German with a licence to kill."

The satirical assault on both French- and English-speaking Canadians continues in the third section of the poem. Together they are referred to as "boobies of the north" and "dead-hearted turds of particular speech." However, an optimistic alternative is also invoked. The speaker proposes the possibility of communication beyond the built-in prejudices of any language and of salvation beyond politics. This positive alternative is sketched in a series of striking sexual, musical, and religious images. The poet suggests that kneeling "between the legs of the moon" and performing a sort of mystical cunnilingus is a better use for the human tongue than speaking either French or English. To escape the respective chauvinisms that are paralyzing Quebec, both francophone and anglophone extremists are invited to lift their voices musically, "like the wind harps you were meant to be." Both sides could then awake into a "state of common grace."

Forms and Devices

The speaker of this poem assumes the first-person point of view, using the personal pronoun "I" throughout. The poem doubtless expresses Leonard Cohen's attitudes and feelings toward the conflict that is its subject. However, Cohen is speaking as it were through an angry puppet: He has adopted an extremely aggressive persona in order to dramatize his theme effectively. The persona of the speaker in "French and English" employs the rhetorical technique of hyperbole. He rants and raves in wild exaggeration, understood as such, in order to depict clearly the warped extremes each side tends to mirror in the other. He subverts the appeal and dissipates the hatred of French and English fanatics by turning them into ridiculous caricatures.

The primary rhetorical mode employed in this poem is satire. Satire was allegedly invented by the Greek cynic Menippus, whose works are lost. Since then it has been written in many formal variations, but the common element in all of them is attack. Public institutions, political parties, fashionable attitudes, even prominent individuals are held up for intense criticism in this way. Perhaps the best-known example of satire in English literature is "A Modest Proposal" by Jonathan Swift. In this parody of a political editorial, Swift proposed a radical solution to the problem of poverty in eighteenth century Ireland. His proposal was to sell the infants of poor Irish people to be cooked and eaten as an exotic delicacy for the tables of the ruling class. His point was to attack the callous attitude of certain people toward the suffering of those less fortunate than themselves.

The structure of "French and English" is based on the dialectical method originating with the Greek philosopher Socrates and developed more systematically in the nineteenth century by Georg Wilhelm Friedrich Hegel and Karl Marx. The three stanzas of the poem correspond to the three stages in the dialectical evolution of an idea: the thesis, antithesis, and synthesis. The first stanza caricatures the attitude of the ruling class in Quebec. (Historically, English dominance dates from the defeat of the French by the English on the Plains of Abraham near Quebec City in 1759.) By virtue of their military dominance and the cooperation of the Roman Catholic Church, the English ruling class was able to prosper disproportionately.

The second stanza caricatures the antithetical reaction of the French majority, which intensified dramatically in the 1960's. The power vacuum left by the declining influence of the Church and the global devolution of the British Empire has been filled to a great extent by the independence movement in Quebec politics. This movement arose in opposition to the thesis of the status quo. The synthesis in dialectical theory is created from the struggle between the thesis and the antithesis. The third stanza of "French and English" calls for a positive and peaceful resolution to the conflict. Such a possibility is imagined through the power of music, love, and spiritual awareness.

Themes and Meanings

This poem focuses on the impasse of linguistic and cultural misunderstanding in Canada. Hugh MacLennan coined the expression "two solitudes" in his 1945 novel of the same title to refer to the psychological distance between the English and French communities. Though this problem, satirically described in parts 1 and 2, has become extremely political, the solution to it evoked in part 3 is not.

Parts 1 and 2 begin respectively with the same line, the last word only being changed: "I think you are fools to speak French/English." Cohen seems to be implying that all people are fools when they depend on the formal peculiarities of any language. No language is adequate, by itself, to effect the miracle of human communication. Words are dead and useless unless they are animated by music, love, and spirit. The third stanza also begins with two practically identical lines, "I hate you but it is not in English/ I love you but it is not in French." The poet is saying that the particular sound and/or written form of a word are incidental to its real significance. Both love and hate are essentially expressed by a language of the heart, which all people share.

Leonard Cohen is better known as a songwriter and singer than as a poet, and his reputation demonstrates his commitment to the musical element in language. His tunes are a protest against the "flat rhythms" of English. Without music, language becomes a trap, and "the lovers die in all your songs." The reader is invited to escape from the trap with the help of "other voices" in order to find a common "mother tongue/ and be awakened by a virgin." The reference to oral sex ten lines earlier is still fresh in the reader's mind when it is extended, transformed, and combined in this line with an image of spiritual reawakening or rebirth. The radical juxtaposition and intertwining of sexual and spiritual images in the third stanza is typical of Cohen's writing. Sexual communication and spiritual awareness are understood as two inseparable aspects of love.

Fanatical French and English partisans in Quebec are attacked in this poem from the point of view of the fundamental force of life, sex, which requires no particular language. They are also attacked from the point of view of the enlightened spirit that can transcend ordinary language. Though Cohen is Jewish and has studied Zen Buddhism for many years, the references here are mainly to the spiritual tradition of Christianity. The poem concludes with the image of prisoners of "particular speech" being resurrected by the intercession of a virgin, presumably Mary. The possibility of political and linguistic peace in Quebec is thereby affirmed as a potential benefit flowing from the "grace" of God.

Steven Lehman

FROM MAN YOU CAME AND TO MAN
YOU SHALL RETURN

Author: Yehuda Amichai (1924-2000)
Type of poem: Elegy
First published: 1985, as "Me-Adam atah ve-el adam tashuv," in *Me-Adam atah ve-el adam tashuv*; English translation collected in *Yehuda Amichai: A Life of Poetry, 1948-1994*, 1994

The Poem

Yehuda Amichai's "From Man You Came and to Man You Shall Return" is a seventeen-line poem in four stanzas, the first consisting of three lines, the second of four lines, the third of seven lines, and the fourth of three lines. The lines are uneven in length and irregular in meter, but the poem may have a different prosody in Hebrew, the language in which Amichai wrote and from which his poems have been translated into at least thirty languages. The title is an integral part of this poem and provides the first surprise for the reader. The phrase "From Man You Came and to Man You Shall Return" strikes the reader with a certain irony; the framework is certainly familiar, one has heard it before, but it seems not quite right. Is this a familiar biblical edict? The reader is immediately drawn into the poem, trying to remember the wording of the original phrase. It does not take long to recall the source of the title, a sentence embedded in Genesis 3:19: "For dust you are,/ and to dust you shall return," which the God of the Hebrew Bible said to Adam when He discovered Adam and Eve had eaten the forbidden fruit.

The three lines of the first stanza form an apparently simple statement,

> Death in war begins
> With one young man
> Descending the stairs.

Readers are far from the field of battle, in the city or village, and one young man is leaving his home, yet the poet says that the casualty of war begins here. Although the statement appears simple, it is really ambiguous. Is Amichai looking at a photograph of a soldier leaving for battle? Is he imagining such a scene? Does he mean that even as young men go about their daily business the seeds of war are carried in their genes? The second stanza continues in this vein; the young man is "closing a door in silence" and "opening a window"; actions performed frequently and even innocently are the beginnings of death.

In the third stanza Amichai addresses the reader with an imperative. "Hence, do not weep for the one who goes," he commands, "Weep for the one who descends the stairs of his house." Weep only for the living, the poet is saying, weep only for those who are still performing the daily gestures of life, although death in war is lurking in their future and every action brings them closer to that fated end. The third stanza ends with three lines that start with the word "weep," exhorting the reader to mourn objects, objects that themselves remember the dead. The fourth and final stanza takes readers back to the title. Amichai's titles are often lines taken from the poem, usually the first line. By using the last line for the title, however, the poet gives this statement, literally, as the last word. Although this stanza contains a question, the brief three lines do not end with a question mark. It is a rhetorical question, "Who will stand up and say to the dust:/ From man you came and to man you shall return."

Forms and Devices

Although Amichai was born in southern Germany, his extended family sailed to Palestine in the mid-1930's, avoiding the Holocaust. Growing up in an Orthodox Jewish family and attending the Orthodox Ma'aleh high school, the poet became accustomed in his youth to the stately cadences of the Hebrew Bible, which had the greatest influence on his own poetry. Typically, Hebrew biblical poetry has little or no metrical scheme but is organized instead on symmetry of units, called parallelism. The main type of parallelism used in "From Man You Came and to Man You Shall Return" is repetition. In much biblical poetry, symmetry is achieved by the repetition of three or more words in each unit or line.

Significantly, given the biblical reference of the title of this poem, the form also echoes biblical technique. "Death in war begins" is the unifying phrase that opens the poem and recurs twice in the second stanza. In the third stanza, the phrase "do not weep for" in the first line is reversed to "Weep for" in the second, creating another type of parallelism, antithesis. "Weep for" is repeated again in the third, fifth, sixth, and seventh lines of the third stanza, and with each repetition the poem grows stronger and more memorable. This third stanza is written in the third person; the poet is speaking directly to the reader and establishes a sense of intimacy enhanced by the simplicity of the vocabulary and references to such humble items as stairs, a door, a key, a pocket, and tears. For years Amichai was Israel's most loved and respected poet, a man who remained aloof from politics and literary cliques but was a familiar sight in Jerusalem's cafes and classrooms. This apparent simplicity was loved by students and soldiers as well as intellectuals, and critics praised his work and considered him Israel's most important poet.

The fourth stanza is also intimate in tone, although it does not continue the use of parallelism. The first line, "And in this spring," establishes the time for the poem. It is the eternal now; it is not some other spring, or some past spring, but "this spring," and as long as the poem is read it will always be now. The second and third line pose the question, "Who will stand up and say to the dust:/ From man you came and to man you shall return." This is a startling departure from the biblical quote it refers to, and here the poem changes from an elegy for those who die in war to a subversive, even revolutionary, work.

Themes and Meanings

Although Amichai was brought up as an Orthodox Jew, he soon gave up the orthodoxy of his parents. His provocative allusions are his way of wrestling with Jewish history, a history in which he played an active role. He made his living as a teacher while becoming a warrior, first as a soldier with the British army in World War II, then with the Palmach in the Israeli War of Independence in 1948 and with the Israeli army in 1956 and 1973. Many of his poems are about war, including the well-known "God Takes Pity on Kindergarten Children," in which God takes no pity at all on adults but leaves them alone even when they are crawling on their hands and knees dripping blood. Even Amichai's poems about relationships with family and lovers often take place against the background of war, such as "I Was Waiting for My Girl and Her Steps Were Absent," in which he hears the shots of soldiers training for war and grows increasingly anxious.

Despite the fact that he writes in Hebrew, a language saturated with Jewish experience from biblical times to the present, Amichai was never at peace with God after his childhood, and the poet's quarrel with God is present as a major theme in his poems. Yet the God of the poems, who seems sometimes a mere figure of speech deeply embedded in the language, makes his presence felt even in his absence, as in "From Man You Came and to Man you Shall Return." The tone of the poem is defiance toward the God who first said "For dust you are,/ and to dust you shall return." God's statement is intended to humble Adam, pointing out that he is no more important than the dust beneath his feet.

Amichai's ironic statement is a statement of pride, for he implies that humanity is the beginning and source of everything, even the lowly dust. The implication is that humanity, not dust, will triumph in the end. Perhaps this note of triumph is the reason that Benjamin Harshaw, who has translated many volumes of Amichai's poetry, chose to read this poem at a memorial service for the poet in the Sifka Center for Jewish Life at Yale University on October 24, 2000, exactly one month after Amichai was buried in Jerusalem, the city he loved.

Sheila Golburgh Johnson

FROM THE BEAM

Author: Paul Celan (Paul Antschel, 1920-1970)
Type of poem: Lyric
First published: 1971, as "Von Querab," in *Schneepart*; English translation collected in *Last Poems*, 1986

The Poem

"From the Beam" is a short poem composed of nineteen short lines of free verse. It is a spare, tight poem, and some of the lines (in the translation) consist of a single word. Poets who compress their thoughts to the fewest possible words, claiming that "less is more"—the less on the surface, the more beneath—are known as minimalists. Paul Celan identified with no school of poetry, but this poem, which uses only sixty-odd words in its nineteen lines, exemplifies the concentration of the minimalist poets.

This poem is one of Celan's last poems and was first published posthumously. Celan's suicide, like that of the American poet Sylvia Plath, was followed by the discovery of a powerful series of poems that the poet had left ready for publication. "From the Beam" illustrates the strong attraction of death experienced by one who had lost so much in the concentration camps and in the war that he could never again participate fully in the life of the world. Celan's final poems are intense expressions of pain that almost defy explication. This poem uses nautical imagery to illustrate the bond the speaker feels with the dead, here depicted as a drowned or submerged "other" whom the poet addresses as "you."

In this difficult poem, the speaker is identified or associated with a ship. At times the speaker seems to be running the craft, but at other points he seems to be almost one with the ship, seeing with its "beacon" and feeling with its "drop-keel." (While in some poems there is reason to distinguish the speaker's thoughts and feelings from the poet's, there is no reason to do so in this one.)

The poem begins with an invitation to an unknown other to come in, down from "the beam"—presumably the crossbeam of the ship. There may be the suggestion of a crucifixion image. In the rest of the poem, the "you" is addressed as down, below, or under, probably under the sea. The "you" has been sacrificed, and the pain of the loss is borne permanently by the speaker, who describes "[the] scream/ enshrined" of the being or person who is "below,/ . . . down below." The speaker is drawn toward the submerged other; as the speaker is still among the living, he is whole-handed, "with fingers"—able to grasp or to write. The other, the submerged one, has arm-stalks which "multiply." The German word *wuchern*, here translated as "multiply," actually means to grow flourishingly, not a characteristic one would ordinarily apply to the dead. Using the word here suggests an unhealthy growth, forms beneath the water suffering sea-changes into monstrous shapes. The "beacon" broods instead of the "one-starred heaven," an obscure reference which may suggest the individual consciousness of the speaker as opposed to the shared consciousness of Jewish heritage. Alternatively, it may suggest simply that the only light is his own, if the beacon is taken to be a part of the ship rather than on land. Interpretations are mainly speculative at this level, but the line evokes the image of a single, "brooding" light: an intensity of mind. The keel of the boat, which draws up, is used to "get a reading from you"—to establish communication with the dead, or with the unreachable other. The horror of the poem is in the image of the speaker reaching out with his fingers toward the figure underneath, who has only arm-stalks to be grasped or with which to grasp.

The identity of the other is never established with any clarity. The "you" addressed is Celan's dead, and perhaps also that part of himself that was lost with his family in the Holocaust. Usually Celan describes the dead as ashes in the air, bringing to mind the Holocaust furnaces. The unhealthy, unearthly "down below" that calls him in this poem is unusual for Celan. These depths which conceal corpses bring a wealth of other associations including Sigmund Freud's description of the unconscious, the deepest part of the psyche; the sea-death-transformation images in William Shakespeare's *The Tempest* (1611); and the Phlebas the Sailor passage in T. S. Eliot's *The Waste Land* (1922).

Forms and Devices

The short, spare lines of "From the Beam" emphasize each image and give the impression that the poem itself is something painful being dredged up, word by word, image by image, from depths more happily left unplumbed. The form is stark and without any ornament at all, let alone the complex elaboration that rhyme and rhythm would provide.

The group of poems from which this work is taken, *Schneepart*, or "Snow-Part," consists of works containing intuitively rather than logically related images in poems of separation and loss. The collection, left ordered as Celan wished them to be published after his death, consists mostly of brief, untitled poems which emphasize isolation, loss, and fragmentation by their disconnected form as well as their images of amputations, breaks, and holes. (These poems are identified by their first lines in lieu of titles.) Celan commented once that language was the only thing which remained whole for him after the war; these late poems show that language, too, can be broken down and fragmented.

The major image of the ship dominates the poem; technical nautical language fine-tunes the metaphor. The "beam" of the first line is the main crossbeam, if literally translated. The drop-keel is a keel that can be cranked up in order to pull the boat ashore; thus the conclusion of the poem, "with the drop-keel/ I get a reading from you," suggests a lowered part of the boat's bottom dragging the depths, feeling for remnants of the lost other, trying to "read" the sea's floor.

The repetition of words in a poem of such brevity and compactness heightens the intensity and places emphasis on the thoughts reiterated. The lines "You are below,/ you are down below" show both the feeling of loss and the distance between the speaker and the "you" addressed. The compulsion of the fatal attraction of the submerged addressee is stressed by "I go, I go." Unable to stay in his own element, the speaker is indivisibly bonded to the one underneath the surface. "With fingers" is another repeated phrase, and it suggests the act of grasping and perhaps of writing. His grasp is an attempt at communication or closure. The speaker wishes to establish a sustaining link with history, but history has no hand with which to clasp his.

Themes and Meanings

"From the Beam" is a poem about loss and about the irresistible pull of the past. For Celan, whose family was killed in the Holocaust and whose losses did not stop when the war was over but continued with the death of his son in childhood, the past was a series of amputations. The horror in this poem is barely suggested but remains a dark presence. "[Y]our scream/ enshrined" suggests that the speaker was never able to go beyond this painful separation, but kept it with him always as a talisman of his life and a guide to its meaning. The "arm-stalks" which "multiply" (or grow luxuriantly) are another reminder of amputations which fester. The poem reflects the inability of one who has experienced such wrenching horror to get free of it and live.

Although this poem is not directly about the Holocaust and the concentration camps, as so many of Celan's poems are, their presence informs the poem. Celan was accused by critics of "aestheticizing" the Holocaust—of turning it into art instead of representing it in the horror of its reality. These poems of loss and of unhealing wounds do nothing to blur or diminish the reality of the Holocaust, however; rather, through the empathy with which they evoke the desolation of loss in the reader, they perpetuate the memory of the death camps as well as more realistic accounts.

"From the Beam" needs to be read together with Celan's other late poems if it is to achieve its full effect. In context with these, it becomes a cry of isolation from one who has had family, friends, country, identity, and faith wrenched away from him. The mysterious other toward whom he gropes "with fingers" becomes lost family, lost love, lost God: All losses merge into the shadowy underwater being that he addresses in German as "du Untre"—"you down there," or "you, the underneath-one." The conclusion of the poem may suggest an attempt at closure through "reading" the past, but the sustained tone of the poem is one of anguish at irrecoverable losses.

Janet McCann

FROM THE RISING OF THE SUN

Author: Czesław Miłosz (1911-   )
Type of poem: Dramatic monologue
First published: 1974, as *Gdzie wschodzi słońce i kędy zapada*; in *Bells in Winter*,
    1978; English translation collected in *The Collected Poems, 1931-1987*, 1988

The Poem

From the Rising of the Sun is a long poem divided into six parts, each part having its own title. Czesław Miłosz has identified the poem's title as coming from a psalm sung at vespers (evening prayers): "From the rising of the sun to the going down of the same." The poet seems to be alluding to the beginning and end of things, to the meaning of existence as it is perceived in the poet's life and in the life of humanity. Written in the first person, the poem is autobiographical, referring to specific events in the poet's life but also to his vocation as a poet, which stimulates him to project into other times and places.

Part 1, "The Unveiling," evokes the universal figure of the poet as he has existed at various times, creating his work with "a stylus, reed, quill or a ballpoint." The poet, the speaker reminds us, has served in religious orders and labored for kings. In both his sacred and secular roles, he has divined the fate of human beings, working under a "dark-blue cloud"—a rather ominous portent of things to come—and "with a glint of the red horse"—a foreboding allusion to the apocalypse of Saint John in the Book of Revelation in the New Testament.

The poet expresses distaste for his vocation, for the "odious rhythmic speech" that grips him. His intuition of disaster is contrasted with a chorus that invokes the longings of humankind for "their day/ Of power and glory." As the poet witnesses the flight of his words, the chorus answers with a plea for an understanding of the meaning of their existence. Returning to the images of the apocalypse, introduced at the beginning of "The Unveiling," the poet wonders whether anything in life can be made clear except its "completed fate."

Part 2, "Diary of a Naturalist," draws directly on the poet's memory of his native Lithuania, of the child's feeling for the forest that surrounds him like a family, impressing him with a sense of comfort and protection not yet shattered by an adult's awareness of fate. Referring explicitly to human sin, to the "tree of Knowledge," the poet launches into a lament for the lost generation, the city (Wilno), and the nation (Lithuania) of his youth. Yet the words he uses to describe his particular lost world remind him that there are other lost worlds in other languages and other places—the loss of the Indian words for places and experiences in southern Oregon, for example. Examining his childhood experience more closely, he finds an incipient awareness of the cruelty and voraciousness of nature: the "rapacious" flies devouring the "fat flesh of caterpillars," which is not so different from the human destructiveness he finds in the image of a "burned-down city." The poet becomes, then, a pilgrim, shuttling from place to place, visiting

Sarlat (near the site in central France of the magnificent cave paintings, the earliest evidence of art), and Roc Amadour (also in France, and once a stop on the journey of medieval pilgrims), as a witness to the human search for meaning; he is also a witness to its denial, for the poet hears "no call," no confirmation of what his mission should be.

In Part 3, "Over Cities," the poet attempts to deny his responsibility for what he imagines happened on planet Earth: "If I am responsible/ It is not for everything." Born at a time when "locomotives ran on rails," he was not a participant in the great trials of human beings, in the controversies over Copernicus's and Galileo's discoveries. As a man of history, he would yet divorce himself from it—even resist his poetic vocation: "I have always lacked words and have not been a poet/ If a poet is supposed to take pleasure in words." Concerned about the experience of the masses in modern cities, the poet complains that the "Universal is devouring the Particular," that individuality counts for nothing. It is a bleak vision of modern times, leavened only by a sense of continuity: "A life unendurable but it was endured," suggests the poet, who is thinking of the fate that bound humanity in past ages as well as at the "end of the twentieth century." The principle of individuality persists in the poet's recollection of his childhood and of his mother offering him to Our Lady of Ostrabrama for her protection. Saved from some destiny the poet does not name, he wonders if he has "fulfilled" his duty and been of use to anyone. Perhaps because of his awareness of having been rescued for something important, the poet imagines the figure of Sir Hieronymus, apparently an eighteenth century nobleman, the cultivated man who takes the poet to a park, tells him of his adventures—opens up the world to the child, so to speak—but then disappears, leaving the poet wondering about the visit he has received, the vocation he pursues without knowing whether his course has been the right one.

Part 4, "A Short Recess," continues to dwell on the poet's childhood, on the "impossible" life that he nevertheless "endured." He thinks of what he might have been, of the other self he would have become, had he been able to stop the rush of the "Heraclitean river"—an allusion to the Greek philosopher who contended it was impossible to step into the same river twice. So it is with the poet's life, which he cannot relive although he can imagine himself remaining in his native city, Wilno, of becoming one of the town's elders, a diplomat concluding an alliance with Ferrara, instead of traveling to "Megalopolis," a modern mass society in which he finds no center to his life, and where he can only wonder whether life "means little/ Or much."

Part 5, "The Accuser," reviews the poet's sense of his own fate, of his place after death in an encyclopedia next to a "hundred Millers and Mickey Mouse." In a dialogue with himself, he questions the usefulness of his existence—even his contention that words have helped him deal with his grief. It is a difficult issue for a poet who sees a man in a barber's chair getting his hair and sideburns trimmed, dreaming of himself as a great man, an emperor or a czar, imprisoned in "Ego." It would be good to have some "ritual of purification through the columns of a temple," the poet suggests, invoking ancient history and humankind's need to find a way out of its own corruption. Yet, the poet ends this part by asking, "Where? When? For whom?—" again implying his doubts about his own authority.

Part 6, "Bells in Winter," again projects the poet into an alternative existence: Traveling in the Carpathian mountains, he is hailed by a man in "Greek raiment," calling himself the man chastised by Saint Paul for having "stolen my father's wife." Explicitly noting that he has not had this experience in actuality, the poet suggests that he "could have," and that he speaks for the imperfectness of human experience. From this hypothetical episode he moves to an account of a real experience of his student days on "Literary Lane" in Wilno. He tells of the old servant woman, Lisabeth, whose religious faith is linked with the "Egyptian division of the Louvre," a grander but by no means more important manifestation of a belief in the hereafter—a belief the poet contemplates, calling it apokatastasis. This word appears in the Bible, signifying "reverse movement" or restoration, a sense that one can return to the past, that the significance of the poet's experience lies both "in time and when time shall be no more." Recognizing that through the ages there has been this faith in eternal salvation, in a time when human experience will be recast and purified, the poet nevertheless admits his failure to accept the end of the world and its renewal, ending his poem with a confession of his doom: "I was judged for my despair because I was unable to understand this."

Forms and Devices

Three devices make this long poem difficult but rewarding reading: the poet's allusions to many different episodes from literature, history, myth, and religion; his manipulation of time; and his division of the poem into six parts, embodying his fluctuating feelings about his life and poetic vocation. To give the flavor of the different times and places and to strengthen the meaning of his allusions, he quotes from old documents, encyclopedias, and other texts. His poem is studded with quotations, emphasizing the written sources his memory draws upon and the bits and pieces of these different worlds that make up the poet's consciousness.

One way to fix an interpretation of the poem is to regard the poet as moving back and forth from his present, in California, to his past, in Lithuania. The complexity of history is filtered between these two different periods in his life as he conflates Lithuania and California, implying that they are all in the eternal present of the poet's imagination, a kind of super-reality that transcends any single place in time.

Thus the poet has in mind more than the boundaries of his personal existence. In part 5, for example, he remarks: "Well, it happened long ago, in Ecbatana/ In Edessa, if you prefer." These two cities, one in Persia, the other in Asia Minor, are the sites of early Christian sects—of disputants, in other words, over the meaning of Christianity. The implication is that the poet's specific experience is actually a part of everyone's experience, and they will find it in one place, if not in the other—in Ecbatana or in Edessa. What happened long ago—the search for faith and meaning—is also happening now, just as the man in the barber chair can imagine himself to be an emperor or a czar.

The opening line of the poem is the key to understanding the poet's sense of time: By picking up various writing instruments developed in different periods of history, he is simultaneously taking on the imagination of those times—the stylus and the reed corresponding to his references to ancient art and writing; the quill to later, but still premodern, periods of history, such as the eighteenth century world of snuffboxes and Sir Hieronymus; the ballpoint pen to the world of "Megalopolis."

Each part of the poem expresses a tension between past and present, between the poet and his past selves, and between the meaning he wishes to find in the world and his lack of faith. Part 1, "The Unveiling," is a statement of the problem: "I begin, though nobody can explain why and wherefore." The poet is described as a diplomat or courier bringing meaning to the world (Miłosz once held such a position in Poland) without being sure of his warrant for doing so. Part 2, "Diary of a Naturalist," literally contains a diary or passage from a naturalist, but it is also a fond memory of childhood, when the bond between the poet's early self and nature had not yet been broken; his feelings about nature are his diary, so to speak. Part 3, "Over Cities," returns the poet to urban experience, to human conflict in which humankind has argued over the nature of the world; it is a world that takes away everything from humans: "Crossed out. All our treasures," the poet concludes. Part 4, "A Short Recess," begins with a vivid image of himself at a school recess, standing under a wall in "chubby meditation," a powerful image of what he was but could not remain. The recess the poet calls is a recess from history, if only momentarily, to contemplate the image of the self he would have become if he had not left Wilno. Part 5, "The Accuser," is built around a dialogue with the poet's challenger, the one who is skeptical that poetry has created order or been "of help," and who can be looked upon as the poet's alter ego. Part 6, "Bells in Winter," is organized around the memory of Wilno's bells, calling people to worship—even in winter, the bleakest of seasons and yet a season of faith—and prompting the poet to express his own sense of the future, while acknowledging the bleakness of his own hopes.

This intricate six-part structure is suggestive of the tensions between hope and despair that inform each part of the poem, for no part of it—even in isolation—is dominated by a single mood; but is rather a microcosm of the whole, of the poet's conflicted feelings about himself and existence.

Themes and Meanings

From the Rising of the Sun is a meditation on the role of the poet and his doubts about the power of his vocation. It is as if he distrusts his facility with words and is resentful of the poetic flowering of language he finds difficult to control. In an interview, Miłosz observed that he regards himself as a "medium" for poetry, "but a mistrustful one."

As part 2 of the poem suggests, the poet's first love is for nature, for the naturalist who can lose himself in the bounty of his environment—a cheerful contrast to the brooding, self-aware poet. Poetry requires memory, a recalling of often painful, destructive experiences, and an examination of nature itself, which destroys the boy's innocence in its merciless exposure of the way nature's creatures prey upon one another. The images of life consuming itself are what the poet can hardly bear and what make him call it "impossible." Only by not dwelling on this aspect of life can he bear to go on.

The poet in *From the Rising of the Sun* is a displaced figure, not really at home in his California setting and unable to return home to the Lithuania he can only imagine as it once had been. He cannot purge himself of his experience so as to relive the past innocently; consequently, there is a bitter, harsh tone to many of the poet's reflections. The compensating factor is that no element, either of the poet's life or of human civilization, is truly lost. It is all potentially, at least, reclaimable—a concept the poet develops in his use of the term apokatastasis—first promulgated by Origen (185?-254?), a father of the Christian church who believed it was possible to restore or reinstate the world as it was before Original Sin. In the poem, this is not so much a religious notion as it is a metaphysical conceit—that there might come an end of time that could serve as a redemption of time, a recovery of the past in a cleansed form.

The idea of redemption is not endorsed by the poem. Indeed, at the end the poet convicts himself of a lack of faith, again emphasizing his ambivalence about his poetic vocation. Poetry has provided him with a conception of a better world, yet he finds it difficult to rise to the occasion of that conception, and he imagines that even should this restored world come to pass, he would be judged wanting, convicted for his despair, rejected because, finally, he could not understand the very world that would fulfill his dreams.

Carl Rollyson

FROST AT MIDNIGHT

Author: Samuel Taylor Coleridge (1772-1834)
Type of poem: Lyric
First published: 1798, in *Fears in Solitude*

The Poem

"Frost at Midnight" is a seventy-four-line "conversation" poem, written in blank verse paragraphs of varying lengths. In the middle of a February night, the poet is sitting alone in his cottage. (The location is Samuel Taylor Coleridge's cottage at Nether Stowey, near Bristol.) His baby son sleeps peacefully by his side; the other members of the household have all gone to bed. The poet watches frost forming silently on the windows and hears the hooting of owls. Apart from that, everything is silent. It is so calm and quiet that it makes the poet uncomfortable. He thinks of all the "numberless goings-on of life" that exist in the nearby village, and in the nearby wood and sea, yet nothing can be heard.

Then his attention is drawn to the fireplace, and he notices a film of soot fluttering on the bar of the grate. He feels a vague kinship with it because it is the only thing he can perceive that seems as restless as he is. Coleridge explained, in a note attached to the poem, that in England such films were often called "strangers" and were thought to announce the arrival of an absent friend. This sends the poet into a reverie in which he reflects on his childhood. He thinks back to how, while at school, he had often gazed at these "strangers" in the grate. Under the intimidating eye of his stern teacher, he would then pretend to study. Whenever the door opened, or even half-opened, he would look up expectantly, hoping to see the "stranger's" face, whomever it might be. Often, too, in school he had daydreamed about the town where he had been born and where he had spent his early childhood. He remembers how entranced he had been by the ringing of church bells, "the poor man's only music."

In the third verse paragraph, the poet's attention turns back to the present, to the sleeping infant at his side. The gentle breathing of the baby punctuates the calm, and the poet is filled with tender feelings for him. Having just looked back at his own life, the poet now looks forward to the future life of his baby. He is elated because he believes that the child will grow up in an entirely different, and far superior, environment than that in which the poet had spent his early days. The poet was reared in the city, but his child will be able to enjoy, and be nourished by, a more natural environment of lakes, sandy shores, and mountains. By learning to appreciate the beauty of creation, he will also learn about God, who can be found in every aspect of the created world.

Finally, the poet evokes the passage of the seasons, using the opportunity to round off the poem where it began, with the silent activity of the frost. He declares to his baby that "all seasons shall be sweet to thee," even the depths of winter, when the "secret ministry of frost" leaves icicles "Quietly shining to the quiet Moon."

Forms and Devices

"Frost at Midnight" is often regarded as the finest of Coleridge's "conversation" poems. It perfects the lyric form that Coleridge had already developed in such poems as "The Eolian Harp" (1796), "Reflections on Having Left a Place of Retirement" (1796), and "This Lime-Tree Bower My Prison" (1800). These poems all possess a circular structure. Coleridge believed that the structure of a poem should reflect the structure of existence, and he saw the latter as cyclic in nature, whether at the macrocosmic or microcosmic level. All things proceed from the universal One, are individualized into the many, but are continually turning backward toward the One, their source and true nature. Ultimately, everything returns to the One. As Coleridge once wrote in a letter to publisher Joseph Cottle, "The common end of all *narrative*, nay of *all*, Poems is to convert a *series* into a *Whole*: to make those events, which in real or imagined History move on in a *strait* Line, assume to our Understandings a *circular* motion—the snake with its Tail in its Mouth."

This is clearly the structural pattern of "Frost at Midnight." The poem begins with a description of an outer scene in which the "secret ministry of frost" is at work. As with all of Coleridge's conversation poems, the outer scene stimulates the poet and sends him on an inward, meditative journey. In this case, he reflects at length on incidents in his childhood before returning to the present with some consoling thoughts about the future of his child. The poem ends where it began, with the "secret ministry of frost," although there has been an enormous growth in the meaning and significance attached to the phrase.

The imagery of the poem carefully interweaves sound and silence, movement and stillness. This is particularly apparent in the first verse paragraph. Only the owlet's cry breaks the "strange/ And extreme silentness" of the night, and there is a comparable emphasis on stillness. There is not a breath of wind, and the flame of the low-burning fire "quivers not." Only the film of soot shows any movement, reminding the poet of the restlessness of his own mind. It is this combination of stillness and motion that sets the scene for the inward direction of the poet's mind, as it seeks to discover more about its own nature. The "gentle breathings" of the poet's son, "heard in this deep calm," continue the image pattern, which is reaffirmed in the final lines of the poem, with the "silent icicles,/ Quietly shining to the quiet Moon."

Themes and Meanings

One of the most important themes is that of the "child of nature," which finds expression in a number of Coleridge's other poems of this period, including "The Dungeon" (1798) and "The Nightingale" (1798). "Frost at Midnight" contrasts the stifling effect of life in the city, where as a child the poet was "Pent in cloisters dim," with the liberating effect of an upbringing in nature. In the city, education is characterized by the "stern preceptor" and the unwilling student. In nature, God himself is the teacher, and he reveals himself through the beauties of his creation.

This suggests the underlying religious, even mystical, theme to the poem: the development of the poet's ability to perceive the eternal, unifying, divine spirit through all the diverse forms of time. This is beautifully captured in the last verse paragraph, beginning "Therefore all seasons shall be sweet to thee," which reveals the growth in the poet's consciousness that has occurred during the poem. In the opening scene, the poet, in his restlessness, felt at odds with the peaceful environment. Now a "sweetness," a sense of quiet communion with the outer world, has been added that was not there before. The "secret ministry of frost" has done its work. This can be understood at both the literal and the symbolic level. At a literal level, the frost has performed its ministry by freezing the water drops into icicles which shine as they reflect the light of the moon. Symbolically, this suggests a kind of spiritual radiance. The frost, which can be taken to symbolize the workings of the creative imagination, has "frozen" a particle of nature so that it is seen to contain or reflect something larger and more majestic than itself, the eternal light of the "quiet Moon." The moon is at once one of the "lovely shapes . . ./ Of that eternal language, which thy God/ Utters" and the quietness of the poet's own mind in his state of meditative illumination.

As this analysis suggests, it is hardly possible in this poem to think in conventional ways about inner and outer phenomena. The two are inseparably interwoven. Coleridge himself said as much in an entry in his notebook:

> In looking at objects of Nature while I am thinking, as at yonder moon dim-gathering thro' the dewy window-pane, I seem rather to be seeking, as were *asking*, a symbolical language for something within me that already and forever exists, than observing any thing new. Even when that latter is the case, yet still I have always an obscure feeling as if that new phenomenon were the dim Awaking of a forgotten or hidden Truth of my inner Nature.

The relevance of this to "Frost at Midnight" can be seen not only in terms of the frost and the moon, which are at once inner and outer realities, but also in the film of soot which Coleridge transforms into an image of the workings of his own mind, which is "every where/ Echo or mirror seeking of itself." Seen in this light, the entire poem is self-referential, an attempt by the poet to probe the nature of his own mind, which is also discovered to be the nature of the universe.

Bryan Aubrey

FUNERAL ORATION FOR A MOUSE

Author: Alan Dugan (1923-   )
Type of poem: Ode
First published: 1961, in *Poems*

The Poem

"Funeral Oration for a Mouse" is a short poem in free verse, its thirty-seven lines divided into three stanzas of unequal length. The title, in comically dignifying a mere mouse with a grand "funeral oration," prepares the reader for the poem's leveling of human and beast. Although at first sight the orator (or the speaker of the poem) may seem lowered in stooping to such a low theme, it becomes clear from the body of the poem that the mouse, in view of its great determination and courage, is indeed the more dignified of the two.

The poem begins as a meditation upon the qualities, both good and bad, of a mouse that the speaker has recently caught in a mousetrap. The speaker addresses himself to his Lord, as befitting a funeral speech, and, though there are no descriptions of the speaker's immediate surroundings, it can be assumed the mouse is either buried, or about to be buried, in the speaker's backyard or else is being laid to rest in the garbage—probably the latter, given Alan Dugan's typically acerbic imagination. The speaker immediately links himself to the mouse as "an anxious brother" and, nine lines down, as "a guest/ who shared our board." He characterizes the mouse as paradoxically combining health and disease and as a quiet, furtive creature which can nevertheless, for "some ladies," cause a stir. In the last two lines of the stanza, he reveals the dual causes of the mouse's demise—the trap and the mouse's "necessary hunger," both of which compose the principal matter of the second stanza.

For the speaker, the essential meaning of the trap has little to do with "humors of love"—that is, with seduction and the attainment of the object of desire. Rather, it is merely his "opinion of the mouse," the simple fact that he wanted the mouse dead. On the other hand, the speaker imagines that for the mouse the trap was the sole symbol of a mouse religion founded upon and driven by hunger, serving as tree of knowledge, true cross, and hell's gate combined. Able to approach its god, even with caution, the mouse proved itself braver and wiser than the speaker, who, though victorious, finds himself unable to delight in his victory.

Indeed, as the last stanza reveals, the speaker is repulsed by what he has accomplished. He realizes that, as the mouse was a pest to him, so he may be to someone else. For a moment, he imagines that the mouse, with its fingers "skinnier/ than hairpins and as breakable as cheese," might become itself a trap, grasping the speaker's "grasping" life, and he trembles lest he, with his "own stolen baits," be pulled "into the common death beyond the mousetrap."

Forms and Devices

In choosing to dignify a dead mouse with the pomp of a funeral oration, Dugan must perform a careful balancing act. On the one hand, if he treats his theme too lightly, his poem becomes a mockery of the mouse and the speaker's own "felt though minor guilt" for killing the mouse. This is hardly Dugan's intention; his meditation is indeed sobering. Yet if he allows too much solemnity, he risks falling into bathos. Dugan manages much of this balancing act through a manipulation of rhythms and rhetoric, undercutting his dignified, classical tone with gently comical touches.

Much of the dignified effect is achieved through the elongation of the sentences. In considering this aspect of the poem, it may seem that Dugan's use of colons is problematic. If this were ordinary prose, four of the poem's five colons would need to be corrected to either periods or semicolons. The only "correctly" used colon occurs at the end of the ninth line. Yet by using colons instead of full or partial stops, Dugan achieves much the same effect as the contemporary American poet A. R. Ammons, who almost invariably uses only colons to divide his sentences and fragments. The colon allows ideas to run together, giving the suggestion that each sentence comments on the previous one as well as making otherwise short sentences seem longer and, as is the case in "Funeral Oration," weightier.

Also, almost every sentence is either complex or, like the massive sentence which makes up the entire third stanza, compound-complex. This in itself adds weight to the poem; here one finds no Hemingwayesque strings of simple and compound sentences. Instead, elegant constructions abound: "full of health himself,/ he brought diseases like a gift"; "Younger by far, in dying he/ was older than us all"; "Why,/ then, at that snapping sound, did we, victorious." Added to this elegance of construction is an elegance of rhythm and sound. The first two words, "This, Lord," being both stressed, demand a slow entrance into the poem. The tempo quickens after the first colon and continues fast and light through the next five lines, during which the mouse is described. Thus, the sound becomes, in accordance with Alexander Pope's famous prescription, "an echo to the sense," with the movement of the verse mimicking the quickness of the mouse. In line 7, this movement suddenly slows with "for whom some ladies stand on chairs." To the ladies the mouse is all too large and slow. Through the manipulation of rhythm and imagery, Dugan undercuts his heretofore self-conscious elegance with some sly comedy.

Dugan also uses assonance and consonance, sometimes to heighten the dignity of his oration, sometimes to render it comical. As examples of the former, there are the assonances of "ignoble foe and ancient sin" and the repeated *o* and *l* sounds in "mobile tail and nose." An excellent example of a comical effect occurs with the near rhyme at the end of the first stanza between "trap" and "back," combined with the almost sardonic alliteration and consonance of the heavily stressed "broken back."

Themes and Meanings

On the one hand, "Funeral Oration" can be read simply as the speaker's exploration of his "felt though minor guilt" for having killed what after all was a brother in the family of life. Thus, he personifies the mouse, making it into "a guest/ who shared our board" and a worshiper of a religion. Braver and older than the speaker, the mouse is also feared bigger and stronger, able to pull the speaker along "into the common death beyond the mousetrap." Not only, then, is the mouse equal to or better than the human who doomed it, it in effect becomes in turn a trap to that human, forcing upon him an acute awareness of how frail his own grasp on life is. Worse, he realizes that the act of killing was itself born of the pettiness of his own "grasping" life, bloated with its "stolen baits"—that is, born from a small-minded desire to rid himself of what to him was a pest, but which indeed was an honorable little beast. His self-centered ego forced into humility, the speaker seems to repent of his act with a larger awareness of the vital connection between all mortal things.

Were this the only theme of the poem, it could be characterized as an elegantly executed, although pedestrian, effort; however, the poem contains more subversive suggestions. How, for example, is the reader to understand the relationship of the speaker to his audience, the "Lord," in light of the relationship between human and mouse? In the traditional view, as links along a great chain of being stretching from most high to most low, God is to human as human is to mouse. Yet the speaker makes clear that the mouse is in many ways superior to the human. Is the reader to assume the same reversal occurs in the relationship of the human being to its God? This possibility seems likely, especially in consideration of the fancifully imagined relationship between the mouse and the mousetrap. If the latter, which to the human is a mere machine with an "effect of death," is the core symbol of a mouse theology, what kind of mousetrap is the human Christian theology with its tree, its cross, its heaven and hell? One wonders what else but a machine might the human theology be to the God which has apparently baited it, set it in place, and now waits for it to snap the spiritual back of a too-venturesome human.

For the modern, secular audience, such considerations might seem to lack impact. Dugan, however, who throughout his work often bitterly defines himself against his Catholic upbringing, is, in a broader view, saying, "define your gods as you will, but beware stooping to that which is actually smaller than you"—a warning well heeded.

Peter Crawford

THE FURY OF AERIAL BOMBARDMENT

Author: Richard Eberhart (1904-   )
Type of poem: Lyric
First published: 1944, in *Poems, New and Selected*

The Poem

"The Fury of Aerial Bombardment" is a short poem of four stanzas. Stanza 1 rhymes *abba*; stanza 2 rhymes *bccb*, although "centuries" rhymes weakly with furies. Lines 1 and 4 rhyme in stanza 3, and in the final stanza, lines 2 and 4 rhyme. The title of the poem defines its subject—aerial bombardment. It also suggests the author's attitude toward his topic: moral indignation toward humankind and God.

The first three stanzas employ a persona who refers to himself as "I" in stanza 4. The poem traces Richard Eberhart's experience as a theoretical gunnery instructor for the United States Navy in 1942. The speaker ventures what "you" or every person who has confronted war thinks and feels about the fury of aerial bombardment.

Stanza 1 uses the subjunctive to point out a discrepancy between what the situation actually is in relation to war and what one would presumably think—that the fury of aerial bombardment "would rouse God to relent." Eberhart states that "the infinite spaces/ are still silent." God's inaction seems incomprehensible. He looks on "shock-pried" faces and does not relent; "History, even, does not know what is meant." Stanza 2 again uses the subjunctive to point out a condition contrary to fact: "You would feel that after so many centuries/ God would give man to repent." "Give" here means "cause," but God has not "caused" humanity's repentance. Cain was allowed to exercise free will. He killed his brother, and humankind is still possessed of ancient furies.

Stanza 3 questions humanity's sensibility. Was humanity "made stupid to see his own stupidity?" Perhaps God permits war. The poet inquires, "Is God by definition indifferent, beyond us all?" No answer is given, and the poet conjectures about eternal truth. Is there a beast in "man's fighting soul" that feeds upon its own desire for profit or gain?

No answer is provided. In the final stanza, the poet turns inward and focuses upon his own human experience. He recalls two names on a list, Van Wettering and Averill, who were recently or "late" in school. Both men had been trained as gunners and had learned to handle weapons of war. They could release the bullet from the "belt feed lever" into the pawl, and that is their only distinction—an ironic one, since the speaker of the poem has no recollection of either man's face. The fury of aerial bombardment is clear; these young men did not live to distinguish themselves. The fury of aerial bombardment has sent them to an "early death."

Forms and Devices

In *Of Poetry and Poets* (1979), a book of lectures, essays, and interviews, Eberhart defines poetry as "a confrontation of the whole being with reality." The soul, the mind, and the body struggle to comprehend life. Aerial bombardment brings untimely and terrible death. The poem is philosophical in its questioning, and the terrible meaning of humanity's failure to live in harmony and peace is revealed through intricate manipulations of meter and rhyme.

Stanza 1 begins with a subjunctive enjambed line that carries through to a caesura after the third foot of the second line. The pause is preceded by the internal rhyming of "relent" in line 2 with "bombardment" in line 1. This pattern is repeated in line 3, where "silent" rhymes with "is meant" at the end of line 4.

Stanza 2 mirrors the pattern of stanza 1. It employs the subjunctive "would feel" in line 1, which matches the "would give" conditional in line 2. Again, a pause comes after "repent" in the middle of the second line. The verb "to repent" stresses humanity's evil in causing mass destruction. The grammatical construction of the poetic lines emphasizes this and causes a further contemplation of humanity's will to kill. Yet war fails to move God so that He "would give man to repent." The first two stanzas establish the problem, "aerial bombardment," and examine its cause. They balance each other in masculine and feminine rhymes, with stanza 2 reversing the pattern of stanza 1.

Philosophical inquiry is typical of much of Eberhart's work. The first two stanzas of "The Fury of Aerial Bombardment" address humanity's fate in relation to God's plan. The probe is rhetorical in nature, and the tone exhibits indignation toward God, who could stop humanity's senseless folly. Stanza 2 shifts from rhetorical statements to a series of questions.

The significant change in the poem comes after stanza 3. The speaker no longer questions God's lack of intervention in tolerating humanity's tendency toward destruction. Stanza 4 is elegiac, a lament over the lost lives of two youths. A conversational tone is used. The speaker switches to the first person and comments that he does not remember the two young faces. The men are mere names on a list. The previous tone of moral indignation changes to an attitude that encompasses sorrow and waste. The poem ends with quiet irony. The men's lives have amounted to the fact that they learned to distinguish the parts of a gun.

Themes and Meanings

"The Fury of Aerial Bombardment" deals with a single subject—war. The poet's consciousness of death, seemingly senseless death, is the focus of the poem. The poem is short and compressed. The theme of death is a common one in Eberhart's poetry, and a number of other poems address the particular issue of war.

The poet claims that "You would think the fury of aerial bombardment/ Would rouse God to relent." "Rouse" is an interesting word, because it points to God's indifference and to His design in creating humanity: Did He make humanity stupid? The topic of war and the theme of death are united in the inquiry that takes place. The poet makes it clear that "the infinite spaces are still silent." Even the sight of "shock-pried faces" fails to move God to relent.

Stanza 2 moves to the world's beginning. Humankind has possessed the will to kill since the days of Cain. Stanza 3 asks why this is so. All stanzas lead to the final lament, which is a recognition of the waste and futility of war.

This poem is one of a series of poems that deal with death and the senseless destruction of war. They reflect Eberhart's assignments as a theoretical gunnery instructor in the naval reserve at Pensacola, Florida, and at Dam Neck, Virginia. The last three lines of a poem entitled "Dam Neck, Virginia" reiterate sentiments expressed in "The Fury of Aerial Bombardment": "The truth of guns is fierce that aims at death./ Of war in the animal sinews let us speak not,/ But of the beautiful disrelation of the spiritual."

"At the End of War" repeats the theme of death in war. Like "The Fury of Aerial Bombardment," the poem addresses God, who sees men fight "in blindness and fury," but in this poem God is asked to "Forgive mankind for its abominable stupidity" and for the "impenetrable fierceness" that God has put into them. Although the poet condemns humanity's actions, there is recognition of the fact that God made human beings this way. The duality of blaming humanity for its tendency to kill and God for allowing it to happen is also examined in Eberhart's poem "God and Man."

Eberhart's themes are philosophical. He is a man who questions how it is to live fully, to be alive in this world, to be a human. Perceptions and reason are components of the ego, of being and becoming. In order to comprehend existence, given the limitations of humanity's vision, it is necessary to examine the problems of life. In a 1986 interview in the journal *Negative Capability*, Eberhart stated: "I am a meliorist, and I judicate between opposite ideas. I don't accept anyone's idea as absolute, or I try not to." This explains Eberhart's approach to poetry and his questioning stance in "The Fury of Aerial Bombardment."

Sue B. Walker

GACELA OF THE DARK DEATH

Author: Federico García Lorca (1898-1936)
Type of poem: Lyric
First published: 1940, as "Gacela de la muerte oscura," in *Diván del Tamarit*; English
    translation collected in *Divan and Other Writings*, 1974

The Poem

"Gacela of the Dark Death" is a short lyric poem in free verse. The poem is composed of twenty-four lines divided into five stanzas. The title, "Gacela of the Dark
Death," identifies the poem as a *gacela*, a form perfected by the fourteenth century
Persian poet Hafiz. *Gacelas* are typically short, usually rhymed, verses that often mix
religious mysticism, eroticism, and daily experience. In Federico García Lorca's
gacelas, images drawn from his surrealistic and folk-inspired imagination figure
prominently. Moreover, "Gacela of the Dark Death" has a place in *Diván del Tamarit*
in that the typical movement of the collection as a whole is from a remembrance of
erotic familiarity to a confrontation with and recognition of the inevitability of death.
Death is the condition most associated by García Lorca with lost love, and water is a
frequent symbol portending death.

The poem is written in the first person. A poet may adopt a first-person narration strategically, to speak through a persona whose outlook on life and point of view may differ
from his or her own. No such difference, however, is implied in "Gacela of the Dark
Death." In the intimate, personal tradition of the lyric poet, the narrator speaks directly
to the reader, establishing a foundation of personal experience. The reader is placed in a
position to experience life as the narrator does, with all of life's immediate sensations.

"Gacela of the Dark Death" embraces a return to nature, and particularly to the spiritual aspect of nature. In the first stanza, the separation implied between human concepts and conventions and natural experience is established. The poet attacks the artificial distinction created by Western civilization, which separates itself from the
natural and spiritual (and therefore eternal) and overly emphasizes mortality. By the
third stanza, the poet has transformed himself through a union with nature, and the
commonplace in nature serves as the catalyst for this transformation. The transformation renders the artifices of civilization, including mortality, superficial.

Throughout the poem, the speaker emphasizes the personal quality of his experience that permits reunification with nature. Having paid close attention to dreams and
learned the lessons offered by everyday experience, the narrator has discovered an alternative—a spiritual, fulfilling alternative—to conventional values. Ultimately, this
alternative leads to a self-actualizing, eternal experience that, by comparison, reveals
the shallowness of a civilization that is predicated on a narrow view of time. Finally,
even such givens as death and time are emptied of their conventional meanings as, in
the alternative experience, they are redefined and become nonthreatening, positive
forces.

Forms and Devices

Repetition is one important element of "Gacela of the Dark Death." Emphasis is continually placed on personal experience through the repetition of "I want." Metaphors of dreams and sleep lend a spiritual, metaphysical quality to the poem; it is through the force of these images that the narrator is able to transcend conventional experience. The image of the child is also central to the poem, in that it is the child's ability to experience nature completely and without reservations and anticipations that allows an awareness of nature as a transforming entity.

References to apples are frequent in García Lorca's poetry, and they usually represent the forbidden knowledge Eve attained. In the first and last stanzas of "Gacela of the Dark Death," the apple is used to confirm the narrator's desire to merge an eternal moment of sexual communication with a sense of eternal time (that is also death). In *Diván del Tamarit* the flow of water, which signals timeless death, is reminiscent of an Arabian, especially Moorish, sensual appreciation of water. This twin dread of and fascination with death is characteristic of García Lorca's poetry.

The sea has usually stood in García Lorca's work for infinity and death. To be touched by the sea in life is to become ready for whatever destiny awaits. Such a readiness enables the recipient to be better prepared for that destiny.

Themes and Meanings

"Gacela of the Dark Death" is probably Federico García Lorca's most complete exploration of the nature of death, an even more complete exploration than *Lament for Ignacio Sánchez Mejias*, perhaps his most famous and ambitious poem. The second stanza is reminiscent of the work of Miguel de Unamuno y Jugo. Human beings, in Unamuno, both need and fear immortality so that fear and desire, the opposing emotions involved, animate human beings through life. In the second stanza, it appears that García Lorca is expressing a wish for a complete death and that he has the courage to accept it.

In "Gacela of the Dark Death," nature is held forth as a fulfilling, if initially fearsome, presence. The initial representation of nature is fluid and antagonistic, mirroring an inward landscape, in the narrator, of unfulfilled desire and passion. The last line of the poem suggests that the very act of lamentation constitutes a victory over mortality. Lamentation is cleansing.

The idea of a person facing up to what is perhaps the most horrifying fact of all—that his body will rot away—is present in the figure of a Dead Boy in García Lorca's play *Así que pasen cinco años* (1937; *When Five Years Pass*, 1941). In that play, a young man is at the center of the action, and all the other characters are, in one way or another, projections of him. The play is also preoccupied with time, and especially with the tendency in Western civilization to live in the present, ignoring the timeless, universal possibilities of time.

Ultimately, in "Gacela of the Dark Death," García Lorca appears to present an indifference to physical death. This indifference is accomplished because the narrator believes that he can be remembered, if people can be reminded of his accomplishments, or if he retains a mystical consciousness which is symbolized by the fruit of knowledge, the apple. In this quest for meaning, the poem takes on a meditative quality. Nature becomes a transforming force, able to strip away the mortal flesh of the narrator and reveal an immortal soul.

David Lawrence Erben

GACELA OF UNFORESEEN LOVE

Author: Federico García Lorca (1898-1936)
Type of poem: Lyric
First published: 1940, as "Gacela del amor imprevisto," in *Diván del Tamarit*; English
translation collected in *Divan and Other Writings*, 1974

The Poem

"Gacela of Unforeseen Love" is the first poem in Federico García Lorca's collection entitled *Diván del Tamarit*. The words *diván* and "Tamarit" both have several meanings. Originally, the Tamarit was the chief administrative office of Arabic power in Spain during the period of medieval Moorish domination. It was also the name of a family home in the country where García Lorca spent summers until the time of his death. "Divan" was the Arabic name for the assembly of governors who held council with the Tamarit; a divan is also a collection of poems. In Spanish, *diván* also means "reunion." By celebrating the spirit of all southern Spain, the collection may be seen as García Lorca's attempt to come to a "reunion" with his past.

García Lorca labeled the twenty-one poems in the collection as either *gacelas* or *casidas*, forms invented by Hafiz, a fourteenth century Persian poet. In Arabic, a *gacela* is a short lyric form, usually with the theme of love; the *casida* is a longer poem of varied elements, one of which is the elegiac reminiscence of love or parting. The *casida* tends to be more abstract than the *gacela*; however, García Lorca neither adhered strictly to their Arabic forms nor made any real distinction between the two forms. García Lorca's language and imagery are drawn from his own surrealistic and folk-ballad styles.

The first poem of *Diván*, "Gacela of Unforeseen Love," is often considered to be the key poem of the collection. It is a short, extremely personal poem written in free verse, and it contains four stanzas. Its theme is that of fleeting love and inevitable separation.

In the first stanza, the speaker (the "I") of the poem addresses his male lover, using the past tense to recall the "perfume" of his lover's body, in particular his "belly's dark magnolia." He reiterates the fact that he alone understood that body and notes how his lover tormented him by taking "love's hummingbird" (an unusual phallic symbol) between his teeth. The speaker goes on to describe that as his lover slept and dreamed of "a thousand Persian ponies," an allusion to Spain's Moorish past, the speaker embraced his lover's waist for four consecutive nights.

In the third and fourth stanzas, the lover's glance is described as "between plaster and jasmine," images connoting hardness and softness; the speaker continues his description, calling the glance "a pale seed-branch," something that can be as transitory or as ephemeral as seeds scattering in the wind. Then, desiring to give his lover a symbol of permanence, the speaker searches his heart and thinks about giving his lover letters carved out of ivory that spell "always." Yet that same word is also the speaker's "garden of agony," because he knows that permanence in love is unattainable and death will overtake both lover and beloved. In the poem, time, as well as love, is fleeting; separation is inevitable.

Forms and Devices

In "Gacela of Unforeseen Love," García Lorca sketches in imagery that is partly Eastern and partly surrealistic his attraction to a young man. In the first stanza, the strange image of "love's hummingbird" also appears in a painting by Salvador Dalí. García Lorca's central image in this stanza is the magnolia, which he has made dark with all the suggestions of the word—the dark night of passion, dark as isolation and oblivion. The speaker tries with all of his being to make his love eternal, but he fails.

It is interesting to note that form illustrates content. The third stanza ends with the word "always." The fourth stanza repeats the word twice more; the form of this broken stanza illustrates the impermanence of love, declaring that permanence was not to be in "the ivory letters saying always." The speaker is writing in the garden of the Tamarit, the same one in which the Arabic poets mused long ago, but it has become for him a "garden of agony."

At the poem's end, images of light and dark prevail: "the blood of your veins in my mouth/ your mouth's light gone out for my death." The sensual connotations of "night" and "darkness" seem to outweigh the foreboding attributes of these words. The speaker seems almost willing to accept the transitory nature of existence: He accepts only "four nights" of love with his lover, and at the end of the poem he accepts the fact that he must die. Thus, in "Gacela of Unforeseen Love" there is a movement from a remembrance of erotic attachment to a recognition of the fact of death.

Themes and Meanings

As the title of the volume suggests, a specific evocation of the Arabic civilization exists in García Lorca's collection. The poet looks back not only at the long years of Spanish decline but also at the agonizing years of the decay of the Arabic civilization in Spain. In mature Arabic literary culture, three distinct themes of love existed: sensual love; a kind of Platonic love, in which the sensual is transmuted into artistic or divine love; and "Greek love," in which the poet extols the beauty and attraction of young men, often of humble station in life. In the *Diván*, the poet projects a form of Greek love, sometimes with Platonic overtones.

The general theme of the *Diván*, as well as the particular theme of "Gacela of Unforeseen Love," centers on the anguish of the memory of love and on the speaker's present despair, which he is struggling to translate into language. The speaker's voice has seemingly become disembodied; he is a universe of presentiment and nostalgia, of dark instincts and faded passions. Time hangs heavy; there is a sense of the poetry as frozen in time, of having no way out, of merely grimly enduring. In García Lorca's personal images and metaphors, there is a threatening desperation that the poet keeps tightly controlled.

The *gacela* as a standard Arabic verse form used for love poetry is used by García

Lorca to sing of a love no longer incarnate, a love that has become almost mystical in remembered passion. He adds to the Arabic theme a heightened sense of sympathy with the mineral, botanical, and animal worlds that create the immortal conflict in nature. This poem, as well as all the poems in the collection, reaffirms the cultural heritage García Lorca had derived from the medieval Arabic poets; the poems also celebrate the aesthetic of sensual form in fleeting time.

Genevieve Slomski

GAMBLING

Author: Charles Baudelaire (1821-1867)
Type of poem: Meditation
First published: 1857, as "Le Jeu," in *Les Fleurs du mal*; English translation collected
in *Flowers of Evil*, 1982

The Poem

"Gambling" (also translated as "Gamblers") is a twenty-four line poem, divided into six stanzas. Each line contains twelve syllables and is thus an Alexandrine, which has been a traditional verse form used by French poets for centuries. Each stanza observes the same *abab* rhyme scheme.

Charles Baudelaire included this poem in the section entitled "Tableaux parisiens" (Parisian Scenes) in *The Flowers of Evil*; "Parisian Scenes" is the second of the six sections in the book. In "Parisian Scenes," Baudelaire described diverse aspects of daily life in Paris from personal perspectives.

This poem is a third-person narrative for the first three stanzas. In the last three stanzas, Baudelaire switches to first-person narration. These two different perspectives enable one to appreciate more thoroughly the complexity of the narrator's subjective perceptions.

In the first three stanzas, one finds an apparently objective description of self-destructive men and women who spend their evenings in Parisian gambling casinos. He compares the women to garishly dressed prostitutes and the men to poets who "squander" their talents in such unproductive activities as gambling.

In the fourth stanza, the narrator informs the reader that this scene seems nightmarish to him. He sees himself in the casino observing the gamblers, he looks at them from a corner of the room. Although he is repulsed by the whores and poets who demean themselves by "selling" their "honor" and "beauty," he is nevertheless envious of these gamblers, who can concentrate their attention so exclusively and so passionately on such a frivolous yet addictive diversion, one which will restrict significantly their personal freedom of action. Although the narrator is revolted by the moral degradation shown by the gamblers, he realizes that their behavior mirrors similar self-destructive tendencies in himself as well.

Forms and Devices

"Gambling" illustrates well Baudelaire's belief that a truly original writer should be a visionary realist who expresses profound insights into everyday scenes and situations which readers can recognize easily. Baudelaire describes the physical and moral degradation caused by the addiction to gambling. In the first three stanzas, Baudelaire states that the poets and aged whores are frequenting a casino whose "shabby armchairs," "dirty ceilings," and "dusty chandeliers" seem to suggest the emptiness in the lives of the gamblers. The gamblers will find neither wealth nor aesthetic pleasure there. In a vain effort to impress their customers, the whores put on excessive mascara and cheap earrings, but their makeup and jewelry make one only more conscious of the lack of moral and physical beauty both in the whores and in the amoral men who purchase their services. The men who frequent this casino are equally superficial. Baudelaire states that the poets are "famous," but their fame is presumably in their own minds. The hours which they spend in casinos could have been used to create poems, but they have chosen to "squander" their talents here.

By the end of the third stanza, it appears that "Gambling" will be a fairly predictable poem about the moral degradation which can result from this addictive behavior. A significant transition occurs, however, in the fourth stanza. The scene in the casino provokes in the narrator a terrifying nightmare. He imagines that he is seeing himself in this degrading scene. Although he claims to be indifferent to the gamblers, he still feels "envious" of their "stubborn passion." Baudelaire stresses the identification which the narrator feels for the gamblers by ending the fourth stanza and beginning the fifth stanza with the same French word, *enviant*, which can mean both "envious" and "envying." Their passion results in nothing worthwhile, but by means of the oxymoron in the words "deadly gaiety" (*funèbre gaïeté* in French), Baudelaire conveys the painful truth that "gaiety" brings both ephemeral pleasure and eternal suffering. Although their lives may seem meaningless to many people, these gamblers may have, in fact, done something positive: They prefer "pain to death, and hell to nothingness." Self-destructive, they are nevertheless still alive, and some hope for moral improvement exists simply because they are not yet dead.

Baudelaire has often been described as a visionary poet because he enables his readers to appreciate more thoroughly the moral and psychological complexity in situations which they might well see with their own eyes. This poem permits and even requires two different interpretations because readers can never determine with certainty whether the depressing casino scene describes people whom the narrator actually saw or whether it is the artistic representation of a nightmare experienced by the narrator. Each of these interpretations, however, complements the other. In the first three stanzas, Baudelaire has his readers "see" the self-destructive behavior of these gamblers, but in the fourth stanza, the narrator "sees" himself "in a corner of that hushed den." This nightmarish vision enables the narrator first to see and then to understand the psychological similarities between himself and these pitiful gamblers.

Themes and Meanings

The very title *The Flowers of Evil* indicates that its main theme will be an exploration of the dark side of the human condition. In the book's prefatory poem, "Au lecteur" ("To the Reader") of *The Flowers of Evil*, Baudelaire states his intention of examining self-destructive tendencies not only in society as a whole but also in himself and his readers. Baudelaire concludes his prefatory poem by addressing his reader thus: "Hypocrite reader,—my alias,—my twin," as Richard Howard translated this verse. Readers should note that Baudelaire ended this poem with the words *mon frère* ("my brother"), but Richard Howard's free translation stresses the fact that both male and female readers can recognize elements of their personality in *The Flowers of Evil*.

The poem "Gambling" reinforces well the general theme in *The Flowers of Evil*, which most critics consider to be the most psychologically profound book of poetry written in France during the nineteenth century. Despite their efforts to hide their mediocrity behind makeup and jewelry, the gamblers still reveal their "pitiless eyes," "colorless lips," and basic insensitivity toward others. Although the readers may not practice gambling or dress in a "garish" manner, they frequently act selfishly and "squander" talents. Baudelaire reminds them of the terrible truth that self-destructive behavior brings them pleasure and yet revolts them simultaneously.

Baudelaire defines the complicated and often contradictory nature of human personality. Like these gamblers, people seek happiness, but these superficial and ephemeral pleasures can produce only "deadly gaiety" which forces them to "sell" their "honor or beauty" in order to obtain these moments of pleasure that will inevitably cause long-term suffering. Whenever humans demean themselves, they behave like dogs "who rush so recklessly into the pit" in which they will be destroyed. Baudelaire encourages his readers to avoid making the terrible error of judgment committed by these gamblers, who believe that the only possible moral choices are between "pain" or "death" and between "hell" or "nothingness." These are false choices. Baudelaire entitled the first section of *The Flowers of Evil* "Spleen et idéal" ("Spleen and Ideal"). In both French and English, the word "spleen" refers to an organ in the upper abdomen, but it also reminds readers of the ancient medical theory of the humors which affirmed that the spleen was the physical source of all negative and depressing thoughts. Although one cannot deny the reality of self-destructive tendencies which were once explained by the psychological effect of the spleen on the personality, the "ideal" also exists. Baudelaire wants his readers to recognize the reality of both "spleen" and "ideal" and to avoid the simplistic moral choices made by the whores and poets in "Gambling." It is a visionary poem which enriches one's insights into the self-destructive tendencies in everyone. "Gambling" is a profoundly moving poem that continues to fascinate readers.

Edmund J. Campion

GARDEN

Author: H. D. (Hilda Doolittle, 1886-1961)
Type of poem: Lyric
First published: 1916, in *Sea Garden*

The Poem

"Garden" is a brief free-verse lyric, divided into two parts. None of the poem's twenty-four lines exceeds seven syllables in length, and many are shorter. The stanzas are of varying length, but each is made up of a single sentence. These formal characteristics reinforce the poem's small scale; H. D. is working on a deliberately small canvas.

Each section begins with an address to an element present in the garden: to a rose in the first part, to the wind in the second. Yet each section then modulates from the prayerlike address into a more meditative consideration of the speaker's relation to what she is describing. The terms used to describe the rose are likely to be surprising to the reader; certainly they deviate from the traditional poetic associations of roses. This rose is "clear" and "hard" and, metaphorically, "cut in rock." the traditionally delicate flower is described as almost unbreakable: "if I could break you/ I could break a tree."

The lines that follow hint at a transition to the description of heat and wind in section 2. The speaker wonders if she can find the strength or will to move: "if I could stir." This lassitude prepares for the summery vision of stillness and heat that dominates the "thick air" of the second section. The wind that is addressed in the first and third sentences of this section seems present only in the speaker's imagination. She longs for a wind to "rend open the heat," and she imagines that the force of the heat shapes the pears and grapes into round forms in the gauzy air. Images of the wind cutting or tearing open this oppressive atmosphere dominate the second section, and the poem concludes with an imagined image of the wind plowing the heat like a field.

The poem does not give a detailed description of the garden it names in the title. Instead, the poet concentrates on a few specific images that suggest a season and a mood more than an elaborate picture. The reader does learn that the garden contains a rose, a pear tree, and some grape vines. If the poet is interested in visual detail or richness, she apparently wishes to communicate it through a few well-chosen images rather than through a descriptive catalog.

This poem is from H. D.'s early and important Imagist period. The term "Imagist" was coined, rather fancifully, by Ezra Pound, specifically in reference to H. D.'s smaller poems. For a brief period in the second decade of the 1900's, imagism became a movement, adopted by others, including Richard Aldington, Amy Lowell, and Pound himself (whose two-line poem "In a Station of the Metro" is a classic example of the style). All these poets sought a clear-cut, direct presentation of simple images in a fresh way; they were reacting against the flowery and elaborate style characteristic of much late nineteenth century verse. H. D. was influenced by her reading of Greek poetry, particularly the poetry of Sappho, which survives only in fragments. These fragmentary bits of lines (often from the middle of lines surviving on torn parchment) seemed to offer intriguingly suggestive possibilities for modern poets seeking a new style.

Forms and Devices

The figurative language used to describe the rose in the first two sentences of the poem is significant in its invocation of the plastic and pictorial arts. The rose is "cut in rock," suggesting sculpture; the brilliant color of the petals can be scraped off "like spilt dye," suggesting painting. These comparisons intimate how Imagist poetry sought the hardness and simplicity of the nonlinguistic art forms. Resisting flowery language, H. D. describes a flower with two references to "rock," the use of "clear" and "hard," and the repetition of "break" four times. The desire to render the soft rose as something hard and unsentimental emerges in the simple diction as well: of the fifty-one words in the first section, all but three are single syllables, and all are common, familiar words.

Word repetition is important in the second section as well, where "rend" and "cut" are both significantly repeated. A contrast emerges between the longed-for, refreshing cutting action of the wind and the still air that generates such verbs as "drop," "fall," "blunts," and "rounds." The hyperbolic assertion that the thick air actually shapes the fruit is reinforced with alliteration: "through this thick" appears in the line before "fruit" and "fall," while the *p* sound unites "presses up," "points," "pears," and "grapes."

"Garden" is essentially a poem of images, and much of the interest in the poem lies in how H. D. keeps those images fresh and intriguing. As well as borrowing imagery from sculpture and painting, she subtly sets in motion unusual connections. The strength of the rose, which the speaker asserts can only be broken with the strength it would take to break a tree, becomes an oppressive heat that can only be broken or torn apart by the natural force of the wind. The imagery suggestive of violent action all exists in the imagined realm of the poem. On the literal level, stasis dominates, with the unbreakable rose and the "fruit" that "cannot drop/ through this thick air."

The use of figurative language is part of the poem's freshness. The addresses to the rose and the wind are implicit personifications, and they locate the speaker as one whose utterance is an appeal to natural forces beyond her control. The hardness of the rose is compared in a simile to "the descent of hail"; the images of cutting apart the heat or "rend[ing] it to tatters" metaphorically turn the concept of heat into a concrete object, like cloth. The final metaphor, asking the wind to "plough through" the heat, combines the personification of the wind (here, appropriately enough, compared to a farmer tilling the soil) with the metaphoric transformation of warm air into something hard (like the very ground of the garden). None of these instances of figurative language is particularly startling in itself, yet the poem creates a surprisingly rich metaphoric field in its brief space.

Themes and Meanings

The very process whereby the poet captures the interaction of observing mind and perceived object through the shifting medium of language is, in a certain sense, the recurring theme of Imagist poetry. It would be a mistake to strive too hard to read the poem symbolically, or to interpret it as a document of an emotional state. Nevertheless, any literary work that invokes a garden invites one to think of the Edenic garden that has so frequently animated the artistic imagination. That the poem is phrased as an invocation or prayer and makes reference to at least one kind of "fall" provides, perhaps, further grounds for this sort of consideration. If the Garden of Eden and the Fall of Man lurk behind this poem, how might it be manifest?

The only viable answer lies in the speaker's weariness and apparent powerlessness. One consequence of the Fall is humankind's entrance into the world of labor, a world in which one must work to make things grow, and struggle against barren soil, drought, and difficult climates. The oppressive heat, which, ironically, keeps the fruit from falling, reminds one that this garden is no Eden. Its hard roses and blunted pears reflect beauty in an imperfect and fallen world in which the human speaker is separate from nature, and even calls on one natural force (the wind) to relieve another (the heat). The poem is not, by any means, an allegory of the Fall. As its title and the word "fall" remind one, however, it is set in the fallen world that humans accept as natural. Some of the natural imagery may appear sexually charged, as well, and that is consistent with a depiction of a garden in the fallen world. The rounded fruits held up by the hot atmosphere are shaped by the forces pressing against them. More suggestively, the longed-for wind is seen as a force which plows open the heat, cuts it open, and rends it. The sense that the play of natural forces in the process of generation is one of violent antagonism suggests the condition of sexuality in the fallen world.

In that world, the poet wrests a momentary fragment or image. And the beauty of the poem lies in that vivid interaction of speaker, nature, and language that shapes the imagery of this deceptively simple poem. "Garden" has a simple integrity of its own, though it owes its shape in part to the poetic traditions H. D. resists or rebels against. For H. D., as for Pound, the Imagist period was an early phase in a rich poetic career; it was an important phase for its cleansing power, for the way it opened English poetry to new possibilities.

Christopher Ames

THE GARDEN

Author: Andrew Marvell (1621-1678)
Type of poem: Lyric
First published: 1681, in *Miscellaneous Poems*

The Poem

"The Garden," which comprises nine eight-line stanzas, opens with the assertion that people ordinarily confuse themselves ("amaze," with a possible pun on the "maze," a common feature of seventeenth century formal gardens) by pursuing recognition in only one field, as represented by wreaths associated with military (palm), civic (oak), and poetic (bay) achievements. Against those conventional modes of activity, the speaker, who enters the poem as "I" in the next stanza, argues for the ease and retirement embodied in the combined vegetation of the garden. Its plants, he offers, will provide the quiet and innocence he has mistakenly sought in the busy world, for such conditions result not from "society," but from "solitude."

In the third and fourth stanzas, the speaker reflects on the destructiveness of lovers, who record their passions by carving their initials on trees. The white and red (pallor and blushing) of the lovers' complexions are not actually as worthy of admiration as is the green of the restful garden. Against the intense pursuits recounted in classical mythology, specifically in Ovid's *Metamorphoses* (c. 8 C.E.), the speaker (now using the first-person plural, "we") proposes love's retreat to the security of the garden.

With the fifth stanza, the speaker exalts in his own sensuous indulgence in the rich fruits of the garden. In an environment without passionate distractions, desire is transferred to the other senses, notably to taste and touch. The next stanza, however, suggests a transition from physical to mental or intellectual fulfillment, as the mind withdraws from lesser pleasures ("from pleasure less") to those of what might be called the creative imagination. The divisiveness of worldly pursuits, whether of ambition or love, resolves to the unity implied by the annihilation of "all that's made/ To a green thought in a green shade."

The seventh stanza opens to a spiritual transcendence, as the speaker, at the slippery ("sliding") foot of a fountain or at the roots of a fruit tree (that is, at the point of origin), discards his physical being. His soul soars upwards and sings in preparation for a "longer flight" (presumably, its eventual glorification).

At this point, however, the speaker steps back from his prophetic speculation and drops into the past tense: Before the coming of Eve, man (Adam) experienced bliss, but it was not his destiny as a mortal to live alone. When he comments, "Two Paradises 'twere in one/ To live in Paradise alone," the speaker may be reasserting his view that this garden must be without the tensions of passion, or he may be restating his preference for total solitude.

The concluding stanza introduces a "skilful Gardener" who creates a sundial of flowers and herbs, thus reestablishing the world of time against the implied claims of eternity and the Edenic past of the previous two stanzas. The only industry in this garden of meditation and reflection, however, is that of the bee, which, unlike the busy humans of the opening sections, moves with the rhythms of nature.

Forms and Devices

Andrew Marvell employs iambic tetrameter in this poem, generally in the form of closed couplets. For a meditative poem, one might expect the lengthier and more formal pentameter (ten-syllable) couplet, but Marvell insists on the lighter and more lyrical line. This is not to imply that the poem is superficial in any way, but it is a reminder that the tone of the poem remains witty and even somewhat playful throughout.

Joseph Summers, in *The Heirs of Donne and Jonson* (1970), argues that Marvell pushes the claims for the superiority of retirement "to their ultimately absurd limits" in this poem. The speaker teases the "fond" (foolish) lovers in the third stanza, and when he stumbles on melons, becomes ensnared in flowers, and falls on the grass in the fifth stanza, one is not reminded so much of the Fall of Adam and Eve as of the antics of a man who has gorged himself and is left staggering drunkenly. This is not to undercut the striking imagery of that passage, with such rich assonance as "luscious clusters" of grapes which "crush" their wine on the speaker's mouth. The consonance that links the *m* and *n* sounds of "Stumbling on melons" assures him a soft fall.

In the metaphors of the sixth stanza, the mind becomes an ocean, and the created world finds complete unity as "a green thought in a green shade." The "green thought" is, presumably, life-giving and "innocent" as opposed to the destructive passions embodied in the colors red and white. Marvell's most elaborate metaphor occurs in the next stanza, where the body is regarded as clothing (a vest) to be cast aside and the soul becomes a bird with silver wings. Both metaphors are conventional enough; their impact comes from the context and from the language that Marvell uses to give them life. (Consider, for example, the verbs associated with the bird/soul: sits, sings, whets, combs, waves.)

The language of "The Garden" is conceptually charged or "loaded." The title itself suggests both a secular garden and the Garden of Eden, and Marvell fully exploits both significations. The "skilful Gardener" of the last stanza may be an ordinary horticulturalist or God Himself, and Marvell, like other poets of his age, delights in the sort of wordplay that would allow the reader to think of the "milder sun" as something other than the star around which the earth rotates. Even "time," by this stage of the poem, may refer as readily to the herb as to the hour.

Themes and Meanings

The celebration of retreat from the cares of the world is a common theme in Roman poetry, particularly that of Horace, and there is evidence that Marvell wrote "The Garden" while serving as tutor to Lord Fairfax's daughter at his country estate, Appleton House. A general of the parliamentary forces, Fairfax had retired following the recent civil war that brought Oliver Cromwell to power.

The question with respect to this theme is whether to take the poem as serious commendation of such a decision or as playful mockery of it. Marvell may well have written this poem the same year he wrote his famous "Horatian Ode upon Cromwell's Return from Ireland," in which he celebrates the "restless Cromwell" for leaving his gardens and urging his "active star." In another poem from the same period, *Upon Appleton House*, Marvell seems almost to be teasing Fairfax when he portrays him as governor of a garden in which flowers are ranked in regiments and bees perform as sentinels.

Marvell's wit clearly runs toward irony and intentional ambiguity, but there is no direct evidence that this poem was intended as anything other than a celebration of the life of ease and leisure, the contemplative life, in the face of distracting ambitions and romantic passions. How seriously, one might ask, is the reader to take the "mystical" or "transcendental" mode of the sixth and seventh stanzas? Is Marvell "anti-woman" in the eighth stanza? Perhaps what makes this three-hundred-year-old poem still worth reading is that such questions remain worth discussing. The answers to those questions, and to many others that spring from "The Garden," very likely follow from the reader's decision as to how seriously Marvell's speaker is committed to the theme of withdrawal. Perhaps it is significant that while the return of time in the closing stanza is witty and pastoral, it returns nevertheless.

Ron McFarland

GENERAL GAGE'S CONFESSION

Author: Philip Freneau (1752-1832)
Type of poem: Satire
First published: 1775

The Poem

Philip Freneau's *General Gage's Confession* is a dialogue in heroic couplets that reveals British general and royal governor of Boston Thomas Gage seeking absolution from a Catholic friar for his sins against the cause of American independence. The poet employs his poem to ridicule Gage, who was recalled to England in 1775 for ineptitude. The arrogant Gage was responsible during his term of office for igniting the Boston Tea Party and for sending of British troops to Lexington, who fired upon American militiamen and initiated the Revolutionary War. The poem lampoons Gage as the feckless instigator of all the above troubles.

The poem's subtitle is *Being the Substance of His Excellency's Last Conference with His Ghostly Father, Father Francis.* In the first of thirteen speeches between Gage and the friar, the British general relishes his recall to England but admits to Father Francis a "burden'd conscience." The friar assures him that his "deepest sins may all be purged away" through confession. In the next six exchanges of dialogue Gage admits that "faultless" young America never deserved his hate and asks if obeying his monarch's wishes was a sin. After Father Francis calmly recounts some of Gage's murderous acts against American patriots, he promises that: "A dozen masses shall discharge you clean;/ Small pains in purgatory you'll endure,/ And hell, you know, is only for the poor." For such absolution the general must "pay well the priest" and need not fear hell.

Gage, remembering that he stole sheep from the colonials, asks if theft with murder will seal his damnation. The friar quickly reminds him that although "some few Americans have bled," it was Gage's soldiers who killed them. Brushing aside Gage's concern that his soldiers murdered by his command, the friar responds,

> Let each man answer for his proper deed,
> From sins of murder I pronounce you freed,
> And this same reasoning will your honour keep
> From imputations of purloining sheep:

Then the friar warns Gage to cut short his transgressions or "the supper will be cold."

In the poem's last three speeches, Gage regrets he has earned purgatory by establishing martial law, which pitilessly imprisoned American captives, and that he had written an invective-filled letter to American general George Washington (which, historically, rejected Washington's written remonstrance about Gage's cruel treatment of American officers). Dismissing Gage's fears as groundless, the friar offers to take the blame for the general's proclamation proscribing American patriots and all Continental Congress members as traitors, and for Gage's letter to Washington. Father Francis avers that fellow "private Papists" will support such acts and consoles Gage with his final words: "Your sins in Lethe shall be swallowed up,/ I'll clear you, if you please, before we sup." In the poem's last speech, the still guilt-ridden Gage rejects the friar's easy absolution for his sins and feels condemned for his prideful, unjust acts against the American cause.

Forms and Devices

Freneau's poem of 151 lines of rhymed couplets in iambic pentameter is a dialogue between two persons: the remorseful questioner Gage, and his confessor, from whom Gage seeks answers. Within the question-and-answer framework, thirteen speeches, ranging from two to twenty lines, disclose a British officer in a supplicator role seeking exculpation of sins from the authority figure of a priest. The point of view is satirical, for contemporary readers knew that the obstinate and prideful General Gage never voiced any misgivings for his actions.

In the first exchange of dialogue, Freneau uses nature images of sailing, wind, and sea to reveal the conscience-stricken Gage being blown home from "friendless shores" while describing him in classical and biblical terms as a "second Nero" and "another Cain." The poet then puts flowery imagery in the friar's mouth, comparing Gage to "yon bright star" that "faints not" when its rays are blunted by "pestering clouds." The friar refers to Gage in slaughterhouse imagery as a "master butcher"; the friar also employs imagistic religious vocabulary ("purgatory," "heaven," "hell") when offering assurance that a "dozen masses" will save Gage from hell. Freneau trained for the ministry at Princeton (then the College of New Jersey) and was no stranger to religious terminology.

Later Freneau describes the general in the concrete imagery of a gluttonous sheep-stealer and murderer spreading "devastation thro' a guiltless land." Later, when the heartless confinement of captives is cited, biblical references are used again, when Gage is equated with Judas tempted by the devil, consigned to purgatory, but not yet punished by a heaven "to mercy swift, to vengeance slow?" Gage describes himself as " a wretched pilgrim" whose sins could not be cleansed even by penance in Palestine tearfully washing Christ's footsteps, or by washing his hands like the self-condemned Roman prelate Pontius Pilate. Like Judas, he avows he will hang himself to gain peace.

The rhythm of the iambic pentameter relentlessly conveys the growing desperation of Gage as he continually rejects the friar's oily promises of absolution and concludes his sins cannot be purged. The friar's sophistic reasoning is accented when he slyly absolves the general and minimizes his deed by placing responsibility for Gage's sins on others, suggesting that money will buy salvation and affirming that fellow Catholics will support his methods. Additionally, the rhyming couplets produce an effect of comically emphasizing the cleric's glibly false reasoning and the satirical observation of Gage disparate from his historical counterpart. Comic detachment is created in the reader, removing any sympathy for either character.

Themes and Meanings

The poem needs to be understood from the historical perspective of its author. Although Freneau's active support of the patriot cause was initially limited to his writing, he knew of events ranging from the siege of Boston and the arrival of British troops to Gage's shameful treatment of Washington's officers, the Battles of Lexington and Bunker Hill, and more. In 1778 Freneau joined the New Jersey militia and served on blockade runners until temporarily imprisoned on a British prison ship.

After his 1768 graduation from Princeton and having given up a career in divinity and teaching, American-born Freneau published in 1775 a series of poems revealing both his commitment to the American cause against Great Britain and his satirical skill. "American Liberty," later published as "The Present Situation of Affairs in North America," reviewed the background of the colonies and the beginning Revolution. Freneau praised General Washington and was contemptful of Tories, General Gage, Catholic Canada, and British king George III. Also in 1775 Freneau published "A Voyage to Boston," which included ridicule of Gage and other British generals in Boston.

After Gage's recall to England, the poet published "General Gage's Soliloquy," in which the title character doubts the future success of the British cause, and "General Gage's Confession." Both, written in heroic couplets, are burlesques of the British leader in Boston. The impetus of the latter poem was to satirize and denigrate British power, which Freneau saw as symbolized by Gage. It reflected the poet's anti-British sentiment, as many of his patriotic poems did. That Gage confesses to a mendacious friar, indicates an added satire of Catholicism probably sparked by Church support of the Loyalist cause and the 1774 Quebec Act, which officially established the Catholic Church there, thus raising fears of an established church in the colonies.

Although known during his lifetime and a century later as a political propagandist and a satirist of Federalist presidents George Washington and John Adams, Freneau became recognized as an accomplished essayist and a gifted, versatile poet. He experimented with forms, favoring the heroic couplet among others; and is considered by some critics the first true poet born on the American continent who could be called the father of American poetry. Freneau authentically led the way by turning from England and introducing a new standard of literary art.

The issue of the poem is the injustice and cruelty of British power and the false rationale of clerical powers supporting the British cause. The poem became an integral part of the poet's oeuvre treating the American cause. "General Gage's Confession" is significant in that it reflects the early and lasting concern of America's first native poet with native themes and introduces readers to not only a significant aspect of early American history and literary satire, but also a highly deserving American poet not adequately known.

Christian H. Moe

GENERAL PROLOGUE TO THE CANTERBURY TALES

Author: Geoffrey Chaucer (c. 1343-1400)
Type of poem: Narrative
First transcribed: 1387-1400, in *The Canterbury Tales*

The Poem

In the early months of 1387 Philippa Chaucer lay ill; she would die that summer or early fall. Her husband of twenty years, the courtier and author Geoffrey Chaucer, may have resolved to invoke spiritual aid for Philippa by journeying some sixty miles from their home of Kent to the cathedral at Canterbury, with its shrine to Saint Thomas Becket, murdered in 1170 and canonized three years later. By the late fourteenth century it had become one of the most popular pilgrimage sites in Europe. As the English winter yielded to spring in mid-April, perhaps Chaucer joined other pilgrims "the hooly blisful martir for to seke,/ That hem hath holpen whan that they were seeke [sick]."

A genuine journey may thus underlie the most famous fictional pilgrimage in English literature, the one recounted in *The Canterbury Tales*. The "General Prologue" sets the scene for this jaunt. The action unfolds in mid-April, a month that inspires both lust and wanderlust. In England both impulses lead people to venture to Becket's shrine.

The tone of the first sentence of eighteen lines of iambic pentameter rhymed couplets, which provides the setting, is formal and objective. Like the pilgrimage itself, this stately mood quickly vanishes in the subjective and colloquial. In homely language, though still in rhymed couplets, the narrator explains that he is preparing to embark on a journey to Canterbury. To that end he has lodged for the night at the Tabard Inn in Southwark, just outside London's walls. In the evening he is joined by "nyne and twenty in a compaignye,/ Of sondry folk," all of whom are also going to Canterbury. If one adds up the ensuing list of travelers, one finds that in fact there are thirty.

Chaucer identifies the pilgrims by their occupations, beginning with the respectable Knight, the Knight's son the Squire, and the Squire's Yeoman, and concluding with an unsavory lot consisting of the Reeve (estate manager), Miller, Summoner, Pardoner, Manciple (college purser), and the narrator himself. In quick, bold strokes Chaucer describes most of the twenty-seven men and three women, noting the most revealing features of each. He mentions the Prioress's golden brooch with its crowned *A*, the Monk's gold pin that fastens his hood under his chin, the Merchant's manner of riding "hye on horse," the Wife of Bath's gapped teeth, the Summoner's baldness.

After everyone has supped, their host, Harry Bailly, who actually owned the Tabard Inn in 1387, proposes that the travelers pass the time by telling stories. The trip to Canterbury from London would require four days, as would the return. Each pilgrim would tell two stories on the way to the shrine and two on the homeward journey.

Bailly would accompany the pilgrims, and whoever, in his opinion, told the best tale would receive a free meal at the Tabard Inn at the others' expense at the end of the expedition.

The next morning the pilgrims and their Host set off. At the "wateryng of Seint Thomas," a brook at the second milestone on the Kent Road, Bailly instructs the pilgrims to draw lots to determine who will begin the story-telling contest. The Knight wins the right to tell the first story, and so the "General Prologue" ends by neatly segueing into "The Knight's Tale."

Forms and Devices

The "General Prologue" is analogous to a Gothic processional with individual portraits. The roll call of characters accords with the medieval dedication to hierarchy, beginning with the Knight, proceeding through those of middle state, and concluding with the corrupt Summoner and Pardoner. This party of some thirty divides into various smaller groups: the Knight, Squire, and Squire's Yeoman; the Prioress, Second Nun, and three priests; the Reeve and Miller; and the Summoner and Pardoner. In some instances the figures in the subgroup coexist peacefully. The Squire carves his father's meat, which the Squire's Yeoman apparently catches. The Summoner and Pardoner may be lovers. The Miller and Reeve, on the other hand, clearly are antagonists. The Miller leads the procession out of town, while the Reeve brings up the rear. The Miller is as fat as the Reeve is lean. These differences foreshadow a future falling out between the two. Chaucer recognized that he could enhance the interest of his anthology by allowing the narrators to interact with each other, to comment on both tales and tellers. No exchanges occur within the "General Prologue," but the groupings here anticipate later affinities and antipathies.

The poet Chaucer places the pilgrim Chaucer at the end of the hierarchically arranged catalogue to suggest that the Chaucer within the poem will not be omniscient. He has total recall of what is said, but he never learns all the pilgrims' names. Further, he is naïve. He imagines that the Physician loves gold because gold is useful in compounding medicines. He calls the Summoner "a gentil harlot [rascal] and a kynde;/ A bettre felawe sholde men noght fynde." What elicits this seeming praise is the Summoner's willingness to overlook sexual indiscretions for a small bribe of wine. The pilgrim Chaucer says that both the Monk and Summoner arrange marriages for young women of their acquaintance. He never suggests what the reader infers—that these churchmen have first made the women pregnant.

Indeed, none of the details that the narrator conveys is as innocent as it seems because to the medieval mind all was symbolic. The gap in the teeth of the Wife of Bath connotes lasciviousness. The bagpipe that the Miller plays indicates from its shape that he is gluttonous and lecherous. Chaucer dresses his Knight in cheap English homespun to imply a forthright simplicity. The Knight is so devout that he has not even taken the time to clean his habergeon (short chest armor) before embarking for Canterbury from his latest foreign combat.

Themes and Meanings

In his preface to *Fables Ancient and Modern* (1700) the seventeenth century poet laureate John Dryden commented that *The Canterbury Tales* offers the reader "God's plenty," that here one finds "the various manners and humours . . . of the whole English nation in [Chaucer's] age." The "General Prologue" does indeed portray a cross-section of fourteenth century England's middle class. Although both Chaucer and his wife belonged to court circles, none of the pilgrims come from the aristocracy, nor are any of them destitute. The picture that Chaucer presents is at least in part painted from life. The Cook who accompanies the five guildsmen bears the name, if not all the traits, of the actual victualer Hodge of Ware. The Merchant may be patterned after Gilbert Mawfield, to whom Chaucer and some of his friends owed money. The Prioress speaks French in the manner of one from Stratford-at-Bow. Near that town was the Benedictine convent of St. Leonard's. Chaucer's first audiences may have recognized the model for his worldly nun.

Realism is not, however, reality. Chaucer made his characters memorable by drawing on literary convention as well as on his own experiences, particularly on estates satire, popular at the time. The late fourteenth century in England witnessed the rise of Lollardism, which attacked clerical corruption. The Prioress of the "General Prologue" shows kindness to animals but not to people. Both the Monk and Friar are lecherous, and the Pardoner is a charlatan who sells pigs' bones as saints' relics. The Reeve and Manciple grow rich by cheating their employers; the Miller steals from his customers.

Even though the majority of the pilgrims here are flawed, Chaucer treats almost all of them kindly. The Prioress's attempt to ape courtly manners has its charm, even its pathos. The Monk appears to have no more real religious vocation that the Prioress, but in the "General Prologue" he seems to be a jolly companion. The Franklin is an epicurean who is perhaps overly concerned with a good meal for himself, but he is also a St. Julian, the patron of hospitality. Most of the failings one sees in the pilgrims are venial rather than mortal. The satire is further tempered by the recognition that corruption is not universal. The Knight embodies the ideals of chivalry. The Clerk (student) of Oxford loves learning. Even if his fellow ecclesiastics do not live up to their vows, the Parson is a model priest, and his brother the Plowman an exemplary layman.

The "General Prologue" re-creates a lively image of Chaucer's world. If the sinners outnumber the saints, the picture is perhaps the truer for this imbalance and certainly more entertaining. Chaucer here weaves a medieval tapestry with characters as eternally vibrant as they were when they assembled at Southwark on that April evening toward the end of the fourteenth century to begin their immortal journey, on which they are forever embarked.

Joseph Rosenblum

GENERAL WILLIAM BOOTH ENTERS INTO HEAVEN

Author: Vachel Lindsay (1879-1931)
Type of poem: Elegy
First published: 1913, in *General William Booth Enters into Heaven and Other Poems*

The Poem

"General William Booth Enters into Heaven" is a short, fifty-six line, rhymed elegy. It is divided into two sections. The first section contains two stanzas, totaling twenty-three lines, and the second section contains five stanzas, totaling thirty-three lines. The title establishes the dramatic setting of the poem—General Booth's ascension into the glory of heaven. The poem makes heavy use of repetition and onomatopoeia.

The poem is written in third-person, omniscient, simple narration. No attention is drawn to the narrator, as the narration is intended to report, rather than interpret, the events of the poem. In the modern tradition of the elegy, "General Booth Enters into Heaven" is a dignified and climactically glorifying chronicle. This form of simple narration is intended to recite events and is largely chronological, creating a you-are-there presentation.

The poem takes as its subject the ascent into heaven of a well-respected, generous, self-sacrificing historical figure; Booth was the founder of the Salvation Army. The qualities that the general possessed in life not only permit his ascension but also, by extension, elevate the status of the street people that surround him and to whom he dedicated his life to helping. Through his intervention, they accompany him to heaven.

Vachel Lindsay based the poem on the cadences and tune of the Salvation Army hymn "The Blood of the Lamb" and included parenthetical instructions for the poem's recitation, such as "Bass drum slower and softer" and "Sweet flute music." The poem combines Salvation Army oratory and lyricism. With its variations of rhythm and volume and its many contrasts, the poem moves between tension and celebration. Lindsay was very proud that his poems could be danced to (yet he repeatedly said that poetry is intended primarily for the reader's inner ear, which is a source of truth). His intent was usually to evoke emotional responses. Lindsay's greatest successes occur when he captures his own excitement concerning his subjects.

"General William Booth Enters into Heaven" is a good example of the simple emotional appeal of Lindsay's poems. The poem is stately and moves inevitably toward its resounding climax, a movement that is accompanied by the sounds of a Salvation Army band. The first stanza begins with the sound of a bass drum booming loudly. In this stanza the reader (or listener) is introduced to the subject, Booth, the people he helped, and the reaction of the saints to his heralded arrival. The second stanza is accompanied by the sounds of banjos, as a catalog of Booth's accomplishments is presented. In the third stanza, Booth's faith is chronicled; his faith persevered despite physical blindness, and, through the image of an eagle, Lindsay makes it clear that his blindness only increased the power of Booth's inner, spiritual sight. The fourth, fifth, and sixth stanzas, accompanied by flute, bass drum again, and then a "grand chorus of all instruments," depict the arrival of Booth at heaven's gate. He is met by Jesus and is accompanied by the unfortunate people he had struggled to help in his lifetime of service. Finally, in the concluding stanza, Booth and "King Jesus" meet face to face. The accompanying music is voice only, no instruments, and is "reverently sung."

Forms and Devices

The first line of the poem is one example of the subtle and intimate qualities of Lindsay's verse. The first metrical foot of the first line is composed of three long syllables. Thereafter, syncopation is achieved through the use of feet composed of two short syllables. Lindsay intersperses trochees (feet of two syllables, of which the first syllable is long or stressed and the second short or unstressed) for vigor and anapests (feet of three syllables, the first two short or unstressed and the last long or stressed) to create the banging drum effects and to imitate marching time. These examples of the noises usually associated with Salvation Army gatherings are also good examples of onomatopoeia in poetry. Under the poem's title, Lindsay wrote in parentheses that it is "To be sung to the tune of 'The Blood of the Lamb' with indicated instrument." Each stanza is preceded by a notation on that stanza's intended accompaniment.

Throughout the poem, Lindsay makes effective use of repetition. A stately, mournful, but triumphant effect is produced by the bass drum, which is parenthetically included as accompanying the first and fifth stanzas. Moreover, the line "Are you washed in the blood of the Lamb?" is repeated throughout the poem. In the first and second stanzas, the line occurs parenthetically, almost as an afterthought. By the conclusion of the poem, the question occupies the critical final line. No longer a parenthetical question, it forcefully stands out after Booth has been depicted entering heaven and being received by Jesus, challenging the reader to address his or her own life in comparison to the self-sacrificing and ultimately rewarding life of William Booth. Repetition of this sort, for emotional effect, is frequent in the poetry of Lindsay.

Themes and Meanings

Vachel Lindsay had the Salvation Army in mind when he wrote "General William Booth Enters into Heaven," and he wanted his readers to hear its noise and activity. Lindsay was not a great technical poet; rather, he was, in the tradition of Walt Whitman, filled with passion regarding America, American heroes, American religion, democracy, and American beauty. His purpose in his poetry, as can be seen in "General William Booth Enters into Heaven," lay in finding and expressing the soul of America and giving it voice.

This poem expresses that purpose and vision. It is a mixture of history and myth, and it works to create a context for an idealized type of American identity. Much of his work was an attempt to break down the regional and group differences that worked against a sense of America and of being American. William Booth was one of Lindsay's heroes whom he attempted to place in an American context, a context designed to create a particularly American history. Lindsay attempted similar projects, for example, with Native Americans, Johnny Appleseed, and Presidents Abraham Lincoln, George Washington, and Andrew Jackson.

Lindsay had experience with the Salvation Army at first hand and did indeed have the great respect for the organization and its founder that the poem shows. Lindsay wrote that when he was "dead broke, and begging" in Atlanta, Georgia, he slept at the Salvation Army shelter there. Lindsay was, for a period of his life, a part of that lowest level of society that Booth had established the Salvation Army to reach and save from degradation. According to Lindsay, he wrote this poem while spending an entire night walking around a park in Los Angeles.

David Lawrence Erben

GEORGIA DUSK

Author: Jean Toomer (1894-1967)
Type of poem: Lyric
First published: 1922; collected in *Cane,* 1923

The Poem

"Georgia Dusk" is a short poem of twenty-eight lines divided into seven stanzas. The basic rhythm is iambic pentameter; in each stanza, the first and fourth and the second and third lines rhyme (*abba, cddc*). The title establishes a specific time of day and geographical location. In the poem, Toomer presents the emotions evoked by the end of a day in the Deep South.

Jean Toomer begins with the sky, herald of sunset. As he paints a picture of the colorful sky, he creates a mood. The sky is too lazy and passive to prolong the splendid sunset. The reader is encouraged to adopt a similar mood, one that is receptive to the sequence of emotions presented by the poem.

The last word of stanza 1 announces the special event of this night, a "barbeque." With this announcement, the mood shifts in the second stanza from indolence and passivity to song and activity. Toomer indicates that the activity is secret and at least partly religious in nature. The night's "feast" will be an "orgy," as people with "blood-hot eyes" express their deepest emotions in song. The reader is invited to watch and listen along with the poet.

After introducing the African Americans who are celebrating, Toomer shifts the mood again in stanza 3, returning to the quiet picture of the Georgia scene. While human activity stops with the sound of the sawmill whistle, the growing season of nature continues. References to "pollen" and "plowed lands" indicate that the time of year is early spring.

The peaceful picture of nature continues in stanza 4. Smoke from the smoldering mound of sawdust lingers close to the ground before rising to join the sunset sky. Stanza 5 returns to the people. The poet now recognizes in their celebration signs of a lost civilization. Recollections of an "ostrich" and a "juju-man" confirm that these are traces of the African societies from which the ancestors of these people were abducted. In the sixth stanza, the natural surroundings complement the songs of the people. Adding to the harmony, the pine trees seem to accompany the voices celebrating the coming of evening.

In the final stanza, the poet directly addresses the singers. As the twin sounds of pine trees and human voices continue to mingle, Toomer calls on the singers to transform the people. Moving away from the pagan connotations of some of the words mentioned earlier in the poem—"orgy," "High-priests," and "juju-man"—Toomer asks the singers to make the "cornfield concubines" sing like virgins and to give the people "dreams of Christ."

Forms and Devices

"Georgia Dusk" is a poem characterized by repetition and regularity. The patterns of rhythm and rhyme are maintained throughout all seven stanzas. The meter, iambic pentameter, is used consistently, with only a few variations. The rhyming pattern (*abba, cddc*, and so on) also remains uniform, and all of the rhymes are true rhymes. This formal regularity reflects a theme of the poem, the persistence of group memory through song and ritual. Repetition plays a key role in the way people use poetry to preserve and pass on their history.

Many sounds are repeated within the poem. Alliteration, the repetition of consonant sounds in neighboring words and syllables, often occurs in the first letters of words. Examples in the first two stanzas are "setting sun" and "moon and men," and, in the last stanza, "cornfield concubines." Sometimes Toomer multiplies this effect by alliterating two or more sounds in a single line. The third line of stanza 3 is a good example: "Soft settling pollen where plowed lands fulfill." In this line, Toomer alliterates the *s* sound of the first two words ("Soft settling"), the *p* sound of two other words ("pollen" and "plowed"), the *f* sound in the first and last words ("Soft" and "fulfill"), and the *l* sound that appears in five of the seven words of the line.

Toomer uses other poetic devices to present the idea that the natural world acts in concert with the human world. One device is personification, attributing human qualities or feelings to an inanimate object or an abstract concept. The opening description of the sky as too proud and lazy to chase the sunset is one example.

In the last two stanzas, Toomer uses another poetic device, metaphor, to connect the natural and human worlds. In metaphor, a word or phrase is applied to something to which it is not applicable literally in order to suggest an imaginative comparison. To show how the sound of the pine trees in the wind seemingly blends with the singing of the people, Toomer calls the trees "guitars,/ Strumming." The pleasant sound created by the wind moving through the pine branches makes the poet think of the strings of a guitar played by a person's fingers.

In the opening line of the last stanza, Toomer reverses the comparison. Now the people's songs are metaphorically compared to two qualities of the pines: "resinous and soft." The songs, in other words, are as pleasant to hear as resin is to smell, and they stick in one's memory. In the last line of the poem, Toomer repeats his earlier description of the people as "cane-lipped." This metaphor is based on the dark, sometimes purplish colors of sugar-cane stalks. One association that the metaphor picks up is that of lips and the sweet taste of sugar cane. In the previous stanza, the song was described as coming from the cane itself rather than from the people in the cane. These repeated metaphorical connections of the people to the cane gain greater significance when they are related to the complete work in which "Georgia Dusk" appears, the book whose title is *Cane*.

Themes and Meanings

On the simplest level, "Georgia Dusk" is a lyrical celebration of the beauty of African Americans singing in a southern landscape. As was previously mentioned,

Toomer uses various formal devices to draw attention to the harmony of song and setting. The second word in the title, "Dusk," not only establishes the time of day, but also, combined with several details in the poem, takes on a deeper symbolic meaning. As a symbol, "dusk" comes to stand for a complex of associated meanings. Uppermost among these is the implication that something is passing away. For this poem, the primary example is the great African cultures brought to America by the slaves. Toomer feels that he is witnessing the "setting sun" of the last remnants of African culture in the lives of the African Americans.

Several aspects of the poem reinforce this theme. In stanza 1, the sky will not or cannot stop the sun's setting. The "tournament" it will not hold recalls the martial glory of medieval African kingdoms. Toomer describes the smoke rising from the mound of sawdust as "blue ghosts of trees." This metaphor reflects the vanishing quality of African civilization in America. Like the countryside surrounding the sawmill, the traces of African culture are "only chips and stumps . . . left to show" the fact of "former domicile" across the Atlantic Ocean.

Stanza 5 states the theme of the surviving "vestiges" of African greatness. Several details carry African connotations: desert "caravan," "juju-man" (a word of African origin for a holy object or fetish), and "ostrich," a flightless bird found in Africa.

The change in characteristics of the ostrich seems to be paralleled by Toomer's thoughts about the history of African Americans. In the last stanza, Toomer speaks directly to the people, asking the singers to give a new content to the songs and thoughts of these people. The poet's first request is to "Give virgin lips to cornfield concubines." This statement calls for a complete transformation, for a concubine is a woman kept by a man for sexual purposes. The phrase "virgin lips" represents the opposite pole from that of "concubines" and implies other meanings. One is an association with Mary, the mother of Jesus. Another is that the changed content of these people's songs will be totally new, virginal material. Toomer has already indicated that much of the little African culture remaining is of a non-Christian religious nature. The "orgy" anticipated in stanza 2 meant originally a form of pagan secret rite, and the phrases "High-priests" and "juju-man" carry pagan connotations.

The last line of the poem is crucial. Its heavy alliteration draws attention to it. (The two accented sounds in the phrase, "dreams of Christ," are repeated in the same order in the next phrase, "dusky cane-lipped.") The content is vital to the meaning of the poem as a whole. As part of a possibly inevitable evolution, Toomer calls on the singers to alter the content of traditional songs, to lead the people to dream of Christ. Song is one of the strongest means of affecting people, with its direct, highly emotional effects on listeners. This song at dusk may be, therefore, a "vesper" in a double sense, a form of worship associated with Christianity and a farewell to the last traces of an old religion.

Samuel B. Garren

GERONTION

Author: T. S. Eliot (1888-1965)
Type of poem: Meditation
First published: 1920, in *Ara Vos Prec*

The Poem

In a letter dated July 9, 1919, to John Rodker, who was preparing T. S. Eliot's volume of poetry *Ara Vos Prec* for publication with his newly founded Ovid Press, Eliot mentions his newly completed poem "Gerontion" for possible inclusion. It became the lead, and perhaps the most significant, poem in the volume, published in February, 1920.

In critical consideration, "Gerontion" has been identified as one of the poems of the so-called Waste Land cycle of poems, the others including "The Love Song of J. Alfred Prufrock" (1917), *The Waste Land* (1922), and "The Hollow Men" (1925). Like these other works, "Gerontion" explores the hollowness of the modern age, the failure of human history to provide firm direction, and the vacuity of a life without passion or belief.

The poem casts the title character, Gerontion, a name derived from the Greek *geron* in its diminutive form, suggesting "a little old man," as reflecting in his room while being read to by a young boy. The name is apt, for Gerontion is an old man who has shrunken in upon himself by virtue of his need to think through, to analyze and scrutinize, all options rather than act upon them. As the boy reads, Gerontion's mind wanders.

Associations occur in his mental wandering. The house is owned by a Jew, which reminds Gerontion also of Christ, who was a Jew. What, Gerontion wonders, has modern humanity made of the Christ? His mind flickers over lessons from human history, all of which reveal a people preoccupied by present concerns and devoid of spiritual passion. His thoughts focus, finally, upon the state of his own mind. Gerontion's mind, too, has become a dry, sterile house of thought, devoid of passion.

Eliot's style in the poem is itself frequently elliptical and fragmentary. He places one directly inside the mind of Gerontion and lets one experience the thoughts with all the randomness with which they occur. This method makes some lines difficult to construe syntactically. For example, lines 19-23, which refer to the Communion or Mass which divides and shares Christ's body and blood, may be construed thus: In the "juvescence" (or springtime) of the year, in depraved May (because there is no rain) with its dogwood and chestnut and flowering judas, Christ the Tiger came to be eaten, to be divided, to be drunk among whispers.

The fragmentary nature of Gerontion's mind is mirrored by the fragmentary form of the poem. Thereby the poem becomes an example of the use of organic verse in modernism, a method whereby the form itself objectifies the ideas expressed. Rather than possessing a clear beginning, middle, and ending, the poem constantly intensifies the activity of the analytic mind. Gerontion is victimized by his rational scrutiny, having to examine something intellectually until the mind itself squeezes all the life and passion out of the thoughts it holds.

Finally, then, "Gerontion" is a kind of tragedy. The character's tragic flaw is the restlessness of his own mind; his tragic ending is the lack of any passionate commitment or belief that might impose some order, direction, or meaning upon such thoughts as he holds. Almost like William Shakespeare's Hamlet, Gerontion finds himself incapable of acting upon what he thinks, allowing his life to slide into futility.

Forms and Devices

T. S. Eliot was one of the pioneers of modernism, a technique whereby images in the poem, frequently discordant and jarring, fuse together to provide an emotion related to, or an insight upon, the modern age.

Significant in "Gerontion" are images of aridity that capture the lack of passionate belief in the modern age. Gerontion is being read to "in a dry month" and he is "waiting for rain." The rain, which signifies for Eliot renewal and redirection, never comes in this poem. Thus the poem is placed in close relation with *The Waste Land*, in which the desertlike aridity mirrors the spiritual and intellectual poverty of the modern age. The dryness, finally, is internal. People lose passion and conviction. In this poem, only the mind, never the heart, works like a spider, spinning webs of thought that the wind tears apart.

Juxtaposed to this lack of vigorous passion is the advent of Christ, imaged in this poem as a tiger in an allusion to William Blake's symbol of the union of God and humanity. The sign for which the people have looked, however, is "swaddled in darkness," unclear and indistinct to modern searching. Since the sign is unclear, modern people decipher it in their own ways, trying to tame the tiger to fit their mental constructs.

Gerontion cautions that all such constructs are futile, for finally the tiger will devour humankind. Gerontion suggests that death—what he describes as stiffening in a rented house—is not the end of the matter. There will also be a judgment. All this he knows intellectually, but he is unable to grasp it with the heart. He has, as he says, lost his passion.

Themes and Meanings

"Gerontion" is structured in six stanzas. The first introduces the narrator, who describes himself as an old man who has never really done much with his life. He has had no passionate involvements, no great battles, and is mindful only of living in a "decayed house," by which he refers both to his physical house and to his aging body.

In the second stanza, Gerontion begins reflecting upon the spiritual poverty of the modern age. People look for signs, an echo of the biblical passage in John 4:48, but do not pay attention to the sign of the Christ who has come. Instead, modern humanity is typified by four characters. For the art dealer Mr. Silvero, Limoges enamels are mere objects to be bought and sold. Their preciousness is reduced merely to a bartering value. Hakagawa bows among the Titian paintings, but he is the outsider, not really a part of their culture. He represents a person simply "going through the motions" without any vital involvement. Madame de Tornquist, who presides over a seance, represents the debasement of religious belief to the occult and the search for immediate signs. Fräulein von Kulp simply walks away, repudiating religious belief altogether. Like the wind, these characters, and Gerontion himself, have no sense of a whole religious passion or pattern.

In the third stanza, Gerontion ponders the course of human history, looking for answers or forgiveness to the knowledge of his and humanity's lack of passion. Yet history itself is a maze, "cunning corridors" of human ambitions, and provides only enough taste of the truth to make one hunger for more. Everything, including the human conception of virtue, becomes relative merely to the age itself. This knowledge of futility, says Gerontion, is shaken from "the wrath-bearing tree," which suggests the cross of Christ, the fig tree cursed by Christ for failing to bear fruit, and the Edenic tree of the knowledge of good and evil.

With this realization of human futility, in stanza 4 Gerontion sees Christ, formerly imaged as a tiger, as a devourer, snapping human hollowness under his jaws. Gerontion feels himself nearing death and claims that he is genuinely struggling with the meaning of Christ in an age without apparent meaning. Forlornly, he claims that he, too, has lost his passion, having forsaken it simply for discursive thought and rational scrutiny.

Finally, in the fifth stanza, he sees the thoughts of the poem itself as cold and sterile, a "chilled delirium." All the thoughts seem to turn inward upon his own mind like "a wilderness of mirrors." They whirl and spin like the constellations above or like the wind blasting across the Horn—the tip of South America. As the winds of modernity blow new socialites—De Bailhache, Fresca, Mrs. Cammel—into oblivion, so too they blow Gerontion into a tiny little speck of humanity.

So the sixth and last stanza, a mere two lines, looks back on the entire poem, the entire process of reflection he has gone through, and announces that it is no more than "Thoughts of a dry brain in a dry season." The final portrait of the poem suggests the complete insufficiency of human reason to locate a way out of the spiritual poverty of the wasteland.

John H. Timmerman

THE GIFT

Author: Jean Burden (1914-   )
Type of poem: Lyric
First published: 1992, in *Taking Light from Each Other*

The Poem

"The Gift" is a twenty-eight-line poem written in free verse. Under the title, Jean Burden dedicates the poem "for Cristy." Writing in the first person, Burden reveals the nature of the gift in the first two lines: "You gave me the socks/ off your feet." Possessing a wry wit, Burden parodies the expression "the shirt off your back" with these opening lines. Although Cristy's age and relationship to the poet are never precisely identified, it seems clear that Cristy is much younger than Burden and that they must be very close friends. In reality, Cristy was a young woman in her twenties and nearly forty years younger than the poet at the time of the poem's writing. Written in 1976, "The Gift" is one of a number of poems that Burden composed while staying at the MacDowell Colony, a colony for artists located in Peterborough, New Hampshire.

The socks, "dark blue, striped in red and white,/ with embroidered clocks of cats," are given to the poet in a restaurant. Cristy states matter-of-factly, " 'Of course you must have them.' " The waitress in the poem is startled by the sight of Cristy removing her socks; "Demure/ in Japanese kimono," she "almost spilled the tea" when Cristy strips "to pink toes." After being given the colorful socks, Burden says, she placed them "in a napkin/ and stuffed them in my Gucci bag." She and Cristy then left the restaurant and "squeaked up Park Avenue." With the identification of Park Avenue, it is clear that Burden and Cristy are in New York City. As they walk, Cristy is wearing her "leather boots" with "sockless feet," and the poet, in contrast, feels "embarrassingly/ over-shod."

Reflecting on how generous Cristy was and how the poet desires to balance the scales, Burden comments, "I never gave you anything/ as right as that/ except once—a fossil polished/ by the sea." Since Cristy has been such a loyal friend and given up even the socks off her feet, Burden understandably wants to do right by her friend. Cristy lets it be known that the socks cost only forty-nine cents. Burden plays on this fact by concluding the poem with the lines "Nothing comes out even./ The stone was free." Without bombast, she has employed subtle humor to talk about the real value of any gift. The appropriateness of a gift is not contingent on its monetary value. It is indeed, as the saying goes, the thought that counts.

Forms and Devices

In numerous other poems Burden has shown herself to be adept at using common speech in original ways. In "The Gift" the poet addresses the reader in a direct manner rather than employing a persona to express some experience that is not her own. What transpires in the poem is Burden's own experience. Cristy is a real person, and she did give the poet her socks in a New York restaurant. Although "The Gift" is written in free verse, there is nonetheless a subtle lyrical rhythm in the poem. The lines of the poem are condensed. Burden is a master of the delicate observation, of creating a well-modulated poem through spare and understated images. Without relying on cliché or worn-out phrases, she uses common language to create fresh images. Although Robert Frost once described writing free verse as "playing tennis without a net," there is a need for discipline in free verse just as there is in any other poetic form. Burden uses precise language to convey sights and sounds. One of the sound devices that Burden employs is alliteration, the repetition of initial consonant sounds of words that are in close proximity. In "The Gift" there are *s* sounds with such words as "socks," "striped," "staid," "stripping," "spilled," "stuffed," "squeaked," "said," and "stone." While in untrained hands alliteration can be over used and thus awkward or ponderous, Burden drops in the appropriate sound precisely where needed.

In her 1966 essay collection *Journey Toward Poetry*, Burden speaks about the need for poems to possess simplicity without being simpleminded, to be stripped of artifice, and to speak in a straightforward manner. As the poetry editor of *Yankee* magazine, beginning in 1955, and a veteran poetry teacher, Burden believes strongly that a poem should be filled with the poet's vision. When a specific event is related honestly and freshly, it can become an experience with which the reader can identify. While "The Gift" may seem slight and does not demand to be seen as a "consequential" poem, its value grows through its quiet use of humor. The idea that humor or wit is employed only by poets who are writing lightweight poems is a severe underestimation of the value of humor in contemporary poetry. Humor is a very human response to many monumental concerns, and it can provide a fresh viewpoint to an age-old problem. In "The Gift" Burden uses a quirky and amusing experience to speak about friendship, sacrifice, and obligation to those one loves.

Themes and Meanings

Although written in 1976, "The Gift" was not collected until 1992 with the publication of Burden's second poetry collection, *Taking Light from Each Other.* Her first collection, *Naked as the Glass,* was published in 1963. *Taking Light from Each Other* is divided into five sections, and "The Gift" is included in the fourth section of the book. As with other poems of the section, it celebrates the value of interpersonal relationships with pointed observation and cunning wit. No matter how serious the topic, Burden never loses sight of the playful ordering of words. She approaches the favor that Cristy did for her without sentimentality. Although unorthodox, the giving of socks is a magnificent gesture of friendship. A true friend will make a sacrifice even in a public place where it could be awkward or embarrassing. While Cristy feels no qualms in giving up her socks, the poet puts them away in a bag. The reader has a sense that these are two unique individuals who express themselves in their own personal ways. Burden recognizes what has been done for her and regrets that she has not done more for her good and loyal friend.

The cost of the socks was forty-nine cents, almost nothing, but in comparison with a stone that was free, they were expensive. As Burden states, "Nothing comes out even." Between friends and between lovers, good deeds cannot be balanced in a ledger. It is self-evident that people who are close will want to help each other when the need arises, and Burden uses one humorous incident to make this larger point. As with many of her poems in *Taking Light from Each Other,* Burden has written freshly, lovingly, humorously, and convincingly about the complexities of human relationships.

Jeffry Jensen

THE GIFT OUTRIGHT

Author: Robert Frost (1874-1963)
Type of poem: Narrative
First published: 1942, in *A Witness Tree*

The Poem

Robert Frost's "The Gift Outright," perhaps most famous for having been read by the author at President John F. Kennedy's inauguration on January 20, 1961, discusses the relationship between Americans and America. In its sixteen iambic pentameter lines, the poem questions and affirms Americans' history as a nation.

Frost begins by setting out the major argument of the poem: "The land was ours before we were the land's." He proceeds to explain and clarify that statement. The physical land of America, the plot of earth itself, acts as a major player in the work, the "she" and "her" of his lines. Personifying the land this way results in making it an equal partner with the "we" and "our," the American citizens who act as the other player.

Frost summarizes the history and politics of the formation of the country by elaborating on this relationship, the "gift" of the title that Americans could not accept without surrendering to it. In the metaphor of the poem, the land gave itself to its citizens while America was still a British colony, so that its people did not "possess" it but merely inhabited it. The first half of the poem sets forth this concept. The second half explains what happened to make Americans "her people." According to the poem, the "gift" of the title had to be earned by both sides before becoming a gift "outright."

In this poem, one sees many distinctive characteristics of Frost's poetry: the conversational tone, the words of everyday speech, and the literary devices that create the meter, rhythm, and "sound" of his poetry. While succeeding in sounding like everyday speech, "The Gift Outright" employs many traditional poetic devices; in fact, one of the greatest achievements of Frost's poetry results in the straightforwardness of its prose and word choices belying the poetic nature of the work itself.

The poem summarizes early American history while also making a political and human statement about the responsibilities of citizenship and ownership. Americans, he argues, cannot claim title to the land without making sacrifices and contributing labor to it. While on one hand citizens "possess" the country, on the other they must assume the responsibilities and commitment to its growth and success. This duality of rights and responsibilities appears in line 10, when he refers to it as "our land of living." Americans not only live there and derive their "living" from it but also must accept the "surrender" implicit in this relationship.

Frost combines the political and the personal, the narrative and the poetic, the historical and the present to create a poem with clear expectations of what being an American entails. While greatly emphasizing the past, Frost ends the poem with a direct relationship to the future—what the country "would become."

Forms and Devices

In its sixteen lines, "The Gift Outright" presents a straightforward commentary on the history of the country, beginning literally with the land, the earth itself. Throughout, Frost personifies the physical earth, the "she" of the poem. Citizens of the country and the country itself engage in a relationship, with each side claiming ownership, although on different timetables, of the other. Frost relies on the argument—the recounting of history—to carry the meaning; therefore, one does not find heavy use of symbolism or double meanings. Given the conversational tone, the choice of straightforward words, and the lack of rhyme, at first glance the poem may seem rather "unpoetic" in its structure and style. However, Frost carefully crafts that very casualness. He combines meter and sound to create memorable and beautiful phrases, such as "vaguely realizing westward" and "unstoried, artless, unenhanced."

The poem has no stanza breaks; however, rhetorically, it can be divided in two. In its simplest terms, the poem says that the land welcomed and possessed settlers for more than one hundred years before they welcomed and possessed the land. Only with "surrender" and the "gift . . . of war" did the relationship become reciprocal. Lines 1-8 set forth the first half of that argument, expanding and explaining his first line. Lines 9-16 set forth the second half. Here Frost develops his narrative to expand and explain the change. While variations occur, Frost uses regular meter (iambic pentameter). One of Frost's greatest achievements was making such regular poetry sound like conversational speech, artistry easy to overlook because of its success.

Frost uses balance in sentences, rhythm, and repetitions of sounds to create the conversational tone of the poem. In the first line, he sets up the two sides: "The land was ours before we were the land's./ She was our land more than a hundred years/ Before we were her people." The narrative goes back and forth between the land's relationship to humans and their relationship to it. Repetitive sentence structure creates balanced sentences and rhetorical oppositions. Examples can be found in lines 1-3 with the "before" clauses, lines 6 and 7 with "possessed," lines 8-10 with "withholding," and lines 12 and 16 with "such as."

Frost also employs repetition of vowel sounds (assonance), beginning with the first lines: "land," "was," "than," and "we," " were," "years," "her." Vowel repetitions are used again in lines 6 and 7: "Possessing what we were still unpossessed by,/ Possessed by what we now no more possessed." The poem uses such repetitions of sounds throughout. Sometimes the same word repeats, as noted above. Other times Frost repeats certain sounds, as the *st* in "still unstoried" in line 15 and the *ou* in "ourselves outright" in line 12. Frost also uses the repetition of initial consonant sounds (alliteration): "possessing" and "possessed" in lines 6 and 7; "we," "were," "withholding," and "weak," in line 8; "land of living" in line 10; and "forthwith found" and "salvation in surrender" in line 11.

Themes and Meanings

"The Gift Outright" serves as history, narrative, metaphor, and political statement. Its subject matter—the origins and future of the United States of America—makes it a logical choice for his presentation at President Kennedy's inauguration. It serves as both a reminder of the past and a call to action for the future.

Frost begins with no proper nouns to orient readers to his subject matter; he draws them in by his use of pronouns—the corporate and individual meanings of "we" and the land as "she." He refers to the "hundred years" preceding the designation as "her people." He next refers to Massachusetts and Virginia, setting his geographical location, and with "we were . . . still colonials" he sets the time. The British colonized what became the United States of America, and the "we" of the poem in turn colonized the "her," the land itself, by inhabiting it without the responsibilities of possession. "Surrender," entering into a reciprocal relationship, required not "withholding . . . ourselves." The first eight lines spell out this unequal beginning. While Americans "possessed" the land, they "still were unpossessed by" it. The weakness was failure to act, to contribute, to shape the land. The first-person narration attempts to pull the reader into the feeling of responsibility and duty.

Lines 9-16 explain what happened to alter the relationship. The "gift" of the title gains complexity throughout the poem; possessing the gift of land required citizens who "gave [them]selves outright" to it, and "The deed of gift was many deeds of war." The last three lines move from the acquisition to the possession. The people gave "to the land vaguely realizing westward." While the earth clearly precedes the country, without citizens to "realize" it, a country does not exist. It remains "unstoried, artless, unenhanced."

In the end, citizens cannot receive without giving, without providing the stories (both narrative and buildings), the art (both knowledge and art forms), and the enhancements to earn title. The poem implies that an imperfect citizenry ("such as we were") must sacrifice to the imperfect land ("such as she was") in order to build something greater than the sum of its parts ("such as she would become").

Caroline Carvill

GIRL POWDERING HER NECK

Author: Cathy Song (1955-　　)
Type of poem: Lyric
First published: 1983, in *Picture Bride*

The Poem

"Girl Powdering Her Neck" is a free-verse lyric poem written in short lines of vary-ing length divided into seven stanzas, also of varying lengths. The title and descriptive subtitle ("from a ukiyo-e print by Utamaro") refer to the Japanese artist Kitagawa Utamaro (1753-1806), the best known of many Japanese printmakers working in the ukiyo-e tradition who produced sensitive studies of a privileged class of highly culti-vated and well-respected courtesans (among other subjects). The Japanese word *ukiyo-e*, commonly translated as "pictures of the floating world," suggests the transi-tory nature of beauty. Like the wood-block print that the poem's third-person narrator is describing and interpreting, the poem is a close-up view of a woman preparing her-self, as she does daily, to be the object of a transitory but beautiful encounter.

The first two stanzas describe the setting in which this woman (or "girl," according to the title) is depicted, but because the setting has already been presented by Utamaro, what the narrator offers is essentially an art critic's view of a fine print. The opening lines—"The light is the inside/ sheen of an oyster shell"—ask the reader to imagine the quality of light in the print as much as in an actual scene, a double pleasure. Yet the poem is more than an art critic's adventurous use of form; the narrator is as entranced by the story this scene suggests as the artist must have been, as can be seen in the poem's interpretation of the oyster-sheen quality of the light as "moisture from a bath." One part of the poem seems to imagine what is beyond Utamaro's print; outside "the rice-paper doors" of the room in which the woman kneels, this being a traditional Japanese house, she has left her slippers. Because everyone in this culture took off their shoes before en-tering a house or a room off a balcony (as the room in the poem probably is), this inti-mate detail portrays the woman as utterly human, ordinary, needful of slippers—hardly the intensely seductive and fragile creature she is about to turn herself into for her day's work. Again, in the last two stanzas of the poem, the narrator imagines the woman as human, as perhaps longing for some break in the facade that she creates daily.

From the setting the narrator moves in the second stanza to the woman herself, briefly describing the color of her hair. The third stanza provides evidence of the woman's occupation as a courtesan, with the phrase "the ritual/ wheel of the body" hinting at the countless days begun with the same ritual application of powder used to whiten and smooth, to make "translucent skins" with many delicate layers of powder. The implications of the double entendre of the next line, that "She practices pleasure," are made clear in the closing lines of the stanza, in which the narrator looks ahead to the movement "some other hand will trace" upon the woman's face, following, as the verb "trace" suggests, her very movements.

The fine kimono, draped open at the shoulders so that the woman can powder her neck without spoiling the silk, is described in stanza 5. From the woman's shoulders and neck the narrator's attention turns to her face reflected in the mirror, a familiar device of ukiyo-e prints that allows the artist to portray two views of a woman's beauty. The narrator compares the mirror to "a winter pond" in which the woman's face can be seen "rising to meet itself." The stanza's comparisons of the woman's shoulder to a snow-covered hill and her face to a reflection in a pond suggest cool appraisal of her beauty, which is indeed what the woman herself bestows upon her reflected beauty in the sixth stanza, where her "eyes narrow/ in a moment of self-scrutiny." The final image of the poem of two chrysanthemums touching and drifting apart "in the middle of a lake" is a metaphoric echo of the woman's futilely parting her lips in the previous stanza, "as if desiring to disturb/ the placid plum face."

Forms and Devices

The poem is rich in visual imagery. The second stanza's deliberately unconventional comparison of the color of the woman's hair—"black/ with hints of red"—to "the color of seaweed/ spread over rocks" picks up the hint of ocean and water imagery begun in the opening stanza's comparison of the scene's light to the "sheen of an oyster shell." This imagery is continued in the fifth stanza with the comparison of the woman's mirror to "a winter pond" and in the last stanza's comparison of her face itself to a still lake. The "floating world" to which this woman belongs, as suggested by this imagery, is not only a quality of experience that she can provide but also an essential part of her own character or person. She exists as part of the natural world, a positive force in it as well as a creature trapped by it.

The richest image comes in the implied metaphor that ends the poem. The striking placement of this metaphor in its own, final stanza creates the same effect as can be achieved in haiku, in which a single image reverberates with meaning barely suggested by a previous line. While more than one interpretation of the metaphor is possible, one possibility is that the two drifting chrysanthemums floating in a lake are the just-parted "berry-stained lips" in the woman's still, white face. The aimless passivity of the flowers' movement echoes the woman's own absolute silence, in itself a part of the stylized "mask of beauty" that she wears, as another, smaller metaphor, "the symmetry of silence," suggests.

The lining of the free verse is fairly simple, with line breaks coming at points suggested by naturally occurring breaks in grammatical units, such as before similes, as in the lines "She dips a corner of her sleeve/ like a brush into water," before prepositional phrases, as in "Her hair is black/ with hints of red," or after verbs:

> The eyes narrow
> in a moment of self-scrutiny.
> The mouth parts
> as if desiring to disturb
> the placid plum face.

Slightly more complex lining is found in stanza 4, with "Morning begins the ritual/ wheel of the body," but this is almost the only instance of an unexpected disruption of a syntactical unit. The effect of this steady pulsing rhythm is to echo the poem's theme, that almost nothing unexpected will ever occur in the ritualized form of beauty this woman inhabits.

Themes and Meanings

"Girl Powdering Her Neck" is both about the girl of the title and Utamaro's depiction of her. As in poems by William Carlos Williams, Cathy Song "reads" the work of a visual artist and finds meaning in it, leading the reader to see beyond the surface of the beauty the print depicts. The "peach-dyed kimono/ patterned with maple leaves/ drifting across the silk" is a lovely image whose surface is so perfect there seems to be no need to look beyond it. Yet Cathy Song offers an interpretation of this beauty that is at odds with its pure serenity. By gazing long enough at the woman preparing to powder her neck, some idea about what is going on in the woman's mind surfaces: She may have something to say but does not. She is so thoroughly masked by the powder, the berry-stain, even the lovely kimono that no disruption of the beautiful surface that she has created can be allowed—either by the conventions of the culture that invented her beauty or by herself, who lives and fulfills those conventions. She thinks ("The eyes narrow/ in a moment of self-scrutiny"), but her lips "do not speak."

Another theme of the poem may be that beauty is as rigorous, demanding, and confining as it is beautiful, but it is not so thoroughly masklike as to forbid any glimpse into the human being behind the facade. Cathy Song brings the humanity of the girl powdering her neck alive by recognizing in Utamaro's print Utamaro's recognition of that humanity. The poem is a tribute both to this girl and those who lived lives like hers and to Utamaro, for his insight into the nature of their beauty.

Lisa A. Seale

GIRLFRIEND

Author: Alan Shapiro (1952-   )
Type of poem: Narrative
First published: 1996, in *Mixed Company*

The Poem

"Girlfriend" is a medium-length free-verse poem with eighty lines divided into three stanzas of twenty-five, twenty-one, and thirty-four lines. The lines of the poem are short: Most of them vary from four to six syllables in length, although some lines have as many as nine syllables. In the first stanza, it almost appears that longer, deca-syllabic lines have been divided in half in order to make up two lines of Shapiro's poem. The title suggests that the poem will focus upon a memory or anecdote about a girlfriend from the speaker's past. The poem is written in the first person, and the voice of the poem's speaker, like most of the other poems in *Mixed Company* (1996), greatly resembles the voice of the poet as he remembers people and events from child-hood and adolescence.

The speaker in "Girlfriend" is an adult male who is looking back fondly, yet ironi-cally, at a relationship that he now calls "The perfect match." The girlfriend, who is unnamed, is slightly more sexually experienced than the young speaker. The speaker recognizes that her experience and knowledge are what attracted him to her. She was able to instruct him as a "school marm" might. Shapiro's speaker shows no regret for this lost love. Instead of lamenting the absence of the girlfriend, the speaker views her merely as someone who guided him through one rite of passage that is associated with coming-of-age.

The second stanza begins with an address to readers that reminds them of their place as observers and informs them that passing time has not allowed the speaker enough distance to judge this story objectively. This stanza also reinforces the anal-ogy to the teacher-student relationship. The speaker remembers being an earnest stu-dent, not in order to please his girlfriend but in order to avoid embarrassment. Shapiro's speaker has an awkward moment of self-awareness when he remembers be-ing lost in his own thoughts: He was so caught up in his own pleasure during inter-course that he was oblivious to the reactions of his girlfriend. He was so absorbed in his own thoughts that he found this intimate moment to be another "way of being left/ alone."

The third and final stanza begins with the end of intercourse and the girlfriend ex-cusing herself. The young speaker is left alone and is wholly overwhelmed by his own thoughts. He is so absorbed in his self-awareness that he reimagines the act that they have just completed over and over in his head. He finds that the reimagination of the sex is better than the sex actually was. He is brought out of his own thoughts by the sound of his girlfriend giggling on the phone in the next room, presumably talking to one of her girlfriends about his poor performance. The poem concludes with the adult speaker stating how her voice continues to haunt him: Whenever he feels too self-confident, it always serves to humble him.

Forms and Devices

Shapiro's diction and syntax often mimic the rhythms of plain, colloquial speech. This is the literary convention that readers will immediately notice as they read this poem. Readers who are familiar with the Romantic tradition in English literature will recognize an adherence to William Wordsworth's instruction in the preface to *Lyrical Ballads* (1800) about how "the language of a large portion of every good poem, even of the most elevated character, must necessarily, except with reference to the metre, in no respect differ from that of good prose."

Although "Girlfriend" resembles the language of prose, that does not mean that it is prose. Shapiro's own comments on James McMichael's "Four Good Things" (1980) in *In Praise of the Impure* (1993) can also be used as an apt description of "Girlfriend": It "seems like poetry on the verge of speech and speech on the verge of poetry." Within this free-verse poem, there are passages in which Shapiro employs a loose iambic meter that makes the reader aware of a heightening formality within the speaker's voice. Most noticeable is the address to the reader in the second stanza. The first two lines of the second stanza ("You'd be, of course,/ a better judge of this"), if combined into one line, would read as iambic pentameter. Allowing meter to enter the poem at this time forces the reader into an awareness that this poem is not a story and that it is instead a crafted and sculpted lyric poem that merely resembles a story. It also creates an odd tension between the speaker and the reader. At the moment that the conversational language of this poem becomes more formal, the speaker invites the reader into the poem to be an observer who should assess the motivations of the poem's characters.

The speaker's conversational voice resembles that of a storyteller who brings all of his experience and personality into the retelling of a personal anecdote, which allows the reader to recognize the poem as the product of a particular individual who speaks from a particular historical moment. The voice of the speaker allows the reader to learn about the narrative in a way that makes the narrative itself seem secondary to the way that it is told. Indeed, one important aspect of this poem is the way that the details come back to the speaker willfully. The speaker always remains in full control of the story that he is telling the reader. There is little free association or wordplay in Shapiro's poem. Instead, the poem is a thoughtful and sober retelling of a memory that often returns to haunt the adult speaker.

There is a sculpted and almost minimalistic quality to the detail; readers know much less about this drama than Shapiro must know. One never learns the girl's name or what she looks like. There is no discussion of the relationship before or after this moment. There is little to prove that the girl exists anywhere in the world outside of this brief drama. Also missing are clues about the poem's location. The spareness of details reminds one that this drama exists in the speaker's consciousness more than it exists in the physical world.

Themes and Meanings

"Girlfriend" is a poem about memory. The speaker is committed to exploring the past and examining how his past actions are revised by his memory. This speaker does not express a desire to change any of the details of this drama about the loss of virginity. Instead, he hopes to come to an understanding of how this one small incident from the past helps make him the person that he is today. Therefore, the work of a poetic project such as this is never finished; it is ongoing because any one person's life has too much complexity to be resolved in one poem. In many of Shapiro's poems, past interacts with present as he engages in his quest to understand all the complex factors that have contributed to his becoming the person that he is today. Thus, the drama that the speaker in "Girlfriend" reveals is more than an anecdotal remembrance of something that once took place. It takes on a dimension of heroic proportions when one recognizes that the adult speaker is wrestling with all of his personal history.

There is also an instructive quality to such a confession. Without telling its readers that similar explorations are necessary in order to understand all the history that goes into the creation of each person's self, it displays a person engaged in such exploration. Readers will realize that if they are to understand themselves they must also engage in a similar exploration of their past experiences and actions. One's whole life is constantly reexamined and explored in order to understand one's experience. Poets such as Robert Lowell, Anne Sexton, and W. D. Snodgrass are famous early examples of the confessional tradition in American poetry.

The poem is notable for what it discovers about the self. Instead of being able to look at this somewhat humiliating experience and laugh at it, the speaker admits that the girl's giggling still haunts him and that he cannot escape the burden of this memory. In this brief drama, the older and experienced speaker remembers one incident that led to his loss of innocence. The loss of innocence that occurs is not necessarily the loss of sexual innocence. Instead, it is the loss of solipsism. The young, virginal speaker was not at all concerned with the pleasure or desire of his partner. In his unwise and innocent state, he was only concerned with his own pleasure. His memory of this experience reminds him that he cannot return to such solipsism, that her reliable "tune/ of scorn" will not allow it. This constant reminder forces the speaker to be wiser. He will always remember the possible pitfalls when he might "grow too free/ in pleasure." This memory of his girlfriend's scorn is an inescapable reminder of the young, overly self-aware, pathetic young boy that he once was. It is the act of remembering this drama that keeps the adult speaker from returning to his youthful, unwise solipsism.

Jeffrey Greer

THE GIRLS

Author: Diane Wakoski (1937-   )
Type of poem: Verse essay
First published: 1986, in *The Rings of Saturn*

The Poem

Diane Wakoski's "The Girls" consists of six verse paragraphs in which the first-person speaker addresses the differences, both physical and intellectual, between herself and other women, whom she labels "the girls." Since "girls" is a term customarily used by male chauvinists to describe females of all ages, Wakoski's poem has a decidedly feminist edge. "The Girls" was written "for Margaret Atwood and Cathy Davidson": Atwood is a Canadian writer and literary critic with feminist views, and Davidson is a feminist literary critic.

In the first two verse paragraphs the speaker stresses the differences between herself and "the girls." While they have thin hips and lemon-scented hands and look like models in fashion magazines, she sees herself with "fat ankles/ And ass as soft as a sofa pillow." She, however, is the "class brain" who answers more questions in class than they do. More significant, she is the "ugly duckling class brain," an allusion to the fable about the seemingly ugly duckling which becomes a beautiful swan. In effect, the speaker envies the girls who torment her (Valerie Twadell, who "chased [her] with worms"), but she also feels superior to them.

The third paragraph continues the description of the physical beauty of the girls and also develops the motif of snakes introduced in the fourth line of the poem. Cathy is slim with a fashionable "Zelda-ish bob," and Peggy is as "slender and chic as Jane Fonda." The use of "now" and the reference to Fonda suggests that at age forty-seven the speaker still sees the same differences between herself and other women. Further, the reference to Cathy's "sorority girl students" raises the issue of the speaker not belonging to a clique.

The focus of the verse paragraph, however, is on the ease with which the girls handle the snakes the speaker fears. The speaker concludes the verse paragraph by alluding to Emily Dickinson's poem about the "narrow fellow in the grass" and stating that she "would have died" if she had seen it. Dickinson's and the speaker's personification of the snake makes it obvious that "snakes" are to be seen not only literally but also metaphorically and symbolically.

In the fourth verse paragraph the speaker begins, "I have never been one of the girls," a line that is repeated twice later in the poem. The "girls" are smart but are not given labels such as "encyclopedia," which dehumanizes the speaker, or "brain," which segments her. They are "graceful" without dieting and are "followed by men." It is the "ease" with which they handle snakes that the speaker most envies. She mentions only dangerous snakes (the python, mamba, cobra, and cottonmouth), but the snakes are seen in intimate contact with the "girls." The skin of the python is "like milky underwear," and the cottonmouth swims "next to you all night/ in muddy fertile loving water."

When the speaker continues the snake imagery in the fifth verse paragraph, she becomes the mythical Medusa "with vipers hissing around my hair" and with the power to turn men into stone, but this is how men regard her, not the way she sees herself. In the last paragraph she repeats, "I have never been one of the girls" and states that if she had seen the phallic snake D. H. Lawrence described in his poem that she would have "turned and run." Unlike Lawrence, who believed "snakes were/ the Lords of Life," the speaker believes that "you pretty girl women" are "the real Gods." In the presence of such "Gods," she is "neither man/ nor woman," essentially deprived of her sexuality.

Forms and Devices

In an interview with Andrea Musher, printed in Wakoski's *Toward a New Poetry* (1980), Wakoski discusses snakes and mythology. She states that the image of the rattlesnake is "basically the phallic image," but she goes on to claim that "snakes were almost always part of the female cult in all religions." The Medusa image, which she uses in "The Girls," is the image "of an intellectual woman that turns the man to stone unless he has a mirror that can reflect it away from himself." This image she considers "the threat of the female mind."

In "The Girls" Wakoski uses the symbolism and mythology of snakes to differentiate herself from other women. These women understand and control the "Lords of Life" (the snakes) because they are at "ease" with phallic power. The passage about the cottonmouth best exemplifies the relationship between the sexes: "the cottonmouth who swims next to you all night/ in muddy fertile loving water." There is no violence, but the swimmers are in "fertile loving water," suggesting a fruitful union of the sexes.

How this control is achieved is explained in the last verse paragraph: "but I know you pretty girl women/ who handle them like hula hoops,/ or jump ropes,/ or pet kittens." To handle a hula hoop is to make it circle one's hips, while maintaining only occasional fleeting contact with it—this is to tease and control through sexuality. To deal with a jump rope is to respond rhythmically to an outside threat without being tripped up or "caught." To handle a pet kitten is to be affectionate to something that has been domesticated. In all three instances the woman knowingly uses her sexuality to control the men who would control her.

The reference to "pretty girl women" implies that women are only pretty "girls" grown older and more adept at manipulation. In contrast, the speaker is the Medusa figure, who becomes in Wakoski's mythology "the threat of the female mind." Men do not adore her, as they do the "girls," when they are turned away. In fact, the only means of protection a man has against Medusa is the mirror, which reflects the gaze away from himself, but since it is a mirror, the reflection itself becomes a self-destructive threat to the Medusa figure.

Themes and Meanings

In "The Girls," Wakoski uses the refrain "I have never been one of the girls" to separate herself from the mainstream, and in so doing she establishes herself as the "other," a marginalized person who does not belong. At first, it is her physical appearance that isolates her and makes her the victim of the girls with Barbie-doll figures and designer clothes. An outsider, not a sorority girl, she is labeled and identified as a nonperson (an "encyclopedia") or as one who is not complete (a "brain" only).

Often things change with time, but in the speaker's case, at age forty-seven, things have not changed. "Now," as she puts it, Peggy looks like Jane Fonda; the speaker does not. The speaker also differs from the "girls" in terms of men, who in this poem are represented or symbolized as phallic snakes—unlike the "girls," who are at ease handling snakes literally (they put one "ritually" in a teacher's desk) and figuratively (they swim with cottonmouths). For the girls, the snakes are intimate, nonthreatening associates personified in one case as a "cobra who sits on the family radio/ in Sri Lanka." These "snakes" are almost domesticated by women, who know how to control the phallic snakes associated with Lawrence, whose fiction depicted castrating women attempting to destroy masculinity.

Compared to these "girl women," the speaker is deprived of her sexuality: "In your presence I am neither man/ nor woman." If to be a "woman" is to be the "girl woman" she has depicted, she is no woman, nor can she be an easily manipulated man with only the semblance of control. She is "simply the one/ afraid of snakes."

The concluding lines do not suggest defeat because the speaker refuses to be labeled or identified in stereotypical gender terms. She will define herself, and when she adds that this fear of snakes is "the one thing/ not allowed," she willingly and defiantly accepts her marginalized position. This tone is consistent with the tone used throughout the poem. While she states that she "envies" the girls and wishes she could shed her Medusa image, there is a kind of bemused contempt for the "girls" and their machinations. The notion of the "girls" being real "Gods" is surely bitterly ironic.

Thomas L. Erskine

GIRLS WORKING IN BANKS

Author: Karl Shapiro (1913-2000)
Type of poem: Lyric
First published: 1967; collected in *Adult Bookstore*, 1976

The Poem

Karl Shapiro's "Girls Working in Banks" presents a detailed bank scene as it might appear on any business day to clients who walk in to take care of their banking needs. The poem consists of twenty-seven lines of irregular meter that move from one image to the next in an apparently casual description of a familiar environment. The first three lines describe the girls themselves and suggest the grandeur of their surroundings with "rather magnificent floors." The next three lines mention the girls walking through "rows of youngish vice-presidents" before they return to their stations to deal with money transactions. One of the features of Shapiro's poems is their immersion in the rituals of American middle-class life. He wrote about Buicks, barber shops, banks, and auto wrecks, topics that were not considered appropriate poetic subjects in the 1940's, when he started publishing.

Lines 9-16 switch suddenly from the lobby scene to the interior vault of the bank, where the assets are kept, presumably large amounts of money and other valuables. The poet depicts the glowing vault in scrupulous detail, yet Shapiro takes care to point out that "If you glance inside it, there's nothing to be seen." These eight lines focused on the interior of the vault suggest there is something important about this unseen space, but it is not yet clear exactly what it is.

Line 17 returns the poem's focus to the girls, moving easily back and forth behind the counter and past the guards with their "almost apologetic" pistols watching people while they conduct their business. The last six lines develop the image of these people who come and go in the bank, make their "papery transactions," and leave finally with a sense of relief. They exit from revolving doors, which suggests that they will return and emerge again in a recurring cycle.

By the end of the poem it becomes clear that the poet is writing about something other than a bank. The eight lines devoted to the vault take on a new meaning: It is a hallowed sanctuary where the most holy dwells, and yet it is "Built out of beaten dimes." There is a strong association between financial and religious institutions. Re- ligious references become more overt as the poem nears its conclusion: People who use the bank write at desks with pens "attached to rosary chains," after which they "stand/ Pious," waiting to complete their business with the girls. "Girls Working in Banks" presents a subversive view of religion, religion carefully monitored by the vice presidents and guards who appear to control a public that needs their services but receives little satisfaction once these services are rendered.

Forms and Devices

A conceit is an intricate metaphor that functions by arousing feelings of surprise, shock, or amusement. The poet compares elements that seem to have little or nothing in common, or juxtaposes images that establish a marked discord in mood. In this case, Shapiro has chosen to talk about a spiritual subject, religion, in terms of the most materialistic feature of society, finance. While this may seem a far-fetched conceit, the opposition of religious and financial qualities sets up an arresting paradox. Yet the conceit works so smoothly that the combination of these opposites in the poem changes after the first or second reading: What seemed paradoxical now seems complementary. After the reader is shocked by the juxtaposition of finance and religion, similarities arise in the poem, and surprise turns to insight. The metaphor brings out aspects of religion that one might not have previously considered.

Irony often defines Shapiro's work, which in this case heightens the readers' surprise. The title is apparently straightforward; the poem will be about "girls working in banks," and the first line bears this out. Yet by the third line the girls are shedding "Tiny shreds of perforated paper, like body flakes," and suspicions are aroused. The rows of vice presidents, who are not even focused on the girls but on something far away, also create an enigma. By the time readers get to the vault, where nothing is to be seen but the formidable steel door bars that safeguard the interior and keep the public out, it is apparent that Shapiro is referring to something else as well as a bank.

In lines 17-19, the girls are moving about inside the bank with "surprising freedom," hinting that they might be angels, and their flakes might be bits of feathers; perhaps they are nuns or vestal virgins, and the vice presidents are priests. The best poetry is open to various interpretations. The irony continues through the poem as the careful choice of religious vocabulary becomes more pointed with the terms "rosary chains," "pious," and "glorious." This irony provides a certain tension as the reader struggles to understand exactly what the poet is saying about the bank, and Shapiro pulls off a stunning example of poetic compression by illuminating two whole and opposing realms of society in twenty-seven lines.

Although the lines do not end in rhymes, "Girls Working in Banks" is distinguished by other euphonic devices. Alliteration, the repetition of the initial consonant or consonants for an artistic effect, occurs in "floors," "flakes," and "flashing," in lines 3, 4, and 6. The word "friendly" appears in line 7, echoing the *f* sound but varying the second consonant for a pleasing variation. Lines 20-25 are tied together by the consonant *p*, as in "past," "pistols," "people," "pens," "pious," and "papery." Assonance, the use of vowel repetition in words whose consonants differ, links lines 10 and 12 with "dimes," "shines," and "inside," while the last two lines resonate with their final vowel sounds of "relief" and "streets."

Themes and Meanings

Confinement is one of Shapiro's major themes, and the great central image of the glowing vault in "Girls Working in Banks" is a perfect vehicle of confinement with its "polished steel elbows/ Of the great machine of the door." Doors are devices that can keep people in or out, and the image works well for both banking and religion; money creates class and sets up barriers between people, just as religion often does. The irony is, however, that nothing is to be seen in this vault: There is a terrible void at the center of the bank or church. Yet in another kind of metaphor, a simile, Shapiro compares the vault to "the best room in the gallery/Awaiting the picture which is still in a crate." The poet seems to be saying that both institutions are empty at the core, yet there is still hope that each will find its own center, just as the picture will be hung one day. A picture is an image, which refers back to the poem itself, a series of images.

The theme of confinement echoes throughout the poem with the armed guards who watch the people doing business, and with the final escape of these people into the "glorious anonymous streets." Within the walls of finance the individuals are known, they have names and numbers, and within the walls of religion they are watched by an omniscient god. Yet once the clients escape these institutions the streets are glorious and anonymous, suggesting that the ordinary people might find glory and fulfillment only outside these institutions of mass control.

Significantly for a master ironist, "Girls Working in Banks" appeared in Shapiro's collection *Adult Bookstore*, a title that hints at sexually explicit material. The poem does contain some suggestive language, primarily in the guards whose pistols watch people bending over, and in the changing addresses of the girls, from "Open" to "Closed" to "Next Counter." These hints go nowhere, however, and in fact seem to emphasize only the impersonal nature of everyone connected to the bank. All the girls perform the same tasks, after all; each one gives the same service.

Critics have often called Shapiro an iconoclast, one who delights in smashing images or who attacks traditional institutions to show they are based on error or superstition. A loner, the poet learned about institutions in his youth as a Jew growing up in the South and wrote many poems about his own place in them. One of his early poems that won fame in the postwar era is "University," a work that attacks the institution of higher education in Virginia as a monstrosity of racism and class privilege. "Girls Working in Banks" falls squarely into the iconoclastic category, and its ruling metaphor works both ways: Banks have become religious institutions where people worship money, and churches, representing religious life, are empty vaults awaiting a true spirit.

Sheila Golburgh Johnson

GIVE ALL TO LOVE

Author: Ralph Waldo Emerson (1803-1882)
Type of poem: Poetic sequence
First published: 1847, in *Poems*

The Poem

In the six-stanza poem "Give All to Love," Ralph Waldo Emerson connects the finite cycles of natural order with the infinite eternal order through individual feelings and experiences that are governed by love. The persona of the poem advises the audience to withhold nothing and to "Give all to love."

The first stanza explains what "all" entails in the context of this poem. It encompasses the entire reality of an individual's experiences: relationships with friends and relatives, the turn of events, ownership of property, recognition and renown, plans for the future, and encouraging sources of inspiration. When love guides one's actions and interactions, human relations and transactions define the very existence and identity of an individual—enfolding both the material and spiritual aspects of reality. In this stanza, the "Muse" suggests a harmonious link between memories of the past and the promising dreams of the future through the poetic language of love.

Love is decribed as a brave "master" and "a god" in the second stanza, connoting a powerful force in the individual's struggles in life. Love functions as the supreme authority, "utterly" controlling the choices of an individual; as a result, this individual's life expands in "scope." Because love "Knows its own path," it offers new possibilities that unfold new heights, which reach out to the "outlets of the sky," displaying hope beyond hope.

The third stanza describes the character of the individual who is willing to give all to love; such giving is not possible for a weak individual, who is "mean," in the sense of lacking in personal strength. This stanza attributes a heroic quality of "Valor unbending" and "courage stout" to one who is willing to take on the challenges posed by the demands of love in an uphill struggle to rise to greater heights.

The opening line of the next stanza, "Leave all for love," is a reminder to pursue the ascending path with "One word more" of caution, which requires "firm endeavor" in preserving the autonomy of an individual. An Arab remains "free" even though his experience of love makes him "cling with life to the maid," yet this love relationship does not compromise the freedom of the beloved. Emerson shows that even though all relations within the natural order are finite and temporal, the individual's autonomy can connect the natural and the spiritual dimensions of human life. This connection bridges the finite and the infinite through feeling and choices of an individual. Although the Arab's separation from the beloved maid "dims the day," the transcending heights revealed by love point to a fuller and better form of spiritual satisfaction as the individual draws closer to divine presence and eternity.

Forms and Devices

In this poem, Emerson uses six strophes of varied lengths with no uniform rhyme scheme to contextualize the theme of love in its varying patterns. He addresses love from a transcendentalist perspective and goes beyond cultural barriers by using the image of an Arab. The poem begins with the personification of love as a leader and a master who guides the individual on an ascending course in all relationships. The "path" represents both the natural and the spiritual journey of an individual enriched by wise choices and rewarding experiences. The last line of the poem evokes a contrast between "half-gods" and "gods" to highlight the varying levels of ascent that progress from demigods to the real gods. Love is "a god" that guides the individual's heart to discover a unique path and new knowledge. Consequently, horizons widen and the person's experience has an expanding "scope" of personal fulfillment. The ascent symbolizes a unique individual experience because it involves spontaneity and "untold intent" of love. At the same time, love adds a heroic dimension and determination to the individual's pursuit in rising "high and more high," aiming for the sky. Thus, the ascent also symbolizes various levels of knowledge that are inspired by love and refined through experience.

The allusion to an Arab empowers Emerson to defy the conventional attitude toward love as a strictly romantic experience that seeks a union of lovers, depriving them of their individuality. In his essay "Self-Reliance," Emerson explains how social "conformity and consistency" are barriers to an individual's self-fulfillment. Here, he departs from the established tradition to emphasize the autonomy of an individual as a precondition for the sovereignty of love. The Arab knows that when the heartbeat and the pulse of the maiden's autonomous being promises "a joy apart from thee," then the heroics of love must gracefully accept the separation. While this separation symbolizes the temporal constraints in the natural order, its transcendent scope symbolizes the love for a Creator who is eternal and infinite and whose presence is manifest in individual experiences.

"Stealing grave from all alive" is an image that sets up the contrast between the living and the dead as well the sorrow of the Arab and the "joy" of the maid. This separation may be caused by another lover, or it may be interpreted as the death of the maid, which echoes the limits of the natural order; however, it also represents a moment of "joy" on the ascending path as it reaches the infinite and the eternal. The reference to gods validates higher levels of experiences that are free of finite limits. In the final stanza, the maid is a metaphor for a powerful relationship at two levels—human and divine: At the human level she can be "loved as thyself," and appears as "a self of purer clay." However, her ascent marks a separation between humans as a reminder of a stronger divine presence. The path of love rises above the limitations of time, where "half-gods" abide, allowing the individual to witness the presence of real gods in the eternal realm.

Themes and Meanings

In this poem, Emerson celebrates the authority and power of love, which is manifest in an individual's quest for perfection in all relationships. In other words, by submitting to a grand design of love, the individual's surroundings transform into beneficial transactions, and personal relations change into investments in the continuum of time. When love governs the individual's faith and vision for the future, personal property is guarded through wise decisions, while family ties extend from generation to generation and friendships are formed through mutual respect.

In the first stanza, the individual is advised to "obey" the heart because it represents the faculty that understands the language of love. This language empowers the individual to submit to love with an open mind, refusing "Nothing" within one's circle of relations and transactions. This dedicated compliance to love echoes Emerson's essay on "Self-Reliance" and his philosophical statement "Trust thy heart" in pursuing the individual path towards perfection, as well as "Accept the place divine presence has found for you, the society of your contemporaries, the connection of events."

Emerson was a graduate of the Harvard Divinity School and well versed in Christian doctrine and scriptures, but he was equally knowledgeable about Eastern religions and belief systems. While Emerson draws upon the Christian tradition to emphasize love as a divine attribute present within the natural and the spiritual realms, he also underscores the transcendentalist concept of a Creator who transcends cultural and finite barriers. The overarching presence of love unfolds a unique path for a unified reality. In his poem "Each and All" Emerson describes the unifying connections within God's creation that come together in the persona's consciousness as "a perfect whole."

In "Give All to Love," Emerson seems to depart from the Western literary tradition that usually refers to three different categories of love: Eros, the love between man and woman; Philo, communal love; and Agape, the love for God. Under the supreme authority of love, all these forms of love become intertwined in an individual's quest for perfection and fulfilling relations. Surpassing the pantheistic approach, Emerson shows how love is instrumental in revealing the divine presence in a pantheistic manner, for it acknowledges a transcendent Creator who guides the individual on an ascending path.

Emerson's transcendental approach to love is similar to the Muslim Sufi poets who celebrate love in their poetry. Emerson admired these poets and refers to them in his translations and verses. He also dedicated a long poem to Saʿdī: "Spin the ball, I reel, I burn." The Sufi poets connect the natural experience of love to the eternal order through the mystical quest to rise higher in pursuit of a transcendental Creator. For the Sufis, the Arab's intensity of love for the maid would mark an important phase in an unfettered ascent that strives to reach the "sky," or the heights of eternity. An individual who fails to experience the divine presence through love in the natural order, with its temporal constraints, circumvents the experience of rising to the spiritual order that is available to humans through feelings and heroic choices.

Mabel M. Khawaja

THE GLASS ESSAY

Author: Anne Carson (1950-   )
Type of poem: Poetic sequence
First published: 1995, in *Glass, Irony, and God*

The Poem

"The Glass Essay" is an ambitious, inventive, thirty-eight-page series of interrelated poetic montages and meditations on the loss of love. This central theme is developed using three interwoven sets of images: memories of the life and works of nineteenth century English novelist Emily Brontë, memories of the author's family, and visions concerning the nature of poetry. Using short prose passages, triplet line structure, one-word subheadings, and short sentences floating in white space, Anne Carson intermingles dreams, memories, family portraits, and quotations from Brontë's letters and diary papers to explore the nature of gender, the artistry of writing, and, most importantly, the painful feelings in the aftermath of lost love. With these juxtaposed streams emphasizing the place of the mind and body in human relationships, the poem begins and ends with two perspectives on the female body, the central image of the poem.

The poem begins at four o'clock in the morning in a dream, followed by the poem's first glass or mirror image: "my face in the bathroom mirror/ has white streaks down it." The setting then moves to the house of the poet's mother where the three central women of the poem—the poet, her mother, and Brontë—are compared and contrasted, showing three generational perspectives regarding self-identity and relationships with men. Carson begins weaving her tropes by stating that visits with her mother make her fear that she is becoming Brontë, and she compares her kitchen to the moors in Brontë's novel *Wuthering Heights* (1847). Kitchen imagery—the dining table, food in the refrigerator, the mother eating toast—represent conventional expectations of women. The narrator's mother believes modern bathing suits arouse men, dislikes feminists, and tells her daughter that she should have worked more on her relationships with men, particularly the poet's five-year affair with the principal lover of her past named Law. This criticism prompts the poet into a meditation on Brontë's interest in "watching" from the cliffs on the moors and feeling imprisoned in a world of men. Brontë, the daughter of a clergyman trapped by strict Victorian conventions, walks the moor, has no friends, has no sexual life, cannot earn her own living, and thus writes poetry about prisons from her "invisible cage." The narrator connects her own life with Brontë's biography and fictional characters, observing that during the long period of grief after the loss of love, her body's needs are also a prison. The poet realizes that resolving these needs will be a major part of her healing process.

The poet sees mirroring characteristics that she shares with Heathcliffe, the male protagonist of *Wuthering Heights*, who is also tormented by his perceived loss of love. The poet recalls the scene in the novel in which Heathcliffe overhears a conversation in the kitchen but only hears the first half of his lover's sentence. Had he not run away, he would have heard her desire for him instead of living a half life as a "pain devil." This fragmented communication is echoed in the poet's life when she goes to the hospital to visit her aging father who can no longer speak full sentences. She recalls previous uncertain meanings when her parents were younger and they exchanged sexual innuendoes beyond their then eleven-year-old daughter's comprehension. Throughout the poem, fragments and unclear meanings are a central motif demonstrated in Carson's images and line structure.

Carson develops her major points, remembering the thirteen pictures of female nudes in Law's house that become artistic muses in separate, numbered sections of the poem. Carson first attempts to perceive the female body intellectually as art, but she then decides that Brontë wrote art she "could neither contain nor control." This lack of control is seen as the link between art and romantic love that leads to loss and despair.

In a pivotal scene, the poem shifts back in time with descriptions of the last meeting between the poet and Law where he tells the writer he no longer desires her. In a last attempt to arouse him, the poet offers him her nude back, his favorite part of her body. Law moves on top of her and the poet realizes "Everything I know about love and its necessities/ I learned in that one moment." Thrusting her "burning red backside like a baboon/ at a man who no longer cherished me," the narrator describes images of coldness, winter, and cruelty. She compares Law with Heathcliffe and juxtaposes images of light and dark, saying she prefers the light of sexless day. Recalling the pictures of nudes, she focuses on nude "#1," a "Woman Caught in a Cage of Thorns." She describes Charlotte Brontë's conventional responses to her sister Emily's poems and compares her own self-expectations with those of the nineteenth century. This connection again becomes personal when the poet returns to the setting of her mother's kitchen where the two women argue about the responsibility of women arousing male sexual desires and the poet realizes her mother is afraid. The poet points to generational differences in their perspectives. Then, in a hospital, "where distinctions blur," the narrator visits her mentally ill father who is strapped to the wall, representing the other side of the glass or mirror. In the guise of her father, males are seen to be equally subject to imprisonment and mental anguish but for different reasons from those suffered by women.

Forms and Devices

In her narrative, Carson uses a number of common poetic techniques such as the repetition of words to emphasize dramatic moments. Many "broken moments" are intentional fragments meant to illustrate "half-lives" as "half-finished sentences." Carson's original imagery and mix of tones and styles move the poem from one theme to another in shifts that keep her three narratives easily understandable. Simultaneously, her images reinforce each other, repeating and underlining her points. For example, transparent images—primarily glass, mirrors, and ice—are both metaphors and euphemisms for sex and interpersonal communications and also serve as vivid, strongly drawn, and primarily quiet settings. Descriptions of the settings illustrate both external and emotional states. Wintery images of ice and cold underscore the poet's feelings of loss and reinforce her glass imagery. Near the poem's opening, Carson states, "It is as if we have all been lowered into an atmosphere of glass./ Now and then a remark trails through the glass." These fragmentary remarks evoke responses from different levels of the poet's consciousness, linking perspectives with experience. These glass images move from weather and the natural world to psychological states, allowing the poet to evaluate moments in her life from an emotional distance as in the lines "the video tape jerks to a halt/ like a glass slide under a drop of blood." Her "atmosphere of glass" is later juxtaposed with Brontë's "electric atmosphere" in which women wrestle with the "pain devil" of love.

Carson also makes use of colors and juxtapositions of light and dark. "Strings of lights" and lamps illuminate dark rooms, blue and black colors are repeated in various settings, and painful memories take place in cold, wintry settings that emphasize the darkness of feelings of loss. She observes that her mother and Law both prefer the dark. Her mother is angry over the poet's unwillingness to close shades and her preference for the morning sun. Carson's use of cool colors, particularly blue, contributes to the tone, mood, and imagery of the poem: Her aloof ex-lover Law lives in a "high blue room," time is described as "blue and green lozenges," and ice pokes through the "blue hole at the top of the sky." Gold is another repeated symbol of irony, including "gold milk," a "gold toothpick," and the "Golden Mile," the name of the chronic wing of the hospital where the poet's father is confined.

Several sets of images unify the different narratives, including visions of the body that begin and end the poem and are recurring images throughout. For example, when Law announces he no longer desires the poet, she realizes "There was no area of my mind/ not appalled by this action, no part of my body/ that could have done otherwise." The poem's final lines return to the author's body, nude "#13" now transformed into a vision:

> trying to stand against winds so terrible that the
> flesh was blowing off the bones.
> And there was no pain.
> The wind
> was cleansing the bones.
> They stood forth silver and necessary.
> It was not my body, not a woman's body, it was the
> body of us all.
> It walked out of the light.

By making her body a symbol of universal pain (literally stripped to the bone), Carson makes her breakup with Law a shared event with her readers, and she counsels them on how to deal with loss. Her reconciliation with loss allows her to create a distance from the pain in the mind, to put feelings in artistic and intellectual terms, and to examine loss and relieve its power.

Themes and Meanings

While most readers of "The Glass Essay" interpret it as primarily a statement of feminist anger against men, Carson's last stanzas broaden her theme of loss and love. Her use of Brontë's work points to a gender-based comment on the separation of the woman artist from cultural conventions and demonstrates the contrasting desires of the body and the intellect. In the opening of the poem, Carson states the importance of her internal conflict, but to "talk of mind and body" begs a series of questions particularly relating to the soul. "Soul is what I kept watch on all that night" and soul is "trapped in glass," she says, seeing family members forced to "tilt" to survive. Surviving and resolving loss take the soul through painful moments, forcing individuals to deal with the necessities of mind and body: "Soul is the place,/ stretched like a surface of millstone grit between body/ and mind,/ where such necessity grinds itself out." As with much of her other poetic work that explores the nature of eros and loss, bodies and boundaries, Carson sees religion as part of the struggle to achieve resolution. The moment of her breakup with Law is centered "between heaven and hell"; the poet connects this to her thoughts on Brontë and states that "one way to put off loneliness is to interpose god." Carson notes that Brontë's poems speak to a biblical, patriarchal "Thou," which prompts the poet to meditate and to chant Latin prayers. However, emulating Brontë, who "has gone beyond religion," Carson says she simply needs someone to talk to at night without "the terrible sex price."

The flesh as prison of mind and body is a dominant theme, from beginning to end a central conflict in the author's identity. At one point, the narrator's psychiatrist asks why she keeps dwelling on the terrible nudes in Law's rooms, but the poet has no answer. Later, reflecting on the first picture, the poet declares that speaking of nudes will perhaps make her points clearer, and she uses the heavily symbolic portraits to examine female psychological states. The grotesque, tortured pictures continually portray women as wounded victims in a series of surreal settings open to a wide variety of interpretations. For example, nude "#3" depicts a woman who is trying to pull out a "single great thorn implanted in her forehead." Nude "#4" shows a woman "on a blasted landscape" with her head covered by a contorting contraption. Women's lives are then symbolized by a white room without planes, angles, or curves (images of order reflecting male "law"). Other nudes return to vivid torture images: green thorns poking through a woman's heart with blood in the air and women under pressure of "bluish-black water." The repeated thorn imagery can be seen in both biblical and Freudian terms, while other images evoke sexual connotations. Nude "#13," which resembles nude "#1," brings the cycle full circle. She is the body stripped of its flesh, the poet herself coming out of the light.

Issues of identity and self-definition, forged in anger, are reflected throughout the poem: The poet sees women shaped by themselves and men linked in the sex acts she resents. "Girls are cruelest to themselves," she asserts, especially virgins such as Brontë, "who remained a girl all her life despite her body as a woman." Love changes girls to women, creating "animal hunger" that leads to "anger dreams" following the loss of love. The narrator believes "anger could be a kind of vocation for women."

This anger comes from the imprisoning "ropes and thorns" of male desires. Only loneliness allows "true creation" for women, and the poet ultimately declares, "I am my own nude and nudes have a difficult sexual destiny." To reach this destiny, a woman travels "From love to anger to this cold marrow,/ from fire to shelter to fire." Concluding "The Glass Essay," Carson discards mortal boundaries and ultimately finds resolution in rejection of gender and the body, peeling away layers of human conditions. Only after being cleansed to the bone can the poet walk out alone from the light in an artistic vision that transcends the needs of the body, images of the body, and mental interpretations of the body.

Wesley Britton

GO, LOVELY ROSE

Author: Edmund Waller (1606-1687)
Type of poem: Lyric
First published: 1645, in *Poems*

The Poem

"Go, Lovely Rose" is Edmund Waller's most notable work. Waller was a prominent figure in seventeenth century England, and his poems circulated widely before they were published in a collected edition in 1645. "Go, Lovely Rose" conveys a *carpe diem* ("seize the day") theme similar to that of two other famous poems of the same era: "To the Virgins, to Make Much of Time" (1648) by Robert Herrick and "To His Coy Mistress" (1681) by Andrew Marvell. The poem, which contains four stanzas, each with five lines, has symmetry in theme as well as form. The rose, addressed in the first line, serves as the unifying image, symbolizing the brevity of youth and beauty.

The poem opens with a conversation of sorts between the speaker and a rose. The rose must relay an urgent request to another: "Go, lovely rose,/ Tell her that wastes her time and me/ . . . How sweet and fair she seems to be." The rose serves as a metaphor for an attractive woman. The speaker hopes that the lesson provided by the rose will prompt the maiden to yield to his advances. There is a sense of impatience in the speaker's tone in line 2; she "wastes her time and me." The term "waste" suggests not only that the girl is careless in squandering time but also that her delay has more serious connotations. The word might also imply exhaustion or devastation, reinforcing the vision of death expressed in the final stanza, when the rose must die. Moreover, the poet uses the pronoun "me" rather than the more predictable "mine" in line 2, suggesting that she is wasting him—not just his time—when she resists his advances.

In the second stanza, Waller reveals that the woman is shy; she's "young/ And shuns to have her graces spied." Yet, such charm will be wasted if it remains cloistered. The strongest admonition regarding the fragility of beauty arises in stanza 2, when the speaker likens her to a rose that blooms in an uninhabited desert and then dies "uncommended." The image of a delicate rosebud withering in the heat of the desert sun reinforces the speaker's directive that time is short. Therefore, the woman must not hide her beauty. If she waits too long, it may be too late, and like the rose in the desert, her "bloom" will be lost.

The focus of a central image continues in the third stanza, when the speaker amplifies the mission of the rose. It must bid the woman to "come forth." She must abandon what the speaker hints is a false modesty and let herself be admired and desired without a blush, for "Small is the worth/ Of beauty from the light retired." Like an unseen rose in the wilderness, her beauty is worthless if it remains hidden.

The object lesson concludes in the final stanza. The rose must die at the completion of its message so that the woman will see for herself "How small a part of time they share/ That are so wondrous sweet and fair." The rose serves as both messenger and metaphor. The commands are given to "Go," "Tell," "Bid," and "Then die." The speaker finds the rose a most effective emissary. Its fragile petals and transient beauty may convince the reluctant woman in a way that an impatient suitor could not.

Forms and Devices

Waller is known for his development of fluid metrical forms. The poet is credited with refining the heroic couplet (two rhymed lines, written in iambic pentameter). His sense of regular rhythms in his lyric poetry inspired later English poets such as John Dryden (1631-1700) and Alexander Pope (1688-1744). "Go, Lovely Rose" contains a regular rhythm and rhyme scheme. The lines are composed primarily of iambic feet—every other syllable is stressed. In the five-line stanzas, the first and third lines are short, only four syllables, while the remaining three lines each contain eight syllables. The short lines, especially those that begin the stanzas, contain commands and interrupt the regular iambic rhythm with the use of strongly accented syllables, as in the lines "Go, lovely rose" in the opening and the spondaic stress of "Then die" in the final stanza. In addition, the rhyme scheme reinforces the metrical structure of the poem. The short lines of each stanza rhyme, as do the longer lines (2, 4, and 5), forming an *ababb* rhyme scheme.

Waller employs apostrophe in addressing the rose in line 1 and commissioning the flower to deliver his message. Such figurative language provides the speaker with a sense of detachment. The woman whom the rose must visit has obviously been unmoved by the speaker's previous advances. He must send a flower to do his bidding. Thus, it will not be the impatient suitor who will try to pry the reticent beauty from seclusion but rather a lovely rose. The beauty of the rose forms the central metaphor for the woman as well as the work. The speaker hopes his love interest will see herself in the rose, and in the same way, the reader comprehends the point of Waller's verse: "Small is the worth/ Of beauty from the light retired." Death is the "common fate of all things rare." If the woman wastes her time, she will also waste her youth and opportunity.

The poem's conceit exemplifies Waller's tendency toward conventional metaphor. In contrast to John Donne's poem "The Flea" (1633) in which the speaker tries to seduce a girl by comparing their lovemaking to a flea bite, Waller uses the more traditional image of a rose in an extended comparison to fleeting beauty and life. Waller's contemporary Robert Herrick employs a similar image in his poem "To the Virgins, to Make Much of Time." Lines 3 and 4 echo Waller's theme: "And this same flower that smiles today,/ Tomorrow will be dying."

Themes and Meanings

"Go, Lovely Rose" has preserved Waller's reputation as a poet, in part, because of its simplicity of language. The poem marks a movement away from the seriousness of metaphysical poetry to a form reflecting less weighty subjects. The rose, personified as a creature able to deliver speeches and die on command, must urge the woman—beautiful but fragile, tangible but tenuous—to "Suffer herself to be desired/ And not blush so to be admired." Waller employs ambiguity in the word "suffer." The young woman must allow herself to be admired, but the word "suffer" also implies that she might feel distress at such a request. The speaker's petition also poses a paradox. The woman who so readily blushes has cheeks the color of roses, but to cease blushing and accept the man's advances readily, as the speaker suggests in line 15, would take away the blush and would make her pale and thus, appear less like the rose.

In the tradition of Cavalier poets, Waller addresses his mistress in a forthright manner. She is not portrayed as an unattainable, chaste goddess, but rather a maiden who must be confronted with her hesitation and chastised for her shyness. Such poetry celebrates the minor pleasures of life and is often more about the speaker than the lady who receives the address. Thus, Waller's gentleman is frank in commanding the rose to die so that his lady may "read" her own fate: "Then die, that she/ The common fate of all things rare/ May read in thee." His urgency in bidding her to "come forth" and permitting herself "to be admired" hints that his regard is fleeting and superficial.

The poem's *carpe diem* theme encourages the young maid to accept the speaker's advances while there is still time. However, Waller's subtle satire also raises questions about love and beauty. The speaker does not assert, as does William Shakespeare in "Sonnet 116," that love does not alter, or that love is not "Time's fool." In fact, the lover in "Go, Lovely Rose" implies that time is beauty's enemy. Death is the "common fate of all things rare." The lover of "Go, Lovely Rose" is impatient. Perhaps his interest in the young woman will be as short-lived as her beauty or as her youth. The poem ends as it began, with an appeal to one who is "sweet and fair." The woman must accept his advances while she can. Time is short, as he reiterates in the closing couplet: "How small a part of time they share/ That are so wondrous sweet and fair." The poem is a call to action, since his interest and her beauty may both be short-lived.

Paula M. Miller

GOATS AND MONKEYS

Author: Derek Walcott (1930-   )
Type of poem: Narrative
First published: 1965, in *The Castaway and Other Poems*

The Poem

"Goats and Monkeys" provides an excellent example of intertextuality—that is, it relies on an earlier text but in itself becomes an altogether new work, sometimes called the "echo-text." The epigraph from William Shakespeare's *Othello* (1604) announces Derek Walcott's source, one he expects the reader to know. The lines come from act 1, scene 1, of the play and are spoken by Othello's jealous ensign, Iago, as he reveals to Brabantio that his daughter, Desdemona, has run away with the "blacka-moor" Othello. In these charged lines, the "black ram" (a male sheep) depicts Othello and the white ewe (a female sheep) Desdemona. "Tupping" means they are "even now" engaging in sexual intercourse; "tupping" is synonymous with "ramming," the kind of pun that would appeal to Walcott, whose poetry abounds in elaborate wordplay.

The poem's title is not altogether clear. Lecherous men are sometimes called goats, and when made to act like fools they are dubbed monkeys; in the play, Iago sees Othello as a lecher, then sets out to make a fool of him. Yet that seems a rather literal and oversimplified reading. Men whose wives are unfaithful to them—as Othello thinks Desdemona is—are derisively called goats. The goat is also part of the zodiac, to which the poem alludes. While Walcott never describes Othello specifically as a goat, he does at one point refer to him as an "ape" and refers to him throughout in bestial terms, most often as a bull. So the title remains elusive, yet extraordinarily suggestive.

In the poem's five stanzas, uneven in length, free in structure, and rich in imagery, Walcott recounts the story of Othello and Desdemona. The first stanza records their sexual union. The next reveals the passion of Desdemona, who has been "Dazzled by that bull's bulk"; still, the poet asks, should not the "poor girl" realize that tragedy awaits her? The third stanza recapitulates the first two, elaborating on their sexual passion and foreshadowing the cruelty that the black Othello will inflict on his white lover. The fourth stanza tells how Othello "arraigns" Desdemona's "barren innocence" by accusing her of infidelity, as though her whiteness "limns lechery"—"limn" meaning to illuminate. In the final stanza, "this mythical, horned beast"—possibly the goat from the zodiac, or maybe the mythological bull—murders Desdemona in a "bestial, comic agony."

While this summary covers the main points of a story already well known, it does little justice to the way Walcott has echoed Shakespeare's text. In fact, he also echoes a number of other texts in a less obvious manner. The sustaining metaphor of Othello as the earth and Desdemona as the moon brings to mind the structure of seventeenth century metaphysical poetry by writers such as John Donne and George Herbert. Walcott also assumes that the reader knows the Greek myths of Pasiphaë and Eurydice.

This poem, though, comprises no mere retelling of the story Shakespeare had already retold, no mimicry of metaphysical poems, no slavish dependence on mythology. Walcott's impressive exercise in intertextuality holds larger intentions.

Forms and Devices

To underscore Othello's blackness and Desdomona's whiteness, the poet transforms Othello into the earth, Desdemona into the moon. The first stanza, when Othello seduces Desdemona, describes an eclipse: The earth (Othello) covers the moon (Desdemona), and "God's light is put out." The poet compares Othello to Africa, as "a vast sidling [furtive or fawning] shadow" that obscures the moon—or the white world represented by Desdemona. Throughout, this black/white imagery, stemming from the introductory metaphor of earth and moon, accentuates the poem's apparent racial overtones. As Walcott extends the elaborate comparison, he refers to "the sun of Cyprus," an apt allusion in that Othello and Desdemona flee to Cyprus once she has left her father's Venetian home.

Then, to make Desdemona's plight more resonant, the poet compares her to doomed women from Greek mythology, Pasiphaë and Eurydice. Pasiphaë, the daughter of the sun god and wife of Minos, fell in love with a bull that Poseidon had given to Minos. Like Othello, Minos brought about his wife's downfall, for he refused to sacrifice the bull; as punishment, Poseidon cursed the faithless Minos's wife Pasiphaë, decreeing that she would unite with the bull and "breed horned monsters." From this union came the Minotaur, a creature with the body of a man and the head of a bull. Walcott turns Othello into another Minotaur, the beast who wreaked havoc on innocents in his labyrinth—an elaborate maze of passageways—until he was slain by Theseus. In the second stanza, the poet speaks of Othello's mind as a "hellish labyrinth" in which Desdemona's soul will be swallowed.

The other allusion recalls the story of Eurydice, wife of Orpheus, who died from a snake bite and descended into the underworld, from which Orpheus almost rescued her. Like Minos—and Othello—he brings about his beloved's destruction, in his case by looking back at her, which he had been forbidden to do until they reached the earth. Eurydice must return to the underworld, and Orpheus loses her the second time. Thus the "hellish labyrinth" of Othello's mind assumes another meaning, compared now to the Hades that swallows Eurydice and, by implication, Desdemona.

Walcott, perhaps taking his cue from the strong sexuality of the passage in *Othello*, fills the poem with charged sexual imagery, which serves to delineate in another way Desdemona's innocence and Othello's corruption. Othello's "earthen bulk" presses against the white Desdemona's "bosom," his "smoky hand" charring her "marble throat." "Virgin and ape," "maid and malevolent Moor" they are called, as the "panther-black" man violates the "white flesh." Othello's sexuality conjures up "raw musk" (the odorous sexual secretions of various male animals) and "sweat," his penis a "moon-shaped sword" girded by fury, while a "white fruit/ pulped ripe by fondling but doubly sweet" describes Desdemona's sexuality.

Themes and Meanings

Walcott deceives the reader of "Goats and Monkeys," for until the last two lines it appears that the poem follows the traditional view that black is evil, white is good; black is corruption, white is innocence; black is the destroyer, white the creator. In the final lines, the poet contradicts what he has seemingly argued. Othello, the "mythical horned beast" so carefully and effectively drawn to this point, the poet states, is "no more/ monstrous for being black." The words "comic," "mockery," and "farcically" appear in the final stanza, perhaps to hint that the reader is not to take literally what has been presented in the first four stanzas. In effect, Walcott subverts his own poem.

Walcott's ancestors were Africans brought to the Caribbean as slaves to work on sugar plantations; he has some Anglo-Saxon blood as well. Several generations later, Walcott grew up in an educated home, aware of his African heritage but thoroughly schooled in the English language and the British tradition dominating his tiny West Indian island. Walcott was in his early twenties when the Caribbean colonial outposts gained independence from Great Britain. As a child of the faded British Empire, he has often addressed the experience of colonialism in his poetry, an experience he describes as divisive. Yet, unlike many other postcolonial writers of non-Anglo-Saxon origin, he has never promoted a back-to-Africa movement as the panacea for this divisiveness or as a form of revenge for the injustice of British imperialism.

Ironically, long after "Goats and Monkeys" was written—it is one of Walcott's early poems—postcolonial literary-political theorists discovered new meaning in *Othello*, and set out to read it as a racial document. Othello represents the innocent black man, seduced and corrupted by the temptress Desdemona, the white world. Seeking revenge on this white villain, whom he believes to be unfaithful, black Othello rejects her whiteness and destroys it.

Long working to overcome the divisions between black and white through art rather than through political revenge and rejection of his white heritage, Walcott in 1965 appears almost to have foreseen the revisionist reading of *Othello* and, in "Goats and Monkeys," pre-answered and pre-disputed its claims from the 1980's. Walcott concludes that black is no worse than white, that human nature possesses the capacity for cruelty no matter the color of skin. At first this may seem a simplistic way to approach the poem, but not when the first four stanzas are reconsidered in light of the final statement—"no more/ monstrous for being black." These words redefine all that has preceded them and turn the old conception of black and white into a "comic agony" and a "mockery," one that can only be taken "farcically."

Robert L. Ross

THE GOBLET

Author: Gabriela Mistral (Lucila Godoy Alcayaga, 1889-1957)
Type of poem: Lyric ballad
First published: 1938, as "La copa," in *Tala*; English translation collected in *Selected Poems of Gabriela Mistral*, 1971

The Poem

Gabriela Mistral's "The Goblet" consists of four stanzas alternating in odd and even lines. The title has also been translated as "The Drink," evoking the elemental nature of water. Its lyrical quality evokes sensory images of the Caribbean islands and lulls the reader into its calm until the final stanza, in which ecstatic energy is transformed into anguish and alienation. The poet describes how she has traveled from island to island with her water-filled goblet, carefully protecting it so as not to spill a drop. If she had lost one drop, she would have lost the grace that it had granted her. If she had spilled all its contents, she would have been left in misery.

The poem continues its journey through the tropical islands. In the second stanza, the poet explains that she did not come to the islands to search for human constructs or civilizations, to visit and praise society's creations, or to establish a family. She seeks to immerse herself in nature and to be granted its grace. The third stanza describes her journey, which takes on the form of a quest or pilgrimage to a holy shrine. The narrator climbs the mountains in order to deliver her goblet. She describes a state of ecstasy, in which she is bathed in sunlight. She is balanced between hillcrests as she rocks between valleys. After offering up her goblet, her arms swing freely as if they were stray clouds. She is immersed in nature's beauty and majesty.

The final stanza abruptly changes the poem's rhythm and tone. The speaker confesses that her epiphany was a false "alleluia." She sees herself as a pathetic, spiritless wanderer, empty-handed and empty-hearted; "anguish and fear" replace joy and elation. She recognizes her alienation from the human and natural as well as the spiritual world. The poem that begins in joy ends in sorrow.

Forms and Devices

Mistral's structure emphasizes the fluidity of language over the formal construct. The poet employs an interruption of the rhyme in one line of each stanza. The rhyme scheme in the original Spanish version is more fluid and consistent with the verse pattern established in the first stanza. Mistral devoted her attention to ideas and their linguistic expression rather than to the formal construction of her poem.

The ballad form contains eight-syllable lines with an assonant rhyme in the even lines. The odd lines are unrhymed. The pattern of the meter is similar to popular Spanish lyrical forms. Two four-line stanzas alternate with a five-line stanza and a final six-line stanza. Other sections contain some irregular unrhymed lines that resemble prose.

Symbols and metaphors appear throughout the poem. The goblet itself is reminiscent of the Holy Grail, which inspires the seeker to search for perfection and reunion in order to restore a paradise lost to peace and harmony. It may also symbolize an offertory cup such as that used in the sacrament of Holy Communion. Her gift of water offered up to the heavens in the first stanza alludes to the transmutation of the chalice of wine into the blood of Christ. It stands in stark contrast to the blood that falls from her chest and through her veins in the final two lines of the fourth stanza. The narrator embarks upon a personal quest in which she seeks communion with nature and a spiritual transformation.

In the first and third stanzas, the seeker transcends human frailties and limitations, completely immersed in the transformational symbols of the natural world leading her to spiritual enlightenment. Water serves as the dominant symbol of purification, baptism and initiation into the spiritual realm, and transformation from flesh into spirit. The goblet's gift to the poet is water. If she had lost it, she would have been in despair. Its life-giving and transformational properties would have abandoned her. In the final stanza, she lowers her eyes to empty hands, realizing, "I walk slowly, without my diamond of water." She is silenced by her spiritual poverty. In her emptiness, she admits, "I carry no treasure." Water is a jewel, a treasure that creates and sustains life. After acknowledging the loss of this precious gift, she falls into the depths of human suffering.

In the second stanza, she cuts herself off from the human world only to find in the fourth stanza that she is dragged back into it. The repetition of her denial is adamant. She declares, "I did not pause to greet cities" or any other human achievements, from a humble family to the Great Pyramid. In her denial of human connections and endeavors, she alienates herself from society as she seeks to elevate herself to a spiritual plain.

Actions not taken in the second stanza find their counterpoint in the third stanza. She does not greet cities, but she welcomes the sun on her throat as she greets it from a greater height than the "flight of towers" in the second stanza. She does not fling her arms out wide in praise of the Great Pyramid but opens her arms like free clouds at play amid the mountaintops. She does not build a home for "a circle of sons" in the second stanza. Rather, she rocks between hillcrests and admires valleys beneath her. The closed family circle is replaced with the open valleys that mirror her open arms, always reaching toward the sky's portal to heaven.

The second stanza lists symbols of human creation tied to the earth: cities, towers, home, and sons. However, the third stanza elevates the goblet-bearer to spiritual union with the elements by bringing its gift of water to air at its purest elevation, cleansed by the sun's fire as she is supported by the summits of hills, the earth's purest rock that touches the sky. The sun's fire also purifies the poet's words as she praises her heaven: "the new sun/ on my throat." This metaphysical transformation of abstract elements into comprehensible objects enables the reader to share in the poet's experience.

The fourth stanza serves as a cruel denouement to the spiritual epiphany of the third stanza. Lowered eyes and fallen blood metaphorically transform her from her high emotional state, represented by open arms, upward climbing, and triumph at the summit. After acknowledging her ephemeral flight, she wallows in misery and self-pity. Most poignant is the first line's sharp contrast in style and tone: "It was a lie, my alleluia. Look at me." Her words are more prosaic and describe the very human state of alienation, sorrow, and fear. Her eyes are lowered, her hands are empty, and she walks slowly and silently in a profound state of depression. In the final line, the blood that falls in her veins is "struck with anguish and fear." It replaces the goblet of water, or the chalice of Christ's blood that had sustained her spirit.

Themes and Meanings

Most critical to the poems collected in *Tala*, translated as "felling" or "harvesting," are the themes of sorrow and recovery, loss of faith and redemption. In its metaphysical thematic schema, Mistral's poem reveals life as a pilgrimage leading to death as a final liberation from the misery of the human world. She searches for universal principles that guide humans through life's sorrows and fears. Abstract universal concepts are conveyed by particular symbols. The symbolic language is a precise tool that transforms simple experiences into divine transcendence. Through it, Mistral expresses the heights and depths of human experience.

The ambience of Puerto Rico attracted Mistral, and the poem intends to convey its exotic tropical atmosphere as well as its purity and simplicity uncontaminated by civilization. The narrative is transformed by poetic language that echoes the movement of the surf's ebb and flow. While the poet sings her praise to Puerto Rico and its natural beauty, her love and awe for the Caribbean islands is overshadowed in the final stanza by a sense of alienation and spiritual duality. The bounty and splendor of nature leads the speaker to a false epiphany. In it, she discovers spiritual emptiness. The song of praise that characterizes the first three stanzas falls into mourning in the fourth stanza as the speaker abandons her hilltop alleluia and departs empty-handed in silence. The speaker laments: "And in my breast and through my veins/ falls my blood, struck with anguish and fear." Despite a temporary flight from her human suffering, she must return to examine and overcome her anguish and fear. Otherwise, a true and enduring spiritual transformation is unattainable.

Carole A. Champagne

GOD'S GRANDEUR

Author: Gerard Manley Hopkins (1844-1889)
Type of poem: Sonnet
First published: 1918, in *Poems of Gerard Manley Hopkins, Now First Published, with Notes by Robert Bridges*

The Poem

"God's Grandeur" is a Petrarchan sonnet describing a world infused by God with a beauty and power that withstands human corruption. The poem begins with the assertion that God has "charged" the world with grandeur. It then describes the implications of this "charge." The grandeur is like a physical force, an electric current, a brightness that can be seen.

The poet questions the human response to this grandeur. Why do humans not "reck his rod?" That is, why do they not recognize and accept divine rule? Instead, humans have dirtied this world by using it for mundane purposes. The images work on both the literal and metaphorical level. The poem may be read both as a literal lament for the destruction of the environment by industry, and as a metaphorical lament that humans are more concerned with the prosaic and utilitarian than with spiritual values. In any event, the world seems tarnished, and humans seem insulated, unable to perceive the underlying beauty and grandeur.

The poem's sestet dispels the gloom evoked in the first part. Even though humans are often insensitive to the glory of the world, "There lives the dearest freshness deep down things." The beauty and power of the world remains inviolable, intact. Though the night seems dark, there is a continuing restoration of the light and morning, because the presence of God, like the dove of peace, protects and restores the world.

Although Gerard Manley Hopkins wrote this poem in 1877, he did not seek to publish his poems; he entrusted them to his friend Robert Bridges. Bridges placed some of these poems in anthologies, but it was not until after the poet's death, in 1918, that Bridges published a volume of his friend's poetry.

Forms and Devices

Sonnets are fourteen-line poems built according to strict conventions in a tightly structured form. Hopkins was intrigued with the sonnet form and used it often, sometimes adding his own variations. His poem "That Nature is a Heraclitean Fire and of the comfort of the Resurrection" is a modified sonnet with twenty-three lines.

"God's Grandeur," however, is written according to the conventions of the Petrarchan sonnet, named for the Italian writer Petrarch. This sonnet form has two parts, the initial eight lines, or the octave (rhymed *abba, abba*), and the concluding six lines, or sestet (which here uses the rhyme scheme *cd, cd, cd*). Typically, the Petrarchan sonnet poses a problem in the octave and presents a resolution in the sestet. Hopkins poses the problem of the human response to the beauty of nature, as created by God. The resolution comes through God's grace, for divine concern preserves the beauty of the world intact despite human despoliation.

Hopkins studied Anglo-Saxon and Welsh poetry and drew from them an interest in alliteration, which he believed was essential to poetry. In "God's Grandeur" the letter *g* is associated with God: "grandeur," "greatness," "gathers," and "Ghost." Each line of the poem is knit together through intricate sound patterns that include alliteration (repetition of consonants at the start of words), assonance (repetition of vowel sounds), and consonance (the recurrence of consonants within words). For example, the second and third lines read:

> It will flame out, like shining from shook foil;
> It gathers to a greatness, like the ooze of oil.

Notice how vowels (the long *i* of "shining" and "like"; the *a* of "flame" and "greatness") and consonants (the repeated *l*, *sh*, *f*, *m*, *n*, *s*, and *g*) are echoed and re-echoed in the lines. Here and throughout the poem, words are repeated as well. In these lines, the simple words "it" and "like" recur. Elsewhere in the poem, words are repeated for emphasis: "have trod, have trod, have trod" suggests the repetitive, almost marchlike tread of generations of trudging people. The assonance of the vowels in "seared," "bleared," and "smeared" again drives home the ugliness of human destruction. The last line of the poem draws together in a complex pattern the consonants *w*, *r*, *b*, *d*, and *s*, which have echoed throughout the sestet and have come to carry the associations of the gentle, protecting warmth of God as a nesting dove. Further, the word "world" itself brings the reader back to the first line.

Alliteration may have had a philosophical meaning for Hopkins. He believed that the universe is built on the unity of God, which finds expression in the diversity of the natural world. Alliteration is a principle of showing the similarity of sounds in words of different meanings. Thus, alliteration becomes a poetic analogy of the unity underlying the diversity of the world.

Drawing again from the Anglo-Saxon and Welsh traditions, Hopkins made significant innovations in poetic rhythm. He was chiefly concerned with intensity, with capturing the essence of an image, idea, or action. To that end, he would often omit inessential words. Rather than using an even rhythm of stressed and unstressed syllables, as in iambic pentameter, he was interested in the number of stressed syllables. He might omit unstressed syllables for effect or use extra unstressed syllables where they seemed useful. One may scan this poem by counting the number of stressed syllables in each line. These vary from five stresses in the first line to six in the last.

Themes and Meanings

The problem that Hopkins poses in the octave is that of the human response to God: Why do people ignore the beauty and grandeur of God's presence in the natural world? The problem of the world's beauty and its divine origin was a central one for Hopkins, who was a talented artist and musician as well as a poet. His sketchbooks are full of detailed drawings of forms he found in nature: shells, twigs, waves, and trees. When he converted to Catholicism in 1866, he gave up his original plan of becoming a painter and decided to become a Jesuit priest. At that time, he worried that his attraction to the natural world and his love of music, art, and poetry was in contradiction to his religious vocation. He feared that his aesthetic impulses would draw him away from the strict asceticism he believed he must practice. He destroyed most of his early poems when he took religious orders.

Hopkins's resolution of his conflict came about when he was deeply moved by a newspaper account of a shipwreck that killed five German nuns. He told his rector about his feelings. The rector remarked that he wished someone would write a poem about the subject, and Hopkins took this casual comment as a personal mandate. He broke his seven-year poetic silence by writing "The Wreck of the *Deutschland*." After that, he continued to write poetry. In his poems, Hopkins explored his complicated feelings of faith and doubt. By celebrating the beauty of the natural world as an expression of God's power and "grandeur," Hopkins could reconcile his religious faith with his love of nature.

Repeatedly in his poetry Hopkins used his deep love of nature's beauty to reaffirm his belief in the God who created and maintained the world. In "God's Grandeur," this theme is developed with a great technical virtuosity to create a passionate poem that is somehow both a warning and a reassurance. Although Bridges delayed publication of Hopkins's work, fearing that readers would find it strange and difficult, contemporary readers find Hopkins an exciting and powerful poet. It is difficult to imagine modern poetry without the groundbreaking work of Gerard Manley Hopkins.

Karen F. Stein

GOLD AND BLACK

Author: Michael Ondaatje (1943-   )
Type of poem: Lyric
First published: 1973; collected in *There's a Trick with a Knife I'm Learning to Do: Poems, 1963-1978,* 1979

The Poem

"Gold and Black" is a short poem in free verse, its twelve lines divided into three stanzas. The title suggests color; its function is to show the color of the bees as well as the light images in the poem: the black night and the gold light. The first two stanzas are written in the first person. In the third stanza, the poem shifts to the third person, which adds a generality to its theme. There are times when a poet uses the first person to speak through a persona, as in a dramatic monologue, but here no distinction is implied between Michael Ondaatje the poet and the speaker of the poem. Yet, as Douglas Barbour writes in *Michael Ondaatje* (1993), "The 'I' that writes in these seemingly 'confessional' poems is purely inscribed, exists in each poem as a subject but alters his subjectivity from poem to poem." The "I" of "Gold and Black" can be seen as a character rather than the poet himself. A lyrical poem is about a subject, contains little narrative content, and addresses the reader directly.

"Gold and Black" begins with a metaphor for a nightmare, something that readers can readily understand. Just as a nightmare comes at night and disturbs the sleeper, so do the bees in the poem "pluck my head away." As the nightmare surrounds him, "Vague thousands drift" over him and "leave brain naked stark as liver." The nightmare, portrayed with the image of the bees, removes integral parts of his identity and creates a kind of spoiling of his thoughts. As the tone here is haunting and frightening, the image of the bees attacking the sleeper and taking away "atoms of flesh" is representative of the speaker's helplessness regarding his own nightmares, products of his unconscious.

In the second stanza, another person, Kim, is introduced; she is outside the speaker and outside the nightmare. The poet is no longer haunted by his nightmare but is instead affected by his lover, who is turning beside him: She "cracks me open like a lightbulb," he says. This action can be seen as Kim breaking the speaker into darkness as the nightmare flies away. As the poet takes readers out of the nightmare of the speaker, he takes them to the external forces in the speaker's world. His lover, too, is "In the black" but seems unaffected by her own nightmares. She is, rather, "a geiger counter" gauging his.

The third stanza shifts to a third-person point of view and describes "the dreamer" from a distance, as opposed to inside his own mind. This shift from the extremely personal first-person point of view to the generalization of the third-person point of view suggests that the problem of nightmarish hidden thoughts is everyone's problem. The shift also implies a universality in the loss of control in a nightmare, and ultimately in the unconscious. As this stanza concludes the poem, the reader is left with the image of "the dreamer in his riot cell," which suggests entrapment in a chaotic stage of sleep.

Forms and Devices

Metaphors are abundant in Ondaatje's work. He works with wondrous imagery and sometimes violent action, which both balance and reflect off each other. The people who inhabit his poems are often verging on madness and trying to deal with the violence and beauty of their worlds. With "Gold and Black," Ondaatje takes the ordinary state of sleep and creates a world of horror and loss of control over the speaker's thoughts, which buzz around him like bees and take parts of him with them.

A metaphor is a direct comparison between two dissimilar things, and "Gold and Black" is a series of images that are compared with one another. Most of the metaphors are implicit—the comparisons are not completely spelled out. For example, the poet never explicitly compares the nightmare to the "gold and black slashed bees," yet the context of the poem clearly suggests the comparison. The metaphors that the poet employs are both surprising (the bees taking the speaker's flesh away) and awesome (the dreamer trapped in the "riot cell" of his own mind), and they work to create the fantastic and private world of the speaker. They aim at mystery rather than explicitness, just as dreams often do.

The metaphors in "Gold and Black" move from the mind of the speaker to his external world and finally to the universal. This pattern is established in stanza 1, where "the gold and black slashed bees come/ pluck my head away." Although at first the image suggests external forces acting on the dreamer, it becomes clear that the bees are internal, as they "drift/ leave brain naked stark as liver." The last line of stanza 1 completes the pattern of the internal, creating a metaphor for the thoughts of the dreamer as rotten meat. Stanza 2 introduces Kim, who is outside of the speaker's mind (and nightmare), and takes the reader from the internal world of the dreamer: "She cracks me open like a lightbulb." The simile indicates that Kim has woken the speaker. She has cracked open the speaker's mind, the bees have flown away, and there is darkness in his mind where there was light.

The sleeper and Kim are surrounded by darkness, and the light in the speaker's unconscious has been put out. Stanza 3 depicts "the dreamer" from outside. The description of the subconscious as a "riot cell" depicts the loss of control in the realm of the subconscious as well as the confines of the "cell," or mind, that encompasses the thoughts. In several poems Ondaatje uses images of animals alongside images of the unconscious, particularly in the section "Rat Jelly" in *There's a Trick with a Knife I'm Learning to Do.* "Near Elginburg," "Spider Blues," and "The Gate in His Head" are other examples of this technique.

Themes and Meanings

"Gold and Black" is a poem about the unconscious, which is portrayed through nightmares and dreams. In one sense, the sleeper's underlying thoughts control the sleeper—as dreams and nightmares are seldom controlled—and illuminate hidden fears and desires of which the dreamer may or may not be aware. When one sleeps, the subconscious surfaces and sheds lights on innermost thoughts. The idea of being surrounded by darkness in order to see innermost thoughts has been explored by many poets. Ondaatje takes a somewhat unusual approach, however, in that here the light illuminates horror and violence, as opposed to beauty and truth, and it leaves the dreamer feeling helpless against his innermost fears. The shift to the third person at the end of the poem suggests, but does not definitively conclude, that all people are prisoners in their unconscious minds.

"Gold and Black" is also about isolation. The dreamer, in his nightmare, is isolated from the world and his loved ones. He must face his unconscious alone. Communication with the outside world is impossible within the nightmare, but as a loved one turns and wakes the dreamer, the nightmare goes dark, the light in the unconscious now out. "Gold and Black" takes the reader into the chaotic world of the senses and illustrates the difficulty that a suffering individual has in communicating his fears to the outside world—and even to himself.

Paula M. Martin

THE GOLD CELL

Author: Sharon Olds (1942-   )
Type of poem: Book of poems
First published: 1987

The Poems

Sharon Olds is among the most highly regarded contemporary American poets. Her work has been described as "haunting" and "striking," and the novelist Michael Ondaatje has said that it is "pure fire in the hands." Like the poet's earlier books *Satan Says* (1980) and *The Dead and the Living* (1984), Olds's third collection, *The Gold Cell*, makes aspects of everyday life—news items, childhood, family, and sexuality—its subject matter. Olds tells her audiences at poetry readings that she did not publish her poetry until late in life (she was thirty-seven years old when her first book was published) because she did not know whether she wanted to make her work public. She also says that when she decided to publish, she considered using a pseudonym. This hesitation to publish may have had something to do with Olds's tendency to blur the lines between the public and the private, for it is never quite clear where she draws the line between what she calls "the paper world and the flesh world."

As a result, many of Olds's readers view her books as "poetic memoirs," comparing her to confessional poets such as Anne Sexton and Sylvia Plath. Historically, American poets have argued that to assume too much of a connection between a poem's speaker and its writer is to commit a "biographical fallacy," though some contemporary American poets, perhaps influenced by a growing tendency in the United States to view public exposure of the private self as emotionally healthy and socially productive, admit to writing highly autobiographical pieces (Linda McCarriston, for example). Olds has been unwilling to publicly discuss the connections between her private life and her poetry, though, so readers must encounter Olds's poems on more universal grounds, taking them as one poet's attempt to see the world clearly and to represent it accurately. In an interview with Patricia Kirkpatrick, Olds says, "We need to know how bad we are, and how good we are, what we are really like, how destructive we are, and that all this often shows up in families." When Olds writes about the difficult aspects of human nature, then, she invites her readers to confront those realities with her, to know that these are the circumstances not only of individual lives but also of life in general.

Olds has been described as a poet of the landscape of time, and *The Gold Cell* traverses that landscape. The book has four parts: The first part is concerned with the relationship of the poet to the world in which she lives, the second focuses on childhood, the third deals with life beyond childhood, and the fourth is about the relationships between parents and children. Among the most frequently discussed poems in the first section are "On the Subway" and "The Girl." In their own ways, these two poems are at once disturbing and redemptive. In "On the Subway," the speaker encounters a black man on the subway and is forced to acknowledge her own racist assumptions. She says, "white skin makes my life, this/ life he could break so easily, the way I/ think his back is being broken." "The Girl" is about a twelve-year-old girl who is raped and left for dead, then must go on with her life: "she does a cartwheel, the splits, she shakes the/ shredded pom-poms in her fists," knowing "what all of us want never to know."

"I Go Back to May 1937," in part 2 of *The Gold Cell*, is about the speaker's desire to communicate with her parents before their marriage to warn them, "you are going to do things/ you cannot imagine you would ever do,/ you are going to do bad things to children,/ you are going to suffer in ways you never heard of,/ you are going to want to die." Initially, the speaker, who has the 20/20 vision of hindsight, wishes she could collapse time in order to influence her life and the lives of her parents; she wants to save herself and her parents by warning them that they are going to make terrible mistakes. In the end, however, the poem declares, "Do what you are going to do, and I will tell about it." In the course of the poem, the speaker—clearly a writer—decides to speak about her life, to answer it in her own words rather than wish it away. This poem's primary goal is to tell about the world as the poet sees it. Olds says that the poet has only what she knows and that the poet's unique experiences are central to her work. The question both the reader and the poet must ask is, "What can this poem tell?"

The title of the book is directly connected to the overriding themes in *The Gold Cell*. The book's cover art, which illustrates the title, is an adaptation of figure 14 from *The Collected Works of C. G. Jung* (1959). The figure is a gold ball surrounded by a snake, and Jung identifies it as an "Indian picture of *Shiva-bindu*, the unexpected point." Jung explains, "The god rests in the point. Hence, the snake signifies extension, the mother of Becoming, the creation of the world of forms." The Hindu god Shiva is the primordial state and the snake encircles that state, indicating both the containment and the continuity of creation and life. Therefore, all life forms connect, and life itself connects with the concept of god and with its own beginnings or source. This reference to creation, and particularly to the feminine aspects of creation, plays itself out in virtually every poem in the book; each of the poems works to examine and elucidate both life's cyclical nature (the connection of every moment to the previous and to the next) and the connections among lives.

Forms and Devices

In *The Gold Cell*, as in most of Olds's work, the metaphor represents the poet's vision and thinking. In interviews, Olds expresses concern with seeing accurately; her poems reveal her commitment to this goal, for their vision is unflinching. Part of what Olds wants readers to see has to do with the connections between endings and beginnings. "Summer Solstice, New York City" has as its narrative core the story of a man threatening to commit suicide by jumping off a building and his interactions with the people who convince him not to jump. However, the poem's metaphors reveal one of its philosophical points: that life's beginning and its end are inextricably tied. That tie becomes apparent when the title, in which the summer solstice represents birth and renewal, comes together with the poem's first image: a suicidal man walking across the roof of a building, then standing with "one leg over the complex green tin cornice." Within the poem, Olds describes the bulletproof vest one "cop" puts on as a "black shell around his own life,/ life of his children's father," an image that illustrates that the police officer, in the middle of his life, is aware of the impact his death would have on the lives of his children who have just begun their lives. Olds describes the net meant to catch the man if he does jump as a sheet "prepared to receive at a birth" and the burning ends of the cigarettes that the man and the police officers smoke as "tiny campfires we lit at night/ back at the beginning of the world." Though the man finally chooses life, the poem is about the possibility of his death. When Olds ends by connecting the image of the men smoking and the image of campfires at the beginning of the world, she implies that there is a connection between the beginning of all time and the beginning created when the man chooses not to jump. One life, the poem seems to imply, can represent all life.

In "Alcatraz," the prison, famous for its remote location and for its reputation as inescapable, becomes a metaphor for a child's shame and for the intense power parents have over their children's sense of self. The connections between humans and other animals and between the manufactured and natural worlds are established as the metaphor deepens; the prison becomes "white as a white/ shark in the shark-rich Bay," and its bars are like the shark's "milk-white ribs." The child sees herself as a shameful creature who will be swallowed whole by the prison shark. She believes she will be trapped there forever with "men" like her "who had/ spilled their milk one time too many,/ not been able to curb their thoughts." "Alcatraz" draws a connection not only between the child's life and that of other animals but also between the female child and the adult men who inhabit the prison when the speaker proclaims, "When I was a girl, I knew I was a man/ because they might send me to Alcatraz/ and only men went to Alcatraz."

If the metaphor reveals to readers the way Olds sees and thinks, then the poetic line helps readers hear how she speaks. Like most American poets writing in free verse during the latter half of the twentieth century, Olds has expressed great concern for the poetic line. Olds is known for her run-on sentences broken into lines and for lines that end in articles and conjunctions. In the Kirkpatrick interview, she publicly analyzes her use of the poetic line in *The Gold Cell*: "As for ending lines on *of the*, I think I did that too much in *The Gold Cell*, so much that the poems as written lack the musical form I hear in them." In spite of the poet's criticism of her own work, the lines as she writes them serve an important function. In "Looking at My Father," for instance, the second sentence spans sixteen-and-a-half lines. There are, in those sixteen lines, fifteen commas, two semicolons, and one colon. The combination of a run-on construction and lines that end in articles and conjunctions lends a breathlessness to the poem that expresses the difficult moment when a child both recognizes the failings of her father and acknowledges her connection to and affection for him.

Themes and Meanings

Olds is known for her frank discussions of sex and sexuality, and poems such as "First Sex," which appears in *The Gold Cell*, illustrate that she sees sexual issues as inextricably tied to other issues related to the human condition. She says, "I'm just interested in human stuff like hate, love, sexual love and sex. I don't see why not." "First Sex" focuses, as the title implies, on the speaker's first sexual experience. It begins with the speaker's confession, "I knew little, and what I knew/ I did not believe—they had lied to me," then goes on to describe in vivid detail a sexual encounter. "First Sex" embodies both the excitement of sex and the youth of its characters in phrases such as "his face cocked back as if in terror" and "sweat/ jumping out of his pores like sudden/ trails." As is the case with many of Olds's poems about sex, "First Sex" is a poem with a punch line, for in the end the speaker proclaims, "I signed on for the duration."

After the first printing of *The Gold Cell*, Olds revised several poems. These revisions seem to be designed to clarify images or reflect the poet's further thinking about an issue. The most significant revisions occur in the poem called "What if God" in which she modifies an entire metaphor. Between the original and final versions of the poem, Olds clarifies the mother's role, changing the lines "when my mother/ came into my bed" to "when my mother/ came into my room, at night, to lie down on me/ and pray and cry" and "like a/ tongue of lava from the top of the mountain" to "like lava from the top of the mountain." Olds says that she made these revisions because readers were interpreting the poem as a piece about the sexual abuse of a female child by her mother, a reading she had not intended. She says that she had not realized her metaphor could be read so literally but that when readers pointed the reading out to her she felt it important to clarify the image.

The revision of the metaphor necessitated a revision of the entire poem, and changes that occur toward the end are perhaps more significant than the changes to the original metaphor. In the first version, the speaker asks, "did He/ wash His hands of me as I washed my/ hands of Him," but in the final version she says, "He/ washed his hands of me as I washed my/ hands of Him." In the first version there is a possibility for hope that God has not abandoned the child, but in the final version that hope is eradicated. In the next two lines, the speaker asks (in both versions), "Is there a God in the house?/ Is there a God in the house?" In the first version of the poem, in which the possibility of heavenly intervention to help the child exists, these are hopeful cries, but in the second version, in which there is no hope of such intervention, they are the futile cries of a helpless child. While Olds removes the disturbing images of the sexual abuse of a child from the poem, the final version is ultimately more hopeless than the original.

Michelle Gibson

GOLDEN VERSES

Author: Gérard de Nerval (Gérard Labrunie, 1808-1855)
Type of poem: Sonnet
First published: 1845, as "Vers dorés"; in *Les Chimères*, 1854; English translation
collected in *An Anthology of French Poetry from Nerval to Valéry in English Translation with French Originals*, 1958

The Poem

Gérard de Nerval's sonnet "Golden Verses" relates humankind to the natural world. In its dual suggestions of the dominance of humanity and the dominance of nature, the poem draws on a conflict that is still very real in modern times, as humanity tries to decide when to control nature and when to leave it alone.

This traditional Petrarchan sonnet in Alexandrine verse concludes Nerval's sonnet sequence *Les Chimères*. The title (chimeras) may refer to the mythological beast or to any imaginary vision. In the light of this definition, one wonders which of the views expressed in his sonnet Nerval held to be true. The first quatrain, with its reference to man as a "free thinker," recalls the scientific positivism of the Enlightenment, when the concept of progress by means of the scientific analysis of nature promised to free humans from the superstitions that free thinkers associated with traditional religious beliefs. Both modern science and the Christian views that had preceded it, however, granted to humankind a special status that made it superior to all other things in nature. Both of these schools of thought pushed aside a much older belief in which ancient peoples had seen divinity in nonhuman forms.

In the first quatrain, Nerval seeks to recall the old belief, asking how humans can believe that they alone are capable of thought when "life bursts forth in all things" around them. When he says that the "universe is absent" from human "councils," Nerval's suggestion of a governmental body invokes an area of thought that gives great attention to the rights of humankind and little consideration to those of nature.

The second quatrain asks man to respect the various elements of nature, but a change occurs in the final line when Nerval asserts that "all has power over you." Up to this point, the power in the poem was human power, the "forces that you hold" of the first quatrain. Now, suddenly, humankind must face a strength that is potentially superior to its own. When the sestet begins with the imperative "Fear," the once secure position of humankind is clearly threatened.

Nerval seeks to restore the respect that was once given to nonhuman things. If a "hidden God" resides within each element of the natural world, humankind has a sacred duty to respect the life and growth of these things. When the final line says that "a pure spirit grows," however, it introduces two new concepts into the poem. First, the pure spirit seems to be of a more transcendent nature than that of the animal or vegetable life to which the earlier lines seem to be referring. If this is the case, the growth of this spirit constitutes a form of theological progress that outweighs the concerns of humanity.

Forms and Devices

Nerval's choice of imagery in "Golden Verses" reflects the context of the nineteenth century, but in a way that is distinctly his own. The Romantic poets' concept of nature was strongly pantheistic. Victor Hugo repeatedly invoked such a world, as he does in his poem "To Albert Dürer" (from *Les Voix intérieures*, 1837) in which the forest, to Dürer's "visionary eye" becomes "a hideous monster." This pantheistic life in nature, apparent only to the artist's penetrating vision, also retained a link with its classical origins. (According to Hugo, Albrecht Dürer "saw . . . the faun . . . the sylvan . . . Pan.") Thus it seems strange that, except for his sonnet's epigraph, which is attributed to Pythagoras, Nerval does not cite explicitly classical sources, but presents his pantheism in an entirely modern context.

Paradoxically, the only special degree of insight to which Nerval's sonnet alludes is not that of the poet as seer, but that of the free thinker who believes that humans alone are capable of thought. The only voice that recalls the insights of a pantheistic world is that of Nerval himself.

In the second quatrain, Nerval's generic imagery leads the reader ever further from the initial focus on humankind, first to the beast, then to the flower, and finally to metal. In his choice of categorical references that do not specify which beast or which flower, Nerval parallels a generic form of expression that Charles Baudelaire would develop later in *Les Fleurs du mal* (1857; *Flowers of Evil*, 1909) in which flowers, almost never a specific variety, become emblems of beauty and poetry.

With the final element named in the second quatrain, metal, Nerval draws especially close to Baudelaire. In his poem "To the Reader," Baudelaire describes moral strength as "the rich metal of our will," and references to metal and gems occur frequently in his work. Despite the similar vocabulary, however, this usage serves to pinpoint the difference between Baudelaire and Nerval in their use of generic nature images. For Baudelaire, the importance of either the metal or the flower comes from its role in representing an attribute or a creation of humankind: will or poetry. For Nerval, the life that exists in natural elements does not depend on humans. It has an independent status, resisting human attempts to dominate it, but can nevertheless influence the world.

Given this subordination of humankind's role, the choice of imagery in the sestet contains an apparent contradiction. When Nerval tells the free thinker to "fear in the blind wall a gaze spying on you," not only does blindness conflict with seeing, but also the wall itself seems an unlikely object for this role. Although they may contain natural stones, walls are human construction, but this exploitation of the material is doubtless what Nerval has in mind in his injunction not to make "any impious image" of it.

In any case, the progression of objects Nerval invokes in this sonnet takes one far from those in which one is accustomed to imagining life. Plant and animal life are not unusual, but to find sentience in metal or stone, even after the latter has been worked by human hands, demands a leap of faith. Thus the "eye" born in the final tercet seems that of a chimeric being.

Themes and Meanings

While with his generic imagery Nerval seems to make a simple statement that is devoid of detail and as spare as the sonnet form is brief, when the poem is considered in its context, a further complexity emerges that is perhaps analogous to the sonnet in its detailed structure. Between its autobiographical opening sonnet, "El Desdichado," and this concluding one, *Les Chimères* devotes five sonnets to figures from pagan antiquity and five to the sonnet sequence "Christ on the Mount of Olives." In the context of "Golden Verses," this pagan/Christian dualism may seem to combine views centered on nature and on humanity. The time sequence of the poems, however, suggests a more coherent view.

Time as it is invoked in "El Desdichado" works backward from the early references to "my only Star," said to be the woman Nerval loved, and the relatively modern Dürer engraving of *Melencolia I* (1514) to classical references to the Acheron and Orpheus. Nerval frequently connected his family to early periods of French history, but here he combines French references with those from a much earlier time. Thus, by the time the first sonnet ends, one is ready to accept Nerval's assertion in the first pagan poem, "Myrtho," that "the Muse made me one of the sons of Greece."

One may wonder how much of Nerval's pagan experience was real and how much was imagined, for while he asserts that he "had drunk the intoxication" of it, the role of the Muse still implies the intervention of imagination. The experience of the sonnet sequence takes Nerval to a number of early cultures, and the nature gods of Egypt in "Horus" parallel the pantheism of the Greeks. In all these settings, however, he finds evidence of a dying world. The "clay gods" of "Myrtho" are broken, and Isis in "Horus" says "the new spirit is calling me." In "Delfica," Nerval seeks consolation: "They will come back, those Gods you weep for!" Inevitably, however, Christ follows the pagan gods.

Nerval shows the reader Christ at his most desperate moment, facing death alone, but his Christ speaks already of a vast experience. Unlike the pagan sonnets, which are rich in flower images that may be linked to the nature invoked in "Golden Verses," "Christ on the Mount of Olives" abandons such imagery for a vaster vision of "worlds," and Christ affirms that "no spirit exists in these immensities." A profusion of life existed in the elements of nature, but it has become invisible to the Christian view that is oriented toward the cosmos but not toward the things of this world.

Thus "Golden Verses" may serve as the moral that concludes the sonnet sequence. Having experienced and compared the cultures of the past, Nerval finds himself in the visionary role of the poet who should advise humanity. The context of the poem may be Greek without specifically Greek references within the text because its message results from the entirety of Nerval's poetic vision. The multiple imperatives of the poem define the poet's role in that it is he who must return humanity to the consciousness of nature.

Dorothy M. Betz

GOLFERS

Author: Irving Layton (Irving Peter Lazarovitch, 1912-   )
Type of poem: Satire
First published: 1955, in *The Blue Propeller*

The Poem

"Golfers" is a short poem in free verse. It comprises three stanzas of three lines each, a parenthetical single-line stanza, and a closing couplet. It belongs to one of the most intensely creative and productive periods in Irving Layton's long publishing career as a poet—the middle to late 1950's and the early 1960's—when he wrote some of the best and most memorable of his poems. Many of his poems of this period celebrate the creative urge so central to Layton's life and writing. The central observation of "Golfers" is one that is voiced over and over in Layton's poetry: contempt for those whom he believes deny the life force by leading lives and taking moral stances that seem to Layton sterile and static.

Of the many volumes in which "Golfers" has appeared since its first publication in Layton's seventh solely authored collection, *The Blue Propeller* (1955), the one that seems best suited to its tone and intent is F. R. Scott and A. J. M. Smith's *The Blasted Pine: An Anthology of Satire, Invective, and Disrespectful Verse*, first published in 1957 and reissued in a second edition in 1967, Canada's centennial year. In both editions, "Golfers" is included in a section entitled "Solid Citizens," in which Canadians, particularly of Anglo-Scottish descent, and their institutions and mores are the chief target of the satirical verse. Though it is nowhere stated in Jewish poet Layton's poem that the golfers depicted are Gentile, they do seem the epitome of the "country-club set": smug and exclusive Gentile materialists and nation-builders that the professedly atheist but strongly Hebraist and socialist Layton abhorred and whom he has pilloried all of his writing life.

In "Golfers," Layton depicts golf, a slow, mannered game of strategy and precision, as the choice of those people who relate not at all to earthy, Dionysian joy—the sensual, creative principle—but who cultivate a cerebral sterility of morality, mind, and spirit. Wynne Frances, in a critical work on Irving Layton, says:

> Philistinism is the name Layton gives to that compound of smugness, rigidity, gentility, complacency, materialism, and moral apathy that he regards as the most insidious threat to the creative spirit. He attacks it wherever he finds it . . . anywhere in the world.

Forms and Devices

The poem's opening three lines are a simile formed on an allusion to Michel de Montaigne (1533-1592), the renowned French essayist unsurpassed for his thorough, enlightened, and lively observation of human nature with all of its idiosyncrasies and folly. Montaigne's "distinction/ between virtue and innocence" differentiates between virtue, a chosen moral position, and innocence, a lack of experience. Layton believes that the creative urge can be best expressed and satisfied through experience, so that innocence is not necessarily a desirable state: virtue seems to him a moral stance that often precludes experience and invites intellectual, moral, and spiritual stasis. The golfers appear to have opted for virtue: irritated, the poet observes, "what gets you is their unbewilderment." The coined word, where "certainty" or "confidence" might have served, implies an attitude of deliberate disengagement from the turmoil and vitality of a headlong encounter with experience, with *life*.

Stanza 2 comprises another simile: The intrusion of the golfers into a pastoral scene is likened to the despoliation of landscape by raw, unfinished houses. The golfers "come into the picture suddenly"; whether this phrase is simply a colloquial expression of the golfers' sudden appearance or is an expression of their assault on the poet's artistic sensibilities and his communion with the natural setting is unclear. In stanza 3, the tone is jeering; the contempt of the poet for these Philistines is intensified. The poem's tenth line, a parenthetical aside, picks up the thread of the moral and spiritual stance that the poet attributes to the golfers in the poem's first stanza, and the reader realizes the extended metaphor on which the satirical structure of the poem is based. "(What finally gets you is their chastity)," complains the poet; the golfers are compared to reluctant virgins, trapped in restraints that prohibit their access to sensual pleasure and fulfillment.

While virtue and innocence can be admired and understood as conditions involving free will or inexperience, chastity is generally viewed as having been imposed and is regarded as an undesirable state. To a poet who embraces Dionysian philosophy with the overt enthusiasm that Layton always has, chastity is practically obscene. Thus in the closing couplet the poet makes a final sardonic observation about the golfers: "And that no theory of pessimism is complete/ which altogether ignores them."

Themes and Meanings

From the beginning of his career as a poet, Layton has defined himself as anti-intellectual, although the profusion of literary, historical, philosophical, and mythological allusion in his poetry speaks to the enormous range of his reading and thinking and belies the anti-intellectual stance he takes. According to critic Eli Mandel, Layton's is "a poetry of profound social and personal concern. . . . Layton belongs with the sort of writer (and artist) [George Bernard] Shaw was prepared to speak of as poet-prophet." In the eloquent "Foreword" to his 1959 collection *A Red Carpet for the Sun*, in which "Golfers" also appears, Layton voices his central concerns, laying out the issues he takes up so aggressively in his poetry. Those concerns are ego- and life-centered; poetry is the artistic medium through which he addresses them:

> The free individual—independent and gay—is farther from realization than he ever was. Still, in a world where corruption is the norm and enslavement universal, all art celebrates him, prepares the way for his coming. . . . Poetry, by giving dignity and utterance to our distress, enables us to hope, makes compassion reasonable.

"Golfers," though ultimately too slight a poem to sustain the weight of Layton's vociferous disapproval, does embody what Mandel cites as Layton's central themes: "[T]he nature of the creative process, . . . and the social implications of both human perversity and creativity. . . . But beyond, . . . is the question of articulation itself, the pattern and meaning of poetic form." If Layton's vision is thus understood, the rationale of "Golfers" 's central simile becomes clear. More than being symbolic of a social and cultural group that Layton abhors, the golfers are anathema to his beliefs as a person and a poet. The comparison of the golfers to the "gaps [in subsequent collections amended to the harsher "gapes"] and planed wood" of unfinished houses depicts them as raw, ungainly, without athletic ability or (more significantly) aesthetic wholeness or satisfaction. The poet invites the reader to share his opinion that "among sportsmen they are the metaphysicians." He dismisses golf as an effete game that is contemplative and bloodless, one in which the golfers may strike poses and take attitudes—just as metaphysicians are often regarded as practitioners of a most abstruse branch of philosophy. The golfers are laughable, in the poet's view, because they are "intent, untalkative, pursuing Unity," an aesthetic structure as artificial, empty, and unsatisfying as an unfinished house. (In his *Gulliver's Travels* (1726), eighteenth century satirist Jonathan Swift similarly mocked the fictitious Laputians, scholars so cerebrally preoccupied that they needed "Flappers" to draw their attention to earthly realities.)

The bitter irony of the poem's closing couplet, then, arises from Layton's view that golfers represent almost everything he abhors as a person and a poet. "Why are people so destructive and joy-hating? Is it a perception of the unimportance of their lives finally penetrating the bark of their complacency and egotism?" he asks plaintively in the "Foreword" of *A Red Carpet for the Sun*. It is above all the misplaced arrogance of the golfers on which Layton focuses his satire and defines his own "theory of pessimism" in "Golfers."

Jill Rollins

THE GOOD-MORROW

Author: John Donne (1572-1631)
Type of poem: Lyric
First published: 1633, in *Poems, by J. D.: With Elegies on the Authors Death*

The Poem

"The Good-Morrow" is a poem of twenty-one lines divided into three stanzas. The poet addresses the woman he loves as they awaken after having spent the night together.

The poem begins with a direct question from the poet to the woman. Deliberately exaggerating, the poet expresses his conviction that their lives only began when they fell in love. Before, they were mere babies at their mothers' breasts or were indulging in childish "country pleasures." This phrase had a double edge in John Donne's time: it would have been understood as a reference to gross sexual gratification. Perhaps, the poet continues, they were asleep in the Seven Sleepers' den (referring to an ancient Syrian legend in which persecuted Christians slept for several hundred years in a cave near Ephesus). He asserts that compared with their true love ("this"), all past pleasures have been merely "fancies," and the women he "desir'd, and got" were only a "dream" of this one woman.

The second stanza opens with a triumphant greeting to their souls as they awaken into a constant, trusting love. They have no need to keep a jealous eye on each other because their love subdues the desire to look for other partners; it is so complete, so self-sufficient, that it "makes one little room, an everywhere."

The emphasis moves to the external world that the lovers have abandoned for each other. The poet contrasts the physical worlds sought by explorers and map readers with the spiritual world of the lovers. When he asserts that each of them is a world in itself, he is referring to the Elizabethan concept of microcosm and macrocosm: the view that every man and woman is a miniature universe, with the same qualities and components as the greater universe.

In the third stanza, the poet's attention focuses even more intimately on himself and the beloved. As they gaze into each other's eyes, each sees a tiny image of the other reflected in the lover's eye, and "true plain hearts" that "in the faces rest." Where, the poet asks, could they find "two better hemispheres"—referring to their faces and to the two lovers themselves as two halves of one world. Their love is spiritual, not earthly, and so is not subject to coldness ("sharp North") or decrease ("declining West").

The concept behind the fifth line is that the earthly sphere is composed of heterogeneous substances which are unstable, ever-changing, and therefore mortal. The heavenly sphere is formed of homogeneous spiritual substance, which is pure and eternal. Sensual love is earthly and subject to change and decay, whereas the love enjoyed by the poet and his beloved is "equal," a state of oneness, a pure and changeless union.

Forms and Devices

Donne is considered an innovator in the area of love poetry. The Renaissance style relied heavily upon convention: the predictable nature of the love affair, the idealized qualities and appearance of the woman, the subservient role of the poet, and the courtly language in which he addressed the woman. Donne broke all these conventions. He shocked readers of his century and the next with his direct, dramatic style, his colloquial language, his open approach to physical aspects of love, and his use of the broken rhythms of real speech. He was also criticized for perplexing the women in his poems (traditionally addressed in terms of uncomplicated emotion) with complex metaphysical matters.

Donne begins "The Good-Morrow" with a typically dramatic opening—no less than three insistent questions to the woman, in the style of everyday speech. The entire poem has the air of being part of an intimate conversation which keeps one always conscious of the immediate presence of the woman. The language and imagery of the poem, however, are deliberately exaggerated, with a strong element of paradox.

For example, love is said to make one small room an everywhere—an image which can be grasped intuitively but which outrages logic. Notice also that the speech rhythms in this phrase work against the basic iambic pattern of a weak stress followed by a strong one: two consecutive strong stresses (a metrical unit called a spondee) fall on the first two syllables of "one little." The effect of this heavy pair of stresses is to undercut the diminution implied by both these words—an effect that is driven home by the most powerful stress of the line, on the first syllable of "everywhere." Another spondee throws into strong relief the first two words of the phrase "true plain hearts"—again, an idea the poet wants to emphasize.

Donne uses strong and weak stresses, and strong and weak verb constructions, to emphasize his thematic contrasts. The "sea-discoverers" and map readers are dismissed in the weak constructions of "Let [them] . . . have gone,/ Let [them] . . . have shown," where the verbs, weakly stressed and in the indirect subjunctive form, allow the ends of the lines to tail off. The threefold repetition of "worlds" also makes the whole adventuring enterprise seem wearisome. In contrast, the lovers "possess" their world—a strong, heavily stressed verb followed by a weighty pause after "world."

The language, line structures, and meter describing the perfection of the lovers' relationship is also worthy of note. The unmusical rhythm and language of "Which I desir'd, and got," contrasts strongly with the lilting rhythm and smooth assonance of "'twas but a dream of thee." The first and fourth lines of the last stanza are divided into two halves, one in perfect symmetrical balance with the other, reflecting the constant, even nature of the relationship described. The structure of these lines reflects the important ideas of the third line, where the lovers are described as two perfect hemispheres making one sphere, and the fifth line, which asserts that "Whatever dies, was not mix'd equally."

Themes and Meanings

The poem is one of contrasts: between gross physical lust and true love; between the poet's profligate past and the lovers' present spiritual awakening; between earthly worlds sought by sea discoverers and the spiritual world discovered by the lovers. These contrasts are brought out in the main themes of sight, awakening from sleep, and earthly versus spiritual worlds.

Renaissance theories saw the sense of sight as central to the birth and continuance of love. In this poem, the sense of sight is seen in two opposing guises: the roving eye of the libertine, and the constant, steady gaze of mature "true" love.

This theme is introduced in the sixth line of the first stanza, where he refers to the attractive women whom he saw, desired, and "got"—a deliberately unsubtle expression. The triumphant opening to the second stanza brings forth the comment that the poet and his lady do not watch each other out of fear, since their true love controls "all love of other sights"—meaning, all interest in the outside world (turning "one little room into an everywhere"). In the third stanza, the lovers gaze into each other's eyes so single-mindedly that they see each other's reflections. Moreover, the steadiness of their gaze is reinforced by the true, plain hearts that "rest" in their faces—an image of openness and trust in each other.

The lovers' lives before they met are discussed in terms of sleep and the unreality of dreams. They were as if asleep in the den of the Seven Sleepers of Ephesus. The pleasures he sought were "fancies," every other woman "but a dream of thee." These images throw into lively relief the radiant greeting that celebrates the lovers' literal and metaphorical awakening into their mature love: "And now good-morrow to our waking souls."

The theme of sea discoverers and map readers pursuing new worlds was topical in Donne's time, as the boundaries of the old world were broken to include freshly discovered continents. Since the dominant contrast in the poem is between true love and false, it is possible that these explorers carry the additional connotation of sexual adventurers. However this may be, the world that the lovers are shutting out is one of high excitement and romance; how infinitely more attractive, then, must be the self-sufficient universe of their love, which is capable of rendering their small room "an everywhere." Theirs is a perfect world, as opposed to the earthly spheres of the explorers. As such, it is not marred by the seasons' inconstancy, and is of such a fine equal spiritual substance, that it can neither weaken nor die.

Claire Robinson

THE GOOSE FISH

Author: Howard Nemerov (1920-1991)
Type of poem: Lyric
First published: 1955, in *The Salt Garden*

The Poem

"The Goose Fish" is a study in irony, and the irony begins with the title. On one level, the title is straightforward and appropriate, because the goose fish occupies center stage in the poem's "story": It is assigned many roles, including onlooker, comedian, optimist, emblem, and patriarch. The irony is that the fish is dead, so one might well wonder how significant any of those roles might be. The poem is in iambic tetrameter and trimeter, in five stanzas of nine lines each (eight lines of tetrameter and the last of trimeter).

The first stanza sets the scene—a moonlit night on the beach—and contains the poem's central action: Two people, believing themselves alone, passionately embrace. For a short time, they believe themselves "emparadised" on the "long shore" where "their shadows [are] as one." In stanza 2, the lovers feel embarrassed afterward, but nevertheless stand united, "conspiring hand in hand." Believing themselves alone, they are shocked to discover that they have been "watched" by a goose fish "turning up, though dead/ His hugely grinning head." This ghoulish discovery not only shocks them but also induces guilt. The presence of the goose fish, in a sense, "gooses" the lovers out of self-centeredness into the realization that their lovemaking did not take place in isolation.

Stanza 3 shows the lovers staring at the dead fish, wondering at its significance. Before discovering it, the lovers had thought that lovemaking would carve for them "a world their own." Having realized that they are not apart from the rest of the world, they try to place a private meaning onto "the observer." Stanza 4 reveals that the lovers, not knowing what the fish symbolizes, decide that its "wide and moony grin" makes it first a comedian, then an "emblem of/ Their sudden, new and guilty love." There is a suggestion in this last line that the fish's observation makes their love "guilty" either because they have been "caught" or because of their modesty at having been watched.

The last stanza ironically stresses the continuing naïveté of the lovers. Not knowing what to make of their grisly audience, the lovers decide that the fish is their friend and their "patriarch," perhaps in an effort to extort a sort of blessing from the fish. The grin, which is so grotesque in death, fails to explain anything. The presence of death, like a bad joke, has accompanied the lovers both before and after their "private" union, just as the moon continues to follow its accustomed path along the sky.

Forms and Devices

The action in "The Goose Fish" is achieved through the lovers' experience of different stages of feeling and knowing, rather than through their experiencing severe external actions. In fact, the movement in the poem is based on their responses after they make love, not on the lovemaking itself. The poem is unified by its images, two explicit—the moon and fish—and one implicit, that of the drama.

This drama image frames the poem. It has been noted that "The Goose Fish" is structured like a drama, with its five verses taking the place of five acts in a play. The lovers are actors upon the "stage" of the long beach. The moon serves as spotlight for an audience of one, the fish. When the lovers are finished with their lovemaking, they are embarrassed, "as if shaken by stage-fright." They stand together "on the sand," "hand in hand" like actors taking a bow on the stage. In this context, the goose fish is considered "a comedian" whose act "might mean failure or success." The moon's decline in the last stanza is like the fall of a curtain on the last act.

Two explicit images dominate and organize "The Goose Fish"—the moon and the fish. "Moon" in some form and the fish appear in each stanza. In the first stanza, the moon is mentioned but not emphasized. The moon serves as a spotlight to convince the lovers that they are alone, as they see no one else in its light. Then the moon becomes "hard" and "bony" in the lovers' perception as they experience embarrassment after their passion; the moon also casts its light upon the macabre fish. Stanza 3 finds the moon also described as hard, although this time it is the hardness of fragile china. Like the moon, the fish is ancient; like the fish, the moon is "bony." This is the beginning of the merging of the images; they blend in stanza 4: The fish has a "wide and moony grin." This merging of the two central images, the earthly and dead with the heavenly and eternal, implies the larger unity of the cosmos, which the lovers finally recognize.

The regular meters of "The Goose Fish" (its iambic tetrameter with each stanza's closing iambic trimeter line) plus its detached, objective narrator give the poem a detached, philosophical tone. Howard Nemerov's successive use of long vowels in the first stanza ("On the long shore, lit by the moon") drags the lines' sounds out in imitation of a stretch of beach. Similarly matching form to content, the energy of the lines increases with the action in his use of shorter, abrupt words, such as "For them by the swift tide of blood" and "But took it for an emblem of." Thus, the metrics of "The Goose Fish" subtly reinforce the content.

Themes and Meanings

"The Goose Fish," a study in irony, deals with the delusions of humankind. On one level, the lovers express the ultimate delusion—that they can make a world apart from the rest of the cosmos. This is what they believe they accomplish by making love unobserved on the sand. Ironically, they are not alone, but are watched by the fish, that simultaneously represents the cosmos and the equally inescapable presence of death. The intruding goose fish, with its oddly comical expression, punctures the romantic mood created by the first stanza, with its description of the moonlit shore. The lovers' queries as to the fish's meaning present further comment on humankind's egocentricity.

From the lovers' discovery that they are not unobserved follows an implicit comment on the deceptiveness of appearances. The lovers think themselves alone, because of the moon's light and because of their passion, but they are controlled by the very forces they believe they can escape. The fish's sudden "appearance" is not actually sudden at all. It has been there all the time, just as death is always present even in the most seminal situations. In fact, "The Goose Fish" concerns an ironic "love triangle," the lovers and the fish, or the lovers and the rest of life and death.

Another contrast between the worlds of appearances and reality is in the soft sweeping beauty of the beach with its underlying hardness. The moon softly lights lapping waves and warm sand. Beneath this scene of supposed privacy and comfort, however, is a dead fish with brittle bones; the moon's light becomes hard, optimism is rigid, and death grins with "picket teeth," as a bony moon goes down its "track."

Although the central delusion is the lovers' belief that they are unobserved and that through mating they can create a separate sphere, they are also deluded in other ways. Never does the poem indicate that they realize that they are as much of a part of the universe as the moon that goes along its "tilted track" and that they are only "doing what comes naturally" by copulating on the sand as would any other species.

The lovers also think that the fish has special meaning for them, and they try to decipher it. They "hesitated at his smile," but once recognizing that they have been wrong in their presuppositions, they again make a mistake in assuming that the fish's presence is a "sign" which will explain "everything." Here, the lovers fall into another egocentric trap. They assume that the outside world revolves around them and is sending messages. They anthropomorphize the goose fish into "their patriarch," after assuming that it must be "an emblem" of their love.

Although the goose fish "never did explain the joke/ That so amused him, lying there," the lovers enshrine him to legitimize themselves. The joke, actually, is on them; the lovers may grasp that they are part of the whole, but they do not see that they are an insignificant part. The universe does not revolve around them; in fact, their behavior is as programmed and as impersonal as the moon's mechanistic route. The lovers show no recognition of their mortality, even when death "grins" at them. Instead, they transform the obvious into a personal emblem.

"The Goose Fish," one of Howard Nemerov's most anthologized poems, illustrates the poet's philosophical side as well as his realistic awareness of nature as entity in itself, not subject to humanity's "pathetic fallacy." The poem also contains, implicitly, a wry comment on humanity's foolishness and life's mystery.

Mary Hanford Bruce

A GRAMMARIAN'S FUNERAL

Author: Robert Browning (1812-1889)
Type of poem: Elegy
First published: 1855, in *Men and Women*

The Poem

Robert Browning's "A Grammarian's Funeral," subtitled "Shortly After the Revival of Learning in Europe," is a funeral elegy in four stanzas. It is written in the first-person plural, suggesting either a group or a single person speaking for a group. It is important to bear in mind the distance between the speaking persona of the poem and the poet himself; throughout "A Grammarian's Funeral," Browning is careful to include elements that make the reader question the objectivity and accuracy of the speaker's (or speakers') observations.

The poem describes a funeral procession for a noted grammarian; the procession leaves a sleeping countryside at daybreak and makes its way to a burial site high on a mountain. The funeral party is composed of students of the grammarian, including the speaker(s), who praise their dead master enthusiastically for his devotion to scholarship and his choice of a life of learning over a more conventional existence.

As the students proceed up the mountain, they describe the grammarian, his early years, his decision to embark on a life of study, and finally, his physical decline and death. They speak with admiration of his contempt for life's more ordinary pursuits and praise his focus on lofty scholarship.

Forms and Devices

Browning uses form and language to heighten the poem's thematic tension between appearance and reality, between the high praise the students lavish on their master and the more shadowy, contradictory portrait of the grammarian that emerges through their posthumous encomium.

The phrasing of the poem is frequently awkward and discordant, and the unusual metrical pattern is distinctly unmelodious: "He ventured neck or nothing—heaven's success/ Found, or earth's failure:/ 'Wilt thou trust death or not?' He answered 'Yes:/ Hence with life's pale lure!'" Such verse seems particularly incongruous in a poem about the great achievements of a man whose life was devoted to the study of the graceful and flowing language of Homer and Sophocles.

The verse seems to undercut the ostensibly serious tone of the poem. The feminine rhymes in the even-numbered lines create a somewhat comic effect, at times resembling strained doggerel more than serious verse. Lines such as "*Calculus* racked him:/ . . . *Tussis* attacked him," and "Fancy the fabric/ . . . Ere mortar dab brick!" are but a few examples of the pat, singsong rhyming found throughout the poem.

Despite the praise of the grammarian's lofty idealism, there is much in the poem that seems to decry his austere way of life. The most apparent is the recurrent imagery of death. In the setting of the funeral, the grammarian is first referred to as "the corpse." He is described rather strangely as "famous, calm, and dead." The students themselves make an unwitting acknowledgment of a connection between death and a life of selfless devotion to scholarship when they say, "Seek we sepulture," implying that the pursuit of knowledge leads to death. It is interesting to note that the only specific reference to the grammarian's field of study (as opposed to more general references to "learning" throughout the poem) occurs at the grammarian's deathbed, as he stammers out Greek grammar through his death rattle.

This physical death, however, is not the only death associated with the grammarian. The life he leads with such singleness of purpose can be seen as a kind of death-in-life in which he rejects the fullness of an ordinary life for the intense but one-dimensional life of a scholar. At the beginning of his career he determined that "before living he'd learn how to live"—but if he follows this plan he will never begin to live, since, as he himself knows, there is "No end to learning." He seems glad to make this sacrifice, saying, "Hence with life's pale lure!"

Other images add to the ambiguity of the grammarian's portrayal. Despite the students' admiration of him as a heroic figure, the grammarian is described as bald, "cramped and diminished," with "eyes like lead." He was racked with physical disease, and by the end of his life he was "dead from the waist down," hardly the "Lyric Apollo" his students describe. Browning uses imagery such as this deliberately to set up tension between the positive and negative aspects of the grammarian and his life's work.

Themes and Meanings

"A Grammarian's Funeral" is marked by ambiguity and division. By contrasting the ideal and the actual and by subtly emphasizing the difference between appearance and reality, Browning creates a shadowy, ambiguous character and leaves the reader to decide whether the grammarian is the hero, as his students see him, or a foolishly overzealous scholar who has rejected life for the pursuit of trivial knowledge.

The grammarian's students praise him as a paragon of scholarship and intellectual vigor, and often he is described as an admirable figure striving for lofty ideals. His complete and wholehearted absorption in his studies seems particularly inspiring when he says, "What's time? Leave Now for dogs and apes!/ Man has forever." The grammarian's life of scholarship in this light seems a noble example of the Renaissance spirit of dedication to the pursuit of knowledge, and Browning's pinpointing of the time in which the poem is set as the beginning of the Renaissance is significant; the grammarian's close study of Greek grammar may well have paved the way for more accessible and practical products of the renewal of classical scholarship.

The grammarian's chosen field of study, however, is treated with some ambivalence. After the students' enthusiastic praise of the grammarian's devotion to an idealized but rather vague "learning," one is surprised to discover that his great achievements are in the realm of particles of grammar. The subject seems comically trivial in comparison with the comprehensive study of "bard and sage" described earlier. Yet, while grammar is perhaps relatively unexciting compared to other aspects of ancient Greek, such as drama or poetry, it is no less valid a field for scholarship, especially in view of the fact that prior to the Renaissance very little was known about the language of the ancient Greeks. Part of the reader's judgment as to whether the grammarian is an admirable or a ridiculous figure rests on this intentionally ambiguous issue of whether the study of Greek particles is a significant or a trivial exercise.

The grammarian's final words on his deathbed further exemplify this ambivalence toward his preoccupation with the minutiae of grammar. In his final moments, the grammarian delivers doctrines on *Hoti*, *Oun*, and *De*. In one sense it is admirable that even at the end of his life he does not waver from his devotion to his subject, instead continuing to the last to contribute to his life's work. At the same time, however, the reader may wonder that at the moment of death the grammarian cannot raise his thoughts to anything higher than prepositions and conjunctions.

The grammarian's choosing "not to Live but Know" is a similarly cloudy matter. He seems to have taken up learning as a prelude to living an enlightened life, only to spurn life after becoming engrossed in his grammar. While his single-mindedness in his scholarship seems laudable, his rejection of a conventional way of life seems foolish and wasteful; the determination is left to the reader.

Browning's equivocal conclusion strikes one last note of ambiguity; the final three lines are capable of multiple interpretations. The grammarian is described as "loftily lying," ostensibly a reference to his burial site, but possibly implying dishonesty— perhaps referring to the grammarian's life of self-denial as he deceived himself about his own human wants and needs. "Leave him," say the students as they depart the summit, possibly a hint that they are rejecting the austere lifestyle of the devoted scholar who renounced life's pleasures. The grammarian was "loftier than the world suspects," "lofty" here implying "noble" or "idealistic," but also perhaps connoting "haughty" or "arrogant," an appropriate term to describe the grammarian's rejection of everything but his studies.

The final image of the grammarian is of him "Living and dying." The two seem inextricably intertwined for the grammarian. During his life he was dead to the world, living a kind of death-in-life, but he lives on after death in his achievements and in the hearts of his students. This paradox is a particularly appropriate finish for a poem that creates, through the use of contrasts and intentional ambiguities, such a complex and enigmatic figure as the grammarian.

Catherine Swanson

GRANDFATHER

Author: Michael S. Harper (1938-   )
Type of poem: Lyric
First published: 1977, in *Images of Kin: New and Selected Poems*

The Poem

Michael S. Harper's "Grandfather" is a celebration of its title character at the same time that it is a recognition of the racism and persecution that were part of the history of many African American families in the United States over the centuries. The poem holds these two subjects together in a delicate balance through its forty-seven-line length.

The first of the two verse paragraphs in the poem (lines 1-22) describes an ugly racial incident from 1915, when a white mob, fueled by a screening of D. W. Griffith's *The Birth of a Nation* (1915), tried to burn out their black neighbor in Catskill, New York. (The film glorified the Confederacy and the Ku Klux Klan during the Civil War, at the same time that it demonized blacks and their struggles.) Even in the midst of this violence, however, the grandfather in the poem achieves a certain dignity, when "he asked his neighbors/ up on his thatched porch" of the house they were trying to burn down. The contrast between the human being here, a man who is both father and grandfather, and the brutal mob is clear.

In the second verse paragraph (lines 23-47), the speaker highlights the course of his grandfather's career over the remainder of his life: first working as a waiter at his son's New York City restaurant and racing, and beating, his grandson in a footrace; then through a series of everyday experiences; then, at last, sitting on a porch dying of cancer. The end of the poem returns to the opening incident, for "the great white nation immovable" is at least symbolically the same mob that tried to burn him out (now metastasized as a killing cancer), and "the film/ played backwards on his grandson's eyes" in the last lines is the racist *Birth of a Nation* again. The grandfather's life, in short, is bounded by acts and artifacts of the racial violence of American history. Put another way, the grandfather, and his grandson after him, are both defined by the particular racial history of this American "nation" or society, and at the end of the poem the film has been "played backwards" but both men know its meaning. Black history, Harper is saying, is highlighted by incidents and attitudes like those in the film and the poem.

Forms and Devices

Sound is important in all Harper's poetry; many of his poems have jazz subjects and modulations, such as "Dear John, Dear Coltrane" and "*Bird Lives*: Charles Parker in St. Louis," and most can best be appreciated read aloud. "Grandfather" is no exception. The enjambment and internal rhymes of certain sections of the poem, for example, as well as the variable rhythms of the whole poem, can most easily be recognized when recited. In addition, the drama and momentum of the poem both benefit from such a reading. Harper's poem is a complex confrontation with ideas, but it is a powerful performance piece as well.

Harper's language and imagery are fresh and stark but often exist on the edges of clarity. Phrases such as "waiter gait" and "blossoms of fire" are vivid images that help to unlock the meaning of the poem, but the sense of the "white jacket smile/ he'd brought back from watered/ polish of my father/ on the turning seats" is not readily clear: Has the grandfather been turning his son on a counter stool in the restaurant where he works? Likewise, what is the crowd doing exactly in "spittooning their torched necks"? Does this translate literally as "rednecks spitting"? Why is *The Birth of a Nation* "played backwards" at the end of the poem? Many poems cannot be reduced to prose statements; Harper's poetry in general, and "Grandfather" in particular, can usually lead, in the classroom at least, to spirited discussions of possible shades of meaning.

What readers often miss in the violence and drama of Harper's poetry is the conscious way that the poem has been constructed. "Grandfather" encompasses the biography of one man, framed not only by the film but also by the "porch": In the first case he tries to defuse the mob with his manners; in the second, he is dying of cancer. This poem bears reading and rereading and yields levels of subtlety and meaning each time it is approached anew. Like a complicated jazz composition, its sound at times disguises its careful craftsmanship.

Themes and Meanings

"Grandfather" is not an easy poem to understand completely, although its basic sense is clear enough; it is almost as if Harper, as in many of his poems, wants his readers to have to work to grasp his meaning. To try to achieve that meaning, it is important to note first that the poem is really about two characters, both the grandfather and the grandson; if it is the former who is the subject of the poem, it is the latter, the speaker of the poem, who learns the most important lessons embodied in his grandfather's life.

The grandfather faces two great battles in his life, according to this metaphorical account by his grandson: the violent racial incident earlier in his history, which perhaps defines it but which he overcomes, and the cancer that will apparently soon kill him. What is curious is that Harper uses the same word—"nation"—to describe both. The mob is a "nation" that tries to burn him out in 1915, and the cancer is a foreign "nation" that has invaded the grandfather's body. Racism, Harper is saying subtly but clearly, is a social disease in the United States that kills just as violently as cancer. Put another way, the white "nation" of the Griffith film at the beginning of the poem has some of the same deadly properties as "the great white nation immovable" in the grandfather's body at the end.

The grandson learns from his grandfather's struggles. He describes the scene from 1915, which he has only heard about, but he clearly imparts the dignity and humanity his grandfather marshaled in the face of the violent forces that were trying to burn him out. Later, the narrator can recount his own childhood knowledge of his forebear, like the footrace the grandfather will win in his "white clothes." In the end, he witnesses his grandfather's struggle with cancer "on a porch/ that won't hold [his] arms."

The last four lines are ambiguous and have led to a number of interpretations of their meaning. The grandfather is in a cancer hospice or hospital, apparently, and perhaps the young speaker—in the ways that hospitals once banned children visitors—is not allowed to see his grandfather. Why then is the film "played backwards on his grandson's eyes"? In a sense this phrase may mean only that the speaker's recounting of his grandfather's life, like this poem, can be run the same way: To capture his grandfather's life, in other words, is to run his story backward—from present to past—to get to that crucial 1915 incident.

The speaker is talking also about *The Birth of a Nation*, and on that level the film is a metaphor for the violent racial history it depicts. To run it backward is to reverse its thrust and escape its racial ugliness, or to cancel out its racist conclusions. The film "played backwards on his grandson's eyes" is thus being replayed from ending to beginning, from the triumph of the Ku Klux Klan in its final scenes back to the introduction of slavery in America in the seventeenth century at its opening. To play it backwards is to cancel out the cancerous "nation" that has been "born" in the film. The narrator wants to learn a positive lesson from his grandfather's life.

The speaker in the poem is paying tribute to his grandfather, describing the racial incident that defined his life but that did not take away his dignity, and at the same time he is commenting on the racist history that most African Americans faced in the past few centuries in one form or another. To tell black history—even personal, family history like this poem—is to identify its defining moments of abuse and discrimination. At the end, the narrator has clearly become a stronger person for the knowledge he has gained from his grandfather's life.

David Peck

GRANDFATHER AND GRANDMOTHER IN LOVE

Author: David Mura (1952-   )
Type of poem: Lyric
First published: 1989, in *After We Lost Our Way*

The Poem

David Mura's "Grandfather and Grandmother in Love" is a poem of thirty lines divided into two fifteen-line stanzas, which celebrates the union of "the bodies that begot the bodies that begot me." The poem is written in the first person and opens with the provocative line "Now I will ask for one true word beyond/ betrayal." This is followed by a scene in which the poet imagines the circumstances of his grandparents in bed between sweaty sheets; the grandfather whispering haiku about clover, signifying good luck; and the cuckoo bird, a symbol of betrayal and cuckoldry. Grandfather also complains of misfortunes such as "blight and bad debts," while both grandparents hear the quavering sound of the *biwa*, a Japanese stringed instrument.

The word the poet seeks is found by line 10, in which the poet cracks the word "like a seed/ between the teeth," to spit it out in the soil of his grandfather's greenhouse roses. Although the word the poet seeks is never stated, it is associated with positive images of sweet *teriyaki* and the smell of *sake*. This longing for the "one true word" leaves the reader to imagine what the word might be and draws the reader into a contemplation of the grandparents' life. Words such as "redemption," "trust," "success," and even "luck" come to mind, but it is fairly certain that the found word is associated with the grandparents' Japanese roots, transplanted to the United States like the seed spit out on the greenhouse loam. Mura's grandfather, an Issei—a first-generation Japanese American—was a grower who lost his greenhouse during the war, but by calling up the past in this poem the poet is able to coax something sweet from the bitter experience.

The second stanza pursues the image of the grandparents in bed but changes focus from the poet's musings to the actions of the lovers themselves as they turn toward each other in the chaos of love, bursting from the alien culture of the United States into their private, shared, Japanese life. In the first line they are referred to by the Japanese names for father and mother, "*otoo-san*" and "*okaa-san*," identifying them in their native tongue and placing them in the Japanese world they inhabit spiritually, if not physically. Afloat on the "ship of the past," the grandfather who has been betrayed regains his manhood. In a stunning metaphor using vivid ocean imagery, he "hauls her in,/ trawling the currents, gathering/ a sea that seems endless." The metaphor builds to a climax in which the grandfather frees the grandmother from the net and dives into the water, where night obscures the couple and they find peace until the inevitable dawn.

This is a poem built on oppositions: between the past and present, between Japanese and American cultures, and even between the grandparents' real life, typified by blight and bad debts, and the imagined one of the sea depths. It is Mura's poetic vision and compression that pull these elements together into a new object: the poem.

Forms and Devices

"Grandfather and Grandmother in Love," written for the ear as well as the eye, is characterized by sound associations that link lines together in the absence of obvious rhyme. The first eight lines use alliteration, the repetition of initial consonants, to create a sequence of labile *b* sounds that create their own irregular rhythm. Starting with "beyond," the poem strings together "betrayal," "buoys," "bedsprings," "begot," "bodies," and many other *b* words, ending with "blight and bad debts, as the *biwa's* spirit/ bubbled up between them." In the last three lines of the second stanza, the poem draws to a conclusion made memorable by the linkage of sibilants in "slipping," "sight," "soft," "shush," and "swells." The word "shush" both contrasts with and highlights the *s* sounds.

The poem is sprinkled with Japanese words that form a bridge to the Japanese past of which Mura writes. The *biwa*, *teriyaki*, and *sake* of the first stanza are words that appeal to the senses: hearing, taste, and smell. It is significant that the poet uses these words in speaking of his grandparents, since science has verified that memory is often triggered by sensual clues. In the beginning of the second stanza, Mura names his grandparents' roles in Japanese words, placing them directly in the context of their own culture as they move close amid the reverberations of the "*ran*/ of lovers." *Ran* means "chaos" in Japanese, and here it implies that only in the throes and the privacy of love's chaos are the grandparents able to return to their genuine selves.

The simile used to give substance to the "word" of the first line, as the poet cracks it "like a seed/ between the teeth," and spits it out "to root in the loam of his greenhouse roses," again recalls the life of the grandparents: the grandfather's greenhouse and the grandmother's rice.

Yet everything in the first stanza is mere prelude to the second, in which Mura creates a stunning metaphor of the grandfather as a fisherman trawling for his wife in a magic ocean "where flounder, dolphin, fluorescent fins, fish/ with wings spill before him glittering scales." Yet there is a suggestion that they cannot sustain either their passion or their return to Japanese culture, for the poem ends with the "knocking tide of morning."

Themes and Meanings

Mura once said, "One of the things my work is about is the conjunction between race and sexuality." Born to parents who were detained in United States internment camps during World War II, he writes poetry that traces themes of racial discrimination and betrayal. His sexual identity is subtly associated with race since even as a young boy he was aware of standards of white beauty and of masculinity to which he could never aspire as an Asian American male. Both these themes are subtly evoked in "Grandfather and Grandmother in Love," written in 1989.

When Mura first imagines his grandparents coupling, he thinks of "the moon bluing the white/ sheets soaked in sweat." "Bluing" is a chemical added to laundry sheets to make them look even whiter, and the word functions here to emphasize the whiteness of the sheets, or of the culture in which his grandparents find themselves. Yet the sheets are stained with the grandparents' sweat, suggesting that the grandparents are not quite as "white" as they are expected to be. The grandparents are not engaged in the sexual act in the first stanza; grandfather is simply complaining of his problems in the brief lines of haiku, immersed in the sounds of the *biwa*, real or imagined, that presumably starts him on his journey back in time to his native culture. The poet, also, is traveling back to his Japanese roots on the "word," poetically transformed into sense impressions of taste and odor.

It is only in the second stanza, when the grandparents come together and the "ship of the past" bursts onto the scene, that they regain their gusto and life force. Their spark of passion now ignites, and in teasing behavior the grandmother swats away the grandfather's grasping hand while he laughs with joy in a surge of renewed manhood. In a luminous metaphor, the lovers now find themselves in a magical sea at "depths a boy dreams of," with grandfather hauling in grandmother, who seems magically transformed into a fish, until he dives under to join her.

This second stanza consists of only one long sentence, which builds in intensity on strong verbs that move from "drift" to "bursts, "swats," and "laughing." The lines build in intensity as images of sea creatures grow more surreal, mirroring the passion of the lovers until they disappear beneath the waves and "drifting ground/ swells."

Many of Mura's early poems grapple with Japanese and Japanese American subjects, partly in an effort to come to grips with a self-hatred and rage he did not understand. Eventually, through membership in several men's groups and therapy groups, he learned that feelings of inadequacy are often found in men who do not fit the cultural ideals by which they are surrounded. He calls these feelings "internalized racism."

In "Grandfather and Grandmother in Love," the poet imagines his grandfather unable to participate fully in an act of love until he returns, if only in his mind, to the Japanese past he has lost. Mura embellishes the poem with Japanese words, but the entire metaphor of the grandparents entering the sea is thoroughly Japanese. Japan is a small island nation to which the ocean is very important as a source of industry, commerce, and food. Mura considers himself very much an American poet, influenced by the tradition of Walt Whitman and William Carlos Williams. In this poem he successfully merges many disparate elements to create a work of great power.

Sheila Golburgh Johnson

GRAPPA IN SEPTEMBER

Author: Cesare Pavese (1908-1950)
Type of poem: Narrative
First published: 1934, as "Grappa a Settembre"; collected in *Lavorare stanca*, 1943;
   English translation collected in *Hard Labor,* 1976

The Poem

Cesare Pavese's "Grappa in September" is a four-stanza, free-verse narrative poem about the state of nature just before harvest. First published before World War II, the poem describes autumn mornings in the northern Italian countryside in the early part of the twentieth century. The land has reached the height of its season, and the women flourish as much as the land; even the clouds in the sky give the impression of being at the peak of perfection. The men, however, are not a part of this autumnal readiness. They watch their land and their women from a distance, enjoying the view, consuming the products of past harvests. The men do not interact with the world around them.

Mornings in this part of Italy "run their course, clear and deserted/ along the river's banks," which turn a darker green just before the fog is burned off by the rising sun. A house that sits close to the edge of a field sells tobacco that "tastes of sugar" and "gives off a bluish haze." The house also sells grappa, a cheap, potent brandy common to northern Italy made from the leftover skins and stems of grapes used to manufacture wine. Distant trees that stand under "occasional" plump clouds conceal "fruit so ripe/ it would drop at a touch." The ripeness of autumn is not confined to the country, however. In the city, houses are "mellowing in the mild air."

The land is lush and fecund, and in the early mornings only women are outside. The women are as lush as the land, as the fruit on the trees, and as the streets that "ripen by standing still." The women "stand in the sunlight,/ letting it warm their bodies." As these women, who "don't smoke,/ or drink," bask in the morning sun, the narrator implies they enjoy the morning. The morning air is like the colorless grappa, so strong it "has to be swallowed in sips." As the sun begins to heat the earth, "everything here" scents the air with "its own fragrance." Even the river's banks carry the scent of the water they contain.

The poet narrator believes that every man should see the countryside at this particular time of the year, should see "how everything ripens." A breeze rises, but it is not strong enough to move the clouds, only to maneuver a blue haze that carries the scent of tobacco and grappa, a sign that men are smoking and drinking in the house at the edge of the field. The men are enjoying the morning too, consuming the products of nature.

Forms and Devices

"Grappa in September" is a free-verse poem; it has no formal meter or rhyme. Most of the lines in the poem are end-stopped; either the poet's thought is completed in each line, causing the reader to pause, or punctuation marks require the reader to pause at the end of the line. End-stopped lines slow down the movement of a poem, and Pavese's use of end-stopped lines contributes to the meditative quality of "Grappa in September." Pavese's lines are similar to prose; his diction instructs his reader to speak the poem quietly.

Pavese admired the work of the early American poet Walt Whitman, whose style Pavese emulates in this poem by relying on editorial omniscience rather than first-person narration to lavish attention on related images of the everyday and the ordinary. The narrator's point of view is clarified in each stanza. In the first stanza, the narrator describes the countryside impartially and hierarchically, from how the sun rises to which house sells grappa and tobacco. Because the poet does not use the word "I," by the second stanza the reader realizes that the narrator is not a part of the scenes being described. The narrator is simply making observations and comparisons. However, in the third stanza the poet uses the second-person singular. Here, Pavese's use of the word "you" to tell his reader he or she will "see only women" so early in the mornings assumes that the reader and the narrator are both spectators who share the same perceptions. However, in the final stanza, the narrator separates himself from the reader by stating an opinion: "This is the time when every man should stand/ still in the street and see how everything ripens."

Like Whitman, Pavese uses implied rather than direct metaphors; that is, he uses metaphors without conjunctions or the verb "to be." For example, lines 19 and 20 (in the third stanza) say, "water in the river has absorbed the banks,/ steeping them to their depths." A comparison is being made between the action of the river on its banks and the process by which the skins and stems of grapes are absorbed and distilled in the manufacture of grappa.

Pavese's similes are direct and provide the reader with a sense of pleasure. For example, women "stand in the sunlight,/ . . . as if they were fruit" and "The streets/ are like the women."

Instead of employing complex symbolism, Pavese structures his poem as a series of images that continually foreshadow and augment each other. In the first stanza, for instance, mornings are as "clear" as the grappa that is "the color of water." The tobacco that is "blackish in color" and "gives off a bluish haze" recalls the dawn that turns "foggy,/ darkening" the green of the river's banks. In the second stanza, trees deepen in color like the green in the first stanza that darkens. The fruit of the trees ripens, as do the "occasional clouds." Even houses in the distant city are "mellowing." Pavese's technique for showing the connection between the different aspects of a September morning develops and underscores the poem's theme of ripeness and waiting, of observation and participation.

Themes and Meanings

Pavese's poems generally concern themselves with the struggle to understand the relationship of the self with other people and the external world. Even in early work, such as "Grappa in September," Pavese presents his idea that the work of poets is first and foremost to convey clarity, or truth, to readers through a sequence of images. In this sense, "Grappa in September" might be misconstrued as simply a series of pastoral descriptions linked to an underlying theme of ripeness. At first glance, the poem does not seem to achieve the clarity important to the poet. However, a deeper reading reveals that the poem does indeed develop a philosophical idea: Women participate in the world, while men observe the world. The exceptionally beautiful images show how the poet assembles his philosophy.

Beginning with a recounting of color in nature (the mornings are "clear," the river banks are "green," the tobacco is "blackish" and gives off a "bluish" haze, the grappa is "the color of water"), and moving to a description of fecundity (fruit is "ripe," clouds are "swollen," and city streets are "mellowing"), the poet then tells of women who are by nature merged with the world, and finally of men who, by contrast, can merge with the natural world only by consuming its products.

The morning, the river, the clouds, the fog, the streets, even the trees ripe with fruit, form the background for Pavese's illustration of women as a passive yet integral part of the natural world. Women are like other objects portrayed in the poem that ripen as a consequence of "standing still." They are a part of a landscape where at daybreak, "you see only women." Men, on the other hand, are removed from the scene. The only evidence that they exist comes from the "bluish haze" that drifts into the countryside. The haze is from tobacco smoke, and, since women "don't smoke," then men must be smoking. The smoke carries with it the smell of grappa, and since women "don't . . . drink" then men must be drinking.

The poet exhorts the men to "stand/ still in the street and see how everything ripens." However, only by smoking and drinking do the men "enjoy the morning" as much as the women do. Only by smoking and drinking can men actively connect with nature at all. Because the men smoke and drink, Pavese's reader understands that men are separate from nature, they are removed from September's profuse ripeness, and they have no need to establish a deeper relationship with it.

Ginger Jones

GRAVELLY RUN

Author: A. R. Ammons (1926-2001)
Type of poem: Lyric
First published: 1960; collected in *Corsons Inlet: A Book of Poems*, 1965

The Poem

"Gravelly Run" is a thirty-line free-verse lyric divided into six stanzas in which the speaker meditates on a small stream, questioning the connection between the world of human thought and the world of nature. The poem is characterized by a struggle between the highly abstract thought processes of the speaker and the concrete imagery of the stream. The poem opens with the speaker wrestling with a problem. The first line sounds as if the speaker has already been pondering the problem for a while. "I don't know," he says, indicating the tentative nature of what follows. The speaker proposes to himself that it is "sufficient" to concentrate only on the natural world, thus losing self-consciousness in nature, in "stones and trees."

In the second stanza, the poet explores the reasons for losing oneself in nature. He says that it is not as important "to know the self" in an absolute sense as it is to know the self as nature ("galaxy and cedar cone") knows it. This second way of knowing the self does not take in the notion of time, the notion that people are born and must one day die. Rather, the "galaxy and cedar cone" approach the self as it is at any given moment, without the intrusion of past or future.

Having come to this conclusion, the speaker turns to the scene at hand, the stream named in the title of the poem, which flows from a swamp and down to a highway bridge, washing the water plants along the way.

At this point, the speaker looks at the banks of the stream, where holly and cedars grow, both trees laden with religious symbolism. The grove of cedars, with their long, "gothic-clustered" trunks, makes the speaker think that they could inspire religious thought in even the coldest heart ("winter bones"). He looks at the trees and tries to evoke that religious sense, but it does not come. There is no revelation. Each distinct object, each tree, each holly leaf remains separate. The natural objects will not be transformed into something spiritual.

In the final stanza, the speaker comes to grips with the realization that the natural world is not a harbor for human emotions or thoughts. He realizes that no systems of thought ("philosophies") can be based on nature, that God does not exist in the holly. The objects of nature, he realizes, are not conscious ("the sunlight has never/ heard of trees"). Therefore, the speaker now sees that the "surrendered self," the self that lost itself among the "stones and trees" in the first stanza, is among "unwelcoming forms" that do not recognize it. The self is therefore a stranger in the natural world, and, since the natural world is not a place for philosophies to be built, the self must take up its burdens (which philosophies might solve) and take them back "down the road" (a human-made object) to civilization.

Forms and Devices

The major device in "Gravelly Run" is the play between abstract and concrete language. The poem itself is about a struggle between the speaker's human self-consciousness and the utter lack of consciousness on the part of the natural world.

The first three lines of the poem contain no concrete visual imagery: The language is abstract, reflecting the speaker's interior monologue. In these lines, the speaker advances the poem, developing his thoughts. Lines 4-6, however, contain only visual imagery. Whereas the first three lines are full of verbs ("know," "seems," "see," "hear," "coming," "going"), the second half of stanza 1 contains none ("bending" acts as an adjective). The language also slows the poem. The repetition of the preposition "of" and the increased number of hard stresses slows readers down, forcing them to dwell on the imagery.

In stanza 2, the poet reverts to the abstract. Lines 7 and 8 are dense and difficult to sort out. Line 8 repeats many of the words used in line 7, and the key word, "know," appears three times. This spare vocabulary forces the reader to go back over the lines to make sense of them. Even readers who know the poem well often stumble over line 8. In contrast, line 9 is effortlessly clear because it refers only to readily comprehensible, concrete objects. In effect, the reader moves from the cramped, restricted space of the mind into the vast reaches of nature. Furthermore, the rhyme of "known" with "cone" gives the lines a feeling of completion. Furthermore, the repetition of "it" (referring to the self) at the end of lines 10 and 11 brings the interior monologue to a close.

Another prominent device in the poem is the use of alliteration. In stanza 3, Ammons uses alliteration and half-rhymes to give the passage the feeling of a meandering stream. The *s*'s and *w*'s in line 12 move the poem along, while "comes," with the *m* and *s* (pronounced as a *z*) causes the reader to pause momentarily. The reader is then hung up again on "Run" in the next line, which forms a half-rhyme with "comes." The *ng*'s and *l*'s in the next line-and-a-half again move the poem forward like liquid. Ultimately, the stanza comes to a halt at the harsh sound of the human-made object, the "bridge."

A third device Ammons uses to great effect in the poem is punctuation. The poem consists of a single sentence broken into sections by colons. Ammons uses the single sentence because the poem elucidates a single thought: The natural and the human are distinct. However, the dominant form of punctuation in the poem is the colon: The poem contains ten of them. There is one at the end of each of the first five stanzas, and there are five in the last stanza. The colons in the poem function as semicolons, linking closely related independent clauses. The semicolon suggests connection, and Ammons's poem is about the separateness of things, and so he uses a colon, an element of punctuation that marks boundaries and separated elements such as hours, minutes, and seconds, leaving "each thing in its entity."

Themes and Meanings

"Gravelly Run" is a poem about the relationship of the world of human thought to the world of nature. American nature writing has long been concerned with this con-

nection. What is the place of the human in the natural world? One of the great paradoxes of this issue is the desire on the part of some writers to be lost in nature, to shed
the concerns and consciousness of the human world for the immediacy of the natural
world. Transcendentalist thinker and poet Ralph Waldo Emerson sought exactly this
kind of experience in nature, describing himself in this state as "a transparent eye-
ball. . . . [T]he currents of the Universal Being circulate through me; I am part or particle of God." Yet, there is a contradiction in Emerson's transcendence: Any attempt to
make the natural world carry the intellectual freight of human consciousness obscures
the natural world. Thus, people who attempt to lose themselves in nature are merely
imposing human meaning on nature.

Like Henry David Thoreau, Emerson's literary heir, Ammons had a lifelong interest in science. As a result, he viewed the natural world with the precision of a naturalist and consistently refused to anthropomorphize nature. Yet, like Thoreau, Ammons
was powerfully drawn to the beauty of nature, which remained always before him like
some Eden. "Gravelly Run" enacts this struggle. The speaker desires to be lost in the
natural world, to lose consciousness, yet that very desire is itself an act of consciousness. The run, coming out of the dark mystery of the swamp and flowing through the
banks of holly and cedar toward the highway bridge, seems to offer a place of refuge,
a place of spirituality. In the end, however, the natural world remains beyond human
thought. Ammons was too much aware of the complexity of the natural world to sim-
plify it into symbols of human consciousness. Each thing, each tree, bush, and rock,
remains sealed in "the air's glass/ jail"; Ammons could not reduce the objects simply
to serve the human desire for spirituality. Ammons recognized that philosophies may
not be grounded in natural facts. The only proper ground for philosophy is human
ground, and so the speaker is told to "hoist [his] burdens," and "get on down" that
other gravelly run, the road.

Andrew C. Higgins

THE GRAVEYARD BY THE SEA

Author: Paul Valéry (1871-1945)

Type of poem: Meditation

First published: 1922, as "Le Cimetière marin," in *Charmes, ou poèmes*; English translation collected in *An Anthology of French Poetry from Nerval to Valéry in English Translation with French Originals*, 1958

The Poem

"The Graveyard by the Sea," written in 1920, is Paul Valéry's best-known poem. It consists of twenty-four stanzas of six lines each. The poet returns in imagination to the cemetery of Sète, a city on a cliff above the Mediterranean, where he was born and where he dreamed as a youth among the tombs of his ancestors. He imagines himself sitting on a tombstone at noon and contemplating the white sails on the calm sea, which he describes as doves pecking on a roof, while he wrestles with the problems of life and death, of being and nonbeing, and thinks about the future course of his life.

In his monologue, Valéry thinks of the sea as the roof of the temple of time sparkling with diamonds, and he enjoys the idea of mingling with the sky and the sea. As his shadow passes over the tombs, he realizes that he himself is subject to change; he recalls his nineteen years of what he calls indolence. (Actually, since 1894 he had been working first in the Ministry of War and later in the news agency Havas. He was a married man and the father of two children, devoting his free time to research on the nature of thought.) He accuses himself of idleness because he has not made full use of his poetic talent.

In stanza 11, the poet imagines himself a shepherd among the quiet white sheep, the tombs. He refuses the Christian consolation symbolized by the marble doves and angels and contemplates eternal nothingness, reflecting in stanza 13 that the dead buried in the cemetery are quite comfortable.

In the next two stanzas the noonday sun, symbol of unchanging perfection, is contrasted with ephemeral man—with the poet himself, who is filled with fear, repentance, and doubt. Man, he decides, is the flaw, the changing element in the perfection of the universe. The dead lose their individuality and return to the great Whole; their bodies feed the flowers.

In the seventeenth stanza, Valéry chides himself for dreaming of a more perfect world and asks himself if he expects to write poetry when he is dead. Immortality is only an illusion; those who compare death to a maternal breast are guilty of a beautiful lie and a pious trick. The empty head of a skeleton laughs forever. Stanza 19 states that the true worm is not that which has destroyed the bodies, but is thought that feeds on life and never leaves man. Even in his sleep, the worm of thought pursues him. Valéry is referring to the dictum of René Descartes, *Cogito ergo sum*: "I think, therefore I am."

In stanza 21, Valéry asks Zeno, a Greek philosopher who denied the reality of movement by asserting that a flying arrow is immobile at each instant, if he has pierced him with the arrow that is killing him. He rejects the idea that time does not pass; movement exists, therefore life and time exist and action is possible.

In the last three stanzas, the poet reacts: The weather has changed, and a breeze has sprung up. Its salty freshness returns his soul to him. Like a man who has plunged into the refreshing sea, he emerges from his reverie filled with a taste for life. He will plunge into action.

Forms and Devices

All six lines in each stanza end with a rhyme in the pattern *aabccb*. This rigidity called for great expertise on the part of Valéry and his translators. If a translator is truly faithful to the thought of a poem, it is the music that suffers most in passing from one language to another. If he must limit each line to ten syllables and adhere to a difficult rhyme scheme, he can hardly hope to imitate the music of the original.

This difficult poem requires the reader to penetrate a host of metaphors. The reader must equate the calm sea with a roof and the sails with doves pecking on the shining roof of the temple of time under a blazing noontime sky while the poet meditates on great philosophical problems and on his own existence. Stanza 5 contains a simile: The poet inhales his future as a hungry mouth obscures the contour of a piece of fruit. This is perhaps the only reasonably simple comparison in a forest of unexpected (and unexplained) images used as symbols.

The theme of the poem rests on these original, complicated, and obscure symbols. One eminent critic insists that the whole poem is a metaphor, to which each image refers. Another famous scholar declares that the noonday sun is the symbol of eternity and the sea is the symbol of human consciousness. Less difficult to conceive is the idea that the sea seen through the trees is a prisoner of the leaves. It devours the graveyard grills because the sea, sparkling in the sun, causes them to seem to disappear.

Comprehensible also is the metaphor of the poet as a shepherd among his sheep, the white marble tombs, and the sea as watchdog. The angels and doves (unfortunately translated sometimes as "pigeons") obviously represent the consolation of the Christian religion. He urges the watchdog to frighten them as a sign that he rejects this idea of life after death.

In the second-to-last stanza, Valéry describes in startling images the sea as it reacts to the rising wind: It is delirious; it resembles a panther's skin and a torn Greek cloak; it is a hydra, the serpent with nine heads which, according to Greek mythology, replaced each lost head with two others; it is a serpent biting its tail.

Valéry employed figures of speech and symbols to express philosophic ideas. The metaphor which unifies the structure of the poem, according to one critic, establishes a parallelism among the three separate elements: the sea, the graveyard, and the poet. Each of these elements has two aspects, one on the surface, the other interior. Other poetic devices, such as alliteration, embellish the original but cannot be preserved in translation. For example, stanza 4 of the French has nine pronounced *t* sounds and eight pronounced *s* sounds; the effect is striking.

Themes and Meanings

Scores of books have been written about Paul Valéry and "Le Cimetière marin," as well as hundreds of articles by critics, teachers, poets. In 1928, Gustave Cohen, a professor at the Sorbonne, gave a series of lectures entitled *Essai d'interprétation du "Cimetière marin"* (attempt to interpret "The Graveyard by the Sea") to a large audience that included Paul Valéry himself. The poet expressed his pleasure at having the intentions and the wording of the poem, reputedly obscure, so well understood. Valéry explained in a preface to the publication of the lectures that he had decided to write a monologue that would be at the same time personal and universal, one that would contain the simplest and most constant themes of his emotional and intellectual life. His poem is a meditation on life and death, on mobility and immobility, on being and nonbeing. Since, in the fashion of his friends the Symbolists, he does not explain his metaphors, the reader must puzzle out the meanings. This is harder to do from a translation than from the original, because the translator has had to incorporate English rhymes and meter as well as preserve the meanings.

The personal problem at issue in the poem is how the poet should spend the rest of his life. For the past nineteen years, his chief intellectual efforts have been directed to mathematics, art, music, and linguistics at the expense of his great poetic talent. He is trying to discover his true self. He meditates on life and eternity. The surface of the sea is calm, but underneath there is turbulence; the poet thinks of the activities of life with philosophic disdain, but behind the disdain there is a living organism. The graveyard offers the immobility of the tombs, but underneath them are the remains of the poet's ancestors. As he looks at the sea he is filled with the idea of changelessness, but his own shadow rejects the light. He needs some assurance of the fact of change to prove his own existence. He cannot accept the idea of immortality. The true irrefutable worm is not in the grave but in life.

The story of Zeno's stationary arrow and the tale of Achilles and the tortoise were meant to illustrate the fact that change is illusion. He must reject this idea, however; he cannot escape from change and action. At the end of the poem, the calm sea becomes turbulent, and with a triumphant cry the poet accepts the prospect of an active life.

Dorothy B. Aspinwall

THE GREAT BEAR

Author: John Hollander (1929-　　)
Type of poem: Sonnet sequence
First published: 1958, in *A Crackling of Thorns*

The Poem

John Hollander's sonnet sequence "The Great Bear" is part of his 1958 volume of poems *A Crackling of Thorns*, which was selected by the distinguished poet and translator W. H. Auden for the Yale Series of Younger Poets in 1958. "The Great Bear" is written in six stanzas. Each of those six stanzas is a technically discrete fourteen-line sonnet in hendecasyllabic meter. A simple narrative unifies the six sonnets that compose "The Great Bear." The speaker describes an imaginary journey with a child or children to search the night sky for constellations, in particular the Great Bear constellation (called Ursa Major in astronomical charts) of the poem's title. Hollander's opening sonnet traces the path of the speaker and his companions "Out onto hilltops," where even in the clearest night sky "by no means will/ They make it out." The speaker regrets that the constellation of Ursa Major is not easy to see, not easy to point out, not easy to imagine. By the final line of this first stanza the speaker is not sure he can see it either.

As the first sonnet yields to the second one, Hollander pauses to contemplate what exactly the experienced adults pointing out the stars have forgotten. Possibly, he suggests, they are only remembering the Great Bear constellation, and memories are notoriously unreliable. Alternatively, there never was more than an innate sense of shape, which the human mind determined to find order in chaos recalls as the image of the bear.

In any case, by the end of the second stanza the speaker despairs of being able to explain the stars at all—much less their shape and relative importance in the universe. The phrase "never to get the point" is emblematic. In the third stanza Hollander concentrates on people's understanding of "any single star," as if to recognize an individual star would make the pattern more perceptible. Thus, the child who fails to see and the star that is not there coalesce into a familiar and universal topic, the conflict between appearance and reality. By the second half of the poem, in the fourth stanza and sonnet, the reader suspects that in "The Great Bear" stars are not as important as what they stand for. Indeed, the speaker insists, people must "understand/ The signs that stars compose" because the stars themselves may be no more significant than the "apparent space between them." That is the dilemma the speaker attempts to resolve for the reader and for himself in the final two stanzas: Hollander calls the dilemma that people confront in seeing and in believing any thing or idea the human mind perceives "Our sense of what is what."

Yet there is no resolution in the poem or in the problem that Hollander presents in this cunningly straightforward narrative of looking for the constellation Ursa Major.

Since the human mind must conceive of things it cannot understand in familiar terms or as "Some Ancients really traced it out," it is impossible to know whether people really do understand or merely imagine that people understand. Even if people did see the constellation, the speaker is afraid that "there still would be no bear."

Forms and Devices

Hollander brings a vast arsenal of weapons to the construction of each sonnet in "The Great Bear." He is a sensitive, thoughtful scholar of philosophy and of literature, with rigorous academic training to augment what nature failed to supply. The poem resonates with meaning. The opening stanza contains the themes of all the sonnets to follow.

"The Great Bear" is written in a traditional accentual syllabic meter, the hendeca-syllabic line, which originated in the love lyrics and satires of the classical Roman lyric poet Catullus. In "The Great Bear" Hollander embraces a formalist model and consequently produces a poem with highly conventional patterns of rhyme and meter. Hollander brings an arsenal of weapons to the construction of each sonnet in "The Great Bear." What is both exciting and surprising about the poem is the way it looks on the page—as though it comprises six simple stanzas (groups of lines with roughly the same length). However, it turns out to be a sonnet sequence intentionally obscured with enjambment between stanzas and caesuras within lines. For example, between the first and second stanzas (each a sonnet, though not entirely independent either syntactically or imaginatively) the grammatical structure reinforces the natural progression of Hollander's narrative line by carrying both sense and sentence over from one sonnet to the next: "Because there is no bear" ends the first stanza; "We blame our memory of the picture" opens the second. The caesura, a rhythmic pause in the center of a line, is achieved occasionally by punctuation but more often by syntactic plan. This creates a shift toward prose rhythm that gives both variety and originality to the sonnet stanza form.

Hollander's choice of language appears more natural and thus suitable to his subject of introducing stars to children, where one would refrain from mentioning such lofty ideas as Einstein's constant or Doppler shift. He can create puns out of thin air, as when he glosses the tired expression "glittering generalities" as "really nothing . . . the bright, simple shapes that suddenly/ Emerge on certain nights." Hollander is fond of the pun as a device for both repetition and allusion. He uses the term "bear" in myriad versions throughout his poem. The stars are "there to take a bearing from"; a child's timidity is framed as "Such a bear,/ Who needs it?"

The bear is a wonderful symbol for this purpose. It is easily recognized as implying intelligence, curiosity, and ferocity. A bear is similar to a human because it can and occasionally does stand and walk on its hind legs. Yet the bear is indisputably a wild animal. The motif of the bear appears in ancient Greek mythology as well as in pre-Columbian Native American legends. The designations Ursa Major and Minor (the Big and Little Dippers) are part of elaborate cosmological explanations from ancient Greece. Zeus, king of the gods, changed a woman named Callisto, who bore him a son, Arcas, and that son, who nearly killed his own mother when she was transformed into a bear by jealous Hera, queen of the gods, into stars and set them into the heavens to protect them from his wife's rage.

Themes and Meanings

Despite its subject of Ursa Major and its focus on the stars, "The Great Bear" is not light verse. This poem is, on an abstract level, about writing poetry, about showing a poem to students and encountering their puzzlement. Words, after all, are like stars in a night sky. Their arrangement can mean different things to different people, and that arrangement can appear very different indeed depending upon where the viewer (or reader) is positioned. Clearly, Hollander substitutes the innocence of a child in his narrative for the immaturity of the emerging speaker. Everything needs to be pointed out.

The bear is also a wonderful symbol for this purpose. It has various meanings as both noun and verb. As an action word "bear" can reflect both what a person is and what a person does—his bearing, or behavior, in battle as well as his bearing of arms. "To take a bearing from" in Hollander's poem implies both to determine one's own position and to confirm the position of things around the earth. The stars in the sky remain in the same place, but the earth revolves on its axis and moves around the sun. So the part of the sky visible at night in any particular location changes as the earth moves around the sun. The sky appears to change because one's location seems much more solid. The appearance and reality motif emerges as a compelling wish to find reassurance and order in a chaotic world.

Moreover, the themes that Hollander explores in "The Great Bear" are equally applicable to a study of the stars or of poetry. These themes include the conflict between freedom and restraint, the inadequacy of language to express truth, and the search for intellectual sources explaining the dilemma of appearance and reality. Hollander must have been intending the allusion to a famous anecdote about the Roman poet Vergil, who compared the slow way he composed verse to the way a mother bear licks her cubs into shape. Indeed, so determined was Hollander to cement his foundation solidly that long after "The Great Bear" was finished he discovered an ancient passage in the *Phaenomena* by Aratus of Soli (270 B.C.) which includes images of the stars nearly identical to his own. With delight he footnotes his poem to the reference.

Kathleen Bonann Marshall

THE GREAT BLUE HERON

Author: Carolyn Kizer (1925-   )
Type of poem: Elegy
First published: 1958; collected in *The Ungrateful Garden*, 1961

The Poem

Carolyn Kizer first published "The Great Blue Heron" in *Poetry* magazine as a poem of fifty-five lines and three irregular stanzas. When it was later reprinted in *Mermaids in the Basement*, she split the middle section, creating a fourth stanza. She has dedicated the poem to "M.A.K." These initials and the dates that follow them, as well as the content of the poem, confirm that this is an elegy, a long, sustained poem of mourning, for her mother, Mabel Ashley Kizer, who died in 1955 in her seventy-fifth year. The tone is serious and melancholy. The speaker in this first-person poem seems to be Kizer herself, as references to "my mother" also suggest. The youthful vision of the heron may likewise be autobiographical.

In the first stanza of the poem, the speaker remembers the day when, as a child on the beach near the family's vacation home "Some fifteen summers ago," she saw a solitary great blue heron standing "Poised in the dusty light" and was struck by this prophetic apparition. Her startled response, "Heron, whose ghost are you?" indicates the intensity of this experience. Her body reacted as if in physical shock as she stood in "the sudden chill of the burned." Even though the child raced to find her mother in the house and bring her back to the beach, "the spectral bird" had vanished from sight. The mother, however, called her attention to the heron in soundless flight above the trees, afloat on "vast, unmoving" wings ("ashen things") that the child beheld as "A pair of broken arms/ That were not made for flight."

Although the child speaker grieved for the loss of the bird, she could not quite comprehend what she had lost. Like little Margaret, who weeps for the falling leaves in Gerard Manley Hopkins's famous poem "Spring and Fall: To a Young Child," the child's heart had intuitively grasped the meaning of an omen that her mind could not yet accept, even as she was aware that her mother understood. The mute vision of the heron is a central metaphor for the child's dawning perception of mortality, to be confirmed in the poem's final lines.

In the last stanza, the adult speaker addresses the heron directly. Now that the years have passed, now that many Fourth of July rockets and pinwheels have fizzled and burned out and the summer house itself has burned to the ground, "Now," she says, "there is only you." Why has the memory of the heron followed her? The somber vision of that moment fifteen years ago has haunted her until this day when, "like gray smoke, a vapor," or "A handful of paper ashes," her mother too has disappeared. It is clear to the adult that the silent heron prefigured death and that the death to come was her mother's. The poem travels from the child's vision to the mother's indirect vision and ultimately to the speaker's mournful recognition.

Forms and Devices

Critic Elizabeth B. House has observed that Kizer uses form in this poem in order to distance herself from the raw pain of her mother's death. Although this relatively early poem may appear to be composed in free verse, it is actually in a form, as is most of her early work. The meter is accentual (of a type sometimes known as "loose iambic"), with the two-syllable iamb as its basic metrical foot. Each line consists of three distinct stresses or beats, with a varying number of unaccented syllables. Both the meter and the device of repetition give the poem an aura of inevitability.

Kizer makes use of repetition through occasional end rhyme and slant or imperfect rhyme, as well as through consonance and assonance (repeated consonant and vowel sounds). Perhaps most significant is her emphasis on key words such as "shadow" and "heavy," which help to establish the poem's mood and tone. First the child feels a premonition like the "sudden chill of the burned"; later the summer house has "burned." She watches the heron "drifting/ Over the highest pines" with its "ashen" wings, and fifteen years later the "ashes" of the mother "drift away." These words were carefully chosen for their connotations, their emotional impact upon the reader, as have such shaded words as "bleaker," "tattered," "ragged," and "decayed."

Kizer's vivid visual imagery is noteworthy. Her contrast of the implied colors of summer and fire with the complete absence of color identified with the heron creates a dramatic tension within the poem. The glow of a past that cannot be recaptured—the warm, bright Fourth of July images of "smokes and fires/ And beach-lights and water-glow/ reflecting pin-wheel and flare"—fades to bleakest ash. That once brilliant, light-drenched past is contradicted by the flat shadow of the heron in its "dusty light." The dark shape of the bird drifting in the sky is echoed by the drab, intangible qualities of gray smoke and vapor.

The great blue heron obviously becomes something more than a bird. It is otherworldly, passionless, almost mechanical in its movements. It appears and vanishes in ominous silence. The fact of its gloomy presence is warning enough. "What scissors cut him out?" asks the child, perhaps echoing William Blake's question of "The Tiger": "What immortal hand or eye/ Could frame thy fearful symmetry?" The poet offers no answer.

Themes and Meanings

Love and death are both major themes in Kizer's work, appearing in multiple variations, but here they are combined in a single poem. "The Great Blue Heron" not only confronts the hard fact of death (specifically of the mother, but by implication of all humankind) but also seems to ask, What is the meaning of death—and, perhaps, of life?

Certainly the poet mourns for her mother, and in that sense this is also a poem of love. Mabel Ashley Kizer was a most uncommon woman for her time. She held two degrees in biology, taught at Mills College and headed the biology department at San Francisco State College, was a radical political activist and organizer, and did not marry until her mid-forties. In "A Muse," the second prose section of her Pulitzer

Prize-winning collection *Yin* (1984), Kizer credits her mother as the source of inspiration for her writing. She notes with deep affection and respect that her "serious life as a poet" began after her mother's death in 1955: "I wrote the poems for her. I still do." Other portraits of her mother appear in the poems "The Blessing," "The Intruder," and "A Long Line of Doctors."

In addition, this poem is an elegy, a serious meditation on the vanishing past and the despoiling of nature: "The pines and driftwood" have been "cleared/ From that bare strip of shore." Kizer's reverence for nature comes partly from her love of its beauty, which was encouraged by her mother; it was also influenced by her love for Chinese poetry, which again was nourished by her mother, who would read to her from translations of Chinese poets by Arthur Waley. In Chinese poetry, images taken from nature, rather than those from religion or myth, predominate.

In her essay "Western Space," Kizer points out some of the differences between poets such as herself who hail from the American West (specifically, Washington State), and poets from the East. Characteristically "there is something about our great spaces . . . that makes us feel small, and fragile, and mortal," she writes. "To live in the midst of this [natural beauty] is to live . . . like a fallen angel who sees paradise taken from him piece by piece." She suggests that the destruction of nature's beauty has created in Western poets "the impulse to conserve, to memorialize what is lost, to elegize what is dying before our eyes." A reader can sense this concern as well in the speaker's awareness of her changing landscape.

Ironically the heron, which in ancient Egypt was believed to be a sacred bird that housed the soul and symbolized the generation of life, serves here as death's indifferent and inexorable messenger. Yet the heron is clearly part of the living world of nature. Perhaps the symbol of the heron has been used to reconcile the opposites of life and death as they coexist in the great cycle of nature. The poem's speaker, whether she realizes this truth or not, remains heavy-hearted in her grief.

Joanne McCarthy

THE GREAT GULL

Author: Howard Nemerov (1920-1991)
Type of poem: Narrative
First published: 1951

The Poem

Howard Nemerov's "The Great Gull" is a twenty-seven-line narrative poem of irregular tetrameter, punctuated with tense trimeter lines. The poem relates the narrator's dawn encounter with a gull who flies in for a brief stop on his lawn. The convergence of human and gull evokes the narrator's reflection upon the relationship of humanity to nature and ends with his sense that humans and their concerns are puny things in contrast to the stern mystery of nature, and by extension, the cosmos.

The opening six lines of "The Great Gull" reveal that the narrator is restless and so gets up at dawn, where he sees the great gull fly in and rest upon the lawn, a sight he would not ordinarily see. The gull's wing is "savage," and the bird must shake it to quiet, a sign of restlessness and power. The bird's stance is authoritative, priestly. Its grey feathers evoke a mantle; his head a mask, a bird mask, like those worn by pagan priests. The gull's "fierce austerity" causes the narrator to bow in humility and wonder, to speculate on the sea-lanes and wild waters the bird not only traveled by but also slept in, "still as a candle in the crypt."

The next two lines focus on the gull's response to the narrator. The bird's stare is noble, not polite or obsequious, indicating he needs no permission to stand on the narrator's territory. The following lines compare the gull to a merchant prince exploring a poor province. The bird surveys the narrator and, presumably, the lawn, the house, and its accoutrements, but finds "no treasure house," nothing that can be made "Delightful to his haughty trade"—nothing worth staying around for. The gull readies himself to fly away, leaving "savage men" to "Their miserable regimen," words indicating its scorn of humanty and its "green concerns."

It takes effort for the bird to hoist his wings like a sail and his body into the air. When he does so, his mighty wings create a wind. As the gull flies away, he lets out an eerie cry. The narrator does not understand the language but comprehends that the bird disdains the narrator's concerns and flies into a cosmos more interesting, mysterious, and profound than any human issues. The cry's tone tells the narrator that he will never understand the universe except to comprehend that it is beyond him and human analysis. The experience leaves the narrator humbled and aware of a strange yet majestic universe in which he plays a tiny part and of which his understanding is fragmentary and myopic.

Forms and Devices

Nemerov uses half irregular iambic tetrameter and half iambic trimeter in this poem. The rhymes are approximate, with the exception of three couplets and two alternating rhymes—the rhyming end words occurring after one or two intervening lines at the beginning and near the close of the poem. The iambic tetrameter lines interspersed with clipped iambic trimeter create the effect of a leisurely story being punctuated by important points or actions. For example, "Restless, rising at dawn" is an abrupt opening line. "Still as a candle in the crypt" is a terse yet powerful line. The longer lines, such as "I saw the great gull come from the mist" and "And vanished seaward with a cry—," have a slowing effect, appropriate to the time it would take to watch a gull sail in and perch upon one's lawn, then fly so far into the horizon that it appears to vanish. The shorter, staccato lines, which include "bird mask," "mantled," and "fierce austerity," convey undisputed authority in their terseness.

Alliteration and assonance substituting for more conventional rhyme schemes follow the alliterative verse tradition of Anglo-Saxon poetry. Alliterative consonants such as "Restless, rising," "great gull," "masked, mantled," "wild waters" "candle . . . crypt," "poor province," "spread . . . sail," "fought . . . freight," and "tongue . . . tongue" create immediacy in the poem. These hard consonant sounds are softened by assonance in almost every line; "stand . . . lawn," "shook . . . stood," "thought bowed down," "wandered . . . waters . . . candle," "down . . . courteous . . . upon . . . concerns," "come . . . some . . . poor," "who . . . looking . . . ," "gull come from," "can . . . made," "miserable regimen," "making . . . gale," "vanished seaward," and "tongue . . . tone." The abundant assonance juxtaposed with hard alliterative beats creates a rhythm suggestive of heavy wings flapping or a bell tolling, an evocation in keeping with the metaphysical simile of priest and crypt.

The imagery and tone of "The Great Gull" also suggest the mournful tone of Anglo-Saxon poetry, such as "The Seafarer." Words such as "sea-lanes" and "wild waters" evoke Anglo-Saxon kennings, such as "whale's road" or "water way." The sea, long a symbol of infinity, contrasts with known "green concerns." The addition of "my" to "green concerns" implies the narrator's naïveté, his being "green," as well as the mundane, earthly issues specified in a "lawn," a tended piece of grass in contrast to a field.

The personification of the gull as priest and merchant prince does more than establish the bird's commanding position. Personifying a bird creates an "Other" that is easier to invest with human qualities than a fish, for example. The story, because it is told from a human point of view, dodges the problem of presenting a gull's consciousness and evokes reader empathy for the narrator.

Themes and Meanings

"The Great Gull" is essentially a religious meditation. It reflects Nemerov's sense of correspondences, an Emersonian belief that nature teaches metaphysical and moral lessons if one observes closely. Unlike Ralph Waldo Emerson, Nemerov does not perceive moral lessons or judgments in nature. Rather, in this poem, his meeting with the gull teaches him that he is inconsequential in the grand scheme of things, that the issues that keep him awake at night mean nothing to the cosmos. Instead of despair, however, the poet's epiphany about his egocentricity and the ineffability of the universe results in reverence, his thought being "bowed down."

The poem's artistic genius resides in its subtlety. Nemerov illustrates the strangeness of the universe by personifying a gull, a being sharing some qualities with humans yet different enough to establish foreignness, thus a symbol of the cosmos itself. Moreover, the bird seems to have some knowledge that the poet does not, a knowledge that allows the gull to disdain the narrator and to fly comfortably into a cosmos that discomforts yet awes the narrator.

The gull, whose color reflects the gray of the sea, descends out of a mist, another symbol of the unknowable, the unclear. Mist metaphorically illustrates the narrator's whole experience with the gull. Even the bird's "strange tongue" has a clear tone, illustrative of a misty experience in which a reality can be glimpsed but not clearly defined. Relating the incident from the point of view of a human put in his place by an unexpected encounter with a strange gull, also reverses the conventional stance of humans as the "highest" form of life. In fact, all the poetic devices serve to establish nature's supremacy to humankind, a view antithetical to the Genesis account of Adam's having dominion over nature and closer to the Native American ideal of human cooperation with nature.

However, "The Great Gull" does not preach either cooperation or conquest. It simply acts as a poetic Galileo to a worldview which, like the ancient Church, is still anthropocentric and still confident that humanity's intellectual, moral powers are competent to deal with whatever arises. The narrative implies humanity's arrogance by showing how humans' "miserable regimen" is easily burst by an encounter with the Other, especially when the narrator perceives the bird as disdaining the narrator and, by implication, the burning issues that prevent the poet from sleeping.

Historically, the "The Great Gull" mixes the Romantic tradition with realism. It is an outstanding example of Romanticism in that it glorifies nature and privileges intuitive knowing over rational analytical thought, much like Walt Whitman in "When I Heard the Learned Astronomer." It differs from nineteenth century Romanticism in that it does not exalt the individual and has no Byronic hero, but instead perceives humans as regular, nonspecial creatures in an intricate, unfathomable order.

Mary Hanford Bruce

THE GREAT HUNGER

Author: Patrick Kavanagh (1904-1967)
Type of poem: Narrative
First published: 1942

The Poem

The Great Hunger is a fine example of the long poem in the twentieth century. Its 756 lines, primarily in free verse, are divided into fourteen sections, varying in length from twenty-two to 125 lines. The poem, with its oblique title reference to the Great Famine of the 1840's in Ireland, examines the life of Patrick Maguire, an unmarried peasant farmer tied to his small acreage. Maguire starves intellectually, psychologically, and spiritually as he struggles against the tyranny of the soil.

In section 1, Patrick Kavanagh sets a dramatic frame for the whole poem as the narrator invites the reader to watch Maguire and his fellow potato gatherers on the hillside for an hour. That hour figuratively spans Maguire's life through the course of the other thirteen sections. In this section, Maguire is fully introduced, and the bleak Donaghmoyne setting is vividly fixed. The time is October, and Maguire and his men are gathering the potato crop—"like mechanised scarecrows." While detailing the men at work, the narrative voice unfolds the complexities of Maguire's present plight. "Too long virgin," Maguire regrets his unfulfilled promise to himself to marry, sighing, "O God if I had been wiser!" As the section closes, the narrator is ready for the curtain to go up: "Come with me, Imagination, into this iron house/ And we will watch . . . the years run back."

In the next twelve sections, the sixty-five years of Maguire's existence is "run back," somewhat like twelve scenes in a play. Kavanagh projects the "drama" of Maguire's personal, familial, and communal activities, as well as his hopes, illusions, and fears, against a backdrop of a seasonal cycle compounded of the growing season of the Irish potato from early spring seeding to October harvest and the varied seasonal toils of Maguire and his potato gatherers.

The narrative segments in the separate sections freely range back and forth over the years of Maguire's life and over his fourteen-hour day. Some of these vignettes depict the daily course of Maguire's activities; others re-create earlier moments of his life. Kavanagh augments these vignettes with broader sketches of key moments (usually of psychological importance) from Maguire's life. As the seasons pass and one potato crop follows the next, Kavanagh reveals Maguire's increasing awareness of time's passage—*his* time. Throughout, Maguire's aspirations for a fulfilling life clash with the reality of his thwarted existence.

The climax of Maguire's drama, such as it is, comes at the end of section 13. At this point it is clear that this is a tragedy without a resolution: "No crash,/ No drama./ That was how his life happened." In the poem's final section, now that the "years run back" have completed their course, the narrator steps out of the iron house (the one into which he had invited the reader in section 1): "We may come out into the October, Imagination." The drama has ended: "Applause, applause,/ The Curtain falls." All that remains is a brief epilogue. The poem has come full circle from the opening "Clay is the word and clay is the flesh"—with all the promise in this variant expression of Christian Revelation—to the utter despair of the conclusion, "the apocalypse of clay/ In every corner of this land."

Forms and Devices

The intense, realistic depiction of peasant life in *The Great Hunger* arises directly from Kavanagh's first-hand knowledge of daily existence on his native Monaghan clay hills. To craft his striking and convincing portrait of Maguire's personal hunger, a blend of memory and imagination, Kavanagh employs the techniques now common to modern cinematography. The poem is a carefully crafted editing of close-ups, long shots, and flashbacks; it employs direct and indirect characterization, dialogue, interior monologue; naturalistic narrative vignettes, dramatic sketches, and reflective passages. The fourteen sections are a cinematographic tour de force in poetry.

Kavanagh's re-creation of the natural speech pattern of the Irish peasants is remarkable—and typical of Kavanagh's sharp detailing of particulars throughout the poem. The total effect of the speech passages is more than that of realistic re-creation and more than the ancillary unity they provide. Almost all the talk is of the land—its grip is figuratively at the very throats of these potato gatherers. Their talk reinforces that theme.

A series of key images, or motifs—dream, gap (in the sense of a "way to freedom"), circle, a stone and a handful of gravel—serve structural and thematic functions. Kavanagh's variations on the dream motif illustrate those functions. The poet uses the dream image twice in the first section and returns to it in later sections, with incremental effect. In section 1, Maguire, on the hillside gathering potatoes, reflects associatively upon the moment. Then a shift occurs in Maguire's mental meanderings:

> His dream changes again like the cloud-swung wind
> And he is not so sure now if his mother was right
> When she praised the man who made a field his bride.

The shift is from Maguire's present casual preoccupations to a more reflective contemplation of his past and the factors that have brought him to his present plight. The passage, with the striking simile "like the cloud-swung wind," also implies that Maguire may be more the recipient than the agent in his relations with his fields. The second dream image in section 1 depicts Maguire's youthful suspicious response to the flirtatious laughter of young girls: "He dreamt/ The innocence of young brambles to hooked treachery."

In section 4, the dream motif exposes Maguire's limited and limiting concept of morality and his inclination to be cautious with girls. In the short sixth section, the dream motif reveals broken idealism and, in particular, Maguire's tendency to dream of life (health, wealth, and love) rather than to live it: "Three frozen idols of a speech-less muse." Kavanagh concludes this interrelated string of dream images in the final section of the poem, where he ironically speculates on the possibility of Maguire real-izing the dream in death: "And the serious look of the fields will have changed to the leer of a hobo/ Swaggering celestially home to his three wishes granted./ Will that be? will that be?"

Themes and Meanings

The Great Hunger is a striking (and necessary) counterbalance to the frequently voiced sentimental, romantic exaltation of the Irish peasant. It is a firm refutation of the 'noble peasant' myth.

The poem is not only the depiction of the "sad, grey, twisted, blind, awful" life of one Irish peasant-farmer; it is also a terrible and moving composite image of human frustration. Held by the "grip of irregular fields," Maguire is emblematic of all human beings in their material and spiritual struggle against squalor, emptiness, and sexual deprivation.

The tyranny of the soil dehumanizes Maguire and his fellow potato gatherers. Time for them is measured by the land and its demands; holidays are remembered by the color of the fields. Maguire, only once removed from the beast he drives in that he, un-like them, is aware of his plight, is, in the end, "a sick horse nosing around the meadow for a clean place to die."

Those tied to the land like Maguire become eunuchs, as youthful dreams of love eventually turn to lust, self-abuse, and finally impotence. Promises to marry "before apples were hung from the ceilings for Halloween" are delayed, and in the delay Maguire dismisses "children as tedious" and becomes lost to "passion that never needs a wife." Such deprivation leads to self-deception as a mechanism of survival. Sitting on the wooden gate one July day and "riding in day-dream's car," Maguire is moved to "high ecstasies" by the glory he beholds while, ironically, "Life slipped be-tween the bars."

Religious strictures and rigid communal standards also stifle one's humanity and sense of divine truth. Symbolically, when Maguire leaves Mass, he coughs "the prayer phlegm up from his throat"; ritual without meaning chokes spiritual truth. A puritanical, overactive sense of sin—a part of the general spiritual condition of Maguire's community—operates in his mind. One day as he eyed a passing young woman, he "rushed beyond the thing/ To the unreal. And he saw Sin/ Written in letters larger than John Bunyan dreamt of."

Excessive idealism and the quest for eternal truths also stirred Kavanagh's satiric ire. Too often, like Maguire, people turn "from five simple doors of sense" to the door "whose combination lock has puzzled/ Philosopher and priest and common dunce." Kavanagh would have his reader probe the everyday and the commonplace with com-mon sense.

Glenn Grever

GREEN CATEGORIES

Author: R. S. Thomas (1913-   )
Type of poem: Meditation
First published: 1958, in *Poetry for Supper*

The Poem

"Green Categories" is one of R. S. Thomas's more complex poems, drawing in part on the ideas of the German philosopher Immanuel Kant that are developed in *Kritik der reinen Vernunft* (1781; *Critique of Pure Reason*, 1838). Thomas blends language and concepts from Kant's work with images of the Welsh countryside, a device that simultaneously raises questions about Kant's ideas and provides a larger context for the representation of a Welsh farmer, Iago Prytherch. The title reflects this blend: "Green" describes the countryside, while "Categories" refers specifically to Kant's divisions of forms of pure understanding.

Stylistically, the poem is not particularly complicated: It consists of two stanzas, a long first one and a shorter second one. It is written in the second person and addressed to Prytherch, who is a character in several of Thomas's other poems, including "Iago Prytherch," "Lament for Prytherch," and "Invasion on the Farm." Thomas introduces Kant in the first line, writing, "You never heard of Kant, did you, Prytherch?" He goes on in the stanza to speculate upon what Kant might have thought of Prytherch's life and draws distinctions between Kant's logic and abstract ideas and Prytherch's life on the farm, a life tied to the natural world and concrete objects. Slightly more than halfway through the first stanza, Thomas takes two of Kant's concepts, space and time, and gives an alternate definition for them in Prytherch's life. He justifies his definition by then asking "how else" Prytherch could live as he does and as the men before him did. The stanza ends as it begins: with a question. However, both questions are rhetorical; the speaker is using them to make assertions about Prytherch's life.

The second stanza is significantly shorter. It begins with a contrast, indicating that Prytherch and Kant would have given pause to each other, then concludes by saying that they "could have been at one." While each one's logic and mind could not stand up to the other's, the two men do share a kind of faith.

Perhaps because of the use of Kant's ideas and terminology, Thomas keeps the rest of the poem structurally simple. He uses no rhyme and, as is typical of his work, does not rely heavily on metaphors or elaborate images, using, instead, simple and plain words. This simplicity of language does not, however, keep the poem from being a difficult one to understand; even a reader who is well versed in Kant's philosophy will probably have to puzzle out what Thomas means by "faith." At the same time, though, the reader can connect to the concrete images of objects belonging to Prytherch's world and, in comparing them to the abstract terms referring to Kant, think about different ways of being. One need not understand Kant to see that the poem contrasts a life shaped by inner logic and mental properties with one formed by external forces upon the body; furthermore, one need not understand Kant to try to find connections between these two lives.

Forms and Devices

Thomas does not use many of the traditional forms or devices associated with poetry in the poem: It has no obvious rhyme or meter, and there are only a few metaphors. Several of them are used to describe the landscape: "the dark moor exerts/ Its pressure," "the moor's deep tides," and the "moor's/ Constant aggression." These representations of the land as a heavy, moving, dangerous force bring home the difficulty of Prytherch's life and its close connections to the natural world. Thomas's other metaphors reinforce this theme: A "green calendar" suggests that Prytherch lives according to the seasons rather than by the arbitrary dates delineated in a calendar, and the phrase "cold wind/ Of genius" reminds the reader of the hostile forces of nature that Prytherch encounters, even while it deepens the contrast between him and Kant.

One of the more interesting stylistic devices in the poem is the linguistic shift between certainty and uncertainty. The first stanza contains three questions, and, while the first and last are actually assertions in question form, the second one, beginning "What would he have said," is a question for the reader to consider. Prytherch, never having heard of Kant, could not speculate on what Kant might say to his life, but Thomas is asking the reader to engage in such speculation: Although the poem is written in the second person to Prytherch, the language requires readers to take parts of the poem as addressed to themselves. The speaker then returns to a descriptive voice, stating as fact that "Here all is sure." This certainty continues through the first stanza, even with the question at the end. The second stanza, however, moves from what is to what is possible, stating that "His logic would have failed" and that "you could have been at one." While neither of these are speculative in the same way that the poem's second question is—indeed, both assert that, given certain conditions, such would have happened—they do ask the reader to imagine a contrary-to-fact situation: a meeting between the philosopher and the Welsh farmer. Thomas moves back and forth in the poem from defining a situation to inviting the reader to reflect on that situation, a move that is, in some ways, parallel to the difference between Prytherch's life of the body and Kant's life of the mind.

Themes and Meanings

Several of the terms in the poem are taken specifically from Kant's work: categories, antinomies, space and time, and mathematics. In *Critique of Pure Reason*, Kant defines the categories as "concepts of synthesis that the understanding contains within itself *a priori*." The categories, which include such thing as "Unity," "Reality," and "Possibility-Impossibility," are ways in which the understanding synthesizes or groups its ideas and which have not been taught to the understanding; they are known intuitively, without benefit of experience. The antinomies consist of the conflicts between different ideas in transcendental philosophy that cannot be proved or disproved experientially; they transcend all experiences. Kant's first conflict, for example, is between the thesis that the world has a beginning in time and the antithetical statement that it has none: Space and time are not concepts that can be derived from experience but are rather a priori concepts upon which a person's intuitions are based (space underlies outer intuitions and time underlies inner ones). Mathematics is an example of a form of synthetic knowledge derived from the a priori knowledge of space and time.

In the poem, Thomas is juxtaposing Kant's ideas of a knowledge that is not based on experience or empirical data with Prytherch's understanding. Prytherch comprehends and understands the world through his experiences, through the flesh, through the things of the natural world around him. When the speaker says, "Space and time/ Are not the mathematics that your will/ Imposes, but a green calendar/ Your heart observes," the distinction being made is between Kant's ideas of space and time as something that leads to a pure science (such as mathematics) and Prytherch's experience of space and time as connected to the physical earth and the seasons. Prytherch's knowledge comes not from intuition but from experience.

In the last stanza, Thomas claims that Kant's logic could not continue in the face of Prytherch's relationship with the world, even while Prytherch's mind would be unable to comprehend Kant's. The speaker does find a connection between them, however, in the faith that they share "over a star's blue fire." What he means by "faith" is not clear; one strong possibility, however, is that both men have a faith in existence itself. While Kant's logic is indeed "remote" to Prytherch's world, it is founded on the idea that one does exist. Space and time are intuitive concepts, and the world's beginning cannot be substantiated through any experience, but the antinomy does not deny the world's existence itself. Thomas imagines Prytherch and Kant together at night with the hostile moor outside, a condition that would make each man aware of his own existence and his desire to continue to exist. Beneath intuition, beneath experience, there is the enduring faith that one is and things are. "Green Categories" uses Prytherch's life to point out the remoteness of Kant's philosophy from everyday experiences, but it does not validate Prytherch's life as the best way to exist either. Instead, the poem moves beyond asking how one knows the world to affirming that one is in the world.

Elisabeth Anne Leonard

GREEN CHILE

Author: Jimmy Santiago Baca (1952-   )
Type of poem: Meditation/ode
First published: 1989, in *Black Mesa Poems*

The Poem

Jimmy Santiago Baca begins "Green Chile" with a distinctly personal statement that establishes his intimate experience with one of the staples of southwestern American cuisine, then expands his meditation on the significance of the chile pepper in the life of the residents of that region throughout the poem. In a conversational address to the reader, Baca declares his preference for "red chile over [his] eggs" in the introductory section of the poem, the first of three parts which convey the poet's lifelong involvement with an agricultural item that has a cultural resonance considerably beyond its delectable properties.

Indicating the central aspect of chile in his life, Baca describes how "Red chile *ristras* decorate [his] door,/ dry on [his] roof, and hang from eaves," before widening the focus to show how forms of the plant are evident throughout the community, lending "historical grandeur" and a "festive welcome" to the market commons. Deepening the description, Baca personifies the plant, claiming that he can "hear them talking in the wind" and likening the sound of their talk to the "rasping/ tongues of old men," evoking the spirit of village elders whose words recall ancient customs and ways.

The poem shifts perspective in the second section as Baca reverses the outward motion of the first part by developing a warmly detailed portrait of his grandmother, who, in contrast to the poet's taste, "loves green chile." In an extended recollection of his visits to her in his youth, Baca describes the ways in which his grandmother prepared a favorite meal, starting with the relationship between the cook and the plant. Here, Baca presents the green pepper as a version of a "well-dressed gentleman" caller to whom his grandmother responds with an enthusiastic combination of appreciation for an impressive physical presence and a robust application of the responsive interaction that a masterful cook brings to the ingredients of the meal. Baca emphasizes the ways in which the physicality of the person and the plant becomes palpable during the process of preparation, envisioning his grandmother "with lust/ on her hot mouth, sweating over the stove," and a "mysterious passion on her face." His retrospective gratitude for "her sacrifice/ to her little prince" concludes this section on a note of satisfaction and achievement.

The third section widens the field again in a conclusive summary of the importance of the pepper for communities "All over New Mexico." Speaking with a sense of a life's observations, Baca identifies "sunburned men and women" in small towns throughout the state—"Belen, Veguita, Willard, Estancia"—who have gathered the crop and who are "roasting green chile/ in screen-sided homemade barrels" to provide a simple, delicious meal for residents and travelers. As a measure of meaning, Baca places himself directly within this "beautiful ritual," in which for "a dollar a bag" he, and anyone who can appreciate the food, as well as its cultural relevance, can be a part of a still-vivid tradition.

Forms and Devices

In accordance with the dynamic physical nature of the plant at the center of the poem, Baca uses sensory images of a particularly engaging nature to convey the prominent qualities of the pepper. Sound, sight, touch, and taste are brought into play, as Baca hears "rasping tongues," sees a "swan-neck stem, tapering to a flowery/ collar," notes his grandmother taking the pepper "sensuously in her hand,/ rubbing its firm glossed sides," and says, "my mouth burns/ and I hiss and drink a tall glass of cold water." These are the components of what appears as a living entity, and Baca turns the chile in his grandmother's hands into a metaphorical version of a romantic visitor. "Ah, voluptuous, masculine," he calls "him," with "an air of authority and youth."

This leads toward an extended image of his grandmother in the act of preparing the meal, which is also designed to be read as an erotic exchange between parties with an open and honest mixture of desire and arousal. The culmination of the relationship is a comparison of the chile to "a tiger in mid-leap," with "Its bearing magnificent and taut," which Baca's grandmother cuts open with a thrust of her blade and "lust/ on her hot mouth."

The personification of the plant is designed to give it a place of prominence beyond an inanimate object, to suggest that it is a sentient being containing the spirit of the culture that Baca is celebrating. In casting himself both as a youthful observer of the power the pepper exercises on the imagination and as a mature adult responding to its allure, Baca maintains a kind of dual narrative with respect to the poem's subject. He also, in his use of a friendly, inclusive conversational mode of speech, is projecting himself as a character in the tableau.

The language that he employs from the start is open and direct, creating a mood of exuberance and permitting the reader to enter the world that the poem re-creates. His exclamation of delight in the line "Ah, voluptuous, masculine," is characteristic of an unabashed pleasure in the word picture he is drawing. His use of familiar words from the Spanish language such as "tortilla" or "con carne," and the less familiar *ristras*, which the glossary in the back of *Black Mesa Poems* defines as "a braided string of *chiles* (peppers)," gives the poem a flavor of a specific locality without restricting its accessibility.

Themes and Meanings

In an interview, Baca described himself as "a detribalized Apache" and explained that his grandparents essentially raised him from infancy to the age of six. From that point, he was shuttled from a broken home, to foster homes, to the streets of the El Paso barrio, to juvenile detention centers, and then to prison. Practically illiterate and totally directionless, he learned to read in jail, and then to write about his life. "Green

Chile" was conceived as a tribute to his grandmother, a special person he trusted and loved, as a demonstration of the endearing qualities he responded to and respected.

Beyond this, the poem presents Baca's grandmother as a representative of a culture that has often been disparaged and stereotyped, and the chile pepper that she so artfully prepares is developed as a symbol of the strength, substance, and style of her community. When Baca describes the red chile he prefers in the first section, he shows how his personal choice is a part of a larger cultural matrix in which the pepper becomes an emblem of cultural pride, signifying "historical grandeur" that carries an image of a vegetable stand into the realm of generational succession, and making its "festive welcome" indicative of a social standard.

The expansion from a single house to the entire state of New Mexico in the third section is a strong expression of pride in simple but basic facts inherent in a way of life. Baca's depiction of the people he has seen who "drive rickety trucks stuffed with gunny-sacks" to carry the chile to the roadside stands across the state where this delicacy is available is like a fond embrace for a fundamental activity rarely celebrated if frequently appreciated. He is functioning here in the classic fashion of the poet as a living voice for a community as his poem permits the reader to "relive this old, beautiful ritual again and again"—his words spurring the imagination to reexperience something special and almost timeless.

"Green Chile" is a meditation on the enduring appeal of an essential element in the life of a community and an ode to spirit of the poet's grandmother. Her wholehearted participation in the preparation of "green chile con carne" is the individual experience that makes the communal vision tangible and affecting. The poem is one among many of Baca's drawn upon and contributing to a cultural heritage that has been largely overlooked in American letters, a condition he points toward in the title of his collection *Immigrants in Our Own Land* (1979). His writing is his own way of taking part in this tradition, a way for him to merge the "authority and youth" that "simmers" from the "swan-neck stem" of the pepper plant in a joining of ancient wisdom with the youthful energies of his poetic power.

Leon Lewis

GREEN ENRAVISHMENT OF HUMAN LIFE

Author: Sor Juana Inés de la Cruz (Juana Inés de Asbaje y Ramírez de Santillana, 1648-1695)

Type of poem: Sonnet

First published: 1690, as "Verde embeleso de la vida humana," in *Poemas*; English translation collected in *Anthology of Mexican Poetry*, 1958

The Poem

"Green enravishment of human life" is a sonnet of the Italian or Petrarchan type. It consists of an octave (eight lines rhyming *abbaabba*) and a sestet (six lines rhyming *cdecde*). The sonnet lacks a title; it is identified by its first line. The octave is mainly descriptive of the theme of the poem: hope. The speaker of the poem emerges in the sestet. After describing the attitude of those who, hoping for change, ignore or distort reality, Sor Juana Inés de la Cruz expresses her own positivist attitude about the world.

Sor Juana spent several years of her life at the court of colonial Mexico. There she wrote many poems of circumstance, conventional pieces in which she praised persons of high rank and love poems that might have been written by request. Another part of her lyric poetry, however, conveys her own feelings and worldview. "Green enravishment of human life" is one of those philosophical or moral poems in which Sor Juana expresses her personal ideas. The poem is a good illustration of Sor Juana's rationalism, an attitude that is obvious at other points in her work. For the poet, to hope is to fool oneself, and she distances herself from those who live in the expectation of future improvements or riches. An even more unfavorable description of hope can be found in another of her sonnets, "Diuturnal infirmity of hope," in which she describes hope as cruel, deceptive, and homicidal, since it "inflicts a more protracted death."

In the first stanza of this sonnet, Sor Juana calls hope the "green enravishment." This metaphor suggests the ability of hope to conquer human will. The second line takes up the notion of the irresistibility of hope and relates it to madness ("smiling frenzy of demented hope"). This association sets the tone for Sor Juana's condemnation of such a feeling. The last lines of the first stanza further underscore the unreality of hope by connecting it with dreams, which, according to Sor Juana, usually turn out to be empty.

The second stanza adds more images that underscore the deceitfulness of hope. Hope provides only a false feeling of strength, an illusion of renewed vigor. The last two lines of this stanza mirror each other. Hope makes one who is happy expect more happiness; it makes one who lives in misery expect happiness in the future.

The poet's skeptical attitude is already betrayed by the associations that are implicit in the octave, but her skepticism becomes explicit in the last six lines of the poem. There is a shift of tone in the third stanza. In the first two stanzas, the poem was static, with the author describing hope by means of a list of paraphrases. The third stanza begins with a direct address to hope in the second person: Let those who view reality as they wish, by looking at it through green glasses, chase your shadow, Sor Juana writes. In the last stanza, the poet places herself in opposition to those who filter reality to suit their fantasies. She considers herself to be more reasonable. Rather than chasing the shadow of hope, she considers only that which is tangible.

Forms and Devices

This sonnet is exemplary in its use of conceits which were characteristic of Spanish Baroque poetry. A conceit always implies ingenuity, striking inventiveness, whether in a single original image or in a series of elaborate and witty analogies. This sonnet utilizes several unexpected pairings of terms to describe hope. Paradox and wordplay are also frequently used in Baroque poetry, and Sor Juana uses here the parallelisms, inversions, and repetitions that were favorite ways of syntactic organization in Baroque poetry.

The recurring image that runs through the poem is the traditional association of hope with the color green; this image appears in the first three stanzas. The roots of this association may lie in the rebirth of the world with the reemergence of vegetation in the spring. Sor Juana, however, undermines the positive connotations of the color green by presenting it in contexts that become increasingly negative. It accompanies "enravishment" in the first stanza, which suggests a deceitful, passing state. The falseness of hope is further stressed in the second stanza, in the seemingly paradoxical juxtaposition of images of weakness and strength: "robust old age," "decrepit vigor" (in Spanish, *verdor*, greenness). In the third stanza, hope is described as making the hopeful wear "green glasses" through which they adapt the real world to suit their personal desires.

Furthermore, Sor Juana accentuates the insubstantiality of hope by associating it with nouns such as "dream," "madness," "imagination," "frenzy," and "shadow." The "I" of the poem emerges strongest in the last three lines, and again takes up this notion of the immateriality of hope to underline the poet's own skeptical attitude toward it. Those who hope live in a world of incorporeal desires, but she is firmly rooted in the world of corporeality. The last stanza ends with a striking image: The poet holds her eyes in her hands and only sees that which can be touched.

The poem also reflects the Baroque "spirit of geometry," the delight in calibrated syntactical organization. The first two stanzas are structured almost identically; a list of paraphrases for hope is followed by two concluding sentences that mirror each other: "inextricable dream of them that wake/ and, as a dream, of riches destitute"; "longing for the happy ones' today/ and for the unhappy ones' tomorrow." The last two stanzas also play on each other by juxtaposing the disapproved behavior (of those who live in hope) with the right attitude (Sor Juana's realistic outlook).

The sonnet's careful syntactic arrangement and interconnected metaphors for hope transcend pure lyric ornamentation and give the poet's argument for reason additional weight.

Themes and Meanings

Sor Juana's condemnation of hope might seem excessive, but the poem can be better understood in the context in which it was produced. "Green enravishment" is representative of the pessimism of the Spanish Baroque. The grim vision of life and obsession with death of the Baroque came as a reaction to the optimism and affirmation of humanistic values of the Renaissance. In the poetry of the Spanish Baroque masters Francisco Goméz de Quevedo y Villegas and Luis de Góngora y Argote, one finds as recurring themes a disenchantment with the human being and a preoccupation with the ephemerality of human existence. In her philosophical-moral poems, Sor Juana elaborates on these typically Baroque ideas; she very often describes a deceptive world, the humiliations of old age, and the evanescence of earthly experience.

Such a grim vision of the world and human life precludes relying on hope or expecting future improvements. Sor Juana clearly reproves such attitudes. In the poem, hope is a state that resembles stupidity or madness, implying a voluntary or involuntary distancing from reality. Reality is the only thing one should consider, as Sor Juana states in the last stanza. One should neither project oneself into the future by expecting a change or improvement of circumstances nor impose one's subjectivity on the world.

The poem reminds one of the Greek myth of Prometheus and Pandora. When the Greek gods created Pandora as the punishment for Prometheus's theft of fire, they gave her a box that contained all the evils that would afflict humanity from that moment on. Included in Pandora's box was hope. The myth leaves many questions open. Why is hope an evil? Why did it stop at the box's rim when Pandora opened it and let the evils loose to roam the world? Hope can be seen as that which fuels human ambitions and keeps people going, but it can also be seen as a delusive, blind force that can prolong human misery, inflicting "a more protracted death," as Sor Juana puts it. Sor Juana seems to believe that hope sets one up for greater disappointments and that a rational, positivist attitude is preferable to the ersatz energy provided by a hopeful attitude.

Carlota Larrea

GRODEK

Author: Georg Trakl (1887-1914)
Type of poem: Lyric
First published: 1915, as "Grodek"; in *Die Dichtungen*, 1918; English translation collected in *Selected Poems*, 1968

The Poem

"Grodek" is a free-verse poem of seventeen lines. The title is highly significant; Georg Trakl served in the Austrian medical services during the World War I battle at Grodek in Galicia in 1914. He was charged with the care of some ninety wounded soldiers at an inadequately supplied field hospital; unable to ease their suffering, he himself broke down and was hospitalized for psychiatric observation. "Grodek" was the last poem Trakl wrote before his death from a cocaine overdose—perhaps a suicide—shortly after his breakdown. It quickly became one of the best-known war poems of World War I.

Though not separated into stanzas, four complete sentences (in the original) divide the poem thematically as well as syntactically. The first six-line sentence describes the close of a day of battle; as evening comes the sounds of combat—tones of "deadly weapons" and the "wild lament" of "dying warriors"—are embraced and surrounded by the approaching night.

Trakl's opening image of the human and mechanical sounds of battle echoing through the woods into the evening twilight is cut off by the "But" which begins the second, four-line sentence: "But," says the poet, even though the battle continues, the spilled blood of the day also "gathers" "quietly there in the pastureland" under the coolness of the moon. This silent return of shed blood to the earth points to the endless circle of life and death, which is at work even on the battlefield. The first ten lines of the poem remind the reader of a pastoral scene because of their familiar nature images such as "autumn woods," "golden plains," "blue lakes," and "pastureland," yet the pastoral allusions are constantly challenged by contrary images. Just as all the warriors' blood runs together in the low-lying meadows, so too do all roads lead to "blackest carrion," and the whole second image is also overshadowed by red clouds, "in which an angry god resides," a presence which further unsettles the poem.

The third, four-line sentence again highlights nature—"golden twigs," "night and stars," "the silent copse"—as the scene through which now "the sister's shade" moves "to greet the ghosts of the heroes." This introduction of the shadow or spirit of an unknown "sister" could imply the soothing touch of an ethereal nurse, or the peaceful greeting of Woman within the violent male world of the battlefield. Yet in the context of Trakl's life and poetic oeuvre, in which his own sister plays a very important role, this "sister" can also represent an intensely personal love, here shared among the bleeding, fallen heroes. The accompanying sounds of "dark flutes" could refer to the whistling of nature's cleansing autumn winds, but it is also a second allusion to the now-distant "deadly weapons" of line 2, that is, the battle's guns. *Tönen* ("to sound," "resound," or "cry out") in line 1 is the same verb Trakl uses in line 14; this repetition, along with the recurrence of "autumn," though as a noun rather than an adjective, signals the closure of the first series of descriptive images.

The vocative "O prouder grief!" serves to set the final sentence apart from the preceding body of the poem. The broken syntax of the last sentence allows for varying interpretations, yet the apostrophized "brazen altars"—for both grieving and sacrifice—seem to be animated by the "great pain" of the tragedy of war. "The unborn grandsons" of the last line serve as a coda to the last sentence and to the poem as a whole; the battlefield images are complete. Yet, the poem implies, what will follow war? Present as well as succeeding generations will be touched by it. The poem's ambiguous attitude asserts itself in the last line, which can mean either "the grandsons yet unborn" or "the grandsons never to be born"; either meaning, however, concludes the poem on a note of mourning and loss.

Forms and Devices

The most obvious formal aspect of Trakl's late poems is their difficult syntax. Like many of his expressionist contemporaries, he bends grammar past the breaking point, a technique which forces the reader to concentrate on the associations between clusters of images. In "Grodek" there is neither a "story" nor pure impressionistic description; instead, Trakl presents a series of images which are at first familiar, then strange to the reader. His images of nature recall a pastoral landscape tradition, yet the traditionally positive connotations of "golden plains" or a "silent grove" are estranged by their unsettling juxtaposition with a "more darkly" rolling sun or warriors'"bleeding heads."

The tradition of the German elegy, a poem of lament for the dead often written in distichs, is recalled by the use of the word "lament" in line 5, as well as by the mention of "grief" and the associations made with sacrifice and mourning through the "brazen altars" in line 15. Yet the poem's free-verse form contradicts the expected metrics of the traditional elegy, and its lack of a dominant personal and subjective voice—an important facet of the modern elegy—defeats further comparison.

The sounds in "Grodek" recall for German ears an important aspect of medieval Germanic heroic poetry, the heroic alliterative line, best known from a ninth century Old High German poem, the *Hildebrandslied* (*The Song of Hildebrand*, 1957). Alliteration—in lines 3 *(Seen/Sonne)*, 5 *(Krieger/Klage)*, and elsewhere—is the oldest form of Germanic rhyme. Through its use Trakl makes reference to the earliest Germanic war poetry, in which were sung the glories of the solitary warrior in his ultimately tragic search for honor through battle. Trakl's allusions to the past serve not only to recall the heroic tradition in poetry but also to ironize it through the all-too-obvious differences between warriors a millennium apart.

"Grodek" introduces and confounds several well-known poetic modes in its attempt to capture the results and implications of this battle. The complex of images the poem presents, then, is left to stand on its own, outside poetic tradition, and the reader sees but this silent progression of pictures, as in a film; only in the final sentence does the voice of a commentator cry out in grief at the momentous loss.

Themes and Meanings

In the highly politicized German literary world between the two world wars, Trakl's "Grodek" was read and claimed by readers both on the right and on the left of the political spectrum. Although expressionism as a school or style of literature was disdained by the National Socialist regime as decadent in its public associations and indulgent in its subjectivity, "Grodek" maintains enough of the tradition of the elegy to have been read by Nazi readers as a memorial to the dead, to the "ghosts of the heroes." At the same time, those who read closely or were privy to Trakl's difficult private language were able to understand the poem as full of resignation and hopelessness, especially because many of them concentrated on the poem's last line: "the grandsons (yet) unborn." Are the grandsons to come being sacrificed on the brazen altars of war? Is some craving "spirit" of humankind being fed these unborn generations through the act of war? Will these "grandsons" ever be born, or have the deaths of their elders, the "dying warriors," foreclosed their existence once and for all? Trakl leaves the interpretation to the reader.

Trakl's poetry has traditionally been read autobiographically, and this poem—occasioned as it was by his own experience at Grodek—is no different. In general, though, most of his other poetry is far more private and intimate and has consequently been subjected to psychological, religious, sexual, and philosophical interpretations. "Grodek" presents readers with something of an exception among Trakl's works since, unlike many of his poems which are grounded in some intensely private ordeal (experiences of religion, drugs, and incest), it has its roots in the common historical experience of World War I.

Because "Grodek" has been anthologized in collections of war poetry so often over the years, readers have been forced to interpret it in this context. So although academic readers and Trakl specialists like to trace the poem's key words and images throughout Trakl's oeuvre—to determine, for example, the various associations of "blue lakes" or of the "sister" in all his other poems—and interpret "Grodek" as the culmination of a consistent poetic journey, the poem actually stands well on its own as perhaps the most important German war poem of all. Within the context of twentieth century German history, Trakl's mourning call, "the unborn grandsons," might force readers to consider all the dead of the next war and to mourn them as well.

Scott D. Denham

THE GROUNDHOG

Author: Richard Eberhart (1904-   )
Type of poem: Meditation
First published: 1934; collected in *Reading the Spirit*, 1936

The Poem

"The Groundhog" is a poem in free verse; its forty-eight lines are marked by no formal divisions. It traces a process of development in four main stages, however; the first stage occupies the first twenty-four lines, while the last three are allotted eight lines each.

The speaker, the "I" of the poem, is never clearly identified but is probably a man of thoughtful, even scholarly, habits. He recounts a series of four encounters with a dead groundhog, ending in the present, three years after his first sight of the lifeless animal.

Strong emotions dominate stage 1, the speaker's first reaction to the groundhog, which has died recently. It is June, the height of the season of fullest life, but the three heavy stresses of line 3, "Dead lay he," arrest and shock the speaker. Senses shaking and mind racing, the speaker nevertheless focuses carefully on the busy, "ferocious" process of the groundhog's decay. He even takes action, angrily poking the body, which is seething with maggots. His anger may stem from his disgust at seeing the maggots or it may be the anger of denial, a cold rage against death. The emotion is pointless, however, for the heat of the localized natural scene becomes generalized and cosmic, as the "immense energy" of nature—from maggots to the sun—dwarfs and disarms the speaker. Standing silently, the speaker tries to make sense of his experience, hoping to balance his initial passion with understanding. He hopes for a spiritual benefit as well, for the first stage ends with the speaker "Praying for joy in the sight of decay."

Stage 2 occurs during the autumn of that same year, when the speaker returns intentionally to see the groundhog's remains. He revisits the scene "strict of eye," but finds only a disappointing, shapeless hulk. Consciousness predominates and seems to have inhibited or destroyed the man's emotional powers. He concedes that he has gained wisdom, but at an excessive cost. The next summer, in stage 3, the speaker chances upon the site of the groundhog's corpse, of which only hair and bones remain. In line 39, the speaker sees the groundhog objectively, "like a geometer." He cuts a walking stick, a steadying contrast to his angry stick of the previous summer.

The speaker reports on his fourth and final stage of development in the present, three summers after his first sight of the carcass. By now, the groundhog has decayed completely, leaving the speaker to recapitulate the whole process. The poem's last six lines summarize the process and compare it to historical figures, from its physical stage of vigorous summer and the conqueror Alexander, through the intellectual stage of withered emotion and the detachment of the ironic thinker Michel Eyquem de Montaigne, to the spiritual stage of Saint Theresa.

Forms and Devices

As a whole, "The Groundhog" is a complex and unresolved metaphor, pairing two processes: the universal mortality of nature and the growth of human awareness. As the carcass of the groundhog decays and disappears, so do the speaker's reactions develop. He moves from initial shock to intellectual paralysis to dispassionate objectivity, then ends with a recognition that combines, but does not wholly reconcile, feeling and thought.

Richard Eberhart reinforces the poem's controlling metaphor with an equally complex treatment of the ancient poetic convention that associates the seasons of the year with the stages of individual human life. Traditionally, this convention matches spring with youth, summer with early maturity, fall with late maturity, and winter with death. "The Groundhog" modifies the convention, since its four main stages enact scenes that take place in summer, fall, summer, and summer, respectively. The sequence is fitting, for the action of the poem encompasses only three years of the speaker's life—most likely, years of early manhood.

Outwardly, the speaker has changed very little. Inwardly, however, the process of growing awareness has been much fuller. Near the end of the poem, the speaker brings both processes together, standing "in the whirling summer" of external nature, his hand capping the "withered heart" of his internal realization that death's power is terrible and complete.

Thus the poem's main metaphor involves both parallels and juxtapositions of humankind and nature. At first, the speaker registers the parallel of shared mortality. Viewing the dead groundhog, he is shocked to note "our naked frailty" in line 4. This early insight, however, is only momentary, as the speaker shifts to intense visualization and desperate action. After he pokes the carcass, the speaker sees the power of nature expand from the tiny maggots to a universal fever, a cosmic power that leaves him feeling powerless. His only refuge is silent contemplation, as he tries to control his emotions, hoping that he will come to understand the relationship of universal death and human awareness.

His return in fall is subdued, since he has allowed his intervening intellectual pursuits to wall out his earlier emotional response. The speaker himself is aware of the seasonal metaphor, for during this stage—the only one not to occur in summer—he recognizes that "the year had lost its meaning" (line 29).

The next summer's visit owes little to conscious effort; the speaker chances upon the site. In this brief scene, the speaker replays his first visit, but with important differences. He views the disintegrating carcass, but his vision is calm and objective. Again, he uses a stick, not as an angry goad, but as a walking stick, an aid to steadiness and direction.

The poem's fourth and last stage recapitulates and combines both metaphorical parallels and juxtapositions. The season is again summer, with the speaker at a new height of awareness, a state that includes both emotional loss and increased but chastened thought. His conclusion, expanded by allusions to human civilizations and exemplary individuals, testifies to the omnipotence of death.

Themes and Meanings

"The Groundhog" is a poem about death. More specifically, its theme may be put best as a question: What does the knowledge of death do to a human being, the only creature blessed and cursed with consciousness? This theme is as ancient as poetry and as persistent as human thought.

As noted above, Eberhart explores and traces the intricate relationship of mortality and awareness, but he does not resolve it. The completed processes of the poem form a neat synopsis—summers whirl, hearts wither, men think—but such a synopsis is only an invitation to further speculation. Such speculation is a recurrent theme in Eberhart's work. In his first book, the long autobiographical poem *A Bravery of Earth* (1930), the poet explicitly describes three levels of "awareness," linking them with "mortality," "mentality," and "coming to understand." Much of his later work, especially "The Groundhog," represents a deepening and enriching of this powerful theme.

Two great principles animate "The Groundhog": the grand mortal energy of nature, and the smaller but equally recurrent energy of human thought. The first three sections of the poem present the reader with two sets of facts: the natural process of decay, and the human task of trying to make sense of mortality from within the larger cycle of death and disintegration.

The reader who notices the repetition of "in" during the poem's last six lines, one long sentence, might come as close as possible to resolving the relationship of death and consciousness. Line 43 presents the last sight of the speaker, "there in the whirling summer," contained within the larger natural process. Line 46 shows "Alexander in his tent," the world conqueror at rest before confronting once again the physical action and death that brought him a short-lived empire. This allusion also echoes the physical action of the speaker's first stage.

Line 47 focuses on the quiet intelligence of "Montaigne in his tower," contemplating life and death. The French thinker also suggests the speaker's "intellectual chains" of stage 2, as well as the "geometer" of stage 3. The poem's last line seems to add a new dimension, spirituality, with "Saint Theresa in her wild lament." In its way, however, this line recalls and extends the prayer that ends the first section, lines 23 and 24. Whether by means of the speaker's quiet prayer or the saint's loud protest, the human being strives to understand the mixed gifts of life and awareness.

Thus the speaker and the reader of "The Groundhog" both achieve a kind of recognition. The dead creature has provided the occasion for recognition. Contemplating dead civilizations and heroic individuals could have done no more. An understanding of death comes only at the end of a complex process of realizing and fusing flesh and spirit, reason and passion, outward and inward nature.

Terry Lass

GUIDE TO THE OTHER GALLERY

Author: Dana Gioia (1950-   )
Type of poem: Dramatic monologue
First published: 1991, in *The Gods of Winter*

The Poem

Like many of Dana Gioia's poems, "Guide to the Other Gallery" is highly struc-tured and traditional. Composed of six iambic tetrameter quatrains, the poem is set as a dramatic monologue reminiscent of Robert Browning's "My Last Duchess" both in its form and its surface subject, a guide showing artistic possessions to a visitor. Un-like in Browning's poem, the guide is not revealing exceptional pieces of art but the castoffs, the broken, useless, decayed, and unidentifiable objects kept in a back room for some unexplained reason, possibly because they were either useful at one time or were a part of someone's life (and therefore memory). Whatever the reason, in this museum "Nothing is ever thrown away." That final line of the first stanza, and indeed the entire first stanza, sets up a central question that plagues the reader throughout the poem: Why does the gallery keep these obviously broken and irreparably damaged or decayed objects?

The poem begins with the guide, as a good docent would, listing the objects and telling why each has been consigned here. The objects he enumerates include the sev-ered marble limbs of athletes and cherubim, butterflies carefully arranged in display cases, framed portraits of unknown people by unknown artists, books crumbling on shelves, empty bottles, and locks without keys. From the manner in which he dis-cusses the contents of the room—"These butterflies," "These portraits," and "Here are the shelves"—the guide and visitor appear to be walking through the gallery, passing by each exhibit as he mentions it. At one point the guide even tells the visitor, "I wish I were a better guide," adding "There's so much more that you should see," indicating they may be moving out of the room.

In the final stanza, though, their situation is clarified to show that the pair have merely been looking into the room. For at this moment, despite the depressing nature of the objects in the gallery, the visitor obviously asks to enter it, only to be told, "I wish you could./ This room has such a peaceful view." Rather than allowing the guest to enter, the guide points out an unlabeled antique wooden box and astonishingly adds, "It's for you."

The last two stanzas of the poem interestingly, but without preparation, move from a focus on the contents of the gallery to the people surveying it, the speaker lamenting his inadequacy as a guide, sorry that he is unable to show his guest everything that should be seen, and the visitor wishing to go farther inside, but instead being shown a box—most likely a coffin—just for her, indicating that this gallery, rather than the "other gallery," presumably the one that holds the whole, classified, and useable ob-jects, will eventually become a holding place for the visitor, too.

Forms and Devices

All the images in Gioia's "Guide to the Other Gallery" are sight images, none particularly concrete. The "splintered marble athletes" and cherubim are undifferentiated, the butterflies unclassified, and the books untitled. Gioia's decision to provide generic images rather than concrete ones appears intended to convey a sense of the leveling quality of time, decay, and death. His ordering of images similarly reinforces this sense. He begins his catalogue of images with the juxtaposition of the human and the divine, strength and delicacy with the broken and dismembered marble statues of the athletes and cherubim now relegated to what William Butler Yeats might have called this "foul rag-and-bone shop." He then moves on to another item often found in museums, a collection of butterflies, ethereal in contrast to the marble substantiality of the statues, but indistinguishable from one another.

The third image is of unidentified portraits. They are, significantly, flat, two-dimensional, unable to embody the "potent soul[s]" who commissioned them, achieving a worthless measure of immortality. The shelves of books, though visual in themselves, take the imagery in a slightly different direction as their covers are not what matters, but what the "Millions of pages turning brown" contain that is really significant. From the portrayal of the human form to the butterflies (symbolic in many cultures of the soul) to the books (the symbol of human thought and knowledge), Gioia moves to empty bottles, useful but unfilled and thus unfulfilled, and keyless locks, conceivably as useless an object as exists. The imagery thus becomes both increasingly mundane and evocative of the futility of accumulation, vanity, knowledge, and perhaps even life itself in the face of eroding time.

This sense of time is reinforced by the meter as well as the rhyme scheme of the poem. The poem is written in extremely regular iambic tetrameter and has a rhyme scheme that varies from *abab* only in the first and fourth stanzas, in both of which it is *abac*. The insistent beat of the lines mimics not only the emotionless, monotonous patter of the guide but also, more elementally, the tick of the clock or the beat of the heart, regular and lulling, just as time itself levels, dulls, and decomposes. An additional effect of the regular meter and rhyme here is that after it leads relatively painlessly and hypnotically through the list of the contents of the room, it continues and almost slips the gravity of the association of the visitor with the artifacts past the reader, adding to the jolt of the final words, "It's for you."

Themes and Meanings

With its focus on useless accumulation, whether of the divine or the mundane, and what that hoarding of the broken and disintegrating has to say about and to humankind, "Guide to the Other Gallery" is reminiscent of several of Gioia's other poems, most notably "Counting the Children." Both collected in *The Gods of Winter*, dedicated to the memory of Gioia's young son, these poems emphasize the ravages that time inflicts on everyone and everything. They also highlight the inability of humans to let go of objects, perhaps even ideas or their own bodies, in the face of the loss of their function and purpose. There is also a central paradox here in that these objects, which are now relentlessly held onto, were previously discarded by someone else. The place in which they now reside is a kind of netherworld, which conveys other, even more archetypal, associations to the poem.

The descent into the underworld—this poem admittedly presents a glimpse of and not a descent into the abyss—is an integral part of epics. Having no pretensions of being an epic—indeed the "you" of the poem comes across more as an Everyman than a heroic figure—this poem nonetheless borrows from that tradition.

Although these conventions hail from at least as far back as the Greek and Roman periods, Gioia's poem, appropriately for the work of a poet known for his translations of Italian poetry, is perhaps most evocative of Dante's *Inferno* from *La divina commedia* (c. 1320; *The Divine Comedy*, 1802). That allusion to Dante is perhaps nowhere clearer than in the guide who brings to mind Vergil conducting Dante through the Inferno; in this case the guide does not allow his companion into the forbidden place but merely grants a glance through its portals. "I wish I were a better guide,/ There's so much more that you should see," he tells the visitor, and in this statement and allusion the guide connects himself to all poets and seers; he should be able to illuminate the dark more fully for everyone but feels somewhat at a loss to do so. Instead, all he is able to do is to glance over the useless objects filling the room and only point to the final holding place of the visitor, the unmarked antique case.

That the guide is of seminal importance to the poem, despite his relative ineffectualness, is clear from the title, which does not focus on the visitor or even the gallery, but the guide. Additionally, the ambiguity of the title—"a guide" as in a guidebook or sign or "the guide" as in the docent—appears deliberate as Gioia omits the article that would provide clarification, further strengthening the allusion and contrast to the much more capable guidance of Vergil.

The ineffectiveness of the guide is in keeping with the lack of usefulness of the objects of the gallery. The statues, useless fragments of the human and divine, are kept for no apparent reason and rest beside rows of butterflies. Discovered after long and often difficult searches and then carefully arranged to show their relationship as well as their differentiation, the butterflies are indistinguishable from one another, made "commonplace" by death. The portraits are of people who intended to immortalize themselves, but their vanity has led to nothing, as their names are now forgotten. Similarly, the unread books accent the pretensions of writers who felt they had something to say and may even represent the futility of all knowledge as well as of all possessions.

The final stanza, with its implication of the desire but inability of the guide to let the visitor in to discover fully the ramifications of the gallery, holds some promise as the gallery supposedly "has such a peaceful view." However, even that promise appears to be thwarted, for when the visitor will be allowed into the room, it will be to be enclosed in an unlabeled wooden box and therefore to be unable to experience the view. In the tradition of ancient and modern poetry, "Guide to the Other Gallery" thus underscores the futility of this life while it points to the potential, possibly unrealizable, of the next.

Jaquelyn W. Walsh

GUNSLINGER

Author: Edward Dorn (1929-1999)
Type of poem: Poetic sequence
First published: Gunslinger I, 1968; *Gunslinger II,* 1969; *The Cycle,* 1971; *Gunslinger Book III,* 1972; collected in *Slinger,* 1975

The Poem

Gunslinger (or *Slinger,* as it is called in the 1975 Wingbow Press complete edition), owes some of its strategies to the modern long poems that preceded it. In particular, its form and perspective derive from an extraordinary new kind of epic poem, *The Maximus Poems* (1953-1975), by Charles Olson. Olson was Edward Dorn's teacher at Black Mountain College, an experimental arts school in North Carolina famous for its stellar faculty and gifted students. The college, under Olson's rectorship, gave its name to a movement in experimental verse that used ancient myth and principles from theoretical science in poetry. Olson's intense relationship with Dorn profoundly influenced Dorn's writing.

Other works that have influenced Dorn's poem include Ezra Pound's formidable epic on twentieth century culture, *The Cantos* (1919-1970), William Carlos Williams's *Paterson* (1946-1958), which celebrates the common man of New Jersey's small towns, and even Hart Crane's lyrical paean to John Augustus Roebling's engineering wonder, the Brooklyn Bridge, in *The Bridge* (1930). All these and other poems turned away from the English literary tradition to forge a new American epic literature based on the materials of modern American life and the symbols and archetypes of ancient Western literature.

Unlike its predecessors, however, Dorn's long poem is explicitly a satire on contemporary Western thinking; its humor and hyperbole distinguish it from the sonority and somber vision of Olson's *The Maximus Poems,* which ends on a note of frustrated hopes and beleaguered visions of the ideal. The American tradition of extended lyric works calls for the probing philosophical analysis of American life, the exploration of religious ideals, and the construction of a utopian republic drawn from elements of contemporary social reality. Dorn departs from these conventions by satirizing the bedrock of American social gospel—the notions of sensible reality and of individual autonomy and privilege that Americans distilled from British and continental thought. Instead of proposing his own ideological program, Dorn punctures the philosophical illusions of empirical causality, simple time and space, realism, and dichotomy, the underpinnings of awareness that Americans have inherited from the European Enlightenment.

Dorn's satirical assault on the social gospel aligns him with a much older tradition of philosophical debunking. *Slinger's* parentage includes Geoffrey Chaucer's *Canterbury Tales* (1387-1400) and Miguel de Cervantes's *Don Quixote* (1605, 1615), works in which a cast of characters set out on a journey and share long humorous tales exposing the foibles of their age. The journey itself is only a pretext for the complex dialogues that ensue among the leading characters.

Dorn's *Slinger* is thus a patchwork of influences that have been combined to form a modern version of the ancient quest narrative. The plot involves a cast of colorful twentieth century stereotypes—among them a talking horse, a talking barrel, a Western saloon keeper named Lil, a poet, an LSD-toting hippie called Kool Everything, and a character referred to simply as "I"—marginal beings who might well populate a George Lucas film, who set out by stagecoach for Las Vegas and after several days' travel stop at Cortez, Colorado, near Four Corners, the common boundary of New Mexico, Colorado, Utah, and Arizona that has long been held sacred by the Hopi Indians as marking the center of the world. Here they say farewell and go their separate ways.

Their journey begins in Mesilla, New Mexico, a small town south of Las Cruces that houses a museum devoted to the cowboy outlaw Billy the Kid. The protagonist of the poem, the Gunslinger, is a campy updated version of Billy, less an outlaw than a philosopher-maverick whose targets are all the dregs of materialism and linear thinking that have been antiquated by the intellectual revolutions of the post-World War II era. His weapon is his quick, aphoristic speech, which he directs at anything that cannot exist on its own terms. His most deadly "shot" is to *describe* a thing, to obliterate its autonomy by drawing it into a sentence, thus imprisoning it in another mind's perspective.

Gunslinger's horse, modeled after Quixote's Rocinante, enjoys its own privileged autonomy as a member of the group; the animal talks a combination of rant and wisdom and calls itself Claude, after the great French anthropologist of primitive culture, Claude Lévi-Strauss. The character "I," who comes into the discourse as the authorial or narrative voice, is "deconstructed" into a hapless minor figure who stumbles about in an LSD-induced daze for much of the poem. At one point, the poet declares, "I is dead," a double entendre referring to the character "I" and to the fate of the imperial ego in literature. These are a few of the upendings or anticonventions that Dorn establishes at the outset of the quest.

The poem opens as Gunslinger, his horse Claude, "I," and Lil set out for Las Vegas by stagecoach. They are soon joined by the poet and Kool Everything as they make their way slowly across New Mexico into southwestern Colorado, the Hopi *axis mundi* (axis of the world), where several of the characters soar off into the Hopi visionary cosmos and return just as the group is breaking up. Their pilgrimage to Las Vegas is diverted to Cortez, the county seat of Montezuma County, Colorado. These names suggest the Spanish Conquest of Mexico by Hernán Cortes, the first imperial soldier of Western expansion into the Indian New World. Montezuma was the last Aztec emperor, who mistakenly trusted the Spanish on their arrival. The Cafe Sahagun is Dorn's allusion to Fra Bernardino de Sahagún, the Spanish monk who feverishly copied down several of the Mayan codicils or parchment scrolls before the whole of Mayan literature was thrown on the fire by the conquistadors.

Thus the journey from New Mexico to Cortez, Colorado, follows a path from white settlement and an outlaw's museum to an Indian shrine shrouded in the symbols of conquest and devastation. Everyone grows in spirit as a result of the journey, though Dorn's use of hyperbole, bombast, ridicule, and comic detachment conceals the serious motives of the poem.

Forms and Devices

Long twentieth century poems are formally eclectic and attach almost any kind of structure to their segmental design. *Gunslinger* is no exception. Among its many forms are those of song, set speech, narrative episode, dialogue, anecdote, and fable. Comedy abounds in all of its tonalities: hyperbole, sarcasm, witty punning, visual wordplay, philosophical in-jokes. Verbal exuberance underscores the work throughout; the poem's comic progenitors include François Rabelais, the sixteenth century French master of broad farce and caustic exaggeration, and even Lewis Carroll and Edward Lear, the great English satirists of social philosophy at the turn of the nineteenth century. The poem is a catchall of erroneous thinking in the century, which it ruthlessly parodies throughout the poem. One is never permitted to literalize the discourse of the poem; it operates on several levels at once to both propose and then explode egocentric intellectualizing and lyric gush.

Slinger is divided into four numbered books, each taking up a segment of the group's journey as its narrative frame. Book I sets up the quest and introduces the main characters, announcing the sudden turns in the plot by imitating an old soundtrack device of cowboy films, in which an ominous guitar chord is struck. "Strum" is posted in bold, silhouetted type at various junctures of book 1. In book 4, the strum turns into a manic "thwang!" Dorn tries out other "dramatic" clichés, such as the use of italics to introduce different voices into the dialogue.

The songs that punctuate parts of the dialogue are broad parodies of Western film songs. Gunslinger's song about the girl from La Cruz proffers such pseudolyrics as "she stood and she stared like a moose/ and her hair was tangled and loose."

One must think of cowboy crooners such as Gene Autry and Roy Rogers to get the full flavor of these burlesques. When nonsense and absurdity reach a peak, Dorn slips in a quasi-serious digression on a point of vision, a sobering comment on contemporary morality, or a surprisingly beautiful snippet of lyric that pulls the reader up short.

Suspense, as in much of Olson's poetry, is rich here, and it is used playfully to distract the reader from "believing" anything in the text. Dorn knows that the reader is well-versed in the clichés and formulaic plots of cowboy stories; he works against them by mockingly following their conventions, turning them inside out when the Gunslinger or his horse Claude or Kool Everything expounds casually and knowledgeably on an obscure point of epistemology or uses an absurdly decorous eloquence in speaking of a trivial matter.

Dorn uses every pretext to spoof, deride, or simply toy with literary monism in this poem. When the Drifter is introduced in Lil's bar, the narrator slips into archaic speech and stiffly describes the guitar-strumming bard, using all the hyperbolic figures of epic poetry. Dorn's humor moves from farce and slapstick to subtle jibing at classic poetry; the reader is always conscious of the poem as a parodic tour de force as well as a brilliantly crafted yarn about the modern West.

"The Cycle," which fills the latter half of book 2, is a stylized sequence of songs delivered by the poet in numbered, unrhymed quatrains that mimic Elizabethan song "cycles." These "heroic" songs, paced out in ragged iambic pentameter, narrate the bumbling adventures of the Cheez, the song's antihero, who is the very opposite of a knight or his cowboy counterpart; instead, he is among the myriad anonymous, faceless citizens in industrial urban life. His name signifies his lowly function as part of a cheeseburger made by the local fast-food franchise.

Book 4 starts with a prolegomenon, an invocation to the muses, and moves on to the narrative proper, a journey into space rendered in computerese and regional slang. The characters stop at the Cafe Sahagun in Cortez, Colorado, the terminus of their journey, and another comic dialogue on contemporary life takes the reader to the end of the poem. The second half of book 4 contains a series of quick comic sketches featuring several new minor characters, including Portland Bill and the "talking barrel." Reality has been transformed by drugs and mind travel into a looking-glass world in which any object can suddenly spring to life and deliver a comic monologue on the absurdities of conventional life. Even these spoofs on reality have their serious purpose, however—showing the "ensouled" world of Indian mysticism against a backdrop of Western skepticism and literal reality.

Themes and Meanings

Slinger takes the cowboy film or story as its subject because it is the essence of modern Western ideology: The subject of the cowboy film is a white male hero who overcomes the forces of evil in other white men, the adversities of the environment (wolves, raging fire, storms) or the perversities of so-called primitive peoples such as American Indians and the "half-breeds" south of the border. What is said to triumph in such heroic tales is reason itself—cold, empirical logic set against wild nature. Dorn's perspective runs directly counter to each of these assumptions. His sympathies are squarely with Indian America, with wilderness, the unspoiled frontiers of the New World that the European immigrants contaminated and largely destroyed.

Dorn's purpose in this mock epic is to puncture his readers' illusory certainties and attack their cultural assumptions. The Gunslinger is modeled on the figure of Charles Olson, a kind of philosophical and ideological outlaw who is opposed to the conventional roots of modern reality. Behind Dorn's beliefs lies the century's heritage of new thinking, which is redefining nature as harmonious balance and creativity, and rediscovering in the primal societies colonialized by Western imperialism secrets to living in harmony with the earth. The new villain of modernism and postmodern writing is not the wild Indian or the savage beast of the forest, but the predatory ingenuity of Western society itself.

The cowboy story is the place to set up Dorn's mocking denials; here is the lode of images and themes by means of which Western society propagandizes audiences, preaches its gospel of progress and rationality. All of Dorn's figures derive from the typical cowboy tale but reverse their stereotypical roles. "I" ceases to be a hero and becomes a mere vessel to hold lysergic acid; he is "retired" from literature in this tale. Even the drifters get a new image; they are not menacing, but rather helpful marginal figures. The horse, Claude, is intelligent, witty, wry, and more rational than a human. Nature itself is intelligent, more balanced in its dynamic than is human thought.

The journey that begins at Mesilla, New Mexico, is intended to reach Las Vegas, the mecca of Western greed and artificiality in the desert, but it gradually turns into a pilgrimage to the Hopi shrine at Four Corners. This shift in goals is the serious point buried beneath the poem's satirical surface: It marks in the characters a turning away from the neon-lit excesses of contemporary urbanism toward the ineffable mysteries of nature encoded in Hopi religion. The characters themselves are a microcosm of fringe culture in America—the hippies, gurus, poets, and artists who have been composing alternative visions since the end of World War II. Indeed, *Slinger* belongs to the "drug culture" of the 1960's, which is now thought to have mocked and satirized rationality itself by means of "trips," descents in the mind, visions, psychedelic hazes, and similar methods.

Slinger's place in contemporary literature is with other bohemian classics of the era: with the work of the Beat writers Allen Ginsberg and Jack Kerouac; with the plays of Sam Shepard, which treat the modern West from a similarly jaundiced viewpoint; and with Thomas Pynchon's satiric novels, all of which explode the underlying psychology of destruction in Western thought and propose antidotes in the form of primitive mysticism and myth.

For a time in the early 1970's, *Slinger* enjoyed the reputation of a cult text and was passed around reverently by younger readers who shared the passionate conviction that the West was hurtling toward technological suicide. *Slinger*'s outrageous satire has faded over the years, and its views seem a bit quaint and light-hearted in an age that is reeling from environmental catastrophes and ravaging plagues. Like many good works of literature, *Slinger* was prophetic in sounding the alarm.

Paul Christensen

THE HABIT OF MOVEMENT

Author: Judith Ortiz Cofer (1952-   )
Type of poem: Lyric
First published: 1987, in *Triple Crown: Chicano, Puerto Rican, and Cuban-American Poetry*

The Poem

"The Habit of Movement" is a short poem of twenty lines divided into two stanzas. It is written in free verse, a style that does not adhere to any regular meter or rhyme scheme. The lines are irregular, some as long as thirteen syllables and others as short as six. The poem is categorized as a lyric because of its subjective, emotional, and personal qualities. Although the poet herself is the speaker of the poem, she uses the first-person plural pronoun "we" as she refers to herself as part of a family.

Judith Ortiz Cofer was born in Hormigueros, Puerto Rico, which served as the archetype for Salud, the imaginary town in her first novel, *The Line of the Sun* (1989), nominated for the Pulitzer Prize in 1990. The title of the poem "The Habit of Movement" refers to the family's practice of moving back and forth between Puerto Rico and Paterson, New Jersey, because of her father's Navy career. Jesús Ortiz Lugo was first stationed in Brooklyn Navy Yard and was then assigned to other places around the world. Because the family was forced to move so often, they never established roots in any one place. This poem reflects Ortiz Cofer's struggle to make a place for herself out of a childhood spent traveling back and forth between cultures. However, the poet moves beyond her own experience as a Puerto Rican immigrant who grew up bilingual and bicultural to voice the collective experience of the Puerto Rican community.

In the first stanza, Ortiz Cofer shows the problems that frequent movement causes the family: loss of identity, a sense of rootlessness, and an inability to feel at home in either culture. Eventually, she and her family lose the will to become part of the new community and accept the transient state that keeps them no more grounded than the library books they borrow and return "hardly handled."

In the second stanza, the meaning shifts and Ortiz Cofer uses the habit of movement as a symbol of safety. Moving from place to place keeps the poet and her family insulated and safe as they continue to relocate without becoming attached to or feeling a part of any particular place. Since they never stay in one place long enough to establish roots, they are also free of any responsibility to a community. The poem reflects Cofer's ambiguous attitude toward a life spent traveling between the United States and Puerto Rico as the family struggles to make a home in the new environment. As a writer, she seeks to create a history for herself out of the cultural ambiguity of a childhood divided between two cultures.

Forms and Devices

By using the pronoun "we" throughout the poem, Ortiz Cofer is able to show her deeply personal attitude toward the nomadic life while, at the same time, giving voice to other immigrants with similar backgrounds. The first-person plural form allows her not only to refer to herself and her own family but also to move outward to include other immigrants struggling to find identity in a foreign setting. The metaphors reinforce the sense of restlessness, of not being grounded in one country or one culture. She compares her family to "balloons set adrift" who have lost their "will to connect." When she says her family "carried the idea of home on [their] backs," she calls up images of refugees fleeing with bundles of their belongings tied to their backs. To show the depth of her feelings of isolation and dispossession, she compares "the blank stare of undraped windows" to "the eyes of the unmourned dead." As the family moves on, this habit of movement not only keeps them isolated but also keeps them safe like "a train in motion" that "nothing could touch."

Instead of a rhyme scheme or regular metrical pattern, Cofer uses other poetic devices as a way of providing a sense of unity in the poem. Here, alliteration, rather than rhyme, is the chief means of repetition. When she suggests that her family's lives are of no more importance than the books they borrow from the library, she uses alliteration to emphasize the comparison: "books borrowed" and "hardly handled." Alliteration also serves as a unifying agent in the repetition of the *c* sound in the following lines: "we lost our will to connect,/ and stopped collecting anything heavier/ to carry than a wish." Through her choice of words, Cofer shows the contrast between the tropics and the new world: The family was "nurtured" in the "lethargy" of the tropics. In the new world, with its "wide sky" and libraries as foreign as Greek temples, the family drifts until they lose the will to connect. She juxtaposes the idea of a rich, full life with her feeling of displacement in the seemingly contradictory phrase, "we grew rich in dispossession."

Themes and Meanings

"The Habit of Movement" is a poem about the difficulties involved in the painful assimilation into another culture. Ortiz Cofer shows the stages along the way as she and her family move away from one culture but are not yet absorbed into another. Ortiz Cofer says she is "a composite of two worlds." Since she speaks English with a Spanish accent and Spanish with an American accent, she feels that she has never completely belonged in either culture. She writes in English, the language of her schooling, but thinks of Spanish as her cultural and subconscious language. She is a mixture of both worlds, constantly straddling two cultures. She has spent too much time in the United States to think of leaving, but she says she becomes melancholy at times as she continues to yearn for Puerto Rico.

In "The Habit of Movement," the poet provides a mental picture of the dichotomy of the immigrant experience. Ortiz Cofer has said that "every time I write a story where Puerto Ricans live their hard lives in the United States, I am saying, look, this is what is happening to all of us. I am giving you a mental picture of it, not a sermon." In this poem, she shows the ambiguous state of immigrants who no longer feel at home in their old culture but are not part of the new one. The images that she uses to illustrate this struggle begin with a feeling of nostalgia for the homeland that nurtured her and quickly move to the feeling of being adrift in a nomadic lifestyle. By using sensuous imagery, she involves the reader in the experience, comparing her family to "red balloons set adrift/ over the wide sky of this new land." Her poetic imagery appeals to the visual sense, and the vivid, concrete details help create the tone and meaning.

To show how little each new place means to her, Ortiz Cofer uses the image of "the blank stare of undraped windows." This failure to connect with new places has an advantage in that the family members never experience a sense of loss when they leave. Again, the poet shows the ambiguity: Her family does not belong to the community, but this same sense of alienation protects them from pain when they leave. As they move, they leave behind places that hold no meaning for them. They never stay long enough in any one place to "learn the secret ways of wood and stone" or become familiar enough to call it home.

The poet's family has lost the feeling of warmth and safety that their home in Puerto Rico had provided. As they drift from one place to the next, the "lethargy" of the life in the tropics gives way to a loss of "the will to connect." Yet the nomadic life offers another type of safety: The constant movement that isolates the family from others also keeps it united. The poet is not alone in this isolation because she is part of a family as well as part of a community of immigrants who share her experience. The poem ends with the image of a train in motion as Ortiz Cofer, knowing the family will continue to move, accepts the safety their habit of movement provides.

Judith Barton Williamson

HALF-HANGED MARY

Author: Margaret Atwood (1939-   )
Type of poem: Narrative
First published: 1995, in *Morning in the Burned House*

The Poem

"Half-Hanged Mary" is a medium-length narrative poem in free verse that has ten sections, each containing one to five stanzas. In it, Atwood reconstructs the hanging of Mary Webster, a woman accused of witchcraft in Massachusetts in the 1680's. Webster was hanged but did not die; thus the title of the poem.

The poem is written in the first person: Mary tells her own story. The ten sections of the poem are titled by time. The first, "7 p.m.," tells of the hour in the evening when authorities come for Mary while she is milking the cows. Her crimes, she deduces, include living alone, owning her "weedy farm," knowing a cure for warts, and, most of all, being a woman: having "breasts/ and a sweet pear hidden in my body." Her specific examples show how well she understands her situation. The times are ripe for witch-hunts, and any woman a bit out of the ordinary is vulnerable. "Rumour," she tells her reader, was "hunting for some neck to land on."

At "8 p.m.," the time of the second section, Mary is hanged. She describes the excitement of the men who hang her; they are excited "by their show of hate" and by "their own evil." At "9 p.m.," she describes the women who watch. She understands that they cannot help her, for they, too, are vulnerable just by being women. Should they choose to help or even acknowledge her, they might be the next to be accused. At "10 p.m.," Mary addresses God. She suggests that now she and God can continue to quarrel about free will, obviously an important subject to her. She searches for some reason for her suffering, and she finds God indifferent to her plight.

At "12 midnight," Mary fights against death. It waits for her and tempts her. She knows that giving in to death means giving up the pain, but it also means "To give up my own words for myself,/ my own refusals." Staying alive is an assertion of her own personhood, of her refusal to accept the allegations and punishment of her society, and she is determined to hold out for as long as she can. The focus of her fight is against oblivion, and this fight carries her through the night. At "2 a.m.," she feebly cries out, a cry that mostly means "not yet." At "3 a.m.," her strength is ebbing, and she feels as if she is drowning. She reiterates her innocence and refuses to give in. By "6 a.m.," although she is still technically alive, she feels that she has already died once, and, in fact, she has.

At "8 a.m.," the townspeople come to cut down the corpse. However, Mary is not dead, and the law prohibits another attempt at killing her. Her tenacity is a mixed blessing, however, for the citizens are more certain of her dark powers now that she has escaped death, and, in her struggle, she has lost much of her own self: "Before, I was not a witch./ But now I am one."

The final section, titled "Later," substantiates these two lines. Now people stay out of her way. Now she can say and do anything without fear. Now she is truly an outcast, surviving on berries, flowers, dung, and mice. She has, in fact, become crazy from the same experience that has made her free. Absolutely mistreated and misunderstood, she speaks "in tongues." The townsfolk have created the witch that they wanted.

Forms and Devices

Margaret Atwood's poems are loaded with imagery, and, in "Half-Hanged Mary," the imagery often disturbs. Atwood forces the reader into what contemporary poet Adrienne Rich calls "re-vision": "seeing with fresh eyes" in order the break the hold of tradition. Her images grab and surprise the reader and insist upon the reader's reassessment of expectations. Some of the images depend primarily on visual surprise. The rope is put around Mary's neck and she is yanked skyward: "Up I go like a windfall in reverse,/ a blackened apple stuck back onto the tree." She later compares her hanging self to "a turkey's wattles." Death is "like a crow/ waiting for my squeezed beet/ of a heart to burst/ so he can eat my eyes." These similes present fresh, startling pictures that require a moment for the reader to take in.

Often, single words or simple phrases form the image. When Mary speaks of the women watching her, she uses synecdoche (the use of a part to represent the whole) to freeze the image. It is the "bonnets," "dark skirts," and "upturned faces" who come to stare. Her images often shock. An aborted baby is "flushed" from the mother. Mary looks down into "eyeholes/ and nostrils" from above. Atwood's angels do not sing, but "caw." This raw imagery pervades the poem, intruding on the reader's sensibilities like static on the radio.

The unexpected word or combination of words creates not ambiguity but clarity. By the last section of the poem, "Later," Mary's lunacy or witchness seems certifiable. She skitters and mumbles, "mouth full of juicy adjectives/ and purple berries." As she scavenges for food because her position and means of self-support are gone, she speaks without fear: "I can now say anything I can say." Yet, in reality, she is voiceless. First, nobody listens to her. Even worse, she has less ability to speak, as indicated by the second "can" in the quote above. She is now limited by her own emotional demise, and the words Atwood uses for her speech are "mumbling," "boil," and "unravels"; she speaks in tongues to the owls.

Throughout the poem, Atwood emphasizes the irony of Mary's situation, often expressing her cynicism in sarcastic renderings of common phrases. In describing herself, Mary mentions her breasts and ovaries, then says that "Whenever there's talk of demons/ these come in handy."

She understands that the women cannot come to her aid because "Birds/ of a feather burn together" and because "Lord/ knows there isn't much/ to go around." She starts a conversation with God because she has "some time to kill," but she later finds him absent from the sky. "Wrong address," she says, "I've been out there." By the end of the night, she is "At the end of [her] rope," and, when she is cut down and gives the onlookers a "filthy grin," she speaks to her reader: "You can imagine how that went over."

The tone of these expressions clearly shows Atwood's attitude toward the whole hanging affair. Seemingly light statements are steeped in sarcasm and thus hang in the air in judgment of the society that does kill the original Mary and reincarnates her as a witch and lunatic.

Themes and Meanings

Atwood revisits a witch hanging, an incident familiar in American history, and forces the readers to revise their understanding of the event by telling the story through the eyes of the accused. Atwood is a feminist who is deeply interested in women's rights and in the plight of women who are held subservient in a male-run society. Her novel *The Handmaid's Tale* (1985) portrays a futuristic society where the men in power control women as completely as Mary Webster's seventeenth century Puritan society controlled her. "Half-Hanged Mary," like much of Atwood's other work, is a political statement.

Telling her own story and expressing her own feelings, Mary challenges many assumptions about the events she narrates. One assumption is that she is, in fact, a witch. The reader sees her as bright (she understands her situation fully), responsible (she cares for herself and others in her town), and strong (she outlasts her own hanging). Her treatment is based primarily on fear. The men fear Mary, her independence, and her powers, and they also fear their own act of violence. When she refuses to die, they fear Mary even more. The women fear connection with Mary because they know that only the slightest circumstances separate them from her: In the most basic way, they are connected because they are women and, as women, they are controlled by men. When Mary looks to her God for help, she only finds indifference. Having practiced faith, charity, and hope, she expects some compassion and understanding. Just as she is shown none from the villagers, she is shown none by God.

Though the hanging does not kill her physically, it does kill her emotionally. The woman who rises from the ground after she is cut down is, in fact, a lunatic—a madwoman. The free will she has questioned God about—a free will that society did not allow her in her first life—is now hers. As long as she stays clear of the society that shuns her, she can, and must, do as she will, using her own resources. But her resources are tremendously limited now—compare the woman struggling to stay alive in earlier stanzas with the woman eating dung in the final section. Mary Webster is, in fact, not alive, as she acknowledges near the end when she asks, "Who else has been dead twice?" Without her sanity, she has been made less than human, and the punishment of her judges is final and terrible.

Janine Rider

THE HAND THAT SIGNED THE PAPER

Author: Dylan Thomas (1914-1953)
Type of poem: Ballad
First published: 1936, in *Twenty-Five Poems*

The Poem

Dylan Thomas's "The Hand That Signed the Paper" consists of four quatrains that deride the cruel impersonality and wholesale destructiveness of modern politics and warfare. It is a universal war protest poem that expresses profound contempt for political leaders as a whole. They exhibit an absence of true feeling for their fellow human beings in their self-interested and pitiless handling of international conflicts and disputes. The poem scorns these irresponsible and coolly malevolent figures who have arrogantly set themselves up as the ultimate authorities over life and death.

The first stanza catalogs how the simple signing of a document sets off a chain of disastrous and irreversible effects. They include the utter annihilation of a city, the taxing to death of a conquered people, the doubling of the worldwide death toll, the splitting up or demarcation of a country, and even the execution of a seemingly invulnerable king. The perpetrator of these calamitous measures is not some mythical monster or demon, but an ordinary human.

The second stanza mocks the "mighty hand" that is responsible for these prodigious outcomes. It leads to a shoulder like any other hand, the poet nonchalantly notes. Also, it is subject to arthritis, like anybody else's, with its joints becoming "cramped" by chalklike calcium. Furthermore, the instrument of this devastation is not some awesome weapon but, as the poet glibly remarks, a mere "goose's quill" that is used to sign a treaty. Though this document may be an armistice or peace treaty to end all the "murder," the poet cannot help but resentfully remember that the potentially productive negotiations that preceded the armed conflict were broken off in favor of widespread acts of violence.

In the third quatrain, the poet stresses that a peace treaty has not really solved anything at all. Indeed, rather than resolving the suffering brought about by war, it has actually caused more havoc, for the hard terms of the compact have created the conditions for hunger, disease, and pestilence in the capitulating nation. All this biblical-scale desolation leads the poet to ridicule the power and dominion of the "almighty" hand that scrawled a name across a page.

The concluding stanza compassionately foregrounds the terrible miseries of the war casualties, while bitterly observing that these five arrogant "kings," who tally the deaths, are powerless or unwilling to console the wounded or heal their injuries. The poet, horrified by this high-handed, pitiless treatment of fellow creatures, reminds the reader that these inhumane, faceless politicians set themselves up as gods, maintaining absolute control over who is to be pitied and who is destroyed. Hands, the poet tragically comments in the final line, cannot cry for others.

Forms and Devices

"The Hand That Signed the Paper" is in the form of a ballad, but a nonlyrical Augustan ballad containing four quatrains with alternately rhyming lines. The first and third lines of each stanza are in fairly regular iambic pentameter, but with an eleventh, unstressed syllable. The use of so-called feminine rhyme (rhyming words that end with an unstressed syllable) is a key stylistic feature of the poem. Insofar as the rhythm seems to trail off rather than end strongly because of them, the feminine rhyme endings give the poem a passive quality not unrelated to the theme of official apathy to humanity's sufferings.

Also of metrical interest is the fact that Thomas adheres rather strictly to an unusual accentual syllabic pattern for a ballad: Except for the opening stanza, in which the syllable count is eleven in the first and third lines and eight in the second and fourth lines, the poem maintains a pattern of syllables in which the first and third lines have eleven, the second has eight, and the fourth has six. Thus, the fourth lines of the second through fourth quatrains are trimetrical, in contrast to the tetrameter second lines. This shortening of the fourth lines in these three stanzas creates a truncated effect. Once again, the meter reflects the content of the poem in that these shorter-than-expected lines seem to suffer from a lack of fullness and completeness; the reader, so to speak, hears a silence, colored by the poet's disillusionment, instead of a fourth metrical foot.

Thomas's key image, the disembodied hand—whether it is signing a declaration of war or a peace treaty—is a synecdoche for an indifferent, ruthless government: The part (the hand that signs the document) is taken to represent the whole (the brutal government perpetrating outrages on humankind). Although this classical rhetorical figure is a central device in Thomas's poem, "The Hand That Signed the Paper" is modern and complex. It is the product not only of Thomas's social consciousness as a concerned citizen between the wars but also of his intensely symbolic and personal vision of the world. The fingers of the offending hand, for example, assume a sinister, dreamlike character; twice they are metaphorically referred to as "five kings," as if they have an independent conspiratorial reality above and beyond the existence of any individual ruler. They are like some diabolical finger puppets meting out arbitrary punishments. As a whole, the imagery in the poem is apocalyptic, combining biblical, medieval, and modern overtones. A "felled" city, a severed country, a globe piled up with the dead, a landscape devastated by locusts and crop failure, all give the poem a nightmarishly familiar quality.

Thomas is famous for his rich, resonant poetic sound. Although this poem is predominantly somber in tone, he effectively exploits the specific expressive value of words to dramatize his disregard for bureaucratic political authority. Dynamic verbs drive the opening stanza: "felled," "taxed," "doubled," and "halved." The latter, mirrorlike verb pair suggests cold, deadly mathematics. The counting of the dead can, in fact, be said to frame the poem, in the sense that it recurs in the last stanza. Furthermore, the *d*'s of "doubled," "dead," " halved," and "did . . . to death" in the first stanza expressively convey the idea of death and destruction. Also of interest is the sheer contempt Thomas expresses by way of the harsh sounding "scribbled name," a belittling reference to the lifeless signature that holds dominion over human beings.

The contiguity of "paper" and "felled" in line 1 also introduces an ironic undercurrent in the poem in that the signed paper—which is the product of a destructive act, namely the felling and processing of a tree—becomes, with a kind of bizarre circular logic, an accessory in further destruction. Similarly ironic is the cramping of finger joints with chalk in stanza 2. Chalk, a medium for communicating signs and symbols, ironically builds up as calcium in the signer's joints, making writing a painful and counterproductive act. The monosyllabic almost matter-of-fact ending line is anything but a rant against authority; rather, it is an almost anticlimactic paradox producing genuine pathos: "Hands have no tears to flow."

Themes and Meanings

"The Hand That Signed the Paper" was written during an amazingly fertile creative period when Thomas was only nineteen. It is one of his relatively few political poems and was dedicated in the August, 1933, notebook in which it was originally written to a Labour Party friend in Thomas's home city, Swansea. For a time Thomas moved in local Welsh socialist circles, but he rejected socialism in favor of individualism. He was suspicious of all ideologies and sought instead to understand the world in terms of a personal mythology that highlighted the dynamic unity of all life. He and W. H. Auden represent two poles of mid-twentieth century poetry in English: Thomas stands for the personal and the visionary, while Auden is identified with political realism.

Thomas inspired the New Apocalypse, a group of poets in the 1940's who revolted against cerebral "classical" verse (which they associated with Auden), and who admired Thomas's romantic, life-affirming poetry. "The Hand That Signed the Paper" lacks the "green" faith in country goodness of his later "country heaven" poems, such as "Author's Prologue" and "In Country Sleep." Its theme is purely apocalyptic without any promise of personal or collective redemption. The supercilious arrogance of leaders who endorse mass destruction is the subject of the poem. Thomas grew up between the world wars and was acutely aware of the havoc caused by modern mechanized armed conflicts. The poem is absolutely cynical about nationalistic power but is not misanthropic.

The last stanza evokes the pity of war in the spirit of hard-won humanism of one of his favorite poets, the war poet Wilfred Owen. Regarding God's role in all this, Thomas declares that "A hand rules pity as a hand rules heaven." The word "rules" would seem to have negative connotations, with God being alluded to as a projection of the rulers who sanction war on earth, but the meaning, like much in Thomas's poetry, is ambiguous.

James J. Balakier

HANGING FIRE

Author: Audre Lorde (1934-1992)
Type of poem: Narrative
First published: 1978, in *The Black Unicorn*

The Poem

Audre Lorde's "Hanging Fire" is a poem of thirty-five lines of free verse. The poem is divided into three stanzas with lines ranging in length from two to seven syllables. The persona, a fourteen-year-old female, uses terse, declarative sentences, speaking directly to her audience, making readers aware of her anxieties, her isolation, and her loneliness. She explains that she is in love with an immature boy who still sucks his thumb in private, that she is worried about her ashy knees and a skin that has "betrayed her," and that she is occupied with death and dying, for she says, "what if I die before morning." While all of these issues worry the teenager, what affects her most is the fact that her mother is unapproachable: "and mamma is in the bedroom/ with the door closed."

In the second stanza the teenager continues her direct address, making readers aware of her social inadequacies and allowing them to see her inner self. She indicates that she needs to improve her social skills by affirming that she has to learn how to dance, yet she states that there is nothing that she really wants to do. However, she admits that there is "too much/ that has to be done." The ambiguous messages that are sent in these lines of needing to learn how to dance, of not really wanting to do anything, and of having too many things that need to be done indicate that the young girl lacks direction and that she truly needs the guidance of an adult, especially her mother, to help her formulate strategies that will see her through these confusing times of her life. She ends the stanza as she does the first one, bewailing the fact that she has no access to her mother, who has gone into her bedroom and has locked her daughter out.

In the third stanza the persona indicts the school system for its sexist attitudes. "I should have been on the Math Team/ my grades were higher than his," she protests, but she is summarily dismissed as a candidate because of her sex. What seems to pain this black girl more than the dismissal is the fact that no one considers the injustice that she suffers, and no one in the school system comes to her defense or champions her cause, for she admits: "nobody even stops to think/ about my side of it." The young girl's preoccupation with death is revisited. This time she wonders: "will I live long enough/ to grow up." She ends the poem by indicating that while she attempts to deal with these issues alone, her mother is still ensconced in her bedroom with the door closed.

Forms and Devices

In several discussions Lorde explained that the poem comprising the text from which "Hanging Fire" comes, *The Black Unicorn*, was never anthologized during her lifetime because she saw the entire text as one entity. Although the poem under discussion is a unified whole, it should be remembered that the author intended it to be read as a part of a whole. (Works from *The Black Unicorn* have been anthologized since Lorde's death.)

"Hanging Fire" is complete in and of itself; there is a marriage between form and content in this work. The titular statement suggests that the teenager's world is aflame and is about to explode and burn, and her short, terse sentences pop from her mouth like bullets aimed at the reader, while the repetitive statement at the end of each stanza suggests that the one person who could and perhaps should be her advocate, the mother, is "in the bedroom/ with the door closed."

Additionally, Lorde has the ability to use structure as a means of creating tension and ambiguity, resulting in several layers of meaning in the poem. For example, the first two lines of the poem state, "I am fourteen/ and my skin has betrayed me." The teenager then goes on to tell the audience about the immature boy "she cannot live without" and the ashiness of her knees. If the word "skin" is understood both figuratively and literally, it is possible that the teenager could be referring to her sexual desires as well as to her being a female in a world dominated by males.

There is also ambiguity in the third stanza, in which the persona is discussing her not getting on the "Math Team." The stanza begins with a simple declarative sentence: "Nobody even stops to think/ about my side of it." The young girl explains her not being a part of the team even though her grades were higher than those of the boy who was selected. Coming at the beginning of the third stanza and prefacing the statement about not getting on the team, the statement that no one thinks about her in this matter might very well refer back to the mother at the end of the second stanza, who has withdrawn to her room, as well as to the school officials, for not being concerned about the choice they have made.

In "Hanging Fire" Lorde also has a penchant for using very little end punctuation, allowing her sentences to flow into one another. This technique is suggestive of the teenager's anxiety and her need to express herself hurriedly. This method also allows the poet to fuse ideas. In the third stanza, for example, the teenager says: "why do I have to be the one/ wearing braces/ I have nothing to wear tomorrow." The lack of punctuation fuses the ideas of wearing braces, which the fourteen-year-old does not want to do, and the wearing of clothes, which she would like to do. It is evident from the poet's use of language and the structure of the poem that language and form function as a unified whole.

Themes and Meanings

In "Hanging Fire" Lorde's focus is on several issues that confront the teenager within the poem and affect teenagers in the extended world: the preoccupation with death, the problem of living in a sexist society, and the fear of isolation within the home. Throughout the entire poem the teenager is preoccupied with death and dying. In the first stanza she frets, "what if I die/ before morning." In the second stanza she worries, "suppose I die before graduation." In the final stanza she is troubled: "will I live long enough/ to grow up." Lorde makes the reader aware of the fact that, like the persona within the poem, some teenagers are preoccupied with thoughts of death.

As a black feminist Lorde believed that she must combat sexism at all levels and at all times, and she does so in this poem. The fact that the young girl in the poem has not become a part of the "Math Team" despite the fact that her grades were higher than those of the male who was selected, is an indictment of the sexist attitudes of society in general and the school system in particular. Society teaches that an individual, male or female, should be evaluated on his or her merit. Yet the reality is that sexism exists. Lorde suggests that while such behavior is painful for adults, it is extremely traumatic to the young. What seems to be worse than the sexist treatment, however, is the fact that no one deplores the act or is concerned about the effects it might have on the girl. The sexist behavior is condoned as though the boy should be preferred simply because he is male, while the girl is summarily dismissed because she is female. Lorde's philosophy is that all people should protest against such sexist attitudes, but she believes that mothers need to protect their children from such sexism.

Finally, there is the problem of isolation and loneliness. The speaker indicates that her social skills are inadequate, for she clearly states that she needs to learn how to dance "in time for the next party." She indicates also that she is not sure of her grooming techniques because her knees are always ashy, and her major social contact seems to be the immature, thumb-sucking boy.

Despite these external inadequacies and isolation, what seems to cause the teenager the greatest anxiety is the isolation that occurs within her home. While the teenager battles the fears of dying, the problems of a love affair, and the pain of discrimination, she realizes that the one person on whom she should rely, the one who should nurture, defend, and protect her, her mother, is "in the bedroom/ with the door closed." The closed door is a symbol of total isolation and loneliness for the teenager.

Ralph Reckley, Sr.

HAP

Author: Thomas Hardy (1840-1928)
Type of poem: Sonnet
First published: 1898, in *Wessex Poems and Other Verses*

The Poem

Thomas Hardy has structured "Hap" to meet all the requirements of the form of an English sonnet: Its fourteen lines are written in iambic pentameter, the rhyme scheme *abab, cdcd, efef, gg* is complied with, and the three quatrains are followed by a rhymed couplet to conclude the poem.

The title suggests all the readily identifiable characteristics connoted by the word "hap" (used as a noun until early in the twentieth century). The word itself has nearly disappeared in modern English except as a clipped form of the verb "happen" (as in "It then came to us to hap upon the drunken sailor"). At the time the poem was written, however, the word still functioned commonly as a noun meaning chance, luck, fortune, or coincidence.

Hardy's use of the first person leaves no doubt about the poem's existence as a personal expression of the author's own attitudes about and experiences with life, here a certain resigned bitterness attributed to chance or bad luck. The poet is posing hard questions about life (particularly humankind's relationship to a possibly existing god).

The poem has an "if-then-but" structure which exactingly adheres to its division into quatrains. Hardy asks an indirect question in the first stanza, gives a "then" answer in the second one; and follows it with a dismissal in the third. The couplet at the end serves to answer the question embedded in the beginning of the poem.

The opening line of the poem is an expressed desire for "some vengeful god" to communicate to him and laugh, at least, at the poet's condition and suffering. The stanza reveals that Hardy would take satisfaction—though assuredly not joy or delight—in knowing that some omnipotent cosmic force was pleasuring itself in his own pain. This expression actually questions whether such a god exists.

In the middle stanza, Hardy indicates that he would accept such cosmic causes of his suffering by embracing death. He wishes to take some intellectual comfort, at least, in knowing that his pain has been willed by entities in the universe stronger than himself and over which he has absolutely no control.

The final quatrain begins with a loud "But not so." Hardy concludes that the gods are not willfully subjecting him to pain and suffering in order to pleasure themselves. His anguish is not manifested in plan or design or thought. Rather, it can be explained only in terms of "Crass Casualty"—a phrase he uses to mean "chance," or, more nearly correctly, "bad luck." The couplet at the end serves to reemphasize this point: "purblind Doomsters" have indifferently, probably unknowingly, given his life "pain" rather than "blisses."

Forms and Devices

The sonnet is basically constructed around a simplistic metaphor: Life is a pilgrimage through which Hardy journeys, experiencing pain and suffering only. While making this journey, the poet is aware of the existence of God, but he is seemingly unable to determine whether he is a "vengeful" one. Hardy refers directly to God four times, citing him first as "Powerfuller than I," a means of recognizing his own hopelessness and helplessness in the face of whatever God has in store for him. He later refers to God as "Crass Casualty," by which, again, he means "chance" or "bad luck." The reference to "Time" is to mention yet another universal force against which he is sheerly helpless. Finally, Hardy shifts to the plural when he writes of "purblind Doomsters" who will manipulate and control his own life yet who are totally devoid of any care or concern for him. Not only are they more powerful than he, but they also outnumber him.

This metaphor is couched in the form of the English sonnet. The content of the sonnet, both structurally and thematically, adheres to the pattern of the form; specifically, the theme and exposition follow requirements of form. The first stanza introduces the subject and the question, essentially, "Life is a pilgrimage of pain—why so?" The answer is that such suffering is not intentionally willed by a "vengeful god." The second stanza elaborates this idea by repetition and denial. One "Powerfuller than I" has not with thought and deliberation "meted" out his tears. In the third stanza, this perception of and explanation for human suffering is finally made explicit: The poet's "joy lies slain," and his hope is gone, the reader is told, after learning "But not so." That is, the denial that the gods are willing this suffering by plan or with reason is made irrevocably clear. Finally, the couplet spells out emphatically that the poet's suffering can only rightly be explained as indifference and blindness on the parts of the gods themselves, now called "Doomsters."

Other than this basic metaphor, which finds a parallel in the sonnet form, the poem is rather straightforward. "Crass Casualty" obstructing both sun and rain suggests that the gods would block out all, good and evil alike, in human nature and environs; "dicing Time" casting a moan functions similarly. A few examples of alliteration appear ("love's loss" and "meted me"), but with no overall discernible purpose.

Themes and Meanings

Hardy's impetus in writing the poem, surely, was to explore and explain the reasons for his own suffering. The poet asks this question explicitly at the beginning of the third stanza: "How arrives it joy lies slain . . .?" The problem is not merely that joy is slain but also that pain is plentiful on his pilgrimage of life. Hardy takes up the question of God's existence, or, more to the point, the nature of the relationship between God and humanity.

He variously describes himself, either directly or indirectly, as a "suffering thing"; as one whose "sorrow" gives the gods "ecstasy"; as bearing "it" (life, and suffering in life), clenching, and dying; as shedding tears; as possessing "slain" joy and "unbloomed" hope. At the same time, he sees himself encapsulated by omnipotent cosmic forces described as "some vengeful god," "Powerfuller than I," "Crass Casualty," "dicing Time," and "purblind Doomsters."

Hardy denies that humans are as flies to wanton boys. He sees his condition as worse: The gods are deriving no pleasure from the pain of humans. If the gods were inflicting, or even permitting, human suffering with some purpose or purposes of their own (even self-indulgence or sadism), then the poet says that he could "bear it, clench [himself], and die." He can find, however, no evidence that this is the case; the universe is malign through chance and indifference—through "hap"—not through any purpose, even an evil one.

One quality of Hardy's poems, also immediately recognizable in his novels, is that they often evidence fatalism. In the classical sense of the word, "fate" would be either good or evil; the gods gave some people one of these, while others received the opposite allotment. Individuals did not always, or even usually, understand how or why, but purpose and design eventually became evident. Hardy's universe, however, is one in which the gods are merely half-blind "Doomsters," inflicting pain and suffering through indifference and total neglect. Human pilgrimages are entirely haphazard.

Fate, then, reigns supreme in Hardy's perception of the universe and in humanity's recognition and acceptance of the lots not assigned but received anyway. The gods seek neither vengeance nor ecstasy. They slay joy indiscriminately and undoubtedly provide pleasure, fulfillment, and meaning to others in the same way. Chance is "Crass," and Time, arguably the most indifferent of all cosmic dimensions, is seen simply as determined by a toss of the die.

The amounts and degrees of human suffering are determined by matters over which individuals have no control or even perspective. Beyond this, humans not only cannot control their own destinies—their cast of the die—but they also cannot even comprehend their destinies. Hardy is left with a total inability to change or to effect changes in his condition, his pain and suffering. He is only partially able to understand it. Finally, he is left with only a fatalistic bitterness. He is evidently not envious of those whose lot is different from his own. He can neither control nor understand his suffering; he can only accept it in order to live with the terms that the "purblind Doomsters" have unwittingly provided him.

Carl Singleton

HAPPINESS

Author: Jane Kenyon (1947-1995)
Type of poem: Meditation
First published: 1995; collected in *Otherwise: New and Selected Poems*, 1996

The Poem

"Happiness" is a short poem in free verse. Its thirty-one lines are arranged in five symmetrical stanzas containing four, eight, seven, eight, and four lines respectively. The last is a quasi stanza, emanating from a dropped line in the previous stanza. Dramatic intensity builds and then subsides; the central stanza is the keystone, carrying the poem's rhythmic and thematic weight. The lines of the first and last stanzas are similar in length and meter, with three or four stresses per line. The three middle stanzas are more irregular, containing lines with five stresses and ending on shortened lines. The final words of the middle stanzas—"alone," "despair," and "night"— precede an emptiness both visual and aural.

The poem is meditative. The "you" of the poem addresses both the general audience and the individual reader. As the poem progresses, it becomes increasingly evident that the "you" also includes the speaker and that the poem is born of the speaker's suffering. The first two stanzas introduce the two driving forces of the poem: parable and paradox. The parable of the prodigal son, as related in the New Testament, tells of a young man who squanders his inheritance in another country. Contrite and destitute, he returns to his father, seeking forgiveness and shelter. The father not only forgives the son but also honors him with finery and a feast. The parable of the prodigal son is presented in the poem virtually intact, dense with words that evoke the Scripture from which it comes—"dust," "forgive," "feast," "garment." The parable becomes a metaphor for the unpredictable extravagance of happiness. However, the return of happiness causes the speaker to "weep night and day"—and therein lies a paradox. The poem, unlike the parable, is spoken from the perspective of the one abandoned, and the effusive generosity of the welcome is unmistakably linked to the pain of the abandonment.

The central stanza introduces another metaphor for happiness, "the uncle you never knew about," who singlemindedly and with great effort seeks out a soul in extremis. In a curious twist, the act of finding suddenly becomes reciprocal. In the first stanza, it is happiness that is lost and then found; in the third stanza, it is the speaker. The prodigal who was found and feasted becomes the uncle who "finds you asleep mid-afternoon/ as you so often are during the unmerciful/ hours of your despair."

The entire fourth stanza is a litany of others who are found by happiness, representing all ages, genders, and classes. Moral judgment is suspended; in a nod to the first line of the poem, "no accounting" is necessary. Happiness, like the proverbial rain, falls upon the just and unjust: a monk, a lover, and a laborer; a man, a woman, and a child; a drunk and a pusher—even a dog. The final stanza is both a visual and a thematic extension of the one before it. The blessed litany continues but now includes inanimate objects: rocks, rain, and a wineglass. At the poem's end, careful layering of images and skillful matching of form to meaning have imbued these things with life and significance.

Forms and Devices

All of the poem's structural elements—rhythm and meter, grammar and syntax, sound and image—serve and preserve its larger themes by a fine manipulation of contrasts and ambiguities. The dactylic waltz rhythm initiated by the title continues throughout, interspersed with hard-hitting iambs that ground the poem and echo a heartbeat heard in solitude. The silences speak as well: The foreshortened last lines of the three middle stanzas and the spaces that follow them are the formal equivalent of existential isolation.

The poem rides on marvelous extended sentences, the clauses rolling after each other like waves toward a shore. The first, third, and fifth stanzas are each one long sentence. The intervening stanzas, ever graceful, also contain jetties that break up the waves. The speaker's question, "How can you not forgive?" and the litany of the forgiven stand out sharply against the flowing tide around them. An uneasy ambiguity surfaces on this syntactical sea in the form of negatives imbedded in phrases that first appear positive: "There's just no accounting for happiness" hints at indiscriminateness; "And how can you not forgive?" begs the question; "an occasion/ you could not imagine" and "you weep . . ./ to know that you were not abandoned" point to a terrible siege of despair. All these statements are found in the first two stanzas. At the extremity of hopelessness, revealed by the juxtaposition of the words "No, happiness" in the pivotal third stanza, help arrives. Contrasting images abound: happiness and weeping, fortune and dust, night and day, losing and finding, solitude and union. Even the prosaic grocery clerk who works the midnight shift is a foil for the prodigal who squanders a fortune.

Perhaps the poem's best example of structure serving meaning is demonstrated by the recurring images of solitude. Over and over, happiness is given and received in solitude. The uncle comes alone and flies a single-engine plane. Each recipient—from the monk to the wineglass—is named in the singular and, at first glance, so too is the "you" of the poem: "happiness saved its most extreme form/ for you alone." However, the ambiguity of the pronoun "you"—its function as either singular or plural—intimates a movement away from isolation and toward a fragile commonality.

Themes and Meanings

From first line to last, "Happiness" is disturbing. The metaphor of the prodigal son is immediately unsettling. The biblical prodigal is a rather callow and wayward young man who was driven back to the comforts of home by hunger and hard labor. This is not a very flattering picture of happiness. The speaker's response—"And how can you not forgive?"—is also problematic. The question simultaneously suggests two possible responses—forgiving without question and choosing not to forgive. Yet the speaker, like the father in the parable, is also a prodigal, lavishing a welcome on wayward happiness: "You make a feast in honor of what/ was lost, and take from its place the finest/ garment."

The metaphor of the uncle contains an ominous undercurrent as well. On the one hand, this intrepid relative echoes the good shepherd of the New Testament, who braves the wilderness in order to find one lost lamb. On the other hand, the questions lurk: Where has he been until now? What does he want? Why would he go to all this trouble? Is he looking for a share of the inheritance as the speaker dies of despair? Happiness's "most extreme form" may, after all, be death, release from a body that is weary of life, "the wineglass, weary of holding wine." The poet Galway Kinnell employs a similar image in "The Striped Snake and the Goldfinch" (*Imperfect Thirst*, 1994): Wine fills "the upper bell of the glass/ that will hold the last hour we have to live." Although Kenyon wrote "Happiness" before she knew of the leukemia that killed her at the age of forty-eight, she fought depression all her life—a battle that shadows and deepens her poetry.

In "Happiness," Kenyon exquisitely describes the human condition. Happiness is neither deserved nor permanent. It is given indiscriminately, not possessed deliberately. At the beginning and the end of happiness there is loss—the loss that recognizes its appearance and the loss that follows its departure. However, those somber brackets lend it meaning and value. "Happiness" also touches delicately upon last things. Co-existing with the "perpetual shade" of death is the mystery that even inanimate entities—a boulder, rain, a wineglass, a despairing soul "asleep mid-afternoon"—can receive the unexpected blessing that renews life and suggests the possibility of an afterlife.

Kinnell's lovely poem "How Could You Not" (1995), written in Kenyon's memory, draws on the devices and themes of "Happiness" and ends thus: "How could you not rise and go, with all that light/ at the window . . . and the sound,/ coming or going, hard to say, of a single-engine/ plane in the distance that no one else hears?" "Happiness" is a rare look into the poetic imagination that sees what others do not, that breathes life into words and significance into life. The "feast in honor of what was lost" and the "finest garment" that honors the return of happiness are also "happiness" itself. The prodigal has become a poem. That is its ultimate paradox and its ultimate gift.

Louise Grieco

HARD ROCK RETURNS TO PRISON FROM THE HOSPITAL FOR THE CRIMINAL INSANE

Author: Etheridge Knight (1931-1991)
Type of poem: Ballad
First published: 1968, in *Poems from Prison*

The Poem

The first stanza of Etheridge Knight's "Hard Rock Returns to Prison from the Hospital for the Criminal Insane" begins the account of the long-term prisoner Hard Rock, who had a reputation for being impossible to bully, for which he suffered great abuse and physical injury, including split lips, cauliflower ears, and a long scar from his temple up through the hair on the top of his head. He has purple lips, yellow eyes, and curly hair.

Stanza 2 tells the story—"the WORD"—going around the prison that since his return Hard Rock is not an unruly person ("mean nigger") anymore, because the doctors performed brain surgery on him and gave him shock treatment. Hard Rock is brought back to the prison handcuffed and chained. The other prisoners watch him, uncuffed and the chains removed, as if he were a stallion that was just castrated. Like Native Americans ("indians") at an area where livestock are fenced in, they wait to see if it is true that Hard Rock is no longer unruly.

The third stanza recalls how they wait in anxiety to see how Hard Rock will act, and they take comfort in memories of his heroically rebellious deeds: To punish him for the last of these "exploits" committed by him before the reprisal surgery on his brain, it took eight prison guards, or "screws," to put Hard Rock into solitary confinement ("the Hole"). Moreover, it is a thrill to remember again when he hit the captain of the prison guards with his dinner tray. For that spectacularly daring act he was punished with a record amount of time in solitary confinement: sixty-seven days. Also, they remember the "jewel of a myth" that Hard Rock once "bit" a prison guard on the thumb and poisoned him with "syphilitic spit."

In stanza 4 various people of the prison population accost Hard Rock to see if he is really no longer unruly. A "hillbilly" calls him a "black son of a bitch," and Hard Rock does not knock his teeth out; a prison guard who knows how dangerous Hard Rock had been before the brain surgery "[shakes] him down" and yells at him roughly. Hard Rock does not respond at all; he "just grin[s]" and looks stupid. His eyes are "empty like knot holes in a fence."

The inmates lie to themselves that Hard Rock is faking his mental diminishment, even after they notice that it takes him three minutes to say his own first name. Finally, they cannot fool themselves, and they stop looking at the brain-damaged Hard Rock, instead, "crushed," looking at the ground. He had been to them a mythic personality—their "Destroyer"—a singular being who did things they fantasized of doing but were stopped by their fear, "a biting whip" that extinguishes their self-esteem and their will to act in their own defense.

Forms and Devices

From the poem's synoptic twelve-word title the audience knows much that has happened before the first line of the poem is read. It is a mythic ballad. Knight himself spent time in prison: The voice of the poem is an authentic first-person plural "we" that allows the poet to endow the prisoners with an identity they are usually denied. This tactic uses direct dialogue from the inmates to recount the deeds of Hard Rock. Thus, the diction of the poem combines literal exposition with the homely patois of the rebellious and the outlawed. In addition, the poem is emphatically oral. A silent reading of the text of a Knight poem cannot render it. His poetry is unusually preliterate and elemental.

The poetics of "Hard Rock Returns to Prison from the Hospital for the Criminal Insane" are a sledgehammer of explicitness and repetition. Of the 341 words of the poem, 286 words are monosyllabic. This monosyllabic diction creates the formal yet mythically emotional declamation of Hard Rock's story, in which Hard Rock's name is repeated ten times; this marginalizes the otherwise remarkable triple repetition of "screws," the prison guards. The effect is that Hard Rock's career is narrated as a litany—a eulogy and a prayer—that almost liturgically repeats the martyred Hard Rock's name. Monosyllabicity deemphasizes feeling and anchors rationality. Thus, the poet is not so overwhelmed by feeling that the poem is denied a precise diction and recitation. This struggle of feeling with reason is always present in Knight's readings: Feeling always wins out.

"Hard Rock Returns to Prison from the Hospital for the Criminal Insane" also proceeds as a discourse of free verse, of five stanzas grouped in syllables of 6-8-8-6 and nine lines of ten to fourteen syllables. The first four look like sonnet stanzas stretched over a slightly larger poetic frame as Knight uses a Petrarchan stateliness for a homely subject—the story of somebody nicknamed "Hard Rock" in prison. Exceptions are an initial metrically skewed couplet ("shit" and "it") in the opening lines and a fourteen-syllable balanced couplet in lines 21 and 22 ("bit" and "spit"), which wire the poem with a blitz of "electricity" in an onomatopoeia that binds with rhyme the institutional violence and impersonally high-tech instruments used in the mental "gelding" of Hard Rock.

The principal image of the poem, Hard Rock, is an ambiguous sobriquet. One of the image's meanings is the archetypal prison experience as old as the fates of the underclasses in ancient Egypt and Rome. "Hard Rock Returns to Prison from the Hospital for the Criminal Insane" also addresses heroic endurance, the first intoning, moreover, of four terrible invocations in the poem: "Hard Rock," "WORD," "Hole," and "Destroyer," one of Knight's few concessions to textual effects.

Simultaneously, an essential counterpoint throughout the poem is the deliberate use of ironic comic detail that constructs a defiance and an anesthetic to the agony and grief in the poem: "A hillbilly called him a black son of a bitch/ And didn't lose his teeth." This humor is Knight's testimony to how bravely people deal with an intractably helpless "status" and persist in hoping anyway. The humor Knight extracted from the print text of his poetry, when delivered in his intimately compassionate baritone voice, always summoned laughter from his audience. It would usually be followed by the momentary silence of audience respect when in a final stanza the message of the poem's resolution was reached.

Themes and Meanings

Perhaps no American poet has written more authentically and compassionately of the inmates of United States prisons than Knight. His premise is that American society produces particular behaviors in the members of its virtually enslaved underclass that criminalize them. This then rationalizes society keeping them in penal compounds. This underclass in the twentieth century was radically overrepresented in prisons by male African Americans. The most resistant inmates are often dehumanized by social and technological behavior modification projects.

One reading of the poem can invoke the "black Prometheus" imagined by W. E. B. Du Bois. Hard Rock and the prisoners are Promethean avatars. "Hard Rock Returns to Prison from the Hospital for the Criminal Insane" invokes the Promethean crime of stealing power—however briefly—the Promethean setting of imprisonment with stone and chains, and the Promethean punishment of repetitive mutilation.

"Hard Rock Returns to Prison from the Hospital for the Criminal Insane" recalls one of just three characters Knight explicitly named in his *Poems from Prison*, in addition to "Ol' Rufus" and "Freckle-Faced Gerald"—both of whom were remarkable for their gentle vulnerability. The African American male prisoner Hard Rock is the persona of the genius of rebellion. He deserves the fear that the current rulers of the establishment accorded him. Above all, he has the reverence of the inmates. He is loved because his resolve is not defeatable by natural forces. Moreover, because his punishment is permanent, the beacon of his example is timeless. He is a "Destroyer" of docile submission to the depraved ingenuities of the penal curriculum. As a "doer" he authors acts of defiance of the malignant culture and legal code of American prisons and the psychopathological punishments his heroic infractions bring down upon him.

To be insane, mad, and wild is to be heroic in a sense that names white, Middle American culture an abomination and privileges the fabulous "status"of divine defiant madness. As a reenactment of the old crime against race and human morality, the poem provides an exorcism of the historic and modern slavery—"The fears of years, like a biting whip,/ Had cut grooves too deeply across our backs"—of African Americans. It is also an insinuation that the "dream of doing," at least, endures. In doing so it nourishes the irrepressible longing for freedom, which is the subject of the poem.

John R. Pfeiffer

HARLEM

Author: Langston Hughes (1902-1967)
Type of poem: Lyric
First published: 1951, in *Montage of a Dream Deferred*

The Poem

"Harlem" is a short, reflective poem, somber in tone, with an ominous, pointedly italicized ending. It appeared originally as the first poem in the last sequence of poems ("Lenox Avenue Mural") in the book *Montage of a Dream Deferred*. Sometimes *Montage of a Dream Deferred* has been reprinted in its entirety (as in Hughes's *Selected Poems*); sometimes "Lenox Avenue Mural" has been reprinted separately; often "Harlem" has been reprinted alone.

The poem can stand alone. Although it is part of a suite of six poems ("Lenox Avenue Mural") and of a book of ninety-one poems (reduced to eighty-seven in *Selected Poems*), it is self-contained and autonomous. It consists of seven short sentences, the last six of which respond to the opening question, "What happens to a dream deferred?" Of the six responses, all but one are themselves framed as rhetorical questions. The whole of *Montage of a Dream Deferred* is set in Harlem, yet only two of its ninety-one poems mention Harlem in their titles ("Harlem" and "Night Funeral in Harlem"). Simply being titled "Harlem" gives this particular lyric a special recognition in the sequence.

The "dream deferred" is the long-postponed and, therefore, frustrated dream of African Americans: a dream of freedom, equality, dignity, opportunity, and success. This particular poem does not define or give examples of the dream (many other poems in *Montage of a Dream Deferred* do this); it concentrates, instead, on possible reactions to the deferral of a dream, ranging from the fairly mild-mannered ("Does it dry up/ like a raisin in the sun?") to the threatening (*"Or does it explode?"*). The first five potential responses to frustration are essentially passive, the last one active.

Langston Hughes first made his home in Manhattan's Harlem in 1922. He was a leading figure in the Harlem Renaissance, the 1920's flowering of African American literature and art. Although he traveled widely and often, he kept circling back to Harlem. He lived there, on a more-or-less permanent basis, from the early 1940's on, maintaining a home on West 127th Street for the last twenty years of his life. *Montage of a Dream Deferred* is a product of the late 1940's, when Hughes had at last settled in Harlem.

The variety of responses that "Harlem" suggests as reactions to the deferring of a dream may be taken as a sort of cross-section of behavior patterns Hughes saw around him among the citizens of Harlem. The poem reflects the post-World War II mood of many African Americans. The Great Depression was over, the war was over, but for African Americans the dream, whatever particular form it took, was still being deferred. As Arthur P. Davis wrote in a 1952 article in *Phylon*, "with Langston Hughes

Harlem is both place and symbol. When he depicts the hopes, the aspirations, the frustrations, and the deep-seated discontent of the New York ghetto, he is expressing the feelings of Negroes in black ghettos throughout America."

Forms and Devices

The most striking features of "Harlem" are the vivid, even startling, metaphors that Hughes introduces as possible answers to the poem's opening question, "What happens to a dream deferred?" Each metaphor could be taken as suggesting a pattern of behavior. Drying "up/ like a raisin in the sun" could refer to the gradual shriveling of a dream or a person, still sweet but wrinkled, desiccated. (Lorraine Hansberry's 1959 play, *A Raisin in the Sun*, ruminates on this sort of response to a dream deferred—taking its title from Hughes's poem.)

To "fester like a sore—/ And then run" suggests something considerably more unappealing—and dangerous—than drying up: a wound not healing. Eventually a limb or a life may be lost. Worse still among its implications is that it will "stink like rotten meat," for now life is gone from the organism entirely and putrefaction has set in. "Stink" is used as an intentionally offensive, vulgar word, suitable for the occasion.

So far there has been a kind of logical progression, from dehydration to localized decay ("fester") to wholesale decomposition, but here the poem takes a surprising turn. To "crust and sugar over—/ like a syrupy sweet" seems anticlimactic at first, after rot; "sugar" and "sweet" recall the concentrated sweetness of a raisin.

Hughes may have been thinking of a false, "syrupy sweet" form of behavior—what Paul Laurence Dunbar, in his poem, "We Wear the Mask," called "the mask that grins and lies"—an outer "crust" that hides. The poem does not say what it hides, but one may be reminded of the narrator's grandfather in Ralph Ellison's novel *Invisible Man* (1952), a grinning, subservient old man who, on his deathbed, "had spoken of his meekness as a dangerous activity"—who had told his grandson "to overcome 'em with yeses, undermine 'em with grins, agree 'em to death and destruction, let 'em swoller you [like too much sugar, perhaps] till they vomit or bust wide open."

Each of the last two answers to the question "What happens to a dream deferred?" is set off from the others. Penultimately, there is the statement, "Maybe it just sags/ like a heavy load"—perhaps the saddest of the responses, suggesting depression and despair. Finally, there is the overtly warning question: *"Or does it explode?"* When violence broke out in America's inner cities in the 1960's, Hughes's poem proved to have been prophetic.

By no means are the metaphors in "Harlem" meant to exhaust the number of possible responses to the deferring of a dream. Indeed, another poem in *Montage of a Dream Deferred*, "Same in Blues," uses a repeated refrain to state that in a dream deferred there is "A certain/ amount of traveling," "A certain/ amount of nothing," and "A certain/ amount of impotence." The poem notes that "There's liable/ to be confusion/ in a dream deferred." Even with "traveling," "nothing," "impotence," and "confusion," the list of responses is nowhere near exhausted. There may be as many dreams deferred as there are residents of Harlem or as there are African Americans.

Themes and Meanings

Although "Harlem" can stand alone, it is best understood in its original context as a key part of *Montage of a Dream Deferred*. Hughes conceived *Montage of a Dream Deferred* as a single, long poem made up of many parts, some as short as three lines (or fewer than ten words), some as long as two pages.

The word "montage" suggests analogies with a visual design consisting of many juxtaposed smaller designs or, better (since a series of poems exists in time more than in space), with a rapid sequence of related short scenes in a film. The most useful analogue of the work is, however, neither pictorial nor cinematic but musical. In a prefatory note to *Montage of a Dream Deferred*, Hughes wrote that "this poem on contemporary Harlem, like be-bop, is marked by conflicting changes, sudden nuances, sharp and impudent interjections, broken rhythms, and passages sometimes in the manner of the jam session, sometimes the popular song, punctuated by the riffs, runs, breaks, and disc-tortions of the music of a community in transition."

Hughes had long been interested in and knowledgeable about African American music. Beginning in the 1920's, he wrote poems about—and sometimes in forms influenced by—the music. His first book, *The Weary Blues* (1926), took its title from such a poem. Bebop, the innovative jazz of the late 1940's, with its emphasis on the successive improvisations of individual instrumental voices, most strongly influenced the form and the flavor of *Montage of a Dream Deferred*.

If the book were conceived as one long bebop tune based on chord changes on the theme of "a dream deferred," then "Harlem," strategically placed at the beginning of the end of the book, marks the point at which the theme is restated in preparation for the end. Dreams are mentioned in more than a dozen individual poems in the book; the phrase "dream deferred" appears in a half dozen poems prior to "Harlem" (and in three poems that follow). "Harlem" is the first poem to ask, "What happens to a dream deferred?" (The succeeding poem, "Good Morning," repeats the question.)

The dream that "Harlem" (and *Montage of a Dream Deferred*, in general) asks about is the African American version of the American Dream: A "Dream within a dream," as "Island" (the last poem in *Montage of a Dream Deferred*) calls it. In the course of the book, individuals imagine the dream in many different ways. Some merely dream of things (a stove, a bottle of gin, a television set, a diamond ring); other dreams also require money, but they are less specifically material (to have a nice place to live, to get an education, to be able to afford a proper funeral). Some intangible dreams require the cooperation of another person or other people (to be fed, to be appreciated, to be respected, to be loved); other intangible dreams can be solitary (to be safe, to be independent, to be happy). Whether one's dream is as mundane as hitting the numbers or as noble as hoping to see one's children reared properly, Langston Hughes takes them all seriously; he takes the deferral of each dream to heart.

Richard Bizot

HARLEM, MONTANA: JUST OFF THE RESERVATION

Author: James Welch (1940-   )
Type of poem: Narrative
First published: 1971, in *Riding the Earthboy 40*

The Poem

James Welch's "Harlem, Montana: Just Off the Reservation" is a four-stanza narrative prose poem in which the narrator reflects on the hopeless lifestyle of many of the inhabitants of the small town of Harlem, a community in northern Montana that borders the American Indian reservation of Fort Belknap. Welch, whose heritage is Blackfeet/Gros Ventre, uses a nameless narrator to examine the struggles of living in a reservation town. The poet also takes an introspective look at his own identity and reflects on how it has been shaped by the town of Harlem.

The poet begins by establishing himself as a member of the Harlem community when in the first line of the poem he uses the word "We." He quickly reveals the tension that permeates Harlem with references to the rampant alcoholism, bigotry, and financial dependancy that many Native Americans "just off" the reservation face daily: "Money is free if you're poor enough." The "white" citizens of Harlem are not portrayed as being any better off than the Native American inhabitants, but they seek positions of authority: "Disgusted, busted whites are running/ for office in this town."

The bigotry in Harlem is widespread. In the second and third stanzas, Welch shows how deeply the social and racial prejudice lies within the Native American community with his references to Turks and Hutterites: "Turks" and their "olive" skin are "unwelcome/ alive in any town." Welch, however, seems to suggest that this prejudice based on skin color is contradicted by the fact that Harlem men are so lonely that they would welcome these same Turks to "rule [their] women."

This contrasting form of bigotry is juxtaposed and further underscored in the fourth stanza, when Welsh states that the "Hutterites out north are nice," but "We hate/ them." This resentment of the prosperous "Hutterites" is heightened when the Native Americans of Harlem accuse them "of idiocy and believe their belief all wrong." By pointing out the many facets of bigotry in Harlem, the poet seems to suggest that the deep-seeded prejudice that exists on the reservation is multifaceted and that it is perhaps even more difficult to understand than it may be in most mainstream American communities.

In stanza 2, when Welch refers to the "Turks" who are "olive" skinned, he suggests that the loneliness of reservation life and the abuse of alcohol provide a backdrop in which bigotry is only superficially revealed by a person's skin color, whether it be red, white, or olive. The resentment the Native American inhabitants of Harlem feel toward people of different color or social status is meshed with the anger they feel when they realize that "whites" and "Turks" alike seek to control their lives through the use of money and alcohol.

In stanza 3, the narrator suggests that the photo in the New England Hotel lobby of men "nicer/ than pie" is a relic that serves as a reminder of the deals that were made by outsiders with "warring bands of redskins/ who demanded protection money for the price of food." The resentment that lies beneath the surface of the bigotry that the Native Americans of Harlem feel is represented by this photo, which remains in the hotel lobby as a symbol of the deceptive greediness of the "whites," "Turks," and even the elder American Indian leaders who benefited financially from the implementation of the reservation system.

In the final stanza, the poet reveals the facade that the people of the community present to the outside world. In ironic fashion Welch contrasts a local establishment named the "New England Hotel" with the "raggedy-assed" children that wander the streets and the "bad food" that is served by the two cafes in town. Finally, the poet reveals that the only pivotal event in the small town that the people of Harlem seem to remember is an episode when "three young bucks" shot up a grocery store.

Forms and Devices

Beginning with the title of his poem, "Harlem, Montana: Just Off the Reservation," Welch uses the voice of his narrator to establish with readers the unique relationship he has with the community of Harlem. It is obvious that the poet Welch, the unnamed narrator of the poem, has not been able to leave behind his memories of Harlem, recollections that go back to the time when as a young boy Welch himself attended school on the Fort Belknap reservation. Although the poet may in many ways be "just off the reservation," the title of the poem perhaps directly refers to the town of Harlem and its close proximity to the Fort Belknap reservation. The fact that the reservation town's name is Harlem also seems to serve Welch well in presenting readers with a place-name that aptly presents a racially charged look at the bigotry that can take place in a small rural community, a place ironically linked with the Harlem district of New York City.

The narrator's dark description of Harlem, Montana, is filled with references to the alcohol abuse, the bigotry, and the hopelessness that has become far too familiar for many people living in reservation towns. Welch creates vivid images that depict the drunken inhabitants of the community who survive from day to day in a world where "Booze is law" and where racial tension is pervasive.

In the final stanza, just as he has done throughout the poem, Welch speaks directly to Harlem: "Harlem, your hotel is overnamed, your children/ are raggedy-assed but you go on." This approach effectively reveals to readers the anger and resentment that the poet feels for a town that seems to have sold its soul, a town that is filled with broken people who have nothing better to do than to drink their lives away.

The one event that seems to symbolize this hopelessness takes place in Harlem when "three young bucks" shoot up a grocery store and hold it hostage for days. After seizing control of the grocery store, these young men consider themselves important and rich. To them, the store represents a place of wealth and power. It is the center of the community, a place where everyone must come to sustain life. By taking over the grocery store, they too can feel important.

Every ethnic group seeks to find some kind of control in Harlem. The grocery store takeover serves as a pathetic attempt on the "young bucks'" part to compete with the "whites," "Turks," and "Hutterites" for their fair share in controlling what little power exists in Harlem. This need to seize control of the local grocery store is what elicits their response, "we're rich,/ help us, oh God, we're rich."

The poet's description of outsiders as olive-skinned "Turks" furthers Welch's theme of bigotry. Unlike the Native Americans and the whites who live in Harlem, the "Turks" come to town to take what they can get from the locals. Welch's use of "Turks," a people who typically reside in the Middle East and have a reputation for cruelty and tyranny, works well to describe the distance the people of Harlem feel between themselves and the outsiders who come hoping to make some fast money: "Turks would use/ your one dingy park to declare a need for loot."

Themes and Meanings

In Welch's narrative poem "Harlem, Montana: Just Off the Reservation," he paints a dismal picture of the reservation town of Harlem, Montana. His portrayal of the hopeless inhabitants of Harlem who are steeped in a world of alcohol and bigotry serves to make readers aware of the plight that many other Native American communities struggle with as they seek to establish healthier environments that will provide hope for future members of North America's Indian tribes.

The narrator himself appears to be saying goodbye to the uncomfortable memories that he associates with his days of living on or near the reservation: "Goodbye, goodbye, Harlem on the rocks,/ So bigoted, you forget the latest joke." Welch carefully describes the underlying bigotry that is a large part of life as he sees it in Harlem. He traces the way in which the whites in the community survive by "running for office" and how the outsiders he calls the "Turks" seek to reap the financial benefits of Harlem by fleecing the town that does not know how to take care of its own people. Welch further labels the many outsiders to the community as "nice." However, the people of Harlem eventually learn to hate them as well, because their money and their lifestyles become visible signs that suggest these outsiders have superior lifestyles. The Hutterites, who are "tough" and who are well respected by the community for their skills as farmers, are labeled "nice," but the narrator goes on to say, "we hate them."

Welch's poem seems to come from the heart of a man who is both angry and ashamed of the impact that the reservation town of Harlem has had and continues to have on the narrator's life. The consistant use of the pronoun "we" suggests that the poet fully realizes he is in many ways still a member of the Harlem community and furthermore that Harlem will probably outlive all its inhabitants, who have tried to escape the hold that the town has had on their lives: "When you die, if you die. . . ." Although Harlem is filled with bigoted people who are half-dead from the effects of alcohol, the reservation town will survive and Harlem will remain ambivalent to the destructive social conditions that define the town and sustain its identity.

Daniel W. Landes

HARLEM SHADOWS

Author: Claude McKay (1889-1948)
Type of poem: Book of poems
First published: 1922

The Poems

With the publication of *Songs of Jamaica* and *Constab Ballads* (both 1912), Claude McKay achieved immediate recognition in Jamaica as a poet of some consequence, especially in the use of dialect, and he was considered a local equivalent of Robert Burns, the Scottish Romantic poet. However, upon his migration to the United States he abandoned dialect, and in *Spring in New Hampshire and Other Poems* (1920) he showed his ability to experiment with rhythm, rhyme, meter, and even poetic structure.

The extent of his willingness and ability to explore new poetic techniques is revealed in *Harlem Shadows*: In the "Author's Word" prefatory to the poems, McKay notes that he adhered to many older poetic traditions (such as the sonnet form) while trying to achieve "directness, truthfulness and naturalness of expression instead of an enameled originality." In 1922 Harcourt, Brace issued both *Harlem Shadows* and Virginia Woolf's *Mrs. Dalloway*, a combination suggesting that the prestigious New York publishing house perceived McKay as a significant and potentially major new voice in contemporary writing. The collection was well received by readers and critics.

Harlem Shadows, a collection of seventy-four poems, brought together what were thought to be the best poems that McKay had written since his arrival in the United States, many of which had appeared in such periodicals as *Seven Arts*, *Pearson's*, the *Liberator*, and the *Cambridge Magazine*. It had an introduction by Max Eastman, the left-wing mentor of many young writers, and consequently achieved some cachet in literary circles. Eastman observed that McKay's poems had an obvious quality, "the pure, clear arrow-like transference of his emotion into our breast, without any but the inevitable words." He continued by saying that this was what John Keats sought to cherish when he said that poetry should be "great and unobtrusive, a thing which enters into the soul and does not startle or amaze with itself but with its subject." This endorsement and comparison was extraordinary yet justified.

The poems can be divided into three groups of about equal number: those about nature (many of which are nostalgic reminiscences of Jamaica); those about love, affection, and attachment to persons; and those that deal in some way with race. Seriousness—even despondency—is a pervasive mood. After such titles as *Songs of Jamaica* and *Spring in New Hampshire*, which exude a bright, happy spirit or tone, *Harlem Shadows* intimates an almost binary polarity; the connotations of the two words are (for both black and white readers) generally negative, bringing to mind overcrowded and dilapidated tenements, unemployed or underemployed menials, and pervasive social problems (including prostitution, gangsterism, illegitimacy, gambling, and drug addiction) existing in the shadow of New York, with its consumerism, wealth, and bright lights.

There is nothing comparable to the optimism and positive outlook implied by the songs and spring of his earlier titles, even though some of the poems are about red flowers, jasmines, and homing swallows. "Wild May" is "weighted down with fetters" and "the victim of grim care"; "A Memory of June" recalls that love is fugitive; even "The Easter Flower" bemoans "this foreign Easter damp and chilly." Other poems that indicate the prevailing tone and attitude of the collection are "In Bondage," "Futility," "Through Agony," "Enslaved," and "Polarity." The poems that have retained their interest for readers, critics, and anthologists are the obviously polemical poems, those that concern race: "Harlem Shadows," "The White City," "If We Must Die," "The Lynching," "America," and "The Harlem Dancer," which remarkably combines lyricism and social protest within the confines of the sonnet form.

While "Harlem Shadows" is affecting in its condemnation of a society that obliges "little dark girls . . . in slippered feet" to engage in prostitution and thus to live lives "Of poverty, dishonor and disgrace," its concluding couplet is almost anticlimactic in moving the focus from the "dusky, half-clad girls of tired feet" to the poet himself ("Ah, heart of me"). The mixture of language registers, exclamations, and changing metonymies diffuses the focus. In "The White City" the passion is forceful, unmuted, pellucid: "I muse my life-long hatred," "this dark Passion . . . fills my every mood," "I hate," yet "I bear it nobly as I live my part." Though readers might be offended by the poet's confession, nonetheless they must admire his candor and forthrightness.

"If We Must Die," indubitably McKay's most popular poem among some radical groups, is commendable for its "transference of his emotion into our breast," as Eastman observed. Yet it is not without its weaknesses: Would any black orator of the period have used the exhortation "O kinsmen" or "let us show us brave"? Nonetheless, the poem is an exceptionally powerful rallying cry.

"The Lynching," which depicts one of the most deplorable practices of southern racism, has exceptional power, which derives from the juxtaposition of "a bright and solitary star" and "the swinging char" and from the representative community crowd of women and children watching "the ghastly body swaying in the sun." None of the women shows sorrow in her steely eyes, "And little lads, lynchers that were to be,/ Danced round the dreadful thing in fiendish glee." This concluding couplet is moving in its simplicity: The black man has been reduced to a thing, and the racial, communal hate will become a social norm. Yet in spite of the terrors and torments of life in the United States, McKay says, in "America," "I love this cultured hell that tests my youth."

Forms and Devices

Whereas McKay's dialect poetry required copious annotations to explain to non-West Indians the meanings of words and the significance of allusions, the poems in *Harlem Shadows* did not. Whereas the earlier verses were mainly written in iambic trimeters and tetrameters, the New York volume is almost all in tetrameters and pentameters—though not exclusively in iambic or trochaic rhythms. So unconventional were some to Max Eastman that in his introductory essay he noted that "One or two of the rhythms I confess I am not able to apprehend at all." He could have been alluding to these lines from "When Dawn Comes to the City": "But I would be on the island of the sea,/ In the heart of the island of the sea." Alternatively, he could have been referring to these from "Exhortation: Summer, 1919" (a year of American race riots): "In the East the clouds grow crimson with the new/ dawn that is breaking,/ And its golden glory fills the western skies." These rhythmic variations were not even then unusual, however: Walt Whitman, Gerard Manley Hopkins, and others had already experimented with half-stresses and outriders in their attempts to capture the essence of speech rhythms.

In fact, in the earlier *Songs of Jamaica* and *Constab Ballads* McKay had taken numerous liberties with standard syllabic (or quantitative) verse and had incorporated numerous modifications of the rather static ballad meter of iambic tetrameters and trimeters in alternation. In *Harlem Shadows* he continued this independent approach to conventional form, even to the point of modifying the sonnet structure to suit his needs, so that in neither the ballad nor the lyric was he a slavish observer of traditions. Some of his sonnets are Elizabethan, some are Italian, some are Wordsworthian. However, it must be conceded that the Elizabethan sonnet form seemed most congenial to him and that most of his best and most memorable poems are in this style. Within the sonnet form McKay generally observed proper rhyme; nonetheless, he is not averse to rhyming "over" with "lover," "souls" with "ghouls," and "love" with "move," a technique often referred to as a visual or eye rhyme.

Generally in the nonsonnet lyrics McKay favored the four-line stanza and most frequently employed closed couplets; however, "A Prayer" is composed in the form of five couplets of seven-beat lines, and "Harlem Shadows" itself is in six-line stanzas of iambic pentameters in which almost all the lines are run-on.

One of McKay's strengths as a poet is his use of a wide range of imagery. Visual imagery predominates, though appeals to the other senses are also common. The very titles of the poems are at times forcefully visual: "The Easter Flower," "Flame-Heart," "The Night Fire," "Birds of Prey," and "A Red Flower." In some poems, olfactory imagery is primary, as in "Jasmines," "Subway Wind," and "The Easter Flower." Kinesthetic imagery is also encountered: "Homing Swallows," "The Tired Worker," and "The Harlem Dancer" employ this device effectively.

While a few of the poems in *Harlem Shadows* can be considered love lyrics ("La Paloma in London," "Tormented," "One Year After," and "A Memory of June," for example), most are poems of place or of protest. In the former category are those that are purely celebratory ("Spring in New Hampshire" and "Summer Morn in New Hampshire" as well as "Winter in the Country" and "Flame-Heart") and those that are reminiscent, such as "The Tropics in New York," in which the sight of Caribbean produce in a New York store window makes the poet "hungry for the old, familiar ways."

The propaganda or protest poems indicate a sea change in the poet's social and political thinking following his emigration from Jamaica a decade earlier. Gone are the flippant, cordial protestations about discriminations; they have been replaced by penetrating analyses of inequalities, injustices, and humiliations, which are laid bare in "The Barrier," in which McKay states without equivocation:

> I must not see upon your face
> Love's softly glowing spark;
> For there's the barrier of race,
>   You're fair and I am dark.

The opening poem in *Harlem Shadows* celebrates Easter, with its "lilac-tinted Easter lily/ Soft-scented in the air" and "its perfumed power." The second one contrasts the "cheerless frozen spots" of New York with the "birds' glad song," the "flowering lanes," and the "vivid, silver-flecked blue sky" of the West Indies. The third poem, "America," introduces the McKay of the Left, of social awareness, of political proclivities. He is no longer the youthful singer of tropical beauties or personal attachments: He is now a fully committed critic of racial discrimination and social injustice. But a certain ambivalence can be discerned beginning with the fourth line:

> Although she feeds me bread of bitterness,
> And sinks into my throat her tiger's tooth,
> Stealing my breath of life, I will confess
> I love this cultured hell that tests my youth!

This ambivalence is also to be found in "The White City," wherein he acknowledges the "life-long hate" that he bears "nobly as I live my part"; he has to make his "heaven in the white world's hell"—"because I hate."

The other deeply passionate poems of protest are equally affective: The reader cannot but be moved by the repetition of such words as "hate," "lynching," "fiery," "fighting," "tears," "dead," and "dying" that permeate them like punctuation marks. Some readers do not respond positively to McKay's lines in "If We Must Die" that propose that, "Though far outnumbered, let us show us brave,/ And for their thousand blows deal one death-blow!" However, their power is attested by the fact that Winston Churchill, the British prime minister during World War II, quoted them to incite his countrymen to rally to defeat Hitlerite Germany.

Themes and Meanings

Harlem Shadows is fundamentally Claude McKay's philosophy of life, even though it was published when he was in his early thirties and had not experienced his infatuation and subsequent disillusionment with communism, had not seen his fame (and subsequent eclipse) as a writer of novels and short stories, and had not suffered poverty, disease, calumny, and ostracism by former friends and colleagues—particularly after espousing Catholicism.

The collection juxtaposes his delight in natural beauty, whether witnessed in individuals, flora, or fauna (and regardless of whether it is to be discovered in the country or the cities), and his despair in discovering the discrimination against the poor, the dark-skinned, and the immigrant in a society that professes itself to be open, nondiscriminatory, and egalitarian. All these negative characteristics of American society he inveighs against, yet not so offensively as to alienate sympathetic liberal or progressive whites. He is aware of and celebrates the achievements of modern American capitalist society, yet he fervently believes that it can be amended to the end of offering all people better lives.

Whites are seen to be in the sun; blacks are presented as in the shadows, both literally—in the crowded streets and buildings of the North—and figuratively. McKay proposes that no group can grow culturally, socially, intellectually, and economically if perpetually assigned to the umbral regions, the Harlems of the nation. While some of his language of protest might seem to be political harangue, it is really not violent in its intent: It is designed to arouse, to foster critical thinking rather than revolt or violence. *Harlem Shadows* is a noteworthy testament to the serious side of the Roaring Twenties that were just under way and also to the Harlem Renaissance.

A. L. McLeod

HASIDIC SCRIPTURES

Author: Nelly Sachs (1891-1970)
Type of poem: Lyric
First published: 1949, as "Chassidische Schriften," in *Sternverdunkelung*; English
translation collected in *The Seeker and Other Poems*, 1970

The Poem

"Hasidic Scriptures" consists of twenty-nine lines divided into tercets, couplets,
and one quatrain, all written in free verse. The title refers to the teachings of Rabbi Israel Ba'al Shem Tov (1700-1760), the founder of Hasidism, and draws the reader immediately into the context of Jewish mysticism. An epigraph preceding the poem
comments on the mystical relationship between the Law of the Commandments and
man's physical experience. The first line, "All is salvation in the mystery," which repeats throughout the poem, indicates Nelly Sachs's belief that it is inappropriate, if
not impossible, to attain spiritual truth through logic. The poem unfolds as a meditation on this relationship between the Creator and the created world, in which Sachs
transforms theological and metaphysical concepts into a deeply personal artistic vision.

The poem's first eleven lines place the reader at the beginning of Creation as light is
born of darkness in the protective, nurturing matrix of the universe. The entire process
is distilled into images of night, stars, water, and sand. For Sachs, who was inspired by
mysticism, the agent which initiates and sustains the Creation is language: "and the
word went forth/ . . . Names formed/ like pools in the sand." These "names" refer to
the formative power of language and recall man's role in naming the animals (Genesis
2:20), which implies a personal participation in language. In the syntax of the poem,
the names' arrival follows an undefined longing felt by all creatures. The reader is led
to make the connection between this longing and the attempt by man to share through
language in the creative process, thereby becoming one with the Creator.

The next eight lines both close the Genesis material and introduce the next phase of
the poem, which depicts the experience of exile and the promise of the covenant (as in
the biblical Exodus and Deuteronomy). This section presents images of death connoting the expulsion from Eden: bones, bleeding veins, sunset, and pain. Yet upon these
images are superimposed the concepts of the Commandments and laws which transcend individual mortality. Memory, the foundation of tradition, offers another way to
transcend death, the death caused by forgetting. In Sachs's poetry, forgetting and remembering are always functions of the Holocaust's historical burden.

The final ten lines interweave images from God's promise to Abraham, Jacob's vision, and the exodus from Egypt into a composite vision of the Jewish experience.
The biblical incidents are arranged in a backward chronological order that represents
the reversal of the journey away from God. Sachs first records the crossing of the Jordan and the transport of the Hebrew laws and Scripture, which together imply the end

of national exile. Following is a description of a barren wilderness of stones, quicksand, and darkness. Even here, God's presence, the flash of revelation, is immanent: "the dwelling place of buried lightning." The poem closes with the image of the sleeping Jacob, known as "Israel, the fighter of horizons," after his battle with God, dreaming the promise of a nation born "with the seed of stars," which signifies the promise to Abraham. The writing of this poem coincided with the development of Israel's nationhood, and the final lines bespeak a political and historical hope as well as a spiritual one.

Forms and Devices

Hans Magnus Enzensberger wrote in his introduction to *O the Chimneys* (1967) that Sachs's poems are "hard, but transparent. They do not dissolve in the weak solution of interpretations." The most powerful aspect of her poetry is her use of symbols and metaphors in which are concentrated layer upon layer of meaning drawn from her life's experiences and Jewish mysticism. The complexity of her system of signs is further enriched by the associations brought to it by her readers. Her translators face the difficult task of selecting words that evoke at least some of the many nuances found in the original texts. They are further challenged by the complicated and ambiguous syntax of her verses: New clauses begin without markers, subjects and objects are blurred, and inserted modifiers distend the sentence's structure. These strategies alter the pace of reading. The reader is sometimes slowed and sometimes propelled by the use of anaphora (here, the repetition of "and" at the beginning of eleven lines) in a chain of associations.

The broken rhythm of Sachs's syntax is replicated in the arrangement of her lines of verse. The repetition of the poem's first line, "All is salvation in the mystery," weaves through an irregular pattern of couplets, tercets, and a single quatrain creating an unpredictable emphasis. Another unifying element is the recurrence of simile after each repetition of the opening line.

The simile is only one of the many forms of metaphor encountered in this poem. Metaphor, especially metaphor developed from biblical or mystical imagery, is the cornerstone of Sachs's system of poetic expression. She has observed of her own poetic craft: "Images and metaphors are my wounds. Death has been my teacher. I wrote to be able to survive." (She escaped the fate of her fellow Jews in the concentration camps by fleeing to Sweden in May, 1940.)

In this poem, darkness and light have universal significance, but Sachs expresses her hopeful belief in transformation when she imagines the night giving birth to the stars. Dark and light, good and evil, are not in perpetual conflict; rather, one can engender the other. Similarly, she transforms the image of the stone—hard, lifeless matter and symbolic of exile in the barren desert—into a petrified darkness that still contains the promise of divine movement and light. Even threatening quicksand becomes a metaphor of the potential for change on the most elemental level. In conjunction with the final images of fertile seeds and stars, sand assumes yet another dimension inspired by the Bible: God promises Abraham, "I will shower blessings on you, I will make your descendants as many as the stars in heaven and the grains of sand on the seashore" (Genesis 22:17). Sachs allows the conventional, sometimes negative connotations of certain images to stand while exploring the promise hidden within.

Themes and Meanings

Nelly Sachs, described as the "poet of the Holocaust" when she was awarded the Nobel Prize in Literature in 1966, challenges the view that poetry is impossible after Auschwitz. To untangle the disorder left in the wake of World War II, she turned to the works of Jewish mysticism. The Book of the Zohar (The Book of Light), a thirteenth century commentary on the Pentateuch, provided a new way to envision the metaphysical order of the world, a way to make sense of a system fallen apart. She posed the essential question: How could the Holocaust have occurred in a world supposedly under the care of a supreme Divinity? Mysticism provided the keys to putting the shattered world back together again. Within the darkest experience had to be found a new light. The alternative would be nihilism or deep pessimism, and both are untenable positions in a theology based on the Covenant.

Sachs was acutely aware of the dilemma that writing in German posed for her. The German language was discredited because it had been the language of the oppressors. She developed a strategy for salvaging her means of expression and communication—her system of metaphors, which is, in effect, a reinvention of language. Her system affirmed the existence of bonds between words and their meanings, while opening up a new range of meanings, and it challenged words to describe what had been termed indescribable.

In view of Sachs's quest to transform her native language into an appropriate vehicle for poetry, her vision of the Creation is striking. In it the world is essentially created through language. In "Hasidic Scriptures," the indescribable is not directly the horror of the concentration camp but the world's (especially man's and specifically Israel's) relationship to God. She envisioned this relationship in terms of Hasidic mysticism infused with elements of Christian mysticism, which seemed to provide answers to the existential questions raised by the events of World War II.

The central aspect of this relationship is the experience of exile, of separation from the Divine. Juxtaposed with this spiritual exile are the historical exiles of the Hebrews and Sachs's own exile in Sweden. Sachs combined the metaphysical, the biblical, and the biographical concepts of exile into a totality of associations. However, just as sand is a metaphor not only for barrenness but also for the constant transformation and movement in the created world, exile contains within it the ever constant hope of return or reunification.

Elisabeth Strenger

HAY FEVER

Author: A. D. Hope (1907-2000)
Type of poem: Meditation
First published: 1973; collected in *A Late Picking: Poems, 1965-1974*, 1975

The Poem

"Hay Fever" was written in the author's maturity, though not in his old age. It demonstrates that A. D. Hope, although he is sometimes considered primarily an imitator of eighteenth century poetic technique and a facile satirist, was also an innovator in structure and a lyricist at heart. While he was perhaps indebted to Alexander Pope and Jonathan Swift in attitude, he was not in method, for he took numerous liberties in both structure and content that they would not have approved. In place of regular stanzas, the closed couplet, and iambic pentameter, Hope freely intermixed stanza and line lengths and uses iambs, dactyls, trochees, and anapests in lines that vary in length from tetrameters to alexandrines; further, he made use of both single and double rhyme in alternating lines or in lines widely separated; the four stanzas of this poem are in eleven, thirteen, eight, and eleven lines. In fact, this poem shows Hope in a somewhat uncharacteristic light, for he was generally observant of the niceties of Augustan poetic technique.

The poem opens with the general observation that "Time," personified as the grim reaper with scythe in hand (a commonplace in art of the Western world as well as in end-of-the-year cartoons), is a mature, skilled workman who is ever alert and at his task of claiming lives, usually without discrimination. The poet expresses his relief that it is not yet his turn to die (though he is "Waiting my turn as he swings"), and then he recalls how he himself learned to use the scythe to harvest lucerne (the Australian term for alfalfa) and hay in his early adolescence. As the neophyte, he took the last position in the row of harvesters, in case he could not keep up with the others or made poor strokes, which could be corrected on the next sweep. This recollection of a youthful apprenticeship conjures up an analogy: The poet sees himself "As though I were Time himself."

The poem proceeds with detailed recollections of the long-ago summer in Tasmania (the small, southernmost state of Australia) when the neighbors of his father, a Presbyterian minister who owned a small farm, came to harvest his crops and brought with them a scythe with which the young man could learn the skill and thus be inducted into the world of farm men. There is a catalog of the grasses, flowers, and weeds that are cut simultaneously during the harvest—an indication that the good and the bad are harvested indiscriminately, a sort of paradigm of life itself. The catalog is more than a Whitmanesque list; it also reveals a fond recognition of the "still dewy stalks" that, personified, "nod, tremble, and tilt aside." Then, almost inadvertently, the boy sees a dandelion "cast up a golden eye" at browsing cows, but the boy does not consider the cows' hay-breath "the smell of death" as the dandelions do.

In the third stanza, as in the first, the point of view moves from that of the omniscient observer to the first person; the boy has become as proficient a harvester as his associates, but he has a poetic response to his task that the others lack: He notes "the sigh/ Of the dying grass like an animal breathing," identifying with the Other, the object of his scythe. This returns him to the question—both literal and philosophical— "How long can I hold out yet?" The concluding stanza reveals the persona noting the passage of time ("obsolete" scythes have been replaced by harvesting machines). He acknowledges that he has metaphorically "made hay" but has stored consoling memories against the inevitable scythe-stroke of Time; he will "lie still in well-cured hay."

Forms and Devices

The principal poetic device in "Hay Fever" is the analogy between Time as a reaper and the poet himself as first a literal wielder of a scythe and then as a reaper of the joys of life, "stacked high," though intermixed with "a thistle or two . . . for the prick of remorse." Other figures and tropes abound: Personification is used to make Time more forceful, as when he "takes a pace forward" and swings "from the hip" like a masterful harvester. It is used again in reference to the still, dewy stalks that "nod, tremble and tilt aside" and the dandelion that "casts up a golden eye"; the dying grass sighs, the steel scythe sings. Time drives a harvester.

Metaphors are used throughout the poem. Almost every line uses them, from the initial image of Time's scythe being honed fine to the last line's image of lying still in well-cured hay and drifting into sleep (death). Other effective devices are the similitude of a barn stacked high with "good, dry mow" and a brain full of pleasant remembrances, and the statement "I am running with, flooding with, sweat"—an illustration of hyperbole, which occurs sparingly. There are also a few similes of merit: the sigh of dying grass like animal breathing, and romping like a boy in the heap of harvest.

As in much of Hope's poetry there is evidence that he values those compositional elements that were especially prized in the eighteenth century and that he, as a professor of English, taught: parallelisms, balanced statements, antitheses, trials, and double elements. Accordingly, one reads "new to the game and young at the skill," "Out of the lucerne patch and into the hay," and "in his hay, in my day," among the balanced items. There is an abundance of dyads: "Crumples and falls," "lucerne and poppies," "place and pace," "arrows and bow," "the grass and the flowers." Effective triads include "By the sound of the scythes, by the swish and ripple, the sigh/ Of the dying grass," which also illustrates the author's penchant for alliteration, particularly sibilance.

In his imagery, Hope makes frequent use of compound adjectives to gain specificity: The dock is red-stemmed, the milk thistle is hollow-stalk, and the oats are self-sown. Not all of the imagery is visual; some is olfactory ("the sweet hay-breath") and some is auditory ("thin steel crunch" and "the sound of the scythes"). Hope also makes use of kinetic imagery, as in "I snag on a fat-hen clump" and "I set the blade into the grass."

One characteristic of Hope's poetry that has frequently been noted is his use of declamation, of unmodified statements. Here one sees ample evidence of this in "the men are here// They have brought a scythe for me. I hold it with pride.// I set the blade into the grass." Related to declamation as a development device is the inclusion of apothegms, or aphorisms, such as "It is good for a man when he comes to the end of his course/ In the barn of his brain to be able to romp like a boy" and "Time drives a harvester now: he does not depend on the weather." The effect of these aphorisms is to endow the poet with a philosophic disposition and acuity.

The mere inclusion of these poetic devices would be insufficient to grant merit, but the long, run-on lines and the almost imperceptible shifts in point of view make it appear that they are organic rather than applied like decorations. That is, the poem's success is in part the result of the rich texture of the prose itself and in part its philosophic content and its stanzaic form. The almost casual, conversational tone, atypical of Hope, adds to the poem's charm.

Themes and Meanings

In "Hay Fever" Hope addresses an issue that has challenged almost all poets of stature: As people age, they wonder when they will die and whether they have had sufficient satisfaction in life to "go gentle into that good night," as Dylan Thomas phrased it. Hope's conclusion is that, though he has "made hay" (or sown his wild oats) in his day, has good and bad memories, successes and failures to acknowledge, life has been good to him and he can leave this world in a state of satisfaction—or even reverie—as he recounts the good times and perhaps forgets the bad.

This summation and evaluation would not have been possible without the recollection of his adolescent participation in haying on his father's farm, which proved to be an induction into the adult world, an initiation that brought him face to face with the similarity between his cutting down everything in his path, whether good or bad, decorative or essential, and death. All are taken, regardless of merit, it seems, and there is no reprieve or deferment when Time "takes a pace forward, swings from the hips" (almost as if in obedience to an instructor).

Because Hope spent his adult life as a teacher and then a professor of English, he was adept at explication and the use of analogy; "Hay Fever" invites his readers to see the analogy that he offers and then offer their own explications, though his concluding three lines are clearly intended to direct them to certain conclusions.

The poem's title, which might well mislead potential readers into believing that the common allergy is the subject of the poem, comports with Hope's practice of being ambiguous at times. Haying can cause discomfort in people who suffer from allergies, causing tears and sweat, but for him haying caused sweat and tears from physical exhaustion. Moreover, the remembrance of those days—and the contemplation of death—may produce some tears of regret and the sweat that comes from apprehension. "How long can I hold out yet?" he asks, and the answer is implicit: until Time, with his scythe or harvester, comes along. "Hay Fever," like the other poems in *A Late Picking* (the title refers to the final harvest of grapes for wine, which are somewhat riper and sweeter than the main vintage) is fuller-bodied, sweeter, and more satisfying than many of Hope's earlier poems, and it appeals to the connoisseur rather than the beginner.

A. L. McLeod

HE WHO DOES NOT HOPE

Author: Gunnar Ekelöf (1907-1968)
Type of poem: Meditation
First published: 1945, as "Den som inte hoppas," in *Non serviam*; English translation
collected in *Songs of Something Else: Selected Poems of Gunnar Ekelöf*, 1982

The Poem

In "He Who Does Not Hope," the simplicity of Gunnar Ekelöf's diction belies a highly dense thought process. It is a brief poem—thirty-two lines of free verse, divided into four eight-line stanzas—which begins calmly and rationally with two statements, the first of which echoes the title. The first four lines state that the absence of hope also means freedom from the despair that comes from disappointed hope; correspondingly, believing in nothing frees one from the torment of doubt. In the second half of the stanza, however, this passive but untroubled view is contrasted with its opposite. As soon as one breaks out of unthinking passivity and tries to find a goal or a meaning in life, one is flung into conflict. One begins an unending struggle with the "dragons" of doubt and despair which breathe their poison into one's consciousness.

Stanza 2 also shifts between opposites. It evokes the picture of a winter day, when snow is falling outdoors and a fire is burning in the hearth indoors. These seemingly contradictory elements, snow and fire, both suggest the brevity of life. The fifth line draws together the contradictory elements of snow and fire, heat and cold. The "play" of life—the double suggestion occurs of the *theatrum mundi* ("world theater") and of aimless movement—is like the play of both the snow and the fire. A renewed paradox ends the second stanza, with the statement that the "meaning" of life derives from its meaninglessness.

The third stanza begins on a profoundly negative note. Life has no inherent plan or order. While the disasters of Greek tragedy can at least be ascribed to the preordained workings of fate, twentieth century life lacks even this order. People are the victims of haphazard "combinations" of circumstances and the undifferentiated actions of natural disasters ("whirlwinds") and the forces of history (worldwinds). Struggle alone is insignificant; the only important aspect is a change from one form of struggle to another.

With the fifth line of the third stanza, the poem takes on an anguished urgency. The images of fire and snow recur; now, however, they suggest the cycle of destructive forces in human life: "Let the fire thaw the drift./ Let the drift put out the fire"—since disintegration and death are inevitable, let them proceed. The two concluding lines of the stanza raise the poem to a crescendo of agonized questioning. The poetic speaker uses second-person address: "Life, where is your meaning now?/ Life, where is your point now?"

The fourth stanza obliquely answers the intense questioning of the previous one. The focus moves inward, and the tone becomes lyrical. The heart and soul are orphans, born without parentage, nurturing, or guidance. In their bond, however, they find the relationship that their orphan birth has denied them, for they are "brother" and "sister." The soul is superior to the heart or emotions, for it fills the yet more important role of "mother."

In the final four lines of the last stanza, the poem rises to its most lyrical and most personal note. The objective tone is now fully shed with the use of the first person— "me" and "my." The poetic voice invokes the sister-mother to rock him back and forth and sing for him. This "song without end," it is implied, counterbalances the meaninglessness and brevity of life with meaning and eternity.

Forms and Devices

In spite of the free verse and the simplicity of the diction, "He Who Does Not Hope" presents a complex use of paradox, tightly bound by metaphorical development and verbal devices. The structure of the stanzas in both the Swedish original and the excellent translation by Leonard Nathan and James Larson reflects this underlying tightness. In each stanza, a major modification in the thought development occurs halfway. In stanza 1, this shift is introduced by "but" and sets apart two contradictory life views. In the second stanza, the last four lines synthesize paradoxical elements only to posit yet another paradox. The role of the mid-stanza shift in stanzas 3 and 4 is that of lyrical reinforcement: The second half of stanza 3 offers an emotional response to the destructiveness and brevity of life, while the concluding lines of stanza 4 address lovingly the sister-mother.

The syntax reflects the above pattern, for in each stanza, a full stop concludes the fourth verse. In addition, the first two stanzas, with their objective tone, form a subunit, as do the more subjective third and fourth stanzas. The first four lines of stanzas 1 and 2 are subdivided into two statements of two lines each, terminated by periods. The final four lines, however, are uninterrupted by stops and propel the thought forward with the smoothness of their flow. Similarly, the third and fourth stanzas are interlinked by a pattern of statement in the first four lines and rhetorical address in the concluding four. The third stanza, in which the content rises to a peak of questioning, is the most fragmented, both in sentence structure and by breaks or caesuras. The first four lines consist of sentence fragments, marked by the repetition of "not" and "but," separated by stops at the end of each line.

In structure as well as in content, the fourth stanza is the point of final synthesis. Thematically, an abrupt shift occurs from images of the outer to images of the inner world, from images of brevity and destruction to images of endurance. The effect of this revelation is epiphanic. To underline the exultation of the conclusion, a marked caesura separates the fourth and fifth verses, as the poem breaks forth into a lyrical address to the soul/sister/mother and, for the first time, first-person pronouns and adjectives are used.

Not only the structure but also the verbal devices reflect the tightness of this free-verse meditation. In lines 5 and 6, the repetition of "he who seeks" causes the diction to linger emphatically before the theme of conflict is broached. The third stanza is a feat of translating skill. Transposed, as noted above, is the repeated "not . . . but"; in a verbal echo of the sweeping forces of disaster, the second line lingers on "whirlwinds and the drift of world winds." Here, as with the transposition of "fire . . . drift" and "drift . . . fire" in the fifth and sixth lines of stanza 3, the all-embracing cycle of struggle is suggested.

Themes and Meanings

"He Who Does Not Hope" is a poetic search for a goal and meaning in life. In this way, the poet is like a knight who, as did the chevaliers of the Round Table, rides forth on his quest. Like them, he has setbacks and fights mightily with poison-breathing dragons before he arrives at his goal. Unlike them, however, his dragons are not supernatural creatures but are inherent in life itself.

The poem shifts between paradox and antithesis. Beginning in stanza 1 with the absence of both search and struggle, it moves rapidly to the opposite state: the search which transforms man into a knight in combat. Another rapid shift in metaphor introduces two natural images, fire and snow. Within the sphere of nature as of man, one finds brevity and the omnipresence of disintegration and death. At the end of stanza 2, the search seems to have ended in failure, for the only "meaning" to be derived from life is that of "meaninglessness"; paradoxically, however, the words also suggest that "meaning" is implicit in its absence.

Heat and cold, fire and water have to this point been the antithetical elements which suggest transience in the natural world as well as in human existence. In the third stanza, however, the elements of air and earth ("whirlwinds" and "world winds"), along with the interaction of fire and snow, epitomize the destruction wasted upon humanity.

The "goal" and "meaning" of the quest are found, the final stanza implies, not in the external world, but in a mystic inner region. Although the heart and soul are "orphans" within the world of physical existence, their cohesion yet provides the meaning and eternity which the outside world denies. With the image of the cosmic mother whose infusion of the outer world can only be accomplished by means of the vision within—a recurrent motif in Ekelöf's poetry—the poem ends in paradox. Even more significant (and here the poet reaffirms the exalted nature of his calling), the eternal meaning expresses itself in the song of the sister/mother/soul.

Anna M. Wittmann

THE HEART

Author: Georg Trakl (1887-1914)
Type of poem: Lyric
First published: 1914, as "Das Herz"; in *Die Dichtungen*, 1918; English translation
collected in *Poems*, 1973

The Poem

"The Heart" is written in thirty-one lines of free verse. Its three stanzas represent
three stages of an emotional experience that moves from fear to a vision and a sense of
reconciliation. The title emphasizes the image that occurs in the first and the last two
lines of the poem and is a metonym for feeling. In the first and third stanzas, the heart
is nevertheless personified. Wild with passion, unruly, and unnerved by fear and anguish, it represents the persona in the first line. In the last two lines, however, it belongs to a female figure, who brings about reconciliation and hope.

In the first stanza, the persona describes feelings that accompany a walk near the
woods on a November evening. The poem begins with the anticipation and fear of approaching darkness and death. As the persona enters the outskirts of town, he observes a group of poor women, who buy cheap food at the slaughterhouse. They receive innards and decaying meat, nourishment that can clearly bring on illness. On the
symbolic level, the nature of this food evokes the inner decay and disintegration of society, because nourishment that sustains life is traditionally blessed, rather than
cursed, as this food is in the persona's thoughts.

Fear, defeat, and mourning for a destroyed past are the predominant feelings of the
second stanza. Instead of experiencing the hoped-for peace of the evening, the persona observes a storm, which he uses as an extended metaphor for war and destruction. Thunder appears as the dark call of a trumpet that runs through the wet, golden
leaves of elm trees, which suddenly appear as a torn flag, yellow as the flag of the
Austrian Empire, the poet's native land. This flag seems to be both bloody and smoking, as if ruined in battle. A man is mourning as he listens to the sounds of the storm in
wild sorrow. The stanza concludes in an exclamation calling for past ages that have
been destroyed and buried following a conflagration, represented by the red evening
sky.

The third stanza is devoted to a vision of a young woman who appears from the
darkness of a door and transforms the devastated environment by means of purity and
love. Sublimation—that is, a vision of her moral elevation and a sense of her supernatural strength—is indicated by the gold that characterizes her figure. The pale moons
that surround her are reminiscent of traditional Catholic light symbolism pertaining to
the Virgin Mary, particularly in her associations with light that shines through the
darkness of the night and suffering. Additional images of nature—of pines felled by
the storm on the side of the mountain, which appears as a fortification—are closely related to the Austrian landscape and suggest a royal court, through which the young

woman attains high social, or even royal, stature. The radiant heart, which illuminates the cool atmosphere of a snowy peak, sharing its clarity, purity, and calm, belongs to her, not to the persona, who nevertheless finds consolation and awe in this vision.

Forms and Devices

"The Heart" consists of a series of brief descriptions of scenes that the persona selects as if to convey a state of mind informed by social and historical awareness of the world. This approach lends expressionistic style to the first two stanzas of the poem, which nevertheless remains primarily symbolistic.

Symbolic dimensions are introduced by means of a fusion of several literary devices—personifications, metaphors, a rich web of adjectives, and color imagery—which resonate with both traditional associations and new connotations acquired through context. Beginning with the "wild heart" of the first line, almost every image is personified. Most images also involve movement and change. Through the multiple associations of the imagery, the poet stresses that traditional associations or expectations no longer hold. Whereas "wild" suggests daring and independence, for example, here it is transformed by fear. Even the evening, presented in the metaphor of a blue dove, arrives without bringing peace or reconciliation.

The interchangeability of inside and outside, observation and feeling, natural phenomenon and historical event, expressed by means of an intricate fusion of imagery, lends the poem emotively rich texture. In the second stanza, for example, a storm is described in metaphors that suggest war, but it is the battle that appears overwhelmingly real, even though it may be only anticipated or feared by the persona. Again, metaphoric structure prevails as historical time, the past that has disappeared, seems to be buried by the evening sky, and the real conflagration of war is suggested.

Color, both named and implied, as in snow, as well as suggested by its absence, as in dark and bare in the first stanza, contributes to the resonance of the poem. The same color tends to recur and absorb new connotative values from the context. Therefore, in addition to their visual effect and symbolic overtones, colors support the poem's movement on the emotive level. For example, in connotations of prosperity and royalty, gold dies into gray in the first stanza and suggests spiritual impoverishment, which is continued in the images of a bare countryside in November and of the group of poor women. In its reference to the monarchy, introduced through the connotations of the golden autumn trees that appear as a torn and besmirched yellow flag, it is destroyed, emphasizing the expected consequences of war. Gold recurs a third time, as a symbol of transcendence brought about by the strength of the human spirit, and contributes to the affirmation of the value of feeling at the end of the poem.

A similar function is performed by the exclamations, which separate descriptive units of the poem, emphasize emotions that accompany the persona's observations, and delineate the poem's structure. Through them, the poem moves from anguish to horror in the first stanza, through intense regret and mourning in the second, to clarification and reconciliation at the end of the poem. The exclamations also add lyric intensity to the poem.

Themes and Meanings

"The Heart" is about social disintegration and the destruction of not only an empire but also a way of life and a historical period, as well as about the strength of the human spirit, which can transcend adversity by means of goodness of the heart. This is the basic theme of the entire oeuvre of the Austrian Georg Trakl, who gave an apocalyptic interpretation of the impending collapse of the Austrian Empire during World War I. In Trakl's poetry, the doom of his native country is foreshadowed by a sense of decay and the social disintegration that affected both the family and the individual.

Trakl's vocabulary denoting decay and his extensive use of color were strongly influenced by the French Symbolist poet Arthur Rimbaud. In the context of Trakl's poems, this imagery acquired new significance, as it came to cluster around his premonitions of the social and political disintegration of his country and his search for personal resolution in poetry and feeling, which he considered redemptive.

Trakl's sense of social disintegration is often conveyed in his presentation of a polarized sister-brother relationship, the friendship, love, guilt, and suffering of two figures who are envisioned as both the same and irrevocably divided. The female figure, which may be associated with the *anima* or spiritual part of a person, is usually sublimated or envisioned as a consoling superior being in Trakl's poems.

This theme is based on the poet's passionate and tragic relationship with his sister, but it is strongly influenced by the Russian novelist Fyodor Dostoevski's figure of Sonia, the heroine of *Prestupleniye i nakazaniye* (1866; *Crime and Punishment*, 1886): Sonia's innate goodness contributed to the preservation of the purity of her heart in spite of adverse and debasing circumstances in her life and to her recognition of the redemptive capabilities of love and the human spirit.

In "The Heart," polarization in the context of the brother-sister theme takes the form of a movement from a wild, fearful, enervated heart that is aware only of decay to the image of a radiant heart that spreads its light over white snow. The associations of redemption touch upon an awareness of the Austrian landscape; the sense of stability and firmness of the past, conveyed by the image of the fortification; and Catholic associations of the pale moons that surround the youthful female figure to whom the radiant heart belongs. Thus Trakl gathers his tradition and heritage in a few lines and extends the hope for personal redemption in spite of a tragic historical event.

Marie Gerenday Tamas

HEART OF AUTUMN

Author: Robert Penn Warren (1905-1989)
Type of poem: Lyric
First published: 1978, in *Now and Then: Poems, 1976-1978*

The Poem

"Heart of Autumn" is a poem of twenty-four lines about an old man who, aware of the limitations of human knowledge, searches for intimations of a divine purpose in the universe. He does this by observing the migrations of wild geese instinctively accomplishing their destiny in the heavens as they fly southward every year in the autumn.

Appearing last in the volume *Now and Then: Poems, 1976-1978*, "Heart of Autumn" was chosen to round out a group of poems in part 2 of the book containing "Speculative" verses, in contrast to "Nostalgic" works in part 1 of the collection. The poem is a compelling exercise in philosophical speculation about the ultimate meaning of human life, in keeping with Robert Penn Warren's remarks about the purpose of literature in his Jefferson Lecture in the Humanities, entitled "Democracy and Literature," delivered in 1975: "What poetry most significantly celebrates is the capacity of man to face the deep, dark inwardness of his nature and fate." The title of the poem bears the double meaning of the ultimate significance of the dying season of autumn for man and nature, and the oneness that the aged speaker comes to affirm between the migratory geese and himself in his pursuit of transcendence at the close of his life.

Stanzas 1 and 2 describe the southward migration of wild geese from the northwest, somewhere in the United States, when suddenly a hunter's shotgun blast violently breaks the V-shaped formation of the birds but cannot for long prevent their recovery of flight and the resumption of the order of nature ("the season's logic").

Stanzas 3 and 4 begin to decipher the lesson of this description of nature for humankind and its mysterious destiny. The aged speaker perceives a difference between unerring brute instinct guiding the geese's heaven-directed flight and his own limited human intelligence in deducing the purpose of his existence.

Stanzas 5 and 6 at first mock human intelligence as a catalyst for error and deception ("Path of logic, path of folly, all/ The same"), contrasting sharply with the laws of nature that govern the instinct of geese on the right "path of pathlessness" in the mysterious beyond. The mocking quickly subsides under the ecstatic experience of the speaker's identification with nature and his transformation into a wild bird winging his way toward the ineffable finality of a heavenly hereafter, in a sunset glow that makes the fall of his life a climactic rising of the human spirit. The mortal words of the poet wind down into a simplicity that is a prelude to the sound of silence ("the imperial utterance" of the geese) in the awesomeness of eternity.

Forms and Devices

"Heart of Autumn" is a lyric poem of six four-line stanzas without end rhymes and without a regular metrical system. Instead, Warren employed relaxed free verse in run-on lines, capturing the speculative, ruminating quality of his exploration of self, nature, and destiny.

Warren's earlier poetry had been strongly influenced by the formal control and the elegant, well-mannered rationality of John Crowe Ransom's verse. Beginning with the volume *Promises* (1957) and revealed fully in the major book-length poem *Audubon: A Vision* (1969), however, Warren's poetic line became more free-flowing and energetic in the modernist mode. A distinguishing mark of his poetry is a passion directed toward the physical world and toward a knowledge of truth. He was a writer full of yearning for more than what life normally discloses and yet full of appreciation of the world that instigated that yearning. In fact, "Heart of Autumn" is the beautiful swan song of a singer who loved life but lusted after intimations of immortality.

Assonance and consonance permeate the poem and help to make up for the absence of metrical rhythms ("Wind-flicker of forest, in perfect formation, wild geese"). An example of metonymy—the use of one word for another, suggesting the effect for the cause—appears in "the *boom*, the lead pellet" (line 4), representing the hunter's shotgun firing at the geese.

Paradox, an apparent contradiction that is somehow true, appears twice: first, in the "path of pathlessness" (line 14), representing the geese's instinctive flight to a mysterious, heaven-directed destiny in accordance with the order of nature; and second, in the "Path of logic, path of folly" (line 17), signifying the error-prone intelligence and foolish wisdom of human beings out of touch with the natural order of things.

The language of the poem alternates between a colloquial informality ("the *boom*") of extreme simplicity ("fall comes") and a philosophical formality ("Process of transformation") that embraces technical vocabulary ("the sounding vacuum of passage"). There are neologisms; Warren turns a noun into a verb ("arrows") and creates other new words by compounding ("Sky-strider," "Star-strider," and "wing-beat"). Warren is also elliptical, reducing the poetic communication of concepts to the briefest spurts of words and phrases, as in lines 4, 14, 17, and 24.

Symbols lie at the heart of the poem's stunning effectiveness. The autumn indicates the speaker's age, the sunset represents death and eternity, and the migratory geese embody the heaven-directed destiny with which the aged speaker identifies through a process of birdlike transformation at the end of the poem.

Themes and Meanings

"Heart of Autumn" is a poem about the discrepancy between the heaven-directed destiny in the natural order of things and a human being's initial ignorance of this eternal fate, which the speaker comes to realize in the end. The poem is a wonderful way for Warren, late in his career, to have presented a statement about the purpose of his long life dedicated to art.

It is, after all, a modern American Romantic poem, following a well-established tradition of searching for meaning about life now and in the hereafter through literary meditations about birds. The motif has been especially popular during the past two centuries in works such as John Keats's "Ode to a Nightingale," Percy Bysshe Shelley's "To a Skylark," Thomas Hardy's "The Darkling Thrush," and Robert Frost's "A Minor Bird."

Particularly close to the subject matter of "Heart of Autumn" is the content of William Cullen Bryant's "To a Waterfowl" and William Butler Yeats's "The Wild Swans at Coole." Unlike Yeats, however, Warren affirmed an identification with the birds being observed to the point of undergoing a birdlike transformation that Keats would have envied. If anything, Warren is more of an escapist Romantic poet than either Yeats or Bryant had been. Bryant may have similarly worried about the hunter's damage to waterfowl but never assimilated himself with the birds. His moralizing observations about God's providence over humans and nature anticipated but did not duplicate Warren's total identification of humans and nature with providence at the conclusion of "Heart of Autumn."

Even before the later poetry appeared, M. L. Rosenthal, in *The Modern Poets: A Critical Introduction* (1960), had noted in Warren's work "a refusal, against the tangible evidence, to accept the tragic irrevocability of the disappointed hope." A hopefulness about human destiny marks "Heart of Autumn," despite the dark notes suggesting a cleavage between humans and nature in the hunter's shooting of geese (lines 4-7) and in the speaker's initial detachment from the geese and his initially limited understanding of them and himself (lines 9-17). Happily, his detachment and ignorance dissolve under a Romantic "Process of transformation," ending the broken bond between humans and nature and speeding the birdlike poet to his rendezvous with destiny in the heavenly beyond.

Thomas M. Curley

HEART'S LIMBO

Author: Carolyn Kizer (1925-   )
Type of poem: Lyric
First published: 1971; collected in *The Nearness of You*, 1986

The Poem

"Heart's Limbo" is written in six free-verse stanzas of varying length. As is typical of a dramatic monologue, the poem's speaker ("I") addresses a silent listener, presumably a potential lover, and through her words reveals her innermost self. From her choice of language ("rolls ready to brown n' serve,/ the concentrated juice"), the speaker appears to be a woman, although she may not necessarily be Carolyn Kizer. She may be a persona, a voice created by the poet.

In Christian tradition, the word "limbo" refers to a place in the afterlife, somewhere between heaven and hell, which is set aside for the innocent souls of the unbaptized. Here the "limbo" of the title carries the more general meaning of a place or state of confinement or neglect, a place where nothing happens. In the poem's central metaphor, the speaker's "maimed" heart has been placed in limbo (literally, in a freezer) for safekeeping and is now being thawed for use.

The poem begins as the speaker tells her listener that she had placed her heart, like a piece of meat, in the frozen food section of her refrigerator to prevent it from spoiling. She has had to remind herself not to snack on it ("It wasn't raspberry yoghurt") and not to give it to the cat by mistake—in other words, to take special care with it. It is not like the other food in her refrigerator. Although she continues to refer to the heart as an object, the rest of the poem makes evident that the heart symbolizes her ability to love.

Someone has come into her life, even though she is not ready: "Suddenly I needed my heart in a hurry." She offers her heart, her frozen love in its "crystal sheath," in its half-thawed, incomplete state, and the prospective lover is not put off by it: "You didn't even wash its blood from your fingertips." He (or possibly she, as the person's gender is not specified) is "not even visibly frightened/ when it began to throb with love." The fifth stanza reveals the speaker's fear. In a series of vivid similes, she compares her heart to an injured animal, a smooth-skinned but treacherous snake, and a defenseless baby bird. The heart is savage, dangerous, yet helpless, even as it lies imprisoned and protected in the warmth of the lover's hands.

The final stanza shifts to a positive note, as the speaker urges her new lover to heal her damaged heart with gentleness and asks in turn for the lover's own heart. It is clear that previous relationships have hurt this woman and that she is now willing to take a great risk in order to encounter love again.

Forms and Devices

When it was initially published in *Poetry* magazine, "Heart's Limbo" consisted of forty-one lines in eight stanzas. Kizer extensively revised the end of the poem before its inclusion in *The Nearness of You*, where she replaced the final three stanzas with a new, succinct quatrain and reduced the number of lines to thirty. Each version ends with a satisfying couplet, one of only two examples of perfect end rhyme in the poem.

Kizer originally began her career as a formalist poet, basing her early poems on strict classical and older Chinese models. In later poems such as this one, she seems to prefer irregular breath lines to the more uniform line created by regular meter and patterned syllables. Yet even though this poem is written in free verse, the iambic foot predominates, which is appropriate for a poem about a heart. The two-syllable iamb, with its accent on the second syllable, has often been identified as a rhythmic echo of a beating heart. In one instance Kizer begins a line with a trochee ("Quicken"), thus shifting the accent to the first syllable and reversing the pattern of the iambs that surround it: "Quicken its beat with your caresses." This shift emphasizes the change in heart rhythm that is being described. When rhyme appears, it is largely incidental, occurring primarily within the lines and emphasized by repeated phrases: "I had to remember not to diet on it./ . . ./ I had to remember not to thaw and fry it."

The image of the frozen heart, that icy organ in stasis, is underscored by words that emphasize its chill: "crystal," "cold and dripping," "numbed." Personified, it appears as a lifeless creature, "not breathing" until the lover's touch restores it. As the heart revives, it begins to "throb" until its final transformation, lying in "your warm fingers' cage." Poet and editor A. Poulin, Jr., has called attention to the "emotional impact" of Kizer's work, "enhanced by her unique intellectual wit and hearty, often stinging, sense of humor," or what Kizer herself has called "the shield of bitter laughter." The image of a wounded heart lying numb among the unbaked rolls and cans of frozen juice is in a sense comic, but her sly humor also serves a serious purpose, to mask and lessen pain.

Kizer employs a related device, her characteristic irony, to highlight the incongruity of everyday household phrases such as "brown n' serve" or "ran out of tuna," as they are placed side by side with more elegant metaphors such as "smooth as a young stone-bathing serpent." One moment the heart is plunged "deep/ among the ice-cubes," and in the next it rests "in its crystal sheath, not breathing," as the language ricochets from the mundane to the (almost) sublime. Through it all, the reader is aware of the speaker's pain.

Themes and Meanings

Certainly "Heart's Limbo" is a poem about the central importance of love in human life, but it seems to focus more on vulnerability—both the risk and pain of love in addition to the intense human need for it. Kizer writes in "A Month in Summer," a long poem that chronicles the end of a love affair, that for her one of the endearing qualities of male Japanese poets is their "overwhelming impulse, when/ faced with hurt or conflict, to stay in bed under/ the covers!" They too understand vulnerability.

Any reader who is familiar with "Pro Femina," Kizer's widely known feminist poem about the status of women, may not at first think of her as a writer who is sensitive to the delicacy of love. However, love has always been one of her primary themes, beginning with her poem "Lovemusic," published in *The New Yorker* when she was only seventeen. Several of the love poems in her first book, *The Ungrateful Garden* (1961), are filled with lush opulence, images from classical mythology, or paradoxes and metaphysical concerns that are vaguely reminiscent of English poet John Donne. "Heart's Limbo," with its contemporary, bloody images, offers an abrupt contrast to the more mannered poems.

    She has written of love in its various guises, including sensuous poems of physical love such as "The Light" and bleak poems of lost love such as "A Widow in Wintertime," where the yowl of mating cats reminds the widow of the fierce animal pleasures to which she "would not return" although she has obviously not forgotten them. Kizer has composed several other poems that might also be identified as love poems and dedicated them to close male and female friends. Still other frequently anthologized poems such as "The Blessing" and "The Great Blue Heron" address the bond that connects mother and daughter. Finally, characteristic of the witty and outspoken author of "Pro Femina" are the tough, ambivalent love-hate poems such as "Bitch," in which she reveals her doggy self.

    In her later work Kizer presents the subject of love directly and without sentimentality. In "Afternoon Happiness," a poem that describes the joy of a happy marriage, she asks, "So how does the poem play/ Without the paraphernalia of betrayal and loss?" She concludes that, in order to be successful, a good love poem must draw on pain rather than happiness as its source. In "Heart's Limbo," which is laden with domestic details such as rolls in the freezer, Kizer opens the poem to the universal experience of love in all its complexity. Her writing is clearly not limited to the lives of women but rather includes them in her observation of the full human condition. Poulin, who published her Pulitzer Prize-winning collection *Yin* in 1984, contends that, "without sacrificing their feminist edge, Kizer's poems are powerful, myth-making hymns" of celebration.

Joanne McCarthy

HEART'S NEEDLE

Author: W. D. Snodgrass (1926-   )
Type of poem: Poetic sequence
First published: 1959, in *Heart's Needle*

The Poem

"Heart's Needle" explores a father's struggle to remain a father to his daughter who, though separated from him by her parents' divorce, maintains regular visits over a two-and-a-half year period. The child is almost three years old at the beginning.

The title comes from an old Irish tale, "The Frenzy of Suibne," about the death of an only daughter, who is "the needle of the heart." In the poem, W. D. Snodgrass suggests that the daughter's presence as well as her absence is a needle in the heart, since both intensify his sense of loss. In a sequence of ten poems, the father speaks to his daughter as she develops into a petulant, asthmatic child whom he must scold. At the same time, her curiosity and independence bring him as much pleasure as pain. In the end, he cannot imagine his world without her.

The poem begins in the winter of 1952, during the Korean War and after the speaker's first marriage has collapsed. Snodgrass is often grouped with the "confessional" poets of the 1960's who wrote autobiographical poems, and parallels with his own marital breakup and separation from his daughter Cynthia are apparent. Throughout the poem, however, Snodgrass clearly establishes that his concerns are as much universal as personal and particular.

In the first four sections, both father and daughter suffer the consequences of the divorce. The daughter (in section 1), once like "a landscape of new snow," gradually forms (in section 2) similarities in behavior with destructive forces (strange dogs, moles). Between a mother who must be appeased and an unhappy father, the child swings like a heavy weight. Her father realizes that she is "love's wishbone" (section 3) and that he, as the seasons pass, remains a nerveless man and an unproductive poet (section 4).

In sections 5 and 6, as a chilling winter turns into spring, the relationship becomes more complex. The child begins to "chatter about new playmates, sing/ Strange songs." He tells her that he has "another wife, another child." As she forgets their old songs, he remembers in more detail—when she was first born, a storm on July 4, a pigeon they caught and let go. The more he remembers, the more he cannot free her, and the more he feels that he should.

The potential destructiveness of this relationship becomes quite evident in section 6. The father says, "You bring things I'd as soon forget"; one of those things is her severe asthma attack one fall. He recalls the scene and believes that she is giving up, passively drowning. He urges her to understand that one is only free when one chooses the time and place for one's death. Yet a major gap exists between what he says and what he does: "Yet I,/ who say this, could not raise/ myself from bed how many days/ to the thieving world." The danger is that they will try to live their lives on ideas unfounded on experience.

Sections 7 through 9 are dominated by increasing emotional contortions for them both. Delightful times remain, but they diminish in number and intensity. The child whines more; she becomes more willful and demanding. He, rising "back from help-lessness," becomes "local law" and punishes her (section 8). In the ninth poem, after a three-month absence from his daughter, the poet/father finds himself writing bitter poems and wandering "among enduring and resigned/ Stuffed animals" of a natural history museum. Among the fixed postures of bobcat, bison, elk, and malignancies encased in jars, the father projects his self-loathing onto the world and its history, wishing that nothing had ever been born. He and the world's "diseased heart" become one.

In the tenth and final poem, the father's experience confirms that only change is permanent: "The vicious winter finally yields/ the green winter wheat." Among the stirrings of spring, father and daughter are together again, briefly but happily. They will not leave each other to separate lives, but like the coons "on bread and water" reach after each other.

Forms and Devices

In an essay on his revisions of "Heart's Needle," particularly of the sixth section, Snodgrass says that he sought a poem that would be both personal and universal, and styles and forms that would adequately express its depth of feeling. The relationship between father and daughter and the considerable grief in the poem, he knew, could lead to sentimentality. He met the challenge, in part, by establishing a formal struc-ture and developing rhymes, accentual syllabics, and varied verse forms that would balance the emotional content. Thus, the poem gives a sense of deep but controlled feeling.

He also made the poem a metaphor. For example, from the outset, section 1, the poet begins to establish the process of seeing one thing as another. The child is born in winter during a war, and her mind is like new snow; here, she is contrasted with the "fouled" snow in which the soldiers freeze. The father's mind is cramped in "that cold war" of marital stand-off, thus connecting him with inert soldiers. Innocence versus experience is suggested. The personal parallels the global. Other images expand this motif: The father is analogous to a tenant farmer viewing his unplowed field or a poet his uncreated drafts. In a world in which survival of the fittest is the norm, the speaker relishes a brief moment of tranquillity before the new variation begins. Throughout the ten sections, the father/child relationship is persistently connected to broad human and natural processes. A matrix of images is established that expands the limits of possible interpretation.

One of Snodgrass's favorite devices is the leitmotif—an image that reappears and becomes more complicated in its associations and meanings. The soldier image, for example, which is identified in section 1 with adults at war and reaffirmed in section 3 through the figure of soldiers grinding their teeth in trenches, reappears in section 8.

This time it is associated with the daughter who, for not eating her evening meal, is sent to her room where, as prisoner, she grates her teeth. The father says that "Assuredly your father's crimes/ Are visited on you." The human and natural processes continue, and she inevitably enters a cold war.

When grinding teeth is linked to cavities, the meaning is modified. The father's reaction to his daughter's pain is as it was for the soldiers—rotting teeth are an expression of sympathy. In section 8, however, when her departure from him as well as her growing independence provide him both pleasure and pain, he says, "Indeed our sweet/ foods leave us cavities." In the civilian world, and especially in that of father/ daughter relationships, cause and effect are more ambiguous than on the frozen turf of war.

Other motifs that Snodgrass develops in this way are the bird, fox, bed, and snow which define event and emotion and provide the sense that meaning evolves from image rather than generalization.

Snodgrass's voice—his tone and attitude toward his subject—is aptly described by critic William Heyen as "urgent but controlled, muted but passionate, unassuming but instructive." To this should be added "reflective but wry." Snodgrass is a witty poet whose language resonates with tropes that deepen one's sense of his sincerity rather than deflect it. His exaggerations—"We huff like windy giants," or "Bad penny, pendulum,/ you keep my constant time," or sitting "like some squat Nero at a feast"—not only are playful but also define mood and relationships at particular moments. Since such figures appear throughout the ten sections and interact with harsher images, the overall tone is not only ironical—balancing between humor and horror—but also consistent with the narrator's search for the basis on which father and daughter can honestly relate to each other.

Themes and Meanings

"Heart's Needle" is about possibilities and limits. On the narrative level, Snodgrass asks if it is possible for a father and daughter to be physically separated, with the attendant distortions of the psyche for both, and still remain a father and daughter. At various points it appears impossible, particularly when the child has asthma attacks, quarrels with her new stepsister, or goes off to another state. Similarly when the father remarries, has a new child, or sinks into paralyzing bitterness, the odds for maintaining a family relationship diminish.

Snodgrass finds that the continuing union, on this level, remains either mysterious, unexplainable, or the result of willful action alone. In section 10, father and daughter go on a picnic and feed the animals, where he reaffirms that "you are still my daughter." The narrative throughout, however, has been sustained by a pattern of interlocking images which from the beginning raises this question: Is it possible in this world for the world to stay together? In Snodgrass's realm, father and daughter are microcosms, parts of a broader network of actions and meanings.

The answer to both questions is finally yes; however, the affirmation is painfully won and quietly expressed. One misses the point of the struggle if one does not understand the connections between different forces at work in the universe. Everything "wails on its oval track." Seasons, war, the food chain, festival holidays, birth and death—all, within the experience of the poet and his daughter, come "back once more/ like merry-go-round horses." That means that shattering storms, frozen soldiers, trapped foxes, cramped minds, and inert emotions—as well as all the viciousness manifested in the fixed, stuffed animals in the museum—are inescapable. "The malignancy man loathes/ is held suspended and persists," the poet says.

The change of seasons brings spring, however; Canada geese return, Easter arrives, peace replaces war, and a child, new seeds, and piglets "come fresh." This, too, remains ineluctable. Monotonous and mechanical the cyclic process may be, but it is experienced reality.

In an early essay, Snodgrass says about ideas in poetry that the discovery of them comes in a variety of ways. The most common and significant ones are inherent in the patterns and language of the poem. To discover that idea, says Snodgrass, "is one of the most exciting events in our world; it has a value quite distinct from any value inhering to the idea *as* idea." He means that paradigms and systems of ideas (political, economic, or theological) are not important, because they are imposed on reality; they frame attitudes and conduct, requiring that a person subordinate individual experience to them. Those ideas that are real and useful actually happen to a person.

The relevance of this observation to "Heart's Needle" is that the experience of father and daughter teaches the father an idea which he applies. He did not come to the relationship with established ideas of The American Family or prescribed codes of conduct. Their particular situation forces them to come to terms with each other. When he tells her that "We try to choose our life" (quite different from saying we are free only when we choose our death), he affirms a range of possibilities that he has discovered: One can choose separation and bitterness, because that is natural and one is free to do so; however, one can also choose union, because that choice is real and as deeply embedded. Thus, the final line, "And you are still my daughter," understood in this context, is both the father's expression of his choice and the undeluded reality that his experience confirms.

Philip Raisor

THE HEAVY BEAR WHO GOES WITH ME

Author: Delmore Schwartz (1913-1966)
Type of poem: Lyric
First published: 1938, in *In Dreams Begin Responsibilities*

The Poem

Delmore Schwartz has been described by the editors of *The Norton Anthology of Modern Poetry* (1973) as a poet concerned about "divisions within his own consciousness," and "The Heavy Bear Who Goes with Me" dramatizes that division. In the poem, Schwartz personifies his own body and gives it a life apart from his consciousness. The speaker of the poem is actually the disembodied mental consciousness of the poet, who offers observations on the physical part of his humanity as if it were a separate being. To dramatize the differences between mind and body, Schwartz describes the body as if it were a bear.

The three irregular stanzas of the poem offer an analysis of the "heavy bear" that seems to accompany the speaker wherever he goes. This "Clumsy and lumbering" creature (line 3) that loves "candy, anger, and sleep" (line 6) carries on an active existence at the speaker's side. The speaker describes the bear as a "factotum," one that acts on behalf of another—in this case, the bear is acting for the speaker, as if the speaker were giving directions but not directly taking part in the experiences which the bear undergoes.

This constant companion that eats and sleeps with the speaker does not seem to be able to communicate coherently; instead, the bear howls to express its feelings. This animalistic cry signals its hunger—for sugar and other sweets—and also its fear. Breaking the spell he has created by suggesting that the bear is simply an unconscious animal who has attached himself to the speaker, Schwartz notes how such fear is engendered by terrifying dreams in which the bear is confronted with notions of death and the nothingness that waits after death. The awareness that "his quivering meat" will one day "wince to nothing at all" (lines 18-19) causes the bear to "tremble"—a word Schwartz uses twice in the same stanza, perhaps to suggest the existential nature of the bear's (and man's) existence.

At the beginning of the final stanza, the narrator stresses that this "inescapable animal" (line 20) which "Moves where I move" (line 22) appears to be a caricature of the self. The flesh-ridden creature is almost an embarrassment to the rather sophisticated narrator, who sees his companion getting in the way when the narrator wishes to be most human. For example, when the narrator's beloved is near, the bear touches her "grossly" (line 30) just at the moment when the narrator wishes to convey some expression of tenderness; the narrator cannot "bare [his] heart" and make his feelings clear to his loved one (line 31). No matter what he does, the narrator is unable to rid himself of his earthy companion, that "drag[s] me with him in his mouthing care" (line 33)—that is, off to satisfy his visceral needs—amid "the hundred million of his kind" (line 34) that have the same bodily desires and demands. The recognition that the bear is but one of so many exactly like him is a subtle reminder that humans, too, no matter how unique they believe they are, share many of their human characteristics with millions of others.

Forms and Devices

"The Heavy Bear Who Goes with Me" is in some ways reminiscent of the short tales that compose the popular medieval *Bestiary*; as the authors of *A Literary History of England, Vol. I: The Middle Ages* (1967) note, in that work descriptions of various animals are "followed . . . by a Christian application or moral." Schwartz uses a similar technique in associating the physical qualities of the bear with those of the human body in order to make a point about the inseparability of the two parts of human nature: the physical self and the spiritual or mental self.

Schwartz follows traditional rules of poetic composition only loosely in this lyric. The irregular stanzas are more like verse paragraphs, each providing separate descriptions of the bear's physical characteristics and his relation to the speaker. Some use is made of rhyme, but no strict patterns emerge; for example, the rhyme scheme of the first stanza is *abcbdeffa*. More common is Schwartz's reliance on some form of stop at the end of each line. All but six of the poem's thirty-five lines are punctuated at the end, and the syntax of the poem demands that the reader pause at the end of three of the unpunctuated lines. This technique mirrors the sense of clumsiness, the halting, lumbering attitude of the bear; readers will find themselves stumbling from line to line, dragged along in the same way the speaker says the bear is "dragging" him along as a constant companion through life.

Schwartz makes extensive use of active verbs to describe the bear's behavior. The animal "climbs," "kicks," "howls," "trembles," "stumbles," and "flounders." He couples these words with nouns and adjectives that further emphasize the bear's physical, brutish nature: The bear is "clumsy," "lumbering," a "central ton" that, wearing a fine suit, ends up "bulging his pants." He is a "caricature," a "stupid clown" that touches someone "grossly." Readers may be reminded of the famous line in Alfred, Lord Tennyson's "Ulysses" in which the hero, back from his twenty years' wandering about the Mediterranean, expresses his disgust with his subjects in Ithaca by calling them "a savage race/ That hoard, and sleep, and feed, and know not me"—the ten monosyllables striking the note of disdain for the same kind of animalistic qualities and lack of consciousness and intellectual sophistication that characterize Schwartz's bear.

The stress on the physical qualities of the bear and the subtle use of end-stopped lines combine to convince readers of the essentially materialistic nature of the body. Schwartz wants readers to understand that the body is different from the spiritual side of man but that there is no way for the spirit or consciousness to escape from its constant companion.

Themes and Meanings

Schwartz provides a clear indication of the theme of "The Heavy Bear Who Goes with Me" in the phrase he affixes to the poem as a kind of subtitle: "the withness of the body." Usually attributed to the philosopher Alfred North Whitehead, this short descriptive epigraph suggests the complex nature of the human condition. Man is a dual creature; he is possessed of a consciousness that gives him a sense of time and of "otherness," but at the same time he is an animal like other animals. Human consciousness exists within a body that demands the same kind of life-sustaining materials and is subject to the same kinds of appetites—for food, for physical comforts—as other, lower creatures. Further, no matter how unique any man thinks he is, he cannot deny that he has bodily needs remarkably similar to the "hundred millions of his kind" (line 34); this sobering thought is meant to counterbalance the vanity men feel in promoting their own individuality.

The poet is dramatizing the long-debated issue of man's dual nature. The only creature on earth possessing a sophisticated consciousness that gives him a moral sense and an understanding of the consequences of his actions, man is nevertheless compelled to exist in a material body that is really as much a part of him as is his higher intelligence. No matter how hard he tries, man is never able to separate his spiritual nature from his physical side.

Schwartz's extended descriptions of the bear are intended to suggest the physical conditions under which the human body exists. All animals—including the human animal—crave the physical comforts that this bear seeks. Further, many of the actions that humans take are indeed reminiscent of the clumsy behavior of this dumb bear; humans, Schwartz is saying, are often embarrassed by their bodies. At those moments when consciousness wants people to be most human—when a situation calls for erudition or sensitivity, for a clear statement to others that would help one express exactly what one thinks or feels—the material side of human nature seems to get in the way, to be like the lumbering bear, a creature that fumbles and gropes in a most unhuman way to make the expressions of consciousness apparent to the outside world.

Laurence W. Mazzeno

HEBREW MELODIES

Author: Heinrich Heine (1797-1856)
Type of poem: Poetic sequence
First published: 1851, as "Hebräische Melodien," in *Romanzero*; English translation
   collected in *The Complete Poems of Heinrich Heine*, 1982

The Poems

"Hebrew Melodies," Heinrich Heine's series of three poems, written in 1851, constitutes the third and final section of *Romanzero*, a collection published that year
and also containing groups of "Historien" (Tales) and "Lamentationen." The title
Romanzero suggests old-fashioned romantic ballads, but the volume is actually a
compendium of sophisticated mid-nineteenth century poetry. The title of the sequence was suggested to Heine by the "Hebrew Melodies" of George Gordon, Lord
Byron (1815), though the two sets of poems have little or nothing in common. Heine's
poems reflect both continuity and change as far as his attitude toward Judaism and his
Jewishness was concerned.

The first poem, "Prinzessin Sabbath" ("Princess Sabbath"), consists of thirty-eight
unrhymed stanzas that present a warmly appreciative picture of the Sabbath observance in a synagogue. On the eve of the Jewish day of rest, Israel—that is, a Jew—is
freed temporarily from the witch's curse that has transformed him into a dog, and he
enters the synagogue as a prince ready to meet his princess, the personification of the
Sabbath, who is as humble and quiet as she is beautiful. The poet describes the richly
symbolic festive bustle in the house of worship as the cantor intones the traditional
chant *L'khah dodi likrat kallah* ("Come, beloved [or my friend] the bride awaits
you"), which Heine erroneously credits to Don Jehuda ben Halevy. (The real author is
Salomo ben Moshe Alkabez.) Instead of a smoke, which is prohibited on the Sabbath,
the princess promises her beloved the culinary delight of *schalet* (or cholent, a slowly
simmered bean stew). Such treats evoke visions of biblical scenes, but the waning of
the Sabbath threatens to force the observant Jew to resume his dog's life. Heine ends
his poem with a description of the traditional havdalah ceremony: Smelling a spice
box keeps the worshipers (whom the need to bid the Sabbath farewell has saddened
and weakened) from fainting, and a few drops from a goblet of wine serve to extinguish the candle and, with it, the Sabbath.

In a letter dated August 21, 1851, Heine called "Jehuda ben Halevy" his most beautiful poem. It is the longest in this sequence—four sections containing twenty-four
stanzas and almost nine hundred lines—yet it is a fragment. The poem has an elegiac
beginning and undertone as the poet, in his mourning for the devastated Jerusalem, invokes the exemplary figure of Jehuda ben Halevy (more properly, Judah Halevy, a
scholar, physician, and poet who was born in Toledo around 1075 and is believed to
have died in Cairo around 1141). In flowery fashion, Heine describes the making of a
poet and his study of the Torah and the Talmud—the latter divided into the polemical,

legalistic Halaka, which is likened to a fencing school for dialectical athletes, and the Agada, the didactic part, which Heine compares to a phantasmagoric garden. Yet Halevy is not viewed as a parochial poet; Heine integrates him into the mainstream of Christian medieval Europe by calling him fully equal to the great Provençal poets—though his muse was not some lady love but Jerusalem, whose destruction he deplores. Following an old legend, Heine has the poet killed by a Saracen horseman while in the holy land as a penitent, but his conjecture that Halevy's killer may have been an angel in disguise sent by God to take the poet to his eternal home is original with him.

In a lengthy digression, Heine concerns himself with jewels found by Alexander the Great after his victory over the Persian king Darius in 331 B.C.E., specifically the wondrous wanderings of a pearl necklace. The poet says that if he owned Alexander's golden casket, he would use it to store the teardrop pearls of lamentations. Another digression involves Heine's French wife, whose limited education did not include the poetic golden age of Spanish Jewry. Heine uses this excursus to pay tribute to the other great poets of that age, Salomon ben Judah ibn Gabirol of Malaga and Moses ibn Ezra of Granada. After musing about the origin of "schlemiel," the word and the concept, Heine ends with the story of Gabirol's death in Cordova at the hands of an envious Moorish neighbor.

"Disputation" consists of 110 rhymed stanzas, the rhyme scheme being *abcb*. The witty narrator gives a grimly hilarious account of a fourteenth century public debate between the Franciscan friar José and Rabbi Juda of Navarre at the Toledo court of King Pedro I of Castile and his queen, the fragile Frenchwoman Blanche of Bourbon (Donna Blanca). The question to be settled is which is the true God, the threefold Christian God of love or the Hebrews' stern one God, Jehovah. Since the loser will have to adopt the religion of the winner, each debater has eleven assistants standing by with baptismal basins or circumcision knives. After exorcising some Jewish devils, the friar gives an absurd account of Christian beliefs, crudely likening Jews to various beasts. His vulgar rhetoric and violent threats conflict with his promises of gentleness and love. Making little more sense, the more rationalistic rabbi emphasizes that Jehovah is a strong, living presence and holds out the prospect of the faithful feasting on the succulent flesh of the legendary Leviathan, God's favorite fish. The arguments and counterarguments of the two zealots having become increasingly heated and vituperative in this twelve-hour marathon, the king asks the queen for her judgment, and her somewhat unsettling decision is that both of them "stink."

Forms and Devices

Writing about "Hebrew Melodies," Louis Untermeyer, one of numerous poets and scholars who have undertaken to render Heine's poetry into English, states that Heine's background, diction, and emotions are characteristically Jewish in his celebration of the senses and that the poet's Jewish flavor is not bittersweet, as has often been observed, but sweet and sour, the heritage of generations of cultural pungency. Such a statement may not evoke universal agreement, but it is suggestive, for these particular poems reflect Heine's complex sense of Jewishness and contain a variety of devices that serve to reveal as well as mask his ambivalence about his Jewish background. The poet does so through exceptionally colorful and luxuriant language and with abundant biblical and broadly cultural allusions. When Heine was working on the "Hebrew Melodies," he had been living in exile for two decades and wasting away in what he called his *Matratzengruft* ("mattress grave," or "crypt") for more than three years, slowly dying of a venereal disease. This circumstance gave his late writings heightened immediacy and urgency. "Jehuda ben Halevy," and to some extent "Princess Sabbath," the only melodious poems of the sequence, were inspired by a book published in 1845, *Die religiöse Poesie der Juden in Spanien*, a magisterial study of the religious poetry of medieval Spanish Jewry by Michael Sachs, a Berlin rabbi and pupil of Leopold Zunz, a scholar to whom Heine had been close prior to his conversion in 1825.

In the "Hebrew Melodies," the mercurial, often impish poet, a practiced dispeller of moods and destroyer of illusions, delights in juxtaposing different worlds in ingenious and amusing, sometimes confusing fashion. Heine's ingenious wordplay, linguistic drolleries, stylistic shifts, discursiveness, abrasive diction, and mixture of the exalted and ironically deflated are deliberate and sometimes brilliant poetic devices. His penchant for digressions and discord is in evidence throughout as Heine superimposes an irreverent nineteenth century perspective on older traditions. Facts and legends, as well as symbols and reality, intermingle wondrously as pathos and trivia alternate, heartfelt sentiments give way to critical comment, and discussions of momentous events and important figures deteriorate into private gossip and satiric sniping. For example, in "Jehuda ben Halevy," Heine, who tended to ridicule his Jewish contemporaries, satirizes Julius Eduard Itzig, a converted Jew (and noted Berlin jurist) who changed his name to Hitzig, and the poet wonders whether the additional letter indicates a pretension to holiness.

Heine's exploration of the luckless schlemiel, an exercise in mock scholarship, leads him to ask whether the poet, particularly the Jewish poet, is not the quintessential schlemiel, the innocent, the scapegoat. In "Princess Sabbath," the poet's praise of cholent, that kosher ambrosia, culminates in a parody of Friedrich Schiller's "Ode to Joy" (known from Ludwig van Beethoven's Ninth Symphony). The reference to *Tausves-Jontof* (more correctly, *Tosafot Yomtov*), a sixteenth century critical commentary, in the context of a fourteenth century disputation may have been a deliberate anachronism, but other slips, such as his reference to a mezuzah (which is not found at the entrance of a synagogue), are indicative of Heine's limited knowledge of Hebrew and Jewish lore. "Disputation," a grotesque variant of a medieval tournament or athletic contest, has a deliberately discordant, sardonic, and sinister tone, because an unsparing exposure of the clerical mind, as bombastic as it is intolerant, clearly calls for black humor. It is hardly accidental that the last word of that poem, and the entire collection, is *stinken*.

Themes and Meanings

In an afterword to *Romanzero*, dated September 30, 1851, Heine says that, like a prodigal son, he has returned to the idea of a personal God and, having dwindled down to a spiritual (as well as physical) skeleton, he is ready to make his peace with God and the world. It is tempting to believe that after yielding to the blandishments of atheism, Hellenism, and polytheism, Heine is returning to his Jewish roots. There is evidence that the ailing Heine did return to monotheism and identify with the suffering Jewish people, but this identification was paralleled by continued inward detachment from significant aspects of the Jewish religion. In "Princess Sabbath" and "Jehuda ben Halevy," Heine gives a sympathetic account of Jewish religious practices and cultural contributions, and he sensitively delineates the tragically dualistic existence of the Jewish people. The second poem contains a paradigmatic picture of an idealized poet with whom Heine seems to feel a spiritual affinity; Jehuda ben Halevy's writings appear to be divinely inspired, and he acts as a pillar of fire in the desert of the Diaspora. "Disputation," however, contains a clear-cut rejection of Jewish (or any other) dogmatism, proselytic fanaticism, and hidebound self-righteousness. As S. S. Prawer has pointed out, "Princess Sabbath" presents a skillful fusion of caricature, allegory, realism, and symbolism, of light and darkness, the poetic and the prosaic—a poignant insight into what centuries of oppression, persecution, and martyrdom have done to the Jewish psyche. "Hebrew Melodies," then, begins with a touching tribute to the spiritual and aesthetic qualities and rewards of Judaism and ends with a condemnation of what may be called an extreme representative of the Jewish faith. The poet was a free spirit and an ambivalent person to the end, and Heine would not have been Heine if he had been otherwise.

Harry Zohn

THE HEIGHTS OF MACCHU PICCHU

Author: Pablo Neruda (Neftalí Ricardo Reyes Basoalto, 1904-1973)
Type of poem: Narrative
First published: 1946, as *Alturas de Macchu Picchu*; in *Canto general*, 1950; English
translation collected in *Pablo Neruda: Five Decades, a Selection (Poems, 1925-1970)*, 1974

The Poem

The Heights of Macchu Picchu is a long narrative poem forming book 2 of Pablo Neruda's monumental choral epic, *Canto general* (general song), a text comprising 250 poems and organized into twelve major divisions, or cantos. The theme of *Canto general* is humankind's struggle for justice in the New World. "The Heights of Macchu Picchu" is itself divided into twelve sections; it is written in free verse.

The poet, adopting the persona of the native South American man, walks among the ruins of the great Inca city Macchu Picchu, built high in the mountains near Cuzco, in Peru, as a last, and vain, retreat from the invading Spanish conquerors. It is a poem of symbolic death and resurrection in which the speaker begins as a lonely voyager and ends with a full commitment to the American indigenous people, their Indian roots, their past, and their future.

The first poem of the sequence opens with the image of an empty net, sifting experience but gathering nothing. This opening reveals that the speaker is drained by the surface of existence; he searches inward and downward for a hidden "vein of gold." He then sinks lower, through the waves of a symbolic sea, in a blind search to rediscover "the jasmine of our exhausted human spring," an erotic symbol associated with a lost paradise.

The second poem contrasts the enduring world of nature with the transitory goals of human beings, who drill natural objects down until they find that their own souls are left dead in the process. The speaker recalls that in his urban existence he often stopped and searched for the eternal truths he once found in nature or in love. In city life, humans are reduced to robotlike machines with no trace of the "quality of life" in which Neruda still believes. The question of where this quality of life can be found remains unanswered for three further poems; the search for truth, in the poet's opinion, is a gradual and humbling process.

This search for truth is the subject of the third poem, which confronts modern humankind's existence directly. This existence is likened to husking corn off the cob; urban dwellers die "each day a little death" in their "nine to five, to six" routine life. The speaker compares a day in the life of the urban people to a black cup whose contents they drain while holding it in their trembling hands. In this poem, Neruda prepares the way for the contrasting image of Machu Picchu, which is later described in its "permanence of stone."

The fourth poem shows the speaker enticed by not only "irresistible death" but also the life and love of his fellow man. This love remains unrealizable, however, as long as all he sees in his fellow man is his daily death. His own experience in the urban context progressively alienates him from others, dragging him street by street to the last degrading hovel, where he ultimately finds himself face-to-face with his own death.

The short fifth poem defines this kind of death even more closely in a series of seemingly surrealistic images, leaving a final vision of modern life with nothing in its wounds except wind that chills one's "cold interstices of soul." In this poem, the speaker is at his lowest spiritual point in the entire sequence.

Then, quite abruptly, the mood of the poem begins to rise in the sixth section as the speaker climbs upward in space toward the heights of Machu Picchu and backward in time toward the moment when that ancient city was created. At that moment in time, all lines converge, past and present. Here, "two lineages that had run parallel" meet and fuse, that is, the line of inconsequential human beings and their petty deaths and the line of permanence in the recurring cycles of nature.

Machu Picchu is the place where "maize grew high" and where men gathered fleece to weave both funereal and festive garments. What endures in this place is the collective permanence those men created. All that was transitory has disappeared, leaving only "the lonely precinct of stone."

Section 7 picks up this contrast between what endures and what has vanished. The speaker sees "the true, the most consuming death" as having slain those ancient men—their death being nobler because it was a collective experience. What they left behind was their citadel "raised like a chalice in all those hands," their blood to make "a life of stone." The speaker believes that he can "identify" with the absolute "Death" he finds on the heights, but his search for this death also has been a search for a more positive kind of identity and for identification through nature with his fellow men. The speaker's journey teaches him—more by means of feeling than by means of thought—to see new facets of the truth, both about himself and about the nature of existence. The journey does not end, however, with the discovery of the city.

The speaker's hopeful mood lasts through the next two poems: the eighth poem, with its vivid evocation of nature, pre-Columbian man, and his gods all fused together in an all-embracing love that the poet summons up from the past to transform the present and to anticipate the future; and the ninth, a solemn chant, building up to a final pair of lines that bring the reader starkly back to both the ancient men who built the citadel and their destination—time.

The poem's last major turning point comes with the question opening its tenth section: "Stone within stone, and man, where was he?" The speaker begins to speculate about whether the people who built ancient America may not have been similar to modern urban people and whether the citadel might not have been erected on a base of human suffering. The speaker wonders in what conditions these people, possibly slaves, lived.

In the eleventh section, the speaker attempts to go beyond the weave of matter until he can hold "the old unremembered human heart" in his hand, seeing behind the "transcendental span" of Machu Picchu to the invisible "hypotenuse of hairshirt and salt blood" implied by the geometry of those ruins. The speaker concludes that humankind is what matters because "man is wider than all the sea"; the poet wishes to acknowledge all the people who died building this city so that they may be reborn with him and through them as his "brothers."

What really matters to the speaker at the end of the poem is that which his own experience has in common with the experience of other human beings. He also needs to reveal people to themselves in such a way that they can feel the identity behind their separate lives and share his insight.

Forms and Devices

The major symbol of the poem is that of Machu Picchu itself. In Neruda's poem, Machu Picchu becomes the center of a tangled web of associations with disparate and intertwining strands. It is by no means a clear-cut symbol, for its meaning shifts as the poem's strong current of emotions alternates between past and present, but the speaker's journey gradually takes on the nature of a highly personal "venture into the interior" in which he explores both his own inner world and the past of the Latin American people. There is no explicit mention of the city until the sixth of the twelve poems that form the sequence, the earlier sections covering not the poet's physical journey but a kind of pilgrimage through human life in search of meaningful truth. When the poet does reach Machu Picchu, its heights turn out to be the place from which all else makes sense, including his own continent.

Machu Picchu as a natural and human symbol is the pivotal force around which both the natural and religious imagery of the poem is focused. During the speaker's descent into the heart of meaning, the presence of matter, both inorganic and organic, is significant as a symbol of inescapable reality. The speaker touches stone, earth, roots, trees, rain, clouds, and space in the course of his journey. Each line of the poem, each metaphor, brings this matter closer to human experience, specifically to human sexuality, until the speaker says, "I sank my tempestuous sweet hand/ into the most genital recesses of the earth."

Christian symbolism and imagery also inform the poem. Yet Neruda does not embrace theology in his epic and philosophical vision. Although the speaker has questions about the nature of humankind during his search for truth, there is no God or gods beside him or above him. He will reach the high stone pinnacles of the sacred city Machu Picchu, a city built by humans to the greater glory of their gods, but the gods have departed. No mention is made of the divine forces that moved the Incas to haul huge stones to build the sacred city as a last refuge from the advance of the Spaniards and the religion they wanted to impose. Only the stones remain, an echo of the ancient fervor of the old faith.

Neruda often uses Christian imagery in the poem to heighten a vital point, bringing in varied associations without implying the literal truth of the concepts. In line with the Christian imagery, the language of the ninth poem of the sequence is that of a solemn chant, or litany, to Machu Picchu, describing the site with eighty-four epithets. Not a single verb appears in this fragment, which is composed in the style of a liturgical litany, with an abundance of repetitive phrases. Also, when in the final poem, the speaker asks the builders of the ancient city to show him the places of their agony, he uses language that links their sufferings to the stations of the cross.

Themes and Meanings

The major themes of Neruda's poem are death and regeneration. These themes are primarily realized through the speaker's cyclic journey (similar to those in the Bible or in Dante's *The Divine Comedy*, c. 1320). The speaker explores the cosmos, penetrates the earth to its secret chambers, ascends toward light from the roots through the stems of plants, and identifies with the stones of the huge sacred city. The speaker serves as primitive human, as prophet, and, ultimately, as semidivinity, searing through space and through history, bringing the reader with him on an incredible voyage, an adventure to the end of the earth. A strange poetic time machine allows the speaker to swim upstream in the flow of time, exploring nature, humankind, history, and visions of the future.

The speaker's magic powers have taken him first down into the earth, through seas of darkness. Then, he ascends the ladder. Climbing, he goes through the thickets toward the tall city rocked in a "wind of thorns," the city that is like a spade buried in primordial sand, the city made out of stone. The speaker beckons to the reader to "climb up" with him.

On this journey, the overwhelming presences are those of nature in all of its power and those of ghostly ancient men who came to terms with nature many centuries ago. Both presences fuse in a moment of love and recognition, and the past becomes the present.

What the speaker finds in his vertical pilgrimage is not God or the gods, however, but the traces of a destroyed civilization: the ashes of a ruined kingdom and the signs of its priests, its women, its children, and its slaves. Everywhere, the footprints of humankind are present: everywhere, matter has been penetrated. Beneath each stone, the speaker senses a presence from the past, and the initial sense of loneliness gives way to joy. The gods may have vanished, but the presence of humankind endures. Identity and brotherhood infuse the key words of the poem's climactic end: "I am here to speak for your dead lips." Only thus are the ancient ghosts placated. In the speaker's identification with his ancestors, he becomes one of them. The speaker has come into contact with death and resurrection. It is the awakening of an identification and a commitment of solidarity with the Americas past, present, and future.

Thus, *The Heights of Macchu Picchu* is a poem of symbolic death and resurrection in which the speaker himself participates as an actor, beginning as a lonely voyager and ending with the manifestation of his full commitment to the collectivity of the American indigenous people: their cultural roots, their past, and their future.

Genevieve Slomski

HELIAN

Author: Georg Trakl (1887-1914)
Type of poem: Lyric
First published: 1913, as "Helian"; in *Die Dichtungen*, 1918; English translation collected in *Modern German Poetry, 1910-1960*, 1962

The Poem

Georg Trakl wrote "Helian" in December of 1912 and January of 1913, in the darkest time of the year. Shortly afterward, he referred to it in a letter as the most precious and most painful thing he had written. As is all of his work, it is highly autobiographical.

"Helian," at ninety-three lines, is Trakl's longest poem. The stanzas are short and of irregular length, ranging from two to seven lines, and are grouped into five main sections. Some of the material from the "Helian" manuscripts subsequently found its way into shorter poems, so critics now speak of the " 'Helian' complex," which consists of "Helian," "Evening Song," "Rosary Songs," and "Decline."

There has been considerable speculation about the origin and meaning of the title, with critics comparing it to names and titles having variant spellings. Only Gunther Kleefeld has been able to relate the name Helian as it stands to a discernible pattern in Trakl's work; namely, the linguistic juxtapositioning of brother and sister pairs. Elis is the brother of Elisabeth, Georg of Georgine, Narziss of Narzisse, and Helian of Helianthus. Helianthus is the botanical name for a sunflower, which Trakl identifies in one poem as Helian's sister. He himself often appears in his poems as the sun god or the sun boy. He expressed the need for the sort of living conditions in which sunflowers thrive: plenty of light, plenty of warmth, and a quiet beach. In reading "Helian," one should keep in mind that it was written at the time of the year when the sun boy would feel most alienated.

The opening lines of the poem establish the positive effects that the sun, its color, yellow, and the summer have on Helian. He is at peace with himself, his friends, and the world. Likewise, the almost parallel account of autumn that follows contains mainly realistic descriptions of the beauty of the season. The sun is still present, shining into storerooms, and one is almost inclined to disregard the few lines that seem ominously out of place.

The second section of the poem, lines 22 through 38, is framed by depictions of a ravaged garden and black November destruction. Nature is no longer beautiful, but threateningly ugly. Only when walking past friendly rooms does Helian experience harmony that is reminiscent of his mood in summer. Once fully inside, however, in the house of his fathers, Helian is horrified by the decline of his family. His sisters are degraded. His soft eyes are beaten with nettles, and he falls ill. Winter follows.

Section 4, lines 60 through 80, is tripartite. Visions of idyllic existences are contrasted with the agonies of the tortured, the leprous, and the decomposed. The poem ends with Helian's madness in black rooms. He ponders the darker end, and God silently sinks his blue eyelids over him.

Forms and Devices

"Helian" is an extraordinarily complex poem. The overall process it describes is one of tragic personal decline. One may assume that the poetic persona is Trakl. In the progression of the poem, there is a complete inversion in outlook. The first section contains only two negative lines, the last only two positive ones. Serenity and clarity give way to horror and blackness. The most beautiful landscapes yield to nightmarish visions. The best of the outer world is replaced by the worst of the inner world. Trakl has carried to extremes the literary convention of using the changing seasons to represent the human life cycle. In "Helian," the warmth and light of summer turns into the cold and dark of winter, forcing the main character from the healthy outdoor environment back into his parents' house, from extroversion to introversion, from sanity to madness.

Walls play a major role in "Helian." The transformation they undergo in the first half of the poem parallels Helian's mental deterioration. Walls are rigid constructions that in Trakl's work represent self-control and the successful repression of certain urges. The fact that Helian is not surrounded by walls but is walking along them indicates that he is continuing to function with a sense of direction.

In the opening lines, the walls are yellow, a reflection of Helian's sunny mood in the summer season. In autumn, he walks along red walls, perhaps a warning signal, since red is the color of fire and of blood. It is not entirely clear that things have gone wrong, however, until in November he walks along walls full of leprosy. Trakl views ugliness as a product of hatred. He is beginning to resent the self-imposed restrictions and describes the veneer of civilization as loathsome. Significantly, there follows a sympathetic reference to the poet Hölderlin, the "holy brother," who became mad. Finally, in the third and central section of the poem, the walls come down. Black walls collapse on the spot. Helian has let down all restraints; he enters the empty house of his fathers, and malign elemental forces are unleashed.

Just as warm, sunny days may occur in late autumn, "Helian" derives much of its poignancy from the fluctuations between sanity and madness within the overall process of decline. Repeatedly, the poet presents the reader with positive images that give rise to the hope that Helian will be able to pull himself back up out of the depths. Each time, however, he sinks back lower than he was before. These are the steps of madness to which he refers in the fifth section. The suspense one feels in view of these sustained vacillations is heightened by Trakl's repeated references to evening and to night, which keep the poem hovering symbolically on the edge of light.

Themes and Meanings

The meaning of Trakl's poetry eluded critics for more than seventy years. His surprising and apparently unconnected images were dismissed by frustrated readers as the word salad of a schizophrenic whose problems were exacerbated by his dependency on cocaine. Yet the poems continued to be read for the compelling beauty of their language, which in the original German is unequalled.

A breakthrough in understanding Trakl came in 1985, with the publication of Gunther Kleefeld's monumental psychoanalytical study *Das Gedicht als Sühne* (the poem as penance). Based on the known facts of Trakl's biography and remarks in his letters, it presents Freudian interpretations of his poetic images as products of conflicting primal forces in Trakl's mind. The recurrent themes that emerge are Trakl's hatred of his mother for withdrawing from her children, his resultant incestuous relationship with his sister, and his criticism of his father for not providing enough guidance and control. Dark thoughts and demoniac actions stem from the id (the unconscious, instinctual area of the psyche), which may be restrained or punished by the superego (the moral, social area of the psyche and seat of the conscience); hence, the extreme contrasts in the imagery.

Applying this schema to "Helian," one encounters the id first of all in line 5, personified as the son of Pan asleep in gray marble. It is impossible for this side of Trakl's personality to be banished completely. The best the superego can do is to encase the demon in stone and hope that he continues to sleep. In this opening description of summer, Helian gets through the evening and even the night safely. In the evening, he drinks brown wine in the company of friends.

Once the season turns to autumn, however, increasing the distance between Helian and the sun, on which he is so heavily reliant, the dark thoughts surface. Line 5 of this part at first seems quite out of place and nonsensical in itself: "In the evening, the white water sinks into burial urns." This, however, is clearly the first resentful reference in "Helian" to Trakl's mother. Reviewing the context of the preceding lines, one sees that Helian actually has three reasons to feel abandoned. Not only is the sun slowly drawing away from him, but Helian has also just witnessed the flight of the birds, who are going south for the winter. Furthermore, although it is evening again, the drinking parties on the terrace seem to have stopped for the year, leaving a void. There is nothing to drink, just as there was nothing to drink when he was denied his mother's milk, when the white water, intended as the food of life, was misdirected to the ashes of the dead, when things went wrong right at the start. Now, everyone is leaving him again, the sun and the birds and his friends. The present emotional state is symbolically associated with a similar emotional state from early childhood. The line makes perfect sense.

As "Helian" progresses, the poem consists increasingly of such images from the subconscious, so that a very close reading is required—one, in fact, that presupposes familiarity with Trakl's oeuvre.

Jean M. Snook

HENCEFORTH, FROM THE MIND

Author: Louise Bogan (1897-1970)
Type of poem: Lyric
First published: 1931; collected in *The Sleeping Fury*, 1937

The Poem

The four brief six-line stanzas of "Henceforth, from the Mind" express a sense of the sublimation of passion and emotion integrated into the life of the mind and imagination. Throughout, an unidentified speaker addresses an unnamed "you": The meditative and contemplative language and tenor of the poem suggest that "you" is really the speaker, addressing his or her interior life.

The first stanza is a single sentence. The first line is the same as the title, and the speaker tells the listener that from this point in time all happiness to be enjoyed will come from the mind. Although the source of such joy may be traceable to material things—which would include the pleasures of the flesh—the future enjoyment of these pleasures will be an imaginative and mental one. The last two lines add an independent clause, making the assertion that it will be the speaker's thought that will endow time and place with significance and honor. The implication is that such time and place may be present in fact, or in memory and imagination; in either case, it is the mind that creates their meaning.

The second stanza makes a parallel statement with regard to language, asserting that language alone will, in the future, produce the kind of happiness that the listener had formerly thought, in youth, would be the concomitant of passionate desire. The speaker elaborates on the youthful illusion of the power of passion in a set of parallel clauses suggesting the violence of emotions that seem to wrench the person physically, to stab one to the heart even to a sense of dying.

The last of the poem's three sentences comprises the twelve lines of the last two stanzas. Here, the speaker varies the "henceforth" that has opened the first two stanzas by introducing the third stanza with "henceforward." The speaker elaborates a description of a seashell, which, held to the ear, seems to reproduce the rhythmic sound of the ocean surging back and forth over the sand. The sound is characterized in an interpolated clause as a subdued, almost suppressed sound that speaks to the listener from profound depths, but that nevertheless marks the changes of time, notes growth and ripening, and brings forth beauty from a state of agitated calm. In the last two lines, the speaker returns from the interpolated clause with two more repetitions of the word "henceforth"; the shell that began the sentence is now seen to be the source of the speaker's mental, emotional, and cognitive life. From this shell, the entire universe will "echo": that is, the listener's world will, henceforth, be one composed entirely of the inner experience of mind and imagination.

Forms and Devices

"Henceforth, from the Mind" has a particularly tight metrical scheme. The basic rhythm is iambic trimeter, with few, but subtle, variations. The first lines of the first and second stanzas, each opening with the word "henceforth," are headless, beginning with a stressed syllable and containing only five, instead of six, syllables. The third line of the last stanza, "Will sound you flowers," and the penultimate line of the poem, "henceforth, henceforth," are iambic dimeter. There is one foot that deviates from the iambic pattern: The antepenultimate line begins with the trochee "Born under," a stressed syllable followed by an unstressed one, reversing the iambic pattern throughout the rest of the poem. The second and fourth lines of the fourth stanza, however, end in feminine rhymes: "wondered" and "sundered." The meter is highly regular and supported by a close rhyme scheme. The first four lines of each stanza rhyme in a quatrain pattern of *abab*, with the last two lines forming a couplet. The only variation is the slight off-rhyme of the last couplet pairing "henceforth" and "earth."

Such a strongly marked rhythmic and rhyme scheme in a poem with very short lines often produces a mechanical, sing-song effect. That rule does not hold true in this poem because of the interplay between long-vowel syllables in unstressed positions. In the second line, "whole joy," and in the third line, "may find," are feet in which the unstressed syllable (whole, may) contains a long vowel: This attenuates the distinction between the stressed and unstressed syllables and makes the rhythm less heavily marked, less "bouncy" than is often the case with a heavily accented trimeter line. The same is true in the second stanza with the foot "you to" in the fourth and fifth lines, and in the third stanza with "wherein" and "you heard." This device—together with the variations in rhythm obtained from lines that employ enjambment, variation in placement of caesura, and slight differences in line length from headless lines and feminine rhymes—creates a graceful, nuanced rhythm with a subtle music.

"Henceforth, from the Mind" is an example of the plain style identified in Renaissance poets such as Ben Jonson and continuing through the tradition of English poetry down to twentieth century exemplars such as Louise Bogan. The style is characterized by controlled emotion—which may nevertheless be extremely intense—by precision of diction and by little or no figurative language or rhetorical ornamentation. Bogan uses only one extended metaphor: the shell of the last two stanzas, which is said to contain the "smothered sound" that acts as a clock, "chiming" the passing of time to the listener and that will "sound" the listener "flowers." What these flowers stand for specifically is never really clear, simply as a single tenor for the metaphorical shell is not explicitly indicated: Whether it is meant to be the listener's ear as the organ of hearing (corresponding to speech implied in the "tongue" of the second stanza), or whether it stands for the whole of the listener's imaginative and intuitive faculties, the poem does not explain.

Themes and Meanings

The theme of renunciation rings strongly in this poem, balanced with equal strength by the sense of peace and dignity that comes with acceptance and knowledge of what is being renounced, and pleasure in the alternative gains that renunciation of physical pleasures may bring. In the first stanza, for example, the speaker may belittle the possibility of finding much joy in "earthly things"; the listener's mind, however, in endowing time and place with the "grace" (of attention, esteem, or memory), which mind and imagination can give, will actually create a much richer experience than the meager joys that any mere "thing" can afford. The contrast being drawn between "thing" and "thought" focuses the speaker's argument. The promise of future serenity emerges through the sentence structure in the description of the speaker's mind as the peaceful ground of an experience that will happen of itself: "Joy" will spontaneously "spring" from the mind, as "time and place will take" the listener's thought in an equally spontaneous experience of "grace."

The second stanza continues the sense of peaceful detachment from struggle, even though the struggle would have brought joy that—in the past, in the listener's imagination—would have had almost physically painful effects. There is the merest hint of the figure of cupid in the figure of joy that could "pierce you to the heart," but the clichéd picture remains entirely subordinated to the more inclusive sense of "joy." Indeed, here the speaker seems to promise that a purer delight may emerge from "shallow speech alone," for such happiness, the speaker says, "will come," and without the wrenching pain of erotic passion.

The last two stanzas are the poem's most complex statement, both rhetorically and grammatically. The powers of the imagination are invoked in the figure of the shell, which can create in the listener's mind a whole universe physically distant from the material world—the "oceans . . . so far from ocean sundered" that seem to roar within the seashell far removed from the actual ocean.

The interpolated clause in the last two lines of stanza 3 and the first four lines of stanza 4 suggests the creation of alternative worlds by the imagination. The sound is "smothered," and "long lost," and the growth and blossoming of the listener's imaginative gifts takes place in a "troubled peace." The metaphor here, and its grammatical placement embedded deep within the speaker's authoritative lecture on the future, suggest something of a poet's life of the imagination. Louise Bogan was troubled at various times in her life with depression and emotional turmoil, and she underwent psychotherapy to confront her emotional and creative demons. The undersea metaphor of the sound that is both "smothered" and deep, that yet brings forth creations of beauty, suggests the concept of the psyche's unconscious, buried, as it were, below the ego's functioning everyday life, but the source of creative and imaginative gifts. The "flowers" in this reading could stand for, among other things, the speaker/listener's own poems, the spontaneous products of imagination.

The poem's last two lines complete the sentence by arriving, finally, at the verb and its subject, and sum up the entire poem. The joy that the speaker will no longer find in external things or in fleshly pleasures comes not from the world and what it gives or shows the listener, but from the echo produced by the listener's own imagination. To renounce the material world, the speaker implies, is to gain the world of the imagination: an echo, perhaps, more than the real thing.

Helen Jaskoski

HERE, BUT UNABLE TO ANSWER

Author: Richard Hugo (1923-1982)
Type of poem: Elegy
First published: 1982; collected in *Making Certain It Goes On: The Collected Poems of Richard Hugo*, 1984

The Poem

Richard Hugo's "Here, But Unable to Answer" consists of four symmetrically arranged stanzas of seven, ten, ten, and seven lines (a total of thirty-four lines), written in unrhymed, accented lines that approximate iambic pentameter. As its dedication implies, the poem is an elegy mourning the death of Herbert Hugo, the poet's father (actually his stepfather). The title echoes a response that is sometimes given during roll call in the military when an individual, ill or indisposed in some way, is for all other purposes present and accounted for. Its use here is ironic, for the father is dead and thus truly unable to answer, even though he is still present symbolically in the speaker's heart.

The speaker in the poem addresses the father directly, as if the father could still hear him. Several details indicate that Hugo himself is this speaker: the dedication, the term "Father," the autobiographical references to Hugo's lonely childhood with his grandparents ("I alone/ with two old people"), with whom he lived while his father, a Navy man, sailed the world, and glimpses of his own career as an Army Air Corps bombardier in World War II, "praying the final bomb run out."

The poem begins at early dawn. "Eight bells" mark the end of the night watch (4 A.M.) as "first light" illuminates the father's face. Hugo imagines him in command on the bridge of his ship, a powerful, almost godlike figure whose "voice rolls back the wind" and whose eyes light up the ship's compass. In the second stanza, however, the poet momentarily seems to take on some of that power. Had the father been lost at sea, Hugo vows he would have rescued him by tearing away the clouds to reveal the north star by which he might safely navigate homeward. They would then have sailed off together. Yet the poet immediately contrasts that dream with the reality of his desolate childhood.

In the third stanza, Hugo reveals that, during the war, more than physical distance separated the two men. In spite of the father's desire to serve in combat, he was assigned to pilot new ships from the shipyards, whereas the son became an unwilling hero who bombed the enemy and returned home after the war, "these hands still trembling with sky." Hugo remarks that their war will go down in history as the last war worth dying for, a comment often made about World War II.

As the poem shifts to the present in the final stanza, the father has died and lies buried "too close" to a modern highway, but the poet still envisions him on the bridge of his ship, a mythic figure "naming/ wisely every star again, your voice enormous/ with the power of moon, of tide." He assures his father that he has become strong enough to assume control of his life: "I seldom/ sail off course. I swim a silent green." He is guided even when asleep by the father's compass, although the father himself is gone. Here the poet seems to experience a symbolic and benign union with the father, one they could not share in life.

Forms and Devices

Hugo's poetic form owes much to the tradition of Anglo-Saxon poetry. While fellow poet and critic Dave Smith has called attention to "the mighty tug of his cadences," which is present in nearly all of his work, Hugo's use of formal meter is seldom strict. In "Here, But Unable to Answer," he employs a characteristic five-beat line that falls somewhere between the purely accentual meter of Anglo-Saxon poetry and a looser version of unrhymed iambic pentameter, or blank verse, the traditional meter that has been called the most natural rhythm in English.

Typically his metrical pattern will vary, influenced, he once said, by the shifting riffs of American swing and jazz. These lines, for example, contain anywhere from six to thirteen syllables, with three to seven stresses. However, in his well-known and widely imitated syllabic "Letter" poems, published in *31 Letters and 13 Dreams* (1977), he created a precise line of fourteen syllables.

Hugo is essentially a poet of sound. He employs repetition as a frequent device. Like the Anglo-Saxon poets, he favors a heavy emphasis on consonance and assonance (the repetition of consonant and vowel sounds) and, to a lesser degree, alliteration (the repetition of beginning sounds), to unify his lines: "A small dawn, sailor. First light glints." He often repeats syllables, whole words, and even phrases, as he does in "Eight *bells*. You *bell*ow orders" and "Even in *war* we lived a *war* apart." Still another type of repetition may be found in the final lines of the poem's first and fourth stanzas, where five words or their variants are echoed: "Your *eyes light* numbers *on the compass* green" and "When *I* dream, *the compass lights* stay *on*." Seldom does he employ end rhyme in his work, creating instead a more subtle internal rhyme:

> Father, now you're buried much too close for me
> to a busy highway, I still see you up there
> on the bridge, night sky wide open . . .

Like the English Romantic poet William Wordsworth, Hugo seems to favor the rhythms of natural speech, although his choice of words is less mellifluous and more direct. He prefers one- and two-syllable words derived from the Anglo-Saxon language to the more ornate, multisyllabic Latinate terms. As Smith has pointed out, "He is, in words, and has always been a meat and potatoes man."

Themes and Meanings

An overriding theme of "Here, But Unable to Answer" is the concept of loss or abandonment, as seen through what poet Marvin Bell has called "the vengeance of time [and] the clarity of failure." The poet mourns not only the loss of the father through death but the loss of a father who was absent in life as well. This idea of loss is pervasive in Hugo's poetry, whether of a lost era or a past that never was, whether of the faded dreams of "Degrees of Gray in Philipsburg" or the collapsing buildings of a "Montana Ranch Abandoned," two of Hugo's best-known poems.

Here he adopts a typical stance, that of a solitary figure with a desire for connection who views past and present with what critic Frederick Garber has identified as a "stereoscopic vision" of what is and was or, more often, what was not but should have been. In this poem, Hugo views the father in his imagination not from memory but on the bridge of his ship. The father stands alone, as does the poet, who envisions a powerful union between them: "what a team/ and never to be." This statement embodies a kind of wishful thinking. The bond between solitary father and isolated son in this poem is a yearned-for relationship rather than a real one. In truth, they have always been separated.

A related theme, again very typical of Hugo's work, is the undercurrent of personal guilt, as if the poet somehow bears responsibility for the physical and emotional distance between the two men. His tone is melancholy and even apologetic. The phrase "Me and my unwanted self" expresses a clear discomfort with his own identity. The poet urges his father to "forgive the bad nerves I brought home," as if the post-traumatic stress caused by his experiences as a bombardier in the war were something for which he was personally responsible. Even in his final vision of the father, there is a stab of regret for a relationship, a love, never fully realized.

The outer landscape of Hugo's poem mirrors the inner psychological landscape of the speaker. The scene is one of vast space and isolation. At the beginning of the poem, dawn is breaking over the ocean; at the end the dead father, who in reality is buried on land, remains alone on the bridge under a night sky studded with distant stars. This is the landscape of solitude, of sea and sky. The poet remains a contemplative observer throughout, his voice thick with sorrow. Even though he expresses his grief and admiration for the father, they do not touch. There is never a physical connection between them.

Close friend and poet James Wright has written of Hugo's work, "The absence of outcry seems . . . deeply significant. It suggests the spiritual silence at the heart of the poet's imagination." Indeed, one often encounters in Hugo's poetry a quiet loneliness, a reaching out, and here it is very appropriate as he mourns the death of his father.

Joanne McCarthy

HERITAGE

Author: Countée Cullen (1903-1946)
Type of poem: Lyric
First published: 1925, in *Color*

The Poem

Countée Cullen's "Heritage," a long (128-line) and intensely introspective lyric poem, has been considered a classic since it first appeared in print. The poem can be read as a soliloquy or monologue of a studious but deeply troubled young person who is tormented by the effort to reconcile his inner desires and the decorous behavior expected of him. The first ten lines of the poem express the speaker's profound feeling of alienation. He is of African ancestry but, as a descendant of people enslaved centuries ago in what is now the United States, he has no actual knowledge of Africa. Because his impressions of the continent and its cultures are limited to images derived from his reading and imagination, the first half of the poem (lines 1-63) constructs a vision of Africa through a series of beautiful, picturesque details: "wild barbaric birds," feral lions and leopards stalking gentle antelopes, herds of elephants parading through the open savannah grasslands. African people are depicted in equally picturesque terms as savage but regal, beautiful and carefree, lovers unashamed of their nakedness. In choosing such images, Cullen deliberately draws upon the view of Africa that would be familiar to his readers since it was a view reflected in the popular press during the first decades of the twentieth century.

Against this vivid visual backdrop, the speaker imagines that he hears the drums of some unknown tribal ritual temptingly calling to him. He understands, however, that it is only his imagination at work, that the drumming is merely his own pulse. Yet rain beating outside his window again reminds him of drums, bidding him to worship "Quaint, outlandish gods." As the poem progresses, the speaker begins to doubt his own faith as a Christian, finding it especially difficult to maintain a faith based on "the golden rule" and to assume the meek and forgiving role preached in Luke 6:20-49 by Jesus Christ. Risking blasphemy, the speaker wonders how a god who is not also black could understand the humiliation and pain that he must face resulting the racial discrimination that epitomizes American society.

In the end, the speaker struggles to remind himself that he is indeed a professing Christian, a "civilized" and intellectual Western man—no longer really related to the free, regal, but "unsaved" Africans of antiquity. The reader of the poem has also been deeply involved in the speaker's crisis of conscience and cannot help but appreciate the profound dilemma of religious faith and social identity that reading "Heritage" has required him or her to share.

Forms and Devices

"Heritage" is meant to be read aloud. Cullen's poem, though carefully constructed in rhymed couplets, nevertheless recalls the hypnotic metrical effect of Edgar Allan

Poe's "The Raven" (1845). That poem—itself based on the meter of a poem by Elizabeth Barrett Browning—employed subject matter, rhyme, and meter in a manner cal-
culated to induce a sense of anxiety in readers or listeners. "The Raven," therefore,
provided a suitable model for the narrative repetition that marks Cullen's own exploration of the physical state of insomnia and the mood of anxious doubt.

  Cullen meticulously crafts simple rhyming couplets for his seven-syllable line. The
skillful employment of alliteration and assonance (repetition of the same vowel
sound) adds to the poem's syncopated rhythmic effect. A good example of this technique is found in lines 23-25:

> So I lie, whose fount of pride,
> Dear distress, and joy allied,
> Is my somber flesh and skin

Cullen's fidgety word music and emphasis on kinetic and visual imagery effectively
highlights the discrepancy between the speaker's uncomfortable awareness of his
physical being and his conflicted spiritual yearnings. The pivot upon which "Heritage" turns is the repeated phrase "so I lie," which requires different inflections according to context. Sometimes the phrase connotes the speaker's restless inactivity
and sometimes his awareness of his own spiritual duplicity in claiming a religion in
which he might not truly believe.

  The poetic images and rhetorical structure of "Heritage"—often actually in opposition to each other—are carefully balanced in order to reinforce the author's message.
The beautiful African python shedding its skin annually so that it can grow is balanced by the insistent tribal drums bidding the speaker to take off the buttoned-up suit
and vest that simultaneously denote his status as an educated middle-class Werstern
man and the repression of his deepest instincts and desires. Like the snake, his natural
impulse is to shed this constricting covering—yet, in this case, that act would represent not growth but rather regression to an uncivilized pagan condition. Similarly, the
speaker's difficult-to-control inner urges are presented using images having to do
with flood and fire, suggesting that his subconscious desires are akin to subterranean
volcanic forces that would cause chaos should they erupt. Throughout the poem Cullen avoids using abstractions by grounding his rhetoric, even his references to emotions, in sensory perceptions or tangible things.

Themes and Meanings

  Cullen's poem reflects ideas about the relationship of the superego's learned behavior and the desires of the subconscious mind that were being considered by many
American intellectuals in the 1920's as they became familiar with the psychoanalytic
theories of Sigmund Freud and his colleagues. "Heritage" also reflects the identity
crisis peculiar to black Americans that W. E. B. Du Bois, in *The Souls of Black Folk*
(1903), diagnosed as a kind of "double consciousness" caused by a racist society's refusal to accept African Americans as citizens and social equals.

In "Heritage" the poet specifically engages the question of how a person's self-esteem is affected by ethnicity and the desire to be proud of one's ancestry. This was a particularly troublesome issue for black Americans. Standard reference authorities such as the 1910 edition of *Encyclopaedia Britannica* contended that, unlike Europeans, Africa's peoples were childlike primitives inhabiting "a continent practically without a history." Such stereotypical images were further propagated by novels, films, and travel articles. The popular *National Geographic Magazine* in particular, with reports of "expeditions" led by luminaries such as former President Theodore Roosevelt, highlighted the primitive and exotic aspects of the continent. Even among African Americans, the militant Universal Negro Improvement Association (UNIA)—launched by the charismatic orator Marcus Garvey in 1914—reinforced earlier efforts by black American churches to provide enlightened and progressive Christian missionary leadership to a continent they viewed as in need of civilization.

"Heritage"—written when the poet was a twenty-two-year-old college student—is also marked by a sense of youthful rebellion as well as the guilt that attends any attempt to break with previously accepted ideas and moral strictures. Cullen's parents were leaders in the black community's struggle for political rights, but inasmuch as his father was also the pastor of New York City's second largest African American church, they were also guardians of the era's Victorian social mores. This may help to explain why the overarching mood of the poem is anxiety as the speaker explores conflicts raised by his fear that atavistic racial traits, bringing with them an involuntary resurgence of the animist beliefs of his distant ancestors, might overwhelm the straitlaced Christian decorum that his middle-class urban upbringing demands.

While the emotional freight carried by "Heritage" is what immediately captures the reader's attention, there is also a quite mature theme of theological doubt in this poem that cannot be separated from an equally serious concern regarding the political status of African Americans in a hostile society. Cullen's skeptical response to the doctrine represented by "Jesus of the twice-turned cheek" (an allusion to Luke 6:29) anticipates debates in the black community about the nonviolent tactics adopted by activists of the Civil Rights movement in the 1950's and 1960's. More important, Cullen's theme of Christian doubt also directly and somewhat boldly confronts the view of older poets such as James Weldon Johnson, who felt that, for black Americans, Christianity adopted during slavery days had fully triumphed over African cultural survivals.

Still, though he felt that religious faith was more deeply expressed in times of adversity than of prosperity, Cullen never actually denies his religion. Indeed, "Heritage" suggests—as do the Gospels' accounts of the experiences of Jesus Christ and his disciples—that the deep-seated doubts it examines might be a necessary trial for those who are not satisfied to merely pay lip service to their beliefs.

Lorenzo Thomas